READINGS IN
HUMAN RESOURCE MANAGEMENT

READINGS IN
HUMAN RESOURCE MANAGEMENT

Raymond A. Noe
University of Minnesota

John R. Hollenbeck
Michigan State University

Barry Gerhart
Cornell University

Patrick M. Wright
Texas A & M University

AUSTEN
PRESS

IRWIN

Chicago • Bogotá • Boston • Buenos Aires • Caracas
London • Madrid • Mexico City • Sydney • Toronto

Publisher: William Schoof
Acquisitions Editor: John Weimeister
Production Manager: Bob Lange

Development, design, and production provided by
Elm Street Publishing Services, Inc.
Developmental Editor: Karen Hill
Project Editor: Phyllis Crittenden
Production Manager: Kelly Spiller
Text and Cover Designer: Melissa Morgan
Permissions Editor: Abby Westapher

Compositor: G & S Typesetters, Inc.
Typeface: 10/12 Palatino
Printer: R. R. Donnelley & Sons Company

Library of Congress Cataloging-in-Publication Data

Readings in human resource management / [compiled and edited by]
   Raymond A. Noe . . . [et al.].
        p.   cm.
     Includes bibliographical references.
     ISBN 0-256-14852-X
     1. Personnel management.   I. Noe, Raymond A.
   HF5549.R381643   1994
   658.3—dc20   93-42315

Printed in the United States of America
   4 5 6 7 8 9 0 DOC 9 8 7 6

Address editorial correspondence:
Austen Press
18141 Dixie Highway
Suite 111
Homewood, IL 60430

Address orders:
Richard D. Irwin, Inc.
1333 Burr Ridge Parkway
Burr Ridge, IL 60521

Austen Press
Richard D. Irwin, Inc.

CONTENTS

NOTE TO THE INSTRUCTOR:

Austen Press texts are marketed and distributed by Richard D. Irwin, Inc. For assistance in obtaining supplementary material for this and other Austen Press titles, please contact your Irwin sales representative or the customer service division of Richard D. Irwin at (800) 323-4560.

INTRODUCTION

/Introduction/

The focus of this book is to show how the management of human resources can help organizations gain a competitive advantage; that is, help them gain a competitive advantage over U.S. and foreign competitors. Managing human resources can help companies gain competitive advantage in many ways, such as (1) selecting employees who will be innovative, creative, and successful in performing their jobs; (2) preparing employees to work with new manufacturing and service technologies; and (3) rewarding good performance. The effective management of human resources also contributes both to customer and employee satisfaction and retention and to the development of a positive reputation in the community in which the company is located.

The effective management of human resources can enhance the operation of the other business functions (such as production, marketing, and information systems) and contribute directly to company profitability. For example, the introduction of a new information system into a company requires that employees be trained to use the new system. Companies that want to be recognized by customers for the quality of the product and services they provide need to reward salespersons for providing high-quality services (a performance management issue). The management of human resources is also critical for helping companies deal with several competitive challenges they will face in the next decade and beyond. These challenges include the global challenge, the quality challenge, the social challenge, and the technology and structure challenge.

THE COMPETITIVE CHALLENGES

The four competitive challenges are shown in Figure 1.

The Global Challenge

Companies are finding that they must compete for foreign markets in order to survive. U.S. companies must expand into foreign markets and do a better job of preparing employees for international assignments. Opportunities for U.S. businesses are available in Eastern Europe and the former Soviet Union. Pending legislation such as the North American Free Trade Agreement (NAFTA) will make it easier for companies to do business in Canada and Mexico. Although U.S. business problems in gaining access to foreign markets are related to differences in economic, structural, historic, and cultural differences between countries,

1

Figure 1

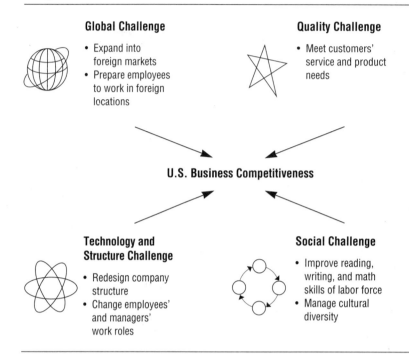

Global Challenge

- Expand into foreign markets
- Prepare employees to work in foreign locations

Quality Challenge

- Meet customers' service and product needs

U.S. Business Competitiveness

Technology and Structure Challenge

- Redesign company structure
- Change employees' and managers' work roles

Social Challenge

- Improve reading, writing, and math skills of labor force
- Manage cultural diversity

a major factor may also be U.S. companies' lack of investment in human resources. For example, Japan and Germany have traditionally invested in new work design and employee training, while U.S. businesses have attempted to improve productivity through cutting costs related to human resources (such as training budgets).

Besides taking steps to ensure that employees are better used, U.S. companies must do a better job of preparing employees for overseas assignments. The failure rate for expatriates (U.S. employees sent to work abroad) is higher than for many foreign competitors. U.S. companies must carefully select employees to work abroad based on their ability to understand and respect the cultural and business norms of the host country, their language skills, and their technical ability.

The Quality Challenge

One of the major reasons U.S. companies have failed to maintain their leadership in many industries (e.g., automobiles, tires, electronics, steel) has been the decline in customers' perceptions of the quality of U.S. products. Quality is defined as the extent to which a product or service satisfies the customer's requirements.[1] Traditionally, U.S. companies have attempted to ensure quality by inspecting products and services after they are assembled or delivered. Foreign competitors have taken a different approach. They emphasize designing quality into a product or service as it is produced or delivered, rather than relying on the inspection process to identify defects and problems.

Recognition for "building in" quality into products or services can help increase companies' U.S. and foreign market share. The Malcolm Baldrige National Award is given by the Department of Commerce to recognize quality achievements of U.S. companies. To become eligible for the Baldrige award, companies must complete a detailed application that consists of basic information, such as location, products, and services. Companies are also required to address seven areas: leadership, information and analysis, strategic quality planning, human resource development and management, management of process quality, quality and operational results, and customer focus and satisfaction. A board of examiners composed of quality experts from business and academia evaluate the companies' applications and conduct site visits. Although only two awards per year are given in three categories—manufacturing, service, and small business—all applicants receive feedback regarding the company's strengths and weaknesses and needs for improvement. Going through the application process for the Baldrige award is a good way for companies to improve the quality of their products and services.

It is important to note that to conduct business in several countries (such as countries of the European Community), U.S. companies must also gain ISO 9000 certification. ISO 9000 is a series of quality standards regarding effective management practices, and guidelines for the design, production, installation, and servicing of products.

To meet the quality challenge, companies must have effective human resource management practices. For example, employees need environments that allow them to be innovative, be creative, and take risks to meet customer demands. Work should be designed so that the skills and talents of many employees can simultaneously be used. Employees need training in statistical process control methods as well as interpersonal skills for interacting with fellow employees and customers.

The Social Challenge

Companies face several challenges as a result of changes in the work force and employment rates in different sectors of the economy. The composition of the

[1] L. B. Forker, "Quality: American, Japanese, and Soviet Perspectives," *The Executive* 5(5) 1991: 63–74.

labor market, projected changes in the structure of the economy, and skill deficits in the labor force will influence company competitiveness in the next decade. The U.S. labor force will be older and more culturally diverse than at any time in the last forty years. One of the challenges that the aging labor force creates for companies is how to create career development systems that utilize and reward older employees. Companies are being challenged to ensure that the talents, experiences, values, and perspectives of all employees are utilized to increase product and service quality and productivity. Employers need to develop safety and health, work and family, and discipline policies that are fair and equitable. Because labor market growth will be primarily in female and minority populations, companies need to ensure that human resource management systems are bias free to capitalize on the talents and skills of these employee groups and help them find fulfillment at work.

Health, business, personal, and recreational services will be the largest growing sectors of the economy. Jobs in these sectors traditionally require more education than those in basic industries such as textiles and automobiles. However, the introduction of new computer-based technology into manufacturing jobs requires employees to collect, retrieve, and analyze production data. An important human resource issue is the projected lack of individuals with the necessary training and education to meet the demands of jobs in the U.S. economy. This means that companies need to provide reading, writing, and computational skill training to large portions of their work forces.

Legislation will continue to influence the management of human resources. For example, as a result of the Americans with Disabilities Act (ADA), employers are required to accommodate known mental or physical disabilities of otherwise qualified employees, unless doing so would result in excessive expense. As a result of the ADA, employers are reevaluating their hiring and training practices, benefit plans, work design, and physical facilities. Similarly, the Family Medical Leave Act (1993) permits employees to take 12 weeks of unpaid leave for birth, adoption, personal illness, or illness of a family member. The FMLA will have a major impact on companies' staffing strategies.

The Technology and Structure Challenge

New technology has caused changes in basic skill requirements and work roles. Advances in computer technology also have made it easier for employees to gain access to information from customers and manufacturing processes at the point of sale or point of production. Computer technology and software is available for managers to track human resources (e.g., skills data bases) or to evaluate alternative human resource strategies.

Because technology has made information more readily accessible for employees, one trend for increasing employee responsibility, control, and use of information is the use of work teams. Work teams frequently assume many of the activities usually reserved for managers, such as work scheduling and coordinating activities with customers and vendors. Work teams also perform inspection and quality-control activities. Work teams have changed the role of the manager. Traditionally, managers control, plan, and coordinate work. In a team environment, managers provide work teams with the resources they need to perform work, facilitate interactions with other departments and vendors, and help alleviate interpersonal disputes that might occur in the team.

To meet the technological challenge, companies need to prepare employees and managers to use new technology and be successful in environments where work teams are used. Companies also need to develop managers' and employees' interpersonal and technical skills so that they can work in teams and utilize computer hardware and software.

ORGANIZATION OF THE READINGS

The collection of readings in this book will help the student understand how the management of human resources can help companies successfully deal with global, social, technological and structural, and quality challenges to gain a competitive advantage. The readings include both academic and practitioner perspectives, and they are organized into six parts:

- I. Managing the Internal and External Environments. The topics in Part I include readings related to the strategic management of human resources, global issues in human resource management, the legal environment, and ethical employee relations.
- II. Assessing Work and Work Outcomes. Part II includes readings that deal with work design, performance management, and employee attitudes that affect productivity and competitiveness.
- III. Acquiring Human Resources. Readings in Part III deal with determining human resource requirements and plans, recruiting, and selecting employees.
- IV. Developing Human Resources. Part IV readings discuss training and developing employees and career management.
- V. Compensating Human Resources. Part V includes readings related to designing pay structures, recognizing employee contributions, and employee benefits.
- VI. Special Topics in Human Resource Management. Readings in Part VI relate to labor and management relations and human resource information systems.

Each topic area begins with a brief discussion of how the topic of the readings can help the company gain a competitive advantage. Brief summaries of each of the articles discuss key points and highlights.

Human Resource Management: Gaining a Competitive Advantage

HUMAN RESOURCE MANAGEMENT:
GAINING A COMPETITIVE ADVANTAGE

INTRODUCTION

As we noted earlier, the management of human resources is expected to play a key role in helping companies gain competitive advantage. Reading 1 by Schuler, "Repositioning the Human Resource Function: Transformation or Demise?" illustrates how the human resource function can help companies gain a competitive advantage. Schuler emphasizes that four issues: managing employee competence, managing work-force diversity, managing for enhanced competitiveness, and managing for globalization are people-related issues that the human resource function should address and view as an asset rather than a business cost. Schuler also highlights the competencies—business focus, change agent, consultant, strategy formulator, talent manager, asset manager—that the human resource manager and function need to help the company successfully deal with the competitive challenges.

To understand how to use human resources to successfully meet the quality challenge, managers must first understand the concept of quality. One commonly accepted definition of quality does not exist. Rather, quality can be defined in terms of customer standards, engineering standards, or the value that a product or service provides. Reading 2, "Quality: American, Japanese, and Soviet Perspectives," by Forker discusses five different approaches to defining quality. The article compares and contrasts the different perspectives of quality proposed by Deming, Juran, Crosby, Taguchi, and L'vov.

Reading 3, "Managing Cultural Diversity: Implications for Organizational Competitiveness," by Cox and Blake illustrates how managing diversity can create a competitive advantage through reducing costs, improving product marketing to minority groups, and generating better quality decisions through capitalizing on the perspectives of individuals with different cultural backgrounds. Cox and Blake suggest that top management leadership, training, research, analysis and change of human resource management systems, and monitoring of results are key factors that are needed to create an organization that successfully manages diversity.

READING 1

REPOSITIONING THE HUMAN RESOURCE FUNCTION
Transformation or Demise?

Randall S. Schuler

Executive Overview

The human resource department is being presented with an opportunity to become a significant player on the management team. This is occurring because the human resource (HR) function is being transformed into a significant management function. Environmental changes are confronting organizations with people issues of great importance and uncertainty. People issues are thus becoming formulated as significant business issues. One result is that line managers are reaching out to take control and ownership over the HR function. This is being facilitated by many HR departments that remain focused on issues involving functional expertise rather than business-relatedness. Examples exist, however, of companies in which the HR departments are seizing the opportunity to become vital members of the management team and working with line managers to tackle the people-related business issues. Doing so, however, appears to require a virtual repositioning of the HR department. This, in turn, involves new roles, new competencies, new relationships and new ways of operating for both HR and line managers. The result is an HR department that is a management team player with a business issue and customer focus and a bottom-line orientation. New roles for both line managers and HR managers and enhanced organizational effectiveness in addressing people-related business issues may result.

"Right now there is a place for corporate HR in company-wide recruiting efforts so it can recruit in one division but with the needs of other areas in mind so there can be company-wide flexibility. Corporate HR is not taking the lead on this situation. Flexibility is needed for worldwide needs but the department does not see themselves as doing this. They see themselves as "doctors" not business managers; not part of the team."

This comment, made by a senior vice president of executive development, points to a general lack of understanding of the business (its strategy, the way it

Source: "Repositioning the Human Resource Function: Transformation or Demise?" by Randall S. Schuler, *Academy of Management Executive*, 1990, Vol. 4., No. 3., 49–60.

works, the dynamics of the industry, etc.) in today's human resource departments. A seeming reluctance to perceive the line manager as customer, prompted Art Maine at Revco, another senior personnel manager to observe:

> The real role of HR is in the areas of human productivity, quality and performance, yet these are being done increasingly by line managers, especially in the highly innovative successful mid-sized companies. The HR staff just do the administrative stuff which could be downloaded someday to the accounting and legal departments.

In this extreme scenario, the HR department is dissolved, and the function split among the accounting and legal departments, outside consultants, and line managers. While this situation has significant implications for HR managers and staff and all line managers, it does not mean that the HR profession is witnessing an irreversible trend. To the contrary, the profession could be seeing through its clearest window of opportunity yet. Taking advantage of this opportunity, however, appears to require nothing less than the total repositioning of the HR department. According to Robert Galvin, CEO of Motorola,

> Generally we're seeing the HR manager and HR department being offered the opportunity to be transformed from a functional specialist to management team member and it is expected that the shift from "employee advocate" to "member of the management team" will continue into the 1990s. Human resource professionals will be called upon to think and act like line managers to address people-related business issues. Managers will increasingly expect HR to think and act, and to view human resource activities from a business perspective.[1]

Having a business perspective means concern with the bottom-line, profits, effectiveness, and survival. It also means addressing human resource issues as business issues—seeing them in the context of business strategies and operation plans, considering the issues at each organizational level, and considering the perspectives of all stakeholders. Thus, rather than being redundant, HR departments could seize the opportunity to be a vital member of the management team.

Whether HR departments seize this opportunity remains to be seen. Failure to grasp it may prophesize the demise of the HR department. However, a virtual repositioning of the HR department will be required to become a member of the management team. Failure to reposition would shift significant HR activities to the line managers. While this may enhance the effectiveness of the line manager, it requires significant understanding of human resource management and commitment of additional time by the line manager.

Dramatic Environmental Changes

Fundamental changes in the business environment have created the sudden shift of importance of the HR function. These changes include:

- Rapid rate of business change; high uncertainty
- Rising costs; increasing competitive pressures on margins

"[T]he real role of HR is in the areas of human productivity, quality and performance, yet these are being done increasingly by line managers, especially in the highly innovative successful mid-sized companies. The HR staff just do the administrative stuff which could be downloaded someday to the accounting and legal departments."

- Rapid technological change; increasing demands for new skills through sourcing, education, and retraining
- Complex organizations; product, geography, technologies, business function, customers/markets
- Flatter, leaner, more flexible organizations
- Changing demographics, limited labor availabilities
- Responding to external forces: legislation and regulation, litigation, union relations and union avoidance, etc.
- Increasing multinational competition and collaboration; multilateral relationships

These environmental changes are leading to the acknowledgement by line management that human resources (i.e., people) are important to the business and growing uncertainty associated with key human resource issues.

People Are Critical

Increasingly organizations such as Federal Express indicate the importance of people by including them in the philosophy of the company. Fred Smith's philosophy, active since day one of Federal Express, is "People, Service, and Profit."

President and COO of Stop and Shop Companies, Carol Goldberg, noted that,

> In most service businesses, but in particular in a business as service intensive as supermarkets, people are a company's most important asset.[2]

As this importance is recognized, people not only get included in the philosophy of the company but in the strategic planning process as well. According to Kathryn Connors, vice president of HR at Liz Claiborne,

> Human resources is part of the strategic planning process. It's part of policy development, line extension planning, and the merger and acquisition processes. Little is done in the company that doesn't involve us in the planning, policy, or finalization stages of any deal.[3]

And it seems that when organizations do strategic planning, line managers are more likely to see the importance of HR issues. According to Revco's Art Maine,

> The problem seems not to be one where line managers don't see HR issues as relevant. Rather it seems that these issues are becoming more important as firms do strategic planning. When forced to do this scenario building, they see that HR issues pop up, especially supply of skilled folks or having people adaptable enough or willing and able to deal with ambiguity. Notice that all these are business issues really: if they are not provided for, the essence of the business is threatened.

Companies are beginning to recognize the importance of people to the business's success. More human resource issues are really "people-related business issues" in that they influence the essence of the business—profitability, survival, competitiveness, adaptability, and flexibility.

People Are Uncertain

There is a growing level of uncertainty surrounding several key human resource concerns. Increasingly, companies can't be certain of:

- a sufficient supply of people
- how to attract, retain, and motivate an increasingly diverse workforce
- getting or having individuals with the right skills, knowledge, and abilities
- employees behaving in ways necessary for the company to be competitive, domestically and internationally.

The two human resource issues together are transforming how the HR function is regarded. They are also causing enough of a problem for organizations to take action—to transform the HR department (manager) from a functional specialist to a management team player with a business understanding.

The transformation of the HR department to management team player is impossible without repositioning. The ideal organization has the HR manager jointly working with the line manager solving people-related business issues.

TRANSFORMING THE HR FUNCTION: PEOPLE-RELATED BUSINESS ISSUES

Issues previously regarded as "people issues" are now being thought of as "people-related business issues" because they very well could threaten the profitability of the business. Although they are strategic, many of these issues call for immediate action and short term resolution. For example, according to Tom Moyers, VP of HR at Perdue,

> What is happening in the entire meat industry is the concern for the repetitive motion syndrome from highly repetitive work. OSHA is trying to get poultry producers to reduce the speed of line work and the firms are trying to get their supervisors to increase the level of job rotation (reducing repetition, etc.). Supervisors are resisting this because this reduces the efficiency of their workers (despite efforts to change the compensation system to reward behavior for HR concerns). Nonetheless, top management is concerned with this issue, because of the immediate threat to profitability and survival of the business and the health of the consumer.

To be certain, not all people issues are being translated into people-related business issues. However, the growing number of them are and line managers are getting involved; even to the point of assuming the HR function. Companies where line managers and HR managers work together on issues generally reflect a situation in which repositioning of the HR departments has occurred or is in the process of occurring.

Because the rise of people-related business issues is having such a profound impact on the behaviors of line and HR managers, it is useful to examine them. There are four major issues that are being regarded as people-related business issues:

- *Managing for employee competence.* Increasingly, individuals coming into the workforce lack sufficient skills or as employees they become obsolete due to technological advances or organizational changes.
- *Managing workforce diversity.* This means attracting, retaining, and motivating individuals with diverse and varied backgrounds regarding race, sex, ethnic origin, age, and language.
- *Managing for enhanced competitiveness.* A major recognition of organizations today is that success and survival depend upon greater levels of operational and strategic effectiveness efficiency. Broadly, this is being translated into restructuring and downsizing operations, reducing costs of operation, enhancing levels of the quality of goods and services and continuous and systematic innovation of new products and services.
- *Managing for globalization.* The entire world is the arena for the purchase of goods and services and for manufacturing. This arena must be understood and mastered by organizations to compete successfully.

Managing for Employee Competence

This major people-related business issue has two targets. One target is the current and projected group of management talent. Employees who suddenly lack appropriate skills because technology changes are the second.

Managerial Talent.   At Allstate Insurance, Frank Berardi of the Corporate HR department believes that HR and line managers have been viewing HR issues as people-related business issues since Allstate started using Michael Porter's competitive strategy framework two years ago. In the process, they identified a concern about managerial talent.

Allstate first identified 14 business groups and then identified if the groups should pursue differentiation or cost strategies. Part of Porter's final analysis is to state the implications for technology and HRM. Because the HR implication section was too brief for Allstate, Berardi used it to build on an HR component. He did a gap analysis with 14 units asking them to identify their current practices and what they would like to and need to have, given their new strategies. At this point, Allstate created the corporate HR planning unit. Each business unit, with its own HR department, tailored or was in the process of tailoring, its HR practices to the businesses. Based on this exercise, line managers saw gaps. For example, lack of management talent in the near future in a rapidly changing world was identified. The need for a new type of manager, who can creatively deal with a diversity of workers and programs was also lacking. While concern for numbers existed, a concern for skills was paramount. Allstate's line managers wanted HR to help them develop management education programs and new succession programs. This is a strategic line issue that is HR in nature.

Current Employees and Technological Changes

The technological revolution has meant major change. Organizations are continually developing plans and philosophies that promote the acceptance of the technological revolution. It brings numerous changes:

- number and types of jobs,
- skills required,
- training needed,
- new organizational structures and reporting relationships,
- supervision form and style adjustment (likely to require major unlearning as well as learning efforts),
- obsolescence fears,
- continual retraining and adjustment,
- organizational flexibility,
- willingness to adapt quickly to unpredictable change.

Thus, technological changes have major implications for the human resource function. But, they are also providing opportunity to both human resources and line managers.

This is the case at the Barden Corporation in Danbury, Connecticut. A manufacturer of precision bearings, the company recognized that they would have to continually install computerized numerical control (CNC) machines. Barden, under the leadership of Donald Brush, vice president and general manager, identified this as a major people-related issue for the business and defined it as follows:

> The technological evolution of increasingly complex machinery and related manufacturing equipment, and the development of trained workers to operate and maintain these machines and equipment.
>
> We perceived this to be a serious problem, and we approached it by creating an ad hoc committee to study the problem and propose solutions. The committee included a senior manufacturing engineer, the manufacturing engineer managers. It was chaired by the director of industrial relations. The committee concluded that CNC machinists would have to be developed in-house, and it blocked in the technical competencies (machining, trigonometry, basic computer programming, etc.) that would be required. The training unit then put together a specific course of training including the hours involved, identified instructors, worked out a full apprenticeship program with the State Department of Labor, and assisted in identifying employees with acceptable minimum qualifications.

A team of line managers, chaired by the HR manager, attacked the people-related business issue of skill shortage. The team identified the strategic and managerial aspects and then handed the operational aspects over to the specialists in training.

This example offers an illustration of the HR department as a management team player and of HR and line managers working together on a people-related business issue.

Managing Workforce Diversity

The radical demographic workforce transformation means that business needs to develop knowledge and understanding in managing a very diverse workforce, i.e., Black, Hispanics, women, Asians, etc. Successful organizations will react to diversity as the important business issue it is by implementing proactive, strategic human resource planning. Short-term strategies designed to circumvent the situation will keep an organization from effectively positioning itself in tomorrow's world of cultural, gender, and lifestyle diversity.[4]

The radical demographic workforce transformation means that business needs to develop knowledge and understanding in managing a very diverse workforce, i.e., Black, Hispanics, women, Asians, etc.

Organizations are casting the topic of workforce diversity in terms of business issues. Bill Fuller, human resources director at the Bank of Boston Corporation, describes companies that value diversity as winners and points out that the costs of programs that support diversity do not compromise a company's ability to maximize profits. On the contrary, companies that value diversity are also financially successful; indeed, some of the companies that lead in valuing differences rank among the United States' most profitable. Fuller said, "In the valuing diversity company, you see employees who are less risk averse, who play to win rather than not to lose, and as a result you see more creativity, more leadership, more innovation."[5]

Businesses are changing in response to this diversity issue. Digital Equipment Corporation now has a manager with the title of manager of valuing differences. Honeywell has a director of workforce diversity and Avon Products has a director of multicultural planning and design.[6] According to Stona Fitch, vice-president of manufacturing for Procter & Gamble:

> The first companies that achieve a true multicultural environment will have a competitive edge. Diversity provides a much richer environment, a variety of viewpoints, greater productivity. And not unimportantly, it makes work much fun and interesting.[7]

Hewlett-Packard conducts training sessions for managers to teach them about different cultures and races and about their own gender biases and training needs.[8] Procter & Gamble has implemented "valuing diversity" programs throughout the company. A mentor program designed to retain black and female managers was developed at one plant, and one-day workshops on diversity were given to all new employees.[9]

At Merck, where the overall recruiting responsibility has shifted from the human resource departments to the line managers, significant progress has been made in hiring and promoting females and minorities. Also, specific hiring and promotion goals have been established during the past two years for blacks in the exempt and professional categories.

To achieve these goals, Merck targets recruiting activities at minority schools. It also offers training programs to executives, managers, supervisors and all levels of employees in affirmative action planning. In these seminars, participants learn appropriate behavior in the workplace, about labor relations as it relates to affirmative action, sexual harassment, and more.[10]

Equitable Life Assurance Society encourages minorities and women to form support groups which periodically meet with the CEO to discuss problems in the company pertaining to them. Avon has several councils representing various groups, each having a senior manager present at meetings. These councils inform and advise top management.

Going beyond programs to recruit and retain black and female managers, companies are also designing programs to manage the diversity of individuals with different language skills. Barden, the precision bearing manufacturer described previously, recently developed a special language program to facilitate the business's opportunity to grow. According to Donald Brush:

> By mid-1988 it had become evident that we had an opportunity to significantly increase our business. In order to achieve otherwise attainable goals, we would need to increase our hourly workforce by a net of about 125 employees (that is, in addition to normal turnover, retirements, etc.) in one year. I asked Personnel to test the waters, recognizing that unemployment in the Danbury labor market had reached an unprecedented low of about 2.5%. The answer that came back to me was a qualified yes. That is, we could do so by using our imagination, (e.g., bounties to employees for successful referrals, imaginative publicity such as an open house) and, importantly, by recruiting workers whose English was very poor.

Managing for Enhanced Competitiveness

As the economy and the nature and level of competition change, jobs and organizations change. The issues described previously are likely to continue to spread to more and more firms in the United States during the 1990s. All the efforts required to create a successful organization depend upon significant changes in human resource management. For example, downsizing efforts involve outplacement, retirement, severance pay, management succession, and better human resource planning programs to reduce the need for further downsizing. Decentralizing involves training employees in decision making, new performance appraisals, changes in compensation, and new leadership skills.

Human resource staff are expected to guide and support company efforts in developing managers as leaders for the new flat, lean, and flexible environments.

"There are no flexible organizations, only flexible people," an executive observed.

Human resource staff are expected to guide and support company efforts in developing managers as leaders for the new flat, lean, and flexible environment. General Electric believes that teamwork, company-wide perspective, global insight, and customer orientation are critical attributes for its leaders. With fewer managers and management levels, management capabilities are more important. Providing challenging and broadening experiences is the key to developing flexible managers. However, in flat and lean organizations, job rotation and mobility are difficult because there are fewer managers—and increased time pressures and demands on unit and individual performance. Business units have little slack and have difficulty releasing talented managers for broadening assignments, even a temporary one.[11]

Mergers and acquisitions create the need for programs in workforce reductions, relations with communities where closed facilities are located, realignment of reporting relationships, and integration of two previously independent and perhaps antagonistic organizations. While all of these efforts have significant implications for human resource management, the following two examples demonstrate how HR and line managers can work (indeed must work) together to sustain programs to make organizations effective.

J. C. Penney.   In service businesses, quality often means improving customer service. In the retail clothing business, getting more cooperation between the clothing buyer and seller means better service. During the past several years, J. C. Penney has identified this need and responded. According to Jim Stahler in the HR department at Penney:

> This is an interesting situation because it was a macro move for the firm and it essentially has been completed. It was certainly long term. The change has been under way for about 10 years.

> During the early mid-1970s, the company started to notice that margins were shrinking due largely to the competition of the Wal-Marts and K-Marts. All the stores here were trying to compete in the full range of goods, including automotive, house and garden, etc. They all wanted to be the one stop shopping place, mostly in a mall environment.

> At this time they discovered the satellite and the ability to link buyer and seller with instantaneous, paperless communication. So the character of the folks needed for buying and selling changed. The buyers needed platform skills (and one thinking more like a customer and having some backshop knowledge) in order to deal with manufacturers and even the sellers. They had to develop a cooperative attitude with the sellers and not be so ready to fix the blame on the sellers. The sellers had to change too. Some sellers went to the buyer organization and vice versa. This was critical to the entire change. Not until the Ford Motor change effort of Quality Is Job 1, were quality and team development seen as critical to the success of or a major turnaround of a large organization.

Grand Union.   Grand Union, the nation's third largest food store chain also decided to become upscale to enhance its competitiveness and profitability. According to Bill Reffett, senior VP of human resources:

> To go upscale meant customer-focused and high quality products. More customer-focused meant more concern for what the customer wanted, more attention to customer complaints and more courtesy from employees (associates). Higher product quality meant better products and more products that they currently didn't have, e.g., their own freshly baked goods.

For Grand Union, the major HR area of impact was training and development. Customer-focused meant paying more attention to management and recognizing performance (previously, there was essentially none of this). The store managers had to be trained in management skills, especially in giving performance appraisals and taking them. Reffett and his team installed a popular performance appraisal system given monthly for the store managers and every six months for other associates.

Managing for Globalization

It is certain that "globalization" will continue to be an inescapable buzzword. Businesses will operate in an interconnected world. With continuing advances in computers and communications, world financial markets are melding. Manufacturing capabilities are appearing almost overnight in new Taiwans and South Koreas.

Managers have to shape organizations that can respond quickly to developments abroad. As speed and agility become critical, we will see even more decentralization, with responsibility closer to the operating level.[12]

Speed, customization, and agility are becoming imperative skills in modern companies. Organizations must develop a world or global structure and perspective.

This global structure is characterized by a decentralized but coordinated framework. Human resource policies need to mirror the necessary organizational characteristics. According to E. Jeffrey Stoll, director of Merck's corporate personnel relations,

Expatriate, third country, and host country personnel policies have to be articulated to create a worldwide workforce.

> Because 50% of our business is from overseas, we must be globally competitive in terms of human resources, internationally and domestically. If not, then we won't be where we want to be five years from now.[13]

Expatriate, third country, and host country personnel policies have to be articulated to create a worldwide workforce. The expatriate assignment needs to be made an attractive one for the best employees to pursue. Assignments anywhere have to be seen as vital components of the whole. According to Jerry Junkins, the CEO of Texas Instruments, overseas managers need to look beyond their own fiefdoms to consider the capabilities and needs of the company as a whole. Junkins now has all the members of its worldwide management group working together. TI's worldwide strategy meetings—

> ensure that the company knows enough about its customers' needs to invest in the manufacturing technologies that will satisfy the greatest numbers of buyers, no matter where they come from. The strategy seems to be working: After steep losses in 1985, TI has posted seven consecutive quarters of profit. In the troubled semiconductor business, that counts as a win.[14]

IMPLICATIONS OF THE HR TRANSFORMATION ON THE HR DEPARTMENT

The potential for the HR department's demise is a major implication of the HR transformation. The examples of Allstate, Grand Union, and the other companies

*What appears neces-
sary, however, is for
the HR manager and
the HR department
to be connected to
and knowledgeable
about the business,
and to be perceived
as credible by line
managers.*

mentioned, however, illustrate that demise is neither necessary nor desirable. In fact, the companies described suggest the opposite. What appears necessary, however, is for the HR manager and the HR department to be connected to and knowledgeable about the business, and to be perceived as credible by line managers.

Repositioning of the HR Department

While a formal process of repositioning is not necessary to ensure that the HR manager and the department are transformed, it can offer suggestions and guidelines that might not otherwise be considered. There are four major phases to any program to reposition an HR department: (1) finding out the current state of things, (2) developing action agendas, (3) implementing the agendas and, (4) evaluating and revising them.[15]

Exhibit 1

- Be a business person
- Function as business executive, not just personnel specialist
- Understand and communicate how human resource programs directly impact business objectives and bottom line
- Be a shaper and agent of change
- Anticipate and focus on the management of change
- Help articulate and build evolving company culture and value system
- Become a driving force in making change happen in attitudes, behavior, skills
- Be a consultant to the organization and act as a partner to line managers
- Become an advisor and counselor on human resource matters to CEO and other senior managers
- Earn acceptance by being a creative problem solver
- Be a strategic planner—formulator and implementor
- Integrate planning into corporate human resource strategic planning process
- Translate specific business strategies into key people requirements and culture
- Identify gaps, evaluate alternatives, develop programs, push delivery
- Be a star talent manager
- Find the best management talent
- Anticipate the human resource needs of the firm
- Do outstanding succession planning
- Be a proactive asset manager, cost controller and server of customers
- Contribute cost-control ideas and programs
- Extend workforce management into productivity improvement
- Develop pay plans that are productivity related and cost-effective

Key New Roles and Competencies for the HR Manager for Transformation

Being a member of the management team and dealing with people-related business issues means that the HR manager assumes some new key roles.[16] Playing these new key roles means several things. One of the most important is that: "HR people have got to stop conceptualizing their role as a 'professional' individual contributor and realize that their job is to help provide corporations with leadership on HR issues."[17] They must acquire the competencies to perform these roles. Because these roles are so important and will continue to be so, the question is: "How can these competencies be attained?" The following represent some possible developmental activities vis-a-vis each of six of the new key roles.

Business Person. (1) articulation and reinforcement of management's expectation to be a business person first—and an HR practitioner next; (2) participation in courses on finance for non-financial executives, as well as marketing; (3) exposure to marketing organization; (4) participation on task forces, business planning teams, acquisition/divestiture teams; (5) rotation of HR and line positions; (6) lunch with "customers"—the line; (7) feedback on performance and HR development needs from the line.

Shaper of Change. (1) participation on teams with outside consultants when change is happening; (2) off-site meetings to visualize possibilities, establish missions, set goals, discuss change process; (3) team-building exercises; (4) formalized mentor relationships; (5) research on change process; (6) courses, such as "The Looking Glass," held by the Center for Creative Leadership; (7) out-of-company work in professional organizations or teams with other companies; (8) outside consulting for non-competitors.

Consultant to Organization/Partner to Line. (1) volunteer work in professional organizations, health care coalition, charities or company consortiums; (2) counselor selling workshops, such as those by Wilson Learning; (3) classes and experience in negotiating; (4) participation in computer systems projects, which are formally documented and show how to structure a large project; (5) proposal preparation; (6) time tracking on a "billable" basis; (7) coaching/performance evaluation; (8) pairing of junior and senior staffers, and consulting with internal staff; (9) seeding of internal staff with those with consulting backgrounds.

Strategy Formulator and Implementor. (1) learn content of business strategy; (2) read business-oriented periodicals; (3) become knowledgeable in the strategies of all the businesses or divisions; (4) describe the human resource implications of these various strategies; (5) articulate these implications in the strategy planning sessions with line management; (6) demonstrate how human resource activities can be used to help valued customers or suppliers; (7) study the human resource practices of successful companies, i.e., engage in benchmarking.

Talent Manager.   (1) constantly talk to all line managers; (2) monitor what the competition is doing; (3) attend conferences to develop network; (4) constantly talk with recruiters and placement firms; (5) attend seminars on succession planning.

Asset Manager and Cost Controller.   (1) take courses on finance and accounting; (2) read journal articles on utility analysis; (3) have conferences with those in the finance and accounting departments; (4) learn the accounting procedures in your firm.

Several organizations have already begun developing these new HR roles. IBM, General Electric, and Digital Equipment are tailoring programs to the needs of their human resource personnel. Some are adapting university programs on human resource topics, and business and strategy perspective. Human resource departments are learning line managers' business needs and tailoring the human resource activities accordingly. The result of this program is better human resource service to the line and also a more excited, challenged, and motivated human resource staff. This is the essence of repositioning the HR department.

SUMMARY AND CONCLUSION

Traditionally human resource departments have been functional specialists, doing staffing, appraising, training, and compensating in the most detailed and professional ways. But they have not done these with the mind set of how they can make the organization more competitive and effective (i.e., they have not treated them as people-related business issues). Consequently, HR departments are not easily assuming the task of becoming business-oriented and a part of the management team.

HR departments (their managers and staff) are in a real dilemma: they can continue in their functional specialists mode or they can reorient themselves and see HR issues as business issues and help line managers solve them.

The former alternative may mean the eventual demise of the HR department while the latter is likely to result in the department being accepted as an active and valued member of the management team. The former route requires no change in behavior on the part of HR departments although line managers assume a greater workload. Taking the latter route, however, requires HR departments and line managers to substantially change. It requires a virtual repositioning of the department and an acceptance by line managers. To reposition, the HR department must treat the rest of the organization as customers and gain a total understanding of business needs.

As previously suggested, HR departments must also learn to play new roles and acquire new competencies. While doing all of this represents a substantial organizational change, it appears necessary if the HR department is to flourish.

The evidence suggests that if the HR department fails to make changes, line managers will assume total control of the HR function relegating perfunctory personnel activities such as payroll and staffing to other departments such as accounting and legal. The organization would then lose the functional expertise of the HR department. Line managers would also be faced with doing a great deal more work. Thus, the stakes involved in who owns and administers the HR function are high for the organization, the line manager, and the HR department.

Endnotes

The author is grateful for the quoted materials used and unreferenced in this paper. They were obtained by the generous cooperation of several individuals. The individuals and their companies include Bill Reffett at Grand Union; Jim Stahler at J. C. Penney; Frank Berardi at Allstate; Tom Moyers at Perdue; Art Maine at Revco; Donald Brush at Barden; Dick Parker at Merck; Jerry Goodman at Swiss Bank Corporation and Jack Berry. The author also thanks Jim Walker, Susan Jackson, Michael Mitchell, Tessa Jolls and several human resource managers, all of whom provided extensive input and commentary for this article.

[1] R. W. Galvin, "Keynote Address," *Human Resource Planning*, March 1989, 3.

[2] J. McCormick, "The Case of the Not-So-Supermarket," *Harvard Business Review*, March–April 1969, 19.

[3] S. Lawrence, "Voice of HR Experience," *Personnel Journal*, April 1989, 61–75.

[4] B. P. Foster, "Workforce Diversity and Business," *Training and Development Journal*, April, 1988, 39.

[5] Lawrence, *op. cit.*

[6] L. Copeland, "Valuing Diversity, Part 2: Pioneers and Champions of Change," *Personnel*, July, 1988, 48.

[7] Lawrence, *op. cit.*

[8] J. Nelson-Horchler, "Demographics Deliver a Warning," *Industry Week*, April 18, 1988, 58.

[9] Copeland, *op. cit.*

[10] Lawrence, *op. cit.*

[11] J. W. Walker, "Human Resource Roles for the '90s," *Human Resource Planning*, March, 1989, 55–60.

[12] "Managing Now for the 1990s," *Fortune*, September 26, 1988, 45.

[13] Lawrence.

[14] Kupfer, *op. cit.*

[15] R. S. Schuler and S. E. Jackson, "Customerizing the HR Department," *Personnel*, June, 1988, 36–44.

[16] ———, "Roundtree Report," *HR Reporter*, December 1987, 3–4.

[17] Walker, 1988, *op. cit.* These ideas and suggestions also find support in D. C. Hambrick, J. W. Frederickson, L. B. Korn and R. M. Ferry, *21st Century Report: Reinventing the CEO*, (New York: Korn/Ferry International and Columbia University School of Business, 1989).

Study Methodology

Extensive mail surveys with these and 250 other human resource managers followed up with telephone interviews were the source of the uncited quotes used in this paper. The mail survey was conducted during 1988 and the interviews were conducted during the first four months of 1989. More extensive case studies with Chad Frost at Frost Inc. and Michael Mitchell at Swiss Bank Corporation, North America were helpful in formulating many of the major ideas here. These were conducted in 1986 and 1988, respectively.

READING 2

QUALITY
American, Japanese, and Soviet Perspectives

Laura B. Forker

Executive Overview

What is quality? Although product quality is recognized as a crucial component of international competitiveness, there is still little consensus about what "quality" really is. Five distinct approaches to defining quality have been identified. The contributions of five major quality experts—from the United States, Japan, and the Soviet Union—are presented and related to the quality definition approaches.

The problems with poor product quality in the Soviet Union are discussed in particular detail to illustrate the consequences of relying on the product-based approach to defining quality and on the use of state standards as a surrogate for consumer preferences. Advantages and disadvantages of the other approaches to quality are also discussed to assist managers in clarifying their strategic focus.

The problems the Soviets face in managing product quality also illustrate some of the consequences that occur when state standards are relied on as a surrogate for consumer preferences.

Quality has become a major focus of manufacturing improvement yet there is no agreement as to what quality actually is and how best to achieve it. Production based on different understandings of quality and divergent quality goals can lead to widely varying outcomes in the performance of finished goods. Executives must have a clear conception of the quality objectives they want their employees to achieve before these goals can be articulated and translated into measurable targets. To achieve this strategic focus, they must first understand what quality is.

This article examines how quality has been characterized by scholars in different disciplines; explores the definitions proposed by five internationally recognized quality experts from the United States, Japan, and the Soviet Union; and reviews the quality management practices advocated by these five authorities.

Quality assurance and the problems with poor product quality in the Soviet Union are examined in particular detail. The Soviet Union has been largely

Source: "Quality: American, Japanese, and Soviet Perspectives" by Laura B. Forker, *Academy of Management Executive*, 1991, Vol. 5, No. 4., 63–74.

Table 1

APPROACHES TO DEFINING QUALITY

Approach	Definitional Variables	Underlying Discipline
Transcendent	Innate excellence	Philosophy
Product-based	Quantity of desired attributes	Economics
User-based	Satisfaction of consumer preferences	Economics, Marketing and Operations Management
Manufacturing-based	Conformance to requirements	Operations Management
Value-based	Affordable excellence	Operations Management

neglected in the quality literature. However, expanding commercial contacts between this country and the West, and the promise of economic and trade reform there, highlight the importance of Soviet product quality to Western trading partners. The quality of Soviet goods purchased by American firms or accepted in countertrade transactions will therefore become a critical issue to American businesses.

The problems the Soviets face in managing product quality also illustrate some of the consequences that occur when state standards are relied on as a surrogate for consumer preferences. They are not alone in their ignorance of customer satisfaction. For example, the Dacia, a Romanian car sold in Western Europe and North America, has suffered from safety problems, poor quality, and outdated technology. Canadian owners of Dacias have experienced problems such as: leaky fuel tanks; gearshifts that fell off in the driver's hand; burnt-out headlights; and batteries, starters, fan blowers, and windshield-wiper motors that failed, all within the first four months of ownership. When confronted with these problems, the Romanian distributor of the Dacia in Canada replied: ". . . North American owners don't really earn the right to drive cars because they aren't first-class mechanics."[1]

APPROACHES TO DEFINING QUALITY

Scholars from philosophy, economics, marketing, and operations management have different opinions on product quality. Garvin classified these viewpoints into five categories of quality approaches: transcendent, product-based, user-based, manufacturing-based, and value-based. These approaches are summarized in Table 1.[2]

These five perspectives highlight distinctive aspects of the quality issue. The transcendent approach points out that quality is difficult to define, yet flawless and universally identifiable. Pirsig expressed the transcendent definition of quality in *Zen and the Art of Motorcycle Maintenance* as: "Quality is neither mind nor matter, but a third entity independent of the two . . . even though Quality cannot be defined, you know what it is."[3] The product-based approach claims that quality can be precisely defined by identifying the product's desired attributes, measuring the amount of the desired characteristic in a given good or service, and then ranking them. K. B. Leffler in the *American Economic Review* gives a typical product-based definition: "Quality refers to the amounts of the unpriced attributes contained in each unit of the priced attribute."[4]

The user-based approach focuses on consumers' individual preferences (demand side) and defines a "high quality" good as that which best satisfies consumer needs or wants. The manufacturing-based approach views quality from the supply side and establishes it as "conformance to requirements," or how well a product meets its engineering design specifications. Finally, the value-based approach defines quality as a measure of excellence and worth. A quality product must conform to its specifications or perform at its intended level but also at an acceptable cost or price.

QUALITY AS DEFINED BY THE EXPERTS

How have the theoreticians writing about quality defined this concept? Do American, Japanese, and Soviet experts share a similar view of quality or do they explain it differently? How is quality assurance practiced in these three countries? A sample of opinions from five quality gurus—three Americans, one Japanese, and one Soviet—is examined in this article to provide a basis for a cross-national comparison of this significant issue.

Deming

W. Edwards Deming is generally considered to be the architect of modern manufacturing quality assurance. In particular, he is associated with the use of statistical process control in production. Deming defines quality by dividing it into three separate categories:[5]

1. *Quality of Design/Redesign.* How well a prototype—created with information from consumer research, sales analyses, and service call analyses—meets consumers' needs.

2. *Quality of Conformance.* How well a firm and its suppliers meet the design specifications required to satisfy consumers' needs.

3. *Quality of Performance.* How well the firm's products or services actually perform in the marketplace (determined through research and sales/service call analyses).

Deming's categorization of quality defines the concept according to how well a good or service meets the user's needs; those products that most successfully satisfy consumer wants are considered to have the highest quality.

Deming emphasizes the use of statistics, control charts, and a reduction of the supply base to achieve the desired quality level. The costs of quality can then be measured by determining: how well a product is designed to achieve the

good's purpose; how well the product meets the design specifications and tolerances; and how well the product performs in the hands of consumers.

Deming also has prescribed 14 steps that management should follow to
direct the company toward the quality goal:[6]

1. Continually improve products and services in order to further the firm's
   competitive position.
2. Adopt the new philosophy; don't accept delays and mistakes.
3. Don't rely on mass inspection to detect defects; use statistical controls to
   assure that quality is built into the product.
4. Discontinue the practice of selecting suppliers based on price; reduce the
   supply base and establish long-term, trusting, single-source partnerships
   where both buyer and seller can pursue quality improvements.
5. Find problems—whether caused by faulty systems or by production
   workers—and correct them.
6. Use modern methods of on-the-job training.
7. Improve and modernize methods of supervision.
8. Drive out fear, so that everyone can work productively for the firm.
9. Open up communications between departments.
10. Stop using numerical goals, posters, and slogans as a way to motivate work-
    ers without giving them the methods to achieve these goals.
11. Don't depend on work standards that assign numerical quotas.
12. Remove barriers that deprive employees of their pride of workmanship.
13. Establish a dynamic program of education and training.
14. Create an executive management structure that will emphasize the above 13
    points each day.

*Meeting and sur-
passing customer
expectations
throughout the life of
the product should be
every firm's goal.*

Deming's approach to quality assurance requires executive management to
balance the needs of employees, customers, suppliers, communities, and
investors in the long run. The customer is the final judge of a product's quality,
however. Meeting and surpassing customer expectations throughout the life of
the product should be every firm's goal.

Juran

Joseph M. Juran, a rival quality consultant and theoretician, also defines quality
from a user-based perspective as "fitness for use." In his opinion, a comprehensive meaning of quality must encompass two dimensions: satisfaction of consumer needs and wants through appropriate product features, and freedom
from defects.[7] Juran includes four considerations in his definition of quality:[8]

1. *Quality of Design.* Quality of market research, concept, and specification.
   Marketing is responsible for the quality of market research, while engineering has the primary responsibility for quality of concept and specification.

2. *Quality of Conformance.* Producing a product to meet its specifications. Quality of conformance is determined by technology, manpower, and management.

3. *Availability.* How much of the time a product is working. Availability is decided by the product's reliability (how long the product can be used before it fails), maintainability (how long it takes to restore service once a product has failed), and logistical support (how fast parts can be supplied when repairs are needed).

4. *Field Service.* Warranty and repair/replacement services of the product after it is sold. Field service effectiveness is determined by promptness (how quickly problems are corrected), competence (how well repairs are performed), and integrity (how honest and courteous service representatives are).

The first three dimensions are essentially the same as those used by Deming. However, Juran incorporates an additional feature—field service. Juran's definition of quality is therefore more complete than Deming's; it considers a firm's willingness to back its products with repair services, once a sale has been made, and considers the value of those services in evaluating quality.

Juran analyzes quality in terms of avoidable and unavoidable costs. Avoidable costs are caused by product defects and failures; these result in scrapped materials and employee efforts spent on rework, repair, and handling complaints. Unavoidable costs are brought about by quality control measures aimed at finding defective items: e.g., inspection, sampling, and sorting. Quality improvement can dramatically reduce the avoidable costs thereby boosting a company's profits.

Juran constructed a "quality trilogy" for organizing quality that is based on the managerial processes used in finance: planning, control, and improvement. Quality planning is used to develop the goods and services desired by consumers; it involves the following steps:[9]

1. Deciding who your customers are.

2. Establishing your customers' needs.

3. Designing the product features that meet consumer desires.

4. Designing the processes that will manufacture these features.

5. Operationalizing the product and process designs.

To ensure the successful implementation of the product and process designs, quality control is employed in the form of a feedback loop. This involves:[10]

1. Evaluation of production results.

2. Comparison of actual results to planned performance.

3. Action to correct the difference.

The last part of Juran's trilogy is quality improvement, where a firm aims to achieve even higher levels of quality than those already reached or planned.

Quality improvement leads to new standards for quality control and future production.

Crosby

Philip B. Crosby, another quality consultant, defines quality from an engineering or operations management viewpoint as "conformance to requirements." According to Crosby, quality can be measured exactly and products can be made error-free. A firm should then strive for "zero defects"—conformance to engineering tolerances by every product. Executive management must be committed to quality and must direct the implementation of quality throughout the firm. Specifically, management is responsible for:[11]

1. Stating its standards regarding quality. Employees must know what requirements they are expected to meet.
2. Supplying the education and tools that employees need to meet the requirements set by management. The role of the quality department also must be clarified.
3. Encouraging, assisting, and training employees to meet the stated quality requirements.

Prevention is the key to establishing quality, according to Crosby or in his words, "doing it right the first time." Managers must understand the processes that their employees work with to be able to identify trouble spots. The costs of errors detected in post-manufacturing inspection and appraisal can then be avoided.

Taguchi

In contrast to American theoreticians, Genichi Taguchi, a Japanese quality engineer, measures quality as a loss to society. Specifically, Taguchi defines quality as "the loss a product causes to society after being shipped, other than any losses caused by its intrinsic functions."[12] This loss can be caused either by variability in the product's function or by adverse side effects. A high quality product, therefore, operates in the manner it was intended to without variability and without causing harm to the consumer. Quality assurance aims at minimizing these two sources of loss that occur after the product leaves its manufacturer.

The variability of a product is determined by first establishing the ideal state, from the consumer's perspective, of each performance characteristic of the product. The ideal state is called the target value of the performance characteristic.

The specifications for the performance characteristic are presented as a numerical value for the ideal state and tolerances around that target value. The loss generated by variability is then measured as a quadratic function whose value continues to increase as the quality characteristic deviates from its ideal state.

In contrast, the typical engineering practice in America is to express the ideal value in terms of interval limits alone. Quality is measured as the percent of items that

Exhibit 1

DISTRIBUTION OF ACCEPTABLE PRODUCT QUALITY: AMERICA VERSUS JAPAN

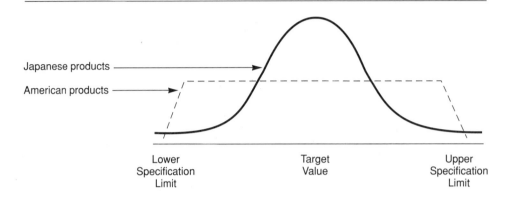

Source: Tang, Kwei, "Economic Design of Product Specifications For a Complete Inspection Plan," *International Journal of Production Research,* Vol. 26, No. 2 (1988), p. 205.

fail to conform to the predetermined product interval. Such specifications imply that a consumer has no preference among the values of the performance characteristic within the specification limits, but becomes totally unhappy as soon as the performance measurement falls outside the demarcated interval.

The divergent distributions of acceptable product quality based on American and Japanese practices are illustrated in Exhibit 1.

Taguchi determines the quality of a product by calculating the performance variation of individual characteristics from their target values during the life cycle of the product, under varying conditions. Variables that can cause a performance characteristic to deviate from its target value are controllable and uncontrollable. Controllable variables can be adjusted easily—for example, parameters of the product's and/or manufacturing process's designs. Uncontrollable variables ("noise" factors) are either impossible or else very difficult and expensive to regulate.

Noise factors can be divided into three types: outer noise, inner noise, and between-product noise. Outer noise consists of variables external to the product's design, components, and manufacturing process, which provoke deterioration in a quality characteristic's performance when the product is used by a consumer. Inner noise is brought about by the decay of a product's parts and materials, or by the degradation of capital equipment used in production, Between-product noise is harder to pinpoint but it shows up as variation among product units or processes where uniformity is supposed to prevail. Examples of controllable and uncontrollable factors are presented in Table 2.

The goal of Taguchi's quality design method is to determine those values of the controllable factors that allow the product to be least responsive to fluctuations

T a b l e   2

EXAMPLES OF UNCONTROLLABLE AND CONTROLLABLE FACTORS

Factors	Product Design	Process Design
Uncontrollable Factors:		
Outer noise	Consumer's usage conditions	Ambient temperature
	Low temperature	Humidity
	High temperature	Seasons
	Temperature change	Incoming material variation
	Shock	Operators
	Vibration	Voltage change
	Humidity	Batch-to-batch variation
Inner noise	Deterioration of parts	Machinery aging
	Deterioration of material	Tool wear
	Oxidation (rust)	Deterioration
Between-product noise	Piece-to-piece variation where they are supposed to be the same	Process-to-process variation where they are supposed to be the same
Controllable Factors:		
	All design parameters such as: dimension material configuration	All process design parameters All process setting parameters

Source: Byrne, Diane M. and Taguchi, Shin, "The Taguchi Approach to Parameter Design", *40th Annual Quality Congress Transactions,* (American Society for Quality Control, 1987), p. 2.

in the uncontrollable variables. Because noise factors are often the cause of performance variation, the removal or reduction of their impact on the product or process will improve the quality level. A high quality product will operate consistently at its target level throughout its life cycle under a variety of environmental conditions.

Taguchi's strategy emphasizes parameter design to achieve high quality without increasing cost.

Taguchi's strategy emphasizes parameter design to achieve high quality without increasing cost. Unlike tolerance design, which involves spending money on higher-grade materials, parts, or machinery, parameter design concentrates on finding those product parameter values or process factor levels that will optimize a given performance characteristic.

Design quality begins with systems design where the most appropriate technology is sought to formulate the basic outline of the product or process. For example, required reaction processes to produce a certain chemical product would be decided at this stage, as would the proper type of circuits for use in converting from alternating current to direct current, or the kinds of machines to be included in a job shop production center.

Table 3

PERCENTAGE OF TIME SPENT ON EACH OF THE THREE ELEMENTS
OF DESIGN OPTIMIZATION IN THE U.S.A. AND IN JAPAN

Design Element	U.S.A.	Japan
Systems Design	80%	40%
Parameter Design	2%	40%
Tolerance Design	18%	20%

Source: Cullem, Joe and Hollingum, Jack, *Implementing Total Quality* (IFS Publications Ltd., UK, 1987), p. 166.

Once the materials, components, and production equipment have been selected, parameter design is used to make the product or process as insensitive as possible to environmental and other noise conditions. In the examples above, means of ensuring the purity of the chemical product (e.g., by designing containers that protect materials from environmental contamination) would be formulated in parameter design. In the circuits example, the proper value for the resistance parameter that minimizes the range of variation of the output voltage would be determined. In the job shop example, the number and layout of the milling machines, drill presses, lathes, and automated guided vehicles that minimize average processing time in the shop and deal most effectively with uncertainties such as arrival rates of parts to the machining center, processing times on each machine, and the part mix to be processed would be decided.

Finally, tolerance design aims at controlling error factors and keeping them within certain tolerance limits. A specified range of acceptable deviation around the target value is calculated on the assumption that the product or process can be inspected to assure conformance to these requirements. Limits on impurities in the final chemical produced, variation in the output voltage, and deviations in total processing time in the job shop would be the tolerances set for the examples mentioned here.

American engineers concentrate on systems and tolerance designs and largely neglect parameter design. They are trained to spend money to improve product and process quality instead of attaining good quality at a low cost through alterations in the product's manufacturing design. Table 3 illustrates this difference in priorities between Japanese and American quality engineering.

L'vov

In sharp contrast to Japan, the Soviet Union has retained a persistent reputation in the West for poor quality in its manufactured goods. Almost no research into Soviet product quality has been performed in the United States. The most in-depth studies have been conducted by researchers in the United Kingdom. Since the Soviet Union is becoming a more active player in international trade, the quality of its export goods is an important concern for Western trading partners.

Table 4

SUMMARY OF VARIOUS APPROACHES TO QUALITY

Expert	Approach	Major Focus of Quality Definition
Deming	User-based	How well a good or service meets consumers' needs
Juran	User-based	Fitness for use
Crosby	Manufacturing-based	Conformance to requirements
Taguchi	Value-based	Operation of product in intended manner without variability
L'vov	Product-based	Totality of a product's properties which determine its usefulness

How do the Soviets define quality? What do they regard as a high-quality item? These questions are addressed by considering the explanation of a prominent Soviet economist, D. S. L'vov.

During the late 1960s, D. S. L'vov examined quality from philosophical, engineering, legal, economic, and social perspectives. L'vov explained one view of quality as "related to research into technical, quantifiable laws covering the formation and manifestation of physical, mechanical, chemical and other properties, of items of identical functional purpose. From this point of view, quality is commonly considered as the totality of properties of a product, which determine the possibility of its utilization in service."[13] A similar definition was offered by a Soviet state standard (GOST 15467-79) ten years after L'vov's publication: "the totality of properties of a product, determining its suitability to satisfy defined requirements in accordance with its purpose."[14] These concepts of quality, which remained consistent throughout the 1980s, are grounded in the product-based approach to quality. Table 4 summarizes the five theoreticians' approaches to quality and the major focus of each of their definitions.

PRODUCT QUALITY IN THE SOVIET UNION[15]

Engineering standards are used by western countries and the USSR to specify dimensions and establish quality characteristics for industrial and consumer commodities. The use of standardization reduces variation in individual items and assigns a minimum level of acceptable quality. Standards also help a firm reduce its costs of production and guarantee the quality of sources of supply.

In the Soviet Union, quality standards are set at the enterprise, ministerial, and national levels. Enterprise standards ("standarty predpriyatiya") can be used to forge the foundation of a purchasing contract, and to ensure the incoming quality of raw materials and other inputs. Industrial ministries may lay out branch standards ("otraslevye standarty") for factories under their authority. However, only the national standards ("gosudsrtstvennye standarty," abbreviated as "GOSTy") provide a legal basis for quality enforcement, since they carry a clause regarding noncompliance. Enterprise profits gained from selling substandard commodities can be confiscated by the state; continued production of sub-standard items can lead to the dismissal of the enterprise's director, chief engineer, and chief quality controller.[16]

National (also called "state") standards can be separated into two types: those that define the general parameters of manufactured (goods) within a generic group of items, and those that specify parameters for particular models of a product, produced at a certain plant. The first type of standards assigns appropriate testing procedures and acceptable tolerances for the class of items produced, in addition to the general parameters of the products. These standards determine the major features of manufactures (goods).

Because Soviet enterprises may only meet the minimum requirements of these state standards, and because additional design and manufacturing features may not be capable of expression in quantitative, measurable terms, the national standards may not capture all the characteristics necessary to assure that the final product *performs* well.

In a market economy, competitive pressures compel firms to produce goods at higher quality levels than those required by the minimum specifications in the national standards. But in the Soviet Union, where consumers face a sellers' market with little or no choice of alternative supply sources, these competitive pressures are essentially missing. The Soviets have attempted to remedy this problem by establishing the "mark of quality" system of state standards.

The mark of quality system is an attempt by the Soviet authorities to raise product quality standards to those found in the Western market. Any product that is judged to be at a similar or higher quality level as its counterparts manufactured in the advanced industrial nations is granted a price increase and the mark of quality stamp (Exhibit 2). Unlike the national standards, whose purpose is to reduce variation and assure some minimum quality floor, the mark of quality system aims at stimulating enterprises to produce items at the highest international quality levels. Specifications are more detailed and product-specific than the national standards (they include product parameters, manufacturing methods, and quality control procedures), and they also provide information on product style and usage. The Soviet authorities have counted on this incentive to raise the quality level of all manufactures (goods).

The State Committee of Standards ("Gosstandart") categorizes products into three levels of quality: highest, first, and second. Products in the highest category are granted the mark of quality based on their compatibility in reliability, durability, style, standardization of parts, and "economic advantage to the purchaser" to similar Western products. Products in the first category conform to the national standards but do not meet the higher requirements for the mark of quality. Second category products are those deemed obsolete, unable to meet

Exhibit 2

THE SOVIET "MARK OF QUALITY"

contemporary needs, and requiring updating or discontinuance. Second category products are being gradually eliminated.

On January 1, 1987, the Soviets launched a new program of quality control—gospriyemka—in 1500 enterprises, involving around twenty percent of industrial output.[17] About two-thirds of gospriyemka's participants were from the machine-building sector. It involves the manufacture of producer and consumer durables, and military hardware and has been targeted as crucial to the country's modernization program by Mr. Gorbachev.

The quality improvements projected for machinery were expected to accelerate production in 1988 and beyond, increase the number of new items in production, and enhance product quality. However, state inspectors from Gosstandart, who were charged with overseeing the manufacturing process and making final judgments about the output's quality, were so thorough in their inspections, that by spring 1987, as much as thirty percent of industrial output was being rejected as unacceptable.[18] Production targets, especially in the machine-building industry, could not be met because resources were diverted to rework rejected items.

In spite of the high rejection rate and new emphasis on quality, leadership speeches and reports from the Soviet press suggest that no large-scale improvement in product quality has occurred.[19] "Many plants were not able to produce equipment that met the standards because production equipment was too old to manufacture high-quality machinery; they lacked test instruments to check the quality of components and final goods; and workers were unfamiliar with the procedures needed to produce high-quality goods."[20] Gospriyemka caused laborers to lose bonus money because targets were not achieved and to put in uncompensated extra hours doing rework. Workers became so frustrated with

Although a few quality gains were achieved in machine building, gospriyemka brought mostly disappointing results: frequent disruptions, reduced output, and little overall quality improvement.

what they saw as unreasonable expectations and an unjustified loss of income, that they staged a three-day strike at a major bus factory in October 1987, and refused to return to work until a more rational approach to quality control was employed.[21] The new quality standards caused so much disruption in manufacturing operations that many were loosened at the end of 1987.

A Soviet economist estimated that thirty-five percent of the 1987 shortfall in plan fulfillment for machinery production was directly affected by gospriyemka, and another forty-five percent was due to supply shortages.[22] Because supplying firms were not always able to manufacture inputs that could pass the tougher quality control standards, gospriyemka was most likely responsible for much of the supply deficiency also. Although a few quality gains were achieved in machine building, gospriyemka brought mostly disappointing results: frequent disruptions, reduced output, and little overall quality improvement.

IMPLICATIONS FOR U.S. MANAGERS

There are several lessons to be learned, from the various approaches to quality, from the suggestions of the quality experts, from the exemplary quality engineering practices of Japan, and from the quality control failures of the Soviet Union.

The user-based approaches of Deming and Juran direct attention to the significance of satisfying consumer needs in determining the quality level of a good or service. Even if a product conforms perfectly to its specifications, it may not have much value if those specifications reflect engineering or managerial requirements rather than consumer wants. This is one shortcoming of Crosby's "zero defects" approach—his assumption that conformance to specifications by every item means that the product is of "perfect quality." There is no guarantee in this manufacturing-based approach that the specifications assigned to products truly reflect what customers desire.

The value-based approach of Taguchi points out another flaw in Crosby's manufacturing-based definition of quality. Referring back to Exhibit 1, if the measured values of a product's attributes all fall within the lower and upper specification limits, then, according to Crosby, those products have "zero defects." A product with measured attributes that are outside those tolerance limits would be rejected. But how much difference in quality is there between a product that falls just within the specification limits and a product that falls right outside them? According to Crosby, the first one is acceptable, the second one is not.

Taguchi highlights the importance of consistently meeting the target value for a quality characteristic as the goal that managers, engineers, and production workers should strive for rather than simply conforming to the tolerance intervals assigned by design engineers. Anything less than the target value is not perfect quality.

Taguchi also emphasizes the fundamental role of design quality in the final product. Even if product parts conform to specifications, and the manufacturing processes stay in statistical control during production, if the original product design did not account for environmental, manufacturing, and consumer usage stresses, the finished good may not ultimately perform well or reliably. American managers should focus far more attention on Taguchi's applications: reduction in variance (around the target value), design of products and processes that are as insensitive as possible to environmental conditions, and the design of products that are robust to component variation.

The Soviets' problems in attaining and maintaining good product quality can be traced to the lack of incentives to produce high-quality items inherent in their state-controlled production system, their reliance on the product-based approach to quality, and to their dependence on state standards to evaluate a product's quality characteristics. While American managers do not have to deal with the inefficiencies of a state-controlled industrial sector, the Soviet experience with poor quality illustrates the outcome of simply adding up an item's properties to determine its value. This is the essence of the product-based approach to quality.

In merely measuring a product's attributes and tallying the scores, no consideration is given to how those attributes interact with each other or at what cost. Adverse interaction effects can cause the final product to malfunction, even if each of its quality characteristics is established as satisfactory. And a high-quality product may be unacceptable to consumers if it has been manufactured at great expense and is sold at an excessive price.

The consumer is the ultimate judge of quality.

The consumer is the ultimate judge of quality. Striving to fulfill consumer preferences with goods and services that operate consistently at their intended level of performance at an acceptable cost or price should be all executives' and employees' goal. Any other standard cheats the customer from obtaining a truly high-quality product.

Endnotes

The author would like to thank the associate editor, the anonymous reviewers, and John N. Pearson for their helpful comments and suggestions on an earlier draft.

[1]"Romanian Dacias Are Cheap Cars in Both Senses, Some Buyers Say," *The Wall Street Journal*, March 14, 1986, A12.

[2]David A. Garvin, "What Does 'Product Quality' Really Mean?," *Sloan Management Review*, Fall 1984.

[3]R. M. Pirsig, *Zen and the Art of Motorcycle Maintenance*, (New York: Bantam Books, 1974), 185 and 213.

[4]K. B. Leffler, "Ambiguous Changes in Product Quality," *American Economic Review*, December 1982, 956.

[5]Howard S. Gitlow, and Shelly J. Gitlow, *The Deming Guide to Quality and Competitive Position*, (Prentice-Hall, Inc., 1987).

[6]*Ibid* and Karen W. Wilson, "5 Factors in the 'Quality Issue,'" *Purchasing*, November 5, 1987, 47–48.

[7]J. M. Juran, "The Quality Function," in J. M. Juran, and Frank M. Gyrna, eds.; *Juran's Quality Control Handbook*, 4th edition (McGraw-Hill Book Company, 1988), 2.2.

[8]J. M. Juran, Frank M. Gyrna, Jr., and R. S. Binghan, Jr. (eds.), *Quality Control Handbook*, 3rd ed. (McGraw-Hill Book Company, 1974), 2–9.

[9]Juran, *op. cit.*, 2.6.

[10]*Ibid.*, 2.6.

[11]Philip B. Crosby, "Management and Policy" in Walsh, Loren, Ralph Wurster, and Raymond J. Kimber; *Quality Management*

Handbook (Marcel Dekker Inc., ASQC Quality Press, 1986), 6–7; and Philip B. Crosby, *Quality Without Tears: The Art of Hassle-Free Management*, (Plume, 1984), 59–65.

[12]Taguchi, Genichi, "The Evaluation of Quality," *40th Annual Quality Congress Transactions*, (American Society for Quality Control Inc., 1987), 8.

[13]D. S. L'vov, in Akademiya nauk SSSR, Institut ekonomik; *Ekonomicheskie problemy povysheniya kachestva promyshlennoi produktsii* (Moscow: Nauka, 1969), 7–8; quoted in Malcolm R. Hill, and Richard McKay, *Soviet Product Quality* (Macmillan Press Ltd., 1988), 1.

[14]Hill and McKay, *Ibid.*, 1.

[15]Parts of this section also appear in Laura B. Forker, "Accepting Soviet Goods in Countertrade: Problems With Product Quality," *Journal of Purchasing and Materials Management*, Vol. 26, No. 2, Spring 1990.

[16]Hill and McKay, *op. cit.*, 184 and 185.

[17]CIA and DIA: "Gorbachev's Economic Program: Problems Emerge," a report by the Central Intelligence Agency and the Defense Intelligence Agency presented to the Subcommittee on National Security Economics of the Joint Economic Committee, April 13, 1988, 9.

[18]"Go, Go Back, Go Gorbachev," *The Economist*, March 25, 1989, 53.

[19]CIA and DIA, *op. cit.*, 13.

[20]Andrew J. Matosich, and Bonnie K. Matosich, "Machine Building: Perestroyka's Sputtering Engine," *Soviet Economy*, Vol. 4, No. 2, 1988, 166.

[21]*Ibid.*, 169.

[22]M. Karpunin, "Ekonomicheskiye Problemy Operezhayushchego Razvitiya Mashinostroyeniya," *Planovoye Khozyaystvo*, 1:16–23, January 1988; in Matosich and Matosich, *Ibid.*, 167.

READING 3

━━▶

MANAGING CULTURAL DIVERSITY
Implications for Organizational Competitiveness

Taylor H. Cox
Stacy Blake

Executive Overview

The recent business trends of globalization and increasing ethnic and gender diversity are turning managers' attention to the management of cultural differences. The management literature has suggested that organizations should value diversity to enhance organizational effectiveness. However, the specific link between managing diversity and organizational competitiveness is rarely made explicit and no article has reviewed actual research data supporting such a link.

This article reviews arguments and research data on how managing diversity can create a competitive advantage. We address cost, attraction of human resources, marketing success, creativity and innovation, problem-solving quality, and organizational flexibility as six dimensions of business performance directly impacted by the management of cultural diversity. We then offer suggestions for improving organizational capability to manage this diversity.

Workforce demographics for the United States and many other nations of the world indicate that managing diversity will be on the agendas of organizational leaders throughout the 90s. For example, a recent report on the workforces of 21 nations shows that nearly all of the growth in the labor force between now and 2000 will occur in nations with predominantly non-Caucasian populations. Behind these statistics are vastly different age and fertility rates for people of different racioethnic groups. In the United States for example, the average white female is 33 years old and has (or will have) 1.7 children. Corresponding figures for blacks are 28 and 2.4, and for Mexican-Americans, 26 and 2.9.[1]

Leading consultants, academics and business leaders have advocated that organizations respond to these trends with a "valuing diversity" approach. They

Source: "Managing Cultural Diversity: Implications for Organizational Competitiveness" by Taylor H. Cox and Stacy Blake, *Academy of Management Executive*, 1991, Vol. 5, No. 3., 45–54.

Exhibit 1

SPHERES OF ACTIVITY IN THE MANAGEMENT OF CULTURAL DIVERSITY

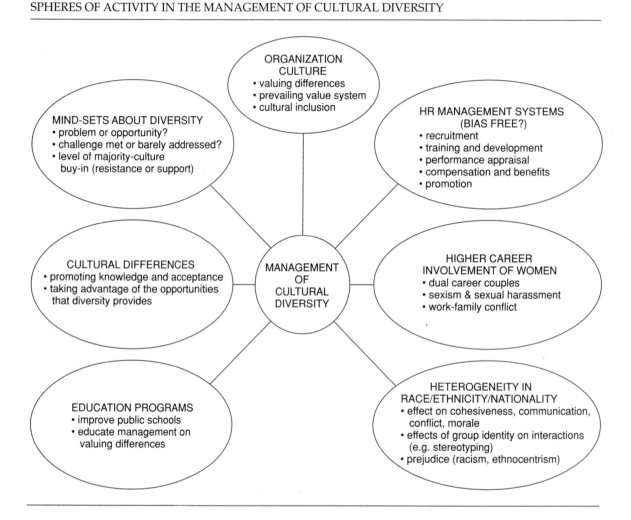

point out that a well managed, diverse workforce holds potential competitive advantages for organizations.[2] However, the logic of the valuing diversity argument is rarely made explicit, and we are aware of no article that reviews actual data supporting the linkage of managing diversity and organizational competitiveness. This article reviews the arguments and research data on this link, and offers suggestions on improving organizational capability for managing cultural diversity. As shown in Exhibit 1, the term *managing diversity* refers to a variety of management issues and activities related to hiring and effective utilization of personnel from different cultural backgrounds.

Exhibit 2

MANAGING CULTURAL DIVERSITY CAN PROVIDE COMPETITIVE ADVANTAGE

1. Cost Argument	As organizations become more diverse, the cost of a poor job in integrating workers will increase. Those who handle this well will thus create cost advantages over those who don't.
2. Resource-Acquisition Argument	Companies develop reputations on favorability as prospective employers for women and ethnic minorities. Those with the best reputations for managing diversity will win the competition for the best personnel. As the labor pool shrinks and changes composition, this edge will become increasingly important.
3. Marketing Argument	For multi-national organizations, the insight and cultural sensitivity that members with roots in other countries bring to the marketing effort should improve these efforts in important ways. The same rationale applies to marketing to subpopulations within domestic operations.
4. Creativity Argument	Diversity of perspectives and less emphasis on conformity to norms of the past (which characterize the modern approach to management of diversity) should improve the level of creativity.
5. Problem-solving Argument	Heterogeneity in decision and problem solving groups potentially produces better decisions through a wider range of perspectives and more thorough critical analysis of issues.
6. System Flexibility Argument	An implication of the multicultural model for managing diversity is that the system will become less determinant, less standardized, and therefore more fluid. The increased fluidity should create greater flexibility to react to environmental changes (i.e., reactions should be faster and at less cost).

DIVERSITY AS A COMPETITIVE ADVANTAGE

Social responsibility goals of organizations is only one area that benefits from the management of diversity. We will focus on six other areas where sound management can create a competitive advantage: (1) cost, (2) resource acquisition, (3) marketing, (4) creativity, (5) problem-solving, (6) organizational flexibility.[3] Exhibit 2 briefly explains their relationship to diversity management.

The first two items of the exhibit, the cost and resource acquisition arguments, are what we call the "inevitability-of-diversity" issues. Competitiveness is affected by the *need* (because of national and cross-national workforce demographic trends) to hire more women, minorities, and foreign nationals. The marketing, creativity, problem-solving, and system flexibility argument, are derived from what we call the "value-in-diversity hypothesis"—that diversity brings net-added value to organization processes.

Cost

Organizations have not been as successful in managing women and racioethnic minorities (racially and/or ethnically different from the white/Anglo majority)

Organizations have not been as successful in managing women and racioethnic minorities (racially and/or ethnically different from the white/Anglo majority) as white males.

as white males. Data show that turnover and absenteeism are often higher among women and racioethnic minorities than for white males. For example, one study reported that the overall turnover rate for blacks in the United States workforce is forty percent higher than for whites. Also, Corning Glass recently reported that between 1980-87, turnover among women in professional jobs was double that of men, and the rates for blacks were 2.5 times those of whites. A two-to-one ratio for women/men turnover was also cited by Felice Schwartz in her article on multiple career tracks for women in management.[4]

Job satisfaction levels are also often lower for minorities. A recent study that measured job satisfaction among black and white MBAs revealed that blacks were significantly less satisfied with their overall careers and advancement than whites.[5]

Frustration over career growth and cultural conflict with the dominant, white-male culture may be the major factor behind the different satisfaction levels. Two recent surveys of male and female managers in large American companies found that although women expressed a much higher probability of leaving their current employer than men, and had higher actual turnover rates, their primary reasons for quitting were lack of career growth opportunity or dissatisfaction with rates of progress. One of the surveys also discovered that women have higher actual turnover rates at all ages, and not just during the child-bearing and child-rearing years.[6]

Organizations' failure to manage women and racioethnic minorities as successfully as white males translates into unnecessary costs. Since eighty-five percent of net additions to the workforce during the decade of the 90s are expected to be women and racioethnic minorities, these costs will escalate in the coming years.

Organizations that fail to make appropriate changes to more successfully use and keep employees from different backgrounds can expect to suffer a significant competitive disadvantage compared to those that do. Alternatively, organizations quick to create an environment where all personnel can thrive should gain a competitive cost advantage over nonresponsive or slowly responding companies.

Cost implications in managing diversity also occur in benefits and work schedules. In one study, companies were assigned an "accommodation score" based on the adoption of four benefit-liberalization changes associated with pregnant workers. Analysis revealed that the higher a company's accommodation score, the lower the number of sick days taken by pregnant workers and the more willing they were to work overtime during pregnancy.[7]

Two other studies investigated the effect of company investment in day care on human resource cost variables. In one study, turnover and absenteeism rates for working mothers using a company-sponsored child development center were compared to those who either had no children or had no company assistance. Absenteeism for the day-care users versus the other groups was thirty-eight percent lower and the turnover rate was less than two percent compared to more than six percent for the nonbenefit groups. The second study showed that in a company that initiated an in-house child care facility, worker attitudes improved on six measures including organizational commitment and job satisfaction. In addition, turnover declined by sixty-three percent.[8]

Greater use of flextime work scheduling is another type of organizational accommodation to diversity. A recent field experiment assessing the impact of flextime use on absenteeism and worker performance found that both short- and long-term absence declined significantly. Three out of four worker efficiency measures also increased significantly.[9]

Cost savings of organizational changes must be judged against the investment. Nevertheless, the data strongly suggests that managing diversity efforts have reduced absenteeism and turnover costs, as cited earlier.

Research evidence relevant to cost implications of managing diversity on some dimensions other than benefit and work-schedule changes comes from a UCLA study of the productivity of culturally heterogeneous and culturally homogeneous work teams. Among the heterogeneous teams, some were more and some were less productive than the homogeneous teams.[10] This research suggests that if work teams "manage" the diversity well, they can make diversity an asset to performance. For example, all members should have ample opportunity to contribute and potential communications, group cohesiveness, and interpersonal conflict issues need to be successfully addressed. Alternatively, if diversity is ignored or mishandled, it may detract from performance.

Actual cost savings from improving the management of diversity are difficult to determine. It is, however, possible to estimate those related to turnover. For example, let us assume an organization has 10,000 employees in which 35 percent of personnel are either women or racioethnic minorities. Let us also assume a white male turnover rate of ten percent. Using the previous data on differential turnover rates for women and racioethnic minorities of roughly double the rate for white males, we can estimate a loss of 350 additional employees from the former groups. If we further assume that half of the turnover rate difference can be eliminated with better management, and that total turnover cost averages $20,000 per employee, the potential annual cost savings is $3.5 million. This example only addresses turnover, and additional savings may be realized from other changes such as higher productivity levels.

Although accurate dollar cost savings figures from managing diversity initiatives of specific companies are rarely published, Ortho Pharmaceuticals has calculated its savings to date at $500,000, mainly from lower turnover among women and ethnic minorities.[11]

A recent field experiment assessing the impact of flextime use on absenteeism and worker performance found that both short- and long-time absence declined significantly.

Although accurate dollar cost savings figures from managing diversity initiatives of specific companies are rarely published, Ortho Pharmaceuticals has calculated its savings to date at $500,000, mainly from lower turnover among women and ethnic minorities.

Resource Acquisition

Attracting and retaining excellent employees from different demographic groups is the second "inevitability"-related competitiveness issue. As women and racioethnic minorities increase in proportional representation in the labor pool, organizations must compete to hire and retain workers from these groups. Recently published accounts of the "best companies" for women and for blacks have made public and highlighted organizations which are leaders in organizational change efforts to effectively manage diversity.[12] In addition to listing the best companies, the publications also discuss why certain companies were excluded from the list.

The impact of these publications on recruitment of quality personnel has already begun to surface. Merck, Xerox, Syntex, Hoffman-La Roche, and Hewlett-Packard have been aggressively using favorable publicity to recruit women and racioethnic minorities. According to company representatives, the recognitions are, in fact, boosting recruiting efforts. For example, Merck cites its identification as one of the ten best companies for working mothers as instrumental in recent increases in applications.[13]

As these reputations grow, and the supply of white males in the labor market shrinks, the significance of the resource acquisition issue for organizational competitiveness will be magnified.

Marketing

Just as people, especially women and racioethnic minorities, may prefer to work for an employer who values diversity, they may also prefer to buy from such organizations.

Markets are becoming as diverse as the workforce. Selling goods and services is facilitated by a representational workforce in several ways. First, companies with good reputations have correspondingly favorable public relations. Just as people, especially women and racioethnic minorities, may prefer to work for an employer who values diversity, they may also prefer to buy from such organizations.

Second, there is evidence that culture has a significant effect on consumer behavior. For example, in the Chinese culture, values such as a tradition of thrift, and teenagers' deference to their parent's wishes in making purchases, have been identified as affecting consumer behavior.[14] While much of the research on cross-cultural differences in consumer behavior has focused on cross-national comparisons, this research is also relevant to intra-country ethnic group differences.

Immigration from Latin America and Asia will continue to be high in the 90s. This represents a large influx of first-generation Americans having strong ties to their root cultures. Acculturation patterns among Asian and Hispanic Americans indicates that substantial identity with the root cultures remain even after three or more generations of United States citizenship. This implies that firms may gain competitive advantage by using employee insight to understand culture effects on buying decisions and map strategies to respond to them.

USA Today provides a good example. Nancy Woodhull, president of Gannett News Media, maintains that the newspaper's marketing success is largely attributable to the presence of people from a wide variety of cultural backgrounds in daily news meetings. Group diversity was planned and led to a representation of different viewpoints because people of different genders and racioethnic backgrounds have different experiences shaped by group identities.

Avon Corporation used cultural diversity to turn around low profitability in its inner-city markets. Avon made personnel changes to give Black and

Hispanic managers substantial authority over these markets. These formerly unprofitable sectors improved to the point where they are now among Avon's most productive U.S. markets. Avon President Jim Preston commented that members of a given cultural group are uniquely qualified to understand certain aspects of the world view of persons from that group.

In some cases, people from a minority culture are more likely to give patronage to a representative of their own group. For at least some products and services, a multicultural salesforce may facilitate sales to members of minority culture groups.

Cultural diversification of markets is not limited to U.S. companies. Globalization is forcing major companies from many nations to address cultural difference effects among consumers. The fact that the U.S. contains one of the most culturally heterogeneous populations in the world represents a possible advantage in "national" competitiveness. Just having diversity, however, is not sufficient to produce benefits. We must also manage it.

Creativity

Advocates of the value-in diversity hypothesis suggest that work team heterogeneity promotes creativity and innovation (see endnote 1). Research tends to support this relationship. Kanter's study of innovation in organizations revealed that the most innovative companies deliberately establish heterogeneous teams to "create a marketplace of ideas, recognizing that a multiplicity of points of view need to be brought to bear on a problem" (p. 167). Kanter also specifically noted that companies high on innovation had done a better job than most on eradicating racism, sexism, and classism and, tended to employ more women and racioethnic minorities than less innovative companies.[15]

Research by Charlene Nemeth found that minority views can stimulate consideration of non-obvious alternatives in task groups. In a series of experiments, participants were asked to form as many words as possible from a string of 10 letters. Individual approaches to the task were determined and then groups formed that were either majority (all members subscribed to the strategy for forming letters advocated by the majority of participants) and minority (non-majority individuals were present in the groups). Nemeth found that the "minority" groups adopted multiple strategies and identified more solutions than the "majority" groups. She concluded that the groups exposed to minority views were more creative than the more homogeneous, majority groups. She further concluded that persistent exposure to minority viewpoints stimulates creative thought processes.

Another experiment compared the creativity of teams that were homogeneous on a series of attitude measures against teams with heterogeneous attitudes. Problem solution creativity was judged on originality and practicality. Results indicated that as long as the team members had similar ability levels, the heterogeneous teams were more creative than the homogeneous ones.[16] If people from different gender, nationality, and racioethnic groups hold different

If people from different gender, nationality, and racioethnic groups hold different attitudes and perspectives on issues, then cultural diversity should increase team creativity and innovation.

attitudes and perspectives on issues, then cultural diversity should increase team creativity and innovation.

> *Attitudes, cognitive functioning, and beliefs are not randomly distributed in the population but tend to vary systematically with demographic variables such as age, race, and gender.[17] Thus, an expected consequence of increased cultural diversity in organizations is the presence of different perspectives for problem solving, decision making and creative tasks.*

Specific steps must be taken however, to realize this benefit. The research shows that in order to obtain the performance benefits, it was necessary for heterogeneous team members to have awareness of the attitudinal differences of other members. Similarly, diversity needs to be managed in part, by informing workgroup members of their cultural differences. In recognition of this, cultural awareness training has become a standard element of organization change projects focusing on managing diversity.

Problem Solving

Diverse groups have a broader and richer base of experience from which to approach a problem. Thus, managing diversity also has the potential to improve problem solving and decision making.

In the 1960s, several University of Michigan studies discovered that heterogeneous groups produced better quality solutions to assigned problems than homogeneous groups. Dimensions of group diversity included personality measures and gender. In one study, sixty-five percent of heterogeneous groups produced high quality solutions (solutions that provided either new, modified, or integrative approaches to the problem) compared to only twenty-one percent of the homogeneous groups. This difference was statistically significant. The researchers noted that "mixing sexes and personalities appears to have freed these groups from the restraints of the solutions given in the problem."[18]

Later studies also confirmed the effects of heterogeneity on group decision quality. The same conclusion is indirectly indicated by research on the "groupthink" phenomenon—the absence of critical thinking in groups caused partly by excessive preoccupation with maintaining cohesiveness. Most of the examples of groupthink cited in the literature, such as the decision of the Kennedy administration to invade Cuba in 1961, portray decision processes as producing disastrous results. Because group cohesiveness is directly related to degrees of homogeneity, and groupthink only occurs in highly cohesive groups, the presence of cultural diversity in groups should reduce its probability.[19]

Decision quality is best when neither excessive diversity nor excessive homogeneity are present.

Decision quality is best when neither excessive diversity nor excessive homogeneity are present. This point has been well summarized by Sheppard: "Similarity is an aid to developing cohesion; cohesion in turn, is related to the success of a group. Homogeneity, however, can be detrimental if it results in the absence of stimulation. If all members are alike, they may have little to talk about, they may compete with each other, or they may all commit the same mistake. Variety is the spice of life in a group, so long as there is a basic core of similarity."[20]

A core of similarity among group members is desirable. This theme is similar to the "core value" concept advocated in the organization culture literature.[21] Our interpretation is that all members must share some common values and norms to promote coherent actions on organizational goals. The need for heterogeneity, to promote problem solving and innovation, must be balanced with the need for organizational coherence and unity of action.

Additional support for the superior problem solving of diverse workgroups comes from the work of Nemeth cited earlier. In a series of studies, she found that the level of critical analysis of decision issues and alternatives was higher in groups subjected to minority views than in those which were not. The presence of minority views improved the quality of the decision process regardless of whether or not the minority view ultimately prevailed. A larger number of alternatives were considered and there was a more thorough examination of assumptions and implications of alternative scenarios.[22]

The presence of minority views improved the quality of the decision process regardless of whether or not the minority view ultimately prevailed.

In sum, culturally diverse workforces create competitive advantage through better decisions. A variety of perspectives brought to the issue, higher levels of critical analysis of alternatives through minority-influence effects, and lower probability of groupthink all contribute.

System Flexibility

Managing diversity enhances organizational flexibility. There are two primary bases for this assertion. First, there is some evidence that women and racioethnic minorities tend to have especially flexible cognitive structures. For example, research has shown that women tend to have a higher tolerance for ambiguity than men. Tolerance for ambiguity, in turn, has been linked to a number of factors related to flexibility such as cognitive complexity, and the ability to excel in performing ambiguous tasks.[23]

Studies on bilingual versus monolingual sub-populations from several nations show that compared to monolinguals, bilinguals have higher levels of divergent thinking and cognitive flexibility.[24] Since the incidence of bilingualism is much greater among minority culture groups (especially Hispanics and Asians) than the majority-white Anglo group, this research strongly supports the notion that cognitive flexibility is enhanced by the inclusion of these groups in predominantly Anglo workforces.

The second way that managing cultural diversity may enhance organizational flexibility is that as policies and procedures are broadened and operating methods become less standardized, the organization becomes more fluid and adaptable. The tolerance for different cultural viewpoints should lead to greater openness to new ideas in general. Most important of all, if organizations are successful in overcoming resistance to change in the difficult area of accepting diversity, it should be well positioned to handle resistance to other types of change.

SUGGESTIONS FOR ORGANIZATION CHANGE

We have reviewed six ways in which the presence of cultural diversity and its effective management can yield a competitive advantage. Organizations wishing to maximize the benefits and minimize the drawbacks of diversity, in terms of workgroup cohesiveness, interpersonal conflict, turnover, and coherent action on major organizational goals, must create "multicultural" organizations. The typical organization of the past has been either monolithic (homogeneous membership with a culture dominated by one cultural group) or plural (ostensively diverse membership but still culturally monolithic and without valuing and using differences to benefit the organization). By contrast, the multicultural organization is one where members of nontraditional backgrounds can contribute and achieve to their fullest potential.

The multicultural organization's specific features are as follows: (1) Pluralism: reciprocal acculturation where all cultural groups respect, value, and learn from one another; (2) full structural integration of all cultural groups so that they are well represented at all levels of the organization; (3) full integration of minority culture-group members in the informal networks of the organization; (4) an absence of prejudice and discrimination; (5) equal identification of minority- and majority-group members with the goals of the organization, and with opportunity for alignment of organizational and personal career goal achievement; (6) a minimum of inter-group conflict which is based on race, gender, nationality, and other identity groups of organization members.[25]

Five key components are needed to transform traditional organizations into multicultural ones.

1. Leadership
2. Training
3. Research
4. Analysis and change of culture and human resource management systems
5. Follow up

Each of these are briefly discussed.

Leadership

Top management's support and genuine commitment to cultural diversity is crucial. Champions for diversity are needed—people who will take strong personal stands on the need for change, role model the behaviors required for change, and assist with the work of moving the organization forward. Commitment must go beyond sloganism. For example, are human, financial, and technical resources being provided? Is this item prominently featured in the corporate strategy and consistently made a part of senior level staff meetings? Is there a willingness to change human resource management systems such as performance appraisal and executive bonuses? Is there a willingness to keep mental energy and financial support focused on this for a period of years, not months or weeks? If the answer to all of these questions is yes, the organization has genuine commitment, if not, then a potential problem with leadership is indicated.

Top management commitment is crucial but not sufficient. Champions are also needed at lower organizational levels, especially key line managers. Many organizations are addressing the leadership requirement by the formation of task forces or advisory committees on diversity, often headed by a senior manager. Some companies also have a designated manager for diversity who oversees the work company-wide (examples include Corning Inc. and Allstate Insurance). We advise using the manager of diversity in addition to, rather than as a substitute for, a broader involvement team such as a diversity task force. This is especially important in the early stages of the work.

Training

Managing and valuing diversity (MVD) training is the most prevalent starting point for managing diversity. Two types of training are popular: awareness training and skill-building training. Awareness training focuses on creating an understanding of the need for, and meaning of managing and valuing diversity. It is also meant to increase participants' self awareness on diversity related issues such as stereotyping and cross-cultural insensitivity. Skill-building training educates employees on specific cultural differences and how to respond to differences in the workplace. Often the two types are combined. Avon, Ortho Pharmaceuticals, Procter and Gamble, and Hewlett-Packard are examples of companies with extensive experience with training programs.

Training is a crucial first step. However, it has limitations as an organization change tool and should not be used in isolation. It is also important to treat training as an on-going education process rather than a one-shot seminar.

Research

Collection of information about diversity related-issues is the third key component. Many types of data are needed including traditional equal-opportunity profile data, analysis of attitudes and perceptions of employees, and data which highlights the career experiences of different cultural groups (e.g., are mentors equally accessible to all members).

Research has several important uses. First, it is often helpful for identifying issues to be addressed in the education process. For example, data indicating differences of opinion about the value in diversity based on culture group can be used as a launching point for mixed-culture discussion groups in training sessions. Second, research helps identify areas where changes are needed and provides clues about how to make them. Third, research is necessary to evaluate the change effort. Baseline data on key indicators of the valuing diversity environment needs to be gathered and periodically updated to assess progress.

Culture and Management Systems Audit

A comprehensive analysis of the organization culture and human resource systems such as recruitment, performance appraisal, potential assessment and promotion, and compensation should be undertaken. The primary objectives of this audit are: (1) to uncover sources of potential bias unfavorable to members of certain cultural groups, and (2) to identify ways that corporate culture may inadvertently put some members at a disadvantage.

It is important to look beyond surface data in auditing systems. For example, research that we reviewed or conducted indicates that even when average performance ratings for majority versus minority culture members are essentially the same, there may be differences in the relative priority placed on individual performance criteria, the distribution of the highest ratings, or the relationship between performance ratings and promotion.[26] The audit must be an in-depth analysis, and the assistance of an external cultural diversity expert is strongly advised.

To identify ways that corporate culture may put some members at a disadvantage, consider a scenario where a prominent value in the organization culture is "aggressiveness." Such a value may place certain groups at a disadvantage if the norms of their secondary or alternative culture discouraged this behavior. This is indeed the case for many Asians and for women in many countries including the United States. While it is conceivable that the preservation of this value may be central to organizational effectiveness (in which case the solution may be to acknowledge the differential burden of conformity that some members must bear and to give assistance to them in learning the required behaviors), it may also be that the organizational values need to change so that other styles of accomplishing work are acceptable and perhaps even preferred. The point is that the prevailing values and norms must be identified and then examined critically in light of the diversity of the workforce.

The results of the audit must be translated into an agenda for specific changes in the organization culture and systems which management must then work to implement.

The results of the audit must be translated into an agenda for specific changes in the organization culture and systems which management must then work to implement.

Follow-up

The final component, follow-up, consists of monitoring change, evaluating the results, and ultimately institutionalizing the changes as part of the organization's regular on-going processes. Like other management efforts, there is a need for accountability and control for work on diversity. Accountability for overseeing the change process might initially be assigned to the diversity task force, or if available, manager of diversity. Ultimately, however, accountability for preserving the changes must be established with every manager. Changes in the performance appraisal and reward processes are often needed to accomplish this.

Follow-up activities should include additional training, repetition of the systems audit, and use of focus groups for on-going discussions about diversity issues.[27]

CONCLUSION

Organizations' ability to attract, retain, and motivate people from diverse cultural backgrounds, may lead to competitive advantages in cost structures and through maintaining the highest quality human resources. Further capitalizing on the potential benefits of cultural diversity in work groups, organizations may gain a competitive advantage in creativity, problem solving, and flexible adaptation to change. We have identified steps that organizations can take toward accomplishing this.

While this article has reviewed a significant amount of relevant research, additional work clearly needs to be done, especially on the "value-in-diversity" issues. Nevertheless, the arguments, data, and suggestions presented here should be useful to organizations to build commitment and promote action for managing diversity efforts in the 1990s and beyond.

Endnotes

[1]See William B. Johnston, Global Work Force 2000, *Harvard Business Review,* March-April, 1991 and "Middle-age at 26," *The Wall Street Journal,* April 10, 1990.

[2]For examples of the competitive advantage argument, see R. Roosevelt Thomas Jr., "From Affirmative Action to Affirming Diversity," *Harvard Business Review,* 2, March/April 1990, 107–117; Lennie Copeland, "Learning to Manage a Multicultural Workforce," *Training,* May 1988, 48–56; Barbara Mandrell and Susan Kohler-Gray, "Management Development that Values Diversity," *Personnel,* 67, March 1990, 41–47; Katherine Etsy, "Diversity is Good for Business," *Executive Excellence,* 5, 1988, 5–6; and A. G. Sodano and S. G. Baler, "Accommodation to Contrast: Being Different in the Organization," *New Directions in Mental Health,* 20, 1983, 25–36.

[3]This focus is not intended to undermine the importance of social, moral, and legal reasons for attention to diversity. We have chosen to address its relevance for other types of goals, such as worker productivity and quality of decision making, because the impact of diversity in these areas has received relatively little attention in the past compared to the equal-opportunity related goals.

[4]See the following sources for details on the turnover data: B. R. Bergmann and W. R. Krause, "Evaluating and Forecasting Progress in Racial Integration of Employment," *Industrial and Labor Relations Review,* 1968, 399–409; Carol Hymowitz, "One Firm's Bid to Keep Blacks, Women," *The Wall Street Journal,* February 16, 1989, Sec. B. 1; Felice Schwartz, "Management Women and the New Facts of Life," *Harvard Business Review,* January/February 1989, 65–76.

[5]Taylor Cox, Jr. and Stella Nkomo, "A Race and Gender Group Analysis of the Early Career Experience of MBA's," *Work and Occupations,* forthcoming in 1991.

[6]These surveys were reviewed by Cathy Trost, "Women Managers Quit not for Family but to Advance their Corporate Climb," *The Wall Street Journal,* May 2, 1990. For additional evidence on this point, including discussions of the cultural-conflict issue, see Schwartz, Endnote 3; A. M. Morrison, R. P. White and E. Van Velsor, "Executive Women: Substance Plus Style," *Psychology Today,* August 1987, 18–25; and Gail DeGeorge, "Corporate Women: They're about to Break Through to the Top," *Business Week,* June 22, 1987, 72–77.

[7]"Helping Pregnant Workers Pays Off," *USA Today,* December 2, 1987.

[8]Stewart A. Youngblood and Kimberly Chambers-Cook, "Child Care Assistance

Can Improve Employee Attitudes and Behavior," *Personnel Administrator,* February 1984, 93–95+.

[9]Jay S. Kim and Anthony F. Campagna, "Effects of Flextime on Employee Attendance and Performance: A Field Experiment," *Academy of Management Journal,* December 14, 1981, 729–741.

[10]Reported in Nancy Adler, *International Dimensions of Organizational Behavior* (Boston: Kent Publishing Co., 1986), 111.

[11]The figure of $20,000 is based on computations of Michael Mercer for turnover costs of a computer programmer. Readers may wish to consult one of the following sources for turnover cost formulas and then use their own job structure to determine cost factors for the actual turnover costs: Michael Mercer, "Turnover: Reducing the Costs," *Personnel,* Vol. 5, 1988, 36–42; Rene Darmon, "Identifying Sources of Turnover Costs," *Journal of Marketing,* 1990, Vol. 54, 46–56. The data on Ortho is provided in Juliane Bailey, "How to be Different but Equal," *Savvy Woman,* November, 1989, 47+.

[12]Examples of these publications include Baila Zeitz and Lorraine Dusky, *Best Companies for Women* (New York: Simon and Schuster, 1988); and "The 50 Best Places for Blacks to Work," *Black Enterprise,* February 1989, 73–91.

[13]Selwyn Feinstein, "Being the Best on Somebody's List Does Attract Talent," *The Wall Street Journal,* October 10, 1989. For other examples supporting the resource acquisition argument, see Joel Dreyfuss, "Get Ready for the New Work Force," *Fortune,* April 23, 1990, 165–181.

[14]S. G. Redding, "Cultural Effects on the Marketing Process in Southeast Asia," *Journal of Market Research Society,* Vol. 24, 19, 98–114.

[15]Rosabeth Moss-Kanter, *The Change Masters,* (New York: Simon and Schuster, 1983).

[16]For details on the research in this section, readers should see: Charlan Jeanne Nemeth, "Differential Contributions of Majority and Minority Influence," *Psychological Review,* 93, 1986, 23–32 and H. C. Triandis, E. R. Hall, and R. B. Ewen, "Member Homogeneity and Dyadic Creativity," *Human Relations,* 18, 1965, 33–54.

[17]Susan E. Jackson, "Team Composition in Organizational Settings: Issues in Managing a Diverse Workforce," in *Group Process & Productivity,* J. Simpson, S. Warchel and W. Wood (eds), Beverly Hills, CA: Sage Publications, 1989.

[18]L. Richard Hoffman and Norman R. F. Maier, "Quality and Acceptance of Problem Solving by Members of Homogeneous and Heterogeneous Groups," *Journal of Abnormal and Social Psychology,* 62, 1961, 401–407. The quote in the text is from page 404.

[19]For reviews of research on the effect of group heterogeneity on problem solving, see M. E. Shaw, *Group Dynamics: The Psychology of Small Group Behavior,* (New York: McGraw Hill, 1981); J. E. McGrath, *Groups: Interaction and Performance,* (Englewood Cliffs, N.J.: Prentice Hall, 1984); and Irving Janis, *Victims of Groupthink,* (Boston: Houghton Mifflin Co., 1972).

[20]C. R. Shepard, *Small Groups,* (San Francisco: Chandler Publishing Co., 1964), 118.

[21]See Ed Schein, "Organizational Socialization and the Profession of Management," in D. A. Kolb, I. M. Rubin, and J. M. McIntyre (Eds.), *Organizational Psychology,* Englewood Cliffs: Prentice-Hall, 1984, 7–21; and Y. Weiner, "Forms of Value Systems: A Focus on Organizational Effectiveness and Cultural Change and Maintenance," *Academy of Management Review,* 13, 1988, 534–545.

[22]See Charlan Jeanne Nemeth, "Dissent, Group Process, and Creativity," *Advances in Group Processes,* 2, 1985, 57–75; and Charlan Jeanne Nemeth and Joel Wachter, "Creative Problem Solving as a Result of Majority versus Minority Influence," *European Journal of Social Psychology,* 13, 1983, 45–55.

[23]See Naomi G. Rotter and Agnes N. O'Connell, "The Relationships Among Sex-Role Orientation, Cognitive Complexity, and Tolerance for Ambiguity," *Sex Roles*, 8(12), 1982, 1209–1220; and David R. Shaffer et al., "Interactive Effects of Ambiguity Tolerance and Task Effort on Dissonance Reduction," *Journal of Personality*, 41(2), June, 1973, 224–233.

[24]These research studies are reviewed by Wallace Lambert, "The Effects of Bilingualism on the Individual: Cognitive and Sociocultural Consequences," in Peter A. Hurnbey (Ed.), *Bilingualism: Psychological, Social, and Educational Implications*, New York: Academic Press, 1977, 15–27.

[25]This discussion of traditional versus multicultural organizations is based on Taylor Cox's article, "The Multicultural Organization," which appeared in the May, 1991 issue of *The Executive*.

[26]For a specific example of race differences in priorities of performance rating criteria, see Taylor Cox and Stella Nkomo, "Differential Performance Appraisal Criteria," *Group and Organization Studies*, 11, 1986, 101–119. For an example of subtle bias in performance rating distributions see Asya Pazy's article: "The Persistence of Pro-Male Bias," *Organization Behavior and Human Decision Processes*, 38, 1986, 366–377.

[27]For additional discussion of organization change processes to manage diversity including specific examples of what pioneering companies are doing in this area, please see Taylor Cox's article "The Multicultural Organization" (endnote 24).

PART I

MANAGING THE INTERNAL AND EXTERNAL ENVIRONMENTS

STRATEGIC HUMAN RESOURCE MANAGEMENT

INTRODUCTION

One key to gaining competitive advantage through human resource management is through linking HRM to the strategic management process. This entails recognizing the organization's human resources (people) issues in the strategy formulation process, developing human resource management programs that aid in implementing the chosen strategy, and evaluating these programs to ensure that they are effective. This set of readings focuses on issues related to the strategic management of human resources.

Reading 4 by Schuler notes that human resource management activities can be the unifying force in helping an organization master strategic change. However, this requires defining the "people related business issues" of the organization and developing activities that effectively manage those issues. The author proposes the "5-P" model of strategic human resources management, which argues the Philosophy, Policies, Programs, Practices, and Processes of HR must be systematically linked to the strategic needs of the business. He then shows how this framework has been applied to a large retail grocery store to gain competitive advantage.

In addition, many HR departments are beginning to recognize the value of a Total Quality Management approach to their own functioning. Reading 5 by Bowen and Lawler discuss how "quality experts" in HRM are pushing companies to make basic changes in recruiting, training, performance appraisals, and merit-pay systems. They show how a total quality approach to HRM requires (1) a focus on the organization, rather than the job (2) support for group performance, (3) egalitarianism as opposed to hierarchy, (4) change as opposed to stability, and (5) participation as opposed to command and control.

READING 4

STRATEGIC HUMAN RESOURCES MANAGEMENT
Linking the People with the Strategic Needs of the Business

Randall S. Schuler

Human resources activities can be the unifying force in helping an organization master strategic change. Here is a model for forging the links between business needs and HR practices.

There really shouldn't be any mystery about the word *strategic* in the phrase *strategic human resources management.*

According to Horace Parker, director of strategic education at the Forest Products Company, a 17,000-person division of Weyerhaeuser in Seattle, Washington, strategic human resources management is about "getting the strategy of the business implemented effectively." For Bill Reffett, senior vice president of personnel at the Grand Union, a 20,000-person supermarket operation on the East Coast, strategic human resources management means "getting everybody from the top of the human organization to the bottom doing things that make the business successful."

The viewpoints of the academics, although stated in slightly different terms, echo the same themes. A composite definition from this source might include the following: Strategic human resources management is largely about integration and adaptation. Its concern is to ensure that: (1) human resources (HR) management is fully integrated with the strategy and the strategic needs of the firm; (2) HR policies cohere both across policy areas and across hierarchies; and (3) HR practices are adjusted, accepted, and used by line managers and employees as part of their everyday work.

Together, these viewpoints suggest that strategic HR management has many different components, including policies, culture, values, and practices.

Source: "Strategic Human Resources Management: Linking the People with the Strategic Needs of the Business" by Randall S. Schuler. Reprinted by permission of publisher from *Organizational Dynamics*, SUM92 © 1992. American Management Association, New York. All rights reserved.

The various statements also imply what strategic human resources management *does*, i.e., it links, it integrates, and it coheres across levels in organizations. Implicitly or explicitly, its purpose is to more effectively utilize human resources *vis-a-vis the strategic needs of the organization.*

While all of this helps us identify the general purview of the subject, it does not provide a framework for melding together the separate components as defined by the practitioners and academics. The purpose of this article is to provide a model for just such an integration, forming a basis for further research as well as more effective practice.

THE 5-P MODEL

The 5-P Model of strategic human resources management, shown in Exhibit 1, melds various HR activities with strategic needs. Viewed this way, many activities within the five "P's" (HR Philosophy, Policies, Programs, Practices, and Processes) can be strategic. Thus, categorizing these activities as strategic or not depends upon whether they are *systematically linked to the strategic needs of the business,* not on whether they are done in the long term rather than short term or whether they focus on senior managers rather than nonmanagerial employees.

One benefit of the 5-P Model is that it shows the interrelatedness of activities that are often treated separately in the literature. This separate focus, perhaps necessary for research purposes, tends to understate the complexity of how HR activities influence individual and group behavior. Thus, by using the 5-P Model, we may gain greater understanding of this complex interaction. Another benefit of the 5-P Model is that it highlights just how significant the strategy-activity link can be, as the case histories included in this article illustrate.

Before we discuss the individual components of the 5-P Model, however, we need to consider the element that sets it all in motion.

DEFINING STRATEGIC NEEDS

Typically, organizations define (or redefine) their strategic business needs during times of turbulence. As such, these needs reflect management's overall plan for survival, growth, adaptability, and profitability. Internal characteristics (e.g., culture, the nature of the business) as well as external characteristics (e.g., the state of the economy, critical success factors in the industry) may well influence the definition of needs. But the biggest factor affecting strategic HR management is not a particular characteristic so much as it is experience with this mode of planning. HR managers who have never before been asked to meld human resources activities with strategic needs will find that the process takes time, persistence, and a detailed understanding of the needs that have been defined. In fact, linkages between human resources activities and business needs tend to be the exception even during non-turbulent times. When such linkages do occur, they are usually driven by the organization's efforts to formulate and implement a particular strategy.

To trigger specific actions, the business needs are generally translated into more actionable statements, which might be called *strategic business objectives.*

Exhibit 1

THE 5-P MODEL: LINKING STRATEGIC BUSINESS NEEDS AND
STRATEGIC HR MANAGEMENT ACTIVITIES

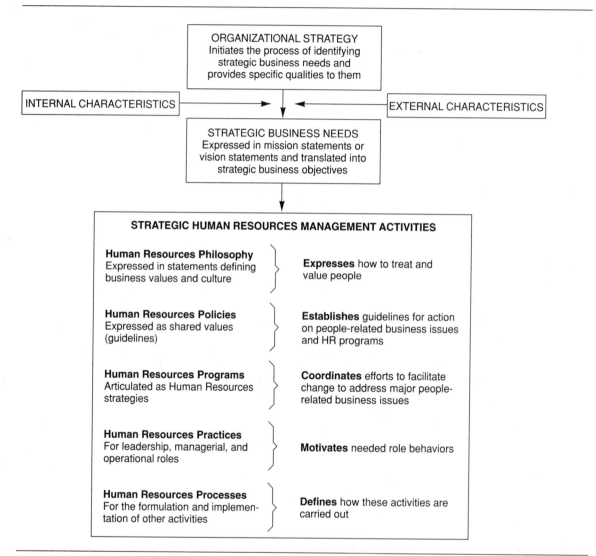

For example, at Pepsi-Cola International, the strategic business objectives are:

• Committed bottling organization
• Uncompromising dedication to quality
• Development of talented people

- Focus on growth
- Quality business plans

For other organizations, these might be called *business vision statements*. By calling them strategic business objectives, Pepsi-Cola believes that the statement conveys a more specific action element, starting with an influence on HR philosophy.

Human Resources Philosophy

This is a statement of how the organization regards its human resources, what role the resources play in the overall success of the business, and how they are to be treated and managed. This statement is typically very general, thus allowing interpretation at more specific levels of action within an organization. A firm's HR philosophy can be found in its *statement of business values*. For example, one of the four value statements used at the Forest Products Company (FPC) describes the company's philosophy of what employees mean to the company and how they are to be managed:

- People are mature, responsible individuals who want to contribute.
- People hold themselves to high standards of integrity and business ethics; they are responsible stewards of the land and environment.
- Our work environment is based on mutual respect, personal satisfaction, and growth opportunities for everyone.
- People recognize that teamwork, cooperation, and a clean, safe, well-maintained work place are essential to fulfilling our customer commitments.
- Continuing education is an ongoing commitment that involves everyone.

Instead of using the terms *HR philosophy* or *HR values* to describe how human resources are regarded, treated, and managed, some organizations use the term *culture*. That is, "We will create a culture that recognizes the importance we place on people, and that builds trust and cooperation." The difference, however, may be more semantic than real. For comparison, here is a statement of the culture at Pepsi-Cola International (PCI):

Leadership in People
We will develop an excellent organization focused on building the business by:

- Empowering people to drive the business from the closest point to the market
- Developing the right skills to be the best in the business
- Building career opportunities
- Building teamwork:
  - With bottlers to ensure that we maintain strong partnerships
  - Among area, division, and headquarters staff to ensure that we coordinate functional strengths to produce the best possible results

- · Across markets to ensure that we share the best practices throughout the enterprise
- · Helping people succeed by building an environment with:
  - · High integrity
  - · Strong and consistent values
  - · Continuous improvement

For both PCI and FPC, these descriptions of HR philosophy are part of a larger statement of *business (corporate) culture* or *business values*. These statements describe the importance to the firm of other, broader aspects of the organization: customers, operations, marketing, products, and general patterns of organization. These generally follow from a statement of the firm's vision or strategic business objectives, and vision and objectives follow from its strategy. For example, PCI's strategy is "Being No. 1 by Creating Value through Leadership and Excellence." This vision includes being:

- · The fastest growing
- · The most committed to customer service and attuned to customer needs
- · The best operators
- · The best selling and marketing company
- · The best people-oriented company

And PCI's business values include:

Leadership in Our Brands
We will achieve brand superiority by:

- · Delivering the best products in the marketplace:
  - · The highest quality
  - · The best tasting
  - · The most consistent
  - · Communicating these benefits in a high-impact, persuasive and consistent manner

Leadership in Marketing
We will build on our brand platforms by:

- · Creating new brand, channel, and package segments that build the business:
  - · Faster off the mark
  - · Better ideas
  - · Quicker to create and take advantage of opportunities

Leadership in Operations
We will build excellence in our own and bottler operations by:

- · Being the low-cost producer
- · Establishing and maintaining a strong focus on customer services and sales management:

- · These cornerstones will make us the best sales company
- • Standardizing operating systems to:
  - · Enhance our ability to provide the highest level of customer service
  - · Develop an ability to measure and manage key parameters of the business in a consistent fashion
  - · Provide a common set of practices and disciplines for the organization

Human Resources Policies

All of these statements provide guidelines for action on people-related business issues and for the development of HR programs and practices based on strategic needs. The term *HR Policy*, as used here, does not mean *HR Policy Manual*. While a policy manual may contain statements of general guidelines, employees often perceive the manual as a "rule book," prescribing very specific actions permitted in very specific situations.

People-related business issues are those that affect the immediate and future success of the business and involve people. Flowing from the strategic business needs, they may include the need to hire skilled workers, the need to improve worker productivity, or the need to reduce health care costs. Other people-related business issues include the need to develop a top cadre of international managers, the need to have an adaptable and skilled workforce under changing environmental conditions, and the need to reduce excessive turnover of younger, talented individuals who are blocked by the limited number of traditional promotion opportunities.

One example, drawn from PCI, illustrates how an HR policy can link values with a particular people-related business need. The value, in this case, is stated in corporate literature as "high standards of personal performance," and the need was to develop communication skills that would foster such performance in a decentralized international environment.

HR Policy at PCI. Communication in an international environment is difficult even under the best of circumstances, as any diplomat knows. For PCI, the overlay of 150 potentially different national cultures makes it likely that some level of misunderstanding on almost any topic will occur on a regular basis.

In the early 1980s, it was clear to almost every manager in Pepsi-Cola International that expectations for individual performance standards varied from country to country. For example, in Eastern Europe it was acceptable for a manager to meet his quota and take the rest of the day off. In Germany, however, managers expected continuous improvement, a more demanding standard. Thus, the company needed a simple yet direct and culturally flexible tool to develop more consistency in managing performance. The answer turned out to be something called "instant feedback"—a device that any sophisticated human resources executive would have called too simple and unstructured to work globally. Stated simply, the principal of instant feedback says that if you have a problem or an idea about any aspect of the business, or about an individual's performance, then the organization demands that you raise the issue appropriately and discuss it maturely. A twenty-minute video tape was used to dramatize and explain how instant feedback could be applied in an international environment. Over time, instant feedback became the connecting link in a chain of feedback systems designed to improve and maintain high levels of personal performance.

Pepsi-Cola International is fundamentally a "feedback driven" organization. This feedback is now mirrored in every tool used to measure and improve performance, and the language of feedback has become part of the everyday vocabulary. It is heard when someone with an issue or problem says to another individual, "Let me give you some instant feedback." With travel schedules, frequent phone contact, and constant time-zone pressures, instant feedback has become a shorthand for getting to the point and communicating clearly.

But perhaps the most fascinating aspect of the concept is that it has worked in every nation, although with some cultural modifications. Americans use it because it fits the fast-paced way we do business. In most Asian cultures, feedback may be tough and direct, but it should never be given in public. Also in Asian cultures, there may be a lot of head nodding during instant feedback, as if signifying agreement. In reality, the nods mean only that the message has been heard. Some Latins will argue very strongly if they do not agree with the feedback, and some nationalities (e.g., Indian) will insist on a great deal of specificity. Canadians will say that Americans are too direct and some Europeans will say that Americans are too demanding and critical.

Instant feedback works amid cultural diversity because the focus is always on how to improve business performance, not on cultural-specific behavior. Some would argue that this method is nothing more than effective communication. This is only partially correct. It is communication directed at solving performance problems, and while total cultural neutrality is not possible, instant feedback says, in effect, "It doesn't really matter *how* you do it, as long as you do it."

This instant feedback example also illustrates the impact of *organization structure* on strategic HR management. PCI refers to its globally dispersed organization structure as "mature decentralization" and considers this structure as a key to success in global markets. Essentially, mature decentralization means that as many decisions as possible be made in the field, as close to the consumer as possible.

Despite the emphasis on decentralization, PCI recognizes the need for operating units to be globally integrated and cooperative. The human resources challenge is to assure that a level of trust and open communication prevails so that needed resources, regardless of their source, can be brought to bear on a given problem. Common business objectives and human resources practices are certainly critical in this. But in the face of diversity, global cooperation is also accomplished by:

- Identifying values that support the objectives of the business, the organizational structure, and the needs of the individual employee, and

- Developing a set of shared understandings concerning individual performance that flow from the values that shape the human resources practices.

Thus, at PCI shared values (reflected in HR policies) result in part from the organization's structure that in turn results in part from the firm's strategic directions. For PCI, policies serve to integrate the company's global operation by providing a basis for the development of HR practices and programs.

HR Programs

Shaped by HR policies, HR programs represent coordinated HR efforts specifically intended to initiate, disseminate, and sustain strategic organizational change efforts necessitated by the strategic business needs. These efforts may begin at the top of the organization and filter down, or they may begin elsewhere. They may even begin in two places at the same time. For example, Ford's early-1980s strategic decision to emphasize quality evolved at the top-management level and the plant level simultaneously, a serendipitous development.

HR programs can be initiated, disseminated, and sustained for many types of strategic organizational change efforts. These efforts, however, have several elements in common. First, they receive their impetus from the firm's strategic intentions and directions. Second, they involve human resources management issues, i.e., they represent major people-related business issues that require a major organizational change effort to address. They also share the reality of having *strategic goals* against which program effectiveness can be measured.

A number of generic questions help to identify the fundamental issues for these types of programs.

- What is the nature of the corporate culture? Is it supportive of the business?
- Will the organization be able to cope with future challenges in its current form?
- What kind of people and how many will be required?
- Are performance levels high enough to meet demands for increased profitability, innovation, higher productivity, better quality, and improved customer service?
- What is the level of commitment to the company?
- Are there any potential constraints such as skill shortages or HR problems?

Programs formulated in answer to such questions are typically associated with the term *HR strategies.* This makes sense because, after all, HR strategies are essentially plans and programs to address and solve fundamental strategic issues related to human resources management. For this reason alone, HR strategies and HR programs are used interchangeably in the framework here. Again, an example from the Forest Products Company illustrates this concept.

In the early 1980s, FPC became aware of a decline in large-volume, commodity lumber businesses and growth among small mills that tailor-made products to meet customers' demands. The small, nonunion, owner-operated, entrepreneurial mills were more market-oriented *and* operated at lower cost.

Deciding that going out of business was not an alternative, Charles Bingham, Forest Product's CEO, suggested that something needed to be done, preferably sooner than later. Together, the top dozen managers decided that a massive reorganization was called for, accompanied by a radical change in strategy. According to Bingham, the change in strategy went something like this:

> Approximately 80 percent of our sales dollars in 1982 represented products sold as commodities. By 1995 . . . we must reverse the proportions.

The result was a decision to dramatically decentralize. The three operating units, of which FPC was one, were given free reign on how to conduct their businesses. In addition, Bingham and his top team split operations into 200 profit centers, each center largely responsible for its own bottom line.

This restructuring proved to be only one step in the right direction. The top team soon realized that there would have to be a total transformation—the corporate culture, knowledge base, skill levels, style of leadership, and team orientation would all have to change. And this change would have to impact everything, from the way business was conducted at headquarters to how a salesperson dealt with customers. To meet this massive challenge, top management established a Leadership Institute. This institute, they felt, could become a powerful catalyst to accelerate the normal process of change.

The institute's first major objective was to develop and implement a four-week HR program for top executives, followed by a similar program for middle managers. A key element in both programs was attention to new HR practices, the fourth component of the Five-P Model.

Human Resources Practices

One useful way to approach this component of HR strategy is from the framework of roles. Generally speaking, the roles that individuals assume in organizations fall into three categories: leadership, managerial, and operational. In each case, behaviors associated with a given role should support strategic needs. The following examples illustrate this concept.

Leadership Roles.   These include establishing direction, aligning people, motivating and inspiring individuals, and causing dramatic and useful change. Within the FPC, *leadership roles* are defined and measured with statements like these:

- Live by the basic values of the Forest Products Company
- Demonstrate honesty and ethical behavior in business transactions
- Show a high degree of personal integrity in dealing with others
- Avoid wasting time or resources
- Strive for continuous improvement in all you do
- Demonstrate confidence in yourself as a leader

By the way, these statements are taken from a more extensive questionnaire used in the company's leadership program. Managers complete the questionnaire (i.e., rate themselves on each point) and ask their employees and customers to provide assessments.

Managerial Roles.   Another part of the questionnaire contains statements on managerial roles. Basically, these are the traditional roles of planning, directing, delegating, organizing and coordinating. Here are some examples:

- Make sure that objectives are clearly understood
- Level with people on what is not negotiable
- Give appropriate orientation to people on new assignments
- Deal effectively with performance problems
- Give people the information they need to be successful
- Give developmental performance feedback in a timely manner
- Give people the freedom they need to do their jobs
- Give co-workers the opportunity to try out their new ideas
- Encourage appropriate collaboration on work assignments
- Encourage people to participate when appropriate

Again, managers use self-assessment and assessment from employees and peers to gauge how well they are playing the roles.

Operational Roles.   These are the roles needed to deliver services or make products. In essence, they are "doing" roles, and as such their content is far more specific than for the other roles. In a service setting, a role statement might be "greets customers as they enter the sales area." In a manufacturing organization, a role might be "reads blueprints accurately" or "performs soldering operations consistent with quality standards."

Roles Can Move.   Although these three roles are labeled leadership, managerial, and operational, this doesn't necessarily mean that only nonmanagers perform the operational roles or only managers perform the managerial and leadership roles. In the process of formulating and implementing new strategic objectives, organizations typically evaluate the "who does what" question. In some cases, this results in a shift of role responsibilities. For example, at the Nissan Motor Manufacturing Plant in the United Kingdom and the Honda Manufacturing Plant in Marysville, Ohio, an analysis of roles and responsibilities performed by first-level supervisors led to a more effective allocation of work. The main activities associated with first-line supervision are identified in Exhibit 2. Many of these activities, it turned out, could be distributed to nonmanagerial employees.

Exhibit 2

MOST COMMON ROLES AND RESPONSIBILITIES OF SUPERVISORS

· Absence control	· Keeping personnel records
· Employee appraisal	· Keeping production records
· Bonus calculations	· Leading quality circles
· Deployment of staff	· Planning/allocating work
· Discipline	· Quality control
· Drawing up shift rotations	· Recruitment
· Employee welfare	· Team briefing
· Handling grievances	· Team building
· Health and safety	· Communicating
· Induction training	

Matching Practices and Roles.   Once the role behaviors, whether leadership, managerial, or operational, are identified, HR practices can be developed to cue and reinforce role performance. While many HR practices are used in organizations without regard to organizational strategy, some practices tie role behavior directly to strategic needs. Consider, for example, a company that has defined a need to improve quality. HR practices might provide cues for group participation in problem solving, training in statistical measures of quality control, and the like.

HR Processes

This area deals with "how" all the other HR activities are identified, formulated, and implemented. Thus, it is a significant strategic human resources management activity. In the FPC situation, the process for establishing the Leadership Institute and the HR programs was accomplished through a great deal of interaction among the director of strategic education and the line managers. According to Horace Parker,

> The trump card in closing the deal [to establish the Leadership Institute and the HR programs] was to involve the executives at various levels of the organization in the planning stages.

This process of involvement at the FPC was not aimed solely at helping executives and HR people understand the organizational change strategy. It also provided opportunity for others to "buy into" the change process. Moreover, involvement is *in itself* consistent with the aims of the programs and the strategic business needs. That is, the executives' participation in change helps orient these individuals toward giving their employees more participation and involvement in devising tactics to meet strategic business needs. (Most quality improvement programs, for example, rely heavily on employee participation.) On the other hand, to the extent that suggestions, commitment, and executive willingness to change are not necessary, the need for a participatory HR process diminishes. These situations are increasingly rare, however, as employees at all levels continue to call for empowerment, ownership, and participation.

Thus, HR processes seem to vary along a continuum of extensive participation by all employees to no participation by any employees. Two continuua could be used to differentiate between the formulation and implementation stages: e.g., high participation/involvement during formulation, but low involvement at implementation. But it appears that there is a need for consistency across these two process dimensions.

This need for consistency becomes evident across *all* the strategic human resources management activities. This need arises because all such activities influence individual behavior. If they are not consistent with each other, i.e., if they are not sending the same messages about what is expected and rewarded, the organization is likely to be an aggregation of people pulling in different directions. This is hardly a situation for the successful implementation of strategic business needs.

Recognizing this need for consistency, then, is an important component. This need, along with an awareness of the other aspects of strategic human resources management, translates into a greater need to be systematic. Strategic human resources management requires consistency and a systematic orientation. An example might illustrate how these two needs actually get played out.

PUTTING IT ALL TOGETHER: THE CASE OF GRAND UNION

The Grand Union is a large retail grocery operation with the majority of stores located in well-established neighborhoods. In the mid-1980s, a new phenomenon appeared in the traditional retail grocery business: the advent of the super store, the smallest of which was about twice the size of Grand Union's largest store.

The Grand Union had always defined itself as a grocery store—a traditional high-volume, low-margin, limited-selection, discount-driven, 40,000 square foot *grocery store.* Five years ago, the top management team decided that competing with the new 100,000 square foot stores (Wal-Mart's largest Hypermart is 260,000 square feet) was not a viable merchandising strategy. A directly competitive strategy would have called for moving stores from their current space-bound locations and uprooting relationships with customers, suppliers, and communities.

New Strategic Business Needs

The top managers found themselves faced with the need to redefine what it meant for Grand Union to be a grocery store. Taking into account both competitive pressures and new customer habits and preferences, the team saw the need for a basic change in direction—from a commodity, undifferentiated business to a high-quality, customer-driven business.

From an individual store perspective, this meant eliminating many of the current items to make room for more national brands and merchandise with higher margins. A major objective was to sell the best quality products, which meant having a deli section (with the smells of barbecued chicken), an expanded fresh fruit section (more tropical fruits), a variety of small, ethnic food booths (for eating in or taking home), and a pastry shop.

The culture of the firm changed to emphasize listening to and serving customers. Store managers and top management started to provide the leadership John Kotter talks about, i.e., articulating and providing excitement, showing confidence in the firm's ability to successfully change in the new, more uncertain environment, and setting objectives that would relate to the new way of doing business.

Linking HR with the Strategic Business Needs

Under the guidance of Senior Vice President of Human Resources Bill Reffett, the firm developed an HR philosophy that said the employee was a valuable, long-term source of competitive advantage, and that all efforts would be made to provide exciting jobs, promotion opportunities, and retraining as needed. The firm described this philosophy as developmental. It was apparent that role behaviors for all employees would need to change to match the needs of the new business.

While the physical size of the stores remained the same, employees were added to staff the new sections. It was important to keep these employees longer so that they could get to know the customer and the store. Consistent with the new business, the traditional command-and-control relationships across all levels were modified to accommodate a more self-directed, self-managed approach. Similarly, an individual orientation gave way to a team orientation.

Major effort was directed toward identifying new role behaviors for supervisors and other staff. This required the intense involvement of the employees, with guidance provided by the senior vice president of human resources. Together, they identified needed supervisory (first-level managerial) and staff role behaviors based upon what they saw as characterizing a customer-driven grocery store. Then they compared these with current role behavior.

This resulted in a critical redistribution of supervisory role behaviors. By recognizing the distinction between supervisors *as an employee group* and *supervisory activities* (responsibilities associated with the supervisory role) it became easier to define role activities in ways that would enhance the level of customer service.

The nonsupervisory employees also addressed the question, "What does this new business orientation mean for us at the store?" Because the focus was on the customer, they first asked, "How do we currently interact with customers?" This resulted in a before-and-after analysis of customer relationships. The "before" analysis produced the following list:

- We do not know customer desires
- We make limited use of customers

Exhibit 3

ORGANIZATIONAL CHARACTERISTICS OF A
CUSTOMER-DRIVEN SERVICE ORGANIZATION

- Just-in-time inventory
- Just-in-time working commitment
- Team-oriented
- Multi-skilled—technical, process, interpersonal
- Flexibility
- Trust, harmonious employee relations
- Communications
- Egalitarianism
- Distributed leadership

- Responsibility for customers
- Standard operating procedures
- Continuous improvement
- No-fault policies
- Job grade reduction
- Rewards for small improvements/suggestions
- Supplier and customer involvement
- Site visits, comparisons, benchmarks
- Customer knowledge

- We are space-driven, not customer-driven
- We have traditional departments, low margins, high turnover rates
- We feel no ownership of service
- We lack managerial skills

In contrast, the employees felt that the new direction would require management to initiate new practices:

- Holding focus groups with customers
- Being customer-driven
- Including service as part of the product
- Adding high-margin departments
- Having stores coordinate efforts; exchanging best practices
- Expanding management skills

In addition, these employees asked, "From the broader, store viewpoint, what are the characteristics that reflect a solutions-oriented, customer-driven service operation?" This question resulted in the list of characteristics for the store shown in Exhibit 3.

Based upon these characteristics, the staff analyzed the needed role behaviors, vis-a-vis the customer, and concluded that substantial changes were in order. The before-and-after role behaviors for the major job categories are listed in Exhibit 4.

In the final stage, the employees identified the HR practices that had to be formulated to match the business, based upon the role behaviors needed from the employees, especially those in direct contact with the customers. The analysis and formulation resulted in several HR practices that represented significant

Exhibit 4

CUSTOMER-DRIVEN EMPLOYEE BEHAVIORS AT GRAND UNION

Employees	Behaviors Before the Change	Behaviors After the Change
Bag Packers	Ignore customers Lack of packing standards	Greet customers Respond to customers Ask for customers' preference
Cashiers	Ignore customers Lack of eye contact	Greet customers Respond to customers Assist customers Speak clearly Call customers by name

Shelf Stockers	Ignore customers
	Don't know store
		Respond to customers
		Help customers with
		  correct production/location
		  information
		Knowledgeable about
		  product location

Department Workers	Ignore customers Limited Knowledge	Respond to customers Know products Know store
Department Managers	Ignore customers Ignore workers	Respond to customers Reward employees for responding to customers

Store Managers	Ignore customers
	Stay in booth
		Respond to customers
		Reward employees for
		  service
		Appraise employees on
		  customer service

change (see Exhibit 5). While these changes in HR practices were prompted by what the employees thought was necessary for the business, they were driven, in large part, by what employees thought would enable them to perform as needed by the customer.

ROLE OF THE DEPARTMENT

As the Grand Union example suggests, the HR department is in an ideal position to take charge of the 5-P's of strategic human resources management. In general it can:

- Assist in the formulation of the firm's strategic direction and needs
- Identify the HR philosophies or culture consistent with the business needs

Exhibit 5

HUMAN RESOURCES MANAGEMENT PRACTICES
AFFECTED BY THE CHANGE AT GRAND UNION

- **Human Resource Planning**
  Longer term focus
  Tie to the needs of the business

- **Staffing**
  More socialization
  More opportunities

- **Training and Development**
  More skill training
  Customer service training

- **Performance Appraisal**
  Customer service measures
  Feedback

- **Compensation**
  Relate to performance appraisal
  Awards and celebration

- Develop and implement HR policies, programs, and practices consistent with the HR culture
- Ensure that the HR process is consistent with the other HR activities

If, as in the case of the Grand Union or the Forest Products Company, the organization must change in response to strategic needs, the HR department can play a critical role as change agent. In this process, the HR department can establish an HR initiative, i.e., a specific HR program to serve as catalyst for change. The initiative can involve:

- Establishing a senior HR council and executive operating committee
- Mounting major activities to rally all employees to the change
- Developing a leadership program to ensure that the change clearly includes top management

In the development of the senior management program (and further programs that facilitate the change throughout the organization), the director of executive development or strategic education can often take the lead. This individual knows the top team perhaps better than any other HR person. This being the case, this person can then be in a position to orchestrate the entire change process—and thus the entire strategic human resources management function.

Within the HR department there can be further division of roles and responsibilities. This can be done by distinguishing between the corporate HR department and the business-unit or division HR departments. Taking a very proactive stance, the corporate HR department can:

- Assist senior managers in formulating change
- Become a model of change
- Develop and guide divisional HR
- Change organizational structure

- Serve as clearing house
- Serve as trainer for other HR personnel
- Do benchmark analysis
- Develop HRIS capability
- Audit competencies

HR activities at the divisional level can then reflect corporate activities. In situations where the corporate HR department abdicates to the divisions, or where the divisions simply seize the initiative, they can essentially perform the roles just ascribed to the corporate HR department. The Grand Union and FPC case studies offer a flavor of both of these situations.

The fact is that while there may be variations in *how* the roles are shared between corporate and divisional HR staffs, there should be little variation in *whether* these roles are performed. Indeed, in the extreme case, many of these roles could be performed by the line managers with or without the assistance of others.

IMPLICATIONS AND SUMMARY

The concept presented here proposes that the framework of strategic human resources management is made up of all activities affecting the behavior of individuals in their efforts to formulate and implement the strategic needs of the business. This rather broad concept carries several significant implications.

First, successful efforts at strategic HR management begin with the identification of strategic business needs. If these needs are important to the success of the business, and if strategic human resources management can be instrumental in meeting these needs, then these needs should be systematically analysed for their impact on human resources management activities, including HR philosophy, HR policies, HR programs, HR practices, and HR processes.

Another implication is that, because all employees are affected by strategic human resources management, participatory processes may help cement the link between strategy and HR practices. At both Grand Union and FPC, employees helped to analyze and define the new roles they would play vis-a-vis the strategic business needs. HR management then developed practices to cue and reinforce role behaviors. While a participatory process may not always be necessary, there is mounting evidence that employees respond favorably to it when it is an option.

A third implication is that strategic human resources management depends upon a systematic and analytical mindset. At Grand Union, Forest Products, and Pepsi-Cola International, the executives formulated and implemented HR activities in a systematic and analytical manner, first identifying strategic needs and then designing HR activities with consistent cues and reinforcements. While the effectiveness of this approach has yet to be formally measured, indicators such as market share, profitability, and productivity suggest a fair amount of success. A fourth implication is that HR departments have a significant opportunity to impact their organizations' efforts to successfully launch strategic initiatives.

This argues strongly for HR's participation in the formulation of strategy—if for no other reason than to get a head start on the systematic analysis of what the strategic needs of the business are vis-a-vis HR.

A final implication relates to the formal study of strategic human resources management. As practitioners do their work, HR academics have a significant opportunity to observe organizations in transition, a real-life laboratory for learning. This paper is evidence of the type of insight such observation can provide. Hopefully it will also stimulate further research, particularly in the areas of identifying employee role behaviors and linking HR practices to them, and in mapping the patterns of consistency within and across the strategic human resources management activities.

Selected Bibliography

Several individuals have written articles relevant to this topic and their ideas have been incorporated here. They include: F. K. Foulkes, *Strategic Human Resource Management* (Englewood Cliffs, NJ: Prentice-Hall, 1986); J. Butler, G. R. Ferris, and N. K. Napier, *Strategy and Human Resource Management* (Cincinnati: South-Western, 1990); and R. Cooke and M. Armstrong, "The Search for Strategic HRM," *Personnel Management,* December 1990, pp. 30–33.

For an insightful discussion of the impact of strategic intent and its implications for strategic human resource management, see G. Hamel and C. K. Prahalad, "Strategic Intent," *Harvard Business Review,* May-June 1989, pp. 63–76; and C. K. Prahalad and G. Hamel, "The Core Competence of the Corporation," *Harvard Business Review,* May-June 1990, pp. 79–91.

For how strategy and strategic directions determine various aspects of human resource management, see D. C. Hambrick and C. C. Snow, "Strategic Reward Systems" in C. C. Snow, ed., *Strategy, Organization Design and Human Resource Management* (Greenwich, CT: JAI Press, 1989); E. E. Lawler III, "The Strategic Design of Reward Systems," in R. S. Schuler and S. A. Youngblood, eds., *Readings in Personnel and Human Resource Management,* 2d ed. (St. Paul, MN: West Publishing, 1984); and J. J. Sherwood, "Creating Work Cultures with Competitive Advantage," *Organizational Dynamics,* Winter 1988, pp. 5–27.

Comments about Pepsi-Cola International are based upon numerous discussions with J. Fulkerson, vice president of HR for PCI. Some of these comments are expanded upon in J. Fulkerson and R. S. Schuler, "Managing Worldwide Diversity at Pepsi-Cola International," in S. E. Jackson, ed., *Working Through Diversity: Human Resources Initiatives* (New York: Guilford Publications, 1992). For further descriptions of international HR issues, see D. Lei and J. W. Slocum, Jr., "Global Strategic Alliances: Payoffs and Pitfalls," *Organizational Dynamics,* Winter 1991, pp. 44–62.

For further examples of people-related business issues, see R. S. Schuler and J. W. Walker, "Human Resources Strategy: Focusing on Issues and Actions," *Organizational Dynamics,* Summer 1990, pp. 5–19.

Descriptions of the HR activities at the Forest Products Company are from conversations with Horace Parker, director of strategic education, and Bill Maki, director of human resources, Weyerhaeuser Company, July 1990; and from J. F. Bolt, *Executive Development: A Strategy for Competitiveness* (New York: Harper & Row, 1989), pp. 139–158. Descriptions of leadership and managerial roles are also in J. Kotter, *A Force for Change: How Leadership Differs from Management* (New York: The

Free Press, 1990). Comments on Nissan and Honda from interviews with Peter Wickens, director of personnel and information systems, Nissan UK, February 1991; and from interviews reported in R. S. Schuler and S. E. Jackson, "Linking Competitive Strategies and Human Resource Management Practices," *Academy of Management Executive*, August 1987, pp. 207–219.

The material describing the Grand Union is based on interviews with Bill Reffett, senior vice-president of human resources, during March 1989 and July 1991. The material here refers only to HR management-related changes; changes, of course, were also made in purchasing, merchandising, and operations. For more detail on using human resource management service organizations, see D. E. Bowen, R. B. Chase, and T. G. Cummings & Associates, *Service Management Effectiveness* (San Francisco, CA: Jossey-Bass, 1990); and S. W. Brown, E. Gummesson, B. Edvardsson, and B. Gustavsson, *Service Quality* (Lexington, MA: Lexington Books, 1991).

A final, but important note: As times change so do companies and individuals. The Forest Products Company was recently divided into two equal-sized groups, Wood Products and Timberland. Bill Reffett is now with Korn Ferry International.

READING 5

TOTAL QUALITY-ORIENTED HUMAN RESOURCES MANAGEMENT

David E. Bowen
Edward E. Lawler III

The "quality experts" are pushing companies to make basic changes in recruiting, train-ing, performance appraisals, and merit-pay systems. But before HR executives can become change agents, they may have to take a hard look at practices within their own departments.

How important are human resources issues in creating quality-oriented organizations? Here is Tom Peters' take on the people-side of quality improvement:

> TQM often looks suspiciously like the latest act in a long-running farce called Revenge of the Number Nerds.

> But the numbers nuts, despite (or because of) the massive Baldrige application (Malcolm Baldrige National Quality Award—or "MBNQA," as one correspondent lovingly labeled it), do not get it. Real participative management, Baldrige categories notwithstanding, is about elusive characteristics such as dignity and worth, much more than computer-aided suggestion tracking systems. Real customer loyalty is as much or more about listening, listening and then listening harder still than it is about zero-variance manufacturing processes.

One major focus in the quality movement is on upgrading technical systems. This attention to process, product, and information technology (and the accumulation of numerical evidence to document quality upgrades in these areas) is necessary—and often yields quality improvement. But it may not be the *key* variable in the quality equation. John E. Condon, immediate past chairman of the board, the American Society for Quality Control, said it succinctly: "People really do make quality happen."

Source: "Total Quality-Oriented Human Resources Management" by David E. Bowen, et al. Reprinted by permission of publisher, from *Organizational Dynamics*, SPR92 © 1992. American Management Association, New York. All rights reserved.

Senior executives across the United States apparently share this belief in the human resources side of the quality equation. Consider the results of a Gallup survey of executive perceptions on a range of competitive issues, conducted for the American Society for Quality Control. The Gallup Organization interviewed some 615 senior executives, 307 representing *Fortune* 1000 companies, the remainder from smaller firms.

The executives most frequently cited quality (service and product) and productivity as the key competitive issues facing them. Asked to rate the relative effectiveness of eight different methods for improving quality, the participants gave top weight to *employee motivation* (85 percent rated it highly effective). *Change in corporate culture* came in a close second (82 percent); followed by *employee education* (74 percent); *process control* (53 percent); *expenditures on capital equipment* (45 percent); *more control of supplies* (36 percent); *more inspections* (29 percent); and *improved administrative support* (28 percent). Clearly, executives are convinced that human resources issues are the most important.

The Baldrige Award (despite Peters' bashing) also highlights the importance of human resources. "Human Resource Utilization" is one of the award's seven examination categories and is weighted with 150 points of the total 1,000. It states:

> This category examines the effectiveness of the company's efforts to develop and realize the full potential of the workforce, including management, and to maintain an environment conducive to full participation, quality leadership, and personal and organizational growth.

This is consistent with the emphasis that most total quality management (TQM) advocates place on employee involvement as an important part of any total quality effort. The other categories are "Leadership" (100 points); "Information and Analysis" (70 points); "Strategic Quality Planning" (60 points); "Quality Assurance of Products and Services" (140 points); "Quality Results" (180 points); and "Customer Satisfaction" (300 points).

Quality guru W. Edwards Deming also focuses directly on human resources issues in his widely cited "fourteen points" for quality improvement. While the exact wording of the fourteen points has changed over the years, the following HR-related directives always appear: (a) institute training on the job, (b) break down barriers between departments to build teamwork, (c) drive fear out of the workplace, (d) eliminate quotas on the shop floor, (e) create conditions that allow employees to have pride in their workmanship, including abolishing annual reviews and merit ratings, and (f) institute a program of education and self-improvement.

TOTAL QUALITY: OPPORTUNITY OR THREAT FOR HR MANAGEMENT?

The importance of the HR side of the quality equation provides HR departments with a golden opportunity. Quality can be the "business issue" that truly brings senior managers and HR execs together to move from *just* HRM to *strategic* HRM. A major role in the quality improvement effort puts HR in a position to contribute directly and visibly to the bottom line, to add value to the company's products and services in the same way that other functions, such as sales, accounting, and production, add value. And HR can gain the heightened status that accompanies a *documented* contribution to the organization's performance.

Many quality consultants, however, are not comfortable about giving HR executives and their staffs a strong hand in the quality improvement effort. As quality guru Philip Crosby observes:

> Most HR execs are still tied up in being a regulatory agency. Many times they act like robots. . . . There are two departments behind the times. . . . One is HR, the other is purchasing. There are enlightened people trying to change this, but most HR execs are their own worst enemy. It's a case of "Physician, heal thyself."

This may explain why few companies have turned to the HR department to lead their quality improvement efforts. Instead, the leadership role usually falls to a newly formed unit. A number of reasons may explain this. First, many senior managers do not understand "holistic quality improvement" well enough to appreciate the critical role of human resources issues in improving quality. Second, most HR functions are so specialized and cut off from the rest of the organization that department members lack the breadth of perspective necessary for total quality. Indeed, these specialists may view the demands of a full-scale quality improvement as a threat to their well-defined, well-guarded domains. Even though the number of top HR executives who report to their CEOs or attend board meetings is increasing, this still is not the case in many organizations. Blocked access denies HR people the opportunity to view the company's overall competitive position. Third, HR departments are frequently autocratic and hierarchical, with strict definitions of responsibility and authority. The participative approach, so necessary for an effective quality improvement effort, can be a tough sell to an autocratic department.

A final reason for HR's minor role in quality improvement stems from its own low self-esteem. There are people *in HR, itself,* who feel threatened by the request to assume a leadership position on an important business issue. They may view themselves as powerless, second-class citizens who really do not know the business. Regrettably, they are often right. As a result, senior managers may conclude that the human resources issues involved in TQM are too important to be left to the human resources department.

Should the TQM effort be run by the HR department, or by a separate TQM office? It is a tough call, and we can only suggest what *not* to do. Do *not* have separate programs—an HR and TQM department acting independently. The more effective approaches create one integrated program that stresses employee involvement and total quality management. In these programs, the HR organization needs: (1) to be redesigned so that the HR function itself practices what is known about quality management, and (2) to institute human resources management practices that support TQM effectiveness throughout the organization.

In what follows we describe how to accomplish these two objectives, creating what might be called total quality-oriented human resources management (TQHRM).

REDESIGNING THE HRM DEPARTMENT TO FIT TQM PRINCIPLES

How should the HRM function define its mission and organize itself to truly become quality oriented? Exhibit 1 presents a typical listing of TQM principles. Putting these principles to work *within* the HRM department provides a first step toward that goal.

Quality Work the First Time.   As is true throughout the organization, the emphasis on quality in the HR department must come from the top. The senior HR executive must truly care that the department delivers only quality services, and this caring must shine through all actions and decisions—instilling a passion for quality among staff members. The HR executive must support his or her staff by giving them the time needed to "do it right the first time"—even when line managers are pressing for a quick fix. He or she must find ways of rewarding HR employees who truly do quality work. And HR managers must insist that less-than-quality work be redone. Nothing leaves the department until it is done right.

What is called "scrap and rework" on the shop floor has a counterpart in HR management. If a bonus system or orientation program needs to be redesigned because employees could not understand it, this is clearly "rework."

The HR department might usefully track the time it takes to do each piece of rework, then compute the percentage of total productive time spent on rework tasks. As HR activities are repeated, staff members can analyze the patterns and identify the causes of poor quality. This parallels the cause-and-effect analysis techniques often applied on the shop floor.

Focus on the Customer.   Quality means more than doing things right the first time; it means first choosing to do the right thing. The HRM department that succeeds in eliminating rework may become more *efficient*, but that does not guarantee it will be more *effective*. It may be doing the wrong things . . . and doing them very well.

Doing the right thing (effectiveness) is a matter of satisfying customer requirements. This translates into making HR departments more service-oriented, and less production-oriented. Production-oriented HR departments are driven more by their own internal technologies and pet programs than by customer needs. Production-oriented departments carry on-the-shelf inventories of canned supervisory skills training programs, or they mass produce the same trait-based appraisal rating forms for all departments, to cite two examples.

Exhibit 1

PRINCIPLES OF TOTAL QUALITY MANAGEMENT

1. Quality Work the First Time
2. Focus on the Customer
3. Strategic, Holistic Approach to Improvement
4. Continuous Improvement as a Way of Life
5. Mutual Respect and Teamwork

A service-driven HR department functions like a high-quality service firm—a world-class resort, a gourmet restaurant, or an elite consulting firm. These firms thrive on satisfying clients. They emphasize the intangibles, customize their offerings to different clients, and involve their clients in decisions that affect the services rendered. HRM must learn to thrive on satisfying its clients (e.g., line managers). Services need to be offered that fulfill the unique and changing needs of different groups of managers and employees.

This argues for more co-design and co-production of services between the HR staff and clients, as when HR staff and line managers work together to develop and teach a training program. It also implies that the HR department should be composed primarily of generalists who act as client executives, rather than staffed with specialists who have a narrow view of the business and champion their various "product lines" (say, MBO or cafeteria-style benefit plans). In sum, service-oriented HR departments get close to their customers and encourage them to help set the department agenda.

Finally, data-based decision making is critical to quality. In this spirit, the HRM department needs to collect data from line managers and others on how well it is doing. Surveys, focus groups, and other ways of listening must keep HRM saturated with client information. In addition, external benchmarking data are critical to keeping the HR department aware of how its performance compares to that of world-class organizations.

Strategic, Holistic Approach to Improvement.   Quality improvement may require changes in mission, structure, job design, management practices, and every other facet of the HR organization. Transamerica Life Companies, Los Angeles, recently overhauled its HR function in a way that exemplifies a strategic, holistic approach to improvement. The process began by asking the employees (customers) served whether HR was doing a good job. The majority revealed *that they did not know what services HR offered or how to access them.* Next, researchers surveyed the HR staff itself, asking them what interfered with their service to customers. Responses indicated that HR jobs were so narrowly defined that people could not see how their work fit into the big picture.

As Transamerica reorganized to better serve internal customers, it created more challenging work in HR. An advisory committee consisting of HR managers and line representatives helped guide the change. Guidance also came from surveying other companies known for effective HR organization (an application of "benchmarking").

The HR staff now has several cross-functional teams (e.g., people from employee relations, employment, and compensation) responsible for key processes and customers. In addition, the department operates a special HR service team trained to provide one-stop customer service by answering 80 percent of the diverse array of questions that come into the department. These teams are being cross-trained to become generalists.

For the first time, HR people are being asked to join strategic planning meetings, and they now maintain ongoing contact with customers. Overall, the HR function serves as a model for innovative work design for the rest of the company.

Continuous Improvement as a Way of Life. A popular tenet in TQM is that continuous improvement must be ingrained as a value in the corporate culture. In other words, it must become part of "how we do things around here," to use one popular definition of culture.

Philip Crosby, despite his reservations about HR executives, believes that "HR should be the architect of corporate culture." It should be the charge of HR departments to build values and practices supporting continuous, incremental improvement in quality throughout the organization. And that emphasis must be applied with equal force within the HR department itself. For example, a small gain of, say, 4 percent in client satisfaction with this year's performance appraisal process needs to be highly valued—even if it comes on top of an already high rating (e.g., 75 percent of the customers indicated they were "highly satisfied" with last year's process). These small gains need to be valued as much as, say, the successful completion of a high-level executive search. Over time, the cumulative impact of endless small improvements transforms the department.

Mutual Respect and Teamwork. W. Edwards Deming talks about driving fear out of the workplace. Much of this fear is tied into the control and hierarchy-dominated fabric of many organizations. The "workers" fear the "bosses," and this fear distracts from high-quality, collaborative work. If HR is to champion such issues as employee involvement and cooperation throughout the organization, it must first champion them internally.

In many organizations, HR is now preaching the importance of supervisors "empowering" their employees by giving them more responsibility, autonomy, and participation in decision making. In one organization, however, a reluctant supervisor responded with, "Why should I stick my neck out and be democratic with my people when the HR people manage their shops as if they were each Attila the Hun?" When it comes to the issue of empowerment, HR must practice what it preaches.

TOTAL QUALITY-ORIENTED HRM PRACTICES

Once the HRM department has learned to make quality a way of life within its own function, it can assume an expanded role: supporting TQM throughout the organization. A long history of research—stretching back much further than the current interest in TQM—has focused on the relationship between product (and service) quality and a number of HR practices and systems. There is no question, however, that the current fascination with quality has brought this relationship into sharper focus. A number of areas in particular—including selection processes, development and training, and reward systems—can have a significant impact on quality performance. As we shall discuss next, the practices recommended by advocates of total quality management fit much of what is known about the relationship between HRM practices and quality. Together, the historical research and the recommendations on "best quality practices" make a strong case for changing the way many HR management systems are designed and operated.

Deming and others in the TQM movement have been outspoken in their criticism of performance appraisal practices. . . . These practices focus too much on the individual. . . .

Selection

For decades, research in the field has validated various selection devices (ability tests, personality tests, interviews, and the like) as indicators of how a candidate will perform on the job, in both productivity and quality. The current focus on total quality management, however, has brought a new dimension into play. Ability testing, in particular, needs to be viewed differently. Organizations that adopt a total quality management approach require individuals who are keen problem solvers and who can perform the type of mathematical work demanded by statistical process control, Pareto analysis, and the like. These abilities need to be tested for during the selection process, to ensure that the candidate has the capacity to learn and apply these methods.

Many Japanese companies that manufacture in the United States place great importance on the whole selection process. For these firms, the process is a long one, with high standards and a much greater emphasis on giving employees a realistic preview of what work will be like. The importance of this is very much corroborated by research findings, which show that realistic job previews help produce a stable workforce that fits the organizational culture. Interestingly, the practices in these Japanese plants are very similar to those now used in plants that have adopted the high-involvement approach to management.

Because of the emphasis on group processes in total quality management (suggestion systems, work teams, etc.), selection tactics must identify candidates who can function well in group settings. This has led to a number of new selection activities, including interviews by teams and the use of assessment centers. One company, Motorola, shows applicants video tapes of problem-solving groups in action and asks them how they would respond to a particular quality issue.

Concern for selecting capable employees is not new, and current practices do not differ greatly from the traditional HR focus. What is perhaps different is the *emphasis on a quality-oriented organization culture* as the desired outcome of selection. This goal requires organizations to commit more resources to the selection process itself, and to structure the process differently so that it includes a realistic preview of expected behaviors and encourages self-selection.

Development and Training

This is a major feature of all total quality management programs. Typically, the training covers problem-solving technologies, problem analysis, statistical process control, and quality measurement—a reach that goes far beyond specific job skills. Predictably, organizations that use problem-solving groups and teams also conduct extensive training in group process and group decision making. Finally, quality programs often call for extensive training programs for managers, to sensitize them to the importance of quality, the cost of poor quality, and the power of their behavior to influence the quality of products and services.

In many respects, a strong emphasis on training is exactly what human resource professionals have been urging for decades. In many cases, however, they have been unsuccessful in getting organizations to commit heavily to such an endeavor. International analyses of training costs show that U.S. corporations spend less on training than do their Japanese and European counterparts. There are some indications that this is, in fact, changing—and the change is long overdue. Motorola and IBM stand out as two companies that have made particularly strong commitments to training. Both encourage extensive training for all employees, mandating a specified number of days annually for all employees.

A strong emphasis on training is also consistent with the high-involvement management approaches that have been advocated for decades. Again, research has clearly shown that if employees at lower levels are to make decisions, they need not only job skills but also team-work skills and decision-making skills, as well as skill in managing their time and the company's resources.

In many respects, total quality efforts recognize the significant value that HR can add by increasing the skill level of the employees in the organization. This value is enhanced if the HR department approaches training needs with a customer service focus, thus becoming a partner in the total quality management effort.

Career Development

Historically, the career development practices of most large organizations have supported linear careers—i.e., career paths that move up the hierarchy through a single function. Assessment centers, management development programs, and a wide range of relatively sophisticated practices have made this path the desired route, ostensibly to insure that the senior managers in an organization are talented, knowledgeable individuals. These hierarchical practices need to be changed significantly.

In order to understand the work flow of an organization, employees need a *systems orientation*, a view of the whole that includes the horizontal relationships between processes. Understanding the horizontal flow requires cross-functional experience; improving the flow often means putting more power and decision-making authority in the hands of individuals at lower levels of the organization.

The career implications of this approach are significant. As a starting point, the systems orientation argues for greater emphasis on cross-functional career moves and, in some cases, purely horizontal reassignments. This type of career move has characterized Japanese organizations for decades, but represents a significant departure for American organizations. Interestingly, the same recommendations that apply here fit with both an emphasis on total quality management and an emphasis on high-involvement management. Both focus attention on horizontal flows and work designs. Understanding and managing these, in turn, require individuals to gain a picture of the whole as well as expertise in particular functions.

Performance Management

Individual performance appraisal is basic to the human resource management systems of most large corporations. Performance appraisals are used to determine reward levels, to validate tests, to aid career development, to improve communications, and to facilitate understanding of job duties. Deming and others in the TQM movement, however, have been outspoken in their criticism of the performance appraisal practices typical of most corporations. Deming and his colleagues point out that these practices focus too much on the individual—and often try to assign blame for quality problems to individuals. Deming argues that most quality problems are the product of systems and processes. Thus, focus on individuals is counterproductive, in that it diverts attention from the root (i.e., systemic) causes of poor quality.

Deming calls for totally scrapping individual performance appraisal systems, particularly those that are based on management by objectives or that encourage competition within the organization. In many respects, his recommendations tend to be consistent with the Japanese orientation toward collective responsibility.

Performance appraisal, then, represents the most significant area of conflict between current and recommended practices. For example, companies frequently try to solve quality problems by putting more emphasis on quality-related measures in the individual performance appraisal process. Although this is easily accommodated within an organization's existing performance management system, it is still *individual* appraisal, and thus at odds with TQM philosophy.

Complete abandonment of individual performance management represents a much more significant paradigm shift, one that, in fact, few organizations are willing to make. But if the goal is simply to align a system more closely with the principle of shared responsibility for quality, a total shift may not be necessary. For example, the performance management system can focus strongly on developing skills and abilities necessary to perform well and, as such, directly support collective responsibility. In addition, performance ratings do not have to be competitive; individuals can compete against absolute standards rather than against each other.

Finally, in participative and team-based organizations, peers can become involved in the appraisal process, and individuals can be evaluated on how much they contribute to team performance and how much they cooperate. This, in turn, can help reinforce the emphasis on collective responsibility and on the horizontal relationships that are needed to get individuals to own systems and collective results. These methods are rapidly becoming common in companies using high-involvement management and team-based approaches.

Overall, there seems to be little question that performance management practices need to change significantly if quality is to be part of the organization's culture. Clearly, traditional performance appraisal systems are more supportive of individual excellence and perhaps high levels of individual performance than they are of a systems-oriented focus on quality. Regardless of an organization's decision—to abandon individual performance appraisal, or to modify the system to gain a better fit with the emphasis on quality—the organization will need to make significant changes. The human resource management department should lead this change process.

Pay Systems

Moreover, job-based pay systems tend to reward individuals for moving up the organizational hierarchy. . . directly counter to the emphasis on horizontal movement . . .

Most pay systems have likewise focused on individuals. Job descriptions spell out what an individual is to do, job evaluation systems suggest how much the job is worth (and thus how much the individual is to be paid), and merit pay increases reflect how well the individual has done the job. Again, there is a strong, direct conflict between these traditional practices and the TQM emphasis on collective responsibility, horizontal relationships, and horizontal learning.

The first conflict is in the area of job descriptions and pay based on job worth. These approaches suggest that an individual's accountabilities and responsibilities are limited to the tasks that he or she regularly performs. Job descriptions, for example, define precisely what an individual is—and is not—accountable for. In contrast, much of the emphasis in the total quality management literature is on flexibility, and on responsibility for an entire production or service process.

Moreover, job-based pay systems tend to reward individuals for moving up the organizational hierarchy. This is directly counter to an emphasis on horizontal movement, and on developing skills related to both upstream and downstream processes.

Interestingly, the body of writing on total quality management contains little discussion of new approaches to pay that are more congruent with TQM. (For an exception to this rule, see Richard Schonberger's "Total Quality Management Cuts a Broad Swath," also in this issue.) Advocates of the high-involvement management approach, however, have suggested substituting skill-based pay for job-based pay. In essence, these systems pay individuals for what they can do by basing increases on the acquisition of new skills and knowledge. The skills may relate to either horizontal or vertical processes. The logic is that individuals with this broader knowledge will be more effective problem solvers, and thus make a greater contribution to quality. Overall, skill-based pay would seem the better fit.

Individual merit pay systems place a strong emphasis on individual performance, almost always creating a competitive situation among employees. (To give a higher increase to one employee, managers must take money from another employee in the form of a lower increase.) Not surprisingly, quality management programs have emphasized abandoning individual-based merit increase systems. Typically, however, they have not suggested an alternative.

This dearth of ideas in the area of pay systems contrasts sharply with the emphasis on gainsharing plans, profit-sharing plans, and stock ownership plans that is present in much of the writing on employee involvement and participative management. This body of literature emphasizes pushing rewards for collective performance throughout the organization and creating a financial reason for employees to be involved in the business and make performance improvements.

In the United States, where rewards for performance are a major cultural value, it is important to create reward systems that not only reward quality improvements but also create a team environment and a group orientation. Creating organizations that focus on collective pay-for-performance is a major challenge for human resource management departments. The evidence on gainsharing plans, profit-sharing plans, and other collective pay-for-performance plans strongly suggests that these tactics work only when they are combined with strong communication programs and relatively high levels of employee involvement.

The implication of this for the human resources function is clear. Not only is it important to support the design of group, plant, and organizational-wide pay-for-performance plans, it is also critical to develop appropriate training and communication activities. In the absence of ongoing training and communication, these programs may simply end up as extra costs that produce few advantages.

Perquisites

Most large organizations tend to be highly stratified. Some stratification is required by law, but much of it occurs—quite simply—because organizations operate hierarchically. And the allocation of perquisites and benefits reinforces the hierarchy. Organizations can do little about the fact that some employees have to be on a nonexempt, overtime-pay basis while others are exempt. However, they can do a lot about who has access to parking lots, dining rooms, and office space. The principle of collective responsibility strongly suggests that organizations need to be much more egalitarian in their personnel and human resource management practices. This point also is highly consistent with the emphasis found in employee involvement programs on non-hierarchical allocation of perquisites, status symbols, and a host of other organizational rewards.

Perquisites are the trappings that go with a position, and in that sense they are simply symbolic and cultural. But, in some respects, the issue goes beyond this. Allocating rewards based on hierarchy can influence how strongly individuals are motivated to seek advancement. Upward mobility is highly attractive in an organization where "the group at the top" is expected to direct the organization, assume accountability for results, and enjoy the perquisites. Again, we see a sharp conflict with the principle of a broad based, multilevel responsibility for quality. Among other things, the hierarchy encourages individuals to listen to people *because they are in a position of power*, rather than *because they have greater expertise*. It also sends a message to individuals at lower levels in the organization: "Sit back and wait for people at the top to take action and solve the problem."

One final point about status symbols and perquisites. They tend to create an environment in which communication channels are easily clogged, especially when communications need to move across functional and hierarchical levels. Differences in office space, accessibility, and visible rewards can block the kind of communication flow and work relationships that are needed to produce systems thinking and solutions.

Labor Relations

Historically, labor relations in the United States have been adversarial, partially because U.S. labor laws were designed to support collective bargaining. There is little doubt that adversarial relationships are the antithesis of the shared responsibility needed to produce high-quality products and services. This is particularly true if the union/management agreements are based on large bureaucratic contracts, carefully specified jobs and accountabilities, and elaborate grievance procedures. There is little room for generating the kind of participation, problem solving, and systems solutions that quality management programs emphasize.

Advocates of employee involvement argue for labor/management relationships that make unions "partners" in the organization's success and regard them as "critical players" in helping the organization achieve its goals—relationships much more compatible with total quality management efforts. The union also assumes responsibility for quality, thus creating opportunity for more systems thinking and more creative problem solving. These relationships also help create a climate in which employees participate in many of the important decisions affecting quality. In the absence of union support for employee problem solving and union/employee participation in improvement groups, there is a danger that employees will not trust the process, and that the union will ultimately reject the activities that are part of the total quality program.

Human resources departments clearly have a central role to play in moving union relationships into a partner mode. More than any other part of the organization, the human resources function deals on a day-to-day basis with the union. It also, of course, handles collective bargaining and indeed, historically, has gained considerable power in organizations because it does so. It needs to play a major role in restructuring the collective bargaining process, turning an adversarial process into one that is more problem-solving and vision oriented. Unfortunately, HR departments sometimes resist this change because they see it as eroding their power and influence. In fact, it may have quite the opposite effect if a more effective labor management relationship is created.

A positive example of this change is represented by the Saturn Corporation's cooperative labor/management relationship. There, the contract has been shortened to just a few pages of general philosophy about how the union and management relate. It clearly states that the company and its union are partners in this venture and that the role of union is one of facilitating employee's involvement in the running of the business and in producing a high-quality product.

Communication

Feedback about quality and information about the strategy and direction of the organization are critical to all quality-improvement programs. The human resources management systems in an organization need to be structured so that they encourage the open flow of information related to quality and business results throughout the organization. The human resources department, of course, is just one component in the organization that needs to support this approach. Nevertheless, because of its presence throughout the organization and its critical role in many of the basic systems that regularly impact on employees, it needs to play a major role in supporting widespread communication of performance results, objectives, and strategic plans. This orientation is a notable contrast to the historical practices in many large organizations.

Secrecy about performance results, business plans, and major changes is the norm for a variety of reasons. In union/management situations, management has assumed that the union cannot be trusted to receive confidential data—or that the information would come back to haunt the company in a collective bargaining session. Many of the same attitudes pertain to information given to employees: They're not interested in it, wouldn't understand it, or can't be trusted with it. The result has been that employees tend not to care about their company's performance.

The evidence from a variety of studies strongly suggests that if employees are going to care about goals and performance improvement plans, they need to receive regular, ongoing communication. In addition, being part of the process that structures communication programs also helps. The human resources function needs to play a role in assuring that employees receive information, have the skills to understand that information, and, where appropriate, participate in developing the communication programs that exist in the organization.

Finally, the human resources function needs to help the organization develop information about how it is doing in establishing a quality culture, improving communication, and involving individuals in the business. Attitude surveys can facilitate this, as can focus groups. The results of these need to be generally distributed and, where appropriate, used as the basis for problem-solving activities.

CHANGE AND HR MANAGEMENT

Five themes emerge across the different quality-oriented HR practices, setting them apart from conventional HR practice: (1) a focus on the organization, rather than the job; (2) support for group performance, rather than individual performance; (3) egalitarianism, rather than hierarchy; (4) change, rather than stability; and (5) participation, rather than command and control.

These five themes represent a radical break with the past as far as HR management is concerned. They demand major changes in both the way HR departments are run and in the type of systems they create and operate.

Major change can be frightening, but it can also be empowering. We believe the opportunity exists for HR departments to become much more important in most organizations if they can change the way they operate. The pursuit of total quality can inspire, guide, and unify this change.

Selected Bibliography

Tom Peters' thoughts on TQM were excerpted from a 1991 Tom Peters Group newsletter. Y. K. Shetty and P. F. Buller, "Regaining Competitiveness Requires HR Solutions," *Personnel* (July 1990, pp. 8–12) was the source for the survey data we reported. Donna Brown, "HR: Survival Tool for the 1990s," *Management Review* (March 1991, pp. 10–14) was the source of Crosby's thoughts on HR executives. Other writings that stress the paramount importance of human resources in quality include: Randall S. Schuler and Drew L. Harris, "Deming Quality Improvement: Implications for Human Resource Management in a Small Company," *Human Resource Planning* (1991, Vol. 14 No. 3, pp. 191–207); William F. Roth, Jr., "Quality Through People: A Hit for HR," *Personnel* (November 1989, pp. 50–52); William N. Yeamans, "Building Competitiveness Through HRD Renewal," *Training & Development Journal* (October 1989, pp. 77–82); Charles F. Hendricks and Arlene Triplett, "TQM: Strategy for 90s Management," *Personnel Administration* (December 1989, pp. 42–48); William F. Roth, Jr., "Dos and Don'ts of Quality Improvement,"

Quality Progress (August 1990, pp. 85–87); and "A Forum for the Power of Quality," *Quality Progress* (February 1990, pp. 19–24).

Articles that describe or imply how to implement TQM principles within the HRM department, itself, include: Clay Carr, "Injecting Quality into Personnel Management," *Personnel Journal* (September 1987, pp. 43–51); "Transamerica Rethinks HR Structure," *HR Reporter*; David Bowen and Larry Greiner, "Moving from Production to Service in Human Resources Management," *Organizational Dynamics* (Summer 1986, pp. 35–53); and William Kahnweiler, "HRD and Empowerment," *Training & Development* (November 1991, pp. 73–76).

References that describe the HRM practices associated with employee involvement and their relationship to total quality include: Edward Lawler III, *The Ultimate Advantage* (San Francisco: Jossey-Bass, 1991) and Edward Lawler III, Susan Mohrman, and Gerald Ledford, *Employee Involvement and Total Quality Management: Practices and Results in Fortune 1000 Companies* (San Francisco: Jossey-Bass, 1992).

GLOBAL ISSUES IN HUMAN RESOURCE MANAGEMENT

INTRODUCTION

A number of factors such as a country's culture, education/human capital, legal/political system, and economic system can affect the desirability of locating facilities in that country, as well as influencing the perceived appropriateness of various HRM practices. It is also important to have internationally oriented management systems if organizations are to effectively compete in today's globally competitive environment. The readings in this section illustrate these issues.

Reading 6 by Hofstede notes the effects of culture on management theories. Hofstede, one of the leading researchers on cross-cultural management issues, points out that in different countries managers have different roles, and these roles are culturally determined. He explores how managers are viewed in Germany, Japan, France, Holland, China, Southeast Asia, Africa, and Russia. He presents a model based on his five dimensions of culture that were discussed in Chapter 3 and uses this model to explain some of the differences in management across culture. This leads to a discussion of the limits to the applicability or appropriateness of management systems developed in the United States.

Reading 7 by Adler and Bartholomew examines some of the ways that firms must develop globally competent managers in transnational firms. These authors examine two basic issues. First, they explore the skills that global managers must have—skills that transcend those of traditional expatriate managers. Second, they examine the changes in management systems that are required to effectively manage people in a global setting. The current state of organizations on these dimensions is then assessed in a survey that the authors conducted. They found that few firms actually exhibit the levels of transnational scope, transnational representation, and transnational process that should characterize successful firms. Finally, they present some of the myths of transnational management processes that exist in today's organizations, exploring how these myths can be destroyed.

READING 6

CULTURAL CONSTRAINTS IN MANAGEMENT THEORIES

Geert Hofstede

Executive Overview

Management *as the word is presently used is an American invention. In other parts of the world not only the practices but the entire concept of management may differ, and the theories needed to understand it, may deviate considerably from what is considered normal and desirable in the USA. The reader is invited on a trip around the world, and both local management practices and theories are explained from the different contexts and histories of the places visited: Germany, Japan, France, Holland, the countries of the overseas Chinese, South-East Asia, Africa, Russia, and finally mainland China.*

A model in which worldwide differences in national cultures are categorized according to five independent dimensions helps in explaining the differences in management found; although the situation in each country or region has unique characteristics that no model can account for. One practical application of the model is in demonstrating the relative position of the U.S. versus other parts of the world. In a global perspective, U.S. management theories contain a number of idiosyncrasies not necessarily shared by management elsewhere. Three such idiosyncrasies are mentioned: a stress on market processes, a stress on the individual, and a focus on managers rather than on workers. A plea is made for an internationalization not only of business, but also of management theories, as a way of enriching theories at the national level.

Lewis Carroll's *Alice in Wonderland* contains the famous story of Alice's croquet game with the Queen of Hearts.

> Alice thought she had never seen such a curious croquet-ground in all her life; it was all ridges and furrows; the balls were live hedgehogs, the mallets

Source: "Cultural Constraints in Management Theories" by Geert Hofstede, *Academy of Management Executive*, 1993, Vol. 7, No. 1, 81–94.

The issues explored here were presented by Dr. Hofstede, the Foundation for Administrative Research Distinguished International Scholar, at the 1992 Annual Meeting of the Academy of Management, Las Vegas, Nevada, August 11, 1992.

live flamingoes, and the soldiers had to double themselves up and to stand on their hands and feet, to make the arches.

You probably know how the story goes: Alice's flamingo mallet turns its head whenever she wants to strike with it; her hedgehog ball runs away; and the doubled-up soldier arches walk around all the time. The only rule seems to be that the Queen of Hearts always wins.

Alice's croquet playing problems are good analogies to attempts to build culture-free theories of management. Concepts available for this purpose are themselves alive with culture, having been developed within a particular cultural context. They have a tendency to guide our thinking toward our desired conclusion.

As the same reasoning may also be applied to the arguments in this article, I better tell you my conclusion before I continue—so that the rules of my game are understood. In this article we take a trip around the world to demonstrate that there are no such things as universal management theories.

Diversity in management *practices* as we go around the world has been recognized in U.S. management literature for more than thirty years. The term "comparative management" has been used since the 1960s. However, it has taken much longer for the U.S. academic community to accept that not only practices but also the validity of *theories* may stop at national borders, and I wonder whether even today everybody would agree with this statement.

An article I published in *Organizational Dynamics* in 1980 entitled "Do American Theories Apply Abroad?" created more controversy than I expected. The article argued, with empirical support, that generally accepted U.S. theories like those of Maslow, Herzberg, McClelland, Vroom, McGregor, Likert, Blake and Mouton may not or only very partly apply outside the borders of their country of origin—assuming they do apply within those borders. Among the requests for reprints, a larger number were from Canada than from the United States.

MANAGEMENT THEORISTS ARE HUMAN

Employees and managers are human. Employees as humans was "discovered" in the 1930s, with the Human Relations school. Managers as humans, was introduced in the late 40s by Herbert Simon's "bounded rationality" and elaborated in Richard Cyert and James March's *Behavioral Theory of the Firm* (1963, and recently re-published in a second edition). My argument is that management scientists, theorists, and writers are human too: they grew up in a particular society in a particular period, and their ideas cannot help but reflect the constraints of their environment.

The idea that the validity of a theory is constrained by national borders is more obvious in Europe, with all its borders, than in a huge borderless country like the U.S. Already in the sixteenth century Michel de Montaigne, a Frenchman, wrote a statement which was made famous by Blaise Pascal about a century later: *"Vérite en-deça des Pyrenées, erreur au-delà"*—There are truths on this side of the Pyrenées which are falsehoods on the other.

FROM DON ARMADO'S LOVE TO TAYLOR'S SCIENCE

According to the comprehensive ten-volume Oxford English Dictionary (1971), the words "manage," "management," and "manager" appeared in the English language in the 16th century. The oldest recorded use of the word "manager" is in Shakespeare's "Love's Labour's Lost," dating from 1588, in which Don Adriano de Armado, "a fantastical Spaniard," exclaims (Act I, scene ii, 188):

Adieu, valour! rust, rapier! be still, drum! for your manager is in love; yea, he loveth.

The linguistic origin of the word is from Latin *manus*, hand, via the Italian *maneggiare*, which is the training of horses in the *manege*; subsequently its meaning was extended to skillful handling in general, like of arms and musical instruments, as Don Armado illustrates. However, the word also became associated with the French *menage*, household, as an equivalent of "husbandry" in its sense of the art of running a household. The theatre of present-day management contains elements of both *manege* and *menage* and different managers and cultures may use different accents.

The founder of the science of economics, the Scot Adam Smith, in his 1776 book *The Wealth of Nations*, used "manage," "management" (even "bad management") and "manager" when dealing with the process and the persons involved in operating joint stock companies (Smith, V.i.e.). British economist John Stuart Mill (1806–1873) followed Smith in this use and clearly expressed his distrust of such hired people who were not driven by ownership. Since the 1880s the word "management" appeared occasionally in writings by American engineers, until it was canonized as a modern science by Frederick W. Taylor in *Shop Management* in 1903 and in *The Principles of Scientific Management* in 1911.

While Smith and Mill used "management" to describe a process and "managers" for the persons involved, "management" in the American sense—which has since been taken back by the British—refers not only to the process but also to the managers as a class of people. This class (1) does not own a business but sells its skills to act on behalf of the owners and (2) does not produce personally but is indispensable for making others produce, through motivation. Members of this class carry a high status and many American boys and girls aspire to the role. In the U.S., the manager is a cultural hero.

Let us now turn to other parts of the world. We will look at management in its context in other successful modern economies: Germany, Japan, France, Holland, and among the Overseas Chinese. Then we will examine management in the much larger part of the world that is still poor, especially South-East Asia and Africa, and in the new political configurations of Eastern Europe, and Russia in particular. We will then return to the U.S. via mainland China.

Germany

The manager is not a cultural hero in Germany. If anybody, it is the engineer who fills the hero role. Frederick Taylor's *Scientific Management* was conceived in a society of immigrants—where large numbers of workers with diverse backgrounds and skills had to work together. In Germany this heterogeneity never existed.

Elements of the mediaeval guild system have survived in historical continuity in Germany until the present day. In particular, a very effective apprenticeship system exists both on the shop floor and in the office, which alternates practical work and classroom courses. At the end of the apprenticeship the worker receives a certificate, the *Facharbeiterbrief*, which is recognized throughout the country. About two thirds of the German worker population holds such a certificate and a corresponding occupational pride. In fact, quite a few German company presidents have worked their way up from the ranks through an apprenticeship. In comparison, two thirds of the worker population in Britain have no occupational qualification at all.

The highly skilled and responsible German workers do not necessarily need a manager, American-style, to "motivate" them. They expect their boss or *Meister* to assign their tasks and to be the expert in resolving technical problems. Comparisons of similar German, British, and French organizations show the Germans as having the highest rate of personnel in productive roles and the lowest both in leadership and staff roles.

Business schools are virtually unknown in Germany. Native German management theories concentrate on formal systems. The inapplicability of American concepts of management was quite apparent in 1973 when the U.S. consulting firm of Booz, Allen and Hamilton, commissioned by the German Ministry of Economic Affairs, wrote a study of German management from an American view point. The report is highly critical and writes among other things that "Germans simply do not have a very strong concept of management." Since 1973, from my personal experience, the situation has not changed much. However, during this period the German economy has performed in a superior fashion to the U.S. in virtually all respects, so a strong concept of management might have been a liability rather than an asset.

Japan

The American type of manager is also missing in Japan. In the United States, the core of the enterprise is the managerial class. The core of the Japanese enterprise is the permanent worker group; workers who for all practical purposes are tenured and who aspire at life-long employment. They are distinct from the non-permanent employees—most women and subcontracted teams led by gang bosses, to be laid off in slack periods. University graduates in Japan first join the permanent worker group and subsequently fill various positions, moving from line to staff as the need occurs while paid according to seniority rather than position. They take part in Japanese-style group consultation sessions for important decisions, which extend the decision-making period but guarantee fast implementation afterwards. Japanese are to a large extent controlled by their peer group rather than by their manager.

Japanese are to a large extent controlled by their peer group rather than by their manager.

Three researchers from the East-West Center of the University of Hawaii, Joseph Tobin, David Wu, and Dana Danielson, did an observation study of typical

preschools in three countries: China, Japan, and the United States. Their results have been published both as a book and as a video. In the Japanese preschool, one teacher handled twenty-eight four-year olds. The video shows one particularly obnoxious boy, Hiroki, who fights with other children and throws teaching materials down from the balcony. When a little girl tries to alarm the teacher, the latter answers "what are you calling me for? Do something about it!" In the U.S. preschool, there is one adult for every nine children. This class has its problem child too, Glen, who refuses to clear away his toys. One of the teachers has a long talk with him and isolates him in a corner, until he changes his mind. It doesn't take much imagination to realize that managing Hiroki thirty years later will be a different process from managing Glen.

American theories of leadership are ill-suited for the Japanese group-controlled situation. During the past two decades, the Japanese have developed their own "PM" theory of leadership, in which P stands for performance and M for maintenance. The latter is less a concern for individual employees than for maintaining social stability. In view of the amazing success of the Japanese economy in the past thirty years, many Americans have sought for the secrets of Japanese management hoping to copy them.

There are no secrets of Japanese management, however; it is even doubtful whether there is such a thing as management, in the American sense, in Japan at all. The secret is in Japanese society; and if any group in society should be singled out as carriers of the secret, it is the workers, not the managers.

France

The manager, U.S. style, does not exist in France either. In a very enlightening book, unfortunately not yet translated into English, the French researcher Philippe d'Iribarne (1989) describes the results of in-depth observation and interview studies of management methods in three subsidiary plants of the same French multinational; in France, the United States, and Holland. He relates what he finds to information about the three societies in general. Where necessary, he goes back in history to trace the roots of the strikingly different behaviors in the completion of the same tasks. He identifies three kinds of basic principles (*logiques*) of management. In the USA, the principle is the *fair contract* between employer and employee, which gives the manager considerable prerogatives, but within its limits. This is really a labor *market* in which the worker sells his or her labor for a price. In France, the principle is the *honor* of each class in a society which has always been and remains extremely stratified, in which superiors behave as superior beings and subordinates accept and expect this, conscious of their own lower level in the national hierarchy but also of the honor of their own class. The French do not think in terms of managers versus nonmanagers but in terms of *cadres* versus *non-cadres*; one becomes cadre by attending the proper schools and one remains it forever; regardless of their actual task, cadres have the privileges of a higher social class, and it is very rare for a non-cadre to cross the ranks.

The conflict between French and American theories of management became apparent in the beginning of the twentieth century, in a criticism by the great French management pioneer Henri Fayol (1841–1925) on his U.S. colleague and contemporary Frederick W. Taylor (1856–1915). The difference in career paths of the two men is striking. Fayol was a French engineer whose career as a *cadre superieur* culminated in the position of Président-Directeur-Général of a mining company. After his retirement he formulated his experiences in a path-breaking text on organization: *Administration industrielle et générale,* in which he focussed on the sources of authority. Taylor was an American engineer who started his career in industry as a worker and attained his academic qualifications through evening studies. From chief engineer in a steel company he became one of the first management consultants. Taylor was not really concerned with the issue of authority at all; his focus was on efficiency. He proposed to split the task of the first-line boss into eight specialisms, each exercised by a different person; an idea which eventually led to the idea of a matrix organization.

Taylor's work appeared in a French translation in 1913, and Fayol read it and showed himself generally impressed but shocked by Taylor's "denial of the principle of the Unity of Command" in the case of the eight-boss-system.

Seventy years later André Laurent, another of Fayol's compatriots, found that French managers in a survey reacted very strongly against a suggestion that one employee could report to two different bosses, while U.S. managers in the same survey showed fewer misgivings. Matrix organization has never become popular in France as it has in the United States.

Holland

In my own country, Holland or as it is officially called, the Netherlands, the study by Philippe d'Iribarne found the management principle to be a need for *consensus* among all parties, neither predetermined by a contractual relationship nor by class distinctions, but based on an open-ended exchange of views and a balancing of interests. In terms of the different origins of the word "manager," the organization in Holland is more *menage* (household) while in the United States it is more *manege* (horse drill).

At my university, the University of Limburg at Maastricht, every semester we receive a class of American business students who take a program in European Studies. We asked both the Americans and a matched group of Dutch students to describe their ideal job after graduation, using a list of twenty-two job characteristics. The Americans attached significantly more importance than the Dutch to earnings, advancement, benefits, a good working relationship with their boss, and security of employment. The Dutch attached more importance to freedom to adopt their own approach to the job, being consulted by their boss in his or her decisions, training opportunities, contributing to the success of their organization, fully using their skills and abilities, and helping others. This list confirms d'Iribarne's findings of a contractual employment relationship in the United States, based on earnings and career opportunities, against a consensual relationship in Holland. The latter has centuries-old roots; the Netherlands were the first republic in Western Europe (1609–1810), and a model for the American republic. The country has been and still is governed by a careful balancing of interests in a multi-party system.

In terms of management theories, both motivation and leadership in Holland are different from what they are in the United States. Leadership in Holland presupposes modesty, as opposed to assertiveness in the United States. No U.S. leadership theory has room for that. Working in Holland is not a constant feast, however. There is a built-in premium on mediocrity and jealousy, as well as time-consuming ritual consultations to maintain the appearance of consensus and the pretense of modesty. There is unfortunately another side to every coin.

The Overseas Chinese

Among the champions of economic development in the past thirty years we find three countries mainly populated by Chinese living outside the Chinese mainland: Taiwan, Hong Kong and Singapore. Moreover, overseas Chinese play a very important role in the economies of Indonesia, Malaysia, the Philippines and Thailand, where they form an ethnic minority. If anything, the little dragons—Taiwan, Hong Kong and Singapore—have been more economically successful than Japan, moving from rags to riches and now counted among the world's wealthy industrial countries. Yet very little attention has been paid to the way in which their enterprises have been managed. *The Spirit of Chinese Capitalism* by Gordon Redding (1990), the British dean of the Hong Kong Business School, is an excellent book about Chinese business. He bases his insights on personal acquaintance and in-depth discussions with a large number of overseas Chinese business people.

If nothing else, the general lack of success in economic development of other countries should be sufficient argument to doubt the validity of Western management theories in non-Western environments.

Overseas Chinese American enterprises lack almost all characteristics of modern management. They tend to be small, cooperating for essential functions with other small organizations through networks based on personal relations. They are family-owned, without the separation between ownership and management typical in the West, or even in Japan and Korea. They normally focus on one product or market, with growth by opportunistic diversification; in this, they are extremely flexible. Decision making is centralized in the hands of one dominant family member, but other family members may be given new ventures to try their skills on. They are low-profile and extremely cost-conscious, applying Confucian virtues of thrift and persistence. Their size is kept small by the assumed lack of loyalty of non-family employees, who, if they are any good, will just wait and save until they can start their own family business.

Overseas Chinese prefer economic activities in which great gains can be made with little manpower, like commodity trading and real estate. They employ few professional managers, except their sons and sometimes daughters who have been sent to prestigious business schools abroad, but who upon return continue to run the family business the Chinese way.

The origin of this system, or—in the Western view—this lack of system, is found in the history of Chinese society, in which there were no formal laws, only formal networks of powerful people guided by general principles of Confucian virtue. The favors of the authorities could change daily, so nobody could be trusted except one's kinfolk—of whom, fortunately, there used to be many, in an extended family structure. The overseas Chinese way of doing business is also very well adapted to their position in the countries in which they form ethnic minorities, often envied and threatened by ethnic violence.

Overseas Chinese businesses following this unprofessional approach command a collective gross national product of some 200 to 300 billion US dollars, exceeding the GNP of Australia. There is no denying that it works.

MANAGEMENT TRANSFER TO POOR COUNTRIES

Four-fifths of the world population live in countries that are not rich but poor. After World War II and decolonization, the stated purpose of the United Nations and the World Bank has been to promote the development of all the world's countries in a war on poverty. After forty years it looks very much like we are losing this war. If one thing has become clear, it is that the export of Western— mostly American—management practices *and* theories to poor countries has contributed little to nothing to their development. There has been no lack of effort and money spent for this purpose: students from poor countries have been trained in this country, and teachers and Peace Corps workers have been sent to the poor countries. If nothing else, the general lack of success in economic development of other countries should be sufficient argument to doubt the validity of Western management theories in non-Western environments.

If we examine different parts of the world, the development picture is not equally bleak, and history is often a better predictor than economic factors for what happens today. There is a broad regional pecking order with East Asia leading. The little dragons have passed into the camp of the wealthy; then follow South-East Asia (with its overseas Chinese minorities), Latin America (in spite of the debt crisis), South Asia, and Africa always trails behind. Several African countries have only become poorer since decolonization.

Regions of the world with a history of large-scale political integration and civilization generally have done better than regions in which no large-scale political and cultural infrastructure existed, even if the old civilizations had decayed or been suppressed by colonizers. It has become painfully clear that development cannot be pressure-cooked; it presumes a cultural infrastructure that takes time to grow. Local management is part of this infrastructure; it cannot be imported in package form. Assuming that with so-called modern management techniques and theories outsiders can develop a country has proven a deplorable arrogance. At best, one can hope for a dialogue between equals with the locals, in which the Western partner acts as the expert in Western technology and the local partner as the expert in local culture, habits, and feelings.

Assuming that with so-called modern management techniques and theories outsiders can develop a country has proven a deplorable arrogance.

Russia and China

The crumbling of the former Eastern bloc has left us with a scattering of states and would-be states of which the political and economic future is extremely uncertain. The best predictions are those based on a knowledge of history, because historical trends have taken revenge on the arrogance of the Soviet rulers who believed they could turn them around by brute power. One obvious fact is that the former bloc is extremely heterogeneous, including countries traditionally closely linked with the West by trade and travel, like Czechia, Hungary, Slovenia, and the Baltic states, as well as others with a Byzantine or Turkish past; some having been prosperous, others always extremely poor.

The industrialized Western world and the World Bank seem committed to helping the ex-Eastern bloc countries develop, but with the same technocratic neglect for local cultural factors that proved so unsuccessful in the development assistance to other poor countries. Free market capitalism, introduced by Western-style management, is supposed to be the answer from Albania to Russia.

Let me limit myself to the Russian republic, a huge territory with some 140 million inhabitants, mainly Russians. We know quite a bit about the Russians as their country was a world power for several hundreds of years before communism, and in the nineteenth century it has produced some of the greatest writers in world literature. If I want to understand the Russians—including how they could so long support the Soviet regime—I tend to re-read Lev Nikolayevich Tolstoy. In his most famous novel *Anna Karenina* (1876) one of the main characters is a landowner, Levin, whom Tolstoy uses to express his own views and convictions about his people. Russian peasants used to be serfs; serfdom had been abolished in 1861, but the peasants, now tenants, remained as passive as before. Levin wanted to break this passivity by dividing the land among his peasants in exchange for a share of the crops; but the peasants only let the land deteriorate further. Here follows a quote:

> (Levin) read political economy and socialistic works . . . but, as he had expected, found nothing in them related to his undertaking. In the political economy books—in (John Stuart) Mill, for instance, whom he studied first and with great ardour, hoping every minute to find an answer to the questions that were engrossing him—he found only certain laws deduced from the state of agriculture in Europe; but he could not for the life of him see why these laws, which did not apply to Russia, should be considered universal. . . . Political economy told him that the laws by which Europe had developed and was developing her wealth were universal and absolute. Socialist teaching told him that development along those lines leads to ruin. And neither of them offered the smallest enlightenment as to what he, Levin, and all the Russian peasants and landowners were to do with their millions of hands and millions of acres, to make them as productive as possible for the common good.

In the summer of 1991, the Russian lands yielded a record harvest, but a large share of it rotted in the fields because no people were to be found for harvesting. The passivity is still there, and not only among the peasants. And the heirs of John Stuart Mill (whom we met before as one of the early analysts of "management") again present their universal recipes which simply do not apply.

Citing Tolstoy, I implicitly suggest that management theorists cannot neglect the great literature of the countries they want their ideas to apply to. The greatest novel in the Chinese literature is considered Cao Xueqin's *The Story of the Stone,* also known as *The Dream of the Red Chamber* which appeared around 1760. It describes the rise and fall of two branches of an aristocratic family in Beijing, who live in adjacent plots in the capital. Their plots are joined by a magnificent garden with several pavilions in it, and the young, mostly female members of both families are allowed to live in them. One day the management of the garden is taken over by a young woman, Tan-Chun, who states:

> I think we ought to pick out a few experienced trust-worthy old women from among the ones who work in the Garden—women who know something about gardening already—and put the upkeep of the Garden into their hands. We needn't ask them to pay us rent; all we need ask them for is an annual share of the produce. There would be four advantages in this arrangement. In the first place, if we have people whose sole occupation is to look after trees and flowers and so on, the condition of the Garden will improve gradually year after year and there will be no more of those long periods of neglect followed by bursts of feverish activity when things have been allowed to get out of hand. Secondly there won't be the spoiling and wastage we get at present. Thirdly the women themselves will gain a little extra to add to their incomes which will compensate them for the hard work they put in throughout the year. And fourthly, there's no reason why we shouldn't use the money we should otherwise have spent on nurserymen, rockery specialists, horticultural cleaners and so on for other purposes.

As the story goes on, the capitalist privatization—because that is what it is—of the Garden is carried through, and it works. When in the 1980s Deng Xiaoping allowed privatization in the Chinese villages, it also worked. It worked so well that its effects started to be felt in politics and threatened the existing political order; hence the knockdown at Tienanmen Square of June 1989. But it seems that the forces of privatization are getting the upper hand again in China. If we remember what Chinese entrepreneurs are able to do once they have become Overseas Chinese, we shouldn't be too surprised. But what works in China—and worked two centuries ago—does not have to work in Russia, not in Tolstoy's days and not today. I am not offering a solution; I only protest against a naive universalism that knows only one recipe for development, the one supposed to have worked in the United States.

A THEORY OF CULTURE IN MANAGEMENT

Our trip around the world is over and we are back in the United States. What have we learned? There is something in all countries called "management," but its meaning differs to a larger or smaller extent from one country to the other, and it takes considerable historical and cultural insight into local conditions to understand its processes, philosophies, and problems. If already the word may mean so many different things, how can we expect one country's theories of management to apply abroad? One should be extremely careful in making this assumption, and test it before considering it proven. Management is not a phenomenon that can be isolated from other processes taking place in a society. During our trip around the world we saw that it interacts with what happens in the family, at school, in politics, and government. It is obviously also related to religion and to beliefs about science. Theories of management always had to be interdisciplinary, but if we cross national borders they should become more interdisciplinary than ever.

Cultural differences between nations can be, to some extent, described using first four, and now five, bipolar *dimensions*. The position of a country on these dimensions allows us to make some predictions on the way their society operates, including their management processes and the kind of theories applicable to their management.

As the word *culture* plays such an important role in my theory, let me give you my definition, which differs from some other very respectable definitions. Culture to me is *the collective programming of the mind which distinguishes one group or category of people from another.* In the part of my work I am referring to now, the category of people is the nation.

Culture is a *construct,* that means it is "not directly accessible to observation but inferable from verbal statements and other behaviors and useful in predicting still other observable and measurable verbal and nonverbal behavior." It should not be reified; it is an auxiliary concept that should be used as long as it proves useful but bypassed where we can predict behaviors without it.

The same applies to the *dimensions* I introduced. They are constructs too that should not be reified. They do not "exist"; they are tools for analysis which may or may not clarify a situation. In my statistical analysis of empirical data the first four dimensions together explain forty-nine percent of the variance in the data. The other fifty-one percent remain specific to individual countries.

The first four dimensions were initially detected through a comparison of the values of similar people (employees and managers) in sixty-four national subsidiaries of the IBM Corporation. People working for the same multinational, but in different countries, represent very well-matched samples from the populations of their countries, similar in all respects except nationality.

The first dimension is labelled *Power Distance,* and it can be defined as the degree of inequality among people which the population of a country considers as normal: from relatively equal (that is, small power distance) to extremely unequal (large power distance). All societies are unequal, but some are more unequal than others.

The second dimension is labelled *Individualism,* and it is the degree to which people in a country prefer to act as individuals rather than as members of groups. The opposite of individualism can be called *Collectivism,* so collectivism is low individualism. The way I use the word it has no political connotations. In collectivist societies a child learns to respect the group to which it belongs, usually the family, and to differentiate between in-group members and out-group members (that is, all other people). When children grow up they remain members of their group, and they expect the group to protect them when they are in trouble. In return, they have to remain loyal to their group throughout life. In individualist societies, a child learns very early to think of itself as "I" instead of as part of "we". It expects one day to have to stand on its own feet and not to get protection from its group any more; and therefore it also does not feel a need for strong loyalty.

The third dimension is called *Masculinity* and its opposite pole *Femininity*. It is the degree to which tough values like assertiveness, performance, success and competition, which in nearly all societies are associated with the role of men, prevail over tender values like the quality of life, maintaining warm personal relationships, service, care for the weak, and solidarity, which in nearly all societies are more associated with women's roles. Women's roles differ from men's roles in all countries; but in tough societies, the differences are larger than in tender ones.

The fourth dimension is labelled *Uncertainty Avoidance,* and it can be defined as the degree to which people in a country prefer structured over unstructured situations. Structured situations are those in which there are clear rules as to how one should behave. These rules can be written down, but they can also be unwritten and imposed by tradition. In countries which score high on uncertainty avoidance, people tend to show more nervous energy, while in countries which score low, people are more easy-going. A (national) society with strong uncertainty avoidance can be called rigid; one with weak uncertainty avoidance, flexible. In countries where uncertainty avoidance is strong a feeling prevails of "what is different, is dangerous." In weak uncertainty avoidance societies, the feeling would rather be "what is different, is curious."

The fifth dimension was added on the basis of a study of the values of students in twenty-three countries carried out by Michael Harris Bond, a Canadian working in Hong Kong. He and I had cooperated in another study of students' values which had yielded the same four dimensions as the IBM data. However, we wondered to what extent our common findings in two studies could be the effect of a Western bias introduced by the common Western background of the researchers: remember Alice's croquet game. Michael Bond resolved this dilemma by deliberately introducing an Eastern bias. He used a questionnaire prepared at his request by his Chinese colleagues, the *Chinese Value Survey* (CVS), which was translated from Chinese into different languages and answered by fifty male and fifty female students in each of twenty-three countries in all five continents. Analysis of the CVS data produced three dimensions significantly correlated with the three IBM dimensions of power distance, individualism, and masculinity. There was also a fourth dimension, but it did not resemble uncertainty avoidance. It was composed, both on the positive and on the negative side, from items that had not been included in the IBM studies but were present in the Chinese Value Survey because they were rooted in the teachings of Confucius. I labelled this dimension: *Long-term* versus *Short-term Orientation.* On the long-term side one finds values oriented towards the future, like thrift (saving) and persistence. On the short-term side one finds values

Table 1

CULTURE DIMENSION SCORES FOR TEN COUNTRIES

	PD	ID	MA	UA	LT
USA	40 L	91 H	62 H	46 L	29 L
Germany	35 L	67 H	66 H	65 M	31 M
Japan	54 M	46 M	95 H	92 H	80 H
France	68 H	71 H	43 M	86 H	30*L
Netherlands	38 L	80 H	14 L	53 M	44 M
Hong Kong	68 H	25 L	57 H	29 L	96 H
Indonesia	78 H	14 L	46 M	48 L	25*L
West Africa	77 H	20 L	46 M	54 M	16 L
Russia	95*H	50*M	40*L	90*H	10*L
China	80*H	20*L	50*M	60*M	118 H

* estimated

PD = Power Distance; ID = Individualism; MA = Masculinity; UA = Uncertainty Avoidance; LT = Long Term Orientation; H = top third; M = medium third; L = bottom third (among 53 countries and regions for the first four dimensions; among 23 countries for the fifth)

rather oriented towards the past and present, like respect for tradition and fulfilling social obligations.

Table 1 lists the scores on all five dimensions for the United States and for the other countries we just discussed. The table shows that each country has its own configuration on the four dimensions. Some of the values in the table have been estimated based on imperfect replications or personal impressions. The different dimension scores do not "explain" all the differences in management I described earlier. To understand management in a country, one should have both knowledge of and empathy with the entire local scene. However, the scores should make us aware that people in other countries may think, feel, and act very differently from us when confronted with basic problems of society.

IDIOSYNCRASIES OF AMERICAN MANAGEMENT THEORIES

In comparison to other countries, the U.S. culture profile presents itself as below average on power distance and uncertainty avoidance, highly individualistic, fairly masculine, and short-term oriented. The Germans show a stronger uncertainty avoidance and less extreme individualism; the Japanese are different on all dimensions, least on power distance; the French show larger power distance and uncertainty avoidance, but are less individualistic and somewhat feminine; the Dutch resemble the Americans on the first three dimensions, but score extremely feminine and relatively long-term oriented; Hong Kong Chinese combine large power distance with weak uncertainty avoidance, collectivism, and are very long-term oriented; and so on.

The American culture profile is reflected in American management theories. I will just mention three elements not necessarily present in other countries: the stress on market processes, the stress on the individual, and the focus on managers rather than on workers.

The ideal principle of control in organizations in the market philosophy is competition between individuals.

The Stress on Market Processes

During the 1970s and 80s it has become fashionable in the United States to look at organizations from a "transaction costs" viewpoint. Economist Oliver Williamson has opposed "hierarchies" to "markets." The reasoning is that human social life consists of economic transactions between individuals. We found the same in d'Iribarne's description of the U.S. principle of the contract between employer and employee, the labor market in which the worker sells his or her labor for a price. These individuals will form hierarchical organizations when the cost of the economic transactions (such as getting information, finding out whom to trust etc.) is lower in a hierarchy than when all transactions would take place on a free market.

From a cultural perspective the important point is that *the "market" is the point of departure or base model,* and the organization is explained from market failure. A culture that produces such a theory is likely to prefer organizations that internally resemble markets to organizations that internally resemble more structured models, like those in Germany or France. The ideal principle of control in organizations in the market philosophy is *competition* between individuals. This philosophy fits a society that combines a not-too-large power distance with a not-too-strong uncertainty avoidance and individualism; besides the USA, it will fit all other Anglo countries.

The Stress on the Individual

I find this constantly in the design of research projects and hypotheses; also in the fact that in the U.S. psychology is clearly a more respectable discipline in management circles than sociology. Culture however is a collective phenomenon. Although we may get our information about culture from individuals, we have to interpret it at the level of collectivities. There are snags here known as the "ecological fallacy" and the "reverse ecological fallacy." None of the U.S. college textbooks on methodology I know deals sufficiently with the problem of multilevel analysis.

Culture can be compared to a forest, while individuals are trees. A forest is not just a bunch of trees; it is a symbiosis of different trees, bushes, plants, insects, animals and micro-organisms, and we miss the essence of the forest if we only describe its most typical trees. In the same way, a culture cannot be satisfactorily described in terms of the characteristics of a typical individual. There is a tendency in the U.S. management literature to overlook the forest for the trees and to ascribe cultural differences to interactions among individuals.

A striking example is found in the otherwise excellent book *Organizational Culture and Leadership* by Edgar H. Schein (1985). On the basis of his consulting experience he compares two large companies, nicknamed "Action" and "Multi." He explains the differences in culture between these companies by the group dynamics in their respective boardrooms. Nowhere in the book are any conclusions drawn from the fact that the first company is an American-based computer firm, and the second a Swiss-based pharmaceutics firm. This information is not even mentioned. A stress on interactions among individuals obviously fits a culture identified as the most individualistic in the world, but it will not be so well understood by the four-fifths of the world population for whom the group prevails over the individual.

One of the conclusions of my own multilevel research has been that culture at the national level and culture at the organizational level—corporate culture—are two very different phenomena and that the use of a common term for both is confusing. If we do use the common term, we should also pay attention to the occupational and the gender level of culture. National cultures differ primarily in the fundamental, invisible values held by a majority of their members, acquired in early childhood, whereas organizational cultures are a much more superficial phenomenon residing mainly in the visible practices of the organization, acquired by socialization of the new members who join as young adults. National cultures change only very slowly if at all; organizational cultures may be consciously changed, although this isn't necessarily easy. This difference between the two types of culture is the secret of the existence of multinational corporations that employ, as I showed in the IBM case, employees with extremely different national cultural values. What keeps them together is a corporate culture based on common practices.

The Stress on Managers Rather than Workers

Managers are much more involved in maintaining networks; if anything, it is the rank-and-file worker who can really make decisions on his or her own, albeit on a relatively simple level.

The core element of a work organization around the world is the people who do the work. All the rest is superstructure, and I hope to have demonstrated to you that it may take many different shapes. In the U.S. literature on work organization, however, the core element, if not explicitly then implicitly, is considered the manager. This may well be the result of the combination of extreme individualism with fairly strong masculinity, which has turned the manager into a culture hero of almost mythical proportions. For example, he—not really she—is supposed to make decisions all the time. Those of you who are or have been managers must know that this is a fable. Very few management decisions are just "made" as the myth suggests it. Managers are much more involved in maintaining networks; if anything, it is the rank-and-file worker who can really make decisions on his or her own, albeit on a relatively simple level.

An amusing effect of the U.S. focus on managers is that in at least ten American books and articles on management I have been misquoted as having studied IBM *managers* in my research, whereas the book clearly describes that the answers were from IBM *employees*. My observation may be biased, but I get the impression that compared to twenty or thirty years ago less research in this country is done among employees and more on managers. But managers derive their *raison d'être* from the people managed: culturally, they are the followers of the people they lead, and their effectiveness depends on the latter. In other parts of the world, this exclusive focus on the manager is less strong, with Japan as the supreme example.

CONCLUSION

This article started with *Alice in Wonderland.* In fact, the management theorist who ventures outside his or her own country into other parts of the world is like Alice in Wonderland. He or she will meet strange beings, customs, ways of organizing or disorganizing and theories that are clearly stupid, oldfashioned or even immoral—yet they may work, or at least they may not fail more frequently than corresponding theories do at home. Then, after the first culture shock, the traveller to Wonderland will feel enlightened, and may be able to take his or her experiences home and use them advantageously. All great ideas in science, politics and management have travelled from one country to another, and been enriched by foreign influences. The roots of American management theories are mainly in Europe: with Adam Smith, John Stuart Mill, Lev Tolstoy, Max Weber, Henri Fayol, Sigmund Freud, Kurt Lewin and many others. These theories were re-planted here and they developed and bore fruit. The same may happen again. The last thing we need is a Monroe doctrine for management ideas.

READING 7

MANAGING GLOBALLY COMPETENT PEOPLE

Nancy J. Adler
Susan Bartholomew

Executive Overview

Transnational firms need transnational human resource management systems. This article recommends global human resource changes at two levels: individual and systemic. First, it presents a set of skills needed by individual managers to be globally competent, highlighting those which transcend the historic competencies required of expatriate managers. Second, it suggests a framework for assessing the global competence of firms' human resource systems. Based on a survey of fifty major North American firms, the authors find today's human resource strategies to be significantly less global than firms' business strategies. To overcome this gap, they identify a series of illusions preventing firms from creating human resource systems which are sufficiently global to support transnational business strategies.

> Top-level managers in many of today's leading corporations are losing control of their companies. The problem is not that they have misjudged the demands created by an increasingly complex environment and an accelerating rate of environmental change, nor even that they have failed to develop strategies appropriate to the new challenges. The problem is that their companies are incapable of carrying out the sophisticated strategies they have developed. Over the past 20 years, strategic thinking has far outdistanced organizational capabilities.[1]

Today, people create national competitiveness, not, as suggested by classical economic theory, mere access to advantageous factors of production.[2] Yet, human systems are also one of the major constraints in implementing global strategies. Not surprisingly therefore, human resource management has become "an important focus of top management attention, particularly in multinational enterprises."[3]

Source: "Managing Globally Competent People" by Nancy J. Adler and Susan Bartholomew, *Academy of Management Executive*, 1992, Vol. 6, No. 3, 52–65.

The clear issue is that strategy (the *what*) is internationalizing faster than implementation (the *how*) and much faster than individual managers and executives themselves (the *who*). "The challenges [therefore] are not the 'whats' of what-to-do, which are typically well-known. They are the 'hows' of managing human resources in a global firm."[4]

How prepared are executives to manage transnational companies? How capable are firms' human resource systems of recruiting, developing, retaining, and using globally competent managers and executives? A recent survey of major U.S. corporations found only six percent reporting foreign assignments to be essential for senior executive careers, with forty-nine percent believing foreign assignments to be completely immaterial.[5]

Which firms are leading in developing globally competent managers and executives, and which remain in the majority and lag behind? That majority, according to a recent survey of 1500 CEOs, will result in a lack of sufficient senior American managers prepared to run transnational businesses, forcing U.S. firms to confront the highest executive turn-over in history.[6]

This article recommends changes in global human resource management at two levels: individual and systemic. First, from an individual perspective, it recommends skills required by individual managers to be globally competent, highlighting those which transcend the historic competencies required of international and expatriate managers. Second, from a systems perspective, it recommends a framework for assessing globally competent human resource systems. It then shows that the majority of North American firms have much room for improvement in developing both globally competent managers and globally effective human resource systems.

By contrast, it describes the approaches of some of the world's leading firms that distinguish them from the majority. There is no question that world business is going global; the question raised in this article is how to create human systems capable of implementing transnational business strategies. Based on their research, the authors support the conclusion of the recent *21st Century Report* that "executives who perceive their international operations as shelves for second-rate managers are unsuited for the CEO job in the year 2000, or indeed any managerial job today."[7]

TRANSNATIONALLY COMPETENT MANAGERS

Not all business strategies are equally global, nor need they be. As will be described, a firm's business strategy can be primarily domestic, international, multinational, or transnational. However, to be effective, the firm's human resource strategy should be integrated with its business strategy. Transnational firms need a transnational business strategy. While superficially appearing to be a truism, transnational firms also need a transnational human resource system and transnationally competent managers.

As summarized in Table 1, transnationally competent managers require a broader range of skills than traditional international managers. First, transnational managers must understand the worldwide business environment from a global perspective. Unlike expatriates of the past, transnational managers are not focused on a single country nor limited to managing relationships between headquarters and a single foreign subsidiary. Second, transnational managers must learn about many foreign cultures' perspectives, tastes, trends, technologies, and approaches to conducting business. Unlike their predecessors, they do not focus on becoming an expert on one particular culture. Third, transnational managers must be skillful or working with people from many cultures simultaneously. They no longer have the luxury of dealing with each country's issues on a separate, and therefore sequential, basis. Fourth, similar to prior expatriates, transnational managers must be able to adapt to living in other cultures. Yet, unlike their predecessors, transnational managers need cross-cultural skills on a daily basis, throughout their career, not just during foreign assignments, but also on regular multicountry business trips and in daily interaction with foreign colleagues and clients worldwide. Fifth, transnational managers interact with foreign colleagues as equals, rather than from within clearly defined hierarchies of structural or cultural dominance and subordination. Thus, not only do the variety and frequency of cross-cultural interaction increase with globalization, but also the very nature of cross-cultural interaction changes.

The development of transnationally competent managers depends on firms' organizational capability to design and manage transnational human resource systems. Such systems, in turn, allow firms to implement transnational business strategies. Before investigating firms' capability to implement transnational business strategies, let us briefly review a range of global business strategies along with each strategy's requisite managerial skills.

THE GLOBALIZATION OF BUSINESS: STRATEGY, STRUCTURE, AND MANAGERIAL SKILLS

Since World War II, industry after industry has progressed from dominantly domestic operations toward more global strategies. Historically, many firms progressed through four distinct phases: domestic, international, multinational, and transnational.[8] As firms progress towards global strategies, the portfolio of skills required of managers undergoes a parallel shift.

Domestic.   Historically, most corporations began as domestic firms. They developed new products or services at home for the domestic market. During this initial domestic phase, foreign markets, and hence international managerial skills, were largely irrelevant.

International.   As new firms entered, competition increased and each company was forced to search for new markets or resign itself to losing market share. A common response was to expand internationally, initially by exporting to foreign

Table 1

TRANSNATIONALLY COMPETENT MANAGERS

Transnational Skills	Transnationally Competent Managers	Traditional International Managers
Global Perspective	Understand worldwide business environment from a global perspective	Focus on a single foreign country and on managing relationships between headquarters and that country
Local Responsiveness	Learn about many cultures	Become an expert on one culture
Synergistic Learning	Work with and learn from people from many cultures simultaneously	Work with and coach people in each foreign culture separately or sequentially
	Create a culturally synergistic organizational environment	Integrate foreigners into the headquarters' national organizational culture
Transition and Adaptation	Adapt to living in many foreign cultures	Adapt to living in a foreign culture
Cross-cultural Interaction	Use cross-cultural interaction skills on a daily basis throughout one's career	Use cross-cultural interaction skills primarily on foreign assignments
Collaboration	Interact with foreign colleagues as equals	Interact within clearly defined hierarchies of structural and cultural dominance
Foreign Experience	Transpatriation for career and organization development	Expatriation or inpatriation primarily to get the job done

markets and later by developing foreign assembly and production facilities designed to serve the largest of those markets. To manage those foreign operations, firms often restructured to form a separate international division. Within the new international division, each country was managed separately, thus creating a multidomestic nature. Because the foreign operations were frequently seen as an extension—and therefore a replication—of domestic operations, they generally were not viewed as state of the art.

During this international phase, a hierarchical structure exists between the firm's headquarters and its various foreign subsidiaries. Power and influence are concentrated at corporate headquarters, which is primarily staffed by members of the headquarters' national culture. It is during this phase that firms often send their first home country managers abroad as expatriates. Cross-cultural interaction

These "inpatriates" are not encouraged to express the diversity of national perspectives and cultural experience they represent. Rather, they are asked to adapt as the firm implicitly and explicitly integrates them into the organizational culture which is still dominated by the values of the headquarters' national culture.

between expatriate managers and local subsidiary staff thus takes place within a clearly defined hierarchy in which headquarters has both structural and cultural dominance.

During this phase, international management is synonymous with expatriation. To be effective, expatriate managers must be competent at transferring technology to the local culture, managing local staff, and adapting business practices to suit local conditions. Specifically, international expatriate managers require cultural adaptation skills—as does their spouse and family—to adjust to living in a new environment and working with the local people. They must also acquire specific knowledge about the particular culture's perspectives, tastes, trends, technologies, and ways of doing business. Learning is thus single country focused—and culturally specific—during the international phase.

Multinational.   As competition continues to heighten, firms increasingly emphasize producing least-cost products and services. To benefit form potential economies of scale and geographic scope, firms produce more standardized products and services. Because the prior phase's multidomestic structure can no longer support success, firms restructure to integrate domestic and foreign operations into worldwide lines of business, with sourcing, producing, assembling, and marketing distributed across many countries, and major decisions—which continue to be made at headquarters—strongly influenced by least-cost outcomes.

During the multinational phase, the hierarchical relationship remains between headquarters and foreign subsidiaries. In addition, with the increased importance of foreign operations to the core business, headquarters more tightly controls major decisions worldwide. However, headquarters' decisions are now made by people from a wider range of cultures than previously, many of whom are local managers from foreign subsidiaries posted on temporary "inpatriate" assignments at corporate headquarters. These "inpatriates" are not encouraged to express the diversity of national perspectives and cultural experience they represent. Rather, they are asked to adapt as the firm implicitly and explicitly integrates them into the organizational culture which is still dominated by the values of the headquarters' national culture. While multinational representation increases at headquarters, cultural dominance of the headquarters' national culture continues, remaining loosely coupled with structure.

For the first time, senior managers, those leading the worldwide lines of business, need to understand the world business environment. Similarly for the first time, senior managers must work daily with clients and employees from around the world to be effective. International and cross-cultural skills become needed for managers throughout the firm, not just for those few imminently leaving for foreign postings. Expatriates and "inpatriates" still require cultural adaptation skills and specific local knowledge, but these are not the dominant international skills required by most managers in a multinational firm. For the majority, learning needs grow beyond local context to encompass a need to understand the world business environment. In addition, multinational managers need to be skilled at working with clients and employees from many nations (rather than merely from a single foreign country), as well as at standardizing operations and integrating people from around the world into a common organizational culture.

Transnational. As competition continues to increase and product lifecycles shorten dramatically, firms find it necessary to compete globally, based simultaneously on state-of-the-art, top quality products and services and least-cost production. Unlike the prior phase's emphasis on identical products that can be distributed worldwide, transnational products are increasingly mass-customized— tailored to each individual client's needs. Research and development demands increase as does the firm's need for worldwide marketing scope.

These dynamics lead to transnational networks of firms and divisions within firms, including an increasingly complex web of strategic alliances. Internationally, these firms distribute their multiple headquarters across a number of nations. As a result, transnational firms become less hierarchically structured than firms operating in the previous phases. As such, power is no longer centered in a single headquarters that is coincident with or dominated by any one national culture. As a consequence, both structural and cultural dominance are minimized, with cross-cultural interaction no longer following any pre-defined "passport hierarchy." It is for these firms that transnational human resource strategies are now being developed that emphasize organizational learning along with individual managerial skills.

To be effective, transnational managers need both the culturally specific knowledge and adaptation skills required in international firms, and the ability to acquire a worldwide perspective and to integrate worldwide diversity required in multinational firms. As a consequence, one of the transnational manager's primary skills is to exercise discretion in choosing when to be locally responsive and when to emphasize global integration.

Moreover, the integration required in transnational firms is based on cultural synergy—on combining the many cultures into a unique organizational culture—rather than on simply integrating foreigners into the dominant culture of the headquarters' nationality (as was the norm in prior phases). Transnational managers require additional new skills to be effective in their less hierarchical, networked firms: first, the ability to work with people of other cultures as equals; second, the ability to learn in order to continually enhance organizational capability. Transnational managers must learn how to collaborate with partners worldwide, gaining as much knowledge as possible from each interaction, and, transmitting that knowledge quickly and effectively throughout the worldwide network of operations. This requires managers who both want to learn and have the skills to quickly and continuously learn from people of other cultures.[9]

TRANSNATIONAL HUMAN RESOURCE SYSTEMS

The development of such "transnationally competent managers," as discussed previously, depends upon firms' capability to design and manage transnational human resource systems. The function of human resource systems, in general, is to recruit, develop, and retain competent managers and executives. Beyond these core functions, we add utilization: human resource systems facilitate the effective "utilization" of those managers who have been recruited, developed, and retained. Therefore, a transnational human resource system is one that recruits, develops, retains and utilizes managers and executives who are competent transnationally.[10]

Three Dimensions of a Transnational Human Resource System

For a transnational human resource system to be effective, it must exhibit three characteristics: transnational scope, transnational representation, and transnational process. We will describe each briefly, and then discuss their implications for recruiting, developing, retaining, and using human resources.

Transnational Scope.   Transnational scope is the geographical context within which all major decisions are made. As Bartlett and Ghoshal have stated, global management is a "frame of mind," not a particular organizational structure.[11] Thus, to achieve global scope, executives and managers must frame major decisions and evaluate options relative to worldwide business dynamics. Moreover, they must benchmark their own and their firm's performance against worldclass standards. They can neither discuss nor resolve major issues within a narrower national or regional context. An example is Unilever's "Best Proven Practices." This British-Dutch consumer products firm identifies superior practices and innovations in its subsidiaries worldwide and then diffuses the outstanding approaches throughout the worldwide organization.[12]

Transnational process, however, is not the mere inclusion of people and ideas of many cultures; rather, it goes beyond inclusion to encompass cultural synergy—the combination of culturally diverse perspectives and approaches into a new transnational organizational culture.

Transnational Representation.   Transnational representation refers to the multinational composition of the firm's managers and executives. To achieve transnational representation, the firm's portfolio of key executives and managers should be as multinational as its worldwide distribution of production, finance, sales, and profits. Symbolically, firms achieve transnational representation through the well balanced portfolio of passports held by senior management. Philips, for example, maintains transnational representation by having "the corporate pool." This pool consists of mobile individuals representing more than fifty nationalities, each having at least five years of experience and ranked in the top twenty percent on performance, and all financed on a corporate budget.[13]

Transnational Process.   Transnational process reflects the firm's ability to effectively include representatives and ideas from many cultures in its planning and decision-making processes. Firms create transnational process when they consistently recognize, value, and effectively use cultural diversity within the organization; that is, when there is "no unintended leakage of culture specific systems and approaches."[14] Transnational process, however, is not the mere inclusion of people and ideas of many cultures; rather, it goes beyond inclusion to encompass cultural synergy—the combination of culturally diverse perspectives and approaches into a new transnational organizational culture. Cultural synergy requires "a genuine belief . . . that more creative and effective ways of managing people could be developed as a result of cross-cultural learning."[15] To create transnational process, executives and managers must be as skilled at working with and learning from people from outside their own culture as with same culture nationals.

TODAY'S FIRMS: HOW TRANSNATIONAL?

A survey was conducted of fifty firms headquartered in the United States and Canada from a wide variety of industries to determine the extent to which their overall business strategy matched their current human resource system, as well as identifying the extent of globalization of their human resource strategies. The results paint a picture of extensive global business involvement. Unfortunately, however, similar involvement in recruiting, developing, retaining, and using globally competent managers is lacking.

Global Strategic Integration

The fifty firms made almost half of their sales abroad, and earned nearly forty percent of their revenues and profits outside of their headquarters' country (the United States or Canada). Similarly, almost two fifths of the fifty firms' employees worked outside the headquarters' country. Yet, when these firms reviewed their human resource systems as a whole, and their senior leadership in particular, they could not reveal nearly as global a portrait.

For example, in comparing themselves with their competitors, the fifty firms found themselves to be more global on overall business strategy, financial systems, production operations, and marketing. However, they found their human resource systems to be the least global functional area within their own organization. Moreover, unlike their assessment in other functional areas, they did not evaluate their human resource systems as being more global than those of their competitors.

Similarly, the senior leadership of the surveyed firms was less global on all three global indicators—scope, representation, and process—than each firm's overall business performance. For example, an average of only eight countries were represented among the most senior one hundred executives in each firm. Half of the companies reported fewer than four nationalities among the top one hundred executives. Firms therefore have less than a quarter of the international representation in their senior leadership (eight percent) as they have in their global business performance (i.e., sales, revenues, and profits: forty percent). Similarly, of the same top one hundred executives in each firm, only fifteen percent were from outside of North America. This represents less than half the

Unfortunately, the results of this study indicate that firms' human resource management systems have not become global either as rapidly or as extensively as have their business strategies and structures.

internationalization of the senior executive cadre (fifteen percent) as of business performance (forty percent). Moreover, using experience, rather than representation, yields similar results. Of the same one hundred leaders, almost three quarters lacked expatriate experience, with only a third reporting any international experience at all. Not surprisingly, less than one in five spoke a foreign language. On no measure of international experience is the senior leadership of these North American firms as international as the business itself.

Transnational Human Resource Integration

Firms' organizational capability to implement transnational business strategies is supported by transnational human resource management systems. As discussed, such systems should exhibit all three dimensions—transnational scope, transnational representation, and transnational process. These three global dimensions are clearly important for each of the four primary components of human resource systems—recruiting, developing, retaining, and utilizing globally competent people. Each will therefore be discussed separately. Unfortunately, the results of this study indicate that firms' human resource management systems have not become global either as rapidly or as extensively as have their business strategies and structures.

Recruiting.   For recruiting decisions, transnational scope requires that firms consider their business needs and the availability of candidates worldwide. Similar to the firm's strategic business decisions, some recruiting decisions must enhance worldwide integration and coordination, others local responsiveness, and others the firm's ability to learn.[16] Local responsiveness requires that firms recruit people with a sophisticated understanding of each of the countries in which they operate; this includes recruiting host nationals. Worldwide integration requires that recruiting be guided by worldclass standards in selecting the most competent people from anywhere in the world for senior management positions. Individual and organizational learning requires that people be selected who are capable of simultaneously working with and learning from colleagues from many nations: people who are capable of creating cultural synergy.

Transnational representation in recruiting requires that firms select managers from throughout the world for potential positions anywhere in the world. In a literal sense, it requires that talent flows to opportunity worldwide, without regard to national passport.

Transnational process in recruiting requires that firms use search and selection procedures that are equally attractive to candidates from each target nationality. Selection criteria, including the methods used to judge competence, must not be biased to favour any one culture.

Similarly, incentives to join the firm must appeal to a broad range of cultures. The antithesis of transnational process was exhibited by one U.S. firm when it offered new college recruits from the Netherlands one of the same incentives it offers its American recruits: free graduate education. The Dutch candidates found this "benefit" amusing given that graduate education in the

Netherlands—unlike in the United States—is already paid for by the government and thus free to all students.

Rather than encouraging high potential candidates, this particular incentive made Dutch students hesitate to join a firm that demonstrated such parochialism in its initial contact with them.

The fifty surveyed firms reported that their recruitment and selection activities were less than global in terms of scope, representation, and process. For a summary, see Exhibit 1: Transnational Recruiting.

Development. In managerial development, transnational scope means that managers' experiences both on-the-job and in formal training situations prepare them to work anywhere in the world with people from all parts of the world; that is, it prepares them to conduct the firm's business in a global environment. Transnational firms search worldwide for the best training and development options and select specific approaches and programs based on worldclass standards.

To achieve transnational representation, training and development programs must be planned and delivered by multinational teams as well as offered to multinational participants. To be transnational, programs cannot be planned by one culture (generally representatives of the headquarters' nationality) and simply exported for local delivery abroad. By contrast, using a transnational approach, American Express created a multinational design team at headquarters to develop training approaches and programs which were subsequently localized for delivery around the world. At no time did American cultural values dominate either the process or the programs.

Transnational process in development requires that the approaches taken effectively include all participating cultures. Thus, the process cannot encourage greater participation by one nationality to the exclusion of other nationalities. Ericsson and Olivetti provide examples of a transnational development approach. Each company created a management development center in which both the staff and executive participants come from all regions of the world. To minimize the possibility of headquarters' cultural dominance, neither company located its management development center in the headquarters' country—Sweden or Italy—but rather both chose another more culturally neutral country.[17]

For transnational firms, foreign assignments become a core component of the organizational and career development process. "Transpatriates" from all parts of the world are sent to all other parts of the world to develop their worldwide perspective and cross-cultural skills, as well as developing the organization's cadre of globally sophisticated managers. Foreign assignments in transnational firms are no longer used primarily to get a job done in a foreign country (expatriation) or to socialize foreign country nationals into the home country headquarters' culture ("inpatriation"), but rather to enhance individual and organizational learning in all parts of the system ("transpatriation"). Using a "transpatriation" approach, Royal Dutch Shell, for example, uses multifunctional

Worldwide integration requires that recruiting be guided by worldclass standards in selecting the most competent people from anywhere in the world for senior management positions.

Exhibit 1

TRANSNATIONAL RECRUITING

The 50 surveyed firms reported that their recruitment and selection activities were less than transnational in terms of scope, representation, and process. In selecting future senior managers, the 50 firms ranked an outstanding overall track record as the most important criterion, with foreign business experience, demonstrated cultural sensitivity and adaptability, and a track record for outstanding performance outside the home country ranked as somewhat, but not highly, important. Moreover, foreign language skills were not considered at all important. Similarly, while considering three out of four transnational scope and process skills to be somewhat important for promotion to senior management (understanding world issues and trends; working effectively with clients and colleagues from other countries; and, demonstrating cultural sensitivity), none was considered highly important. Once again, foreign language skills were not considered important for promotion. Similarly, on transnational representation, only a third of the 50 firms stated that they "recruit managers from all parts of the world in which . . . [they] conduct business."

and multinational experience to provide corporate wide, transnational skills. Shell's "aim is that every member of an operating company management team should have had international experience and that each such team should include one expatriate . . . [Similarly, at IBM], international experience is [considered] indispensable to senior positions."[18]

In the survey, the fifty firms reported that their training and development opportunities were less than global on all three dimensions of human resource strategy: transnational scope, transnational representation, and transnational process (for a summary of the research, see Exhibit 2: Transnational Development). Similar to recruitment, training and development approaches currently are not nearly as global as are overall business strategies. To reduce the gap between the relative globalization of firms' strategies and their less-than-global human resource systems, firms must learn how to recognize, value, and use globally competent managers. As one surveyed executive summarized, closing the gaps begins by having "the key organizational development activity . . . focused on allowing people of different nationalities to meet and to get to know each other, and, through these linkages, to meet the needs of the company."

Retaining.   Transnational scope in retaining managers means that decisions about career paths must consider the firm's needs and operations worldwide.

Performance incentives, rewards, and career opportunities must meet worldclass standards such that the firm does not lose its most competent people. Firms must benchmark excellence in their human resource systems against their most significant global competitors in the same ways that they assess the relative competitiveness of their research and development, production, marketing, and financial systems.

Transnational representation requires that organizational incentives and career path opportunities be equally accessible and appealing to managers from

Exhibit 2

TRANSNATIONAL DEVELOPMENT

In the survey, the 50 firms reported that their training and development opportunities were less than transnational on all three dimensions of human resource strategy: scope, representation, and process. Fewer than one in four of the firms reported that the content of their training programs was global in focus, that they had representatives of many nations attending each program, or that their programs were designed or delivered by multinational training teams. Only four percent reported that cross-cultural training was offered to all managers. However, the firms did report offering a greater number of general development opportunities worldwide than specific international training programs. A third of the firms provide equivalent development opportunities for managers worldwide and 42 percent provide such opportunities for managers of all nationalities.

In reviewing foreign assignments, the 50 firms report using expatriates primarily to "get the job done abroad," not to develop the organization, nor to develop the individual manager's career. Given their emphasis on getting the immediate job done, it is not surprising that they did not report consistently selecting the "stars" (either high potential junior managers or very senior, top-performing executives) for expatriate positions. To increase globalization in their development programs, the surveyed executives strongly recommended "transferring different nationalities to different countries several times in their career" and "making it clear to these employees that international assignments are important to career development." However, to date, the majority of the surveyed firms do not have such recommended programs in place.

---

all nationalities. Firms with transnational human resource systems do not create a glass ceiling beyond which only members of the headquarters' nationality can be promoted.

Transnational process requires that the performance review and promotion systems include approaches which are equally appropriate to a broad range of nationalities. The process by which promotion and career path decisions are made should not be innately biased towards any one culture, nor should it exclude particular cultures. The underlying dynamic in transnational process is not to institute identical systems worldwide, but rather to use approaches which are culturally equivalent. Shell for example, ensures this transnational orientation by having managers' "career home" be in "a business function rather than a geographical place."[19] As one surveyed senior executive summarized, firms considered to be outstanding in transnational human resource management are "flexible enough in systems and practices to attract and retain the best people regardless of nationality."

Firms must benchmark excellence in their human resource systems against their most significant global competitors in the same ways that they assess the relative competitiveness of their research and development, production, marketing, and financial systems.

Utilizing. Transnational scope in utilization means that managers' problem solving skills are focused on the firm's worldwide operations and competitive environment, not just on the regional, national, or local situation. To assess the competitive environment in transnational human resource management, the fifty surveyed firms identified leading North American, European, and Asian companies. The top North American firm was perceived to be IBM, followed by General Electric, and Citicorp. The surveyed firms identified Royal Dutch Shell as the leading European firm, followed by Nestle and Philips, along with British Petroleum and Unilever. Sony was selected as the leading Asian firm, followed by Honda, Toyota, and Mitsubishi. Yet, in reviewing the pattern of responses, a significant proportion of the surveyed firms do not appear to be benchmarking excellence in global human resource management at all, and an even greater number appear to be geographically limiting their perspective to a fairly narrow, parochial scope. For instance, almost a fifth of the surveyed firms (all of which are North American) could not name a single leading North American firm. Even more disconcerting, more than a third could not identify a single excellent European firm, and half could not name a single excellent Asian firm.[20]

Beyond scope, transnational representation in utilization means that managers and executives of many nationalities are included in the firm's critical operating and strategic planning teams. Managers from outside of headquarters are not "out of sight and out of mind"; rather they are integrated into the worldwide network of knowledge exchange, continual learning, and action. For example, as Unilever's director of management development explains:

> In recent years, I have had several product group directors . . . [want] an expatriate on the board of the local company. Not just because they haven't got a national, not just because it would be good for the expatriate, but because it would be good for the company to have a bit of challenge to the one-best-way of doing things.[21]

Transnational process in human resource utilization means that the organization culture does not inherently bias contributions from or towards any particular cultural group. The human resource system recognizes the firm's cultural diversity and uses it either to build culturally synergistic processes that include all cultures involved or to select the particular process that is the most appropriate for the given situation.

ILLUSIONS AND RECOMMENDATIONS

From the prior discussion, it is clear that transnational human resource systems are both fundamentally important for future business success and qualitatively different from prior approaches to human resource management. Equally evident is the fact that North American firms' human resource systems are not nearly as global as their business operations on any of the three fundamental human resource dimensions: transnational scope, transnational representation, and transnational process. Competitive demands appear to have "outrun the slow pace of organizational change and adjustment . . . [with] top management beginning to feel that the organization itself is the biggest barrier to competitive and strategic development."[22] It is telling that in most cases the respondents found the survey itself to be important and yet very difficult to complete, primarily because their firms did not systematically collect or keep data on any aspect of global human resource management.

The remaining question is why. There appears to be a series of illusions—of mind traps—that are preventing firms from acting in a global manner, including recognizing the mental gap between their current human resource approaches and those necessary to succeed in a highly competitive transnational business environment. Many of the surveyed executives recognized that their firms simply "lack global thinking" and "lack global business strategies," largely due to the "massive U.S. imprint on human resource practices." According to many of the American executives, firms must "stop thinking that the world begins and ends at U.S. borders," "stop having a U.S. expatriate mentality," and begin to "realize that the world does not revolve around us." This pattern of responses suggests the following seven illusions.

Illusion One: If business has gone well, it will continue to go well

No, today is not like yesterday, nor will tomorrow be a projection of today. Business has fundamentally changed, and human resource systems must undergo similar transformational changes to stay relevant, let alone effective. As Kenichi Ohmae has pointed out, "Today and in the twenty-first century, management's ability to transform the organization and its people into a global company is a prerequisite for survival because both its customers and competitors have become cosmopolitan."[23]

Illusion Two: We have always played on a level playing field and won

No. The North American economies (and therefore North American firms) have had an advantage: they were the only developed economies left intact following World War II and were thus "the only game in town." Today, Asia, Europe, and the Americas each have highly competitive firms and economies, none of which will continue to prosper without being excellent at including people and business worldwide. As Ohmae has observed, "The key to a nation's future is its human resources. It used to be its natural resources, but not any more. The quality and number of its educated people now determines a country's likely prosperity or decline"; so too with global firms.[24]

Illusion Three: If we manage expatriates better, we will have an effective global human resource system

No. Doing better at what was necessary in the past (expatriate management) is not equivalent to creating systems capable of sustaining global competitiveness today. Whereas the temptation is to attempt to do better at that which is known (in this case, the simple expatriation of managers), the real challenge is to excel at that which is new. Transnational firms need transnational human resource systems to succeed. Better managed expatriate transfers will only improve one small aspect of existing human resource management, not create an overall transnational system.

Illusion Four: If we're doing something, we must be doing enough

No. Focusing on only one of the three transnational dimensions—scope, representation, or process—is not enough to transform domestic, international, or multinational human resource approaches into truly transnational systems. Bringing a "foreigner" onto the board of directors, for example, gives the illusion of globalization, but is insufficient to underpin its substance.

Illusion Five: If "foreigners" are fitting in at headquarters, we must be managing our cultural diversity well

No. This is a multinational paradigm trap. In multinationals, foreigners must adapt to the headquarters' culture, including learning its native language. Multinationals typically see cultural differences "as a nuisance, a constraint, an obstacle to be surmounted."[25] In transnational firms, all managers make transitions, all managers adapt, and all managers help to create a synergistic organizational culture which transcends any one national culture.

Illusion Six: As national wealth increases, everyone will become more like us

No. To the extent that the world is converging in its values, attitudes, and styles of doing business, it is not converging on a single country's national pattern, even that of the world's wealthiest nation. "The appealing 'one-best-way' assumption about management, the belief that different cultures are converging at different paces on the same concept of organization, is dying a slow death."[26] Moreover, transnational firms need to create transnational cultures that are inclusive of all their members, not wait for the world to converge on a reality that looks like any particular firm's national culture, even one that looks "just like us."

Illusion Seven: If we provide managers with cross-cultural training, we will increase organizational capability

No. Increased cognitive understanding does not guarantee increased behavioral effectiveness, nor is enhanced individual learning sufficient for improved organizational effectiveness. Simply increasing the number of cross-cultural training programs offered to individual managers does not ensure that they will actually use the skills on a regular basis, nor that the firm as a whole will benefit from the potentially improved cross-cultural interaction. To benefit, the individual must want to learn that which is not-invented-here and the organization must want to learn from the individual. To enhance organizational capability, managers must continually work with and learn from people worldwide and disperse that knowledge throughout the firm's worldwide operations.

Despite the seemingly insurmountable challenges, firms are beginning to address and solve the dilemmas posed by going global. To date, no firm believes it has "the answer," the solution to creating a truly transnational human resource system. However, a number of firms are currently inventing pieces of the solution which may cohere into just such a system. For example, as John Reed, CEO of Citicorp, describes:

> There are few companies in the world that are truly global. . . . Our most important advantage is our globality. Our global human capital may be as important a resource, if not more important, than our financial capital. Look at the Policy Committee, the top thirty or so officers in the bank. Almost seventy-five percent have worked outside the United States; more than twenty-five percent have worked in three or more countries. Half speak two or more languages other than English. Seven were born outside the United States.[27]

Perhaps, then, a primary role of transnational human resource executives today is to remain open to fundamental change and to continue to encourage the openness and experimentation needed to create truly global systems.

Endnotes

The authors would like to thank the Ontario Centre for International Business for generously funding this research. See "Globalization and Human Resource Management," (Nancy J. Adler and Susan Bartholomew) in *Research in Global Strategic Management: Corporate Responses to Global Change*, Alan M. Rugman and Alain Verbeke (eds.), Vol. 3, (Greenwich, Conn.: JAI Press, 1992) for further details of the research design and results of the study.

[1]Christopher A. Bartlett and Sumantra Ghoshal, "Matrix Management: Not a Structure, a Frame of Mind" *Harvard Business Review*, July-August 1990, 138.

[2]See Michael E. Porter, *The Competitive Advantage of Nations* (New York: The Free Press, 1990).

[3]Paul A. Evans, Yves Doz, and Andre Laurent, *Human Resource Management in International Firms* (London: Macmillan Press, 1989), xi–1.

[4]Ibid.; also see Gunnar Hedlund "Who Manages the Global Corporation? Changes in the Nationality of Presidents of Foreign Subsidiaries of Swedish MNCs During the 1980s, "Working Paper, (Institute of International Business and the Stockholm School of Economics, May 1990).

[5]See Donald C. Hambrick, Lester B. Korn, James W. Frederickson, and Richard M. Ferry, *21st Century Report: Reinventing the CEO* (New York: Korn/Ferry and Columbia University's Graduate School of Business, 1989), 1–94.

[6]Ibid.

[7]Ibid., 57.

[8]See Nancy J. Adler and Fariborz Ghadar "International Strategy from the Perspective of People and Culture: The North American Context," in Alan M. Rugman (ed.), *Research in Global Strategic Management: International Business Research for the Twenty-First Century; Canada's New Research Agenda*, Vol. 1, (Greenwich, Conn.: JAI Press, 1990) 179–205; and "Strategic Human Resource Management: A Global Perspective," in Rudiger Pieper (ed.), *Human Resource Management in International Comparison* (Berlin, de Gruyter, 1990), 235–260.

[9]See Gary Hamel, Yves Doz, and C. K. Prahalad "Collaborate With Your Competitors and Win," *Harvard Business Review*, 89(1), 1989, 133–139.

[10]For a review of international human resource management, see Nancy J. Adler, *International Dimensions of Organizational*

Behaviour, 2nd ed. (Boston: PWS Kent 1991); Peter J. Dowling "Hot Issues Overseas," *Personnel Administrator,* 34(1), 1989, 66–72; Peter J. Dowling & R. Schuler, *International Dimensions of Human Resource Management* (Boston: PWS Kent, 1990), Peter J. Dowling & Denise E. Welch, "International Human Resource Management: An Australian Perspective," *Asia Pacific Journal of Management,* 6(1), 1988, 39–65; Yves Doz & C. K. Prahalad "Controlled Variety: A Challenge for Human Resource Management in the MNC," *Human Resource Management,* 25(1), 1986, 55–71; A. Edstrom & J. R. Galbraith "Transfer of Managers as a Coordination and Control Strategy in Multinational Firms," *Administrative Science Quarterly,* 22, 1977, 248–263; Evans, Doz, & Laurent, (1989) op. cit.; Andre Laurent "The Cross-Cultural Puzzle of International Human Resource Management," *Human Resource Management,* 25(1), 1986, 91–101; E. L. Miller, S. Beechler, B. Bhatt, & R. Nath, "The Relationship Between the Global Strategic Planning Process and the Human Resource Management Function," *Human Resource Planning,* 9(1), 1986, 9–23; John Milliman, Mary Ann Von Glinow, & Maria Nathan, "Organizational Life Cycles and Strategic International Human Resource Management in Multinational Companies: Implications for Congruence Theory," *Academy of Management Review,* 16(2), 1991, 318–339; Dan A. Ondrack, "International Human Resources Management in European and North American Firms," *Human Resource Management,* 25(1), 1985, 121–132; Dan A. Ondrack, "International Transfers of Managers in North American and European MNEs," *Journal of International Business Studies,* 16(3), 1985, 1–19; Vladimir Pucik, "The International Management of Human Resources," in C. J. Fombrun, N. M. Tichy, & M. A. Devanna (eds.), *Strategic Human Resource Management* (New York: Wiley, 1984); Vladimir Pucik & Jan Hack Katz, "Information, Control and Human Resource Management in Multinational Firms," *Human Resource Management,* 25(1),

1986, 121–132; and, Rosalie Tung, *The New Expatriates: Managing Human Resources Abroad* (New York: Harper & Row 1988), and "Strategic Management of Human Resources in Multinational Enterprises," *Human Resource Management,* 23(2), 1984, 129–143; among others.

[11]Op. cit., 1990.

[12]Unilever's "Best Proven Practice" technique was cited by Philip M. Rosenzweig and Jitendra Singh, "Organizational Environments and the Multinational Enterprise," *Academy of Management Review,* 16(2), 1991, 354, based on an interview that Rosenzweig conducted with Unilever.

[13]See Paul Evans, Elizabeth Lank, and Alison Farquhar, "Managing Human Resources in the International Firm: Lessons from Practice," in Paul Evans, Yves Doz, and Andre Laurent, 1989, op. cit., 138.

[14]Kenichi Ohmae, *The Borderless World: Power and Strategy in the Interlinked Economy* (New York: Harper Business, 1990), 112.

[15]Andre Laurent, op. cit., 1986, 100.

[16]See C. K. Prahalad and Yves Doz, *The Multinational Mission: Balancing Local Demands and Global Vision,* (New York: Free Press, 1987); also, for a discussion of global integration versus local responsiveness from a business strategy perspective, see Michael E. Porter, "Changing Patterns of International Competition," *California Management Review,* 28(2), 1986, 9–40; and Christopher A. Bartlett, "Building and Managing the Transnational: The New Organizational Challenge," in M. E. Porter (ed.) *Competition in Global Industries* (Boston: Harvard Business School Press, 1986), 367–401, who explicitly developed the concepts, along with initial work and elaboration by: Christopher A. Bartlett & Sumantra Ghoshal, *Managing Across Borders: The Transnational Solution* (Boston: Harvard Business School Press 1989); Yves Doz, "Strategic Management in Multinational Companies," *Sloan Management Review,* 21(2), 1980, 27–46; Yves Doz,

Christopher A. Bartlett, & C. K. Prahalad, "Global Competitive Pressures and Host Country Demands: Managing Tensions in MNCs," *California Management Review,* 23(3), 1981, 63–73; and Yves Doz & C. K. Prahalad, "Patterns of Strategic Control Within Multinational Corporations," *Journal of International Business Studies,* 15(2), 1984, 55–72.

[17]See Evans, Lank and Farquhar, op. cit., 1989, 119.

[18]Ibid., 130–131; 139.

[19]Ibid., 141.

[20]An even more disconcerting display of ignorance was that four surveyed firms listed 3M, Citicorp, Ford, and General Motors as European firms, and in another four responses, Dupont, Eastman Kodak, Coca-Cola, and Wang were identified as leading Asian firms.

[21]Evans, Lank, and Farquhar, op. cit., 122.

[22]Paul Evans and Yves Doz, "The Dualistic Organization," in Evans, Doz, & Laurent, op. cit., 1989, 223; based on the earlier work of Doz, "Managing Manufacturing Rationalization Within Multinational Companies," *Columbia Journal of World Business,* 13(3), 1978, 82–94; and Prahalad and Doz, op. cit., 1987.

[23]*Beyond National Borders* (Homewood, Illinois: Dow Jones-Irwin, 1987), 93.

[24]Ibid., 1.

[25]Evans, Lank & Farquhar, op. cit., 115.

[26]Ibid., 115.

[27]Noel Tichy and Ram Charan, "Citicorp Faces the World: An Interview with John Reed," *Harvard Business Review,* November-December, 1990, 137.

THE LEGAL ENVIRONMENT AND EQUAL EMPLOYMENT OPPORTUNITY

INTRODUCTION

Complying with the legal system is necessary for gaining competitive advantage. The U.S. legal system sets up a number of requirements regarding how organizations must provide equal employment opportunities to individuals—regardless of their race, sex, color, religion, national origin, age, or disability status. These legal requirements aim to provide all individuals access to the benefits of employment in our country, and as a result, more and more people are able to achieve the American dream. However, the effort to provide such opportunities has resulted in what many believe is a maze of laws, executive orders, federal guidelines, state statutes, and court decisions with which managers must comply. This section provides some readings that are especially of interest to managers who are concerned about legal compliance.

Reading 8 presents a speech made by Evan Kemp to the National Press Club on November 24, 1992. Mr. Kemp replaced Clarence Thomas as the chairman of the U.S. Equal Employment Opportunity Commission and completed his term at the beginning of 1993. Mr. Kemp, a disabled individual himself, discusses the philosophy of the Civil Rights Movement and distinguishes between group and individual rights. He points to the Americans with Disabilities Act as a model for civil rights legislation because it prohibits discrimination against individuals. He also discusses the evolution of affirmative action and the need for diversity in today's society. He presents an agenda for the national debate on civil rights.

As mentioned, equal employment laws have provided many minority individuals access to the mainstream of private enterprise. However, providing this access has entailed some costs, particularly in terms of meeting the paperwork requirements of governmental regulatory agencies, and in some cases has resulted in quota hiring. Reading 9 by Brimelow and Spencer explores the estimated regulatory costs of equal employment legislation. These authors conduct an extensive examination into all of the costs that are incurred, both at the societal and organizational level. They also present some individual case examples of firms that have come face-to-face with the regulatory apparatus. This article is ideal for thinking about the relative trade-offs between social responsibility and organizational survival in a globally competitive world.

READING 8

▸

HAVE CIVIL RIGHTS BECOME
GROUP RIGHTS?

EEOC Chairman Kemp

It's a pleasure to be here at the National Press Club. Most of you probably watched President-elect Clinton's first press conference. There, the Governor pledged to the nation that his administration would look like America, that it would reflect the racial and ethnic diversity of our country. Yet during the campaign, candidate Clinton had made vehement statements opposing quotas, opposing group preferences.

That the President-elect used the term "diversity" is not surprising. Though diversity used to bring to mind the image of the melting pot, the richness of America today, diversity is a code for group entitlement, preferences, division—the very quotas candidate Clinton said he opposed, the very quotas the American people oppose.

I have faced this dilemma as Chairman of the U.S. Equal Employment Opportunity Commission, as did Eleanor Holmes Norton and Clarence Thomas before me. And it is the dilemma that the new Chairman of the EEOC will face. I have felt, as will my successor, the pressure to use our employment discrimination laws to turn the goal of diversity into a prescription for group entitlement. President-elect Clinton's promotion of diversity and opposition to group entitlement must be reconciled. And I can tell you from experience that this is nearly an impossible job—nearly impossible because we have not told the truth about what's really happening in universities, in the work force, in our cities. We have not told the truth about what words such as "diversity" and "affirmative action" have come to mean.

I am glad to have the opportunity to be here today, as my time as Chairman draws to a close, to reflect on this dilemma, as well as on what the future may hold.

Twenty-eight years ago, Americans confronted the unequal status of blacks in this country. The Civil Rights Act of 1964 prohibited discrimination based on race, religion, color, national origin and gender in public accommodations and

Source: Reprinted with permission from *Daily Labor Report*, No. 228, pp. D–1—D–2. (Nov. 25, 1992). Published by the Bureau of National Affairs, Inc. (800-372-1033).

employment. Later, Congress passed the Age Discrimination in Employment Act. And in 1990, on the 25th anniversary of the EEOC, Congress made illegal discrimination on the basis of disability.

These laws, based on a strong consensus, a firm belief in equal opportunity for all, and on the primacy of individual rights, have brought about unprecedented change. America is far better for honoring our commitment to the fundamental principle that all are created equal, that everyone is entitled to the opportunity to compete for jobs for which they qualify, to gain those qualifications through education, to travel, to use public accommodations and to live wherever they can afford.

I believe that the civil rights movement of the 1960s succeeded because we were forced to acknowledge that one group of Americans has been excluded from these entitlements. Dr. Martin Luther King, Jr. made us acknowledge that the great American melting pot had grudgingly, but unfailingly, absorbed refugees from Europe and Asia, but had miserably failed to do the same for blacks. King's simple, but eloquent, message stirred and unified the nation.

But while King suffered insult, even imprisonment, because of his race, he did not ask for reparations or for special privileges. His dream was for a nation where his children—where all children—would be judged by the content of their character, not by the color of their skin. The Civil Rights Act of 1964 realized King's dream of inclusion. The Civil Rights Act of 1964 gave every American the right to be judged by what they can do, not by someone else's stereotypes. Most recently, Americans with disabilities demanded, and won, this right.

Tragically, for us all, Dr. King's assassination robbed the civil rights movement of his leadership and his vision. Others have used his dream of equality to gain power through group entitlement, promoting distrust and resentment among racial and ethnic groups. Notions of individual responsibility and the duties of citizenship have been subsumed by assertions of rights by virtue of victim status. As author Shelby Steele explains: "We have taken our power from our history of victimization, which gave us an enormous moral authority and brought social reforms, to the neglect of self-reliance and individual initiative."

Once group entitlement became the driving force, the consensus of the Civil Rights Act of 1964 began to erode. Politicians bowed to the politics of pigmentation. The policies of pigmentation were sold as equal justice for all. Employers installed quotas and called them "goals and timetables," colleges lowered entrance standards in the pursuit of fairness, and "race norming" was used to achieve a balanced work force.

This was the well from which animosity among groups began to spring. This animosity can be seen in the charges brought to the EEOC, in the news from Los Angeles to Crown Heights. What part did actual or perceived preferences play in the Los Angeles riots? People are frightened by what columnist William Raspberry has described as, "an increase in disputes, claims and counter-claims across ethnic, geographical, gender and economic lines."

The best advice I can offer my successor is not to give in to those who would carve up American society along ethnic, racial and gender lines. Because if we do, we will tragically shortchange minority youths by assuming that because they do not do as well, on a group basis, as others, they will never do as well. We have already lowered standards and expectations. The individual who does succeed is stigmatized. The others are told that they cannot hope to compete as individuals, only as members of a subgroup. Still others get the message, "Don't even try to compete; success is beyond your reach."

The focus on groups over individuals has translated into favoritism of one group at the expense of another, creating division and resentment. This country is home to some 150 ethnic and racial groups. How do we divide the pie? Indeed, what exactly do we mean by affirmative action? Because if affirmative action is going to be based on group entitlement and proportional representation, an impossible task lies ahead for President-elect Clinton, for the new Chairman of the EEOC, for the entire nation. And why are we suddenly hearing about "diversity"? I'm afraid that the term "diversity" is an effort to make permanent what we had before been assured by the U.S. Supreme Court was temporary.

I remember remarking to a friend of mine how impressed I had been by a recent article by Thomas Sowell that examined the use of group preferences in other countries. I told her, "Now here's a guy who really understands disability!" Sowell never mentioned disability in his article. But he talked about the fact that in Sri Lanka, in India, or wherever preferential treatment has been tried, those who needed it the least got all the benefits. That is the reality of preferences with respect to disability as well.

Entitlements in the guise of quotas have always benefitted those persons with the least severe disabilities, or with what I like to call the three H's: hemorrhoids, hangnails and halitosis. Employers will do the minimum necessary to comply with the law to meet their quotas. And those with the most serious disabilities are never used to fill a quota. Moreover, preferential treatment for persons with disabilities raises other questions. How would it apply to the hundreds of subgroups of disabilities? Should the blind be favored over the deaf? Does hiring one person in a wheelchair excuse a company from considering a qualified applicant with a learning disability?

These were among the questions debated in the 12 years leading up to the passage of the Americans with Disabilities Act. I was part of that process, and I can tell you that it wasn't easy, that not everyone liked the answers. But the debate was an honest examination of the fears of employers and the desires of Americans with disabilities. And when we were finished we had a strong consensus that the entire nation would benefit from including Americans with disabilities in the American dream.

I believe the ADA can and should be a paradigm for the future of civil rights because it is based on individual rights. The ADA charges employers to look at an individual's abilities, rather than disabilities. But, most importantly, under the ADA, employers are not required to hire an unqualified applicant simply because that applicant has a disability. The Act ensures that persons with disabilities who are qualified to do a job no longer will be locked out by discrimination. But it does not mandate that employers use statistics and other group-based numbers to make hiring decisions.

Would that were true under the Civil Rights Act of 1991. That legislation certainly was hard fought. Unfortunately, most of that fight took place behind closed doors, where the politics of pigmentation could be openly pursued. During the private debates over the Civil Rights Act of 1991, so-called civil rights leaders went so far as to plead with the White House for one more generation of quotas for blacks. And yet publicly they proclaimed, "This is not a quota bill."

The fight was over the theory of disparate impact. That theory came from a highly ambiguous 1971 Supreme Court decision in *Griggs vs. Duke Power Co.* It had come to be understood to mean that neutral employment practices that did not involve intentional discrimination, but disproportionately operated to exclude blacks would nevertheless be found to violate the Civil Rights Act of 1964 unless they were justified by "business necessity." Never mind that the 1964 Act had rejected this theory.

As a result, employers came to understand that one way to avoid lawsuits over whether their hiring practices operated in this manner was to hire by group preferences. And colleges and universities changed their admissions policies to do the same.

Civil rights leaders also became quite attached to this system. But the rhetoric of civil rights has never reflected that reality. That was my great frustration during debates over the Civil Rights Act of 1991. No one involved in those debates should claim this law was passed with a broad consensus, other than the stated desire of politicians to "get the quota issue behind us." But did we get it behind us? Absolutely not. Executive Order 11246, which is the father of quotas and group preferences, was never even discussed in the two years of debate on the Civil Rights Act of 1990 and 1991. Some readers of the Act, like the worried business leaders who have embraced quotas and preferences to avoid lawsuits, and Fred Barnes of the *New Republic*, believe the Act's prohibition of race as a "motivating factor" in employment decisions, may outlaw quotas and preferences. Others, like Paul Gerwitz of the *New Republic*, believe it protects them. The EEOC eventually will have to address this issue and the Supreme Court ultimately will decide it.

We need an honest examination of the policies championed by those well-meaning do-gooders who would protect and patronize the victim, who would base our civil rights laws on the very stereotypes they were meant to dispel. We need to get back to discussions of individual ability and merit versus group stereotypes and entitlement. We must stop viewing our civil rights laws as the solutions to educational and economic disparity.

And we must return to merit, to values. Values, that much maligned concept from the recent election. People poked a lot of fun at the discussion about values. Yet our values have eroded to the point where studies show that children are cheating more and more in school and thinking that they are doing nothing wrong. How can we instill the importance of merit and respect for individuals if we ignore our values?

We must begin honest debate about these issues. The *Washington Post* took a step in that direction a few months ago in a provocative series on race. The newspaper sponsored two focus groups: one all-black and one all-white. The groups then mixed for a frank discussion about blacks' perceptions of whites and whites' perceptions of blacks. That discussion became explosive at times. Just as there will be animosity as we focus on topics that many are afraid to discuss except among members of their own group. Senate Democrats were afraid to initiate discussion of these topics when Clarence Thomas was considered for the Supreme Court.

It is time to ask: What does affirmative action mean today? Is it more than the removal of unlawful or artificial barriers? Do we owe something special to present-day African Americans—as opposed to Korean-Americans, Chinese-Americans, Hispanic-Americans, Irish-Americans—because blacks have suffered a history of slavery and discrimination? And, even if we own reparations, can that debt ever be repaid in the devalued coin of racial preferences? In fact, monetary reparations might be far less costly to society than racial preferences.

It is time to ask: What does diversity mean today? Is it inclusion in that melting pot that made our nation great? Is it divisive preservation of ethnic or racial heritage to the exclusion of others?

It is time to ask: Can we afford in today's highly competitive world to discount the importance of merit in the guise of fairness?

This is the challenge we face in the years ahead: to heal a nation torn asunder by tension among groups. That healing can only begin when we face the reality of civil rights in America with honest debate and frank talk. I thank you for giving me the opportunity to contribute to the debate in this most important of forums.

READING 9

‒

WHEN QUOTAS REPLACE MERIT, EVERYBODY SUFFERS

Peter Brimelow
Leslie Spencer

"Quota games . . . math games . . . bean counters!"

President-elect Bill Clinton had every reason to lash out at feminist groups at his Dec. 21 news conference. In fact, he had been bean-counting busily himself: According to widespread reports, some of his original Cabinet picks were bumped because they were the wrong sex or race, key constituencies like urban Catholics and supporters of Israel have been crowded out, and his entire appointment process has been seriously slowed. But now mindless feminist pressure was forcing him to admit the ultimate contradiction of all such affirmative action policies: "Diversity" can conflict with merit.

Above all, the President must know the issue is death for the Democrats: His own pollster, Stanley Greenberg, conducted the post-1984 focus group interviews that found opposition to quotas was key to the defection of white working-class voters. (The party promptly suppressed Greenberg's report and now uses only happy-talk such as "looking like America." But a quota by any other name is still a quota.)

If quotas are clogging the Clinton transition, what are they doing to the economy? The subject went unmentioned, needless to say, at Clinton's two-day economic summit in Little Rock. In fact, it has gone virtually undiscussed throughout the quarter-century of bureaucratic and judicial decrees that have effectively transformed the color-blind 1964 Civil Rights Act into a pervasive quota system.

Ironically, just as socialism has collapsed across the globe, the leading capitalist power has adopted a peculiarly American neosocialism, putting politics (and lawyers) in command of its workplace, albeit on the pretext of equity rather than efficiency. Says Edward Potter of the Washington, D.C.-based Employment Policy Foundation: "We have, without doubt, the most far-reaching equal employment laws found anywhere in the world."

Before applauding Potter's sweeping statement, stop for a minute and ponder this question: What does the replacement of merit with quotas cost the American people? The answer is: plenty. The impact may easily have already depressed GNP by a staggering four percentage points—about as much as we spend on the entire public school system.

Quotas are not the law of the land, exactly. They are explicitly banned in both the 1964 and 1991 Civil Rights Acts. Nevertheless, corporate America has been terrorized by the legal legerdemain whereby any statistical disparity between work force and population is equated with intentional discrimination. Throughout American business, newly entrenched affirmative action bureaucrats are enforcing discrimination by race and sex—in favor of the "protected classes" (women, minorities, and, most recently, the disabled)—as decreed by Washington.

One such bureaucrat, Xerox Manager of Corporate Employment Theodore Payne, puts it bluntly: "We have a process that we call 'balanced work force' in Xerox, everybody understands that, and it's measurable, it's goals. . . . *Relative numbers. Relative numbers. That's the hard business, that's what most people don't like to deal with, but we do that all the time.*"

"Balanced work force" is, of course, yet another euphemism for quotas. Payne is apparently saying that Xerox discriminates against white males in favor of the "protected classes." He says it without apology. But, if anyone cares, white males have feelings (and families to support), too.

"To cut whites out of the entire process is racism pure and simple," laments a white male reporter for the *San Antonio Light,* which is due to close down any day. He says Gannett and other major news organizations are showing interest in his Hispanic colleagues exclusively. But he adds: "I don't want to be quoted. I'll never find another job if I am."

In a blistering 1987 article in *Society* magazine, the late Professor William Beer of Brooklyn College described his fellow social scientists' attitude to affirmative action as one of "resolute ignorance." *Forbes'* search of academic journals and Ph. D. theses confirms that ignorance has remained resolute. What little work has been done tends to focus only on whether affirmative action policies have benefited the "protected classes." (Have they? For an answer, see below.)

Corporate America contributes to this resolute ignorance by declining to disclose its costs. "Our members would never say," the National Association of Manufacturers' Diane Generous predicted (rightly). "They would be concerned they might be accused of complaining about how much money they had to spend on this."

Another big business lobby, the Business Roundtable, did publish a study by accountants Arthur Andersen more than a decade ago on how much its members spent to comply with federal regulation, including specifically the Equal Employment Opportunity Commission (EEOC). But today a Roundtable spokeswoman says the organization has no plans to update the study—and that it no longer even possesses any copies.

Sure, measuring the costs of regulation is difficult. But it can be done. For example, the Environmental Protection Agency is required by executive order to make regular estimates of its economic impact.

Competition forces people to face costs, and therefore reduce the amount of discrimination when compared with monopolistic situations.

THE QUOTA ICEBERG

DIRECT COSTS $17 to $20 billion

COST OF REGULATION	Equal Employment Opportunity Commission $202 million	Office of Federal Contract Compliance $53 million	Department of Education $48 million	Other federal agencies $122 million	State and local agencies $120 million
COMPLIANCE COSTS	Federal government *	State and local government $167 million	Education (schools and colleges) $11 billion	Private sector $5 to 8 billion	

INDIRECT COSTS $96 billion

	Federal government ($1 billion in set-asides)	State and local government *	Education (schools and colleges) *	Private sector $95 billion

Total direct and indirect $113 to $116 billion

OPPORTUNITY COSTS $236 BILLION

	Bad hiring	Effect on morale	Misallocation of financial resources
	Total 1991 GNP shortfall 4%		

Direct dollars spent on "civil rights" law enforcement and compliance is only the tip of the quota iceberg. Below water, the indirect costs—resources diverted from other activities—are even larger. And this causes an accumulating GNP shortfall.

*Areas where data were insufficient to make estimates.

So here is a rough but reasonable try at figuring the cost of quotas. That funny noise you hear from now on is economists gritting their teeth. Our response to them: Go make your own estimates. And remember—the truth shall set you free.

Two points about quotas emerge immediately:

Quotas are a very big deal. All employers with more than 15 staff, public, private or nonprofit, come under the EEOC's Uniform Guidelines on Employee Selection Procedures. All can be sued by the EEOC for "discrimination" if the racial, ethnic and sex mix of new hires diverges sufficiently from that of all other qualified applicants—for example, if the percentage of blacks hired is lower than the percentage of blacks applying. That covers 86% of the entire nonfarm private-sector work force.

Additionally, more than 400,000 corporations doing business with the federal government, covering about 42% of the private sector work force, have to file with the Office of Federal Contract Compliance Programs (OFCCP). This process is so onerous that the OFCCP's explanatory manual is about 700 pages long. Corporations with contracts of $50,000 or more must develop an "affirmative action plan" aimed at achieving staffing at all levels that is proportionate to the composition of the qualified work force.

Many colleges and universities are subject to no fewer than three federal agencies: EEOC, OFCCP and the Department of Education's Civil Rights Office. And finally, there are federal, state and local governments. Here a racial and gender spoils system has effectively subverted the merit hiring rules so painfully established by Progressive Era reformers at the beginning of the century.

All of which means that the 1984 poll that found one in ten white males reporting they had lost a promotion because of quotas was quite possibly accurate. Indeed, it could be an underestimate. Quotas have been implemented with extraordinary secrecy and deceptiveness, in part because of their dubious legal status.

"Word comes down, but it does not go out," says Claremont McKenna College sociologist Frederick Lynch, author of the only study on the impact of quotas on white males, *Invisible Victims*. He cites a Los Angeles manufacturer whose receptionist was instructed to accept but quietly shelve employment applications from whites and Hispanics—after they had left the room—because the plant did not have "enough" blacks.

Typical of the secrecy and scale of quotas: the "race-norming" saga. EEOC Vice Chairman R. Gaull Silberman—a Reagan appointee—says that until she read it in a newspaper in 1990, she and EEOC Chairman Evan Kemp had "absolutely no idea" that their own agency was pressing for aptitude tests to be race-normed. This bit of bureaucrat-speak refers to the practice of radically adjusting scores to compensate for minorities' systematically lower results. Yet race-norming had been going on throughout the 1980s. It reportedly subjected at least 16 million test-takers to a quota system they knew nothing about.

After public outcry, race-norming was banned in the 1991 Civil Rights Act. But quotas, like vampires, have proved virtually impossible to kill. Now they seem to be rising from the grave in the shape of a new test-twisting technique called "banding"—concealing differences in performance by lumping ranges of scores together.

The second point about quotas:

Quotas are very expensive. There's surprising denial about this. University of Chicago free market economist Gary Becker, a 1992 Nobel laureate, wrote the standard analysis, *The Economics of Discrimination* (1957). But Becker recently shrugged off affirmative action in a *Business Week* column. He argued that although affirmative action "does hurt some individuals, as it caters to minorities with political clout," it "probably causes less harm than many other programs," such as farm supports.

Strangely, however, Becker tells *Forbes* that in fact he has no idea what quotas cost ("I think it's an important subject for research"). But we do know what farm supports cost: about $9.7 billion in 1992, which is substantially lower than our estimate of $16 billion to $19 billion for private-sector and education compliance costs alone.

Nevertheless, Becker's analysis of discrimination remains the best framework for assessing the economic impact of quotas:

In a free market, Becker argued, there is an inexorable tendency for everyone to receive the marginal value of his or her labor. This means that ultimately, you are likely to be paid something like what your work is worth. If you belong to an unpopular group, employers may pay you less. But that means that they will make more money off you. Because you are such a profitable hire, you will come into demand, and your labor will be bid up. This process can only be prevented by monopoly or government intervention—both of which happened, for example, in South Africa under apartheid. And now in the U.S. under affirmative action.

Relative numbers—
that's what most
people don't like to
deal with, but we do
it all the time.

Talking to *Forbes*, Becker is very anxious to stress that he is *not* saying discrimination will be *completely* competed away. But there is a *tendency* for it to be competed away. "Competition forces people to face the costs, and therefore reduces the amount of discrimination, when compared with a monopolistic or noncompetitive situation," Becker says.

If you believe that racism stalks America like the Angel of Death and that only federal force can keep it in check, you won't like what Becker is saying. But the evidence clearly supports him.

"Once adjustments are made for factors like age, education and experience, 70% to 85% of the observed differences in income and employment between the various groups in America disappears," says economist Howard R. Bloch of George Mason University. "That's been shown by studies dating back to the mid-1960s. And you can't even be sure that the residual gap is due to discrimination. It could be due to factors we haven't controlled for."

Indeed, Harvard economist Richard Freeman found blacks and whites with the same backgrounds and education had achieved wage parity by 1969, well before quotas had America in their grip.

Even the recent much-touted Federal Reserve Bank of Boston study claiming to prove the existence of racial discrimination in mortgage lending turns out to have made a basic methodological error in its handling of default rates (*Forbes*, Jan. 4). Perhaps significantly, its coauthor, Boston Fed Research Director Alicia H. Munnell, was a featured speaker at the Clinton economic summit.

All of which shows the fallacy of two common arguments for government-imposed quotas: that they are necessary to force corporations to tap new pools of labor, and that corporations need a diverse work force to service an increasingly diverse population. Both simply assume that markets don't operate—that corporations couldn't figure this out themselves.

In fact, it's hard to see any benefits contributed by quotas to the overall economy—as opposed to the benefits they channel to the "protected classes." "Affirmative action is a fairly pure form of rent-seeking," says the University of Arizona's Gordon Tullock, using the concept he developed for special interests' use of political power to extract subsidies for themselves from the economy. "There simply isn't any other economic rationale."

In 1987 EEOC's local field office wrote me a letter saying they had reason to believe I didn't have enough women "food servers" and "busers." No woman had complained against me. So the EEOC advertised in the local paper to tell women whose job applications we had rejected—or even women who had just thought of applying—that they could be entitled to damages. Twenty-seven women became plaintiffs in a lawsuit against me. The EEOC interviewed me for hours to find out what kind of person I was. I told them in Sicily where I came from I learned to respect women. I supplied them with hundreds of pounds of paper. I had to hire someone full time for a year just to respond to EEOC demands. Six months ago I finally settled. I agreed to pay $150,000 damages, and as jobs open up, to hire the women on the EEOC's list. Even if they don't know what spaghetti looks like! I have to advertise twice a year even if I have no openings, just to add possible female employees to my files. I also had to hire an EEOC-approved person to teach my staff how not to discriminate. I employ 12 food servers in these two restaurants. Gross sales, around $2 million. How much did it all cost me? Cash outlay, about $400,000.

I wouldn't wish this on my worst enemy.

What the government's done to me—devastating. I wouldn't wish it on my worst enemy.

> —Thomas Maggiore,
> Owner of Tomaso's and
> Chianti restaurants, Phoenix, Ariz.

Economists break the cost of regulation into three parts:

1. *Direct Costs:* the EEOC's outlay of taxpayers' money in regulating and suing Thomas Maggiore, and the money he spends in fines, damages, filling in forms, advertising and otherwise complying with EEOC demands.

2. *Indirect Costs:* the time and overhead Maggiore has to divert from other activities to argue with the EEOC, do the continuing paperwork, sit through sensitivity training, reorganize his workplace and his methods of operating.

3. *Opportunity Costs:* what Maggiore might have achieved if he had been allowed to invest his time and money as he wanted; the loss to the Phoenix-area economy if he gives up and goes back to Sicily.

Remember: Thomas Maggiore is precisely the kind of small business person the politicians claim they want so badly to help.

Let's look at some numbers.

Direct Costs.   One guess of private sector compliance costs for affirmative action: In 1977 Business Roundtable members spent $217 million complying with equal opportunity regulations. They employed 5% of the nonfarm work force; OFCCP regulations cover 42% of the private workforce, implying total costs of $1.8 billion. Adjusted for inflation, that's a current $4.2 billion.

Second guess: In 1981 a study by the Senate Labor & Human Resources Committee suggested compliance costs for the largest 500 companies of about $1 billion. That's $1.8 billion extrapolated over the OFCCP universe. Adjusted for inflation: $2.8 billion.

Neither of these figures includes the EEOC's impact, although it is by far the larger bureaucracy. But the guesstimates are in line with the rule of thumb developed by regulation-watchers from the Center for the Study of American Business at Washington University in St. Louis: Every dollar spent on regulatory enforcement inflicts about $20 in compliance costs. By *Forbes* count, the federal government spent some $425 million on civil rights oversight in 1991, of which about $303 million appears to be directed at the private sector. Implied private-sector compliance cost: $6 billion.

To get an estimate of compliance costs in colleges and universities, *Forbes* turned to John Attarian, a writer and economics Ph.D. who has analyzed the budget of his alma mater, the University of Michigan. Under its "Michigan Mandate," the university is devoting much effort to the recruitment and retention of the "protected classes."

Attarian says about 2.5% of the University of Michigan at Ann Arbor's general budget appears to be devoted to this cause. This does not capture costs buried in department budgets, such as for recruitment. (Minor example: Advertising faculty posts in special minority-oriented publications costs over twice the usual rate.) Still, extrapolated across the estimated $164 billion spent on U.S. higher education in 1992, this suggests total compliance costs of $4.1 billion.

If the same relationship holds true for the $261 billion spent on public and private schools in 1992, their compliance costs would be $6.5 billion. Of course, the problems of schools are different from those of colleges. They may be worse. Busing for racial balance has reportedly caused some school districts to spend over a quarter of their budgets on transportation.

Quotas are just another excuse for the American academic establishment to eschew scholarship for social engineering. Thus, a long survey of "minorities in science" in the Nov. 13 issue of *Science* magazine reported that the National Science Foundation, which is supposed to be funding research, has spent a staggering $1.5 billion in the last 20 years on fostering black scientists. The magazine describes the results as "dismal."

State and local governments also face compliance costs—and they also inflict them on the private sector. New York State, for example, spent $10.5 million complying with its own and federal laws last year, and $7.5 million on "civil rights" enforcement. In 1990 state and local governments spent some $835 billion. Implied total expended on quota compliance and coercion, given New York's rate: $287 million. Additional private sector compliance costs, given New York's enforcement costs and applying CSAB's 20-to-1 rule of thumb: $2.4 billion.

Note that we include no estimate of what it costs the federal government to comply with its own regulations.

We like to be moderate.

Private-sector compliance costs are apparently much exacerbated by the federal enforcers' arbitrary and erratic behavior. Some rare case studies appeared in the September 1992 issue of the American Academy of Political & Social Science's journal *Annals*. One victim reported supplying documents nine times because the OFCCP kept losing them. Another, the National Bank of Greenwood, Ind.—$117 million assets, 138 staff, full- and part-time—was subject to a grueling and chaotic two-year audit, costing more than $100,000 and 4,000 staff hours, although no complaint had apparently been lodged against it. Later the bank was audited twice more, again apparently without any complaints being lodged. Typically, the Indianapolis-based Merchants National Corp., which has meanwhile taken over the National Bank of Greenwood, refused to allow its officers to talk about the experience.

Total direct costs: $16.5 billion to $19.7 billion. Or about $300 per family of four. Compare it with the $20 billion of "infrastructure spending" Clinton has promised to kickstart the economy. And this is just the tip of the iceberg.

Indirect Costs are the part of the iceberg just under the water—easily-seen but involving no direct cash outlay.

"It takes me 50 extra hours to make every faculty hire because of the need to comply with affirmative action rules," says Professor Herbert London, formerly Dean of New York University's Gallatin Division, "even when I end up hiring the person I wanted to hire in the first place."

Naturally, this cost does not appear as a cash item in NYU's operating budget of $627 million, excluding the medical school. (The two-person affirmative action office costs just $172,000— or about $6.50 per full-time student—although a spokesman tells *Forbes* that over a hundred people deal with minority recruitment every day.) Nevertheless, the cost is real.

A measure of these indirect costs is provided by the single Ph.D. thesis *Forbes* found that investigated costs, by Peter Griffin, now assistant professor at California State University at Long Beach. Griffin's rarefied econometric analysis concluded that by 1980, OFCCP regulation had increased federal contractors' labor and capital costs by an average of 6.5%. (As compared with noncontractors—although actually their costs would also have been increased by EEOC requirements.)

The implications of this are substantial. OFCCP regulation covers about 42% of the civilian work force. The contractors' cost of labor alone exceeded $1.4 trillion. The minimum cost of quotas to them, based on Griffin's methodology: about $95 billion—1.7% of GNP.

And the cost to the federal taxpayer is heavy. In 1991, $211 billion was expended on federal contracts with non-government entities. The additional costs inflicted by affirmative action regulation that Griffin's work suggests this sum incorporates: some $13 billion.

Which is on top of the damage inflicted on the taxpayer by "set-asides," the reserving of some portion of federal work entirely for contractors from the "protected classes." About $10 billion of federal contract monies were chan-neled in this way last year. The premium paid is not supposed to go over 10% (although *Forbes* has heard of premiums as high as 25%). Additional quota tax: perhaps $1 billion.

Ironic set-aside fact: The law is confused about this type of quota too. In Richmond v. Croson (1989), the Supreme Court ruled that many of the 234 state and local government set-aside programs were unconstitutional, unless actual discrimination could be proved. Local politicians, anxious to continue handing out the pork, instantly created a minor "disparity studies" industry to make the case that discrimination against minorities was widespread. In a detailed account in the January 1993 issue of *Public Interest* magazine, University of Maryland at Baltimore Professor George La Noue estimates that at least $13 million of taxpayers' money had been fed into this young industry by June 1992, with another $14 million commissioned by the federal Urban Mass Transit Authority alone. Atlanta spent $532,000 for a 1,034-page report coauthored by Ray Marshall, the Carter Administration's Secretary of Labor.

Expensive? Well, proving discrimination is hard work. Most localities have long been legally required to accept the lowest bid—a Progressive-era reform aimed precisely at patronage-hungry politicians. And, significantly, cities like Atlanta, which now want to claim they discriminated, have actually been under black political control for years.

Even more ironic set-aside fact: This type of quota has created another industry—corruption. A prime contractor can set up his black electrician, for instance, in "business" as a purchaser. The electrician needn't have credit or contacts with suppliers. He just takes 5% off the top. One "native American" contractor in Tulsa reportedly had blue eyes and an Irish name but had managed to join the Cherokee Nation of Oklahoma on the strength of an alleged great-great-great-great grandparent.

These abuses can only be checked by more supervision. But minority contractors have been quoted complaining the program is too bureaucratic already.

Astoundingly ironic set-aside fact: According to Professor La Noue, over one-half of the Small Business Administration's set-asides go to groups that are composed largely of first- or second-generation immigrants. He suspects the same is likely to be true for all set-asides. In Washington, D.C.—where an amazing 90% of the city's road construction contracts have been set aside—one of the largest beneficiaries has been the Fort Myer Construction Corp., owned by a family of Portuguese origin who qualify as Hispanics because they emigrated from Argentina.

Absurdly, all immigrants who fall into the "protected classes" qualify for all U.S. quota programs. Which is a pretty clear indication that quotas are not about righting past wrongs at all, but about asserting political power over the economy.

A further indirect cost of the affirmative action system: litigation. (You thought massive regulation would preclude litigation? This is America!)

The number of discrimination suits in federal courts is rising astronomically—by 2,166% between 1970 and 1989, when some 7,500 were filed, versus an increase of only about 125% in the general federal caseload.

Significantly, suits about discrimination in hiring used to outnumber suits about firing. Today it's the reverse, by a factor of three or more. It's obviously absurd to suppose the same employer discriminates in firing but not in hiring.

The civil rights frenzy has simply led to a more litigious, as well as politicized, workplace.

Example: Alabama state law required the Lamar County Board of Education to fire a black teacher after she failed a mandatory competency test five times during the three years allowed. She alleged discrimination because the test failed a disproportionate number of blacks. A judge reinstated her with three years' back salary.

And it's going to get much worse. Preliminary reports are that since the 1991 Civil Rights Act and the 1990 Americans with Disabilities Act (which few people yet realize is also a quota bill) filings have jumped some 30%. Both acts for the first time allow punitive damages, an explicit incentive to contingency-fee trial lawyers.

Opportunity Costs are the base of the quota iceberg, down in the murkiest depths. Unlike the direct and indirect costs of regulation, they don't show up in GNP statistics. They represent what GNP could have been if these more tangible costs had been spent differently—for job-creating investment, say, or for education. But these indirect costs are the most massive of all. For example:

Having the wrong people in the wrong jobs.   Corporate America seems to have resigned itself to quotas as yet another tax. But they are a peculiarly debilitating sort of tax, levied not on the bottom line but on every phase of the corporation's activities, increasing inefficiency throughout. Most taxes are a burden to be shouldered. This is an enfeebling drug.

That affirmative action quotas lead to lowered standards is all but guaranteed by the fact that all standards are suspect to Equal Employment enforcers. "Many of these people believe there really is no such thing as job performance or productivity objectively defined, that it's really just a matter of one's cultural definition or cultural orientation," says Frank Schmidt, a University of Iowa industrial psychologist. Increasingly, they have been able to impose this view on American business.

The civil rights revolution has also virtually aborted the use of tests devised by industrial psychologists, which in the 1950s promised to make employee selection a science. Tests came under attack because minorities typically scored lower on them. Today there are only used, if at all, after work-related validation studies that can cost millions of dollars.

Industrial psychologists, however, have gone on believing in their work. Schmidt and John Hunter of Michigan State University have produced numerous studies showing that hiring the able results in enormous productivity increases. Today, Hunter estimates that total U.S. output would be about $150 billion higher if every employer in the country were free to use tests and select on merit. That's about 2.5% of GNP.

Effect on morale.   Poor hiring shows up not merely in poor decisions but also in poor morale. Quotas, like income tax (and unlike farm supports), have an immediate and dramatic impact on incentives.

Frank Schmidt put it like this: "When the less competent employees reach a critical mass, their lower performance standards become the standards of the organization." The longer-established employees who are equipped for the job abandon their old high standards and conform to the new, lower ones.

Schmidt and Hunter made no estimate of the impact of this phenomenon. But they have speculated that it lay behind the U.S. productivity stall of the 1970s, as the first effects of the war against testing were being felt.

Misallocation of resources.   Monies expended to meet the costs of affirmative action cannot be spent on research and development and plant modernization. The effect of this is cumulative: The growth path of the economy diverges, permanently and increasingly, from its potential. Thus we estimate that an extra $113 billion in direct and indirect costs have been inflicted on the economy annually since 1980. A standard calculation converts this into an estimate of GNP shortfall because of affirmative action: about 1.5 percentage points by 1992.

GNP in 1991 was about $5.7 trillion. The total shortfall quotas may already have caused comes to some 4%. That's well over $225 billion, money that could buy a lot of social programs. Or finance a good deal of job-creating investment.

So quotas cost a lot. But do they do any good at all?

Quotas have obviously failed to prevent continuing catastrophe in much of black America. Prevailing taboos make this subject difficult to discuss. But the distressing facts are powerfully summarized in a remarkable new book, Jared Taylor's *Paved With Good Intentions: The Failure of Race Relations in Contemporary America* (Carroll & Graf). In 1950 only 9% of black families were headed by a single parent; in 1965, 28%; now, fully half. In 1959 only 15% of black births were illegitimate; in 1992, 66%. One in four black men in their 20s is either in jail, on probation or on parole. Clearly, affirmative action has done nothing to reverse the dismal trends.

Quotas have not decisively improved overall black employment. "Despite all the controversies surrounding affirmative action," says Queens College Professor Andrew Hacker, a supporter of quotas, in his bestselling *Two Nations: Black and White, Separate, Hostile, Unequal,* "fewer blacks now have steady jobs of any kind and their unemployment rates have been growing progressively worse relative to those recorded for whites."

Quotas' effect on black incomes appears at best mixed. Between 1970 and 1990 black median family income, adjusted for inflation, crept snail-like from $21,151 to $21,423. But the proportion of black families earning above $50,000 jumped sharply, from about 10% to nearly 15%. Dragging down the median: the increase in black families receiving below $15,000, now nearly 40%. So quotas may have helped create a black middle class (although educated blacks might have done well anyway; after all, the proportion of white high income families also rose in this period). But the black poor have not benefited.

Quotas in colleges have not prevented the gap between black and white college participation from widening in the 1980s. By 1976 some 22.6% of black 18-to-24-year-olds enrolled in college, compared with 27.1% of whites. Thereafter black participation declined, then recovered. In 1990, 25.4% blacks enrolled, but meanwhile white participation had grown to 32.5%.

And although crude enrollment numbers are dear to the hearts of college admissions officers, they conceal tragic differences in attrition. For example, only 37.5% of blacks enrolling at Berkeley in 1983 had graduated five years later, compared with 72% of whites. Critics argue that top colleges burn out black students by irresponsibly recruiting them to fill quotas, when they could be successful at less high-pressure schools.

Quotas may have improved the status of women—or they may not. It's easier to show that women have prospered in the last decades—ironic, because their plight was hardly as serious as that of blacks, with whom they are now competing. Women's share of professional degrees grew from 2.7% in 1960 to 36% in 1990, and their average earnings as a percentage of men's has increased from 61% to 72% over the same period.

But quotas may not be responsible. Female participation in the work force has fluctuated widely for generations, correlated with demographic factors like marriage and fertility rates. For example, the Hoover Institution economist (and *Forbes* columnist) Thomas Sowell has noted that women earned 17% of Ph.D.s in 1921 but only 10% in the early 1960s. Amazingly, as long ago as 1879 women constituted 40% of all college faculty and administrators. Many of these colleges were women-only, but they could still be highly competitive: In 1902 the proportion of women listed in *Who's Who* was more than double that in 1958.

This problem of apportioning credit bedevils the whole quota debate and, indeed, the entire subject of government-mandated social change. Looking back on the 1964 Civil Rights Act and its controversial enforcement, the American Enterprise Institute's Charles Murray, author of *Losing Ground* and *In Pursuit*, offers this startling thought: "There's hardly a single outcome—black voting rights, access to public accommodation, employment, particularly in white-collar jobs—that couldn't have been predicted on the basis of pre-1964 trend-lines." That's pretty devastating. It suggests that we have spent trillions of dollars to create an outcome that would have happened even if the government had done nothing.

From an economic standpoint, quotas work rather like an older form of American neosocialism: price and wage controls. They may seem to produce the desired result. But they could equally well just be simulating it, or even smothering it.

Meanwhile, of course, the economy suffers.

It may be that before America can talk rationally about race, the generation that remembers segregation will have to die off. And we're not talking about liberals. *Forbes* asked Gary Becker, 62, what he thought would be the ideal public policy in this area.

Becker: I prefer to pass on that one. I have views on it, but I don't want to talk about it at this moment.

Oh. Why not?

Becker: Well, let me just make that judgment. I prefer not to.

Becker's University of Chicago colleague Richard A. Epstein, 49, seems to be less nervous about his popularity in the Faculty Club. His book *Forbidden Grounds: The Case Against Employment Discrimination Laws* argues that the modern civil rights laws are flawed to their heart because in negating freedom of association they have inexorably led to government coercion that threatens markets and, ultimately, liberty.

"At bottom are only two pure forms of legislation—productive and redistributive," Professor Epstein argues. "Antidiscrimination legislation is always of the second kind. The form of redistribution is covert; it is capricious, it is expensive and it is wasteful."

And Epstein makes the key economic point: If we want to subsidize a "protected class," he writes, it can be done more efficiently by just giving grants.

"I have a dream," Martin Luther King Jr. said 30 years ago, "that my four little children will one day live in a nation where they will not be judged by the color of their skin, but by the content of their character."

As bean-counting has displaced merit in America, that day is further off than ever.

EMPLOYEE RELATIONS

INTRODUCTION

Employers and employees each have their own sets of needs and values, and the role of human resource management is to help strike some sort of balance between these two sides. The term employee relations is used for the set of activities generated by companies that attempt to meet the needs and values of employees. In some areas, like employee safety, employers' actions are regulated by federal laws, leaving them less latitude. In other areas, however, employers have the discretion to choose how benevolent they wish to be in terms of providing for employee health, employment security, working conditions, and assistance with nonwork problems. Many employers feel that they can gain competitive advantage by recruiting and retaining the best personnel and that this can only be accomplished by establishing a strong, positive image in employee relations.

The readings provided in this section focuses, not on federally regulated areas of safety, but instead on issues where there is some degree of employer discretion. Specifically, we focus on steps that organizations can take to improve employee health, enhance employee perceptions of job security, and promote the interests of individuals by consideration of nonwork problems.

The first reading in this section is titled "Employment at Will: Options for Managers." In this article, authors William Fulmer and Ann Wallace Casey discuss the employment at will doctrine and argue that this idea, born at the turn of the last century, is no longer viable for companies hoping to still be competitive by the turn of the current century. Historically, employment at will has implied that in the absence of a specified contract, either the employer or the employee could sever the employment relationship at any time. The severing of this relationship could be for "good cause," "no cause," or even "bad cause." Fulmer and Casey discuss the costs associated with trying to uphold this doctrine, especially in light of litigation following the precedent established in the 1983 Pine River State Bank case, and conclude that these costs far outweigh any benefits from such policies.

The second reading, Charlene Solomon's, "24-Hour Employees" article examines how many organizations are trying to help their employees better manage the pressures associated with balancing work and non-work issues. Solomon notes that the "traditional" family was typically managed by a mother who was not employed outside the home, but she notes that this is an accurate description for less than 10 percent of current U.S. families. Organizations are now moving in to help out employees with the problems created by this change in family structure, and Solomon discusses the successes and failures of firms entering this challenging new world of employee relations.

READING 10

EMPLOYMENT AT WILL
Options for Managers

William E. Fulmer
Ann Wallace Casey

Executive Overview

This article explores the concept of "employment at will." In addition to examining recent court decisions on the subject, with special attention to a 1983 court decision that is the most significant ruling to date on the subject, this article also argues for U.S. managers to give up the fight to hang on to the "employment at will" concept and devote energies to dealing with the root causes of poor performances.

Employment at will generally is defined as the right of an employer to fire an employee without giving a reason and the right of an employee to quit when he or she chooses. What was once a doctrine that made it easy for employers to fire employees without cause is increasingly being weakened. In some cases, current interpretation of the doctrine of employment-at-will is now causing employers to think twice before discharging even the most unproductive employees. Paranoia has replaced power and employers often seem confused about their rights where employee termination is concerned.

The primary thesis of this article is that the "employment at will" concept is no longer appropriate or useful. In fact, it often is a crutch for poor management. It should be replaced with human resource practices that deal more effectively with potential and actual problem employees. This article briefly explores some recent important court decisions on the subject and attempts to offer some concrete ways to improve managers' abilities to handle problem employees and thereby eliminate the need for employment at will.

THE "COST" OF AT WILL

The employer's "at will" right has become an area of increasing litigation. Jury awards in "wrongful discharge" suits to individual employees have exceeded the

Source: "Employment at Will: Options for Managers" by William E. Fulmer and Ann Wallace Casey, *Academy of Management Executive*, 1990, Vol. 4, No. 2, 102–107.

$1 million mark in some states. In 1986 alone, plaintiffs received favorable verdicts in 78 percent of wrongful-discharge cases that went to California juries and the average total award was $424,527.[1]

Even taking actions to avoid making an implied contract of job security is not without a price. The existence of safeguards like disclaimers, where employees sign statements acknowledging that nothing management has said or done is to be considered a binding contract between employer and employee, may make sense from a legal point of view but one has to wonder what the impact will be on prospective employees. A reasonable person may interpret such disclaimers as meaning that the employer wants to be free to act in a capricious manner. When a prospective employee has other job options, other things being equal, it is reasonable to assume that good employees will reject an employment opportunity at a firm with such a disclaimer.

Some companies have carefully reviewed all materials that are made available to employees to eliminate any reference to job security. By eliminating any reference to employment security, the risk is run of adversely affecting the psychological contract management and employees often want. In general, there may be several unintended costs associated with eliminating any references to employment security.

A few companies have gone so far as to eliminate personnel handbooks for fear that they will be construed as granting contractual rights to employees. As understandable as this management response may be in light of the current judicial climate, it is a bit like throwing the baby out with the bathwater. Employee handbooks can serve a critical function in the workplace. Many employers have discovered that handbooks are invaluable in creating a positive image with employees and publicizing favorable benefits and working conditions provided by the company. A secondary benefit is that they establish the parameters of employee conduct and describe the policies that govern the work environment.

Exceptions to "At Will"

A few companies have gone so far as to eliminate personnel handbooks for fear that they will be construed as granting contractual rights to employees.

In the U.S., employment at will was an element of the laissez-faire philosophy of the industrial revolution. However, by the 1930s, but especially since the mid-1960s, exceptions to the doctrine of employment at will have surfaced. The first major exceptions were statutory. Federal legislation prohibited discharge for such things as participation in union activities (National Labor Relations Act); the exercise of rights guaranteed by minimum wage and overtime provisions (Fair Labor Standards Act); race, color, religion, national origin or sex (Civil Rights Act, Equal Employment Opportunity Act, etc.). Many state laws cover the same issues and in some cases also protect employees from termination for other activities—filing for workers compensation, complaining about safety conditions, refusing to take pre-employment lie detector tests, or "whistleblowing."[2]

Since the 1970s state courts increasingly have restricted the "at will" doctrine. Although there is great variation from state to state, the following are examples of some areas where employees were found to have a right to take legal action against their employer when their termination violated "public policy"; refusing to commit an unlawful act (e.g., perjury or price fixing); performing an important public obligation (e.g., jury duty); exercising a statutory right or privilege (e.g., filing for workman's compensation); exercising the rights of shareholders (e.g., refusing to support a merger); and "whistleblowing," (i.e., reporting alleged employer violations of statutory policy).

In general, when discharge can be shown to be motivated by the requirements of business or the incompetence of the employee, the discharge is generally accepted without question by the courts. Yet, when the motive has been found to be "malicious," the courts have found that in all employment contracts "the employer's interest in running the business as he sees fit must be balanced against the interest of the employee in maintaining a proper balance between the two." Furthermore, the courts also have held "that a termination by the employer of a contract of employment at will which is motivated by bad faith or malice or is based on retaliation is not in the best interest of the economic system or the public good and constitutes a breach of the employment contract.[3]

Not only are courts finding that employees have the right to challenge the employment at will doctrine but some court decisions have awarded damages if the employee can prove that the employer had a motive other than what was stated. Increasingly, the courts seem to be looking more closely at the disparity between what the employer said was the cause and what the employee claims was the true reason for termination.

IMPLIED CONTRACTS

Perhaps the most controversial area of emerging wrongful discharge law is in the area of contracts. Under contract law, the terminated employee must prove:

1. A legally enforceable contract did exist with the employer, and
2. The termination decision was a breach of that contract.[4]

In a 1977 case the court dealt with an employee at will who had a written contract that expressly permitted discharge without just cause. The court found that "the written contract contains an implied covenant of good faith and fair dealing and a termination not made in good faith constitutes a breach of the contract."[5]

Even in situations where a written contract does not exist, the courts now are finding that a contract between the employee and employer is implied by language in company documents, such as a personnel handbook that states that an employee will be fired only for just cause or after a disciplinary procedure outlined in the handbook has been followed. In two 1980 companion cases, the Michigan Supreme Court found that based on statements in company manuals employees could be terminated only for cause and only after being warned.[6]

This trend seemed to take a further step in a 1981 California Appeals Court ruling that allowed a suit to be maintained even though a provision in the state labor code entitled either employer or employee in a noncontract employment arrangement to terminate the employment relationship at will. The court stated that there was sufficient evidence from which a jury could find existence of an implied promise on the part of the employer not to act arbitrarily in dealing with employees. The court's conclusions were supported by the duration of employment, recommendation and promotion received, lack of direct criticism of work, assurances given, and the employer's acknowledged policies.[7]

In what may prove to be the most important employment at will court decision since 1908, when the U.S. Supreme Court upheld and seemingly imbued the "at will doctrine" with constitutional status[8] in 1983, the judge in *Pine River State Bank v. Mattille* used as a standard for determining whether a proposal was meant to be an offer of a contract the "outward manifestations of the parties, not their subjective intent" and that employment documents, such as a personnel handbook, could be the means of communicating a contractual obligation, the acceptance of which by an employee completed the contract.[9]

Once it was established that an employment document constituted an offer, the next question was whether the employee had furnished the necessary acceptance and consideration to make the contract enforceable. The judge in Pine River found that the mere act of taking or retaining the job showed acceptance and that an employee's continuing to work though he or she was free to leave at any time constituted consideration.

It is important to note that in the cases to date regarding implied job security contracts, the courts have been very clear in stating that employers have the right and the ability to enter into such contracts. The courts uphold the employer's prerogative to refrain from making any promises to employees concerning how a termination will be conducted or under what conditions employees may be fired. What the courts do say is that if the employer makes such a promise of job security whether implied, verbally, or in writing in an employment document or personnel handbook, he or she is bound by that promise.

Clearly then, employers can eliminate any reference to job security in their employment documents. For example, some companies have rewritten their manual and application forms, eliminating the word "permanent" from employee descriptions. Other employers have rewritten the manuals, making them much more detailed.

What the courts do say is that if the employer makes such a promise of job security whether implied, verbally, or in writing in an employment document or personnel handbook, he or she is bound by that promise.

Some employers have gone a step farther and chosen to have employees sign disclaimers upon hiring which clearly state management's intention that nothing in the personnel manual or other related material is to be considered a binding contract between employer and employee. Sears has been very successful in winning summary judgments for dismissal of employee termination cases as a result of their disclaimer document.[10] Although other courts have ignored these clauses some employers feel it is safer to have it in both the personnel manual and the application form.

As mentioned at the beginning of this article, a few companies have eliminated employee handbooks out of fear that they might grant contractual rights to employees. Others use outplacement firms to handle dismissals. NAS Insurance Services Inc., of Santa Monica, California, now offers insurance for companies sued by employees for wrongful discharge.[11]

HR PRACTICES THAT MAKE AT WILL UNNECESSARY

If companies really are concerned about the ability to deal with problem workers, they should devote their energies to training managers to do a better job of hiring, training, performing evaluations, making promotion decisions, and dealing with disciplinary problems. These activities are much more at the heart of good management and can contribute far more to the success of the organization than defending an antiquated "right."

Managers need to examine their personnel practices so as to strengthen employee relations and thereby greatly reduce the need for "at will."

Hiring.   Obviously if management could hire the "right" person, an employee is unlikely to become a "problem" employee. Not only do numerous managers follow unsystematic approaches in hiring employees but in an effort to have the "right" person accept, some managers make promises that the organization may not be able to fulfill. It is critical for managers to understand and abide by the constraints under which an offer of employment can be made as well as follow clearly established procedures in the hiring process.

Training and Orientation.   In the orientation of new hires, employees should be given clear expectations about what the organization considers appropriate and inappropriate performance. This needs to be reinforced in subsequent training for employees. Perhaps more important, managers need to be trained in how to handle problem employees.

Performance Appraisals.   It is essential that employees be provided with timely and accurate feedback about their performance and that this feedback be well documented. Not only is it important for high performance employees but it is especially important for "problem" employees. Without being given constructive feedback—a clear statement of their level of performance and suggestions for how to improve—there is at least a possible perception of unfairness about the process. Furthermore, management loses out on a valuable technique for improving the level of everyone's performance.

Promotions.   Promotions cannot be viewed as a reward for seniority or loyalty. To continue to promote a person and then discharge that person cannot help but raise the question of why the person was so good as to warrant promotion and then so quickly became bad enough to warrant discharge. In those unusual cases where, in fact, such dramatic deterioration of performance occurs, it is essential that the situation be well documented.

Discipline.   Too many organizations fail to provide adequate warnings and fail to document the warnings made to "problem employees" before disciplinary action is taken. The result is that the employee may not know that he or she is in danger of discharge. When the discharge occurs, there is an appearance of, if not an actual case of, the employee not being given an opportunity to correct the situation. Such a situation certainly raises the question of fairness.

CONCLUSIONS

Japan, Great Britain, France, Germany, and Canada all require an employer to show just cause in terminating an employee. Unlike other industrialized, especially western, countries, in the U.S. employers are allowed a great deal of power in "at will" firings. Traditionally in the U.S. only those employees protected by collective bargaining contracts had any enforceable protection from summary dismissal. In more recent times, cohesive interest groups, such as unions, veterans and minorities, have been protected from summary dismissal, while "random individuals who are unjustly terminated are isolated and without organizational or political voice."[12]

. The time has come for employers to stop spending so much time, energy, and money trying to protect the employment at will "right."

From an employee-relations perspective, it is time for managers to at least consider the benefits that might be gained from giving up the "at will" right—a right that increasingly is being interpreted as a right to be capricious. In return, they might be able to obtain some things that are more valuable—a more cooperative employee relationship and perhaps a limit on the amount of damages that can be sought when the system does break down.

The fight to hang on to a turn of the century "right" is not worth the effort. It is little more than a "band-aid" solution to the problem of poor performers. It addresses only symptoms and does not get at root causes of problematic employee relations. In fact, it often seems to be used in cases where discharge is appropriate—but management has done such a poor job in executing the discharge, management often has to fall back on the at will argument.

The time has come for employers to stop spending so much time, energy, and money trying to protect the employment at will "right." Given the practices in other developed countries and the trend in recent court decision and especially the strong ruling in the Pine River State Bank case, one has to wonder if in the U.S. it is not just a matter of time until the principle is firmly established in legal precedent or even in legislation. Perhaps the time has come for managers to encourage legislation prohibiting arbitrary discharge. If employers move quickly, they may be able to obtain limits on the damages available. Recent developments in Montana (a law protecting employees against arbitrary dismissal but limiting the damages available) and a California Supreme Court ruling restricting large punitive damages for wrongful discharge may signal that the time is right for managers to move.[13] Employers will be better off to concede its demise and devote management attention and resources to improving the management of human resources.

In summary, in this increasingly litigious society, employers who fire without just cause are finding it difficult to estimate their potential liability in this changing area of the law. Furthermore, employers using this approach to human resource management in the 1990s are likely to find themselves with poor employee morale in the best case and before a jury in the worst case.

Endnotes

The authors wish to acknowledge the assistance provided by Professor Carolyn Hotchkiss of Babson College in reviewing an early draft of this paper.

[1]"The Checkoff," *The Wall Street Journal,* March 3, 1987, 1.

[2]Jerome B. Kanaff and Harry H. Weintraub, "Increasing Restraints in Terminating the Employment Relationship," in Unjust Dismissal and at Will Employment, Practicing Law Institute, 1982, 23–63.

[3]Monge v. Beebe Rubber Co. 114 N.H. 130, 316 A. 2nd 549 (1974).

[4]Lawrence E. Dube, Jr., "Planning for Defensible Discharges," *Management Review,* 1986, vol. 75, no. 3, 45.

[5]Fortune v. National Cash Register Co., 373 Mass. 96, (1977).

[6]Toussaint v. Blue Cross and Blue Shield of Michigan and Ebling v. Masco Corp., 292 N.W. 2nd 880, 892 (Michigan, 1980).

[7]Pugh v. See's Candies, Inc., 161 Cal. App. 3rd 311, 171 Cal. Rqtr. 917 (1981).

[8]Adair v. U.S. 208 U.S. 161 (1908).

[9]Pine River State Bank v. Mattille, 333 NW 2nd 622 (Minn. 1983).

[10]John D. Feerick and Roberta V. Romberg, "Practical Issues of Employment Documents and their Implications for At Will Employment," in Unjust Dismissal and at Will Employment, Practicing Law Institute, 1982, 111–129.

[11]"Firing Rights," *The Wall Street Journal,* October 1, 1985, 1.

[12]Clyde W. Summers, "Protecting all Employees Against Unjust Dismissal," *Harvard Business Review,* January–February 1980, 132–139.

[13]Brenton R. Schlender, "California Ruling Curtails Damages in Dismissal Suits," *The Wall Street Journal,* December 3, 1988.

READING 11

24-HOUR EMPLOYEES

Charlene Marmer Solomon

Balancing business goals with employees' total lives means changing corporate culture. Even the most progressive companies are finding that it takes a serious, long-term commitment.

For many people, 5 p.m. is the end of the workday. They go shopping, out to dinner or to the gym to work out. But for a larger number of working men and women with families, their workday is nowhere near finished. They go home to another shift—a shift of soccer practice, car pools, care for an elderly relative, orthodontist appointments, school events, in addition to marketing, cleaning and errands. Millions of workers go home to several hours of additional work—to a "second shift," in the words of Arlie Hochschild, in her book of the same name.

With the "traditional" family (a family in which the mother is not employed outside the home) accounting for less than 7% of all American families, there's simply more and more to do everyday—both at the workplace and at home. According to many experts, progressive companies are wrestling with the fact that their employees have lives outside the workplace and that their personal concerns often create additional demands on their time at work. Recognizing the employee as a 24-hour human being and translating that into the corporate culture is an enormous undertaking that requires a serious, long-term commitment by the company.

Balancing work and family, and being sensitive to time demands are complex issues that affect some of the most basic assumptions we hold about the workplace: Are traditional work schedules counterproductive in some cases? Is the workplace an appropriate sphere for family problems—and solutions? Is the traditional view of employees too narrow and rigid for today's society?

A more holistic view of employees is crucial if companies are to attract and retain talented individuals. What's now being referred to as a "life cycle" approach to employees goes far beyond dependent care referrals.

A life cycle view of an employee means that the corporate culture responds to an individual's changing needs throughout that employee's life, recognizing in a fundamental way that the employee's personal life strongly influences his or her effectiveness at work, and that the corporation must play an active role in alleviating some of the external pressure. For example, employees don't stop having child care concerns when their children reach elementary school age or become teenagers. Their concerns simply change.

A few pioneer companies already have begun to explore this complex arena. Some businesses are experimenting with ideas and programs that may seem radical to us today: new forms of flex time, career breaks and sabbaticals; phased retirement; and exhaustive employee surveys they will use as scaffolding for future strategic planning.

Some companies even contract with frequently used services—such as banks, dry cleaners, barber shops and hair dressers—to open retail outlets when they design or relocate their offices. The key is that services and programs are part of an integrated approach to solving this overwhelming problem.

"One step in the right direction would be trying to move away from segmentation of work versus non-work roles and recognize that these domains are not mutually exclusive," says Eleanor Haller-Jorden, founder of the Paradigm Group, an international human resources consulting firm that specializes in corporate change and managing diversity.

"Companies stand to realize significant benefits from the standpoint of their own bottom line if they don't persist in this thinking. There's tremendous interdependency. Behaviors and attitudes in one domain impact behaviors and attitudes in the other."

Companies are aware of the facts. They know the demographic projections of *Workforce 2000;* they know that two-thirds of the new workers between now and the year 2000 will be women (who'll have vast numbers of preschool and school-age children as well as responsibility for aging parents); they know that programs that support families boost morale.

Studies show that tension between work and family life is a major source of stress for many workers. They also point to the drop in productivity when employees have difficulty with dependent care. For example, Bank Street College found that problems with child care caused absenteeism and unproductive time. In a study conducted by the Families and Work Institute in New York City, employees who have latchkey children missed 13 days of work per year as compared to an average of seven to nine days. Another survey conducted found that more than 50% of men and women report being interrupted at work because of elder care responsibilities.

"Companies can no longer hire more people when they need to increase production; they must get more out of the people they hire," state Ellen Galinsky and Dana Friedman, co-founders and co-presidents of the Families and Work Institute in New York City in a recent study. "The corporate culture is being re-examined and work-family issues are an important area for exploration in that restructuring."

"A lot of companies have recognized they are losing about twice as many high-potential women as men," says Galinsky. "They're finding that untenable and realize it can't be fixed simply with child care programs. It has to do with the culture of the workplace. I think we're at a point in which the family has shouldered most of the change, and the workplace is going to begin to take some share in that.

"We're at the cutting edge here. If you're going to say that 'face time' [when employees are present at their desk at their office] equals productivity or commitment, then you are going to squeeze yourself out of a part of the work force in which you have invested a lot."

Galinsky thinks we are at a "barrier-breaking" stage, but changes are coming along quite slowly. "We're at a stage in corporate America in which very few pioneering companies are trying to define a new vision," she says. Galinsky and Friedman call these companies, "Stage Three" companies (see sidebar).

Defining that vision is a complicated, arduous task. Many companies already have a whole host of programs that respond to one or another of these needs, including: child care centers; resource and referral programs for dependent care; financial assistance for dependent care; family leave for childbirth, adoption and care of an ill family member; parenting and stress-management seminars; flextime; job sharing; and part-time work. But only a few have a comprehensive, integrated approach, or are "Stage Three" companies.

According to the Conference Board, about 5,000 major U.S. firms offer some form of child care: dependent care assistance programs—about 2,500; resource and referral—about 1,200; near- or on-site child care centers—about 1,200; and special financing—about 100 companies.

"We're seeing a lot of consolidation of efforts," says Christine Scordato, director of research at Catalyst, a national, non-profit organization working with business to affect change for women through research, advisory services and communication. "Some of the largest, most progressive companies are pulling all of these components together into a strategic effort. They recognize that no one program is going to solve employees' needs, but a range of work-family policies is going to help recruit and retain employees."

The family has shouldered most of the change, and the workplace will begin to share in that.

According to Scordato, more companies are looking beyond the one end of the life spectrum that needs child care; they're looking at elder care and recognizing that there's an enormous number of people who are of the sandwich generation. They're recognizing the need for flexible work hours and benefits programs for employees.

"Increasingly, companies are recognizing that the traditional way work has been structured no longer meets the needs of today's working families. They're beginning to see that needs won't go away. They just have to give people the time to deal with them," says Scordato.

DuPont is one company that's consolidating the effort. Its approach to work and family is to have an internal champion where all work and family issues coalesce.

But DuPont is a pioneer on several fronts. In 1989, the company created a work force partnering division. Under the umbrella of corporate human resources, this division combines the affirmative action programs, valuing diversity education and the responsibility for work-family issues, and acts as a champion for all three.

"Each has to do with meeting the new needs of a changing work force," says Faith Wohl, DuPont's director of work force partnering. "There's good synergy and common threads that make them belong together. We've done affirmative action successfully for 30 years, but as the work force changes, we really need to change the culture within the company. That's where a lot of our diversity education is focused—and in the area of family—to make it easier for people to integrate work and family responsibilities. That's also part of the new work force."

This is really quite radical—addressing these multi-faceted issues from one centralized place. It also begins to address the issue of gender equity for women who want both a family and high-powered career.

The work force partnering division was created initially to implement the recommendations of two massive corporate work and family studies (done in 1985 and 1988). In 1985, a committee of 16 employees researched for one year and made approximately two dozen recommendations to senior management.

In response to the 1985 survey, its first work-family survey, DuPont created a child care resource and referral agency in Delaware—the first in the state. It was a non-profit agency to serve the whole community, not just DuPont employees. The company extended the service in 1988 to include child care and elder care referral nationwide.

In addition, DuPont extended family leave to include men, as well as including birth, adoption or serious illness of a parent, spouse or child in their leaves. The company started "School-Match," (a program that helps employees assess different school systems or individual schools with regard to the needs of their children), and provided more than $1.5 million to build and renovate child care centers that are near its major locations.

The second survey was very broad-based, with recommendations so comprehensive that it became clear the company needed an organization with a permanent base. "We couldn't depend on commissioning employee committees every time we suspected the world had changed that much," says Wohl. It required an internal organization whose job it was to stay focused strategically on the changes that existed in the world that would effect employees in the workplace. As a result, the company created work force partnering.

Since its creation, work force partnering has done several things. In addition to adding referral services, investing in expanding community child care facilities and extending family leave, the 1985 survey indicated that 30% of the employees felt the child care they used was inadequate. The company initiated a program to provide incentive grants to child care providers to become professionally accredited through the National Association for the Education of Young Children or the National Association of Family Daycare Homes. (There are 62 providers in the process of receiving accreditation, 25 that have received it, 12 of which are in

THE WORK-FAMILY EVOLUTION OF COMPANIES

Companies evolve in a somewhat predictable (if not always sequential) pattern when initiating work-family policies. That's the discovery Ellen Galinsky and Dana Friedman, co-founders and co-presidents of the New York City-based Families and Work Institute, made while doing research for their upcoming book, *The Corporate Reference Guide to Family-Friendly Programs and Policies.*

During the *first stage* the company takes the programmatic approach. During this phase, programs are developed—typically child care, other dependent care alternatives and seminars to help employees understand some of these issues—and management believes the problem is settled.

In the *second stage* the company moves into an integrated approach. At this point of the evolution, executives at the highest levels of the company begin to become involved in the issues because they see work-family balance as a bottom-line business issue.

Work-family programs are no longer farmed out to a variety of different departments, but rather are guided by one employee or group dedicated to the issue. Upper management—senior vice presidents and the CEO—become involved, and systematic evaluations are undertaken about the effects of other aspects of the workplace. When companies are at this stage, they typically begin to explore the wide range of flextime alternatives and other flexible work arrangements, not for the convenience of company business, but specifically to help employees lessen stress and manage the burdens of combining professional and personal lives.

The *third stage* is the most progressed. It's when a company knows that programs won't suffice, and looks toward changing the corporate culture.

A company may develop a vision or mission statement that says it will be supportive of families and acknowledges the importance of quality-of-life issues. Furthermore, these companies promote the policies to employees so they know what's available, and sensitize supervisors so they support company policies.

Finally, some of these companies broaden their scope to improve the world outside of their own spheres. Some fund dependent-care resource and referral programs; others offer grants to improve the quality of child care; others have become advocates in the public sector.

Delaware.) The company has provided more than $1.5 million to build and renovate child care centers that are near its major locations.

Another major effort has been to continue to encourage good research, particularly at some of the plant sites away from Delaware. This serves to "take the temperature" of local populations and see if anything has changed. It also gives local administrators fresh data about their own employees relevant to their local situations. This is important. For example, at the Wilmington headquarters, 76% of the employees are men but in the Athens, Georgia plant 65% of the plant are women. In Beaumont, Texas, only 10% of the employees are women. Some site populations are older, so they wouldn't be likely to be as interested in child care but might be more interested in elder care.

DuPont has encouraged the development of work and family committees at sites across the country. Currently there are 50 of them. "We see them as the grass roots monitors of what's happening within a specific part of our population, as a very energized communications network," says Wohl.

The corporate work force partnering group puts the corporate programs in place and is a resource to those local committees that are to respond to local needs. These committees have done a variety of things, such as:

- Create parenting days or fairs
- Develop parent support groups for different age children or different problems
- Work with local hospital or governmental agencies to create small, near-site child care centers
- Create on-site summer day camp for children and grandchildren
- Arrange with local summer day camp programs for pick-up and delivery of children to the work site

It was clear to Wohl and others at DuPont that employees need to have a corporate environment that's responsive to these concerns. Wohl's department is now looking at a range of flexibility options. As Wohl points out, none of these are radical; all are in the predictable range. However, trying to drive these options as part of the culture other than individually negotiated arrangements will be fundamentally difficult for the company.

"DuPont has a very old and well-established corporate culture," declares Wohl. "For us, flexibility is going to be not only the biggest need we can address, but in some ways the hardest hurdle for us to overcome."

They'll be examining part-time work with benefits, reduced hours with benefits, adjustable work hours, flex time, longer leaves, sabbaticals and job sharing.

DuPont even is looking at phased retirement. Illustrating a sensitivity to a life cycle perspective, Wohl explains that it's just another period of life—similar to when children are small—when people may want to reduce their hours but don't want to lose their benefits or their professional status or connections. They may need the flexibility of a reduced-hours schedule.

"I think time is probably the biggest problem we all have," she states. "If employers can give the gift of time to their employees, they would be very appreciative.

"The answer is flexibility, helping people use the time they have more effectively—when it's most useful to them. If you can't go to the doctor's office except during the day, we need to give people time to do that. If the school is open during the day and that's when teachers' conferences or school plays take place, people need the flexibility to decide if they want to do that—obviously, consistent with the needs of the business.

"We're experiencing a big change in the nature of our work force—not only in who those people are, but more importantly in what kind of life they live. What the HR organization in total is all about is empowering, enabling, helping employees to be productive and to create a work climate in which they can be productive."

Catalyst agrees with Wohl. In fact, these researchers view flexible work arrangements as the single biggest thing companies can do—if they can only do

THE NARROWING GAP BETWEEN MEN AND WOMEN

Although it's clear that women do a majority of the work at home, it's equally clear that this gap between men and women is narrowing—possibly because more men have employed wives; possibly because more men are involved in childrearing.

A 1990 study by DuPont proved this point with startling results that showed that men are concerned about dependent care issues and want flexibility in the workplace. In addition, men and women professionals were equal in declining jobs that required relocation or heavy travel. And in other surveys conducted by the company, men and women reported stress from the difficulties of managing their personal and work responsibilities.

DuPont began tracking the attitudes of its male employees in 1985, when it conducted its first work-family survey. Focusing on 20% of its domestic work force, the most compelling need expressed was information about child care. A full 70% of the employees (three-fourths of whom were male) who had children under 13 were using some form of care outside the home.

"The data told us that this wasn't strictly a women's issue," says Faith Wohl, DuPont's director of work force partnering. "Although that was only six years ago, it was a very different point in history. So much has happened in the work-family field so quickly that it's sometimes hard to remember."

According to Wohl, the second survey conducted in 1988 revealed that the issue was moving so quickly that DuPont hadn't done nearly enough to help its employees the first time around, although it had made major changes.

In 1985, the company realized quantitatively that men were significantly affected, but by 1988 men were telling the researchers just how much the care of their families was affecting the way they thought about their careers, their jobs and their lives in general. The men reported high stress in their families, indicated that they had turned down promotions, diminished their

Companies recognize that one program isn't going to solve employees' needs

one thing—to help employees manage their personal and professional lives. This includes flexible hours, telecommuting, part time with benefits, compressed work weeks and job sharing. There has been an enormous influx of companies interested in working with Catalyst to implement these types of programs.

In a recent survey of 645 companies published by *Nation's Business*, the following alternatives were offered: flexible time—50%, part-time work—47%, job sharing—22%; compressed workweek—16%; part-year work—7%, and school day only schedule—4%.

According to Catalyst, flexible work arrangements are a key part of the answer. In a recent study, Catalyst conducted extensive research regarding part-time work, job sharing and telecommuting at the professional and managerial levels. The research consisted of literature review, and interviews with 50 human resources professionals and 150 employees. Initially 41% of human resources administrators reported resistance from middle managers, but even with that resistance, the results were impressive.

- 68% said it positively affected retention
- 58% said it had a beneficial impact on recruitment

THE NARROWING GAP BETWEEN MEN AND WOMEN (*continued*)

travel and were not encouraged to take relocation.

"Men were talking much the same as we would have expected women to report from the survey," says Wohl. Because the gap between men's attitudes and women's attitudes had narrowed significantly in four years, this led her and others at DuPont to believe that they really were tapping into a profound social change that was occurring everywhere.

"We are an old and relatively conservative manufacturing company," says Wohl. "If it's happening here to a population that's mostly men, tell me the industry in which it's not happening."

In 1990, DuPont commissioned a third study, this time of 8,500 employees: 70% men, 60% from dual-career households, 20% dependent on outside child care.

The survey results showed a strong desire for flexible work options to balance both home and work responsibilities. The fascinating aspect of these results is the degree to which men expressed interest,

again illustrating the narrowing gap between men's and women's attitudes toward business travel, relocation and care for sick children.

- 56% of men are interested in flexible work hours compared to 37% in 1985, but 76% of women favor the option (which was the case before, too)
- 62% of employees who have or plan to have children, place great value for job flexibility to balance work and family duties better
- 64% of men are interested in sick child leave policy compared to 40% in 1985
- 35% of men favor transition time to care for a newborn compared to 15% in 1985
- 40% of men have considered another employer who offers more job flexibility, up from 25% in 1988
- Men and women professionals were equal in the percentage declining jobs requiring relocation or heavy travel
- 50% of employees who have children 10 to 13 years old leave their children home alone after school.

- 65% reported higher productivity from workers who used flex time
- 70% reported it had a positive effect on morale

Levi Strauss & Co., the San Francisco-based apparel manufacturing giant, is recognized as one of the most progressive companies for quality-of-life issues. Its culture actively advocates flexible work arrangements. Its policies acknowledge that the traditional view of family—and the traditional work force—are changing.

Long acknowledged as a leader in flexibility, the company began experimenting with job share, part time and flex time in the early 1980s.

"With the increased pressure of business demands and limited child care facilities in some field locations, we began to find that we needed to examine how we as a company could help our employees better balance their work lives with their personal lives," says Jenny Crowe-Innes, director of employee relations, employment and EEO.

In 1989 the company created an 18-member work/family task force whose mission was to create a more supportive work environment to help employees balance their professional and personal responsibilities. Headed by CEO Bob Haas, it was a year-long, businesswide effort, with task force representatives

One step in the right direction is moving away from segmenta-tion of work versus non-work roles.

from all levels of the company charged with investigating the issues, crafting the company's vision and presenting a series of programs that would address the current needs.

Working with Galinsky and Friedman at the Families and Work Institute, the company surveyed 13,000 employees to assess their needs. One outcome of the study was a mission statement that says Levi Strauss wants to create an environment that's supportive of employees balancing their work and personal lives, involving all aspects of work, not just child care or elder care. It would include policies, travel norms within the company, anything that puts pressure on the employees.

"We want to break some of the paradigms that we've had before about the very rigid, traditional schedule," says Crowe-Innes. "We realize that doesn't work for everybody. People have differing needs, and at certain times in people's lives, one may need some degree of flexibility."

Levi's is starting to change its culture. As a starter, the firm is piloting a one-day training program for all managers and supervisors about managing a flexible workplace, which according to Crowe-Innes, has been a difficult process.

"We feel we need to educate supervisors and managers, as well as employees on what this means for the company," says Crowe-Innes. "We're not changing our business, we're just trying to change the way we deliver it and still give people some flexibility. We need to be available to the retailing community with customer service eight hours a day, five days a week."

Levi Strauss has several programs:

1. It has a telecommuting pilot underway for 6 months in which 40 personnel from management and different functional levels were provided full equipment. The task force will study the results and come out with parameters so telecommuting can be instituted more fully.

2. In the manufacturing plants, the company is pioneering a model flexibility program. The six-month pilot concept allows the sewing machine operators to come in up to four hours late or leave four hours early as long as they put in their day's production. There are core hours from 10 a.m. to 2 p.m., but flexibility from 6 a.m. to 10 a.m. and 2 p.m. to 6 p.m. to accommodate child care needs, doctor appointments and so on.

   "This is just about unheard-of in a production environment," says Crowe-Innes. So far it seems very successful "We'll be evaluating that. If it's successful, we'll tell other plants about it and if it makes sense at their plants, they can adopt it."

3. The company has just launched a new paid time-off concept. The work-family survey indicated that employees wanted to be able to have more flexibility and manage their time better. In response, TOPP (Time Off with Pay Program) was designed to include the old vacation policy, sick policy and floating holiday policy. It gives employees a bank of days they can use at their discretion for whatever they want. It gives employees more control over their time with the collaboration of the supervisor. Noteworthy is the fact that employees would be able to use time in two-hour increments.

"We're experiencing departments' coming to us saying they want to pilot programs that allow people to get off early one day if they're covered. The idea of work groups is helping individuals manage their time," says Crowe-Innes.

As Levi's begins to train managers in these areas, the company emphasizes to employees and managers alike that it's a partnership arrangement. The employee is responsible to the business, as well as the business and supervisor providing for the employee. It's a partnership approach.

Levi Strauss has two large projects in the planning stages for 1992. The company will set up a foundation to increase the quality of child care. In 1993, it will set up a similar situation for quality elder care. This year, a subcommittee will examine travel norms to see how they might be inconsistent with a balanced viewpoint. The committee will make recommendations about how to make travel policy more compatible with family life.

Concludes Crowe-Innes, "Levi Strauss is driven by a desire to provide employees an environment where they can learn and grow. It's an employee-relations company; it's a family company, the Haas family has very strong values about how to treat people and people are the most important asset. We believe that by helping our employees, we can improve productivity and the bottom line. If you treat people well and give employees more control over their lives, we'll see a real pay-back on that."

PART II

ASSESSING WORK AND WORK OUTCOMES

THE ANALYSIS AND DESIGN OF WORK

INTRODUCTION

The role of designing and analyzing work plays a part in gaining competitive advantage. Increasingly firms are engaging in "reengineering" in an effort to streamline work processes while gaining higher quality and flexibility. This requires an extensive reorganization of the way that work is performed and is usually accomplished through the processes of work and job redesign. However, various approaches to job design exist, and there are trade-offs that managers have to be aware of when designing or redesigning jobs.

Reading 12 by Schneider and Konz explores the problems that occur when analyzing jobs that might change in response to strategic changes. These authors discuss how strategic issues can impinge on the skills, tasks, and responsibilities required in jobs. They present a method for performing "strategic job analysis," which is a technique for performing job analysis that attends to anticipated future events that might affect the job. They then describe how this technique was used in one organization to illustrate the process.

In Reading 13 by Campion and Thayer, the four approaches to job design are examined in detail. These authors present the results of a rather extensive study examining the various approaches to job design. They explore the philosophical and scientific foundations of each approach and examine the outcomes that each approach focuses on maximizing. The authors also present some practical implications for managers who are seeking to understand and weigh the trade-offs inherent in favoring one job design approach over another.

READING 12

STRATEGIC JOB ANALYSIS

Benjamin Schneider
and Andrea Marcus Konz

The application of job analysis techniques makes the implicit assumption that information about a job as it presently exists may be used to develop programs to recruit, select, train, and appraise people for the job as it will exist in the future. Given a rapidly changing internal and external world it is likely that many jobs will change in the future. This article reviews some new techniques that, when added to traditional job analysis procedures, may facilitate strategic planning for the development of personnel procedures such as selection and training. Examples of the new technique are presented, followed by a discussion of some topics requiring future thought and research.

An important, yet frequently overlooked assumption that underlies the use of job analysis as a basis for the development of personnel practices concerns the stability of the job in question. The implicit assumption has been that specification of the tasks to be performed, and the knowledge, skills, and abilities required for job performance are for a job as it *currently* exists, and/or *has* existed in the past. This assumption implies that the job in question is static, a stance that is inconsistent with the need to develop human resource systems for the future (Hall, 1984). Given factors such as the increased use of computers, the expanded capacity of electronic communication systems (Lund and Hansen, 1986), and the need for strategic redirection (Hall, 1984; Schuler, 1988) and the globalization of the U.S. economy, it is unlikely that many jobs will remain static.

The importance placed on job analysis in human resources management has not merely been a function of its multiple uses. The courts have played a role in establishing its importance. In *Albemarle v. Moody* (1975), for example, the Supreme Court disallowed the use of selection tests that were designed without supporting job analysis data. The centrality of job analysis to especially personnel selection was fully documented with the publication of the Uniform Guidelines on Employee Selection Procedures (Federal Register, 1978). It is clear that the courts have subsequently been following the Guidelines' requirement for a job analysis that establishes the framework for selection programs.

The purposes of this article are to (1) integrate different literatures that have addressed the need for strategic job analysis and, (2) describe our experience to date with a procedure to define jobs as they are likely to exist in the future.

WHY STRATEGIC JOB ANALYSIS

Tichy (1983, p. 3) has noted that, with respect to human resources management in general, ". . . that no longer were we asking the question: Are human resources important? Rather, the question for the 1980s is: How will we integrate human resource issues into the strategic management of the firm?" Indeed, the 1980s has seen an explosion of the involvement of human resources issues with business strategy. Meshoulam and Baird (1987) note, for example, that compensation systems, staffing practices, and performance management systems all have evolved to become more integrated with corporate strategy. Schuler and Jackson (1987) have gone so far as to chart the kinds of strategic human resources choices organizations need to make including choices regarding staffing, planning, appraising, compensation, and training and development.

There now appears to be some progress in the integration of human resources management with business strategy, although continued progress is needed (Schuler, 1988). For example, few researchers appear to be concerned with the effects on human resources issues of organizational disruptions such as downsizing, mergers and acquisitions, and so forth (for exceptions see Bastien, 1987 on mergers and Sutton, 1983 on downsizing).

From the innovation/technology literatures comes a clearly specified need for addressing organizational disruptions. For example, in Lund and Hansen's (1986) discussion of the emerging computer and telecommunications technologies, they note that the effects of these technologies will be enormous because they are universal; they apply to all industries. Their research indicated that there will be changes in the nature of the skills demanded by advanced technology. The level of skills required for any job, however, will depend on which elements of the work are combined to make up the job (see also Marjchzak and Klein, 1987).

But if technological change and human resources management is all about people working at jobs, then jobs need to be *a*, if not *the*, focus of strategic human resources management. Here the literature appears to be quite silent. Thus, while there is a relatively comprehensive literature being produced on the need for a strategic approach to human resources (Schein, 1977), and while there is specification that recruitment, staffing, and training issues need to be addressed (e.g., Latham, 1988), precisely what *kinds* of people need to be recruited and selected and the *kinds* of training they should actually receive are not identified.

Hall (1984, p. 159) put the issue of strategic human resource development this way: "[It] is the identification of needed skills and active management of employee learning for the long-range future in relation to explicit corporate and business strategies." In what follows we present our attempts to design a process through which the skills required by jobs in the future can be identified.

STRATEGIC JOB ANALYSIS

The goal of a strategic job analysis is specification of the tasks to be performed and the knowledge, skills, and abilities (KSAs) required for effective performance for a job as it is predicted to exist in the future. Any time frame for the future may be an appropriate frame of reference since this may vary as a function of the job in question and as a function of known or predicted strategic redirection of the organization.

The approaches to strategic job analysis described in this article build on traditional job analysis procedures like those described by Goldstein (1986), Levine (1983), and Schneider and Schmitt (1986). The approach taken here is called "Multimethod Job Analysis" and it is summarized in Table I.

Because there is little that is particularly unique about the multimethod job analysis approach until the stage of collecting information about the future, we describe that step and subsequent steps.

Gather information on the future. To incorporate strategic issues into a "present" job analysis we first gather information about the kinds of issues in the job, the company, and/or the larger environment that may affect the job in the future. This is accomplished in a workshop composed of subject matter experts (e.g., job incumbents, supervisors, managers, human resource staff, strategic planners) and job analysts. The participants might also include experts in a relevant technical field, economists, demographers, and so forth, depending on the specific job of interest.

Some examples of futures issues that may impact the job that have been suggested in past workshops include changes in: state and federal government legislation, labor markets and demographics, computerization of the job and the company, the predicted state of the general economy, changes in the nature of the physical work environment, improved training, and increased supervisor-subordinate interaction. Obviously this list is not exhaustive. Companies can experience changes in jobs and, thus, requirements for people with particular KSAs for many reasons: mergers and acquisitions, downsizing, automation, and such organizational transformations as a move from a quantity to a quality strategy or a change in emphasis from production to service (Schneider and Rentsch, 1988; Tichy, 1983). In the futures workshops that have been conducted to date, SMEs (subject matter experts) have consistently mentioned changes in each of the five facets of the environment Katz and Kahn (1978, p. 124) suggest are important features to monitor if an organization is to be effective:

1. Societal values
2. Political/legal
3. Economic/markets/labor
4. Information/technological
5. Physical/geography.

The issues emerge from a general brainstorming session that includes 6–10 persons and takes about two hours. Notes are recorded on large pads of

Table I

STEPS IN THE MULTIMETHOD JOB ANALYSIS APPROACH.

- Conduct interviews (incumbents and supervisors) and on-site observations of the job in question
- Specify job tasks and build task clusters based on expert judgments of task statements
- Develop and administer task surveys; surveys are of tasks not task clusters; tasks rated for importance and time spent
- Conduct statistical analyses of task survey responses:
  - Technical (means and standard deviations; internal consistency analyses of *a priori* task clusters)
  - Comparative (incumbents vs. supervisors; regional or departmental variations for the "same" job)
- Conduct knowledge, skills, and abilities (KSAs) process:
  - Specify KSAs through interviews with incumbents (when feasible) and supervisors based on task data
  - Build KSA clusters based on expert judgments of KSA statements
- Develop and administer KSA surveys:
  - Rate KSAs for importance, difficulty to learn, and when learned for KSA clusters (selection purposes) *or* rate individual KSA statements (training purposes)
- Gather information on the future
- Revise tasks and/or task clusters, and KSAs and/or KSA clusters in light of expected future changes

newsprint so that all participants have access to the futures issues being generated. The issues emerging from a project designed to understand how the job of a first-line supervisor might look in the future are shown in Table II.

Revise tasks and KSAs in light of expected future changes. Listing the futures issues for all participants provides a shared framework for the workshop participants to then make a series of ratings about the target job in the future: (a) the *importance* and *time spent* on each task or task cluster, (b) the *importance* of the KSAs, the *difficulty to learn* the KSAs, and *when the KSAs will be learned.* Thus, the task information and KSAs developed based on the present job are rerated in the light of the changes the workshop participants identify.

A comparison of present and future ratings allows an assessment of the extent to which changes in the internal and external environment of an organization yield significant task and KSA changes for the job of interest. The re-rating process also provides an opportunity for workshop participants to add to the list of tasks and/or KSAs. Thus, jobs may not only change in how important a task or a KSA is but new tasks and/or new KSAs may emerge in the future. These new tasks and KSAs need to be identified and discussions during the re-rating process provide an opportunity for them to emerge.

It may be clear from the different rating options listed in this section (e.g., rate task statements or task clusters) that the process involved in generating information about the future and then using this information to modify an existing job

Table II

FUTURES ISSUES THAT MIGHT CHANGE A SUPERVISORY JOB.

- Computerization of the job being supervised:
  - Changes in report preparation procedures
  - Changes in work group size
  - Changes in monitoring capability
  - Changes in personal contact
  - Changes in location of where workers work
  - Changes in speed of, and amount of, work done
- Installation of new subordinate selection and training programs; Changing demographics of subordinates:
  - Changes in competencies (skills and abilities)
  - Changes in attitudes/needs (other characteristics)
- Corporate culture change from service provider to sales organization
- Increased rules and regulations (State and Federal) requiring strict adherence to laws governing the business (e.g., financial services laws)

analysis has yet to be finalized. Given the novelty of this futures approach some variations have been tried to facilitate the generation of future issues and to facilitate the re-rating and updating of tasks and KSAs.

For example, in one project SMEs were asked to fill out a job analysis survey for the way the job presently exists and one for the job of the future, prior to attending a workshop to discuss futures issues. So, in this particular variation, the workshop participants were "primed" to discuss futures issues, since they had already been required to independently make the futures ratings. At the actual workshop, generating the futures issues proceeded very quickly. A second workshop was held to further discuss possible changes in the future and then the SMEs, led by one of us, produced consensus ratings of the tasks and KSAs for the job of the future. In this process, group discussion of the implications of the futures issues for tasks and KSAs generated a rich description of what the future is likely to look like, as well as the numerical ratings of tasks and KSAs necessary for the design of human resources programs.

An Example of a Strategic Job Analysis

This example is taken from a job analysis of a first level supervisory position. The task clusters developed on the basis of the standard job analysis were:

1. Sets goals with subordinates (GOALS)
2. Plans and schedules (PLANS)
3. Informs and advises subordinates (INFORMS)
4. Monitors results and updates management (MONITORS)

5. Supervises staff and resources (SUPERVISES)
6. Gives feedback and counsels staff (FEEDBACK)
7. Appraises subordinate performance (APPRAISES)
8. Trains and develops subordinates (TRAINS)
9. Staffs the unit (recruits, selects, terminates) (STAFFS)
10. Handles customers (CUSTOMER)

These clusters are listed in Table III along with mean ratings of *importance* and *time spent* made by incumbents who rated the job as it presently exists and by workshop participants (SMEs) who rated the job of the future.

It is clear from Table III that there is high agreement among incumbents (in this case supervisors) and SME workshop participants on the rank ordering of the *importance* of task clusters ($r = .95$). At first glance this would suggest that little if anything about the job is likely to change in the future (in this case "future" meant three to five years). However, notice that the SMEs see a much greater range of *importance* for task clusters of the future (2.17 – 5.00 as opposed to 3.18 – 4.53 for incumbents). Thus, "goals," "feedback," "appraises," "trains," and "staffs" are predicted to be more important in the future, while "plans," "monitors," "supervises," and "customer" are predicted to be less important in the future. (Only the "informs" task cluster appears highly stable in light of expected environmental changes.) These results indicate a change in the relative importance of different task clusters in the future.

The *time spent* ratings by incumbents (present) and SMEs (future) differ both in terms of means and ranks ($r = .42$). Because the rank order for the future job is not the same as for the present job, knowing where time is spent today provides little information about where time will be spent in the future. According to Table III, the most time will be spent on "feedback" (i.e., Gives feedback and counsels staff) and little time will be spent on "customer" (i.e., Handles customers) and "monitors" (i.e., Monitors results and updates management).

A similar comparative analysis (between present and future) may be conducted for the KSAs necessary to carry out these tasks. An example of these data are shown in Table IV for the Knowledge clusters that emerged from the standard job analysis.

The labels in Table IV for the Knowledge clusters represent seven kinds of knowledge required for this supervisory job:

1. Personnel—knowledge of the personnel and human resources policies and practices of the organization.
2. Budget—planning for budget issues and items in the unit.
3. Product—familiarity with the products and services offered by the company (and sold and serviced by the unit).
4. Rules/Regs—Company guidelines for dealing with the public.
5. CRT—familiarity with the capabilities and operation of the CRT.

Table III

TASK CLUSTER IMPORTANCE AND TIME SPENT RATINGS BY
INCUMBENTS (PRESENT JOB) AND SMES (FUTURE JOB).

Task Cluster	*Importance*[a]				*Time Spent*[b]			
	Incumbents[c]		*SMEs*[d]		*Incumbents*		*SMEs*	
	Mean	*Rank*	*Mean*	*Rank*	*Mean*	*Rank*	*Mean*	*Rank*
Goals	4.39	2	4.80	2	3.36	3	2.67	7
Plans	3.62	7	2.66	8	3.15	4	2.88	8
Informs	3.82	5	3.77	6	2.92	6	3.22	2
Monitors	3.18	10	2.56	9	2.58	9	2.00	9.5
Supervises	3.54	8	3.04	7	2.84	7	3.18	3
Feedback	4.24	3	4.73	4	3.46	2	4.27	1
Appraises	4.53	1	5.00	1	3.47	1	3.00	4
Trains	3.64	6	4.17	5	2.71	8	2.90	5
Recruits	3.87	4	4.75	3	2.38	10	2.42	8
Customer	3.45	9	2.17	10	2.97	5	2.00	9.5

[a]Five point scale used (1-5) where 1 = Not at all important, 2 = Slightly, 3 = Moderately, 4 = Very, 5 = Extremely important.

[b]Six point scale used (1-6) where 1 = No time spent, 2 = Very little time compared to other tasks, 3 = Somewhat less time, 4 = Same amount of time, 5 = Somewhat more time, 6 = A great deal more time compared to other tasks.

[c]N = 59 supervisors

[d]N = 10 SMEs

6. Competition–knowledge of what competitors were offering.

7. Selling—knowledge of selling techniques and sales principles.

The data in Table IV may be summarized as follows. First, the data for *Difficulty to Learn the Knowledge* shows that the present (supervisors) and future (SMEs) estimates are highly correlated ($r = .79$) although the means are elevated for SMEs for five of seven kinds of knowledge. Second, the data for *When Learned* also revealed strong relationships between the present (supervisors) and the future (SMEs), with $r = .85$. For these latter ratings, it is clear that SMEs expect future Supervisors to come to the job already knowledgeable in four domains: Product, Rules/Regs, CRT, and Competition.

SUMMARY

The data presented in Tables III and IV reveal two findings that we have consistently observed: (1) incumbents' views of tasks and KSAs for today's job are generally highly correlated with SME's projections of the future, and (2) high correlation does not equal agreement. This means that while the rank orders of

Table IV

KNOWLEDGE CLUSTER RATINGS OF DIFFICULTY TO ACQUIRE AND
WHERE ACQUIRED BY INCUMBENTS (PRESENT JOB) AND SMES (FUTURE JOB).

| Knowledge Cluster | Difficulty to Learn[a] | | | | When Learned[b] | | | |
| | Incumbents[c] | | SMEs[d] | | Incumbents | | SMEs | |
	Mean	Rank	Mean	Rank	Mean	Rank	Mean	Rank
Personnel	2.4	5	3.0	4	4.0	2	4.0	2
Budget	3.4	3	4.0	2	4.6	1	5.0	1
Product	3.5	2	5.0	1	1.6	6	1.0	4
Rules/Regs.	2.6	4	3.0	4	2.0	5	1.0	4
CRT	2.4	5	2.0	5	1.6	6	1.0	4
Competition	2.0	7	3.0	4	2.6	3	1.0	4
Selling	4.0	1	4.0	2	2.2	4	3.0	3

[a]Difficulty to Learn knowledge is rated on a five-point scale where 1 = very easy, 2 = easier than most, 3 = average, 4 = harder than most, 5 = most difficult.

[b]When Learned is rated on a five-point scale where 1 = prior to job, 2 = minimal after job entry, 3 = some after job entry, 4 = normally acquired after job entry, 5 = only acquired after job entry.

[c]N = 59 Supervisors

[d]N = 10 SMEs

means for tasks and KSAs for incumbents (present) and SMEs (future) are similar, the means themselves may differ. Sometimes the means differ in their dispersion (e.g., greater variability in the future than present) and sometimes the means have a ceiling or basement effect (e.g., a particular kind of knowledge is assumed to exist prior to job entry).

These findings caution against using only correlations as a basis for judging the similarity between present and future ratings. As in all profile analysis techniques, similarity in shape (what a Pearson *r* reveals) is only one index of similarity; the others are elevation and dispersion (Nunnally, 1978). Examination of elevation and dispersion can identify tasks that will become more (or less) important or take more (or less) time or a knowledge that potential supervisors will need to acquire before they are considered for the supervisory role. The latter finding has obvious implications for training.

There are a large number of questions still to be answered about our strategic job analysis process:

1. What is the validity of SME predictions of the future? The issue here is the accuracy of the projections of the future. If the futures ratings made by SMEs turn out to be accurate predictions, then selection and training programs can truly be designed for jobs of the future. Indeed, a validity study that yielded positive findings might also remove the possibility of attacks on an approach

to job analysis that is non-traditional and, therefore, potentially not sanctioned by existing standards and guidelines. Of course, the *Guidelines* do permit the adoption of new procedures where circumstances dictate them [See PP 1607.6 (B)] but it is also important to establish their validity.

2. Who are the most accurate judges of the future? In all forms of job analysis the specification of who the SMEs should be is problematic; the issue is not resolved in strategic job analysis. The approach taken in our work to date is to consult with a variety of individuals and solicit names of people who seem particularly knowledgeable and prescient. These people are then nominated to play the SME role. We have now used a very wide variety of SMEs in our application of the procedure to jobs as different as telephone salespersons, auto repair shop damage adjusters, the first line supervisors described earlier, and the highest levels of management in a telecommunications company. Each time, the SMEs have provided extraordinary insight into how and why the tasks in jobs, and the KSAs required to do them, may or may not change. Our present thoughts suggest a few principles to follow in selecting SMEs for the futures workshop: (1) Choose at least one person who is responsible for corporate strategy most closely tied to the job in question; (2) Choose at least one person who is responsible for monitoring how the competition structures (both technologically and from a human resources standpoint) the tasks done by incumbents in the job in question; (3) Choose at least one incumbent who is known for his/her willingness to suggest and/or try new ideas; (4) Choose a so-called "efficiency expert" in the company (who may be the internal technology/communication expert); and (5) Choose a person in management who worked him or herself up from the job in question.

3. When SMEs make their judgments about how the job of the future will look (tasks and KSAs), on which facets of the future are they focusing and what is their reasoning? This question is amenable to answer through policy capturing studies but, to this date, such studies have not been accomplished systematically. When informally asked to provide their bases for judgments in the projects conducted to date, SMEs are able to tell us why they think a job and its KSAs will change. For example, in Table III it was shown that the time spent on the task cluster *monitors* is predicted to drop in the future. The reason SMEs gave for this judgment of a decrease in time spent on *monitors* was that workers would be monitored by computer in the future.

4. Should more formal techniques for group discussion be used by SMEs? To date, the approach used here has been a roundtable brainstorming discussion with free-flowing conversation for both the identification of futures issues and the subsequent ratings of tasks and KSAs. Perhaps other strategies such as the nominal group technique, or synectics would generate more useful data (see Guzzo, 1982).

5. What role does job analysis play in the larger fabric of organizational effectiveness and the management of human resources? The implicit assumption

in the work presented here is that job analysis is critical for the development of personnel practices such as selection, training, and appraisal. But jobs do not exist alone in organizations; jobs exist as parts of total organizational systems. Indeed, when asked to discuss futures issues that might affect jobs, SMEs raised classic systems issues, including both internal organizational and larger environmental concerns (Katz and Kahn, 1978).

The idea that jobs are part of a larger organizational system suggests a number of issues. First, even current, descriptive, job analysis information may play a larger role in the total organization than most current theories of organizational functioning give it. Thus, except for the job characteristics (Hackman and Oldham, 1980) and socio-technical systems approaches (cf. Miller, 1976) to understanding organizational functioning, facets of people's jobs and the KSAs required to perform them seem to only be of concern to more personnel-oriented psychologists and human resource professionals. Second, results of the application of our procedure presented here, as well as others we have collected, suggest that organizations are essentially *tabulas rasa* regarding the anticipation of changes required in human resources as a function of changes *known* to be planned. Thus, the SMEs who participate in the futures workshops are familiar with many changes that will occur, yet the human resources implications of these changes have rarely been systematically identified. Running the futures workshop sensitizes people in the organizations to the utility of careful specification of these human resources issues. In one company, the data provided have been used in business planning, budget preparation, and the design of systems for choosing participants into the "fast-track" executive program.

6. Can this procedure be applied to jobs that do not yet exist? The job analysis procedure described here is for how an existing job may change in the future. However, many companies start up new plants to produce new goods or deliver new services. Can a job analysis be accomplished for a future job? The same techniques described here could be employed, with special emphasis on the selection of participants for the task and KSA workshops. Because these SMEs would be literally starting from scratch they would need to be intimately familiar with the goals of the new jobs so they can make projections about what the tasks are likely to be; it is task specification that provides the raw input for specification of the KSAs required.

7. Can the strategic job analysis process be useful for more than selection, training, and appraisal purposes? Hall (1986), in fact, proposed a futures-oriented job analysis process as an aid to career planning for individuals. That is, Hall saw the need for organizations to be able to anticipate future jobs so that the likelihood of different career opportunities could be identified, thus facilitating realistic career planning. Obviously, strategic planning of all kinds takes place in organizations but it is generally at a more macro level. Strategic job analysis brings these macro level plans to the micro, job, level from which specific human resources procedures can be developed.

We are sure the reader can generate additional questions. Our purpose here was to introduce practitioners and researchers to the potential importance of doing strategic job analysis. The ideas and early data presented here strongly suggest the need for research on an approach to job analysis that recognizes the changing nature of work and the possibility of anticipating KSA requirements prior to a crisis. Hopefully some curiosities have been twinged and the needed combinations of research and practice will emerge.

Notes

This research effort was supported by an organization that shall remain nameless at its request. We want to thank the people there, especially P. E. W., E. M., N. M., and D. C. who helped us. Others have also been helpful, especially Joe Schneider, Anne Moeller, and Dan Schechter. We received useful comments on earlier versions of this article from Pete Dachler, Kevin Ford, Irv Goldstein, Mirian Graddick, Tim Hall, Paul Hanges, Gary Latham, and Vicki Vandaveer.

References

Albemarle Paper Company v. Moody. 1975, 10 FEP 1181.

Bastien, D. T. Common patterns of behavior and communication in corporate mergers and acquisitions. *Human Resource Management,* 1987, 26, 17–34.

Goldstein, I. L. *Training in organizations: Needs assessment, development, and evaluation,* 2nd ed. Monterey, CA: Brooks/Cole, 1986.

Guzzo, R. A. (Ed.). *Improving group decision making in organizations.* New York: Academic Press, 1982.

Hackman, J. R., and Oldham, G. R. *Work redesign.* Reading, MA: Addison-Wesley, 1980.

Hall, D. T. Human resource development and organizational effectiveness. In C. J. Fombrun, N. M. Ticky, and M. A. Devanna (Eds.), *Strategic human resource management.* New York: Wiley, 1984.

Hall, D. T. Dilemmas in linking succession planning to individual executive learning. *Human Resource Management,* 1986, 25, 235–265.

Katz, D., and Kahn, R. L. *The social psychology of organizations,* 2nd ed. New York: Wiley, 1978.

Latham, G. P. Human resource training and development. *Annual Review of Psychology,* 1988, 39, 545–582.

Levine, E. L. *Everything you always wanted to know about job analysis.* Tampa, FL: Mariner Publishing Co., 1983.

Lund, R. T., and Hansen, J. A. *Keeping America at work: Strategies for employing the new technologies.* New York: Wiley, 1986.

Marjchzak, A., and Klein, K. J. Things are always more complicated than you think: An open-systems approach to the organizational effects of computer-automated technology. *Journal of Business and Psychology,* 1987, 2, 8–26.

Meshoulam, I., and Baird, L. S. Proactive human resource management. *Human Resource Management,* 1987, 26, 483–502.

Miller, E. J. (Ed.). *Task and organization.* New York: Wiley, 1976.

Nunnally, J. C. *Psychometric theory,* 2nd ed. New York: McGraw Hill, 1978.

Schein, E. H. Increasing organizational effectiveness through better human resource planning and development. *Sloan Management Review*, 1977, 19, 1–20.

Schneider, B., and Schmitt, N. *Staffing organizations*, 2nd ed. Glenview, IL: Scott, Foresman, 1986.

Schneider, B., and Rentsch, J. Managing climates and cultures: A futures perspective. In J. Hage (Ed.), *The futures of organizations*. Lexington, MA: Lexington Books, 1988.

Schuler, R. S. Personnel and human resource management choices and organizational strategy. *Human Resource Management Australia, Feb.* 1988, 81–100.

Schuler, R. S., and Jackson, S. E. Linking competitive strategies with human resource management practices. *Academy of Management Executive*, 1987, 1, 207–219.

Sutton, R. I. Managing organizational death. *Human Resource Management*, 1983, 22, 391–412.

Tichy, N. M. (Ed.). Foreword: Strategic planning and human resource management. *Human Resource Management*, 1983, 22, 3–8.

Uniform Guidelines on Employee Selection Procedures. *Federal Register*, 1978, 43, 38290–38315.

READING 13

JOB DESIGN
Approaches, Outcomes, and Trade-offs

Michael A. Campion
Paul W. Thayer

Badly designed jobs are actually the cause of far more performance problems than managers realize. The authors present a way of analyzing job designs to make sure they encourage the outcomes managers want.

Although the nearly catastrophic Three Mile Island incident was attributed to human error, it's clear that the poor design of the control room operator's job was the primary cause of the disaster. Operators had to monitor hundreds of poorly designed displays, controls, alarms, and lights. Because controls and related gauges were physically separated, operators could not respond quickly and accurately to danger signals. Emergency procedures were inadequately designed. In brief, the information and control systems for which the operators were responsible created overwhelming mental demands that quickly overloaded their capabilities. The operator's job was actually (though inadvertently) designed to be error-prone—that is, designed for disaster.

The initial conclusion, however, was that human beings were entirely at fault. People have a natural tendency to conclude that the design of a job is a "given" dictated by the technology, and that poor performance on the job *must* be the fault of the worker.

In a recent study of job design in the wood-products industry, we found two examples that illustrate this point. Although our analysis of the jobs quickly pointed to design problems, in each case the supervisor accepted the job as given and blamed the incumbent for poor performance.

1. *A dryer-feeder job in a plywood plant.* In this job, the incumbent had to align strips of wood just before they entered a dryer on a moving belt so that maximum

Source: "Job Design: Approaches, Outcomes, and Trade-offs," by Michael A. Campion, et al. Reprinted by permission of publisher from *Organizational Dynamics*, WIN87 © 1987. American Management Association, New York. All rights reserved.

This paper is based on a study that won the 1983 S. Rains Wallace Dissertation Award sponsored by the Society of Industrial and Organizational Psychology, a division of the American Psychological Association. The opinions expressed belong to the authors, not necessarily to their affiliations.

drying coverage would be achieved. Because dryer coverage was not up to standard, the supervisor concluded that the incumbent was lazy and negligent and considered filing a written reprimand. However, we found the job to be poorly designed from a biological perspective. The incumbent had to operate a foot pedal while standing and thus spent all day with most of her body weight on one foot. She also had to bend over frequently and extend her arms to adjust the strips of wood, which resulted in biomechanical stresses on the arms, legs, and back. Everyone hated the job, and it was almost impossible to staff. Despite that, the incumbent was blamed.

2. *A puller job in a sawmill.* In this job, the incumbents pulled 2-by-4s from a moving belt and placed them in racks. When production was low, employees were characterized as apathetic, lazy, and lacking a work ethic. However, the job itself was totally unattractive from a motivational viewpoint: It provided hardly any feedback and no variety, and it involved no significant skill. The task seemed unimportant and monotonous—a boring, thankless, dull job.

We, as managers, tend to blame the worker rather than the job despite the many attempts to point out that job design may be the problem. Early in this century, Frederick Taylor and Frank Gilbreth developed a concept called "scientific management" that stressed specialization of duties, time and motion study, and work simplification. This approach to job design permitted employers to staff jobs with almost anyone and still hold down training costs. However, many viewed scientific management as dehumanizing because it assumed that workers were lazy and dull and that tight controls and manipulation were required.

Eventually theorists such as R. N. Ford, Frederick Herzberg, Arthur Turner, and Richard Hackman stressed the desirability of enlarging and/or enriching the job to enhance its motivational potential. They viewed the worker as creative, self-motivated, and responsive to a stimulating environment.

More recently, specialists have been pointing to the need to minimize the physical costs and biological risks of work, and they have emphasized occupational safety and health. A related school of thought is concerned with cognitive and perceptual-motor abilities. It suggests that a human being can absorb only so much information in a given time span and that a job design must recognize that limit. The jobs of the Three Mile Island operator and an air traffic controller are good illustrations of positions that must be designed with careful attention to the limitations of human perceptual capacities.

Which job design approach is best? Advocates of each school point only to the strengths or advantages of their method. Can a job that has been designed from a motivational perspective have characteristics that make it bad from another standpoint? And if a job is designed well from one perspective, does that mean it cannot be designed well from another? What are the costs and benefits of the various approaches? Job enrichment may be the current "in" approach, but what are the costs of this approach? Are the other approaches really so bad?

We tried to answer these questions through a study that attempts to assemble all the available approaches to job design and then determine which approaches produce which job outcomes.

THE STUDY

"We found that there are four different approaches to job design and that each approach is actually geared toward a different set of outcomes. Each approach has its own costs and benefits, and no single approach is best; trade-offs will be required in most practical situations."

We conducted an exhaustive search of the literature and extracted specific "rules" on how to design jobs. We found rules for everything: equipment, facilities, and environments, as well as job content and methods. These rules were then analyzed and sorted into distinct groups based on their underlying theoretical orientation. Four job-design approaches resulted; these approaches then formed the basis for a job analysis questionnaire.

Using that questionnaire, we analyzed more than 120 jobs. We also collected information on a broad spectrum of job outcomes including job satisfaction, absenteeism, training time, staffing difficulty, physical effort required, injury rates, error rates, job stress, and mental demands.

The technical details of this study are presented in the February 1985 issue of *Journal of Applied Psychology*. We found that there are four different approaches to job design and that each approach is actually geared toward a different set of outcomes. Each approach has its own costs and benefits and no single approach is best; trade-offs will be required in most practical situations.

What follows is a description of the content and theoretical orientation of each approach and the associated positive and negative outcomes of that approach. So that readers may analyze jobs in their organizations, we have presented sets of questions to determine how well jobs match each of the different approaches. Answers to these questions will suggest what costs and benefits can be expected from jobs as they are currently designed, as well as how jobs may be redesigned.

FOUR APPROACHES TO JOB DESIGN

Mechanistic Job-Design Approach

This approach stems from the scientific-management school of thought, time and motion study, and work simplification and specialization. Its primary scientific basis is classic industrial engineering. (The term *classic* is used because many contemporary writers include a variety of job design approaches under the label of industrial engineering.)

Exhibit 1 presents the questions one might ask to determine whether a job fits the mechanistic approach. Jobs high in mechanistic features can be staffed by almost anyone, and training time is typically very short. Because mental demands are minimal, stress and overload are unlikely. Errors are less common because mistakes are less likely to occur.

The disadvantages of the mechanistic approach include less satisfied, less motivated employees and higher absenteeism. Sometimes mechanistic work can lead to health complaints and injuries caused by the physical wear and the carelessness that can result from highly repetitive and machine-paced work.

Most low-level factory jobs are designed from a mechanistic perspective. Assembly-line jobs epitomize this approach because they are analyzed and carefully constructed to maximize productivity and efficiency.

Exhibit 1

THE MECHANISTIC JOB-DESIGN APPROACH

1. *Job specialization:* Is the job highly specialized in terms of purpose and/or activity?
2. *Specialization of tools and procedures:* Are the tools, procedures, materials, etc. used on this job highly specialized in terms of purpose?
3. *Task simplification:* Are the tasks simple and uncomplicated?
4. *Single activities:* Does the job require the incumbent to do only one task at a time? Does it *not* require the incumbent to do multiple activities at one time or in very close succession?
5. *Job simplification:* Does the job require relatively little skill and training time?
6. *Repetition:* Does the job require performing the same activity or activities repeatedly?
7. *Spare time:* Is there very little spare time between activities on this job?
8. *Automation:* Are many of the activities of this job automated or assisted by automation?

The nuclear power plant operator's job, on the other hand, would get a very low score on the mechanistic questionnaire because of the complex nature of many of the tasks involved and the corresponding training requirements. In fact, simplified procedures for nuclear power plant operators have been established as a result of the Three Mile Island incident.

Many jobs would get a low score on the mechanistic approach questions simply because of their inefficient nature. Such jobs include many sales and negotiating positions, which have a less than optimal probability of success, and jobs that are needed only in emergency situations (such as the job of a fire fighter). Many office jobs are also poorly designed from a mechanistic point of view. However, the concepts of specialization and simplification of tasks and skill requirements have been applied to some office jobs to reduce staffing difficulties and training requirements.

Motivational Job-Design Approach

This approach stems from the work on job enrichment and enlargement and from the major theories of work motivation and organizational behavior. Its basis is organizational psychology.

Exhibit 2 shows the content of this approach. In addition to taking into account those characteristics that make jobs meaningful from a task-oriented perspective (such as variety, feedback, and achievement), this is the only approach that takes into account the social or people-interaction aspects of job design (including participation, communication, and recognition). Positive responses to the questions in Exhibit 2 are associated with jobs that have more satisfied, more motivated, and more involved employees. Absenteeism tends to be lower and job performance higher among employees whose jobs can be characterized as high in motivational job-design approach. The converse is true for jobs that are low on this approach.

Exhibit 2

THE MOTIVATIONAL JOB-DESIGN APPROACH

1. *Autonomy:* Does the job allow freedom, independence, or discretion in work scheduling, sequence, methods, procedures, quality control, or other decisions?
2. *Intrinsic job feedback:* Do the work activities themselves provide direct, clear information about the effectiveness (in terms of quality and quantity) of job performance?
3. *Extrinsic job feedback:* Do other people in the organization (such as managers and coworkers) provide information about the effectiveness (in terms of quality and quantity) of job performance?
4. *Social interaction:* Does the job provide for positive social interaction (such as teamwork or coworker assistance)?
5. *Task/goal clarity:* Are the job duties, requirements, and goals clear and specific?
6. *Task variety:* Does the job have a variety of duties, tasks, and activities?
7. *Task identity:* Does the job require completion of a whole and identifiable piece of work? Does it give the incumbent a chance to do an entire piece of work from beginning to end?
8. *Ability/skill-level requirements:* Does the job require a high level of knowledge, skills, and abilities?
9. *Ability/skill variety:* Does the job require a variety of types of knowledge, skills, and abilities?
10. *Task significance:* Is the job significant and important compared with other jobs in the organization?
11. *Growth/learning:* Does the job allow opportunities for learning and growth in competence and proficiency?
12. *Promotion:* Are there opportunities for advancement to higher-level jobs?
13. *Achievement:* Does the job provide for feelings of achievement and task accomplishment?
14. *Participation:* Does the job allow participation in work-related decision making?
15. *Communication:* Does the job provide access to relevant communication channels and information flows?
16. *Pay adequacy:* Is the pay for this job adequate compared with the job requirements and pay for similar jobs?
17. *Recognition:* Does the job provide acknowledgment and recognition from others?
18. *Job security:* Do incumbents on this job have a high degree of job security?

On the negative side, jobs that match the motivational approach tend to have longer training times and are more difficult to staff because of their greater mental demands. Furthermore, given the more stimulating nature of highly motivational jobs, the employees are more prone to suffer stress and mental overload, and errors are more likely to occur.

Many executive, managerial, and professional jobs would score well from a motivational point of view. They are satisfying, rewarding, and highly motivating. Many craft and technical jobs would also score well because of their highly skilled nature. On the down side, all of these jobs require extensive training and experience, and major errors are a regular possibility.

Jobs low in the motivational elements tend to be those same jobs that received high scores on the mechanistic approach: low-level factory jobs, laborer

Exhibit 3

THE BIOLOGICAL JOB-DESIGN APPROACH

1. *Strength:* Does the job require fairly little muscular strength?
2. *Lifting:* Does the job require fairly little lifting, and/or is the lifting of very light weights?
3. *Endurance:* Does the job require fairly little muscular endurance?
4. *Seating:* Are the seating arrangements on the job adequate (with ample opportunities to sit, comfortable chairs, good postural support, etc.)?
5. *Size differences:* Does the workplace allow for all size differences between people in terms of clearance, reach, eye height, leg room, etc.?
6. *Wrist movement:* Does the job allow the wrists to remain straight, without excessive movement?
7. *Noise:* Is the workplace free from excessive noise?
8. *Climate:* Is the climate at the workplace comfortable in terms of temperature and humidity, and is it free of excessive dust and fumes?
9. *Work breaks:* Is there adequate time for work breaks given the demands of the job?
10. *Shift work:* Does the job *not* require shift work or excessive overtime?

jobs, and other unskilled jobs. They are not particularly satisfying or motivating; however, their training times are very short, and they can be staffed easily.

From a practical perspective, managers can enhance the meaningfulness of many office, factory, and service-oriented jobs by applying motivational principles. The positive benefits may include higher satisfaction and improved performance. But there are limits: The jobs may become much more expensive to staff, or the incumbents may pay an undue price in job stress or demand higher wages for more mentally demanding work.

Biological Job-Design Approach

This approach is derived from the sciences of biomechanics (the study of body movements), work physiology, occupational medicine, and anthropometry (the study of body measurements). It is often called ergonomics, and its main thrust is to minimize the physical costs and biological risks of work. The goal is to ensure that people's physical capabilities and limitations are not exceeded by the design of their jobs (a consideration that is frequently ignored).

Not surprisingly, jobs rating high on the biological approach (Exhibit 3) require less physical effort, result in less physical fatigue, create fewer health complaints, and cause fewer injuries than other jobs. They may even be associated with lower absenteeism and higher job satisfaction because they are less physically arduous than other jobs.

The biological approach might appear to have no drawbacks because the biological aspects of jobs are largely unrelated to other aspects of job design. However, changes in equipment or job environments needed to implement these principles may be prohibitively expensive. In addition, it is possible to design a job with so few physical demands that the workers become drowsy or lethargic.

Exhibit 4

THE PERCEPTUAL/MOTOR JOB-DESIGN APPROACH

1. *Lighting:* Is the lighting in the workplace adequate and free from glare?
2. *Displays:* Are the displays, gauges, meters, and computerized equipment used on this job easy to read and understand?
3. *Programs:* Are the programs in the computerized equipment for this job easy to learn and use?
4. *Other equipment:* Is the other equipment (all types) used on this job easy to learn and use?
5. *Printed job materials:* Are the printed materials used on this job easy to read and interpret?
6. *Workplace layout:* Is the workplace laid out so that the employee can see and hear well enough to perform the job?
7. *Information input requirements:* Is the amount of attention needed to perform this job fairly minimal?
8. *Information output requirements:* Is the amount of information that the employee must output on this job, in terms of both action and communication, fairly minimal?
9. *Information processing requirements:* Is the amount of information that must be processed, in terms of thinking and problem solving, fairly minimal?
10. *Memory requirements:* Is the amount of information that must be remembered on this job fairly minimal?
11. *Stress:* Is there relatively little stress on this job?
12. *Boredom:* Are the chances of boredom on this job fairly small?

The biological approach has been extensively applied in the redesign of equipment used in physically demanding jobs so that women can better perform them. For example, ladders and other equipment have been changed for the telephone installer job, and handles on many assembly tools have been made smaller to better accommodate the female grasp.

These principles obviously apply to traditionally "heavy" industry jobs that involve difficult physical tasks and environmental stressors, such as jobs in the coal, steel, oil, forest, and construction industries. But some considerations are also important to many "lighter" jobs. For example, many light assembly positions require excessive wrist movements that can eventually lead to a chronic wrist condition. As another example, seating, anthropometry, and posture are important factors to consider in the design of an increasingly common office position, the video display terminal operator. In fact, the influence of proper seating design on long-term musculoskeletal health is an important concern for nearly all office jobs.

Perceptual/Motor Job-Design Approach

The main contributors of principles to this approach are the many human-factors engineering guidelines and the research on skills and how people mentally process information. Its basis, with its emphasis on perceptual and motor abilities, is experimental psychology.

In contrast to the biological approach, the perceptual/motor job-design approach ensures that people's mental capabilities and limitations are not exceeded. The two approaches are similar in that they both suggest that job-design principles can extend beyond the content of the job to the equipment and work environments involved.

The goal of designing jobs around people's perceptual/motor limitations (Exhibit 4) is to decrease the likelihood of errors and accidents. However, another result is to reduce the general mental demands of a job. Thus, like the mechanistic approach, the perceptual/motor approach decreases the chances of mental overload and stress, reduces training times, and improves utilization levels (i.e., percentages of workers who can perform the jobs with little or no training).

On the negative side, the perceptual/motor approach may lower satisfaction and motivation because jobs can be less mentally stimulating.

The nuclear power plant operator's job, previously described, would get a low score on this job-design approach. The air traffic controller's job would also get a low score because of the amount of information the controller must attend to and remember and because of the stress of knowing the potentially devastating consequences of an error. Other jobs that would score low for the same reasons include most jobs that involve the operation of complex machinery, such as flying a jet aircraft or operating heavy construction vehicles. Other, less obvious jobs that can tax people's perceptual and motor capabilities include many product-inspection or equipment-monitoring positions. Not only must much information be taken in and processed in these jobs, but the vigilance requirements can also be mentally draining.

Jobs that would get a high score on the perceptual/motor questionnaire are best described as not overly demanding in terms of concentration or attention. These jobs would include many administrative and clerical or service and custodial positions.

Some of the perceptual/motor elements, such as information processing and memory requirements, are relevant to nearly all jobs, both in the factory and in the office. No matter what the job, then, managers should always ask how much information employees must attend to, think about, remember, and communicate. They should also ask whether these requirements are within the capabilities of the least capable potential incumbent.

SOME PRACTICAL IMPLICATIONS

The four job-design questionnaires can measure existing jobs or help managers design new ones. The questions can be used in a simple checklist fashion to measure quickly the quality of a job's design in terms of the four approaches. The greater the number of affirmative responses to the questions for one of the approaches, the better that job is designed in terms of that approach and the more likely it is that the job will produce the outcomes that approach is intended to maximize.

For example, if you see that employees are not motivated, that job satisfaction is low, that absenteeism is high, or other similar symptoms, perhaps you

"The four job-design questionnaires can measure existing jobs or help managers design new ones. The questions can be used in a simple checklist fashion to measure quickly the quality of a job's design in terms of the four approaches. The greater the number of affirmative responses to the questions for one of the approaches, the better that job is designed. . . ."

should examine the motivational characteristics of the job's design. If you have difficulty staffing a job, if training times are high, if many errors are being committed, or if employees are stressed, consider the mechanistic or perceptual/motor aspects of the job. Likewise, if there is evidence of excessive physical toil and fatigue, look to the biological approach for potential solutions. The questions in Exhibits 1 through 4 will not only point out a problem, they will also lead to recommendations for improvement.

These job-design measures can actually be used in at least three different ways. First, they can be useful as a means of diagnosing organization problems. Only rarely is a job recognized as a potential problem source; as noted earlier, the most common explanation is that there is a "problem person." Along with other means of exploring the situation, the job-design questions can be used to determine if any significant problems exist with the job.

A second use of the job-design questions is in job-redesign projects. They can be used to identify jobs that need redesign, to indicate what redesign is needed, and to evaluate the jobs after they have been changed.

A third use is in developing new facilities or work organizations. The questions can be used as guidelines for providing job-design recommendations during the design phase, as a checklist for evaluating equipment and job descriptions during the development phase, and as an evaluation instrument once the system is developed. The questions may have their greatest positive impact in the area of development, since they can lead to proper job design from the outset and help a manager avoid problems later.

Up to this point, we have not explicitly recognized the role of the incumbent in the job-design process. This is because most jobs exist before the employee arrives on the scene, and they will probably be filled by more than one person over the course of time. Initial job designs must be completed under the assumption that the job will be occupied by an average person. However, with time the incumbent can significantly influence the design of the job—by seeking out additional tasks, ignoring tasks, focusing on the interesting activities, changing the physical environment to reduce discomfort (through homemade padding or extra lighting, for example), or developing a job aid (such as a chart of commonly used numbers). The incumbent is actually an expert who can provide critical job-design information and recommendations. In fact, the incumbent is the primary source of information for the questions in Exhibits 1 through 4. We feel incumbents should be consulted much more often than they usually are.

A FEW CAVEATS

Job-design approaches have many similarities and differences, and no one approach can satisfy all criteria. Exhibit 5 summarizes the pros and cons of each approach. The perceptual/motor and mechanistic approaches tend to produce the same types of outcomes, both positive and negative. The biological approach is quite independent; it produces no outcomes in common with the others.

Exhibit 5

SUMMARY OF OUTCOMES FROM THE JOB-DESIGN APPROACHES

Job-Design Approach	Positive Outcomes	Negative Outcomes
Mechanistic	Decreased training time Higher utilization levels Lower likelihood of error Less chance of mental overload and stress	Lower job satisfaction Lower motivation Higher absenteeism
Motivational	Higher job satisfaction Higher motivation Greater job involvement Higher job performance Lower absenteeism	Increased training time Lower utilization levels Greater likelihood of error Greater chance of mental overload and stress
Biological	Less physical effort Less physical fatigue Fewer health complaints Fewer medical incidents Lower absenteeism Higher job satisfaction	Higher financial costs because of changes in equipment or job environment
Perceptual/motor	Lower likelihood of error Lower likelihood of accidents Less chance of mental overload and stress Lower training time Higher utilization levels	Lower job satisfaction Lower motivation

However, some distinct conflicts do exist. The motivational approach produces outcomes that are almost opposite to those produced by the mechanistic and perceptual/motor approaches. This opposition occurs because the mechanistic and perceptual/motor perspectives strive to design jobs that are simple, easy to learn, safe, and reliable, with minimal mental demands on workers. The motivational approach encourages more complicated, challenging, and rewarding jobs. Furthermore, the motivational approach is the only perspective that encompasses the social aspects of job design.

Regardless of these conflicts, jobs can often be improved in one area and still maintain their high scores in other areas. Sometimes, however, trade-offs will be necessary. Fortunately, physical job demands, best understood in terms of the biological job-design approach, are independent of mental job demands. Employers can reduce physical demands without sacrificing the mental quality of a job's design. The cost of equipment may, however, be a significant deterrent to implementation, and designing jobs with too little physical activity may also be unpleasant for the worker.

Exhibit 6

MENTAL-DEMANDS CONTINUUM

Motivational-Designed Jobs	Mechanistic- and Perceptual/Motor-Designed Jobs
←	→
• High satisfaction	• Low training times
• High motivation	• High utilization levels
• Low absenteeism	• Low likelihood of error
(Individual outcomes)	(Organizational outcomes)

On the other hand, major trade-offs may be necessary in the mental demands of jobs. A mental-demands continuum, such as that depicted in Exhibit 6, illustrates the potential trade-offs. At one end of the continuum are jobs high in motivation features. They are mentally demanding and they attempt to maximize such individual outcomes as job satisfaction, motivation, and lower absenteeism.

At the other end are jobs designed in terms of mechanistic and perceptual/motor principles. They are less mentally demanding and attempt to maximize such organizational outcomes as higher utilization levels, lower training times, and lower likelihood of errors.

Most of the trade-offs in job design will involve this mental-demands dimension. Which trade-offs will be made depends on which types of outcomes a manager wants to maximize; the choice depends on one's values. Our research indicates that managers most often make compromises between an individual-outcomes orientation and an organization-outcomes orientation. (Some readers may have suspected this already.)

In other words, practitioners of the motivational approach are obviously concerned with organizational goals since they are interested in enhancing job performance, improving quality, and reducing costly absenteeism through job redesign. However, enhancing a job's motivation aspects may result in more errors, more stress, or more staffing difficulties. On the other hand, simplifying the job to enhance efficiency may make it less meaningful for the employees.

Since job redesign may have unintended consequences, all job-design approaches must be considered. Knowing all the approaches and their outcomes may help employers make more intelligent job-design decisions.

A FINAL WORD

Too often, jobs are developed haphazardly; they become arbitrary groupings of activities that our machines cannot do. Little consideration is given to the mental and physical capabilities, limitations, and needs of the workers who must perform them.

If any consideration is given, it is likely to be from a partisan perspective. Because of the academic discipline bases of the various job-design approaches, each approach tends to be owned by a different staff specialty or profession within an organization. Industrial engineers are typically located in manufacturing departments, ergonomists in industrial hygiene or safety departments, human-factors engineers in research and development labs, and organizational psychologists in personnel or human resources departments.

Universities have more cross-fertilization, but they do not have complete integration. Industrial engineers will usually learn the mechanistic approach and perhaps be exposed to the biological. Ergonomics and human-factors engineering are frequently combined in the same program, and students will study both the biological and perceptual/motor approaches, but the program will be primarily aligned with either the industrial engineering or the psychology department. Thus, students will get additional exposure to either the mechanistic or motivational approach, but probably not to both. Psychologists usually receive training only in the motivational approach, with perhaps some exposure to the perceptual/motor.

This compartmentalization in both industry and academe tends to work against the interdisciplinary perspective we encourage. We hope that exposure to all approaches will bring about an awareness of people's multidimensional needs. Through the use of tools such as the questions in Exhibits 1 through 4, we can ensure that all critical considerations are recognized in the design of jobs.

"Too often, jobs are developed haphazardly; they become arbitrary groupings of activities that our machines cannot do. Little consideration is given to the mental and physical capabilities, limitations, and needs of the workers who must perform them."

Selected Bibliography

The technical details of this study are published in "Development and Field Evaluation of an Interdisciplinary Measure of Job Design" by Michael A. Campion and Paul W. Thayer (*Journal of Applied Psychology,* February 1985). Other published work on job design by the first author includes "Biomechanics and the Design of Industrial Jobs" by Michael A. Campion and Eileen J. Phelan (*Personnel Journal,* December 1981).

A great number of literature references were drawn upon in the design of this study, and they were taken from a variety of different academic disciplines. In fact, there are literally hundreds of written works on the broad topic of job design in each of the relevant disciplines. Therefore, we will provide only citations to the more contemporary writings and to books that summarize the literature. For the interested reader, the books listed will contain references to the classic works and to the research articles in each of the areas.

A good contemporary book on the mechanistic approach to job design is *Motion and Time Study: Design and Measurement of Work* by Ralph M. Barnes (John Wiley & Sons, 1980). Another good description of the mechanistic approach that also addresses the biological features of job design is *Work Design* by Stephan Konz (Grid, 1979).

The most widely recognized version of the motivational approach is found in *Work Redesign* by J. Richard Hackman and Greg R. Oldham (Addison-Wesley, 1980). An excellent document that addresses the motivational approach from a broader perspective is *Task Design: An Integrative Approach* by Ricky W. Griffin (Scott-Foresman, 1982).

A well-known book on the biological approach is *Fitting the Task to the Man: An Ergonomic Approach* by Etienne Grandjean

(Taylor & Francis, 1980). Grandjean also treats the perceptual/motor approach to job design. Another good book on the biological approach that focuses mainly on the biomechanical aspects is *The Biomechanical Basis of Ergonomics: Anatomy Applied to the Design of Work Situations* by E. R. Tichauer (John Wiley & Sons, 1978).

An excellent reference source on the perceptual/motor approach, *Human Engineering Guide to Equipment Design*, was written by a variety of authors and edited by Harold P. Van Cott and Robert G. Kinkade (U.S. Government Printing Office, 1972). Another well-recognized book on the topic is *Human Factors in Engineering and Design* by Ernest J. McCormick (McGraw-Hill, 1972).

Finally, *Design of Jobs*, edited by Louis E. Davis and James C. Taylor (Goodyear, 1979), is a novel book that includes the unusual combination of articles on both the mechanistic and motivational approaches and that provides a historical perspective on job design.

PERFORMANCE MANAGEMENT

INTRODUCTION

Performance management is the process through which companies ensure that employees are working toward organization goals. This certainly serves as one of the means available to organizations to gain competitive advantage. This process entails (1) specifying the types of performance that are necessary for effective organizational functioning, particularly in accordance with the strategy, (2) measuring that performance accurately, and (3) feeding back the performance information to employees in a way that encourages continuous improvement.

Reading 14 by Schneier, Shaw, and Beatty provides an examination of the role of performance measurement and management (PMM) in strategy implementation. As opposed to the common establishment of performance measurement systems as a simple human resource bureaucracy, these authors point out how an effective PMM system can link employee performance to the strategy of the organization. They note that most attempts to fix PMM systems focus on the rating forms when, in fact, these problems usually stem from the organization's culture. The authors propose the use of "critical success factors," which are the specific operational embodiment of what it takes to win. By linking the PMM to these critical success factors, they demonstrate how organizations have gained a competitive advantage.

The performance management process is one that entails a constant day-to-day feedback to employees regarding their performance, rather than a simple once-a-year activity. Reading 15 by Meyer reexamines the performance appraisal feedback process in light of organizations that are leaning away from authoritarian management practices and toward an involvement-oriented climate. He proposes adding employee self-reviews that provide more involvement of the subordinate in the appraisal process as well as forcing the manager to emphasize his or her counseling, rather than judging, role.

READING 14

PERFORMANCE MEASUREMENT AND MANAGEMENT
A Tool for Strategy Execution

Craig Eric Schneier,
Douglas G. Shaw,
and Richard W. Beatty

In many organizations performance measurement and management (PMM) systems are little more than human resource bureaucracies with forms, rules, and review layers. These paper-driven systems are burdens to managers and hence are completed marginally, if at all. They are typically seen by raters as extra work and by ratees as at best irrelevant, at worst demotivating. Most PMM improvement efforts center on the most visible aspect of PMM—the form. But these quick fixes attempt to treat symptoms (e.g., leniency), while diseases (e.g., lack of managerial accountability for performance improvement or development) go unchecked. Rather than periodic revisions to the rating scales, PMM can be made relevant by linking it to strategy execution. PMM can be a vital tool for strategy execution by signaling what is really important, providing ways to measure what is important, fixing accountability for behavior and results, and helping to improve performance. In this article a PMM process is described which begins with identification of Critical Success Factors (CSFs) derived directly from business strategy. These are the basis for a PMM process that is a welcome managerial tool. The successful use of PMM as a device for strategy execution is illustrated via a case study. © 1992 by John Wiley & Sons, Inc.

As business strategies become increasingly generic (e.g., customer service; penetration of global-markets), the execution of strategy distinguishes high-performing from average companies. Leaders of America's best-known companies are increasingly aware of the need for execution:

> At best the plan is 20 percent of the game. Execution is 80 percent of it. (John Trani, head of GE's medical systems business [reported in Huey, 1991]).

Source: "Performance Measurement and Management: A Tool for Strategy Execution" by C. E. Schneier, D. G. Shaw, and R. W. Beatty, from *Human Resource Management*, Fall 1991, Vol. 30, no. 3, 279–301. © 1992 by John Wiley & Sons, Inc. Reprinted by permission of Wiley-Liss, a division of John Wiley & Sons, Inc.

It is my absolute conviction that you can outmanage your competition by having brilliant strategies, but those brilliant strategies have to be executed brilliantly. (Leo Gerstner, CEO of RJR Nabisco [reported in Irvin and Michaels, 1989]).

Strategy execution has been operationalized as reduced cycle time (e.g., Stalk & Haut, 1989), better customer service (e.g., Zeithaml et al., 1990; Schlesinger & Heskett, 1991), superior quality (e.g., Crosby, 1979; Juran, 1989), flexible manufacturing (e.g., Hayes, et al., 1988), an empowered workforce (e.g., Block, 1987), effective management of change (e.g., Beer et al., 1991), or responsive organization structures (e.g., Bartlett & Shoshal, 1989; Charan, 1991), among other concepts. Each view of better execution advocates a strong measurement emphasis, from 3M's "Project '95," aimed at reducing all manufacturing cycle times by 50%, to Motorola's "six sigma," aimed at improving all products' quality to 99.9997% defect-free.

Yet, as organizations struggle to reduce their cycle times or improve their products' reliability, their performance measurement and management (PMM) systems offer little help. At the macro (organization) level they have been maligned for concentration on short-term, period-to-period financial performance measures to the exclusion of qualitative data and comparisons to competitors (Eccles, 1991). At the micro (individual) level, they have been maligned for a concentration on psychometric nuance, such as the number or title of rating scale categories which lead to no real improvement in rating accuracy (Landy & Farr, 1980; Austin et al., 1991). They are either ignored by senior executives or so lenient as to be useless as a basis for reward allocation (e.g., Longenecker & Gioia, 1991). IBM's experience is indicative:

> Under the new guidelines, IBM will more strictly enforce a system under which it ranks employees on a numerical scale. Few employees now carry a rank below three (on a four-point scale), but the guidelines will force managers to rank people as fours. Anyone with a rank that low will face pressure to resign, and quickly. (*The Wall Street Journal*, October 1, 1991, parentheses added).

IBM's PMM system was obviously not facilitating strategy execution.

It is argued here that PMM is critical to strategy execution and an approach is described that has elevated PMM beyond a personnel *form* to a strategic *tool* in several companies.

PMM: WHAT EXISTS IS NOT WHAT IS NEEDED

The Wrong Measures

Many have detailed the inadequacies of PMM systems (Schneier, 1992; Carroll & Schneier, 1982; Bernardin & Beatty, 1984; Mohrman et al., 1989). As a tool to help execute strategy, most PMM systems are woefully deficient (see Fig. 1). Companies need a process to help identify and measure "what counts"—those few activities that lead to success of individuals, teams, units, and the organization. Most

Figure 1

PERFORMANCE MEASUREMENT AND MANAGEMENT (PMM):
WHAT EXISTS IS NOT WHAT IS NEEDED

What Most Companies Have . . .		*What Most Companies Need . . .*
1. A staff-driven rating *scale* and *forms*	→	1. A management *tool* and *process*
2. Supervisor-driven *ratings*	→	2. Subordinate, supervisor, team member, customer-driven *assessment*
3. A focus on evaluating performance *after* the fact	→	3. A focus on setting expectations *up front, coaching, developing* and *improving* performance *continually*
4. Measuring *generic* aspects of people or jobs	→	4. Measuring those *"Critical Success Factors"* that assure goal attainment, strategy execution
5. Consequences of performance centered around *base compensation*	→	5. *Positive and negative, financial* and *nonfinancial* consequences of performance utilized effectively
6. *Human resources accountability* for *"fixing"* the *system*	→	6. *Managerial accountability* for *designing, operating,* and *improving* the *process,* with human resources technical assistance
7. *Ambiguity and inconsistency* around "what it takes to make it" in different units, at different levels, for different managers; uneven expectations	→	7. *Clarity* about success for individuals, teams, units, across the Company
8. Performance *hurdles set too low,* or *not set at all,* given what is required for the organization to compete successfully	→	8. Performance *hurdles set to stretch* people, *ever-increasing,* reflecting customers' ever-increasing demands and competitors' ever-increasing skills

PMM systems measure performance only at the individual level and measure a set of undefined, generic personal characteristics (e.g., "initiative") or a set of specific, yet narrow technical skills (e.g., "financial analysis") derived from job descriptions. These sets of criteria rarely track with the company's strategy or even with what is truly important for success in any given position.

Consider the recent experience of the procurement function of a division of a Fortune 50 company. An analysis of slipping market share pointed to poor product quality. Quality breakdowns were traced to raw materials. The division attempted to implement a sourcing strategy that included developing partnerships with a select few suppliers in order to focus on product quality and reliability in use. Despite its rhetoric, the number of suppliers and their materials' quality remained constant. The single largest impediment to this major, crossfunctional effort was that the procurement people interacting with the suppliers on a daily basis were still being measured on the discounts they were able to obtain from suppliers. In other words, their success was assured if they dealt with numerous, competing suppliers and pressured them for discounts, with little regard to material quality. Subsequent costs related to downtime from the failure of the product were not on the procurement unit's measurement "screen."

The Wrong Judgments

In addition to measuring the wrong aspects of performance, PMM systems typically require numerous, finite evaluations that too many managers are unwilling and/or unable to make on a performance scale. Leniency, as in the IBM example described above, becomes the norm. Research (e.g., Landy & Farr, 1980) has shown that changes in scale definitions, labels, "anchors," or examples, or even the number of scale points lead to little that is definitive regarding rating accuracy. Further, it has been argued, as well as empirically demonstrated, that a performance rating is more reflective of the *rater's* personality or judgment style than the *ratee's* actual performance (e.g., Borman, 1983). Hence, the emphasis is on *rating* performance, not improving it.

The Wrong Owners

The PMM system is too often viewed as the province of the human resources unit, not the manager's accountability. It is likely that human resources designed and implemented the system. PMM is hence seen as extra work by managers, who resent completing forms merely to process a salary increase and are not skilled at providing constructive performance feedback. Lack of managerial accountability for PMM leads to perhaps the system's most telling deficiency: PMM is routinely ignored. In one recent study, almost half of the executives interviewed indicated they did not receive performance reviews, and those that did described them as rushed and vague (Longenecker & Gioia, 1988).

The Wrong Impact

Most researchers and practitioners agree that the impact PMM systems should have is on performance—to develop it and to improve it. The typical PMM policy statement or CEO's exhortation in the front of the managers' PMM Guide usually contains a direct reference to improved performance as the key objective of PMM. While the evaluative and developmental impacts of PMM are different and hence difficult to reconcile in practice, the facts are that individual-level, hierarchically based performance appraisal has been a failure: it has not improved performance (see e.g., research cited in Mohrman et al., 1991), and it is not a viable force for development in most organizations, according to survey after survey (see e.g., *Training*, 1988).

What has the PMM system impacted, if not performance? The impact of individual-level PMM has been most notable on the merit pay system, where a rating is used to derive and justify (albeit weakly due, for example, to extreme leniency) a base salary increase.

PMM STRATEGY EXECUTION: A FRAMEWORK

Both discussions of strategy execution (e.g., Schneier, 1991; Hrebineak & Joyce, 1984; Ulrich & Lake, 1991), and executives' own experiences (e.g., Rodgers, 1990; Tichy & Charan, 1990) suggest the importance of PMM. T. J. Rodgers is founder and CEO of Cypress Semi-conductor, whose 1991 return on equity is over twice its industry's average. He discusses PMM as follows:

> All of Cypress' 1,400 employees have goals, which, in theory, make them no different from employees at most other companies. What does make our people different is that every week they set their own goals, commit to achieving them by a specific date, enter them into a data base, and report whether or not they completed prior goals. In any given week, some 6,000 goals in the database come due. Our ability to meet those goals ultimately determines our success or failure. (Rogers, 1990, p. 87)

At Cypress, PMM is not merely a paperwork exercise for managers based on a rating scale; it is a key to business performance. At Federal Express a Service Quality Index (SQI) measures 10 key aspects of overall company performance and is flashed daily via closed-circuit television to all employees. At Johnson and Johnson adherence to its famed "Credo" is measured via employee surveys and used to help determine executive compensation. For these companies, PMM is central to business operations and critical to success, both individually and organizationally.

PMM facilitates execution of business strategies by:

1. signaling what to measure;
2. determining appropriate ways to measure; and
3. fixing accountability for performance on the measures.

Unless all three of these activities occur, strategy execution is in jeopardy. People will focus on the wrong measures, fail to know when or agree if targets are reached, aim too low and achieve too little, and/or see no consequences for missing the targets (or perhaps for hitting them). (See Fig. 2.)

Each aspect of a PMM strategy execution model is described below, as is the importance of aligning key organizational capabilities—structure, skills, style, and systems—with strategy to assure execution.

Figure 2

PERFORMANCE MEASUREMENT AND MANAGEMENT
AND STRATEGY EXECUTION

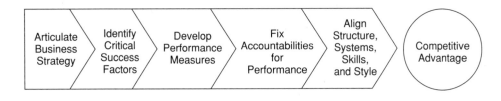

IDENTIFYING CRITICAL SUCCESS FACTORS (CSFs): THE FIRST STEP TOWARD STRATEGY EXECUTION

Regardless of how formally a business strategy is documented, the essence of the strategy can be distilled into the few factors that must be executed with excellence to gain and sustain competitive advantage. For example, many companies' strategies speak to cost-competitiveness: Wal-Mart competes on "everyday low prices." But a key to success for Wal-Mart is its superior capability in purchasing and logistics, enabling low prices everyday (Stalk et al., 1992). While many companies have a customer service strategy, a CSF for Domino's Pizza is custom order processing and, of course, delivery, given its 30-minute delivery time guarantee. These CSFs are strategy-driven, and they are specific, operational embodiments of what it takes to win. They are neither always obvious nor generic.

Two frameworks are useful to assist in identifying critical success factors (CSFs), Rockhart's (1979) MIT study, and Tregoe et al.'s (1989) "driving forces."

Rockhart (1979) advocates the following as sources of CSFs:

1. **The characteristics of an industry.** There are specific factors that must be addressed in a given industry to survive and prosper. For example, hotels and airlines must ensure that their fixed assets are well-utilized (i.e., high occupancy rates), or they will face severe cash crunches, to say the least.

2. **An organization's competitive strategy and industry positioning.** Within an industry, competitors may have different business strategies and typically will not enjoy the same position. In its early years, for example, Compaq Computer could not rely on customer service to gain a fast hold in the marketplace; they chose to fill a niche—"portable" computers—as an entry strategy. Hence, in the early 1980s, innovation was a CSF for Compaq, whereas for IBM, market dominance was critical.

3. **Environmental factors (i.e., economic and political).** Prior to the mid-1970s, few companies worried about the availability of energy supplies. With the oil embargo, securing oil became a CSF for companies in several industries. In another industry, setting up and operating efficient overseas (i.e., US)

manufacturing plants became a CSF for Japanese automobile companies as they encountered more and more resistance from the public and governments in the US and Europe.

4. **Temporal factors.** Specific circumstances may give rise to temporary critical success factors that may become less critical once a crisis is averted. Companies that have just completed a leveraged buy-out may see the ability to generate cash as a CSF. Cash flow may not take on this heightened importance once the debt is paid down.

Just as two companies in the same industry may not have the same CSFs, two divisions or businesses in the same corporation may have different CSFs. For example, the private banking, commercial banking, and investment banking units in a large money-center bank have some overlap, but some unique CSFs. In one of the nation's largest bank corporations, the private bank uses personal service, leading to the cache' that attracts moneyed clientele. For the investment bank, a network of investors able to commit hugh sums on a telephone call is critical. For the commercial bank division, success has followed strong analytical capability and a conservative leading policy (see Bullen & Rockart, 1981, for a review of CSF generation).

Tregoe & Associates (1989) have developed the notion of "driving force," used to generate a strategic vision. There are eight key variables that serve as the source of strategic vision, but each has also helped companies see the CSFs which fall from their strategy (see Fig. 3). The sources of the driving force provide a lens through which a company can view and assess its ability to execute a strategy.

Core Skills, Core Competencies, Capabilities, and CSFs

Like the driving force, notions of core skills (Irvin & Michaels, 1989), core competencies (Prahalad & Hamel, 1990), and capabilities (Stalk et al., 1992) help a company point to what it must do exceptionally well to execute strategy and sustain competitive advantage. Each concept is somewhat different, but each is essential for successful strategy execution.

For Irvin and Michaels (1989) core skills:

> Link strategy (thinking) and execution (doing). If you want brilliant execution, strengthen the right core skills, the ones that provide the most economic leverage. If you do a good enough job, the core skills themselves, even more than the strategy, will become the basis for your continued success.

Irvin and Michaels (1989) discuss Marriott's ability actually to provide high quality service to business travelers (i.e., execution) as a core skill leading to its success, as opposed to merely a stated strategy of providing excellent service to the business traveler. Other companies in Marriott's industry fail to execute as well. Like CSFs, core skills are strategy-driven and specific; they must be operationalized for key positions and reinforced by those at the top.

Core competencies, as defined by Prahalad and Hamel (1990), have three acid tests:

Figure 3

SOURCES OF STRATEGY AND CRITICAL SUCCESS FACTORS (CSFs)

After Tregoe et al. (1989); driving forces are not mutually exclusive in that companies address several simultaneously to develop strategy and CSFs.

1. Products/Services Offered
   Common characteristics of products/services described, but subject to expansion.
   Objective is to rapidly develop/acquire new products/services that fit the profile, seeking broader markets to exploit.
   Product/service value/differentiation sought.
   Product development and marketing emphasized.
   Example: J. M. Smucker

2. Markets-Served
   Strong, well-defined relationships with customers.
   Objective to identify and fill customer needs.
   Marketing and marketing research, along with R&D, are emphasized.
   Example: Consumers Packaging

3. Return/Profit
   Ability to meet return and profit goals determines business portfolio; asset divestiture/acquisition.
   Example: Variety Corporation

4. Technology
   Body of knowledge or technological capability leads to success.
   Objective is to leverage technological expertise, applying it to products/services.
   Example: 3M

5. Low-Cost Production
   Production of products/services is lower than competitors.
   Cost-efficient operations, from economies of scale superior manufacturing processes, and/or ability to match utilization of productive facilities to their capacity.
   Customers buy on price; typically commodity businesses.
   Example: International Paper

6. Operations Capability
   Flexible use of productive capacity as in "job shop" manufacturing and/or unique products/services, is critical to success.
   Specialized target markets must be identified and penetrated.
   Scheduling, expediting, coordinating human and material resources, and budgeting are emphasized.
   Example: Bechtel Group

7. Method of Distribution/Sale
   Distribution channels and/or sales capability allow for large market share and competitively advantaged pricing.
   Additional products/services may be added to exploit the channel.
   Example: Book-of-the-Month Club

8. National Resource
   Ownership/control over a natural resource leads to success, as well as the ability to process the resource into more and more marketable products/services.
   The quality, quantity, or location of the resource may lead to an advantage.
   Example: Shell Oil

Figure 4

THE POWER OF CRITICAL SUCCESS FACTORS (CSFs)

	McDonalds was relentless in adhering to CSFs, Burger King less so . . . *	
Fast Food CSFs	*McDonalds*	*Burger King*
Site Selection	"Penchant for finding the plum"	"Generally good locations"
High Quality Service	"Unparalleled consistency"	"Suffers from operational sloppiness"
Product Innovation	"A knack for product development"	"Spotty record with new products"
Communications	"Surrogate mom"	"Comes off as aggressive, masculine and distant"

* Irvin & Michaels, 1989; p. 7.

1. Provide access to a wide variety of markets.
   Example: Casio's expertise at display systems leads to calculator, miniature TV, dashboards, etc., markets.

2. Contribute significantly to customers' perception of products' benefits.
   Example: Honda's engine expertise helps assure that its engines are a core product, viewed favorably by customers, hence contributing heavily to its end-products' (e.g., lawn mowers) success.

3. Not easily copied.
   Example: 3M's expertise in "sticky tape," leveraged via a culture that reinforces innovation and risk-taking, leads to numerous successful products.

Stalk et al.'s (1992) notion of capabilities is very similar (some would say the differences are semantic) to the concepts described above. Capabilities are critical to strategy execution, and strategy execution, as argued above, is the key to competitive advantage:

> . . . the essence of strategy is *not* the structure of a company's products and markets, but the dynamics of its behavior. And the goal is to identify and develop the hard-to-imitate organizational capabilities that distinguish a company from its competitors in the eyes of its customers. (p. 62)

Processes, particularly those that cross business units and/or functions and are linked to customers, provide strategic capability. Wal-Mart's capability in warehousing—the continuous delivery of goods to warehouses and the continuous dispatching of these goods to stores—almost eliminates inventory. Transportation, buying, information systems, financial analysis (regarding investment decisions), logistics, and asset (e.g., warehouse) management are a few of the

Figure 4

continued

	And McDonalds' resultant financial performance reflects the difference.†	
Performance	McDonalds	Burger King
Royalties Paid By Franchisee	3.5%	3.5%
Number of Employees‡	60	60
Average Cost of Hamburger	$.63	$.63
Average Start-up Cost*	$435k	$1MM
Average Annual Revenue*	$1.5MM	$1MM
Average Annual Profit*	$234k	$140k

* Irvin & Michaels, 1989; p. 7.

† Heskett et al., 1990; p. 207.

‡ Per restaurant.

functions that come together to make the warehousing process a competitive advantage for Wal-Mart. They are able to replenish store shelves twice a week, versus once every two weeks for their competitors (Stalk et al., 1992).

The Power of CSFs: Fast Food

A striking illustration of the power gained by identifying and utilizing CSFs to execute strategy can be seen in a comparison of McDonalds and Burger King. Experts have pieced together a set of CSFs for these "fast food" retail stores (see Fig. 4). In the late 1960's both Burger King and McDonalds had approximately 100 stores, essentially no rivals, and a similar strategy, but over the next two decades McDonalds was relentless on its adherence to the CSFs, arguably executing its strategy much better than Burger King, and growing and profiting handsomely. The size and profitability of the two chains are very different today.

DEVELOPING PERFORMANCE MEASURES THAT DRIVE STRATEGY EXECUTION

Once CSFs (or driving forces or core competencies) have been identified, the second key step in the development of a PMM process to enhance strategy execution is to develop performance measures for the CSFs. CSFs tell *what* must be done to win; performance measures are needed to determine *how well* we must perform and how we will know if we succeeded. Strategies are rarely executed if a general mandate or vision (e.g., "compete globally") is not operationalized via CSFs (e.g., speeding the right financial and sales data to offices all over the world simultaneously). But measures to determine the necessary speed and right data are also needed. These, of course, determine and communicate performance targets and bring the CSF to bear on specific positions, both prerequisites for effective strategy execution. Figure 5 provides illustrative performance measures for a set of CSFs. Some are obvious, some less so, but if the CSFs do not have predetermined, specific measures, and/or if the measures derived from CSFs are not in the PMM system, PMM becomes an administrative exercise, not managers' "real work." Measuring procurement managers on raw material cost, but not on quality in the case of the manufacturing company cited earlier, is an example of a PMM system incompatible with company CSFs.

Another common PMM problem is the system's reliance on duties derived from a job description. One financial service company's PMM system tracks and evaluates analysts on how well they productively prepare reports, because the job description contains a duty called "report writing." However, internal customers, when asked said that the reports provide only redundant data and should not be written by financial analysts, but by the accounting unit. As long as the analysts' PMM measures report writing, the analysts write reports. A worldwide consumer goods manufacturer has shifted to a CSF of product line extensions. Its PMM system rates, but does not define, initiative, motivation, and task knowledge, among other generic criteria, for every position. These characteristics may be admirable, but their relation to executing strategy (more line extensions) for each position is unclear. That is, what does the staff accountant do differently to take initiative and what task knowledge is now important, given the line extension CSF? That many managers fail to complete appraisal forms in this consumer goods manufacturer, and that most who do complete them do so in a "perfunctory" (to quote one executive) manner, is not surprising. Yet the company measures numerous aspects of its operation in detail. The PMM process is not related to strategy and hence is not used in its execution. It is seen as an HR system, not a managerial tool.

A Company's Use (or Misuse) of PMM Is Determined by Its Culture, Not Its Appraisal Forms or Rating Scales

Leniency, leading to inaccurate assessments, is a longstanding problem in PMM systems, particularly at the individual level (see e.g., Austin et al., 1991). This problem has been researched as a psychometric one, but the causes perhaps stem more from a company's culture than the psychometric properties of its appraisal forms.

PMM systems are a reflection of the values a company has around performance and the performance culture is illustrated not by value statements but by action (see Fig. 6). Key questions that are used to assess a performance culture are:

- How hard do people actually work?
- Are performance expectations explicit?
- How high are the expectations for performance?

Figure 5

DEVELOPING PERFORMANCE MEASURES FOR CRITICAL SUCCESS FACTORS (CSFs)

Company	Illustrative CSF	Illustrative Measure/Goal
Rubbermaid	New Products	Reduce new product development cycle
Alcoa	Safety	Improvement in safety rewards(?)
Federal Express	Customer Service	12-factor Service Quality Index (SQI) covering measures such as late deliveries, lost and damaged packages, missed pick-ups
Hewlett-Packard	Innovation	Percent of revenues from products that are two years old or newer
Xerox	Customer Service	Service call measures: frequency, responsiveness, length, copy quality
Domino's Pizza	Home Delivery Time	Percent deliveries within 30 minutes
3M	Manufacturing Cycle Time	Reduce cycle time by 50% within five years
Nissan Motor (Infiniti)	Customer Service	Increases in customer satisfaction survey scores and $100,000 bonus to dealers
Bell Atlantic	Develop, install network allowing advanced services	Percent of phone lines equipped with "Signalling System 7"
Coca Cola	Penetrating and operating in foreign markets	Number of days to set up operating/ bottling in a country
GM	Operating efficiency	Reduce number of direct labor hours to produce a car
Motorola	Quality	Six sigma quality (99.9997% defect-free) products by 1992

Based on company documents, reports in business press.

- Is failure to meet expectations noticed and tolerated?
- What is the relative importance of effort expended and of outcomes (results) attained?
- What happens to those who exceed expectation versus those who merely meet them?
- Do people receive candid performance feedback?
- Are developmental needs identified, discussed, and acted upon?

As Figure 6 describes, companies with an "Up or Out" culture around performance communicate high expectations and do not tolerate failure to meet

Figure 6

PERFORMANCE CULTURES AND PERFORMANCE MEASUREMENT
AND MANAGEMENT (PMM) IMPLICATIONS

Performance Culture	*Competitive: Up-Or-Out*	*Selectivity: Hire the Best, Push Them, Develop Them*
Illustrative Key Practices Related to Managing People, Performance	· Hire only those with high potential · Cultivate an individual "star system" · Tell people early if they'll make it; remove ones who won't · Turnover encouraged · Set extremely high expectations	· Retain people as long as contribution is increasing · Provide first-rate development, not just training · Cultivate teams, synergies · Set high expectations, clear accountabilities · Provide performance feedback regularly · Set high standards
Competitive Environment that Enables Companies with Philosophy to Win	· Image and name of key people bring sales · Highly competitive industry · Dominating companies prevail · Aggressiveness well rewarded financially	· Synergies, innovations lead to sales · Highly competitive, dynamic industry · Leading companies have superior core competencies visible to customers

them. Poor performers are routinely dismissed. In these cultures, leniency on appraisal forms is not a serious problem and measures are plentiful and visible. In contrast, companies with an "Entitlement" ("Hire Adequate, Retain, Redeploy") performance culture typically have inflated ratings. Managers who are brutally frank about performance would violate the performance culture norms. Dismissing people for failure to perform is also taboo. Those who meet and those who exceed performance expectations are treated essentially the same regarding rewards.

The PMM System Must Fit the Performance Culture—Or Help Change It

Different performance cultures can be described and can lead to success, given certain competitive, economic environments (see Fig. 6). As Figure 6 indicates, competitive environments facilitate or deter survival in each performance culture. Many heretofore successful companies are finding it difficult to remain in the "Competence" culture due to increased competitive pressures, higher cost structures, and higher customer expectations. They are moving to "Selectivity" cultures by necessity as an assurance against an eroding competitive position. Companies in transition from a Competence to a Selectivity culture have problematic PMM systems. Old performance expectations were too low, measures too ambiguous, rating too lenient, feedback too sugar-coated, and rewards too homogeneously administered to reflect today's competitive realities. IBM, noted earlier, is a case in point, as it has mandated a less lenient performance rating distribution and a "get tough" policy with regard to poor performers. The recent popularity of downsizing, particularly at the white-collar level, is evidence of

Figure 6

continued

Performance Culture	Competence: Hire Well, Keep as Long as Contributing	Entitlement: Hire Adequate, Retain, Redeploy
Illustrative Key Practices Related to Managing People, Performance	· Hire good people, potential unsure · Provide opportunity to improve, develop · Cultivate a "family," avoid confrontations, dismissals · Turnover avoided · Performance standards vary in degree of rigor · Provide "benefit-of-the-doubt" in ratings	· Move people to a job of best fit, given capability · Promote cooperation, loyalty, security, "family" · "Sugar-coat" or do not offer performance feedback · Provide continual training opportunities · Routes to the top well-known and inflexible · Time in grade, not high performance, brings rewards
Competitive Environment that Enables Companies with Philosophy to Win	· Leading companies have market dominance, slack resources · Industry not highly volatile · Slow growth, yet returns available over time	· "Regulated" and/or "protected" industry · Leading companies have a "franchise" (e.g., size, location) that funnels sales to them · Core technology is not quickly obsolete

companies' attempts to shift to more rigorous performance cultures. PMM systems can assist in this shift and hence can be a powerful lever for change.

FIXING ACCOUNTABILITIES FOR PERFORMANCE: ASSURING EXECUTION

As Figure 2 notes, the final key step in developing a PMM process to drive strategy execution is to hold performers accountable. CSFs and measures must be operationalized at the unit, team, and individual levels. Specific outcomes and behaviors can be specified and then linked to consequences. Most PMM systems fail as tools for strategy execution because managers have not determined what people and teams must actually *do* and *achieve*, given the company's set of CSFs. Johnson and Johnson specifies what people must do via its Credo survey and fixes accountability via compensation. GE's Chairman has publicly described negative consequences (i.e., termination) for those who not only do not achieve business results but also fail to show behavior consistent with GE's values. Those who exhibit the desired behaviors and attain the results are rewarded differentially. Recent actions make the system real.

PMM AS STRATEGY EXECUTION: A PHARMACEUTICAL CASE STUDY

A Fortune 100 East Coast pharmaceutical company (here called Global Health) had a typical PMM system. Their system for managers, technical experts, and

Figure 7

HOW PERFORMANCE MEASUREMENT AND MANAGEMENT (PMM) FACILITATES STRATEGY
EXECUTION: GLOBAL HEALTH CORPORATION (NOT THE COMPANY'S ACTUAL NAME)

Business Strategy	Critical Success Factors	Performance Measures
Penetrate, then dominate North American market for dermatology compounds	Shortened cycle for discovery to FDA approval	Number of compounds submissions
		Number of compound approvals
	R&D talent attraction/retention	Project/team leadership
	Successful worldwide (chemical) compound teams	Turnover of senior scientists
		Collaboration

professionals contained a series of five-point scales measuring various types of
knowledge, several skills, and about a dozen personal characteristics. In addition,
each manager had a set of goals to attain. But the results of all of these measurements and appraisals were boiled down to a single score on a five-point scale.
Over 70% of all those rated received the rating (one below the highest), called
Excellent. The score was forwarded to the Compensation Department to determine merit increases. Over two-thirds of Global Health's employees received a
five percent base salary increase, interestingly enough, the exact amount of the
merit budget. A survey indicated considerable dissatisfaction with the PMM system: almost no performance feedback was provided to those rated; top performers were discouraged as they received the same salary increases as those rated
lower or who had done little; and managers complained bitterly about completing the long, complex forms and the trite, meaningless narrative they were forced
to produce for each subordinate. After offering several voluntary training courses
(run with only a handful of attendees), making numerous attempts at increasing
or decreasing the number of scale points, deciding on a "forced" distribution, and
selecting new titles for the scale values, it was decided that a new PMM approach
was needed.

A line management Global Health task force revised the process along the
lines of Figure 2. Once the company's CSFs were identified, performance measures were developed. Finally, accountabilities for individuals and teams—those
behaviors, outcomes, and consequences for performance required to assure the
CSFs were met—were developed (see Fig. 7).

Test Top Management Support by Deriving
Concrete Implications of Principles

How did the Task Force operate? They provided the basis PMM framework and
assisted managers and their subordinates in developing measures and accountabilities. The company's top executive group identified the CSFs. The task force
ran into one problem however. Top management at Global Health had readily
agreed to support line management, as opposed to human resources, account-

Figure 7

continued

Mechanisms for Measuring Performance	Team/Individual Manager Accountability
Team member surveys of leaders	Annual incentive (partially) based on:
FDA decisions	Reduction in (unwanted) turnover of senior staff
Team member feedback	FDA submission of three compounds
Turnover rates	FDA approval of three compounds
Superior's observations	Job rotation, promotion (partially) based on:
Self-assessment	Team member, subordinate, leadership assessment
	Verbal praise, spot bonus awarded for:
	Team leadership effectiveness
	Hiring new senior technical talent

ability for PMM. The task force decided to test this support by developing a set of PMM principles and related implications (see Fig. 8).

Once the top executive group approved the implications, the PMM process could be designed and implemented. For example, the executive group supported the notion that collaboration is important. But heretofore, those who were not collaborative team leaders were still highly compensated and promoted. Hence top managers' support was nominal, and the principle of accountability had no credibility. Once the executives agreed to the principle, however, they were also now agreeing with the task force's implication for that principle: assessments of team leaders in writing would be obtained from team members and would be used as input for promotion and compensation decisions (see Fig. 8). Such agreements paved the way for managerial accountability for PMM and hence for effective PMM implementation at Global Health.

A CSF for Global Health was shortened cycle time for approval of its products. The PMM process helped identify specific performance measures, mechanisms for measuring performance, and accountability targets for this CSF (see Fig. 8). Direct ties to Global Health CSFs moved PMM out of the category of extra work for managers. Operational performance measures for key jobs helped assure that PMM focused behaviors and outcomes on what counts. The implications for the PMM principles further operationalized PMM and gave it "teeth."

The Global Health task force needed very little debate concerning whether and how to deliver PMM training: managers whose incentive pay is based on their subordinates' assessments of their PMM practices *want* PMM training. The task force trained a cadre of interested managers and HR professionals to deliver practical assistance to "natural" teams. They were credible and did not need canned classroom training. The task force also spent very little time deciding on rating categories. They saw no need for such categories except to send an overall message about performance. They quickly settled on three performance levels:

Figure 8

GLOBAL HEALTH CORPORATION'S* PERFORMANCE MEASUREMENT AND MANAGEMENT (PMM)
PRINCIPLES AND IMPLICATIONS LEAD TO EFFECTIVE PMM PROCESS DESIGN AND IMPLEMENTATION
(*Not the company's actual name)

Sample PMM Process Principles	Illustrative Operational and Design Implications
Managers have accountability for performance measurement, management, and development	Each manager's success is (partially) based on his/her performance management effectiveness No manager receives a higher overall performance evaluation, used for incentive pay allocation, than the evaluation received for performance management skills/duties Subordinates will provide input into their managers' evaluation
Not only results obtained, but behavior exhibited, is evidence of successful performance and is manageable via the performance management process	Poor performance of subordinates reflects adversely on their managers' performance Both behavior and results will be measured Each manager specifies and communicates behavioral performance expectations for subordinates Relative weighting of results and behaviors can vary across positions and/or over time
Teamwork and collaboration is a key to success in the business	Self-assessments will be used as input into an overall evaluation "Skip level" discussions (managers talking to their subordinates' subordinates) and customer and supplier input will be used to assess performance Team leadership and performance will be tracked and will be used in conjunction with individual performance to determine compensation
Performance measures and the measurement process are driven by business strategy and goals	Results and behaviors, based on critical success factors, will be developed initially for each key position by managers and incumbents The top executive team will prepare their performance measures and accountabilities with the CEO

exceeds expectations, meets expectations, does not meet expectations. Most people are doing well and meeting expectations, but could use some development. A minority are truly stellar or very poor performers. Why have more rating categories than the three groups to further separate people? Specific, candid feedback, not rating, is what was needed at Global to improve performance. Since the PMM measures drive the business results, they, not ratings, were the focus of the PMM process.

Making Change Last: Structure, Systems, Skills, and Style

Global Health was able to overcome some tough PMM hurdles—measurement relevance, managerial accountability, top executive participation—because its process was driven by and seen as a mechanism to execute business strategy. However, in order for the PMM process to facilitate strategy execution on an ongoing basis, important aspects of Global Health had to change: structure, systems, skills, and style. For example, effective world-wide chemical compound teams were a Global Health CSF. These teams, composed of people from sales, marketing, research, manufacturing, finance, and government relations were given the awesome responsibility of marshalling Global's resources around the world to turn a chemical compound into a drug, refine it, test it, obtain FDA approval for it, manufacture it, market it, and sell it. The teams became a reality only when the traditional functional, hierarchical structure in Global Health was altered (DeVanna & Tichy, 1990). In some cases, team leaders were taken out of the hierarchy and in others they had network reporting relationships.

Many of Global's senior scientists, appropriate candidates for worldwide compound team leaders, had marginal leadership and management *skills*. Some were coached and improved. Their team leadership skills were enhanced and their managerial style (e.g., verbal communication, listening, participative decision making, tolerance for other cultures) was altered to fit a collaborative model. Other obvious candidates, due to their experience, visibility, level, and expertise were passed over as team leaders because they could not function well in a collaborative setting.

Finally, Global's *systems*—such as budgeting, planning, compensating, staffing—were called into question by the emerging PMM system. In order for worldwide compound teams to succeed, a PMM process identified appropriate performance measures linked to CSFs and built accountability in key jobs for high performance. But appropriate rewards for performance were necessary. Under the old performance appraisal system, most of Global's employees received the same rating and hence the same compensation increase. A revised reward system was proposed. Based on the collaboration PMM principle (see Fig. 8), the entire compound team's performance was measured, not merely individual member's performance. The PMM system facilitated the relevant quantifiable (e.g., speed of FDA approval) and qualitative (e.g., effective collaboration) measures based on the CSFs (see Fig. 7). All members of teams which succeeded were given bonuses. Individual performance was rewarded with job assignments, promotions, and recognition, important to the highly skilled, marketable Global scientists.

DESIGN PMM PROCESSES TO EXECUTE STRATEGY, NOT MERELY TO APPRAISE PERFORMANCE

Global Health was not dissimilar from many of today's companies. It had reorganized and downsized. Its overseas market offered growth potential, but it faced unrelentless competitive pressure both abroad and at home. Its internal functional boundaries were loosening, and it was attempting to push decision making down. But Global knew the keys to its sustainable competitive advantage: deep scientific talent that could fill its pipeline with new drugs and teams of specialists working together who could quickly get the drugs approved and to market.

Like many companies, Global had a PMM system that was not part of the essence of its business. PMM was a paperwork exercise, perceived to be the province of human resources, containing forms with numerous ratings on overly general aspects of jobs, and used primarily to assure essentially a cost-of-living merit increase. Global's task force did not attempt to fix the PMM system by substituting new scales for old, by shrinking the space for comments on the forms so they could be completed quicker, by mandating forced rating distributions because managers were not rigorous enough or candid enough, or by requiring managers to attend training classes. None of these treatments will cure the PMM disease of irrelevance. Simply put, what Global did was to consider how its business strategy could be better executed. It found that identifying what counts, measuring it, holding people accountable for it, coaching them to get better at it, and rewarding it were the simple, yet powerful solutions.

References

AMA (1991). *Blueprints for service quality: The Federal Express approach.* New York: American Management Association.

Austin, J. T., Villanova, P., Kane, J. S., & Bernardin, H. J. (1991). Construct validation of performance measures: issues, development, and evaluation of indicators. In G. R. Ferris and K. M. Rowland (Eds.), *Research in personnel and human resource management* (Vol. 9, pp. 159–234). Greenwich, CT: JAI Press.

Bartlett, C. A., & Ghoshal, S. (1989). *Managing across borders.* Boston: Harvard Business School Press.

Beer, M., Eisenstate, R. A., & Spector, B. (1990). *The critical path to corporate renewal.* Boston: Harvard Business School Press.

Bernarden, H. J., & Beatty, R. W. (1984). *Performance appraisal.* Boston: Kent.

Block, P. (1987). *The empowered manager.* San Francisco: Jossey-Bass.

Borman, W. C. (1983). Implications of personality theory and research for the rating of work performance in organizations. In F. Landy et al. (Eds.), *Performance measurement and theory* (pp. 128–165). Hillsdale, NJ: Erlbaum.

Bullen, C. V., & Rockart, J. F. (1981, June). *A primer on critical success factors.* Boston: Center for Information System Research (MIT).

Buzzell, R. D., & Gale, B. T. (1988). *The PIMS principles.* New York: Free Press.

Carroll, S. J., & Schneier, C. E. (1982). *Performance appraisal and review systems.* Glenview, IL: Scott Foresman.

Charan, R. (1991). How networks reshape organizations—for results. *Harvard Business Review, 69*(5), 104–115.

Conference Board (1989). *Current practices in measuring quality.* Research Bulletin No. 234, NY.

Crosby, P. B. (1979). *Quality is free.* New York: McGraw-Hill.

Deming, W. E. (1986). *Out of the crisis.* Cambridge, MA: Massachusetts Institute of Technology Press.

DeVanna, M., & Tichy, N. (1990). Creating the competitive organization of the 21st century: The boundaryless corporation. *Human Resource Management, 29*(4), 455–472.

Drucker, P. (1992). New strategies for a new reality. *The Wall Street Journal,* October 2.

Eccles, R. G. (1991). The Performance Measurement Manifesto. *Harvard Business Review, 69*(1), 131–139.

Hayes, R. H., Wheelwright, S. C., & Clark, K. B. (1988). *Dynamic manufacturing.* New York: Free Press.

Heskett, J. L., Sasser, W. E., & Hart, C. W. L. (1990). *Service breakthroughs.* New York: Free Press.

Hrebiniak, L. G., & Joyce, W. F. (1984). *Implementing strategy.* New York: Macmillan.

Irvin, R. A., & Michaels, E. G. (1989, Summer). Core skills: Doing the right things right. *The McKinsey Quarterly,* 4–19.

Juran, J. M. (1989). *Juran on leadership for quality.* New York: Free Press.

Landy, F. J., & Farr, J. L. (1980). *Performance rating. Psychological Bulletin, 87,* 72–107.

Longenecker, C. O., & Gioia, D. A. (1988, Winter). Neglected at the top—Executives talk about executive appraisal. *Sloan Management Review,* 41–47.

Longenecker, C. O., & Gioia, D. A. (1991, Fall). SMR Forum: Ten myths of managing managers. *Sloan Management Review,* 81–90.

Lovelock, C. H. (1991). *Federal Express quality improvement program.* Lausanne, Switzerland: International Institute for Management Development (IMD).

Maskell, B. (1991). *Performance measurement.* Cambridge, MA: Productivity Press.

Mohrman, A. M., Resnick-West, S. M., & Lawler, E. E. (1989). *Designing performance appraisal systems.* San Francisco: Jossey-Bass.

Mohrman, S. A., Mohrman, A. M., & Cohen, S. G. (1991). *Human resource strategies for lateral integration in high technology settings.* Los Angeles: Center for Effective Organizations, University of Southern California, CEO Publication 691–11 (196).

Prahalad, C. K., & Hamel, G. (1990). The core competencies of the corporation. *Harvard Business Review, 78*(3), 79–91.

Rockhart, J. F. (1979). Chief executives define their own data needs. *Harvard Business Review, 57*(2), 81–93.

Rodgers, T. J. (1990). No excuses management. *Harvard Business Review, 68*(4), 84–98.

Schlesinger, L. A., & Heskett, J. L. (1991). The service-driven company. *Harvard Business Review, 69*(5), 71–81.

Schneier, C. E., Beatty, R. W., & Shaw, D. G. (1992). Why measure the CEO's performance. In R. J. Niehaus & K. F. Price (Eds.), *Bottom line results from human resource planning* (pp. 247–260). New York: Plenum.

Schneier, C. E. (1991). In executing strategy: The new battleground in business competition. In C. E. Schneier (Ed.), *Human resource strategies for the '90's: A basis for competitive advantage* (pp. 3–11). New York: AMACOM.

Schneier, C. E. (1991). Measuring and assessing top executive performance. In M. L. Rock & L. A. Berger (Eds.), *The compensation handbook* (pp. 520–532). New York: McGraw-Hill.

Schneier, C. E. (1989). Implementing recognition and rewards at the strategic level. *Human Resource Planning, 12*(3), 205–220.

Stalk, G., & Hout, T. M. (1990). *Competing against time.* Free Press.

Stalk, F., Evans, P., & Shulman, L. E. (1992). Competing on capabilities: The new rules of corporate strategy. *Harvard Business Review, 69*(2), 57–69.

Stanich, P. J. (Ed.) (1982). *Implementing strategy: making strategy happen.* Cambridge, MA: Ballinger.

Tichy, N., & Charan, R. (1989). Speed, simplicity, and self-confidence: An interview with Jack Welch. *Harvard Business Review, 66*(5), 112–120.

Tichy, N., & Charan, R. (1990; Nov.—Dec.). Citicorp faces the world: An interview with John Reed. *Harvard Business Review,* 135–144.

Training (1988, June). Appraising performance appraisals, 16–17.

Tregoe, B. B. et al. (1989). *Vision in action.* New York: Simon & Schuster.

Ulrich, D., & Lake, D. (1990). *Organization capability.* New York: Wiley.

Zeithaml, V. A., Parasuraman, A., & Berry, L. L. (1990). *Delivering quality service.* New York: Free Press.

READING 15

A SOLUTION TO THE PERFORMANCE APPRAISAL FEEDBACK ENIGMA

Herbert H. Meyer

Executive Overview

It is hard to dispute the value of the ubiquitous formal performance appraisal programs used in almost all large organizations. In theory, these programs should serve important organizational objectives. Each employee should be evaluated at least annually and be given feedback to communicate how he or she is performing. In practice, however, most managers find these feedback interviews distasteful. Unless constrained by some sort of administrative pressure, like a subordinate sign-off requirement, managers are likely to ignore the responsibility.

The traditional manager-to-subordinate performance appraisal feedback interview is becoming anachronistic in our culture. The appraisal feedback interview is a very authoritarian procedure—a parent-child type of exchange. Most modern organizations are moving away from authoritarian management toward an involvement-oriented working environment. A performance review discussion based on the subordinate's self review fits an involvement-oriented climate much better than the traditional top-down performance review discussion. It also has the advantage of forcing the manager into a counseling mode, rather than serving as a judge. Research has shown that performance review discussions based on self-review prove to be more productive and satisfying than traditional manager-initiated appraisal discussions.

To say that the performance appraisal feedback problem has been an enigma for managers and personnel specialists is probably a glaring understatement. Formal programs to evaluate and document the job performance of subordinates and then provide feedback to the respective subordinates have been around at least as long as there have been personnel departments in organizations. The appraisal and feedback program is one of the psychologists' and personnel specialists' popular topics in the personnel literature. There have been literally thousands of articles on this topic in journals in their personnel field during the last seventy-five years. Most of these articles generally applaud the virtues of the performance

Source: "A Solution to the Performance Appraisal Feedback Enigma" by Herbert H. Meyer, *Academy of Management Executive*, Feb., 1991, Vol. 5, pp. 68–76.

appraisal and feedback process, lament their lack of success, then present suggested solutions to the program. This format has not changed much over the years.

Problems experienced with performance appraisal programs are myriad. Significant evidence has shown that most managers find the program onerous and distasteful.[1] The following scenario depicts a situation that many managers have probably faced in dealing with the performance appraisal feedback problem:

> Jane Novak was preparing for the annual performance appraisal review discussion scheduled with Henry Buckner. She remembered the unpleasant experience she had in a similar discussion a year ago. Henry's performance since that discussion had been tolerable, but mediocre at best. While there were many aspects of the job where Henry's performance could be improved, she planned to focus on only two or three areas where improvement was especially needed.

> Last year in her first appraisal discussion with Henry, he reacted very defensively to any suggestions she made for improving performance. He was especially annoyed by the fact that the overall rating she had assigned was only "Very Satisfactory." In fact, he appealed the rating, but fortunately Jane's boss supported her judgment. Customarily, most professionals in the company were rated as either "Outstanding" or "Excellent." While distributions weren't published, it was generally known that only a small percentage received ratings below "Excellent" on the scale. Yet, Jane couldn't in good conscience rate Henry above "Very Satisfactory," which was the midpoint on the scale.

> Jane hated to conduct these annual review discussions, especially with those for whom she couldn't justify an "Outstanding" overall rating. The discussions often seemed to do more harm than good. Her relationships with Henry, for example, had been strained since their annual review discussion last year.

Is Jane's experience with the annual performance review discussion unusual? Do her reactions indicate that she is a poor manager? The answer to both questions is no.

Experience with appraisal programs shows that unless administrative pressures are applied to ensure that people are appraised and feedback given, the programs invariably die out very rapidly. Managers just do not carry out the process, even though departmental policy may call for it. Most organizations have found that a subordinate sign-off procedure must be used to guarantee that appraisals are completed and feedback is given.

IS APPRAISAL FEEDBACK USEFUL?

Starting about 30 years ago at G.E., we carried out an intensive series of studies on the performance appraisal and feedback process. Followup surveys showed that the majority of employees expressed more uncertainty about the status of their performance in their managers' opinions after a performance appraisal interview than before. Evidently, in many cases the manager's formal feedback was discrepant with the informal signals they had been receiving about his or her view of their job performance. As Dave DeVries observed in a newsletter published by the Center for Creative Leadership a few years ago, most people get the feedback they consider to be really reliable in indirect, obscure ways. They judge the boss's mood, talk with the boss's secretary, note whether or not they are invited to important meetings, whether or not their opinion is sought on important matters, and so on.

A great deal of evidence, from our General Electric research and that reported in the literature, has shown that there is a strong tendency to distort appraisals toward favorable reviews when feedback must be given. For example, the federal government introduced a merit pay plan for mid-level employees about ten years ago. A rating of "fully successful" or better is needed to qualify for a merit increase. A recent study showed that 99.5 percent were eligible.[2]

Managers learn through unpleasant experience that negative feedback not only results in the employee having negative feelings, but it also too often results in deteriorated rather than improved performance. Consequently, because of this positive distortion, subordinates may get misleading information which is often inconsistent with administrative decisions such as salary actions, promotion, and demotions. Such distorted ratings sometimes cause trouble when the manager wants to fire a poor performer. The manager may decide that a certain employee who has consistently performed inadequately should be demoted or fired. Yet, the record may show that this employee's performance has been consistently rated as "very satisfactory."

FEW "GOOD" PROGRAMS

Surveys of companies with appraisal programs have repeatedly revealed that few are satisfied with its performance appraisal program. A survey of 200 large companies conducted by Psychological Associates showed that 70 percent of employees said they were more confused than enlightened by the performance appraisal feedback they received. Similarly, an American Society of Personnel Administrators survey concluded that less than ten percent of companies have reasonably successful performance appraisal programs.

A recent nationwide survey of 3,500 companies showed that the most frequently mentioned human resource concern was the organization's performance appraisal system. Based on another survey reported in *Industry Week,* the author summarized that, "The handling of performance reviews is little short of disastrous—a periodic agony thrust on both bosses and subordinates."[3]

In a recent article in *Personnel Management,* after an exhaustive study of appraisal programs in the public sector the author observed, "The chances of failure in operating appraisal schemes far outweigh the chances of success. Many

The manager may decide that a certain employee who has consistently performed inadequately should be demoted or fired. Yet, the record may show that this employee's performance has been consistently rated as "very satisfactory."

organizations have failed. Many others have systems which have degenerated into sterile paper chases, satisfying personnel departments' thirst for forms and justifying their existence but contributing little to the quality of organizational performance. Appraisal in practice tends to become a grand annual convulsion, more of a bureaucratic colossus than a means of insuring continuing development of people."[4]

R. E. Kopelman, in his book *Managing Productivity in Organizations* noted that most managers regard the performance appraisal interview as a fundamentally unpleasant situation—one to be avoided, postponed, or handled hurriedly.[5] A similar conclusion was reached by Napier and Latham based on their survey of appraisal programs in practice. They found that most appraisers saw little or no practical value in conducting performance appraisal interviews. No potential positive or negative consequences were generally foreseen, unless negative information was fed back and in those cases, the appraiser usually experienced aversive consequences.[6]

WHY ARE PROGRAMS RETAINED?

If the results of appraisal and feedback programs have been so negative, why have they persisted? Why do we keep butting our heads against the wall and continue the search for a solution when the quest for this utopia seems so hopeless? I am sure we persist because the idea seems so logical, so common-sensible. Appraisal and feedback should serve important administrative and developmental objectives.

Feedback regarding job performance seems necessary to justify administrative decisions, such as whether a salary increase is awarded and the size of the increase, or whether an employee should be transferred to another job or scheduled for promotion. Feedback should contribute to improved performance. The positive effect of feedback on performance has always been an accepted psychological principal.

It is also well established that feedback designed to reinforce or alter behavior is most effective if provided when the behavior occurs. Daily coaching is more valuable for this purpose than a once-a-year discussion. However, most personnel managers insist that their managers schedule an annual, formally documented review to ensure that every employee gets at least some feedback about his or her job performance. This annual feedback interview is intended to provide a clear message to employees about their performance and to motivate them to improve.

SPLIT ROLES

In some organizations, administrative feedback, such as communicating planned salary action, is separated from motivational and developmental feedback. Norman Maier, a noted industrial psychologist, recommended this more than thirty years ago. He ascertained that when the supervisor appraises a subordinate for administrative purposes, he or she is serving as a judge. If the supervisor is to effectively motivate a subordinate and provide guidance for development, he or she must serve as a counselor. Maier maintained that being both judge and counselor is incompatible. A person being judged is likely to be defensive. For counseling to be effective, the employee must be receptive to advice and suggestion, not defensive.[7]

One of our G.E. studies in which almost 100 actual appraisal interviews were observed, supported Norm Maier's contention.[8] Managers were required to communicate a salary decision and suggestions for performance improvement in the same interview. We observed that subordinate's defensive reactions were so common, and the ego involvement in the salary decision so powerful, that attempts to counsel the employee about needed performance improvement were mostly futile.

Our recommendation that salary action appraisal and motivational and developmental appraisal be accomplished in separate programs has not been widely accepted—at least not in the United States. Surveys show that in most organizations, both types of appraisals are covered in the same interview. Evidently this is not true in Great Britain where a recent survey of appraisal practices in large companies revealed that appraisals for the two different purposes were separated in 85 percent of the responding companies.[9]

Commitment is not likely to be engendered in today's employees by interacting with them in a control-oriented manner.

Based on my experience, I still maintain very strongly that appraisal for the two different purposes should be separated. I will focus here principally on motivational and developmental appraisal discussions. How can the process be more effective? I think the answer is to change our approach to the process.

CONTROL VERSUS INVOLVEMENT-ORIENTED MANAGEMENT

The traditional workforce management approach is to achieve efficiency by imposing management control over workers' behavior. However, it is becoming clear that a control-oriented approach to management is less effective. Our culture has changed. To remain competitive, organizations must elicit the commitment of employees at all levels. Commitment is not likely to be engendered in today's employees by interacting with them in a control-oriented manner. Employees want to be respected, to be in the know, involved, and to be treated as important individuals rather than as "hands."

The conventional approach to performance appraisal and feedback is certainly consistent with the control-oriented approach to management. It fits perfectly in a bureaucratically run organization. It is incompatible with an involvement-oriented management style.

A CHANGED APPROACH

The traditional approach to appraisal—where the manager completes an evaluation form and meets with the employee to communicate the appraisal—is becoming *anachronistic* in our culture. Performance appraisal conducted in the traditional manner is highly authoritarian. When a manager sits down with an employee for an appraisal, there is no doubt about who is the "boss" and who is in the subordinate or dependent role. It is a *parent-child* type of exchange.

Our culture has been moving away from authoritarianism for at least the last fifty years. Few people like a dictatorial boss and no one wants to have his or her dependence accentuated. People want to be involved, respected, treated as equals and for this reason, involvement-oriented management has become popular. Most performance appraisal programs are inconsistent with this management style.

THE USE OF SELF APPRAISAL

The conventional approach to performance appraisal is sometimes appropriate when the subordinate is dependent on the supervisor—for new employees, trainees, or perhaps for people in highly structured jobs. It is not appropriate, however, for most employees. It is certainly inappropriate for professionals and administrators. For employees who are not in an obviously dependent role, an appraisal discussion designed to serve communication, motivation, and development purposes should be based on the subordinate's *self appraisal*.

About twenty years ago, Glenn Bassett and I conducted another study at G.E. which demonstrated that appraisal discussions between manager and subordinate based on the subordinate's self-review, were significantly more constructive and satisfying to both parties than those based on the manager's appraisal. It also resulted in significant improvement in job performance. Even though these discussions also communicated a salary decision, focusing on the subordinate's self-review was definitely more favorable.[10]

ADVANTAGES OF SELF-REVIEW

Self-review has several advantages. First, it enhances the subordinate's dignity and self respect. The employee is not forced into a dependent role. Second, it places the manager into the role of counselor, not judge. Third, it is more likely to elicit employee commitment to any development plans or goals formulated in the discussion. That is, the subordinate is more likely to develop a feeling of ownership in plans and goals which he or she helped to create.

A fourth and major advantage of the self-review approach to the appraisal discussion was mentioned previously. That is, discussion based on the subordinate's review of his or her own performance is likely to be more satisfying to both parties and more productive than is the more traditional manager-to-subordinate review. Indeed, a number of studies seem to support that satisfaction with appraisal discussion results is strongly related to subordinate contribution and participation in the discussion.[11]

The biggest problem with this approach is that it violates traditional mores regarding the proper relationship between boss and subordinate. This is probably why the results of our experiment on self appraisals have not been widely applied. Certainly, supervisors participating in appraisal discussions based on subordinates' self-review have to some extent lost the value of their acquired credentials as the "superior."

Another disadvantage of self-review is the self-serving bias expected to inflate the self-appraisal. However, research has shown that this "leniency error" can be minimized by orienting the self analysis toward self development rather than appraisal for administrative purposes. In fact, self reviews have proved to be superior to supervisory reviews in identifying individual strengths and shortcomings.[12]

ELIMINATE THE "GRADING"

To improve the value of a feedback discussion based on self-review, the "grading" aspect should be eliminated. Assigning a numerical or adjectival grade, such as "satisfactory," "excellent," "adequate," "outstanding," or "poor" to overall performance or specific performance tends to obstruct rather than facilitate constructive discussion.

In addition, I recommend eliminating the formal grading aspect of a performance appraisal program used for administrative purposes. Most people in business find grading somewhat demeaning. It treats a mature person like a school child. The administrative action taken, such as the amount of salary increase or a promotion will communicate an overall appraisal better than will a grade. Recognition can certainly be given and improvement needs discussed without necessarily assigning grades to performance.

CONTENT OF THE DISCUSSION

Usually, formal performance appraisal discussions are scheduled annually. The major purpose is to provide a periodic summary of job performance and future possibilities. This discussion, if based on self-review, will provide the supervisor with the *subordinate's perspective* of the job, goals, problems, and responsibilities. Specifically, this annual discussion might cover:

1. Overall progress—an analysis of accomplishments and shortcomings.
2. Problems encountered in meeting job requirements.
3. Opportunities to improve performance.
4. Long range plans, opportunities—for the job and for the individual's career.
5. General discussion of possible plans and goals for the coming year.

To be effective, a goal-setting program must be a continuous process.

If a goal setting program is being used, such as Management by Objectives, this annual review discussion is not the best place to establish detailed job goals for the year. To be effective, a goal-setting program must be a continuous process. Several meetings may be needed to propose, negotiate, and agree on goals. Review discussions should be held more than once a year. In many jobs, quarterly reviews may be appropriate, while in other jobs progress review discussions may be needed monthly or weekly.

THE SUPERVISOR'S ROLE

Even though the subordinate has the lead role in the annual review discussion, the supervisor is not passive. The supervisor should prepare by noting the points he or she would like to make and how to present them. Actually, the supervisor is in a better position to give the employee recognition and suggest changes in activities or behavior when reacting to instead of initiating all input. The supervisor's role becomes that of "counselor" rather than judge or "the boss."

NEED FOR TRAINING

If self-review is adopted as the medium for an annual review, it will not obviate the need for training. Training supervisors to handle this type of discussion could be valuable. It need not be any more extensive than the training given for conventional appraisal programs. I can envision, for example, a behavior modeling training program which covers such topics as how to deal with an overly favorable self appraisal, an unrealistically self-deprecating review, an important problem or development need not brought up by the subordinate, and so on.

In addition, employees will need guidance on how to prepare for and conduct a self-review discussion. As a minimum, instructional materials, perhaps in the form of a brief manual, should be provided.

HOW WILL ADMINISTRATIVE DECISIONS BE MADE?

Performance appraisal programs are often used as the basis for compensation and promotion decisions. If the type of performance review discussion proposed here is directed only to communication and development objectives, how should those administrative decisions be made and communicated?

> *As indicated earlier, I strongly believe that appraisal for development should be separated from appraisal for compensation or promotion. The annual discussion based on a self-review is designed to stimulate self development and to open communication channels to improve the working relationship between supervisor and subordinate. A performance appraisal discussion in which salary and/or promotion decisions are communicated does not provide a desirable climate for achieving communication and development objectives.[13]*

Administrative decisions pertaining to merit raises or promotions are too important to the organization to be made by supervisors alone. Few supervisors are all-seeing, all-knowing persons. They have their own idiosyncrasies, failings, biases. In some cases, a supervisor may hide an especially effective employee to ensure continued achievement of his or her unit's objectives. Sometimes a supervisor is threatened by an unusually effective subordinate.

An administrative decision, such as on merit pay or promotion, almost always constitutes a zero-sum game. If differentiations are made, for each winner there must be one or more losers. Identifying the winners is extremely important to the organization as a whole, and therefore these should be organizational decisions, not decisions made by individual supervisors.

A growing trend in large organizations is to use an "annual human resources review" procedure to appraise the performance and potential of all employees. Peer-level managers in each division meet as a team with their manager to discuss the performance and potential of all employees who report to them. Using a team of people to evaluate individual performance provides a broader perspective in appraising employees than individual assessment. It not only provides a more comprehensive and objective evaluation of each employee's performance, potential, and development needs, but it also minimizes the effects of individual biases based on distorted emphases, prejudicial viewpoints, and limited perspectives.

Even though some of the managers in this process may have minimal exposure to some of the employees, they can contribute by insisting that judgments are backed by objective and behavioral evidence. After all, each participating manager has an important stake in the process. If another manager's employee is identified as a winner, one or more of his or her "winners" might become losers.

Appraisals resulting from a team meeting of this kind are more likely to be accepted by employees. It is more difficult to challenge an appraisal formulated by group consensus. Moreover, when a supervisor communicates a merit pay decision to a subordinate, it is less likely that their working relationship will deteriorate. This is not the case when a merit pay decision is made by the supervisor acting alone.

The annual human resources review process has additional benefits that more than justify the investment of time. Each participating manager will become thoroughly familiar with the responsibilities and performance characteristics of each employee in the department. It may clarify expectations regarding responsibilities of specific individuals or positions. It often defines and solves departmental workflow problems. The participating managers may formulate strategy and action plans for more effectively using human resources to achieve department objectives.

SUMMARY

I think the administrative and developmental objectives of the performance appraisal process should be addressed in separate programs. To achieve communication, counseling, and development objectives, I believe very strongly that our traditional top-down approach to performance appraisal is anachronistic, passé, and obsolete. It is a parent-child type of exchange that is inconsistent with cultural values that have evolved in modern organizations. It often proves to be an embarrassing experience for both parties involved and it accentuates the dependent role of the subordinate. This relationship is appropriate only in a control-oriented management environment. Effective organizations are moving away from the control-oriented approach toward an involvement-oriented climate designed to elicit commitment on the part of employees at all levels. Even the term "subordinate" is eschewed in modern organizations.

In most organizations, if supervisors are constrained to use the traditional supervisor rating and feedback approach to the annual review discussion, it would be better to abandon the program altogether. Conversely, if one concedes that it is desirable for supervisors to have some sort of annual review discussion with each of their direct reports, a discussion based on self-review can be valuable and constructive.

Endnotes

[1] See David De Vries comments in the June 1978 Center for Creative Leadership Newsletter regarding his survey of 1,450 managers on their experiences with the communication of performance appraisals.

[2] This finding was based on a federal government study which was cited in an article entitled, "Grading 'Merit Pay'," in the November, 1988 issue of *Newsweek.*

[3] The four survey results described here were cited in an article entitled "Performance Review: Examining the Eye of the Beholder" by Berkeley Rice in the December 1985 issue of *Across the Board* (a journal published by the Conference Board in New York).

[4] J. George, "Appraisal in the Public Sector: Dispensing with the Big Stick," *Personnel Management,* May, 1986, 32–35.

[5] R. E. Kopelman, *Managing Productivity in Organizations: A Practical, People-Oriented Perspective,* (New York: McGraw-Hill, 1986).

[6] N. K. Napier and G. P. Latham, "Outcome Expectancies of People Who Conduct Performance Appraisals," *Personnel Psychology,* 1986, Vol. 39, No. 4, 827–837.

[7] Norman Maier's 1958 book on this subject, *The Appraisal Interview: Objectives, Methods, and Skills,* published by Wiley, is still widely used in training programs and frequently referred to by writers in the field.

[8] This study was reported in a 1965 *Harvard Business Review* article entitled, "Split Roles in Performance Appraisal." A shortened version of the article was republished in 1989 as an *"HBR* Retrospect," since the original 1965 article was one of HBRs ten best-selling reprints.

[9] This finding was reported in a 1985 article in the British journal, *Personnel Management.* The article, by H. Murlis and A. Wright, was entitled, "Rewarding the Performance of the Eager Beaver."

[10] This study was reported in a 1968 article in *Personnel Psychology* entitled, "Performance Appraisal Based on Self-Review." Incidentally, recently a student, P. R. Simmons, in our Ph.D. program in industrial/organizational psychology at the University of South Florida, replicated this study with a few modifications for a dissertation project. His study sample consisted of clerical workers. I would expect their jobs to be fairly highly structured, so that perhaps the traditional top-down approach to appraisal might be appropriate. As an added twist, he obtained a measure of the degree to which each of the participating departments was run in a democratic or authoritarian manner. He found the self-review approach to appraisal to be especially effective in democratically run departments. Subordinate motivation to improve performance and supervisor satisfaction with the results of the appraisal program were significantly more favorable under the self-review condition.

[11] The positive effects of subordinate participation in appraisal discussions have been documented in a number of articles relating to performance appraisal, including: D. J. Campbell and C. Lee, "Self-Appraisal in Performance Evaluation: Development Versus Evaluation," *Academy of Management Review,* 1988, Vol. 13, No. 2, 302–324; D. M. Herold, R. C. Liden, and M. L. Leatherwood, "Using Multiple Attributes to

Assess Sources of Performance Feedback," *Academy of Management Journal,* 1987, Vol. 30, No. 4, 826–835; J. M. Ivancevich and J. T. McMahon, "The Effects of Goal Setting, External Feedback, and Self-Generated Feedback on Outcome Variables: A Field Experiment," *Academy of Management Journal,* 1982, Vol. 25, No. 2, 359–372; R. L. Dipboye and R. de Pontbriand, "Correlates of Employee Reactions to Performance Appraisals and Appraisal Systems," *Journal of Applied Psychology,* 1981, Vol. 66, No. 2, 248–251; C. C. Manz and H. P. Sims, Jr., "Self Management as a Substitute for Leadership: A Social Learning Perspective," *Academy of Management Review,* 1980, Vol. 5, No. 3, 361–367; R. J. Burke, W. Weitzel, and T. Weir, "Characteristics of Effective Performance Review and Development Interviews: Replication and Extension," *Personnel Psychology,* 1978, Vol. 31, No. 4, 903–919; H. H. Meyer, "The Annual Performance Review Discussion—Making it Effective," *Personnel Journal,* October 1977; and M. M. Greller, "Subordinate Participation and Reactions to the Appraisal Interview," *Journal of Applied Psychology,* 1975, Vol. 6, No. 5, 544–549.

[12]The superiority of self reviews over supervisory appraisals for self-development purposes was well documented by Paul Mabe and Stephen West in a June 1982 article in the *Journal of Applied Psychology* (Vol. 67, No. 3), which presented a summary of the results of 55 studies in which self-evaluations were compared with other measures of performance. In a similar survey of research on self appraisal, George Thornton found that self-appraisals showed less "halo" than ratings made by supervisors. In other words, subordinates rating their own performance identified specific strengths and shortcomings better than did their respective supervisors. This study was reported in an article entitled, "Psychometric Properties of Self-Appraisals of Job Performance," in the Summer 1980 issue of *Personnel Psychology* (Vol. 33, No. 2).

[13]The study referred to in endnote 8 showed quite clearly that the supervisor's role as "judge" in communicating an administrative decision, such as a scheduled merit raise, created an almost impossible climate for providing counseling or development planning effectively. More often than not, the subordinate's evaluation of his or her supervisor actually declined as a result of the dual-purpose appraisal discussion. This was probably because in the great majority of cases, the planned administrative action communicated, such as the size of the scheduled merit raise, fell short of the subordinate's expectation.

WORK ATTITUDES AND JOB WITHDRAWAL

INTRODUCTION

Individuals at work can either be satisfied or dissatisfied with their job and/or their organization. The attitudes these people bring to their work can have a profound impact on the effectiveness of their organization. In this section we present readings that explore how one's feelings at work affect the organization and how these feelings can be monitored and managed by organizational leaders—especially those responsible for human resource management.

Our first reading by Reichheld focuses on the impact that worker attitudes have on behavior related to one group of people external to the company—customers. In the article "Loyalty-Based Management," Reichheld argues that developing loyalty among customers is the key to gaining and maintaining competitive advantage in the ever-expanding service sector of the economy. To build loyalty among customers, however, one must first develop loyalty among employees who will be delivering that service to customers. Customers build their trust with a company's employees, not its executives, and when employees leave because they are dissatisfied with the organization, this severs the link between the organization and its customer base. Reichheld then goes on to delineate the steps organizations need to go through to become "loyalty leaders" and documents the benefits of this status in terms of superior financial performance and competitive position.

Our second reading by Jerald Greenberg provides further guidance for companies that wish to generate loyalty and commitment from their employees. In his article, "Looking Fair versus Being Fair: Managing Impressions of Organizational Justice," Greenberg notes the central importance of perceptions of fairness in organizational life. Employees who feel they have been treated fairly are much more likely to respond positively to organizational requests and maintain membership in the organization. Greenberg notes that "acting fair" in one's own mind is simply not enough; those managing human resources must engage in impression management to make sure employees are convinced of the fairness of various acts or policies. Greenberg discusses several tactics for managing these impressions. Some of these tactics (e.g., excuses, justifications, and apologies) are defensive in that they try to directly change perceptions of an employee who has had a negative outcome (e.g., failure to gain a promotion). Other tactics (e.g., entitling, enhancements, and reputation building) are assertive, in that they try to establish a perception of goodwill on the part of the employer prior to any negative outcome occurring. In this way, when something negative does happen to the employee, he or she will be less likely to perceive this as a major injustice. Together, the readings present a strong case for why companies should care about employees' work attitudes, and also give clear guidance to those in human resource management who might want to enhance worker attitudes.

LOYALTY-BASED MANAGEMENT

Frederick F. Reichheld

Despite a flurry of activities aimed at serving customers better, only a few companies have achieved meaningful, measurable improvements in customer loyalty. In manufacturing as well as services, business leaders intuitively know that when customer loyalty goes up, profits do too. Yet few companies have systematically revamped their operations with customer loyalty in mind.

Instead, most companies adopt improvement programs on an ad hoc basis. Hearing about the success of a loyalty leader such as MBNA's credit card business, which loses customers at half the industry rate, companies copy one or two of MBNA's practices. They set up customer-recovery units, for instance, that try to save defecting customers—who, because they are probably less homogeneous than MBNA's customer base, may or may not be profitable. Or they adopt MBNA's policy of delivering employee paychecks in envelopes labeled "Brought to You by the Customer"—while failing to base the bonuses inside those envelopes on incentives that enhance customer value and loyalty. Not surprisingly, payoffs don't materialize.

Building a highly loyal customer base cannot be done as an add-on. It must be integral to a company's basic business strategy. Loyalty leaders like MBNA are successful because they have designed their entire business systems around customer loyalty. They recognize that customer loyalty is earned by consistently delivering superior value. By understanding the economic effects of retention on revenues and costs, loyalty leaders can intelligently reinvest cash flows to acquire and retain high-quality customers and employees. Designing and managing this self-reinforcing system is the key to achieving outstanding customer loyalty.

The economic benefits of customer loyalty often explain why one competitor is more profitable than another.

The economic benefits of high customer loyalty are considerable and, in many industries, explain the differences in profitability among competitors. When a company consistently delivers superior value and wins customer loyalty, market share and revenues go up, and the cost of acquiring and serving customers goes down. Although the additional profits allow the company to invest in new activities that enhance value and increase the appeal to customers, strengthening loyalty generally is not a matter of simply cutting prices or adding

Source: Reprinted by permission of *Harvard Business Review* "Loyalty-Based Management," by Frederick F. Reichheld, 71, no. 2 (March–April 1993): 64–73. Copyright 1993 by the President and Fellows of Harvard College; all rights reserved.

product features. The better economics mean the company can pay workers better, which sets off a whole chain of events. Increased pay boosts employee morale and commitment; as employees stay longer, their productivity rises and training costs fall; employees' overall job satisfaction, combined with their knowledge and experience, leads to better service to customers; customers are then more inclined to stay loyal to the company; and as the best customers and employees become part of the loyalty-based system, competitors are inevitably left to survive with less desirable customers and less talented employees.

The forces in a loyalty-based system are cumulative. The longer the cycle continues, the greater the company's financial strength. At MBNA, a 5% increase in retention grows the company's profits by 60% by the fifth year. And at State Farm Insurance Companies, another champion of customer loyalty, small increases in retention create substantial benefits for the company and its policyholders.

Learning how to compete on the basis of loyalty may be complex, but it is not mysterious. It requires, first of all, understanding the relationships between customer retention and the rest of the business and being able to quantify the linkages between loyalty and profits. Only then can daily decisions reflect systematic cost-benefit trade-offs. It involves rethinking four important aspects of the business—customers, product/service offerings, employees, and measurement systems. To get the full benefit of a loyalty-based system, all these facets must be understood and attended to simultaneously because each is essential to the workings of the whole. If any area is overlooked or misunderstood, the system will underperform. When all areas are aligned, they reinforce each other, and the results are outstanding.

THE "RIGHT" CUSTOMERS

Customers are obviously an essential ingredient of a loyalty-based system, and success depends on their staying with the company a long time. But not all customers are equal. Companies should target the "right" customers—not necessarily the easiest to attract or the most profitable in the short term but those who are likely to do business with the company over time. For various reasons, some customers don't ever stay loyal to one company, no matter what value they receive. The challenge is to avoid as many of these people as possible in favor of customers whose loyalty can be developed.

Demographics and previous purchase history give some indication of a customer's inherent loyalty. People who buy because of a personal referral tend to be more loyal than those who buy because of an advertisement. Those who buy at the standard price are more loyal than those who buy on price promotion. Home owners, middle-aged people, and rural populations also tend to be loyal, while highly mobile populations are inherently disloyal because they interrupt their business relations each time they move.

Finding loyal customers means taking a hard look at whom a company can deliver superior value to.

But generalizing about the right customer fails to take into account the fact that a customer who is disloyal and therefore expensive for one company may be valuable for another. USAA, a loyalty leader with a remarkable 98% retention rate in its field of auto insurance, has created a steady client base among military officers, a group known for frequent moves. Military officers are not very profitable for most insurers, but by developing a system tailored to that group's particular needs, USAA has made it possible and economical to keep them.

The heart of USAA's system is a centralized database and telephone-sales force that customers can access from anywhere in the world. The system itself rather than the insurance agent provides continuity with the customer. That continuity works to the customer's and company's advantage. The military officer doesn't have to find a new agent every time he or she is redeployed, and USAA doesn't have to transfer records or create new ones. More important, USAA avoids having to lure a new customer to replace the one it would have lost.

Finding loyal customers requires taking a hard look at what kinds of customers a company can deliver superior value to. If the analysis is done well, that customer segment will be fairly homogeneous, and that homogeneity improves the economics of serving the segment. MBNA, a loyalty leader in the credit card business, provides cards primarily to members of affinity groups such as the American Dental Association or the Georgetown University Alumni Association. Because members in these groups share important qualities, MBNA has been able to understand their common needs and has made adjustments to serve them well. Its data-processing systems are designed so every group can receive customized packages of services. As a result, MBNA keeps its customers once it gets them. When AT&T introduced its Universal Card, other credit card companies lost market share, but MBNA held its ground.

Historical attrition rates can also point the way to the most promising customer segments. Direct marketers such as L. L. Bean have accounting systems that track individual customers year by year. Other companies can get similar information by asking a sample of customers to reconstruct their purchase patterns from various suppliers over the past five years. This will reveal attrition rates and lifetime value for each type of customer.

Investments in improving service quality may be wasted if they are focused on customers the business should lose.

With knowledge of which customers are likely to be loyal comes knowledge of which customers are not. Companies can then direct resources away from customers who are likely to defect and toward those likely to stay. Special promotions and other kinds of pricing strategies aimed at acquiring new customers often backfire. Companies typically use pricing as a blunt instrument to bring customers in indiscriminately, when instead, they should use pricing to filter out precisely the customers unlikely to be loyal. Cable television companies talk about increasing retention rates but then recruit new customers via price promotions and free sampling—techniques that draw out of the woodwork precisely those customers hardest to keep. Those recruitment efforts merely load the pipeline with people who are inherently disloyal.

Even attempts to recover customers who threaten to leave are often a waste of resources. Investments in service-quality improvements may be counterproductive when they are focused on customers the business actually should get rid of. Auto insurers discovered that certain segments of young drivers were a drag on profits. It took ten years to break even on them, but due to high attrition, only

10% to 15% would stay that long. The industry also realized that it took at least four years before most companies could break even on the average customer, in part because of the high front-end commission paid to salespeople for signing new customers. If the customer didn't stay with the same insurer for four years, the company never recouped those costs.

LIFETIME PRODUCTS AND SERVICES

Once a company has identified the customers it should keep, it has to go about the business of keeping them. Often that means adding new products and services to meet customers' evolving needs. Companies that fail to use their knowledge of customers to develop the product or service those people will need next are leaving the door open for another company to lure them away. Although it is tempting to use new products to win whole new markets, it almost always makes better sense to stick with existing customer segments. Over time, the company develops intimate knowledge of those people, and then can make good intuitive market judgments. Also, it is easier to build sales volume with customers who already know the company than it is with newcomers. USAA, for example, having come to understand one narrow market segment inside and out, found it relatively easy to go beyond auto insurance to offer mutual funds, life insurance, health insurance, and credit cards.

When Entenmann's of New York, a loyal leader in specialty bakery products sold through grocery stores, saw its sales leveling off, it monitored customer purchase patterns in each local market. It discovered that as its core customers aged, they were looking for more fat-free and cholesterol-free products. Through direct contact with customers via telephone surveys and focus groups, the company found that consumers would buy those products from Entenmann's if they were available.

So the company had a choice. It could create a new line of products to serve those customers, or it could search for a whole new market segment. Ultimately, the company determined that it was much more economical to develop new fat- and cholesterol-free products than to go with another group of customers. Entenmann's new product line has been highly successful. It addressed the changing needs of the company's core clientele and even attracted new customers.

In yet another industry, Honda has emerged as the loyalty leader in the midpriced U.S. auto market. Life-cycle marketing has helped propel Honda's owner repurchase rate to 65%, versus an industry average of 40%. After the success of the subcompact Civic, Honda's next car, the Accord, was designed to meet the needs of Civic owners, who continued to care about reliability, conservative design, and value as they moved from their early twenties to marriage and family. Honda added the Accord wagon when it noticed customers defecting to other brands as their families grew.

By growing through the repeat purchases of its core customer base, Honda has maintained a relatively simple product line, and its manufacturing economics have benefited from this low product complexity. Honda's dealer and distribution system also benefits from low customer complexity in equally important, if less well-understood, ways.

One of the largest multifranchise dealers in the United States described this advantage as he saw it: "My Honda dealership is my most profitable because the company makes it so simple. There are fewer models and option packages. The key is the customers, who are very similar to one another." His sales and service operations are geared to the "Honda" customer. In contrast, he described his Mitsubishi dealership as a real challenge: "Salespeople have to deal with a lawyer buying a $30,000 Diamonte one minute, a construction worker buying a pickup truck the next." How can one salesperson (or service representative) develop proficiency with such customer complexity?

Curiously, Honda has had a tougher fight in Japan, where it remains a small player. Even though Honda had the same product advantages that resulted in its strong U.S. position, Toyota remains the dominant player in Japan because of its strong dealer network. In Japan, dealers don't have a lot of showrooms but instead rely on a direct sales force. Because sales-force turnover is low (less than 10% per year for Toyota), they get to know customers very well. It is this enduring bond that has outmuscled Honda. In the United States, where car salespeople turn over quickly (60% to 100% annually) and customers have virtually no relationship with the sales force, Honda's product advantage blasted right through to put it out ahead.

LOYAL EMPLOYEES

Many companies diminish their economic potential through human resource policies that ensure high employee turnover, in part because they can't quantify the economics of retaining employees. Executives might say they want to keep employees, but if doing so means raising salaries, their conviction soon fades. They question the wisdom of increasing pay by, say, 25% in order to decrease employee turnover by 5%. Yet the fact is that employee retention is key to customer retention, and customer retention can quickly offset higher salaries and other incentives designed to keep employees from leaving.

Customers build trust with a company's employees, not its executives; when the employees leave, that bond is broken.

The longer employees stay with the company, the more familiar they become with the business, the more they learn, and the more valuable they can be. Those employees who deal directly with customers day after day have a powerful effect on customer loyalty. Long-term employees can serve customers better than newcomers can; after all, a customer's contact with a company is through employees, not the top executives. It is with employees that the customer builds a bond of trust and expectations, and when those people leave, the bond is broken.

Companies wanting to increase customer loyalty often fail because they don't grasp the importance of this point. While conducting customer focus programs, they may be terminating or rotating the people who have the most influence on the customer's experience. While they are reengineering their business processes, they are failing to reengineer career paths, job content, and compensation so that employees will stay with the company long enough to learn the new processes.

Just as it is important to select the right kinds of customers before trying to keep them, a company must find the right kinds of employees before enticing them to stay. That raises the issue of hiring. The goal is not only to fill desks but also to find and hold onto workers who will continue to learn, to become more productive, and to create trusting relationships with customers. State Farm, the loyalty leader among auto insurance companies that sell through agents, has a distinctive agent-appointment strategy. Prospective agents may spend a year or more in a recruiting and selection process. During this time, they are in competition with several other well-qualified candidates. The lengthy process enables the company's field managers to select the best qualified person. State Farm often looks for candidates with roots in the community who are already likely to have long-term relationships with prospective customers.

One way for any company to find new hires who will likely stay is to look at the patterns of their own employees who defected early. Had they found the job at your company through newspaper ads, college recruiting, or personal referrals? Equally important, how long had they stayed with employers before coming to you? In a loyalty-based system, skills and education are important, but not as important as how long a prospective worker is expected to stay and grow with the business.

Although longevity deepens familiarity, some company policies render familiarity useless. Banks, for instance, are notorious for offering branch managers career paths that rotate them through a series of branch offices. Each time managers move, they take with them the knowledge learned at the branch where they put in their time. They have to start over again in each branch, building a network with the customers and the other employees. Their incentives to acquire the right customers and employees are reduced since it is their replacements who will reap the benefits. In a major bank with several hundred branches, branch managers who had been in the system an average of 12 years stayed at a given branch for only 2 years. Only one branch manager had remained in place and, not surprisingly, his office had the highest customer-retention rate in the entire system. It's worth noting that most banks have 50% to 100%-a-year teller turnover, which is also costly. Because most bankers cannot quantify the systems costs of these policies, they cannot justify the investments required to fix the situation.

Olive Garden managers' most valuable asset: the community knows and trusts them.

But not all businesses follow those practices. The highly successful Olive Garden restaurant chain goes against the industry norm of moving successful managers to open new restaurants or to run bigger ones every few years and letting assistants take over. The chain hires local managers whose major asset is that they are known and trusted in the community. These managers are then kept in place so their asset appreciates in value. Learning accumulates as people stay on the job. By becoming intelligent about the business, getting to know customers, and providing the advantages knowledge gives, long-time hires add value to the company.

Leo Burnett Company's strong position in the advertising industry is largely attributable to its slavish devotion to employee retention. Most advertising firms experience high turnover of their creative people, and they make a point of rotating people through various accounts. They also experience constant client churn accompanied by massive layoffs and severe downturns in revenues and profits. At Leo Burnett, in contrast, new staffers are assigned to their first account "for life," in the words of one executive. Layoffs are rare, and customer retention is high.

All other things being equal, the best people will stay with the company that pays them the most.

Even businesses that don't rely on direct relationships between customers and employees can benefit from boosting employee retention. USAA has an information system that lets any employee pull up a customer's records instantly, so customers don't have to speak with the same employee every time. But USAA's employee turnover of around 7%—one-third the industry average—is one of the most important reasons its productivity is the best in the business. The learning unleashed by employee retention helps in other ways. When the marketing department wants to know more about customer needs or reactions to a new product, they can hold a focus group meeting of employees, whose daily customer contact provides powerful insight.

Of course, employees won't stay and apply their knowledge unless they have an incentive to do so. All other things being equal, the best people will stay with the company that pays them the most. Loyalty leaders know this, and they share their "loyalty surplus" with employees as well as stockholders. They view their best employees as they do their best customers: once they've got them, they do everything possible to keep them. And they provide incentives in the form of higher salaries or bonuses and commissions that align the employees' self-interest with the interests of the company. Bonuses can be based on aggregate customer retention rates, and commissions can be designed to be small initially but grow the longer the customer stays with the company.

There are many ways reward programs can be structured to recognize loyalty. Olive Garden found that its experienced waiters and waitresses resented the fact that new hires were receiving the same base wage as they did, so management established a slightly higher base wage for employees who had served $25,000 of meals.

If employees are expected to be long-termers, companies can justify investing more in them. It becomes worthwhile to teach employees to do the right thing for the customer, which in turn leads to happier customers and ultimately to increased profits, which can be put toward the higher salaries of long-term employees. And the commitment to creating a loyalty-based system has spillover effects. Employees take pride in delivering value to a customer time and again. Their satisfaction in contributing to a positive goal is another thing that induces their loyalty to the company.

MEASURES OF LOYALTY

Even the best designed loyalty-based system will deteriorate unless an effective measurement system is established. Competitors, customer preferences, technologies, and employee capabilities are constantly changing. Measures establish the feedback loops that are the foundation of organizational learning. Only through effective learning can an organization consistently deliver value in an ever-changing world.

Unfortunately, most accounting systems do not measure what drives customer value. They can show the benefits of the one-year magic cure but not of programs and practices that take three to five years or longer to affect profits. Managers who have a year to earn a bonus or two years to turn a business around are forced to think of the usual shortcuts to higher profits: raising prices and cutting costs. Those actions alone rarely create value for customers, and although customers don't all leave at once, if they are not getting the best value, they will eventually turn to a competitor. To make matters worse, the best customers are often the first ones to go.

The first step in developing effective measures is to understand the cause-and-effect relationships in the system. The primary mission of a loyalty-based company is to deliver superior value to customers. Success or failure in this mission can be clearly measured by customer loyalty (best quantified by retention rate or share of purchases or both). Customer loyalty has three second-order effects: (1) revenue grows as a result of repeat purchases and referrals, (2) costs decline as a result of lower acquisition expenses and from the efficiencies of serving experienced customers, and (3) employee retention increases because job pride and satisfaction increase, in turn creating a loop that reinforces customer loyalty and further reducing costs as hiring and training costs shrink and productivity rises.

As costs go down and revenues go up, profits (the third-order effect) increase. Unless managers measure and monitor all of these economic relationships, they will default to their short-term, profit-oriented accounting systems, which tend to focus on only the second- and third-order effects. Focusing on these symptoms—instead of on the primary mission of delivering superior value to customers—often leads to decisions that will eventually reduce value and loyalty.

In the life insurance business, for instance, a five percentage point increase in customer retention lowers costs per policy by 18%. However, very few companies have quantified this relationship, and as a result, they focus their cost-reduction efforts on process reengineering and layoffs, which appear to lower costs but in fact lower employee motivation and retention, leading to lower customer retention, which increases costs!

When life insurers want to grow, they hire more agents, raise commissions, drop prices (to new customers only, if possible) and/or add new products. The result: more inexperienced salespeople (low productivity and high cost) bringing in the wrong kind of customer (disloyal price shoppers) with escalating costs of product-line complexity. The only way to avoid these mistakes in insurance, or any business, is to develop systems that allow employees to track and understand the cash-flow consequences of changing customer loyalty.

Between 65% and 85% of customers who defect say they were satisfied with their former supplier.

It is only the true defection of the target customer that should be of concern because that means something may have gone wrong, and if it has, it's worth a considerable amount of effort to find out what. It could mean that another company has done something innovative that gives customers a better value.

It is important to define customer retention carefully and what it means in a particular industry. In the auto business, for instance, a manufacturer should worry about a customer who switches to another brand—but not about a customer who sells his or her car and takes public transportation. In an industrial setting, customers might shift a percentage of their purchases to competitors, so changes in purchase patterns should be watched as carefully as customer defections.

Customer satisfaction is not a surrogate for customer retention. While it may seem intuitive that increasing customer satisfaction will increase retention and therefore profits, the facts are contrary. Between 65% and 85% of customers who defect say they were satisfied or very satisfied with their former supplier. In the auto industry, satisfaction scores average 85% to 95%, while repurchase rates average only 40%. Current satisfaction measurement systems are simply not designed to provide insight into how many customers stay loyal to the company and for how long.

STATE FARM'S LOYALTY-BASED SYSTEM

State Farm insures more than 20% of the nation's households. It has the lowest sales and distribution costs among insurance companies of its type, yet its agents' incomes are generally higher than agents working for the competition. Its focus on customer service has resulted in faster growth than most other multiple-line insurers, but rather than being consumed by growth, its capital has mushroomed (all through internally generated surplus) to more than $18 billion, representing the largest capital base of any financial services company in North America. Because of careful customer selection and retention, State Farm is able to price below the competition and still build the capital necessary to protect its policyholders in years such as 1992 when they incurred $4.7 billion in catastrophe losses.

These impressive achievements can be traced to State Farm's well-designed loyalty-based system. State Farm began by choosing the right customers. The company was founded more than 70 years ago to serve better than average drivers, first in farming communities and now throughout suburban and urban markets across the United States and in three Canadian provinces. State Farm agents work from neighborhood offices, which allows them to build long-lasting relationships with their customers and provide the personal service that is the basis of the corporate philosophy.

This kind of personal service can start at an early age. Teenagers in State Farm households are usually written while still under the umbrella of their parents' policies. Many State Farm agents routinely sit new drivers down in their offices for a "dutch uncle" speech about the responsibilities of driving and the impact an accident or ticket—particularly for drunken driving—would have on their rates. Also, in an effort to educate all teens on safe driving, agents have available company-produced safe-driving materials for high schools. All these efforts tend to make the young drivers that State Farm insures more careful, and their parents grateful for the interest and help.

When agents are rooted in the community, they often know who the best customers will be. For example, they can scan the local newspaper for the high school honor roll and be sure that their young customers' good grades are recognized with premium discounts. Agents make it their business to get to know the people they insure. The most powerful computer and the brightest underwriter at headquarters simply can't compete with that level of customer insight.

Pricing policies work as a magnet to retain good customers. At the end of three years, accident-free customers get a 5% discount, followed by another 5% decrease three years later. The discounts make customers feel they've earned special status and value, and they create a disincentive to jump to another company, where they might have to start all over again.

State Farm agents not only want to attract and keep good customers, they also have the incentive to do so. Commissions are structured to encourage long-term thinking. Agents receive the same compensation rate on new auto and fire policies as for renewals, thus rewarding agents for serving existing customers, not just for drawing in new business. Unlike organizations that say retention is important while pushing salespeople to find new customers, State Farm consistently conveys the message that both are important.

Remaining focused on its target customers, State Farm provides a full life-cycle product line. Rather than bringing in lots of new customers, the company's marketing efforts encourage existing customers to buy additional products, like home and life insurance. The homogeneity of their market means that one agent can sell and service everything. The full product line preserves the agent's relationship with the customer and allows the agent to learn more about the customer's needs. In addition to benefiting the policyholder and company, this approach serves the agent well, as multiple-line customers are less expensive for the agent to service than are single-line customers. Multiple-line customers have also proven to stay with the agent longer.

State Farm agents are also loyal. According to industry studies, more than 80% of newly appointed agents remain through their fourth year, compared with 20% to 40% for the rest of the industry. And the average agent at State Farm has 13 years of tenure, compared with 6 to 9 years for the industry. This retention advantage can be attributed both to the lengthy recruiting and selecting process before appointment and to the fact that State Farm agents are independent contractors who sell and service State Farm products exclusively. Because agents have built and invested in their own businesses, they are more likely to remain with State Farm than their counterparts representing other companies. In return, State Farm is loyal to its agents and distributes its products only through them. The company has built a marketing partnership with its agents and involves them in key decisions that affect them or their customers.

State Farm's loyalty-based system means its agents earn high compensation— though the company actually pays lower commissions.

Agent retention and customer retention reinforce one another. The agent who is committed to a long-term relationship with the company, and indeed, to his or her own business, is more likely to build lasting relationships with customers. In addition, loyal customers make life easier for the agents, who spend more time working with people they know and like and far less time chasing new customers. Finally, agents like being part of a system that consistently delivers superior value to customers. Agents' experience, plus the fact that they spend more time servicing and selling to proven customers, raises agents' productivity to 50% above industry norms.

State Farm's business systems support its focus on loyalty. Measures of customer retention and defections are distributed throughout the organization. Agents and employees at all levels know whether the system is working and can adjust their activities. Agents find a list of their nonrenewing customers each morning when they switch on their computers, which they can use to prompt telephone follow-ups to try to retain the account. And management can use the same kind of information as a check against policyholders' satisfaction with the service, product, and price they receive.

State Farm's success in building customer loyalty is reflected in retention rates that exceed 90%, consistently the best performance of all the national insurers that sell through agents. State Farm agents make more money by operating in a business system engineered for superior loyalty. And they are more productive, which makes it possible for them to earn superior compensation (after adjusting for the fact that State Farm agents pay their own expenses) while the company actually pays lower average commission rates. The result is a 10% cost advantage. The company also keeps its costs relatively low because it avoids excessive administrative and claims costs associated with acquiring and servicing a large percentage of new customers. State Farm's system provides outstanding value to its customers, benefits for its agents, and has created a company that is a financial powerhouse.

MANAGING FOR LOYALTY

The success of State Farm and other loyalty leaders shows the direct linkages between providing value for customers and a superior financial and competitive position. Doing the right thing for customers does not conflict with generating substantial margins. On the contrary, it is the only way to ensure profitability beyond the short term.

Creating a loyalty-based system in any company requires a radical departure from traditional business thinking. It puts creating customer value—not maximizing profits and shareholder value—at the center of business strategy, and it demands significant changes in business practice—redefining target customers, revising employment policies, and redesigning incentives.

Most important, if companies are really serious about delivering value and earning customer loyalty, they must measure it. And while senior executives may be daunted by the time and investment required to engineer an entire business system for high retention, they may have no alternative. Customer loyalty appears to be the only way to achieve sustainably superior profits.

Managing for loyalty serves the best interests of customers, employees, and investors. The only losers are the competitors who get the leftovers: an increasingly poor mix of customers and employees and an increasingly less tenable financial and market position. As loyalty leaders refine their ability to deliver value by more effectively harnessing the economics of loyalty, their advantages will multiply. Competitors must respond, or they will find it increasingly difficult to survive on the leftovers of the marketplace.

READING 17

LOOKING FAIR VS. BEING FAIR
Managing Impressions of Organizational Justice

Jerald Greenberg

Abstract

This paper conceives of organizational justice as an impression management process. Evidence is presented arguing that fairness is a desired social identity, and that people seek to present themselves as fair to themselves and others. Tactics used to cultivate an image of fairness are presented as they may be used in organizations. These include behaviors designed to mend a spoiled identity—"defensive tactics," such as accounts (including excuses and justifications) and apologies, and those intended to establish a particular identity—"assertive tactics," such as entitlings and enhancements. A discussion of the implications of this analysis focuses on the sincerity of fair impressions, organizational influences on fair identities, the benefits and liabilities of fair impressions, and provides cases of the management and mismanagement of impressions of fairness in and by organizations. In concluding, a plea is made for re-directing future research and theoretical efforts toward an impression management perspective of organizational justice.

In conjunction with a training exercise on developing managerial skills, I recently asked a group of managers, "What should your subordinates think about you in order for you to function effectively as a supervisor?" As evidenced by the following sample of responses, one of the most commonly expressed themes centered around the importance of being perceived as fair.

> To close a sale I have to get both the salesman and the customer to think they're being treated fairly.
>
> Used-car sales manager

> Almost anything I decide about office policy can be accepted if the staff thinks I've treated them fairly.
>
> Office manager at an insurance company

> If my crew doesn't think I'm fair, it's all over, I can't get anything done.
>
> Crew chief for a rural electric cooperative

> My teachers and students can think whatever they want about me, so long as they think I'm fair.
>
> Assistant principal of a high school

Even those who would prefer to dismiss these self-reports as unscientific data would have to admit that the sentiments expressed reflect a concern about the importance of fairness that is commonly espoused. Indeed, if news headlines of the late 1980s linking certain political and religious figures to morally unethical behaviors have taught us anything, it is that the mere *appearance* of an impropriety may be sufficient to erode a powerful figure's base of support, precipitating a fall from grace. What the managers in my training class seem to be saying is very similar—appearing to be fair helps get the job done.

Although the importance of looking fair on the job was expressed prominently by my managerial sample, the theme of impression management has been given little attention by the prevailing "reactive content" theories of organizational justice (Greenberg, 1987a), such as equity theory (Adams, 1965) or relative deprivation theory (e.g., Crosby, 1984), which traditionally have focused on the reactions of workers paid more than or less than comparably qualified others (e.g., for reviews, see Greenberg, 1982, 1987a; Mowday, 1987). This is not to say that purely anecdotal evidence provides the only inspiration for studying the appearance of fairness in organizations. On the contrary, a shift has been noted in recent social science theorizing away from intrapsychic theories (such as equity theory) toward more interpersonal approaches—both in reports of social psychological processes (e.g., Tetlock, 1985; Tetlock & Manstead, 1985) and organizational phenomena (e.g., Chatman, Bell, & Staw, 1986; Gardner & Martinko, 1988; Giacalone & Rosenfeld, 1987, 1990). As theorists (e.g., Bies, 1987a; Reis, 1981) begin to explore justice from an impression management perspective (Schlenker, 1980), it would appear that the study of organizational justice is beginning its journey along this tide.

The present paper advances an impression management orientation toward organizational justice. Such an approach is offered in the interest of promoting "theoretical pluralism" (Feyerabend, 1970), encouraging the study of organizational justice from more than one point of view. As such, it is not intended to completely supplant more traditional approaches, but rather, to provide an alternative that accounts for a broader array of organizational justice concerns. Toward this end, the paper will examine research and theory relevant to three core issues within the impression management literature (Tetlock, 1985; Tetlock & Manstead, 1985). Specifically, the paper will consider: (a) the extent to which fairness is a desired social identity, (b) the possible targets of fair impressions, and (c) the tactics used to achieve a fair identity. Following this, the implications of these analyses for future research and theory development will be considered. Before turning to this, however, I will begin by reviewing some germane background issues.

BACKGROUND: JUSTICE AS AN IMPRESSION MANAGEMENT ISSUE

To set the stage for the presentation to follow, three background issues will be discussed. First, I will review the intrapsychic tradition of studying organizational justice and point out some of its limitations. Then, the alternatives offered by an impression management approach will be outlined. Finally, earlier conceptualizations of justice showing an appreciation for impression management processes will be reviewed.

The Intrapsychic Tradition of Equity Theory and its Limitations

According to Greenberg's (1987a) taxonomy of organizational justice theories, the predominant approach to studying justice in organizations has been Adams's (1965) equity theory. Rooted in the tradition of psychological balance theories (e.g., Festinger, 1957; Heider, 1958), equity theory offers an intrapsychic explanation of behavior that focuses on the cognitive and motivational processes of the individual. Specifically, the theory proposes that workers will experience a state of inequity whenever they perceive that the ratios of their own job rewards (termed "outcomes") to job contributions (termed "inputs") are unequal to the corresponding ratios of some comparison others. The person favored by any imbalance is expected to feel guilty from the resulting "overpayment inequity," whereas the under-benefited worker is expected to feel angry from the resulting "underpayment inequity." These negative states are theorized to cause tension, motivating attempts to restore a more desirable, balanced condition—equity (Walster, Walster, & Berscheid, 1978). Such efforts may be behavioral (such as, by raising or lowering one's work contributions; e.g., Pritchard, Dunnette, & Jorgenson, 1972) and/or psychological (such as by re-assessing the perceived value of one's work outcomes; e.g., Greenberg, 1989)—both of which have been studied in organizations (for reviews, see Greenberg, 1982; Mowday, 1987).

The research inspired by equity theory has left a formidable legacy in the archives of organizational behavior (e.g., see Adams & Freedman, 1976; Greenberg, 1982). However, in recent years, interest in equity theory has waned (Greenberg, 1987a; Reis, 1986), with one observer relegating it to the ranks of the "not so useful" theories of organizational behavior (Miner, 1984). One likely reason for equity theory's decline in popularity may be the acceptance of accumulated criticisms regarding its internal validity (e.g., Furby, 1986; Greenberg, 1984; Schwab, 1980). For example, the theory has been criticized on the grounds that: (a) the conceptual status of many job elements as outcomes or inputs (e.g., decision-making power, status) is ambiguous (e.g., Goodman & Friedman, 1971; Tornow, 1971); (b) the experimental procedures commonly used to manipulate states of inequity are confounded and subject to alternative explanations (e.g., Pritchard, 1969); (c) the hypothesized mediational role of the affective state, "inequity distress," is unsupported (e.g., Greenberg, 1984); and (d) the interrelationship between modes of inequity resolution are conceptually ambiguous (e.g., Adams & Freedman, 1976; Greenberg, 1989). Such criticisms have resulted in some proposed structural re-formulations of equity theory (e.g., Cosier & Dalton, 1983; Harris, 1976) and the introduction of derivative approaches (e.g., Berger, Zelditch, Anderson, & Cohen, 1972; Folger, 1986).

A more frequently expressed reason for disenchantment with equity theory (e.g., Bies, 1987a; Greenberg, 1987a)—and one more relevant to the present paper—is its limited capacity to explain the broad array of factors that define justice as a concern in organizations (Folger & Greenberg, 1985; Greenberg, 1987a). One particular criticism is that equity theory fails to consider how perceptions of justice are influenced by the procedures through which outcomes are determined (Leventhal, 1980). This limitation has resulted in many attempts to broaden the domain of organizational justice (Greenberg, 1987a) to include *procedural justice* variables focusing on *how* outcomes are determined (for reviews, see Folger & Greenberg, 1985; Greenberg & Tyler, 1987; Lind & Tyler, 1988). For example, recent research has shown that the procedures used to appraise employees (Greenberg, 1986a, 1986b, 1987b), supervise them (Sheppard & Lewicki, 1987), and resolve conflicts between them (Sheppard, 1984, 1985) are at least as important as determinants of perceived fairness and job satisfaction as the outcomes resulting from these procedures (see also, Alexander & Ruderman, 1987).

Equity theory also has been cited for ignoring the social contexts in which assessments of fairness are made. For example, although research derived from equity theory has focused on reactions to payment inequities (Greenberg, 1982) and on allocations of organizational resources (Freedman & Montanari, 1980), more recent research has revealed that people think of fairness in terms of behaviors that go far beyond these limited responses, and focus on interpersonal considerations, such as the things people say to one another (Messick, Bloom, Boldizar, & Samuelson, 1985). In this regard, Bies (1987a) has characterized people making fairness judgments as "intuitive jurists" (Hamilton, 1980; Fincham & Jaspars, 1980), seeking to understand *why* certain events occurred, instead of dispassionate, "intuitive scientists" (Kelley, 1967), or "intuitive accountants" (Bies, 1987a), analytically balancing their mental ledgers of outcomes and inputs. This approach is used to introduce the notion of *interactional justice*—the fairness of the interpersonal treatment people receive (Bies & Moag, 1986)—as the basis for studying the role of information presentation of perceived justice. To date, research inspired by the interactional justice approach has found that the explanations given for why outcome decisions are reached may influence workers' reactions to the perceived fairness of layoffs (Brockner & Greenberg, 1989), hiring decisions (Bies, 1986a; Shapiro & Buttner, 1988), performance ratings (Greenberg, 1988a), and the acceptance or rejection of proposals (Bies & Shapiro, 1987, 1988; Bies, Shapiro, & Cummings, 1988).

It may be concluded from this brief review that whereas equity theory, with its emphasis on intrapsychic processes, has fallen into disfavor among organizational scholars, interest in the topic of organizational justice remains very much alive, and has seen a resurgence, stimulated largely by the social context-sensitive procedural and interactional approaches (for a review, see Greenberg, 1987a). The present paper proposes a thematic focus to the study of organizational justice based on the concept of impression management.

An Impression Management Alternative

Schlenker (1980) has defined impression management as, "the conscious or unconscious attempt to control images that are projected in real or imagined social interactions" (p. 6). We will argue in this paper that workers are concerned about projecting an image of themselves as fair, and that they engage in many tactics to do so. In so doing, impression management will be presented as an explanatory concept that helps integrate disparate issues and approaches to organizational justice at the same time it broadens the core knowledge of research on impression management (Tetlock & Manstead, 1985).

The idea that people say and do things to create desired identities in the eyes of others has a rich tradition in the social sciences (e.g., Cooley, 1902; James, 1890; see also, the historical review by Scheibe, 1985). The theme of impression management has evolved in contemporary times from the observational research of the sociologist (e.g., Austin, 1961; Goffman, 1959) to the laboratory of the experimental social psychologist (Schlenker, 1980; Tedeschi, 1981), most recently to the field studies of the organizational psychologist (Gardner & Martinko, 1988; Giacalone & Rosenfeld, 1987). Basic to the impression management approach is Tetlock's idea that people operate as "intuitive politicians" (Bell & Tetlock, 1990; Tetlock, 1985; Tetlock & Manstead, 1985) who seek to convince themselves and others that they possess desired characteristics. As Moberg (1977) put it:

> politicians must avoid having their behavior attributed by others to a particular intent (illegitimate or self-serving motives). They may do so first by "creating the impression" that they have legitimate motives (p.1).

Such political astuteness may be keenly important in organizations. Indeed, the importance of cultivating a proper image has been associated with organizational phenomena as widespread as leadership (Tedeschi & Melburg, 1984), performance appraisal (Longenecker, Sims & Gioia, 1987), goal setting (Huber, Latham, & Locke, 1990), and career development (Chatman et al., 1986). With the present work, the field of organizational justice may be added to those in which an impression management perspective has been introduced.

The impression management approach to organizational justice explicitly recognizes that fairness is in the eye of the beholder. In hierarchical organizations the different interests, goals, and access to information of individuals at different levels are likely to lead to different beliefs about what constitutes fair procedures and outcomes (Greenberg, 1987a). Accordingly, a manager who does what he or she believes to be fair—whatever that may be—may learn that others are not necessarily likewise convinced. To some extent, organizational justice may require impressing others with one's fairness. If different organizational perspectives offer different views of morally, ethically, and socially appropriate behaviors (Cavanagh, Moberg, & Velasquez, 1981), it may be in the best interests of effective management to sensitize oneself to others' perspectives on fairness. As I noted elsewhere, "even the best-intentioned, most "fair-minded" manager may fail to win the approval of subordinates who are not convinced of his or her fairness" (Greenberg, 1988a, p. 155). Thus, the impression management view of organizational justice conceives of fairness as a label for a set of attributions regarding adherence to appropriate standards of conduct that enhances one's self-image and/or one's projected social image. How these images operate, and their value as a managerial tool will be discussed in this paper.

Earlier Applications of Impression Management to Justice

Impression management interpretations of justice behavior are not completely new (e.g., see Bies, 1987a; Reis, 1981). The theme of impression management has been introduced indirectly to the justice literature on several earlier occasions—once as an alternative interpretation of equity theory findings, and once as the result of a movement to study justice as a normative value.

The Self-esteem Challenge to Equity Theory.   Ironically, although not always characterized as such, some of the earliest and most persistent critiques of equity theory research were predicated on an impression management interpretation. Specifically, the prototypical early experimental tests of equity theory (e.g., Adams & Rosenbaum, 1962) manipulated overpayment by leading subjects to believe that they were unqualified for the job they were about to do, but that they would be hired anyway and paid at the advertised rate (which, of course, was inappropriately high). This manipulation has been criticized on the grounds that it may have threatened workers' self-esteem (Lawler, 1968; Pritchard, 1969). Accordingly, the possibility cannot be ruled out that the high levels of performance that followed this manipulation were the result of workers' attempts to demonstrate to themselves and their employers that they were actually quite capable despite their apparent under-qualifications. In other words, subjects' reactions to the inequity may have been caused by attempts to manage impressions of themselves (to both themselves and their superiors), rather than attempts to minimize distress resulting from the inequity.

Support for the self-esteem explanation is provided in a role-playing investigation by Andrews and Valenzi (1970). Participants in this study were asked to report how they would feel if they were involved in a qualifications-challenging situation like that in the Adams and Rosenbaum study. It was found that while none of the subjects expressed awareness of a wage inequity, approximately 44% noted that their self-esteem would be threatened. Although further debate on the construct validity of inequity manipulations has continued (for reviews, see Greenberg, 1982; Schwab, 1980), the self-esteem criticism was an important one. It represents the earliest efforts to propose an impression management explanation for what was initially theorized as an intrapsychic process.

Normative and Instrumental "Uses" of Justice.   An analogous appreciation for impression management influences on justice behavior followed in the 1970s as theorists began to conceive of justice as a social norm. Spearheading this movement, Sampson (1975) argued that, "By nature, man is not an equity theorist" (p. 49). Specifically, eschewing the intrapsychic perspective, he contended that "equity is not as much a psychological law about human nature as it is a psychological outcome of the culture's economic socialization practices" (p. 58). This theorizing ushered in the beginning of a series of conceptualizations about *justice norms* guiding the allocation of resources—social rules specifying "criteria that define certain distributions of rewards and resources as fair and just" (Leventhal, 1976, p. 94). Initially, to the norm of equity, Sampson (1975) added a second justice norm—equality. Later theorists added a third norm—need (Deutsch, 1975; Leventhal, 1976), and the list of justice norms proliferated to 6 (Lerner, 1977), 9 (Lerner, 1980), and 17 (Reis, 1984, 1986).

Such efforts were, in part, directed toward answering the question, "which norm, when?" Such research has shown that the selection of a justice norm often depends on the goal of the allocator (for a review, see Greenberg & Cohen, 1982). At the risk of oversimplifying the conclusions of this line of research, it has been found that a preference for *equitable* allocations (to each according to his merits) predominates when an allocator's goal is to foster economic productivity, *equal* allocations (to each the same) are made when the preservation of harmony is the desired goal, and *need*-based allocations (to each according to his legitimate need) result when the allocator's goal is to foster personal welfare and development (see Deutsch, 1975, 1985; Leventhal, 1976). This line of investigation helps underscore the point that prevailing social rules help define actions made in the name of justice.

Implicit within the normative approach to justice is the idea that adherence to normative standards is dictated by prevailing social forces. The person who follows a normative prescription may be motivated reactively, out of recognition of the pressures to conform to justice norms (Allen, 1982). It also has been postulated that such behavior is motivated proactively—by the belief that behaving in a certain manner provides a path toward attaining other goals. Writing on this topic, Ronald Cohen and I (Greenberg & Cohen, 1982) have argued that many acts performed in the name of fairness actually may be motivated by the desire to attain other goals—what we called *instrumental* acts.

Drawing a parallel to prosocial behaviors, which are not necessarily motivated by an underlying concern for altruism (Schwartz, 1977), we posited that ostensibly fair behaviors may not necessarily be motivated by an ultimate concern for justice. Justice may be a penultimate state on the way to an ultimate goal (Greenberg, 1986c). Leventhal (1976) articulated this point clearly when he asserted:

> it is likely that an allocator who distributes rewards equitably does so more because he desires to maximize long-term productivity than because he desires to comply with an abstract standard of justice. His decisions are based on an expectancy that equitable distributions of reward will elicit and sustain high levels of motivation and performance (p. 96).

As such, he distinguishes between acts motivated out of a concern for justice per se, "fair behavior," and those derived from other motives, "quasi-fair behavior" (Leventhal, 1980). The possibility that the justice-restoring effects of an action may be epiphenomenal, motivated apart from moral or ethical considerations, is basic to our argument that people may internalize expectations about the effects of behaving fairly, and do so in order to meet these expectations. In other words, justice may be "used" as the mechanism for attaining other goals. Although it is difficult to prove the existence of a specific motive underlying behavior, there is evidence to suggest that people sometimes engage in ostensibly "fair" actions for expressed reasons that do not reflect any concern for fairness at all. For example, Greenberg (1978) found that equitable divisions of reward were made by persons claiming to be trying to be maximizing their own gain or the gain of others. Thus, people may be implicitly aware that their adherence to a justice norm may reflect "an attempt to gain the unique pattern of instrumental benefits that is associated with following that norm" (Leventhal, 1976, p. 95).

The underlying point is that many acts are performed behind a "veneer of justice." If so, then one may ask how norms of justice are sustained. It may be argued that justice norms remain intact *because* of their instrumental value. Norms of justice facilitate social system goals (Greenberg & Cohen, 1982). Justice norms may be "used" to promote the social welfare of individuals and society by providing an orderly way for resources to be distributed. As Cohen and I noted elsewhere, "justice works" (p. 457); norms create explanations that guide behaviors in directions that are reinforced by society. Moreover, justice is socially rewarding; people are rewarded for treating others fairly (Walster et al., 1978). Indeed, research has shown that people often closely adhere to justice standards whenever they believe that others can reward them socially for doing so (e.g., Morse, Gruzen & Reis, 1976; Reis & Gruzen, 1976; Rivera & Tedeschi, 1976). Such conformity to justice norms is not only individually rewarding (Allen, 1982), but also facilitates social interaction in general by making interaction more predictable (Thibaut & Kelley, 1959).

Given this background, the stage is now set for analyzing the role of justice in some of the core questions of the impression management literature.

FAIRNESS AS A DESIRED SOCIAL IDENTITY

Probably the most basic core question asked among impression management theorists is: what types of identities do people seek (Tetlock, 1985; Tetlock & Manstead, 1985)? Although it may be tempting to answer this question by positing that people seek "socially desirable" identities, such a response fails to consider the broad cultural and historical differences that may exist in definitions of desirability (Schlenker, 1980). Moreover, it is overly simplistic in that people sometimes seek identities that are not positive. Even identities emphasizing toughness, dangerousness, helplessness, weakness, and dependency, Jones and Pittman (1982) claim, may be effective as means of gaining social approval and power.

There can be little doubt that the characteristic of fairness is recognized as desirable. Probably the most basic evidence in support of this idea is provided by Anderson's (1968) study in which students rated 555 personality traits on scales ranging from 0 ("least favorable or desirable") to 6 ("most favorable or desirable"). Although the trait "fair" was not among those rated, it was found that related traits received very high ratings of favorability (e.g., "honest," $M = 5.55$; "honorable," $M = 5.07$; "ethical," $M = 4.76$). Moreover, the trait, "unfair," was rated as extremely undesirable ($M = 1.07$). Such evidence clearly reflects the abstract positive connotations of fairness and the negative connotations of unfairness as personal characteristics.

Beyond such abstractions, a case can be made for fairness as a social identity. As Reis (1981) has noted, the desire to be seen as virtuous and fair is implicit within Jones and Pittman's (1982) class of self-presentational strategies known as *exemplification*. An exemplifier is one who "seeks to project integrity and moral worthiness" (Jones & Pittman, 1982, p. 245). Because of the conceptual overlap between fairness and exemplification as identities, it has been claimed that perceiving oneself as an exemplifier may be understood as an attempt to project an image of fairness (Reis, 1981).

More direct evidence of a widespread motive to shape dispositional beliefs about fairness is provided by survey research highlighting the central position of fairness as a work value. For example, recent survey research has shown that a concern about fairness on the job is one of the most prevalent life values noted among a wide variety of workers (e.g., Cornelius, Ullman, Meglino, Czajka & McNeely, 1985; Ravlin & Meglino, 1987). Although more recent investigations reveal individual differences in the specific structure of fairness values (e.g., Rasinski, 1987), it appears safe to claim that fairness is a desired value. Identities that are valued on the job may well be those that stimulate the greatest efforts to be attained.

Another line of evidence that fairness is a social identity comes from the finding that people perceive themselves as fairer than others. In six studies conducted in the United States and the Netherlands, Messick and his associates (Liebrand, Messick, & Wolters, 1986; Messick et al., 1985) found that subjects reported behaviors thought to be fair as more characteristic of themselves than of others, believing that they more often did fair things and less often did unfair things. Given the general tendency for people to attribute desirable characteristics to themselves (Miller & Ross, 1975), such self-serving perceptions of one's own fairness may be taken as evidence of the social desirability of fair identities.

The most direct evidence of fairness as a desired identity in organizations is provided by Greenberg's (1988b) survey of 815 managers. Participants were asked two sets of questions: one set inquiring how concerned they were about *actually being fair* on the job, and another set asking how concerned they were about *appearing to be fair* on the job. It was found that the managers expressed greater concern about appearing to be fair than actually being fair. Moreover, the two sets of questions were not significantly correlated with each other, suggesting that managers distinguished between "looking fair" and "being fair".

These findings provide a useful adjunct to the present analysis by directly revealing that the desire to cultivate an impression of fairness is of great concern to managers. Moreover, the findings suggest that this concern operates at the level of conscious awareness. This is not to say, however, that such self-consciousness is a necessary precondition for fair impression management to occur (Schlenker,

1980; Tetlock & Manstead, 1985). Indeed, theorists have contended that impression management efforts may be the result of well-learned scripts (Jones & Pittman, 1982; Schlenker, 1980), and that ostensible reactions to inequities may be the result of enacting such scripts (Greenberg, 1984). Furthermore, it may be argued that questionnaire responses regarding the importance of fairness may themselves represent attempts on the part of participants to present themselves favorably to an authority figure (Alexander & Rudd, 1981). Notwithstanding these limitations, it appears safe to assume that the attribution of fairness is a desired individual identity in organizational settings.

TARGETS OF FAIR IDENTITIES

Accepting that fairness is a desired social identity, I continue my analysis by asking: To whom are identities of fairness presented? At the risk of over-simplification, it may be answered: oneself, and others. Although external audiences (such as bosses, teachers, and judges) are usually emphasized in the study of impression management (e.g., Baumeister, 1982; Jones & Pittman, 1982), there is also widespread acceptance of the idea that people seek to cultivate certain impressions of themselves for themselves (e.g., Greenwald & Breckler, 1985; Schlenker, 1986). As I will review here, the justice literature has recognized the importance of both internal and external targets of an image of fairness.

In keeping with the distinction that justice norms may be either normative or instrumental (Greenberg & Cohen, 1982), Tetlock (1985) has drawn a parallel distinction between impression management efforts that are *principled* (i.e., intended to satisfy internalized standards) and those that are *pragmatic* (i.e., concerned with establishing good relationships with others). As I will review here, many of the same situational variables (e.g., degree of public scrutiny) and dispositional variables (e.g., self-consciousness) identified as mediating the choice of principled vs. pragmatic goals (Greenwald & Breckler, 1985; Tetlock, 1985) also have been identified as moderators of both reactions to inequity and the choice of a justice standard (Reis, 1981).

Others as Targets: Pragmatic Identities

One such situational variable concerns the public scrutiny of one's behavior. A commonly used experimental technique to distinguish intrapsychic explanations from impression management explanations of behavior involves manipulating the degree to which subjects believe their behavior is under public scrutiny (Tetlock & Manstead, 1985). The underlying rationale is that behaviors designed to impress others would occur only when people believe that others can observe their behavior.

Several studies of reactions to inequity have relied on this manipulation (for a review, see Reis, 1981). For example, Rivera and Tedeschi (1976) compared subjects' reactions to overpayment inequity using a simple paper-and-pencil measure and an elaborate lie detector (the "bogus pipeline"; Jones & Sigall, 1971). It was found that overpaid subjects reported feeling more guilt than equitably paid subjects when they believed their true feelings could not be detected (in the paper-and-pencil condition) than when the lie detector encouraged them to express their true feelings. Had the overpayment inequity induction actually led to feelings of guilt, there would have been no reason to suspect that differences in the face validity of the instrument used to measure such guilt would have made any difference. Yet, because the socially desirable guilt response (one *should* feel guilty for being overpaid) was more prevalent when subjects believed they could misrepresent their true feelings with impunity, it appears that the reactions expressed may be more the result of the desire to appear socially acceptable to the experimenter than the desire to express their true feelings. Such findings have been taken as support for the idea that responses to equitable treatment may be based on people's impression management concerns, "contrary to the postulated intrapsychic processes that have been proposed as mediating post-allocation responses" (Rivera & Tedeschi, 1976, p. 899).

A similar tendency for verbal reactions to overpayment to reflect impression management interests has been found by Morse, Gruzen, and Reis (1976). Subjects in this experiment justified overpayment conditions by exaggerating claims of task difficulty to a greater degree when they expected their self-reports to be shared in the experimenter than when they expected them to remain anonymous. Several additional studies (reviewed by Reis, 1981) likewise show that publicly visible reactions to overpayment take the socially desirable form of ostensibly demonstrating dissatisfaction with overpayment more than responses made in private.

Analogous evidence using the public-private distinction is found in the literature on the allocation of reward. By comparing the responses of subjects made publicly and privately, this literature has repeatedly found that "subjects incorporate the perceived standards of significant others who are aware of their behavior" (Reis, 1981, p. 276). For example, Lane and Messé (1971) found that dyad members who expected to be introduced to each other were less likely to take advantage of each other by taking self-interested shares of reward than those who were not identified. Related research has found that allocators attempt to present themselves favorably to recipients by dividing reward equally among them (Leventhal, Michaels & Sanford, 1972), especially when they expect recipients to be aware of their decisions (Reis & Gruzen, 1976). Expecting to meet the recipient of an allocation decision also leads people to favor equal allocations, even when an equity-based allocation may be justified by their higher inputs (Austin & McGinn, 1977; Shapiro, 1975). Equal divisions of reward also tend to be made whenever allocators expected to be evaluated by another whose impressions are valued, such as one's spouse (Schoeninger & Wood, 1969), coworkers (Friedman & Goodman, 1974) or friends (Austin, 1980). Presumably, making a more self-serving response would be antagonistic to an interest in making a favorable self-presentation. Summarizing, studies of reward allocation behaviors suggest that equal divisions of reward are made in the interest of promoting favorable impressions of oneself.

It is important to point out that such favorable impressions may not necessarily be impressions of fairness. By not taking advantage of others, and not wishing to confront those they have harmed, subjects are at least demonstrating an interest in avoiding conflicts likely to arise from discriminatory behavior (Deutsch, 1975; Leventhal, 1976). That they are trying to impress others with their fairness is less apparent. For this to be the case, subjects would have had to internalize the normative appropriateness of equal allocations. To the extent that their behaviors may have been motivated by an interest in avoiding conflict, their impression management interests, although considerable, may have focused on identities other than fairness. However, accepting the inherent ambiguities regarding exactly what behaviors may be fair in any situation (e.g., Reis, 1986), it is possible that subjects in these studies just may be seeking to minimize their costs in the experimental situation, to "get out of it" as inexpensively as possible. Given the low value of the stakes involved, it is not surprising to find experimental subjects willing to forego financial reward in favor of social reward—especially when they can do so by following a justice norm, such as equality (Greenberg, 1978).

Despite this caveat, there is evidence that certain justice behaviors may be the result of specific attempts to cultivate impressions of fairness. Rather than dealing with the impressions created in the minds of others, the investigations examining explicit attempts at cultivating impressions of fairness have focused on the self as a target of fair impressions.

Oneself as Target: Principled Identities

Experimental research making the self salient as a target of impression management typically follows the practice of making subjects "objectively self-aware" (Duval & Wicklund, 1972; Wicklund, 1975) by having them confront their reflections in a mirror. According to the theory of objective self-awareness (Duval & Wicklund, 1972; Wicklund, 1975), the self-focused attention created by this manipulation heightens self-critical judgments; people become more aware of the discrepancies between their own behavior and ideal standards, thereby making them more sensitive to normative values (Vallacher & Solodky, 1979).

Evidence that self-awareness moderates reactions to inequity has been found by Reis and Burns (1982). These investigators found that overpaid subjects were more productive when they performed a task in the presence of a mirror than in the absence of a mirror. Related findings were also obtained by Gibbons and Wicklund (1982, Experiment 4). Given that equity theory predicts increased outputs in response to overpayment inequity, the higher level of inputs following overpayment by self-aware subjects than by not self-aware subjects suggests that reactions to overpayment inequity are heightened by states of self-awareness. Being self-aware heightened subjects' sensitivity to the state of inequity they experienced. Although these findings show that self-awareness increases responsiveness to states of inequity, they do not reveal anything about subjects' proactive concerns about adhering to justice standards.

Such a connection has been established, however, in several studies investigating the role of self-awareness on adherence to justice standards. In one study, Greenberg (1980) found that subjects who were made self-aware while dividing earned rewards between themselves and a competitor showed greater concern for making equitable allocations (i.e., divisions proportional to inputs) than subjects who were not self-aware. The mirror-induced self-awareness led higher-input subjects to keep more reward for themselves and lower-input subjects to keep less reward for themselves than those not self-aware. Moreover, self-aware subjects expressed greater concern over having made the appropriate allocation response than those who were not self-aware. In another study by Greenberg (1983a), subjects rated making fair payments as being more important when they were self-aware than when they were not self-aware. Self-aware subjects in this study were more prone than those who were not self-aware to reject as unfair all inequitable allocation decisions, even those that benefited themselves.

Thus far, it has been established that states of self-awareness enhance adherence to personal standards of justice. In the previous section of this chapter, it was reported that people are also concerned with creating a favorable impression on others. As a result, it is possible that the two interests may conflict. Indeed, the inherent ambiguity associated with the fairness of any given response may make different reward allocation norms (e.g., equity, equality, need; Deutsch, 1975) justifiable as normatively appropriate (Leventhal, 1976). As a result, a potentially fair response may not necessarily be one that is best accepted. For example, although conditions may be such that the prevailing standard of justice is the equity norm (such as when competitive, profit-oriented conditions exist; Deutsch, 1975), it cannot be assumed that the most favorable impressions may be created by adhering to this norm. This would be the case when a reward allocator expects to have future interaction with a poor-performing co-recipient. Impressing such individuals, research has shown (Austin & McGinn, 1977; Reis & Gruzen, 1976; Shapiro, 1975), dictates the use of equal allocations—responses that promote interpersonal harmony (Leventhal, Michaels, & Sanford, 1972). As a result, the normative behaviors required to satisfy one's internal standards of justice may be inconsistent with those needed to cultivate a favorable self-image. The resolution of such conflicts appears to be based on the relative strength of the various forces.

Testing this notion, Greenberg (1983b, Experiment 1) studied how subjects respond to such conflicts by manipulating self-awareness (mirror presence or absence) in conjunction with impression management concerns (expectation of meeting a lower-input person). In keeping with the Greenberg (1980) study, subjects who were self-aware tended to make equitable allocations and to report that behaving fairly was more important to them than those who were not self-aware. Also as predicted, those who expected to meet their low-input competitors tended to make equal allocations (Shapiro, 1975). However, when self-aware subjects expected to meet their low-input competitors, a conflict occurred between making a favorable impression on oneself (by allocating the reward equitably—that is, in proportion to relative contributions) and on the other person (by allocating the reward equally). Subjects tended to resolve this conflict by favoring either one norm or the other; they were almost equally divided in their preference for equity and equality, making very few compromise solutions. Apparently, subjects were divided as to the relative strength of their impression management targets—some adhered to self-standards by allocating rewards equitably; others presented themselves favorably to recipients by allocating rewards equally.

The possibility of an individual difference variable moderating the choice of competing allocation rules is suggested by the attention given to the distinction between public and private self-consciousness in the impression management literature (e.g., Greenwald & Breckler, 1985; Tetlock & Manstead, 1985). The self-consciousness scale developed by Fenigstein, Scheier, and Buss (1975) distinguishes between public self-consciousness—a concern for oneself as a social object (high scorers are concerned about the impressions they make on others), and private self-consciousness—awareness of the covert, personal aspects of oneself (high scorers are attuned to their internal standards) (for a review, see Carver & Scheier, 1981).

Reasoning that differences in public vs. private self-consciousness may have moderate reactions to the self-image vs. impression management conflict in Experiment 1, a follow-up study was conducted (Greenberg, 1983b, Experiment 2). This investigation recreated the conflict conditions for subjects who were highly public self-conscious (scored high on public self-consciousness and low on private self-consciousness) and those who were highly private self-conscious (scored high on private self-consciousness and low on public self-consciousness). It was reasoned that persons in these extreme groups would resolve the conflict between internal standards of justice and the pressure to present oneself favorably to others in ways commensurate with their predispositions. As expected, it was found that subjects followed the equity norm most closely when they were made highly self aware (by the presence of a mirror) *and* were dispositionally predisposed to follow their internal standards (the high private self-conscious group). Analogously, the strongest adherence to the equality norm occurred when highly public self-conscious subjects were not made self-aware. Interestingly, subjects in this condition expressed less concern over doing what seemed fair to themselves than subjects in any of the other conditions. Accordingly, it appears that concerns for fairness and adherence to justice norms are influenced by *both* personal and situational factors operating additively to dictate the salience of justice norms.

What is interesting about these findings is that they have been conceptually replicated in a study obtaining opposite behavioral results. Creating a situation in which equality was normatively appropriate instead of equity (joint cooperation was emphasized; Deutsch, 1975), Kernis and Reis (1984) had subjects allocate rewards after performing a task on which they were led to believe they were more productive. They found that the equality norm was followed by subjects who were highly private self-conscious, but that the equity norm was followed by subjects who were highly public self-conscious. Although these findings are behaviorally opposite Greenberg's (1983b, Experiment 2), they are conceptually identical.

The reason has to do with the fact that manipulations used in the two studies dictated the appropriateness of different norms of justice to fulfill internal and external standards. Specifically, to make salient internal standards. Greenberg (1983b) used a competitive context that made the equity norm appropriate, whereas Kernis and Reis (1984) used a cooperative context that made the equality norm appropriate (for a discussion of the situational factors dictating the appropriateness of various justice norms, see Deutsch, 1975; Greenberg & Cohen, 1982; Lerner, 1977; Leventhal, 1976). Furthermore, to make salient external standards, Greenberg (1983b) led subjects to believe that they would get to meet a low-input co-recipient, thereby encouraging the use of equal allocations in order to avoid conflict and cultivate that person's favor (Reis & Gruzen, 1976; Shapiro, 1975). By contrast, Kernis and Reis (1984) explicitly encouraged subjects to consider each person's relative contributions when allocating the money between them; that is, equity was encouraged to please the experimenter. Despite these different sets of internal and external standards, both studies yielded conceptually identical patterns of results. To wit, both studies show that private self-consciousness enhanced adherence to internal standards and that public self-consciousness enhanced adherence to external standards. The fact that these findings were obtained in two separate studies in which situational factors defined different justice standards as normatively appropriate provides the kind of experimental convergence that enhances confidence in the underlying theoretical interpretation (for further discussion, see also, Carver & Scheier, 1985).

To summarize, the research reviewed here makes a clear case for the importance of the self as a target of identities of fairness. People like to think of themselves as fair, particularly those who are predisposed to think about their personal standards and/or when discrepancies from those standards are made salient situationally. Taken together with the evidence showing people's sensitivity toward impressing others with fairness, it appears safe to conclude that concerns about fair impression management are directed both inward, toward one's self-image and outward, toward one's social image.

TACTICS OF PROMOTING FAIR IDENTITIES

Having established that people are interested in impressing both themselves and others with their fairness, a question arises as to how they go about creating such impressions. Although, "Almost all behaviors and appearances potentially convey information about the self and may be used as a self-presentational strategy" (Schneider, 1981, p. 26), theorists have concentrated on studying the influence of verbal claims about the self. Particularly in organizations, language is recognized as the tool through which managers explain and rationalize their actions (Pfeffer, 1981), and has been studied as such (e.g., Garner & Martinko, 1988). The potential influence of statements about oneself has been noted explicitly by Schlenker (1980) in his treatise on impression management: "Through public descriptions of the traits they possess, the things they are accountable for, and the ways they view the world, people can secure identities that maximize the public esteem in which they are held and the outcomes they receive" (p. 91). Similarly, survey research on the tactics of organizational politics likewise has noted that managerial personnel explicitly identify things said to cultivate and maintain a favorable image in organizations—such as sensitivity to organizational norms—as a popular tactic of gaining organizational influence (Allen, Madison, Porter, Renwick, &

Mayes, 1979). Apparently, people seek to "explain themselves" to others by presenting themselves in ways that create, promote, and maintain desired social identities (Tedeschi & Reiss, 1981a).

What I am alluding to here is known as *self-presentation,* "a set of behaviors designed by an actor to establish particular identities in the eyes of various audiences" (Tedeschi & Norman, 1985, p. 293). Following Tedeschi's lead (e.g., Tedeschi & Norman, 1985; Tedeschi & Melburg, 1984), the present discussion of impression management tactics will distinguish between self-presentations that are *defensive* (i.e., designed to mend a spoiled identity) and *assertive* (i.e., initiated to establish a particular identity). The next two sections will discuss the defensive and assertive tactics used to manage impressions of fairness.

Defensive Tactics: Identity-Threatening Predicaments

Theorists have conceived social situations as involving challenges to people's self-images, raising questions about the legitimacy of one's claim to an image. For example, as Schlenker (1980) put it, "Life is a constant series of tests in which we are called on to substantiate our claims through personal performance or some other means" (p. 99). When an event occurs that casts unwanted aspersions on someone's character, that person is said to be in a *predicament.* Specifically, predicaments have been defined as "situations in which events have undesirable implications for the identity-relevant images actors have claimed or desire to claim in front of real or imagined audiences" (Schlenker, 1980, p. 125). In keeping with the recent work of Bies (1987a), situations in which an injustice is perceived to have occurred may be characterized as "predicaments of injustice" for those associated with it. The severity of a predicament depends not only on the undesirability of the event, but also the actor's responsibility for the event (Bell & Tetlock, 1990; Tetlock, 1985). Schlenker expressed this clearly when he characterized responsibility as "the adhesive that links an actor to an event and attaches appropriate sanctions to the actor that deserves it" (p. 126). Given this, it is not surprising that the major tactics for extricating oneself from social predicaments are attributional in nature (Synder, 1985).

Building on the pioneering sociological work of Austin (1961) and Scott and Lyman (1968), Schlenker (1980) identified two broad classes of remedial tactics used to reduce the negative repercussions of a predicament—*accounts* and *apologies.* Although Tedeschi and his associates (e.g., Tedeschi & Melburg, 1984; Tedeschi & Norman, 1985; Tedeschi & Reiss, 1981a) have expanded this list, accounts and apologies remain the most commonly researched tactics for defending against social predicaments. Accordingly, I will now consider how accounts and apologies may be used to help minimize threats to one's self-identity as a fair person.

Accounts.   Accounts are explanations designed to remove an actor from a predicament. They provide information about an event that either lessens one's responsibility for it, and/or lessens the apparent severity of the consequences (Schlenker, 1980; Tedeschi & Reiss, 1981b). Two types of accounts have been identified—excuses and justifications. An excuse allows actors to deny or minimize responsibility for a predicament; a justification attempts to reduce the negative consequences of a predicament (Austin, 1961; Scott & Lyman, 1968).

More precisely, *excuses* are "explanations in which individuals acknowledge that their conduct was somehow bad, wrong, or inappropriate, but attempted to minimize their personal responsibility or culpability for it" (Tetlock, 1985, p. 215). Several theorists (e.g., Fincham & Jaspars, 1980; Snyder, 1985; Snyder, Higgins, & Stucky, 1983) have claimed that excuses will lessen one's apparent responsibility for an event if it can be demonstrated that the causes of the event were external and/or unintentional. Both internality and intentionality have been studied as general attributional categories (e.g., Weiner, 1974), and they have been shown to influence justice behavior (Greenberg, 1984; Kidd & Utne, 1978; Utne & Kidd, 1980).

Explanations suggesting that an actor's behavior was not volitional, but the result of externally-imposed demands (e.g., "my hands were tied by economic pressures") tend to minimize one's perceived responsibility for the effects of that behavior (Heider, 1958). Moreover, events believed to be externally caused (such as competitive events won as a result of luck as opposed to skill) tend *not* to be rewarded in a manner that credits people differentially for their inputs—that is, equitably (Cohen, 1974; Greenberg, 1980; Witting, Marks, & Jones, 1981). Furthermore, reward distributions following from externally-caused outcomes are perceived to be less fair than those resulting from conditions in which people are responsible for having caused their outcomes (Greenberg, 1980). Similarly, research has found that people are more responsive to inequities that others have intentionally created than those that are unintentional (e.g., Greenberg & Frisch, 1972; Leventhal, Weiss, & Long, 1969). For example, it has been reported that subjects are more likely to re-allocate rewards so as to redress overpayment or underpayment inequities if these were believed to be intentionally rather than unintentionally created (Garrett & Libby, 1973). Taken together, these findings suggest that attributions of internal and intentional causality heighten people's sensitivity to injustices.

In keeping with this, a stream of research by Bies and his associates has examined the influence of claims of mitigating circumstances on feelings of injustice (for a review, see Bies, 1987a). A mitigating circumstance lessens one's responsibility for an event, often by imposing explanations of external and unintentional causality (Weiner, 1974), thereby excusing an actor for any resulting injustice. Research by Bies, Shapiro, and Cummings (1988) content analyzed the retrospective accounts workers gave of their bosses' reasons for denying their requests, revealing six distinct types of mitigating circumstances. The most frequently cited mitigating circumstance was the worker's own behavior (e.g., incompetence), followed by claims of budgetary constraints, controls imposed by higher levels of management, limitations of a political nature, restrictions due to formal company policy, and inconsistencies with company norms. The mitigating circumstance judged most adequate had to do with company norms (e.g., "traditionally, our company has never allowed this"). Judged least adequate were explanations based on the current political environment (e.g., "it would be politically incorrect to do this now")—in fact, claims of mitigating circumstances based on such political considerations were judged no more adequate than reports of no mitigating circumstances at all.

In several laboratory studies Bies and Shapiro (1987, Studies 1 and 2; 1988, Study 1) studied the effects of claims of mitigating circumstances (e.g., an economic depression) on reactions to unfavorable organizational events (e.g., budget cutbacks). Such accounts were found to reduce people's feelings of having been unfairly treated relative to others receiving the same outcomes but who were not given accounts of mitigating circumstances. Follow-up research in field settings also has found that accounts of mitigating conditions enhanced perceptions of fairness of naturally-occurring negative outcomes, such as the rejection of a proposal of organizational funding (Bies & Shapiro, 1987, Study 3; 1988, Study 2; Bies et al., 1988), rejection of an application for employment (Bies & Moag, 1986), poor performance ratings (Greenberg, 1988a), and layoffs (Brockner & Greenberg, 1989). It is the point of these studies that accounts of mitigating circumstances discourage persons disappointed by managerial decisions from attributing malevolent motives to the decision-maker (i.e., eliminating a worst-case reading of the situation), thereby facilitating acceptance of the outcomes (Bies, 1989).

Further research has shown that excuses may most effectively facilitate outcome acceptance when they are perceived to be adequate. For example, Bies and Shapiro (1987, Studies 2 and 3) found that the perceived adequacy of the reasons for claiming mitigating circumstances was significantly more important as a determinant of perceived fair treatment than the claim itself (e.g., an explanation couched in terms of adverse economic conditions). Similarly, Folger and his associates (e.g., Folger, Rosenfield, & Robinson, 1983; Folger & Martin, 1986) found that the feelings of discontent resulting from procedural changes creating unfavorable outcomes were reduced only when an adequate explanation was given for the changes. Recent evidence also suggests that "good" excuses (e.g., claims of mitigating circumstances) were more effective than "bad" excuses (e.g., no mitigating circumstances) or no excuses at all in alleviating the anger of victims of another's harm doing (Weiner, Amirkhan, Foles, & Varette, 1987). These findings are consistent with evidence from the impression management literature showing that the acceptance of excuses requires them to be perceived as genuine (Jones, 1964) and not habitual (Snyder et al., 1983).

What constitutes an adequate excuse? Several recent studies shed light on this question. For example, Shapiro and Buttner (1988) found that explanations for rejected loan requests that were *logical* (i.e., based on relevant financial information) were perceived as adequate, and that such explanations enhanced perceptions of procedural justice. Several additional studies have found that the apparent *sincerity* of an excuse is another determinant of its perceived adequacy. For example, Bies (1987b; Bies et al., 1988) found that the greater the perceived sincerity of a supervisor's reasons for rejecting workers' requests, the more liked the supervisor was, and the more fair those supervisors' actions were perceived to be. Additional research has shown that sincere explanations were found to facilitate social exchange in another way—by discouraging the use of disruptive conflict (Baron, 1988). Indeed, organizational explanations perceived to be ungenuine and manipulative in intent have been found to be associated with disliking for the person offering the explanations, and the unfairness of the resulting actions (Greenberg & Ornstein, 1983). As such, explanations that are based on logical information, and which show sincerity appear to be the most effective in enhancing the perceived fairness of outcomes and the procedures that led to them. Although several additional factors may moderate these effects (Bies, 1987a), the recent studies reported here suggest some promising candidates for refining our conceptualizations of adequate excuses.

To summarize, evidence supports the idea that excuses can influence the perceived fairness of events. People are most likely to redress inequities that are believed to be under internal control and the result of intentional acts. Additionally, the perceived fairness of undesirable outcomes has been found to be enhanced by claims of mitigating circumstances. Verbal excuses—specifically, those perceived to be adequate—enhance perceptions of fairness. Adequate excuses are ones that are logical and which are believed to be sincere.

Another category of accounts is *justifications*. In contrast to excuses, in which one dissociates oneself from a predicament, justifications are "explanations in which the actor takes responsibility for the action, but denies that it has the negative quality that others might attribute to it" (Tedeschi & Reiss, 1981a, p. 281). Predicaments can be resolved if the actor's blameworthy behavior has been explained away in an acceptable manner. Hence, justifications also have been referred to as "techniques of neutralization" (Sykes & Matza, 1957). Schlenker (1980) describes several ways of reducing the severity of a predicament. Among these are: (a) changing the focus of social comparisons, and (b) appealing to superordinate goals. The justice-related implications of each of these tactics will be discussed.

People often justify identity-threatening actions by claiming that "everyone else does it." Individuals making such a claim seem to be implying that their actions are normatively acceptable, and that singling them out for their behavior would be unfair. Although reference standards are emphasized in many theories of organizational justice (e.g., Adams, 1965; Crosby, 1976; for a review, see Greenberg, 1987a), Bies (1987a) reminds us that only a few studies have examined the effects of justifications based on social comparisons—what he terms "referential accounts" (p. 301).

Two studies focused on social comparisons that were temporally-based (Albert, 1977). For example, Bies (1986b) found that people who had proposals rejected by their bosses were more likely to accept this outcome as fair if they believed the boss might approve their proposal subsequently. Future comparisons apparently facilitated workers' acceptance of the fairness of negative outcomes. Similarly, Greenberg (1988a) found that references to future outcomes (e.g., "I hope you will do better next time") were made by managers in 16.22% of the narratives they gave to explain their subordinates' performance ratings. Compared to subordinates receiving no such messages, those who received messages making reference to future outcomes rated their performance evaluations as being more fair. Apparently, communications raising the prospect of future positive outcomes were effective in enhancing the perceived fairness of current negative outcomes.

An alternative source of temporal comparisons is information regarding what *could* have happened (Kahneman & Tversky, 1982). For example, some of the managers in Greenberg's (1988a) study informed subordinates that their outcomes could have been worse (e.g., "I could have given you a lower rating"). Research by Folger and his associates (e.g., Folger & Martin, 1986; Folger et al., 1983) has found that people's reactions to injustices are influenced by their beliefs about outcomes that could have occurred (for a review, see Folger, 1986). Specifically, when subjects were told that a change in procedures could have led to lower outcomes than they currently received, they reported less discontent than when more desirable outcomes could have resulted. Apparently, believing that "things could have been worse" was accepted as justification for the procedural changes that adversely affected their outcomes.

Another technique of justification calls for presenting the incident in the context of attempts to achieve superordinate goals. A father who claims to punish his children "for their own good," for example, may be seen as justifying his actions by embedding them with a more desirable or acceptable context. Likewise, organizations faced with having to layoff employees may justify the decision on the grounds of economic necessity and ostensibly display their good intentions by promoting their re-training or outplacement services. Such "reframing" in terms of "ideological accounts" (Bies, 1987a, p. 300) helps redefine questionable actions or outcomes as morally acceptable (Lofland, 1969). Tedeschi and Reiss (1981a) note that events may be justified by appealing to: higher authorities (e.g., organizational policies), loyalties (e.g., group norms), humanistic values (e.g., peace), ideology (e.g., nationalism), and—of current interest—norms of justice (e.g., equity).

How are appeals to norms of justice used to justify one's actions? Tedeschi and Reiss (1981a) explain that someone's failure to work as contracted or failure to pay for work done may be justified on the grounds that such acts could exacerbate unfair conditions. For example, workers who believe they have been underpaid may seek to restore an equitable state by lowering their performance or going on strike (Greenberg, 1982). Indeed, evidence that such labor actions are justified by recourse to superordinate goals of justice is readily provided by the words often seen on the picket signs carried by striking workers: "Justice on the job," "a fair day's pay for a fair day's work," or most simply, "unfair!"

In a recent study, Greenberg (1988a) found that managers gave ideologically-based explanations of performance to 11.22% of the subordinates whose work they evaluated. An explanation such as, "This rating is good for you; it'll show you there's room for improvement" fits into this category. Such explanations were given primarily to subordinates whose work was rated as average or good, and less frequently to those rated either higher or lower than this. It was found that such ideological justifications enhanced workers' perceptions of the fairness of the evaluations they received relative to those who received no descriptive explanation for their performance ratings. Similarly, Bies (1986b) found that workers' willingness to work harder for bosses who rejected their proposals was facilitated by the use of ideological-based accounts.

To recapitulate, people attempt to justify unacceptable actions by getting others to believe that the future holds more favorable outcomes and that these outcomes are required to attain superordinate goals. Such beliefs facilitate the perceived fairness of unacceptable outcomes.

Apologies.   In addition to accounts (excuses and justifications), apologies are also used to extricate oneself from an impression management predicament. Following from Goffman (1971), Tedeschi and Norman (1985) define apologies as "confessions of responsibility for negative events which include some expression of remorse" (p. 299). Apologies are designed to convince an audience that although the actor accepts blame for the undesirable event, any attributions made on the basis of it would not be accurate. According to Schlenker (1980), successful apologies convince others that the harmdoer's actions "should not be considered a fair representation of what the actor is 'really like' as a person" (p. 154) and permit them to "leave the undesirable event behind and present a reformed identity to the audience" (p. 157). The mechanisms of apology can range from a perfunctory saying "pardon me," typically for very minor harmful acts, to complex statements adding expressions of remorse, offers of help, requests for forgiveness, and the use of self-castigation, usually reserved for acts with more serious consequences (Schlenker & Darby, 1981).

One mechanism for gaining the acceptance of one's apologies is to perform penance and offer to compensate one's victims (Goffman, 1971). In a series of studies, O'Malley and Greenberg (1983) found that persons who admitted their harmdoing and voluntarily offered to compensate their victims were believed by female subjects to require smaller payments as fair restitution than those who did not offer any such penance. The act of voluntarily admitting responsibility was apparently accepted as a "down payment" toward undoing wrongdoing, thereby necessitating smaller amounts of additional compensation. In other words, lower amounts of compensation were believed to be fair costs to be borne by those who already partially compensated their victims by voluntarily admitting their wrongdoing. The tendency for other acts of remorse to induce leniency has been shown in several additional studies (e.g., Austin, Walster & Utne, 1976; Schwartz, Kane, Joseph, & Tedeschi, 1978).

How accepting others are of one's apologies depends, no doubt, on the severity of the deviation from acceptable standards. Kelman (1973) has distinguished between deviations from standards of *morality* (e.g., harming others or society in general), likely to elicit feelings of guilt and remorse, and deviations from standards of *propriety* (e.g., failing to behave in accord with one's particular position or role identity), likely to elicit embarrassment and shame. Evidence from simulated legal settings suggests that harsher fines may be administered to deter moral violations than to deter violations of standards of propriety (Kalven & Zeisel, 1966). Similarly, post hoc analyses of sporting events suggests that more serious penalties (e.g., suspensions) are reserved for unfair acts (i.e., procedural justice violations) that threaten the moral character of the game (e.g., recruitment violations and serious fights), whereas more lenient penalties (e.g., foul shots in basketball) are used to regulate the orderly progress of the game (Brickman, 1977; Greenberg, Mark, & Lehman, 1985; Mark & Greenberg, 1987). Such sanctions may be understood as society's mechanisms for institutionalizing restitution from those who do not voluntarily yield to more subtle social pressures.

In organizations, apologies (also referred to as "penitential accounts" by Bies, 1987a) have been studied by Greenberg (1988a) in his investigation of the explanations given for performance evaluations. Apologies (e.g., "I am sorry to have to give you such a low rating") were given as the prevalent explanation of performance ratings in 13.41% of the cases studied. These represented the most popular category of explanation given to workers in the lowest performance categories ("poor" and "needs improvement"). Although workers receiving such low ratings tended to be dissatisfied with their evaluations, it was found that an apologetic explanation for the rating enhanced workers' feelings that their ratings were fair, relative to those who were not offered any such apology.

To summarize, both accounts (including excuses and justifications) and apologies have been shown to be effective mechanisms for defending against the threat of an identity of unfairness. Verbal behaviors offered to excuse, justify, or apologize for one's actions can enhance the perceived fairness of those actions and the social acceptance of the actor.

Assertive Tactics: Identity-Enhancing Situations

As noted earlier, self-presentational efforts are not only directed toward defending against identity-threatening predicaments, but also promoting identity-enhancing situations. Variously referred to as *assertive* tactics (Tedeschi & Norman, 1985), *offensive* attributions (Tetlock, 1985), and *acclaiming* tactics (Schlenker, 1980), impression management theorists have recognized the existence of proactive efforts directed toward seeking approval for behavior in a meritorious way. Following the lead of D'Arcy (1963), theorists have distinguished between *entitlings*—attempts to gain responsibility for positive events and their consequences, and *enhancements*—attempts to augment the positive implications of one's actions (e.g., Schlenker, 1980; Tedeschi & Norman, 1985; Tedeschi & Reiss, 1981b; Tetlock, 1985). As will be argued in the following sections, both entitling actions and enhancements are used as tactics to enhance one's image of fairness.

Entitlings.   Imagine a supervisor who believes she behaved responsibly by appraising her subordinates' performance following all the procedural rules (e.g., giving worker input into the decision) and distributive practices (e.g., rating commensurate with work performed) recognized as prerequisites for fair performance appraisals (Greenberg, 1986a, 1986b). However, she feels her praiseworthy actions are not being recognized by her subordinates or her superiors. This situation may be said to create a "predicament of image projection" (Tedeschi & Reiss, 1981b, p. 8) for the supervisor, who will desire to gain credit for her actions by getting others to attribute the characteristic of fairness to her. The behaviors directed at prompting these attributions are referred to as *entitlings*

(D'Arcy, 1963). As such, entitlings are the opposite of excuses: the former actions attempt to maximize one's responsibility for positive events, whereas the latter attempt to minimize one's responsibility for negative events (Tedeschi & Reiss, 1981b).

What do managers do to enhance their perceived responsibility for fair outcomes? What fairness-entitling actions do they engage in? Some answers are provided by Greenberg (1988a), who asked a sample of 815 managers to describe one thing they thought they could do to make their subordinates think they treated them fairly. The responses fell into four categories derived by crosscutting things done to look fair (*behavioral acts*) and things said to look fair (*social account*) with the means by which things are done (*process*) and the end results themselves (*outcomes*). Specifically, 81% of the respondents reported that they could enhance their image of fairness by "publicly announcing all pay raises and promotions"—a behavioral act focusing on outcomes. "Allowing workers to participate in decision-making," a response reported by 55% of the sample, exemplifies a behavioral act focusing on organizational processes. Social accounts also focused on outcomes, such as "explanations of why certain work assignments must be made" (43% frequency), and processes, such as, "how pay raises are determined" (76% frequency). Managers were apparently aware of several tactics they could use to promote fair self-attributions. Although it remains to be determined how often managers actually use these tactics, and how effective these tactics ultimately may be in cultivating fair impressions, it is instructive to note the range of potentially entitling actions managers believed were possible.

Whereas earlier research has focused on various organizational outcomes and processes perceived as fair (for a review, see Folger & Greenberg, 1985), the Greenberg (1988a) findings extend this work by showing that managers are aware of the things they can do to promote the *impression* of fairness. In other words, managers appear to be aware of what they have to do or say to *look fair*. Entitlings may be understood as representing tactics for promoting one's image of fairness—*intuitive self-marketing plans*, if you will.

Astute managers who plan to reap the benefits of fair dispositional characteristics may carefully select behaviors that help cultivate desired impressions in the minds of relevant others. Allen et al. (1979) implicitly make this point in reporting their findings regarding the popularity of various techniques of organizational politics (which they conceive of as tactics for gaining organizational influence). Among the most frequently-obtained responses were "attempts to create and maintain a favorable self-image." These included responses such as developing a reputation for being thoughtful and honest—attributions similar to those in Jones and Pittman's (1982) exemplification category, as well as less cognitive acts, such as good grooming.

The organizational politician was also noted for drawing attention to successes, including ones for which the individual was not directly responsible (Allen et al., 1979). Schlenker (1980) refers to this as the "association principle," the tendency to associate oneself with desirable images. Managers claimed this was done sometimes by taking credit for another's accomplishments, often by making misleading statements or not crediting the appropriate source of one's ideas. It is indeed a curious (and, to my knowledge, untested) possibility that one may use a practice of such a dubious ethical nature to foster an image of oneself as a "fair" individual. However, given the importance of justice as a tool of organizational politics (Cavanagh et al., 1981), it would not be surprising to find people attempting to solicit at least partial credit for implementing well-received organizational plans. In fact, anticipating this, team leaders may well wish to gain their team members' support by allowing them to share the credit for their group's accomplishments—thereby giving them an opportunity to "bask in the reflected glory" of their joint accomplishments (Richardson & Cialdini, 1981).

Enhancements.   In addition to attempting to credit oneself with positive events, people also attempt to persuade others that an ambiguous event was positive, or that an ostensibly positive event really was *very* positive. Such efforts at augmenting the positive implications of one's actions are known as *enhancements,* and represent a second category of assertive impression management tactics (Tedeschi & Norman, 1985). Just as entitling actions are the opposite of excuses, enhancements may be understood to be the opposite of justifications (Tedeschi & Reiss, 1981b).

The key to enhancing self-presentations is information. It is therefore not surprising that in their study of managers' use of organizational politics, Allen et al. (1979) found that "information presentation" was one of the most popularly reported techniques. Managers claimed to selectively withhold and distort information in order to influence others. In the case of influence through fair self-promotion, managers may be likely to take advantage of inherently ambiguous consensual definitions of fairness by presenting information that enhances the perceived fairness of their actions (Backman, 1985). By selectively presenting information about an ambiguous event, managers may be helping consensually define the "truth" about it for those who are involved with interpreting it. In other words, managers may attempt to "negotiate" an impression of themselves as fair (Backman, 1985; Schlenker, 1980). This possibility is in keeping with the idea that social constructions help define moral conduct—including a sense of fairness (Backman, 1985). Similarly, the concept of leadership also has been presented as a "negotiated identity," that is socially constructed (Tedeschi & Melburg, 1984). The underlying idea is that many salient realities confronting people in organizations are socially constructed (Weick, 1979). People respond to what they believe, and information is the key to manipulating beliefs. Therefore, it is not surprising that the selective presentation of information—enhancement behavior—is such a useful tool of organizational politics.

There appear to be many ways organizational agents can enhance the ostensible fairness of their intentions—thereby helping others define their perceived reality as fair. For example, public pronouncements (such as through press releases, policy statements, and advertising campaigns) or internal memoranda (such as announcements made in writing or at meetings, and statements in company newsletters) may be recognized as tools used to promote fairness at the organizational level. Similarly, annual reports have been interpreted as tools to influence interested parties in an organization's image (e.g., Salancik & Meindl, 1984; Staw, McKechnie, & Puffer, 1983). At the individual level, managers may behave analogously—by selectively detailing their decisions, and by feeding leaks of fair actions through opinion leaders and informal channels of communication (Katz, 1957). The organizational performance appraisal interview may be understood as another vehicle through which the fairness of a manager's actions may be communicated (Greenberg, 1986b).

It is, in fact, quite likely that an organization that institutes an ostensibly fair, nuturant policy (e.g., a non-layoff agreement) may seek to enhance the intended benefits by promoting it—both internally, to employees, and externally, via institutional advertising. Advertising also may be used by organizations to promote their good-will gestures toward their customers. For example, one large word processing software firm has reproduced in print ads its monthly telephone bills totaling $169,848.22 for toll-free customer support lines ("What's So Special," 1988). Juxtaposing the bill with a check for the amount signed by the company president, the ad may be understood as an attempt to enhance the company's image of concern for its customers. The benefits to be derived from the "we're fair, we care" image may well rival, if not exceed, those directly associated with the administration of the policy itself (Greenberg, 1988b). The possibility that such efforts represent intentional attempts at impression management is inherent in Thompson's (1967) notion of *prospective rationality:* "organizations act rationally to increase their evaluations or ratings by others on whom they are dependent" (p. 65.).

Impression Management Strategies: Reputation-Building

Before concluding this part of the chapter, a final point needs to be made. All the impression management tactics described here are designed to have an immediate, short-term effect on one's perceived identity. Tedeschi and his associates (e.g., Tedeschi & Melburg, 1984; Tedeschi & Norman, 1985) distinguish between these short-term "tactics," and *strategies*—behaviors designed to have long-term consequences on impressions.

Strategic impression management "typically involves a variety of tactical behaviors cumulatively directed toward establishing a particular identity in the eyes of others" (Tedeschi & Norman, 1985, p. 296). As such, impression management strategies have the effect of *reputation-building.* One who repeatedly convinces others of his or her fairness eventually may develop a reputation as a fair person. Relative to the person-specific and transitory identities resulting from the tactics described to this point, reputations are "typically functional for multiple audiences (or targets), [and] are effective across various situations" (Tedeschi & Norman, 1985, p. 297). They are, therefore, much more powerful tools, opening up a wider world of influence. For this reason, a person's acquisition of a good reputation may be seen as an investment that yields long-term gains in social influence (Schlenker, 1980). Accordingly, the benefits of behaving fairly may not only be derived from the immediate impact of the actions themselves, but the cumulative impact of the impression that the actor is himself or herself "a fair person." To my knowledge, there are, unfortunately, no direct empirical tests of this process as it applies to the development of reputations of fairness. Given the likely impact of reputations of fairness, such research would appear to be quite useful.

IMPLICATIONS OF AN IMPRESSION MANAGEMENT VIEW OF ORGANIZATIONAL JUSTICE

The issues discussed thus far have some interesting implications and raise some important questions for the study of organizational justice. Implications and questions focusing on four issues will be raised here: (a) the sincerity of fair impressions, (b) organizational influences on fair identities, (c) the benefits and liabilities of fair impression, and (d) the management of impressions of organizational justice.

On the Sincerity of Looking Fair: Hollow Justice?

If the research and conceptual ideas introduced in this chapter combine to make any single point, it is surely that *looking fair* is a distinct concern from *being fair*. Certainly, people may behave fairly because they are motivated out of an interest in doing the right thing, believing that the cumulative effect of fair behavior benefits everyone in the long run (Lerner, 1977; Walster et al., 1978). Indeed, the value of justice and morality at the organizational level has been expressed eloquently by the philosopher, John Rawls (1971), who referred to justice as, "the first virtue of social institutions, as truth is of systems of political thought" (p. 3), and equally powerfully by the sociologist Charles Perrow (1972):

> The common purpose of an organization must always be a moral purpose,
> and to inculcate this moral purpose into the very fiber of the organization and
> into the members of it is the only meaningful task of the executive (p. 77).

I do not challenge this position. Rather, I seek to expand the point by noting that people may facilitate the process of fostering morality by promoting their own fairness. Such a sentiment is not completely new to management thinking, as Chester Barnard, the former president of AT&T argued over a half-century ago, "wholesale general persuasion in the form of salesmanship and advertising" (Barnard, 1938, p. 144) is needed to persuade employees of the moral character of executives' actions. The various assertive tactics described in the present chapter may be understood as mechanisms for ensuring agreement about the importance of one's fair actions.

It also should be added that people may strive to attain the benefits of being recognized as fair, but without actually behaving fairly. Such self-promotions of fairness lacking in substance may be referred to as *hollow justice*. Any mere "veneer of fairness" may function as effectively as any more deeply-rooted concern for moral righteousness as long as it is not perceived to be manipulative. A perceived intentional "using" of fairness as a tool of manipulation is likely to backfire when such insincerity is suspected (as indicated by research on the ingratiator's dilemma; e.g., Jones, 1964; Liden & Mitchell, 1988; Ralston, 1985). Demonstrating this effect, subjects in two experiments by Greenberg and Ornstein (1983) reported feeling equitably paid when they were compensated for added job responsibilities by being given a high-status job title. However, when they suspected that their supervisor may have given them the title to trick them into thinking they were fairly compensated, they rebelled—attributing malicious motives to the supervisor, perceiving they were underpaid, and dramatically lowering their job performance.

Although some may seek to further their selfish interests by wrapping their malevolent motives around the mantle of justice—particularly political leaders (DiQuattro, 1986)—it is not necessary to assume deceptive motives in order to embrace an impression management view of justice. In this regard, I should not be represented as echoing the sentiments of his honor, Philip Stanhope, the Earl of Chesterfield, who in 1749 said, "Without some dissimulation, no business can be carried out at all" (cited in Rheingold, 1988, p. 88). Impression management theorists are quick to point out, and I would agree, that people's tactical efforts at presenting themselves favorably to others should *not* be confused with lying (Schlenker, 1980; Tedeschi & Rosenfeld, 1981). The image one puts forth may be sincere, in that it accurately reflects the actor's self-image, or it may represent dissembling. However, not all inaccurate self-presentations may be consciously duplicitous; some may represent identities actors believe they have, if only through wishful thinking (Baumeister, 1982). Generally speaking, "people need to believe attributions designed to protect their sense of self-worth (otherwise the attributions do not serve their 'intended' motivational function), but people do not need to believe attributions designed to protest their public or social identities (we can offer explanations for conduct that impresses others favorably, but that we do not really believe to be true)" (Tetlock, 1985, p. 222).

A key determinant of the sincerity of one's projected image is the degree of clarity surrounding the appropriateness of the behavior in question (Baron, 1988; Snyder, 1985). The inherent ambiguity regarding what constitutes fairness makes it possible for many actions to be presented as fair. The very ambiguous nature of fairness has been established in several open-ended questionnaires focusing specifically on organizational behaviors (e.g., Greenberg, 1986a; Sheppard & Lewicki, 1987) and general social interaction (Liebrand et al., 1986; Messick et al., 1985). This condition makes it possible for people to couch their behaviors (including their verbal remarks) in terms of justice without intentional dishonesty. People may well believe that certain acts are fair that others cannot accept as such (Baumeister, 1982). In other words, *fairness may be a socially constructed reality* (Bies, 1987a; Weick, 1979). The idea that fairness is a desired *label* that people seek to attach to their behaviors is one of the most important implications of an impression management interpretation of justice (Bies, 1987a). Understanding the processes through which labels of fairness are attached and removed (an approach that has been recommended for the study of leadership by Tedeschi & Melburg, 1984) opens up an entirely new direction for research on organizational justice. Such an approach clearly identifies a host of different research questions than an approach assuming that the underlying motive behind an act of justice is the desire to relieve the negative emotions brought on by an inequitable payment (Greenberg, 1987a).

As one example of the kind of new questions likely to emerge, we might see a shift in research on individual differences in justice behavior. Traditionally, researchers have studied how differences in such variables as sex, personality, and nationality relate to intolerance for inequities and the preference for various normative standards of justice (for a review, see Major & Deaux, 1982). An impression management perspective would suggest the introduction of variables based on *self-presentational styles* (Arkin, 1981), such as: determinants of sensitivity toward engendering disapproval for unfairness relative to garnering approval for fairness, and preferences for various defensive and assertive techniques of fair impression management. Knowing about such variables would further our understanding of the mechanisms by which impressions of fairness are cultivated.

Organizational Influences on Fair Identities

It has been shown that people seek to present themselves as fair to others and to themselves. Superimposing these findings on organizational contexts identifies some interesting and important unanswered questions.

For one, it would be instructive to know if certain organizational figures are more salient than others as sources of self-presentational concerns. Typically, higher-status persons are more inclined to be targets of impression management efforts (Gardner & Martinko, 1988). In organizations, this phenomenon is complicated by the fact that one's actions are likely to have impact on—or, at least, be known by—multiple constituencies (Ralston, 1985). In many cases, what may be done to impress one party with one's own fairness may be antagonistic to cultivating another's impressions of fairness. For example, in keeping with the research reviewed here, a manager may seek to divide available monies for pay raises equally among his subordinates in order to minimize the interpersonal strain merit-based, equitable divisions may create (Leventhal, 1976). However, in so doing, managers run the risk of displeasing other workers, particularly high-input workers who would have benefited from equitable divisions of reward. To impress such an individual with one's fairness may require making a different response. Further complicating the example, supervisors also may face pressure from their own superiors to follow other rules of fairness. In cases of conflicting expectations among multiple constituencies, it may be expected that the target selected for impression management purposes will be the target whose impressions are most highly valued (Schlenker, 1980). In organizations, this may well be that person believed to control the most valued resources.

This situation is complicated by the possibility that different organizational constituencies may be sensitive to qualitatively different manifestations of fairness. In other words, the aspect of one's behavior needed to cultivate an image of fairness may be different for different target persons. For example, a middle manager may seek to convince subordinates that he behaved fairly by giving them a voice in the decisions regarding the manning of office telephones during lunch hours (e.g., "Someone has to monitor the phones during lunch, and rather than assign one of you to do so, I'll let you decide among yourselves who should do it."). This same manager may have to convince his superiors that he behaved fairly by presenting his personnel-assignment decision in a manner consistent with other organizational units (e.g., "As done elsewhere in our company, I delegated this decision to the workers themselves."). Thus, managers may be able to satisfy the fairness demands of multiple constituencies by simply focusing their explanations on different aspects of the same behavior. In this example, the manager would emphasize to the subordinates the fact that he allowed them to make the decision themselves (i.e., emphasizing the procedural fairness criterion of voice in decision making; Greenberg & Folger, 1983), whereas to the superior, the manager would emphasize the fact in performing the same behavior he conformed to organizational policy (i.e., emphasizing the distributional equality of the outcome). By selectively reporting one's behavior, it may be possible to convince several targets of one's fairness. (Of course, to the extent that an actor's image of fairness is reputational, persons interacting with that actor are likely to attribute his or her actions to fair motives simply because of that person's reputation. He or she would receive "the benefit of the doubt" about being fair.)

Finally, it is interesting to consider how social pressures in organizations impose subtle limitations on efforts at positive self-presentation. In particular, the tendency to play up one's organizational fairness may be limited by fears of presenting oneself immodestly. The practice of immodestly attempting to manipulate desired impressions may sometimes backfire (such as when the actions are perceived as exaggerated and ethically inappropriate), resulting in an undesirable image—a self-promotor's paradox (Ashforth & Gibbs, in press). As a result, the risks of being caught in the act of ostensibly manipulating impressions may be especially likely to be accepted by those who believe their potentially positive impression-forming actions would otherwise go unnoticed. Persons who believe that others will come to know of their desirable actions tend to be less self-aggrandizing than those who do not (Baumeister & Jones, 1978). To the extent that existing mechanisms of organizational communication (e.g., the announcement of one's actions in a company newsletter) ensure the transmittal of a manager's fair actions, managers may be reluctant to engage in further self-promotional efforts. Instead, managers convinced of public acceptance of their actions may reinforce their subordinates' attributions of their fairness through their humility. In so doing, they may be benefiting from the "secondary impression" of modesty as well as the "calculated impression" of fairness (Schneider, 1981). As Schlenker (1980) put it, "successful people can afford to be modest and thus acquire images of success and humility" (p. 193).

Benefits and Liabilities of Fair Impressions

Impression management theorists (e.g., Tedeschi & Reiss, 1981b; Tetlock & Manstead, 1985) have pointed out several benefits of favorable self-presentations that apply quite well to self-presentations of fairness (Greenberg, 1988b). There are also several possible liabilities and limitations associated with attempting to cultivate an image of fairness.

Benefits.   One benefit of a fair identity is that it may reinforce a person's self-identity and sense of self-esteem (Greenwald & Breckler, 1985). People sometimes do things to convince themselves of their fairness (Greenberg, 1983a), particularly those individuals who strongly endorse the Protestant work ethic

(Greenberg, 1979). An internalized belief in a just world (Lerner, 1980) is likely to be reinforced by actions that help define oneself as fair. Indeed, research has shown that self-image maintenance is a very potent determinant of fair behavior (Greenberg, 1980, 1983a, 1983b).

In addition to these intrapsychic benefits, fair identities also may help individual organizational functioning by enhancing a manager's power base. In fact, Tedeschi and Norman (1985) explicitly contend that self-presentations may be interpreted as influence attempts. Managers perceived as fair may gain power advantages through several mechanisms. To the extent that fair behaviors are admired (Messick et al., 1985), and liking encourages compliance with managers so as to gain their approbation (French & Raven, 1959), attributions of fairness may strengthen a manager's power base. Similarly, managers' power may be enhanced by their subordinates' beliefs in their fairness because of widely held associations between fairness and credibility (Liebrand et al., 1986; Messick et al., 1985). Just as the power of a fair judge is derived from his or her perceived lack of ulterior motives and consistent application of the law, so too may a manager's reputation for credibility and trustworthiness facilitate his or her power to supervise (Tedeschi & Melburg, 1984; Tedeschi & Norman, 1985; Tedeschi & Reiss, 1981b).

An indirect power advantage also may be gained by managers believed to be fair. As has been noted earlier in this chapter, the fairness of many managerial decisions is ambiguous to subordinates because they are made on the basis of unknown information. Managers with reputations for fairness (or, at least, those who have temporarily impressed others with their fairness) may meet fewer challenges to their authority than others who lack the reputational power of fairness. In ambiguous situations, managers may rely on their reputations for fairness to convince subordinates of the fairness of their actions. Managers who have demonstrated themselves to be fair in the past may well derive power from the acceptance of their admonitions to "trust me, I'll be fair." In other words, a reputation for fairness may help give managers the benefit of the doubt in situations in which judgments of fairness may not be easily made—a process similar to the issuance of "idiosyncrasy credit" (Hollander, 1964) noted in the study of leadership emergence in small groups.

Finally, I should note that fair social identities also may facilitate functioning at the organizational-level. As Greenberg (1988b) discusses, an organizational-level image of fairness—that is, a corporate culture of fairness—may help attract and retain the best qualified job candidates, as well as customers who are attracted by the company's positive image. Indeed, it has been argued that the public will recognize and support "socially responsive firms"; that is, those that fulfill society's moral and ethical expectations (Murray & Montanari, 1986). To the extent that this is true, then benefits of identities of corporate fairness may also be realized in terms of marketing indicators (e.g., percent of market share) as well as management indicators (e.g., degree of job satisfaction). Promotional efforts that position corporations as fair-minded to their employees, the surrounding economic community, and the ecology may be the result of efforts to cultivate a corporate image of fairness (Greenberg, 1988b). (As an example, one may note the frequent advertisements by large oil companies promoting their efforts at eliminating, rather than contributing to, environmental pollution.) Recent research by Schwoerer and Rosen (1989) has found that job applicants' impressions of prospective employers were enhanced by brochures promoting the organizations as being committed to a doctrine encouraging "fair treatment to all employees." Corporate values, including those emphasizing justice and morality, have been recognized as core elements of organizational culture (Deal & Kennedy, 1982).

In addition to individuals seeking to convince themselves (the private self) or specific external audiences (the public self) of their fairness, organizations provide an opportunity for people to seek adherence to superordinate goals, norms of justice accepted collectively by reference groups. Greenwald and Breckler (1985) use the term *collective self* to refer to an individual's internalization of the goals of a group with whom he or she is identified, the "we-aspect" of one's identity. Although it is often assumed that internalization of reference groups' standards account for public self-presentations (a "situated identity" position; Alexander & Rudd, 1981), the possibility that workers directly may seek to impress the collective self with their fairness remains untested. Some relevant research has shown that people may frame accounts of their behavior in highly ideological terms (e.g., "this is the right thing to do because it helps us—the company"), making reference to loftier collective goals in order to meet more immediate needs (see Bies, 1987a).

Sensitivity to the collective self might not be equal at all organizational levels. Specifically, it may be speculated that higher-level organizational officials, presidents and CEOs, would tend to be held most responsible for achieving collective standards of fairness. The perspective afforded by their positions may empower them to consider justice from a collective viewpoint more than others whose lower levels in the hierarchy encourage them to focus on more individual-level concerns. Position power, in fact, may well reflect one's level of interest in collective concerns about justice (Tedeschi & Norman, 1985).

Liabilities. In addition to the benefits associated with an image of fairness, there also may be some liabilities that are not immediately obvious to those who strive to attain that image. For one, the "responsibilities" of one's image sometimes may jeopardize one's social standing (Schlenker, 1980). Consider, for example, the plight of certain political and religious figures (former President Nixon and TV evangelists Bakker and Swaggart come to mind) whose alleged indiscretions have publicly disgraced them. Because these individuals' identities were defined primarily in terms of their lofty moral standing, it would not be surprising to find them more disgraced for their actions than others who never sought, by virtue of their position or their actions, a reputation for moral purity.

A challenged identity is, perhaps, most threatened when it forms the core of one's public image. A parallel to the concept of "status liability" (Wiggins, Dill, & Schwartz, 1965) is apparent. Just as a high status person may receive the most credit for positive outcomes and take the most blame for negative outcomes, a similar process may be operating with respect to self-presentations. That is, persons whose primary social identities are invested in a certain image may not only receive the most approval for events affirming that identity, but also may receive the most disapproval for events challenging that identity (Schlenker, 1980). Thus, although images of fairness may be quite valuable organizational tools, there also may be some costs associated with maintaining them.

Just as individuals may bear costs associated with having a fair identity, so too may institutions bear similar costs—and in an analogous manner. For example, because the American news media is expected to fairly and dispassionately report stories to the public, it is sometimes found that press accounts of news events that are biased, or which proactively create rather than reactively report stories instigate public outcries of injustice. Such was the case, for example, when press reports surfaced prior to the 1988 U.S. presidential election that questioned Republican Vice Presidential candidate Dan Quayle's motives for joining the National Guard (allegedly, to avoid being drafted and serving in a military unit in Vietnam). One poll taken at that time found that 55% of those surveyed believed the press coverage was unfair ("Poll," 1988). Such assessments may well be partly responsible for growing public disenchantment with the mass media (Roberts & Maccoby, 1985). Given that the American press is an institution historically associated with safeguarding justice and democracy, public sensitivity to potentially unfair actions on its part (e.g., claims of overzealously "hounding" a political candidate) may be readily understood as an instance of an institution's liability for its reputation. In other words, just as the "holier than thou" individual might be held to a higher moral standard than mere mortal souls, so too may institutions sanctioned with responsibility for assuring public well-being be expected to face harsh disapproval when they appear to have violated the very rights they are empowered to protect.

Another personal liability associated with having a reputation for being fair may be the burden of having to justify one's actions in terms of fairness rather than any other criteria, such as one's own preferences (B. R. Schlenker, personal communication, June 26, 1988). If a "fair person" is who you *are* in the eyes of others, your projected identity, then it may be seen as insufficient for you to account for your actions in terms that do not assert this identity. Others will be looking for and expect to find an explanation couched in terms of fairness and may be dissatisfied by any other type of explanation. In fact, it is an intriguing possibility that failure to assert the identity regularly may actually weaken the identity itself. Such obligations to justify one's actions as fair (i.e., pressures to live up to one's reputation) may be burdensome in that they force the actor to couch his or her actions in the language of justice (e.g., "I did it this way because it took everyone's relative contributions into account."), and may restrict the use of other explanatory mechanisms (such as personal choice; e.g., "I did it this way because I wanted to."). In other words, to reap the benefits of a fair identity, one may have to pay for it in terms of the restricted behavioral (or at least, rhetorical) options required to maintain that identity. (This process is analogous to the press agent's efforts to put his client into situations that help reassert his or her public image— such as getting the playboy millionaire to be seen in the presence of a beautiful starlet at a chic night spot. To maintain his appeal as a box office draw, the playboy is expected to present himself in a manner consistent with the image created for him—whether he wants to or not!)

Managing—and Mismanaging—Impressions of Organizational Fairness: Case Studies

Given the fact that scientists and practitioners have only recently begun to recognize and appreciate the full range of organizational behaviors associated with organizational justice, it is not too surprising to find very few published cases in which issues of fair impression management are explicitly analyzed. Yet, with increased frequency, recent treatises on corporate morality are beginning to pay attention to the matter of impressions of fairness, if only in passing (e.g., Jackall, 1988; Walton, 1988). In addition, two recent cases may be identified as explicitly focusing on concerns about fair impressions created in organizations. One highlights the successful management of fair impressions, and the other, unsuccessful management.

Successful Impression Management: Introducing a New Performance Appraisal System at Cyanamid. In 1986 the American Cyanamid Company introduced a new performance appraisal system company-wide following a successful experiment in the company's Medical Research Division during the previous three years (Gellerman & Hodgson, 1988). After reducing an unworkable 10-point scale to an easier 3-point scale and eliminating forced-distribution expectations, claims that the scale was unfair were greatly reduced. In fact, during the last year of the study (1986), 63% of the workers using the new system reported that it fairly assessed their performance, compared to only 24% in a control group using the old system. On the basis of such findings, the new system was adopted in 1986 for all of the company's 11,500 U.S. employees.

Interestingly, although the company planned on introducing the new system company-wide regardless of the study's findings, the positive reaction of workers in the company's Medical Research Division was cited as justification for introducing the system. These findings were then widely disseminated throughout the company in an attempt at publicizing the new system's fairness—and the company's fairness in basing the system's introduction on such successful trial outcomes. Such an ostensible effort at showing the company's concern for introducing an established perceived-fair practice was seen as consistent with CEO George J. Sella Jr.'s commitment toward humanizing the corporate culture and improving the quality of life for the company's employees. These actions also have been credited for fostering workers' acceptance of the new system. (Indeed, it is difficult to ascertain the extent to which acceptance of the new system is based on employees' genuine regard for the system's own characteristics uncontaminated by the company's ballyhoo regarding its greatness.) Cyanamid's efforts at impressing its workforce with the company's interest in introducing proven-fair procedures provides an excellent example of the concern for cultivating fair impressions described in this chapter.

Unsuccessful Impression Management: The Firing of the Ohio State University's Football Coach.   By contrast to the Cyanamid case, not all organizational changes are managed in a manner perceived as fair. An excellent example is provided by Lewicki's (1988) analysis of claims of unfairness resulting from the firing of the Ohio State University's head football coach, Earle Bruce, in November, 1987.

The case begins when the University's President, Edward Jennings, fired Coach Bruce in the middle of Bruce's contract, one week before the 1987 season's final game (against its arch rival, the University of Michigan). Claiming that such personnel matters required secrecy, President Jennings gave little or no information to the public regarding his reasons for Coach Bruce's surprise dismissal (the coach had repeatedly led his team to 9–3 seasons—a good, but not impressive record). The firing subsequently led the University's Athletic Director to resign in protest, Coach Bruce to bring suit against the University (resulting in a $471,000 settlement), the University President to lose a great deal of good will for his actions (publicly decried as unfair), and Coach Bruce to emerge as a sympathetic, victimized hero.

In analyzing this incident, Lewicki (1988) noted that public organizations with highly visible performance and large public constituencies (such as in this case) need to be sensitive to the perceived fairness of their actions. Clearly, in this case the University President was not sensitive enough to issues of perceived fairness. Specifically, by failing to disclose adequate reasons behind the Coach's firing, the university may be seen as violating the public's consensually perceived "rights" of full disclosure, and its "right" to question undesirable actions. Although there are no actual legal rights to such information in this case, the disclosure of such information would have been useful in facilitating the public's acceptance of the decision as a fair one. Lewicki (1988) claimed that by not providing such information, the University violated the public's "right to know," thereby providing an incident of ineffective management of social accounts resulting in perceptions of unfairness. Certainly, the effects of such actions on alumni donations, fan support, and the recruitment of future players and coaches—although unknown at the present time—may be taken as useful indicators of the long-term impact of such mismanagement.

Synthesis.   Despite their many differences, the Cyanamid case and the Ohio State University case clearly underscore the importance of impressions of fairness in organizations. It was the promoted appearance of fairness that facilitated acceptance of Cyanamid's new performance appraisal system, and the ostensible unfairness of the manner of Coach Bruce's firing that led to public disapproval of the University President Jennings. Just because Cyanamid's new performance appraisal system does a better job of evaluating workers, or even if President Jennings actually had just cause for firing Coach Bruce, it was the *way* in which the information was presented in both cases that appears to have been so responsible for the reactions that resulted. Thus, as I have been saying throughout this chapter: it is the management of an impression of fairness that is so greatly responsible for the reactions that result from one's behavior.

CONCLUSION

Can it be said that concerns about impressing others with one's fairness are pre-eminent in organizations, or that fairness is the most important attributional goal sought by subordinates, managers, or organizations? Although any claims to these effects may represent overstatements, the salience of concerns about fairness cannot be ignored. Unfortunately, organizational scientists have largely overlooked impression management issues as they pertain to organizational fairness. Long limited by the domination of a narrow perspective about justice, they have not been able to capture the richness of this topic. With these remarks, it is hoped that the field of organizational behavior will expand its views of organizational justice and re-direct at least some of its efforts away from "being fair" and toward "looking fair."

As in the case of earlier efforts at applying an impression management perspective to social phenomena traditionally studied by intrapsychic theories (Tetlock & Manstead, 1985), my interest has been in encouraging the study of organizational justice from an alternative point of view. I believe the departure from the historically prevalent reactive content frameworks (e.g., equity theory and relative deprivation theory) for studying organizational justice (Greenberg, 1987a) outlined here provides a more insightful approach into a broader range of issues of organizational justice than heretofore may have been considered. As such, the time appears to have come for equity theory, the reigning theory of organizational justice to release its hegemony over the field. Such a shift in paradigms would be in keeping with a reorientation that took place in social psychology from the 1960s to the 1970s, "a shift from motivational/drive models of cognitions, behaviors, and internal states to information processing, attribution models of such phenomena" (Bem, 1972, p. 43). This shift that Bem referred to is also in evidence in the field of organizational behavior (e.g., Salancik & Pfeffer, 1978). However, the field of organizational justice has been slow to catch up with this movement (Greenberg, 1987a). Hopefully, the impression management orientation advanced in this chapter will encourage some new directions in organizational justice research and theory development that embrace the intrapsychic orientation.

Before concluding, I must caution readers against the temptation toward interpreting an element of irony in this paper—namely, that one would act manipulatively in the name of fairness. To be sure, there is nothing inherently Machiavellian about wanting to appear fair. Concerns about the perceived fairness of one's own actions reflect a social sensitivity that may be no more deceitful than any other self-presentational efforts (such as dressing to impress others, or treating people in a kind manner to win their friendship). Of course, whereas any calculated impression may be motivated by unethical interests (e.g., the slick con job of the snake oil salesman), there is no reason to suspect that fairness as a desired identity is any more likely to be associated with the deceitful intentions of those who pursue it than any other identity. To the hopefully many readers to whom this caveat may seem unnecessary and overly defensive, my reply is that it is not aimed at you. Rather, it is intended to reassure those inclined to treat justice as a cherished virtue that risks tarnishing by tampering with it (Bellah, Madsen, Sullivan, Swidler, & Tipton, 1985) that any concern for nurturing justice fails to render it less pure.

I opened this chapter by arguing that practicing managers may have greater awareness of the importance of fair social identities than most organizational scientists who study fairness. In closing, it is hoped that the impression management perspective advanced on these pages will stimulate the efforts of those who study organizational behavior to catch up with the consensual beliefs of those who practice it.

References

Adams, J. S. (1965). Inequity in social exchange. In L. Berkowitz (Ed.), *Advances in experimental social psychology,* Vol. 2 (pp. 267–299). New York: Academic Press.

Adams, J. S., & Freedman, S. (1976). Equity theory revisited: Comments and annotated bibliography. In L. Berkowitz & E. Walster (Eds.), *Advances in experimental social psychology,* Vol. 9 (pp. 43–90). New York: Academic Press.

Adams, J. S., & Rosenbaum, W. B. (1962). The relationship of worker productivity to cognitive dissonance about wage inequities. *Journal of Applied Psychology, 46,* 161–164.

Albert, S. (1977). Temporal comparison theory. *Psychological Review, 84,* 485–503.

Alexander, C. N., Jr., & Rudd, J. (1981). Situated identities and response variables. In J. T. Tedeschi (Ed.), *Impression management theory and social psychological research* (pp. 83–103). New York: Academic Press.

Alexander, S., & Rudeman, M. (1987). The role of procedural and distributive justice in organizational behavior. *Social Justice Research, 1,* 177–198.

Allen, R. W., Madison, D. L., Porter, L. W., Renwick, P. A., & Mayes, B. T. (1979). Organizational politics: Tactics and characteristics of its actors. *California Management Review, 22,* 77–83.

Allen V. L. (1982). Effect of conformity pressure on justice behavior. In J. Greenberg & R. L. Cohen (Eds.), *Equity and justice in social behavior* (pp. 187–215). New York: Academic Press.

Anderson, N. H. (1968). Likableness ratings of 555 personality-trait words. *Journal of Personality and Social Psychology, 9,* 272–279.

Andrews, I. R., & Valenzi, E. R. (1970). Overpay inequity of self-image as a worker: A critical examination of an experimental induction procedure. *Organizational Behavior and Human Performance, 5,* 266–276.

Arkin, R. M. (1981). Self-presentational styles. In J. T. Tedeschi (Ed.), *Impression management theory and social psychological research* (pp. 311–333). New York: Academic Press.

Ashforth, B. E., & Gibbs, B. (in press). The double-edge of organizational legitimation. *Organizational Science.*

Austin, J. L. (1961). *Philosophical papers.* London: Oxford University Press.

Austin, W. (1980). Friendship and fairness: Effects of type of relationship and task performance on choice of distribution rules. *Personality and Social Psychology Bulletin, 6,* 402–407.

Austin, W., & McGinn, N. C. (1977). Sex differences in choice of distribution rules. *Journal of Personality, 45,* 379–394.

Austin, W., Walster, E., & Utne, M. K. (1976). Equity and the law: The effects of a harm-doer's "suffering in the act" on liking and assigned punishment. In L. Berkowitz (Ed.), *Advances in experimental social psychology*, Vol. 9 (pp. 163–190). New York: Academic Press.

Backman, C. W. (1985). Identity, self-presentation, and the resolution of moral dilemmas: Toward a social psychological theory of moral behavior. In B. R. Schlenker (Ed.), *The self and social life* (pp. 261–289). New York: McGraw Hill.

Barnard, C. (1938). *The functions of the executive.* Cambridge, MA: Harvard University Press.

Baron, R. A. (1988). Attributions and organizational conflict: The mediating role of apparent sincerity. *Organizational Behavior and Human Decision Processes, 41,* 111–127.

Baumeister, R. F. (1982). A self-presentational view of social phenomena. *Psychological Bulletin, 91,* 3–26.

Baumeister, R. F., & Jones, E. E. (1978). When self-presentation is constrained by the target's knowledge: Consistency and compensation. *Journal of Personality and Social Psychology, 36,* 608–618.

Bell, N. E., Tetlock, P. E. (1990). The intuitive politician and the assignment of blame in organizations. In R. A. Giacalone & P. Rosenbeld (Eds.), *Impression management in the organization.* Hillsdale, NJ: Lawrence Erlbaum Associates.

Bellah, R. N., Madsen, R., Sullivan, W. M., Swidler, A., & Tipton, S. M. (1985). *Habits of the heart.* New York: Harper & Row.

Bem, D. J. (1972). Self-perception theory. In L. Berkowitz (Ed.), *Advances in experimental social psychology*, Vol. 6 (pp. 42–66). New York: Academic Press.

Berger, J., Zelditch, M., Anderson, B., & Cohen, B. P. (1972). Structural aspects of distributive justice: A status-value formulation. In J. Berger, M. Zelditch, & B. Anderson (Eds.), *Sociological theories in progress.* Vol. 2 (pp. 21–45). Boston: Houghton Mifflin.

Bies, R. J. (1986a, August). Identifying principles of interactional justice: The case of corporate recruiting. In R. J. Bies (Chair), *Moving beyond equity theory: New Directions in research on organizational justice.* Symposium presented at the meeting of the Academy of Management, Chicago.

Bies, R. J. (1986b). *The delivery of bad news in organizations: Strategies and tactics.* Unpublished manuscript, Northwestern University.

Bies, R. J. (1987a). The predicament of injustice: The management of moral outrage. In L. L. Cummings & B. M. Staw (Eds.), *Research in organizational behavior*, Vol. 9 (pp. 289–319). Greenwich, CT: JAI Press.

Bies, R. J. (1987b). Beyond "voice": The influence of decision-maker justification and sincerity on procedural fairness judgments. *Representative Research in Social Psychology 17,* 3–14.

Bies, R. J. (1989). Managing conflict before it happens: The role of accounts. In M. A. Rahim (Ed.), *Managing conflict: An interdisciplinary approach* (pp. 83–91). New York: Praeger.

Bies, R. J., & Moag, J. S. (1986). Interactional justice: Communications criteria of fairness. In R. J. Lewicki, B. H. Sheppard, & M. H. Bazeman (Eds.), *Research on negotiation in organizations: Vol. 1* (pp. 43–55). Greenwich, CT: JAI Press.

Bies, R. J., & Shapiro, D. L. (1987). International fairness judgments: The influence of causal accounts. *Social Justice Research, 1,* 199–218.

Bies, R. J., & Shapiro, D. L. (1988). Voice and justification: Their influence on procedural fairness judgments. *Academy of Management Journal, 31,* 676–685.

Bies, R. J., Shapiro, D. L., & Cummings, L. L. (1988). Causal accounts and managing organizational conflict: Is it enough to say it's not my fault? *Communication Research 15,* 381–399.

Brickman, P. (1977). Crime and punishment in sports and society. *Journal of Social Issues, 33,* 140–164.

Brockner, J., & Greenberg, J. (1989). The impact of layoffs on survivors: An organizational justice perspective. In J. Carroll (Ed.), *Advances in applied social psychology: Business settings* (pp. 45–75). Hillsdale, NJ: Lawrence Erlbaum Associates.

Carver, C. S., & Scheier, M. F. (1981). *Attention and self-regulation: A control-theory approach to human behavior.* New York: Springer-Verlag.

Carver, C. S., & Scheier, M. F. (1985). Aspects of self and the control of behavior. In B. R. Schlenker (Ed.), *The self and social life* (pp. 146–174). New York: McGraw Hill.

Cavanagh, G. F., Moberg, D. J., & Velasquez, M. (1981). The ethics of organizational politics. *Academy of Management Review, 6,* 363–374.

Chatman, J. A., Bell, N. E., & Staw, B. M. (1986). The managed thought: The role of self-justification and impression management in organizational settings. In D. Gioia & H. Sims (Eds.), *The thinking organization: Dynamics of organizational social cognition* (pp. 191–214). San Francisco: Jossey-Bass.

Cohen, R. L. (1974). Mastery and justice in laboratory dyads: A revision and extension of equity theory. *Journal of Personality and Social Psychology, 29,* 464–474.

Cooley, C. H. (1902). *Human nature and the social order.* New York: Charles Scribner's Sons.

Cornelius, E. T., Ullman, J. C., Meglino, B. M., Czajka, J., & McNeely, B. (1985, November). *A new approach to the study of worker values and some preliminary results.* Paper presented at the meeting of the Southern Management Association, Orlando, FL.

Cosier, R. A., & Dalton, D. R. (1983). Equity theory and time: A reformulation. *Academy of Management Review, 8,* 311–319.

Crosby, F. (1984). Relative deprivation in organizational settings. In B. M. Staw & L. L. Cummings (Eds.), *Research in organizational behavior,* Vol. 6 (pp. 51–93). Greenwich, CT: JAI Press.

D'Arcy, E. (1963). *Human acts: An essay in their moral evaluation.* New York: Oxford University Press.

Deal, T. E., & Kennedy, A. A. (1982). *Corporate cultures.* Reading, MA: Addison-Wesley.

Deutsch, M. (1975). Equity, equality and need: What determines which value will be used as the basis for distributive justice? *Journal of Social Issues, 31,* 137–149.

Deutsch, M. (1985). *Distributive justice.* New Haven, CT: Yale University Press.

DiQuattro, A. (1986). Political studies and justice. In R. L. Cohen (Ed.), *Justice: Views from the social sciences* (pp. 85–116). New York: Plenum.

Duval, S., & Wicklund, R. A. (1972). *A theory of objective self-awareness.* New York: Academic Press.

Fenigstein, A., Scheier, M. F., & Buss, A. H. (1975). Public and private self-consciousness: Assessment and theory. *Journal of Consulting and Clinical Psychology, 43,* 522–527.

Festinger, L. (1957). *A theory of cognitive dissonance.* Evanston, IL: Row, Peterson.

Feyerabend, P. K. (1970). How to be a good empiricist—A plea for tolerance in matters epistemological. In B. A. Brody (Ed.), *Readings in the philosophy of science* (pp. 55–77). Englewood Cliffs, NJ: Prentice-Hall.

Fincham, F. D., & Jaspars, J. M. (1980). Attribution of responsibility: From man the scientist to man the lawyer. In L. Berkowitz (Ed.), *Advances in experimental social psychology.* Vol. 13 (pp. 81–138). New York: Academic Press.

Folger, R. (1986). Rethinking equity theory: A referent cognitions model. In H. W. Bierhoff, R. L. Cohen, & J. Greenberg (Eds.), *Justice in social relations* (pp. 145–162). New York: Plenum.

Folger, R., & Greenberg, J. (1985). Procedural justice: An interpretive analysis of personnel systems. In K. Rowland & G. Ferris (Eds.), *Research in personnel and human resources management,* Vol. 3 (pp. 141–183). Greenwich, CT: JAI Press.

Folger, R., & Martin, C. (1986). Relative deprivation and referent cognitions: Distributive and procedural justice effects. *Journal of Experimental Social Psychology, 22,* 531–546.

Folger, R., Rosenfield, D., & Robinson, T. (1983). Relative deprivation and procedural justifications. *Journal of Personality and Social Psychology, 45,* 268–273.

Freedman, S. M., & Montanari, J. R. (1980). An integrative model of managerial reward allocation. *Academy of Management Review, 5,* 381–390.

French, J. R. P., Jr., & Raven, B. (1959). The bases of social power. In D. Cartwright (Eds.), *Studies in social power* (pp. 118–149). Ann Arbor, MI: University of Michigan Press.

Friedman, A., & Goodman, P. S. (1974). *The effect of individualizing pay and secrecy about pay on salary allocations.* Unpublished manuscript, Hebrew University.

Furby, L. (1986). Psychology and justice. In R. L. Cohen (Ed.), *Justice: Views from the social sciences* (pp. 153–203). New York: Plenum.

Gardner, W. L., & Martinko, M. J. (1988). Impression management: An observational study linking audience characteristics with verbal self-presentations. *Academy of Management Journal, 31,* 42–65.

Garrett, J. B., & Libby, W. L., Jr. (1973). Role of intentionality in mediating responses to inequity in the dyad. *Journal of Personality and Social Psychology, 28,* 21–27.

Gellerman, S. W., & Hodgson, W. G. (1988, May-June). Cyanamid's new take on performance appraisal. *Harvard Business Review,* pp. 36–37, 40–41.

Giacalone, R. A., & Rosenfeld, P. (1987). Impression management concerns and reinforcement interventions. *Group and Organization Studies, 12,* 445–453.

Giacalone, R. A., & Rosenfeld, P. (Eds.) (1990). *Impression management in the organization.* Hillsdale, NJ: Lawrence Erlbaum Associates.

Gibbons, F. X., & Wicklund, R. A. (1982). Self-focused attention and helping behavior. *Journal of Personality and Social Psychology, 43,* 462–474.

Goodman, P. S., & Friedman, A. (1971). An examination of Adam's theory of inequity. *Administrative Science Quarterly, 16,* 271–288.

Goffman, E. (1959). *The presentation of self in everyday life.* Garden City, NY: Anchor Doubleday.

Goffman, E. (1971). *Relations in public.* New York: Basic Books.

Greenberg, J. (1978). Effects of reward value and retaliative power on allocation decisions: Justice, generosity, or greed? *Journal of Personality and Social Psychology, 36,* 367–379.

Greenberg, J. (1979). Protestant ethic endorsement and the fairness of equity inputs. *Journal of Research in Personality, 13,* 81–90.

Greenberg, J. (1980). Attentional focus and locus of performance causality as determinants of equity behavior. *Journal of Personality and Social Psychology, 38,* 579–585.

Greenberg, J. (1982). Approaching equity and avoiding inequity in groups and organizations. In J. Greenberg & R. L. Cohen (Eds.), *Equity and justice in social behavior* (pp. 389–435). New York: Academic Press.

Greenberg, J. (1983a). Overcoming egocentric bias in perceived fairness through self-awareness. *Social Psychology Quarterly, 46,* 152–156.

Greenberg, J. (1983b). Self-image versus impression management in adherence to distributive justice standards: The influence of self-awareness and self-consciousness. *Journal of Personality and Social Psychology, 44,* 5–19.

Greenberg, J. (1984). On the apocryphal nature of inequity distress. In R. Folger (Ed.), *The sense of injustice* (pp. 167–188). New York: Plenum.

Greenberg, J. (1986a). Determinants of perceived fairness of performance evaluations. *Journal of Applied Psychology, 71,* 340–342.

Greenberg, J. (1986b). Organizational performance evaluations: What makes them fair? In R. J. Lewicki, B. Sheppard, & M. Bazeman (Eds.), *Negotiation in organizations* (pp. 25–41). Greenwich, CT: JAI Press.

Greenberg, J. (1986c). The distributive justice of organizational performance evaluations. In H. W. Bierhoff, R. L. Cohen, & J. Greenberg (Ed.), *Justice in social relations* (pp. 337–351). New York: Academic Press.

Greenberg, J. (1987a). A taxonomy of organizational justice theories. *Academy of Management Review, 12,* 9–22.

Greenberg, J. (1987b). Using diaries to promote procedural justice in performance appraisals. *Social Justice Research, 1,* 219–234.

Greenberg, J. (1988a, August). Using social accounts to manage impressions of performance appraisal fairness. In J. Greenberg & R. J. Bies (Co-chairs), *Communicating fairness in organizations.* Symposium presented at the meeting of the Academy of Management, Anaheim, CA.

Greenberg, J. (1988b). Cultivating an image of justice: Looking fair on the job. *Academy of Management Executive, 2,* 155–158.

Greenberg, J. (1989). Cognitive re-evaluation of outcomes in response to underpayment inequity. *Academy of Management Journal, 32,* 174–184.

Greenberg, J., & Cohen, R. L. (1982). Why justice? Normative and instrumental interpretations. In J. Greenberg & R. L. Cohen (Eds.), *Equity and justice in social behavior* (pp. 437–469). New York: Academic Press.

Greenberg, J., Mark, M. M., & Lehman, D. (1985). Equity and justice in sports and games. *Journal of Sport Behavior, 8,* 18–33.

Greenberg, J., & Folger, R. (1983). Procedural justice, participation, and the fair process effect in groups and organizations. In P. B. Paulus (Ed.), *Basic group processes* (pp. 235–256). New York: Springer-Verlag.

Greenberg, J., & Ornstein, S. (1983). High status job title as compensation for underpayment: A test of equity theory. *Journal of Applied Psychology, 68,* 285–297.

Greenberg, J., & Tyler, T. R. (1987). Why procedural justice in organizations? *Social Justice Research, 1,* 127–142.

Greenberg, M. S., & Frisch, D. M. (1972). Effect of intentionality on willingness to reciprocate a favor. *Journal of Experimental Social Psychology, 8,* 99–111.

Greenwald, A. G., & Breckler, S. J. (1985). To whom is the self presented? In B. R. Schlenker (Ed.), *The self and social life* (pp. 126–145). New York: Academic Press.

Hamilton, V. L. (1980). Intuitive psychologist or intuitive lawyer? Alternative models of the attribution process. *Journal of Personality and Social Psychology, 39,* 767–772.

Harris, R. J. (1976). Handling negative inputs: On the plausible equity formulae. *Journal of Experimental Social Psychology, 12,* 194–209.

Heider, F. (1958). *The psychology of interpersonal relations.* New York: Wiley.

Hollander, E. P. (1964). *Leaders, groups, and influence.* New York: Oxford University Press.

Huber, V. L., Latham, G. P., & Locke, E. A. (1990). The management of impressions through goal setting. In R. A. Giacalone, & P. Rosenfeld (Eds.), *Impression management in the organization.* Hillsdale, NJ: Lawrence Erlbaum Associates.

Jackall, R. (1988). *Moral mazes.* New York: Oxford University Press.

James, W. (1980). *The principles of psychology,* Vol. 1. New York: Henry Holt & Co.

Jones, E. E. (1964). *Ingratiation.* New York: Appleton-Century-Crofts.

Jones, E. E., & Pittman, T. S. (1982). Toward a general theory of strategic self-presentation. In J. Suls (Ed.), *Psychological perspectives on the self,* Vol. 1 (pp. 231–262). Hillsdale, NJ: Lawrence Erlbaum Associates.

Jones, E. E., & Sigall, H. (1971). The bonus pipeline: A new paradigm for measuring affect and attitude. *Psychological Bulletin, 76,* 349–364.

Kahneman, D., & Tversky, A. (1982). Availability and the simulation heuristic. In D. Kahneman, P. Slovik, & A. Tversky (Eds.), *Judgment under uncertainty: Heuristics and biases* (pp. 201–208). Cambridge, UK: Cambridge University Press.

Kalven, J., & Zeisel, H. (1966). *The American jury.* Boston: Little, Brown.

Katz, E. (1957). The two-step flow of communication. *Public Opinion Quarterly, 21,* 61–78.

Kelley, H. H. (1967). Attribution theory in social psychology. In D. Levine (Ed.), *Nebraska symposium on motivation,* Vol. 15 (pp. 55–88). Lincoln, NE: University of Nebraska Press.

Kelman, H. C. (1973). Violence without moral restraint: Reflections on the dehumanization of victims and victimizer. *Journal of Social Issues, 29,* 25–61.

Kemis, M., & Reis, H. T. (1984). Self-consciousness, self-awareness, and justice in reward allocation. *Journal of Personality, 52,* 58–70.

Kidd, R. F., & Utne, M. K. (1978). Reactions to inequity: A prospective on the role of attributions. *Law and Human Behavior, 2,* 301–312.

Lane, I. M., & Messé, L. A. (1971). Equity and the distribution of rewards. *Journal of Personality and Social Psychology, 20,* 1–17.

Lawler, E. E., III. (1968). Equity theory as a predictor or productivity and work quality. *Psychological Bulletin, 70,* 596–610.

Lemer, M. J. (1977). The justice motive: Some hypotheses as to its origins and forms. *Journal of Personality, 45,* 1–52.

Lemer, M. J. (1980). *The belief in a just world.* New York: Plenum.

Leventhal, G. S. (1976). The distribution of rewards and resources in groups and organizations. In L. Berkowitz & E. Walster (Eds.), *Advances in experimental social psychology,* Vol. 9 (pp. 91–131). New York: Academic Press.

Leventhal, G. S. (1980). What should be done with equity theory? In K. J. Gergen, M. S. Greenberg, & R. H. Willis (Eds.), *Social exchange: Advances in theory and research* (pp. 27–55). New York: Plenum.

Leventhal, G. S., Michaels, J. W., & Sanford, C. (1972). Inequity and interpersonal conflict: Reward allocation and secrecy about reward as methods of preventing conflict. *Journal of Personality and Social Psychology, 23,* 88–102.

Leventhal, G. S., Weiss, T., & Long, G. (1969). Equity, reciprocity, and reallocating rewards in the dyad. *Journal of Personality and Social Psychology, 13,* 300–305.

Lewicki, R. J. (1988). The public face of justice: Ineffective management of an organizational justice problem. In J. Greenberg & R. J. Bies (Chairs), *Communicating fairness in organizations.* Symposium presented at the meeting of the Academy of Management, Anaheim, CA.

Liden, R. C., & Mitchell, T. R. (1988). Ingratiatory behaviors in organizational settings. *Academy of Management Review 13,* 572–587.

Liebrand, W. B. G., Messick, D. M., & Wolters, F. J. M. (1986). Why we are fairer than others: A cross-cultural replication and extension. *Journal of Experimental Social Psychology, 22,* 590–604.

Lind, E. A., & Tyler, T. R. (1988). *The social psychology of procedural justice.* New York: Olenum.

Lofland, J. (1969). *Identities and deviance.* Englewood Cliffs, NJ: Prentice-Hall.

Longenecker, C. O., Sims, H. P., Jr., & Gioia, D. A. (1987). Behind the mask: The politics of employee appraisal. *Academy of Management Executive, 1,* 183–193.

Major, B., & Deaux, K. (1982). Individual differences in justice behavior. In J. Greenberg & R. L. Cohen (Eds.), *Equity and justice in social behavior* (pp. 43–76). New York: Academic Press.

Mark, M. M., & Greenberg, J. (1987, January). Evening the score. *Psychology Today,* pp. 44–50.

Messick, D. M., Bloom, S., Boldizer, J. P., & Samuelson, D. C. (1985). Why we are fairer than others. *Journal of Experimental Social Psychology, 21,* 480–500.

Miller, D. T., & Ross, M. (1975). Self-serving biases in the attribution of causality: Fact or fiction? *Psychological Bulletin, 82,* 213–225.

Miner, J. B. (1984). The unpaved road over the mountains: From theory to applications. *The Industrial Organizational Psychologist, 21*(2), 9–20.

Morse, S. J., Gruzen, J., & Reis, J. T. (1976). The nature of equity restoration: Some approval-seeking considerations. *Journal of Experimental Social Psychology, 12,* 1–8.

Moberg, D. J. (1977, April). *Organizational politics: Perspective from attribution theory.* Paper presented at the meeting of the American Institute for Decision Sciences, Chicago.

Mowday, R. T. (1987). Equity theory predictions of behavior in organizations. In R. M. Steers & L. W. Porter (Eds.), *Motivation and work behavior* (4th ed.) (pp. 89–110). New York: McGraw Hill.

Murray, K. B., & Montanari, J. R. (1986). Strategic management of the socially responsible firm: Integrating management and marketing theory. *Academy of Management Review, 11,* 815–827.

O'Malley, M. N., & Greenberg, J. (1983). Sex differences in restoring justice: The down payment effect. *Journal of Research in Personality, 17,* 174–185.

Perrow, C. (1972). *Complex organizations.* Glenview, IL: Scott, Foresman.

Pfeffer, J. (1981). Management as symbolic action. In L. L. Cummings & B. M. Staw (Eds.), *Research in organizational behavior,* Vol. 3 (pp. 1–52). Greenwich, CT: JAI Press.

Poll: News on Quayle is unfair. (1988, August 29). *Columbus Dispatch*, p. 2A.

Pritchard, R. (1969). Equity theory: A review and critique. *Organizational Behavior and Human Performance, 4*, 75–94.

Pritchard, R., Dunnette, M. D., & Jorgenson, D. O. (1972). Effects of perceptions of equity and inequity on worker performance and satisfaction. *Journal of Applied Psychology, 56*, 75–94.

Ralston, D. A. (1985). Employee ingratiation: The role of management. *Academy of Management Review, 10*, 447–487.

Rasinski, K. A. (1987). What's fair is fair—or is it? Value differences underlying public views about social justice. *Journal of Personality and Social Psychology, 53*, 201–211.

Ravlin, E. C., & Meglino, B. M. (1987). Effects of values on perception and decision making: A study of alternative work value measures. *Journal of Applied Psychology, 72*, 666–673.

Rawls, J. (1971). *A theory of justice.* Cambridge, MA: Harvard University Press.

Reis, H. T. (1981). Self-presentation and distributive justice. In J. Tedeschi (Ed.), *Impression management theory and social psychological research* (pp. 269–291). New York: Academic Press.

Reis, H. T. (1984). The multidimensionality of justice. In R. Folger (Ed.), *The sense of injustice* (pp. 25–61). New York: Plenum.

Reis, H. T. (1986). Levels of interest in the study of interpersonal justice. In H. W. Bierhoff, R. L. Cohen, & J. Greenberg (Eds.), *Justice in social relations* (pp. 187–209). New York: Plenum.

Reis, H. T., & Burns, L. B. (1982). The salience of the self in responses to inequity. *Journal of Experimental Social Psychology, 18*, 464–475.

Reis, H. T., & Gruzen, J. (1976). On mediating equity, equality, and self-interest: The role of self-presentation in social exchange. *Journal of Experimental Social Psychology, 12*, 487–503.

Rheingold, H. (1988). *They have a word for it.* Los Angeles: Jeremy P. Tarcher.

Richardson, K. D., & Cialdini, R. B. (1981). Basking and blasting: Tactics of indirect self-presentation. In J. T. Tedeschi (Ed.), *Impression management theory and social psychological research* (pp. 41–53). New York: Academic Press.

Rivera, A. N., & Tedeschi, J. T. (1976). Public versus private reactions to positive inequity. *Journal of Personality and Social Psychology, 34*, 895–900.

Roberts, D. F., & Maccoby, N. (1985). Effects of mass communication. In G. Lindzey & E. Aronson (Eds.), *Handbook of social psychology* (3rd ed.), Vol. 2 (pp. 539–598). New York: Random House.

Salancik, G. R., & Meindl, J. R. (1984). Corporate attributions as strategic illusions of management control. *Administrative Science Quarterly, 29*, 238–254.

Salancik, G. R., & Pfeffer, J. (1978). A social information processing approach to job attitudes and task design. *Administrative Science Quarterly, 23*, 224–253.

Sampson, E. E. (1975). On justice as equality. *Journal of Social Issues, 31*, 45–64.

Scheibe, K. E. (1985). Historical perspectives on the presented self. In B. R. Schlenker (Ed.), *The self and social life* (pp. 33–64). New York: McGraw Hill.

Schlenker, B. R. (1980). *Impression management: The self-concept, social identity, and interpersonal relations.* Belmont, CA: Brooks/Cole.

Schlenker, B. R. (1986). Self-identification: Toward an integration of the private and public self. In R. Baumeister (Ed.), *Public self and private self* (pp. 21–62). New York: Springer-Verlag.

Schlenker, B. R., & Darby, B. W. (1981). The use of apologics in social predicaments. *Social Psychology Quarterly, 44,* 271–278.

Schneider, D. J. (1981). Tactical self-presentations: Toward a broader conception. In J. T. Tedeschi (Ed.), *Impression management theory and social psychological research* (pp. 23–40). New York: Academic Press.

Schoeninger, D. W., & Wood, D. W. (1969). Comparison of married and ad hoc mixed-sex dyads negotiating the division of a reward. *Journal of Experimental Social Psychology, 5,* 483–499.

Schwab, D. P. (1980). Construct validity in organizational behavior. In B. M. Staw & L. L. Cummings (Eds.), *Research in organizational behavior,* Vol. 2 (pp. 3–43). Greenwich, CT: JAI Press.

Schwartz, S. (1977). Normative influences on altruism. In L. Berkowitz (Ed.), *Advances in experimental social psychology.* Vol. 10 (pp. 222–279). New York: Academic Press.

Schwartz, G., Kane, T., Joseph, J., & Tedeschi, J. T. (1978). The effects of remorse on reactions to a harm-doer. *British Journal of Social and Clinical Psychology, 17,* 293–297.

Scott, M. B., & Lyman, S. M. (1968). Accounts. *American Sociological Review, 33,* 46–62.

Shapiro, D. L. & Buttner, E. H. (1988, August), *Adequate explanations: What are they, and do they enhance procedural justice under severe outcome circumstances?* Paper presented at the meeting of the Academy of Management, Anaheim, CA.

Shapiro, E. G. (1975). Effect of expectation of future interaction on reward allocation in dyads: Equity or equality? *Journal of Personality and Social Psychology, 31,* 873–880.

Sheppard, B. H. (1984). Third party conflict intervention; A procedural framework. In B. M. Staw & L. L. Cummings (Eds.), *Research in organizational behavior,* Vol. 6 (pp. 141–190). Greenwich, CT: JAI Press.

Sheppard, B. H. (1985). Justice is no simple matter: Case for elaborating our model of procedural fairness. *Journal of Personality and Social Psychology, 49,* 953–962.

Sheppard, B. H., & Lewicki, R. J. (1987). Toward general principles of managerial fairness. *Social Justice Research, 1,* 161–176.

Snyder, C. R. (1985). The excuse: An amazing grace? In B. R. Schlenker (Ed.), *The self and social life* (pp. 235–289). New York: McGraw Hill.

Snyder, C. R., Higgins, R. L., & Stucky, R. J. (1983). *Excuses: Masquerades in search of social grace.* New York: Wiley.

Staw, B. M., McKechnie, P. I., & Puffer, S. M. (1983). The justification of organizational performance. *Administrative Science Quarterly, 28,* 582–600.

Sykes, G., & Matza, D. (1957). Techniques of neutralization: A theory of delinquency. *American Journal of Sociology, 22,* 664–670.

Tedeschi, J. T. (Ed.), (1981). *Impression management theory and social psychological research.* New York: Academic Press.

Tedeschi, J. T., & Melburg, V. (1984). Impression management and influence in the organization. In S. B. Bachrach & E. J. Lawler (Eds.), *Research in the sociology of organizations,* Vol. 3 (pp. 31–58). Greenwich, CT: JAI Press.

Tedeschi, J. T., & Norman, N. (1985). Social power, self-presentation, and the self. In B. R. Schlenker (Ed.), *The self and social life* (pp. 293–322). New York: McGraw Hill.

Tedeschi, J. T., & Reiss, M. (1981a). Verbal strategies in impression management. In C. Antaki (Ed.), *The psychology of ordinary explanations of social behavior* (pp. 271–309). London: Academic Press.

Tedeschi, J. T., & Reiss, M. (1981b). Identities, the phenomenal self, and laboratory research. In J. T. Tedeschi (Ed.), *Impression management theory and social psychological research* (pp. 3–22). New York: Academic Press.

Tedeschi, J. T., & Rosenfeld, P. (1981). Impression management theory and the forced compliance situation. In J. T. Tedeschi (Ed.), *Impression management theory and social psychological research* (pp. 147–177). New York: Academic Press.

Tetlock, P. E. (1985). Toward an intuitive politician model of attribution processes. In B. R. Schlenker (Ed.), *The self and social life* (pp. 203–234). New York: McGraw-Hill.

Tetlock, P. E. & Manstead, A. (1985). Impression management versus intrapsychic explanations in social psychology: A useful dichotomy? *Psychological Review, 92*, 59–77.

Thibaut, J. W., & Kelley, H. H. (1959). *The social psychology of groups.* New York: Wiley.

Thompson, J. D. (1967). *Organizations in action.* New York: McGraw-Hill.

Tornow, W. W. (1971). The development and application of an input-outcome moderator test on the perception and reduction of inequity. *Organizational Behavior and Human Performance, 6*, 614–638.

Utne, M. K., & Kidd, R. F. (1980). Attribution and equity. In G. Mikula (Ed.), *Justice and social interaction* (pp. 63–93). New York: Springer-Verlag.

Vallacher, R. A., & Solodky, M. (1979). Objective self-awareness, standards of evaluation and moral behavior. *Journal of Experimental Social Psychology, 15*, 252–262.

Walster, E., Walster, G. W., & Berscheid, E. (1978). *Equity: Theory and research.* Boston: Allyn & Bacon.

Walston, C. C. (1988). *The moral manager.* Cambridge, MA: Ballinger.

Weick, K. E. (1979). *The social psychology of organizing* (2nd ed.). Reading, MA: Addison-Wesley.

Weiner, B. (1974). Achievement motivation as conceptualized by an attribution theorist. In B. Weiner (Ed.), *Achievement motivation and attribution theory* (pp. 3–48). Morristown, NJ: General Learning Press.

Weiner, B., Amirkhan, J. Folkes, V. S., & Varette, J. A. (1987). An attributional analysis of excuse giving: Studies of a naive theory of emotion. *Journal of Personality and Social Psychology, 52*, 316–324.

What's So Special About WordPerfect? (1988, March). *Personal Computing,* pp. 100–103, 107–109, 113, 115–116.

Wicklund, R. A. (1975). Objective self-awareness. In L. Berkowitz (Ed.), *Advances in experimental social psychology,* Vol. 8 (pp. 233–275). New York: Academic Press.

Wiggins, J. A., Dill, F., & Schwartz, R. D. (1965). On "status liability." *Sociometry, 28*, 197–209.

Wittig, M. R., Marks, G., & Jones, G. A. (1981). The effects of luck versus effort attributions on reward allocations to self and other. *Personality and Social Psychology Bulletin, 7*, 71–78.

PART III

ACQUIRING HUMAN RESOURCES

HUMAN RESOURCE PLANNING

INTRODUCTION

Changes in the labor market create both constraints and opportunities for employers, and there are many different responses that an organization can take when confronting these challenges. This variation creates an important arena in which an organization can gain a competitive advantage in its particular market. The key to effectively utilizing labor markets to one's competitive advantage is to be able to avoid discrepancies between the present demand for labor and one's current supply of labor. When these discrepancies cannot be avoided, a company must at least be able to eliminate the problem in a manner that promotes, rather than detracts, from the organization's ability to compete. The set of readings provided here examines issues related to this task, focusing first on using downsizing as a means of reducing a labor surplus and then second at using part-time employees as a means of eliminating a labor shortage.

Our first article focuses on downsizing among white-collar employees. The 1980s recession was often referred to as the "white collar" recession, because the unemployment it triggered occurred among this group of employees rather than blue-collar employees, who are the traditional victims of economic downturns. The article by Kim Cameron, Sarah Freeman, and Aneil Mishra, entitled "Best Practices in White-Collar Downsizing: Managing Contradictions," discusses six specific strategies that distinguished firms that successfully downsized from those that failed. This article notes that successfully managing downsizing forces the company to come to grips with several contradictions, and sincerely try to help those whom the organization just terminated.

Our second article also focuses on downsizing but examines the problem from a more legalistic perspective. Balkin argues that companies trying to downsize should do so in a manner that least hinders their ability to compete. One partial means of doing this is to ensure that high performers are retained at a higher rate than low performers. However, the U.S. legal system makes discharging employees more risky than has traditionally been the case, and layoffs that are "performance contingent" are from a legal perspective identical to discharges. Balkin focuses on several strategies that employers can use to try to get voluntary attrition among low-performing employees so that unilateral discharges, and the resulting legal quagmires can be minimized.

READING 18

BEST PRACTICES IN
WHITE-COLLAR DOWNSIZING
Managing Contradictions

Kim S. Cameron
Sarah J. Freeman
Aneil K. Mishra

Executive Overview

It is no secret that U.S. industry, once the most productive in the world, is now lagging behind its global competitors. What is not well known is that blue-collar productivity is not necessarily the problem. Between 1978 and 1986, for example, the number of production workers declined by six percent while real output rose 15 percent. White-collar productivity decreased six percent while the number of workers increased by twenty-one percent.

Downsizing, which involves reducing the workforce, but also eliminates functions and redesigns systems and policies to contain costs, is becoming more common in U.S. companies. Despite its pervasiveness, however, downsizing has rarely been investigated by organization and management researchers.

This article seeks to identify the processes used in effective downsizing as well as the consequences that result. The authors studied organizational downsizing and redesign for four years in thirty organizations in the automobile industry. Six general strategies are presented that highlight the best practices of these firms that are downsizing effectively.

Once the most productive nation in the world, the U.S. now lags most of its global competitors in productivity growth.[1] For example, private sector productivity growth slowed from 3.3 percent per year between 1948 and 1965 to 0.1 percent today for the entire economy. Worse still, productivity for nonfarm businesses declined 0.3 percent.[2] A good share of the blame for this decline rests squarely on white-collar employees and management. To illustrate, consider that between 1978 and 1986 the number of production workers in the U.S. declined by six percent

Source: "Best Practices in White-Collar Downsizing: Managing Contradictions" by Kim S. Cameron, Sarah J. Freeman, and Aneil K. Mishra, *Academy of Management Executive*, 1991, Vol. 5, No. 3, 57–73.

while real output rose fifteen percent. That represents a 21 percent gain in blue-collar productivity, or a 2.4 percent annual growth rate. During the same period, however, U.S. manufacturing firms expanded the number of white-collar, non-production workers by twenty-one percent, representing a six percent decrease in productivity.

The trend toward a disproportionate expansion in the number of white-collar workers is also illustrated by the fact that in 1950, twenty-three percent of U.S. manufacturing industry employees were nonproduction workers. By 1988 that figure had risen to forty-seven percent. At the same time that production worker employment was decreasing in the 1980s, nonproduction worker employment was increasing dramatically in the manufacturing sector. The good news is that approximately seventy percent of the increase in America's GNP in the 1980s was accounted for by an expansion in the number of jobs. The bad news is that this growth of our major global competitors was accounted for by increases in employee productivity, not merely job growth.

DOWNSIZING AS A RESPONSE

Declining white collar productivity is reflected as a cost disadvantage. Overhead rates reflecting excess white-collar employees have created a cost structure in many U.S. companies that limits global price competitiveness and, consequently marketshare growth. It is not surprising, then, that organizational downsizing has become a common cost reduction strategy in U.S. companies.

More than eighty-five percent of the Fortune 1000 firms, for example, downsized their white-collar workforce between 1987 and 1991, affecting more than five million jobs. More than fifty percent downsized in 1990 alone. Major reductions occurred in firms such as ITT (more than forty percent of the company's workforce), K-Mart (more than 20 percent), Peat Marwick (more than 20 percent), IBM (more than 10 percent), AT&T (more than 10 percent), Eastman Kodak (more than 10 percent), and Sears (more than 10 percent). Almost a million American managers with salaries exceeding $40,000 lost their jobs last year, and between one and two million pink-slips have been handed out each year for the past three years. (More than half of those employees took pay cuts of thirty to fifty percent to obtain new jobs.)

Yet, even with the extensive downsizing implemented in U.S. firms, white-collar productivity has not improved significantly. Overhead rates and costs remain significantly above the best global competitors in many industries.[3] One explanation is that downsizing has not been managed effectively in many firms and, therefore, the intended cost reductions and efficiencies have not materialized. Another is that downsizing has created resentment and resistance in firms, thus hindering rather than helping U.S. competitiveness. Unfortunately, not enough is known about the implementation processes associated with downsizing to identify best practices. Despite its pervasiveness, downsizing has rarely been investigated by organization and management researchers. Few systematic studies have been published of the precursors, effects, and strategies associated with organizational downsizing.

One reason is that downsizing has often been confused with two other organizational phenomena: layoffs and decline. Organizational downsizing involves many alternatives beyond just laying off personnel. Organizations may get smaller, for example, through headcount reduction strategies such as attrition, early retirements, or outplacements. Downsizing may occur by reducing work, not just personnel, by eliminating functions, hierarchical levels, or units. And it may also occur by implementing cost containment strategies that simplify processes such as paperwork, information systems, or sign-off policies.

Organizational decline is also different than downsizing. Decline refers to the *involuntary* loss of resources, generally revenues or marketshare. Downsizing refers to *intended* reductions of personnel. Organizational decline often leads to what Cameron, Kim, and Whetten[4] called "the dirty dozen"—that is, twelve dysfunctional effects in organizations. These include decreasing levels of morale, trust, communication, and innovation as well as increasing levels of conflict, scapegoating, threat-rigidity reactions, and conservatism. Whether these same phenomena occur when organizations are downsizing was an important question in the study reported here. Because downsizing may be implemented when the organization is growing as well as when it is declining, downsizing and decline are not the same phenomena.

ISSUES FOR INVESTIGATION

This article reports some of the findings from a four-year longitudinal study of organizational downsizing and redesign in thirty organizations in the U.S. automobile industry. Some organizations were plants within parent corporations (for example, assembly plants or stamping plants); some were independent firms (supplier businesses). The study focused on white-collar downsizing (as opposed to hourly employee reductions) because productivity declines and non-competitiveness are attributed mainly to excess white-collar positions. Moreover, these positions are often the most attractive positions in organizations. Their attractiveness makes them difficult to eliminate, although they may be the most redundant.

One primary intent of the study was to identify the processes used in effective downsizing as well as the consequences that resulted from downsizing. More precisely, this article reports "best practices"—the downsizing strategies that were associated with the most effective organizational outcomes. In brief, the major question being addressed is: When organizations engage in downsizing, what strategies are most likely to be associated with organizational effectiveness?

METHODOLOGY

Firms in the auto industry were selected because of the extensive downsizing that is occurring in that industry and because of its size and importance in the American economy. For example, more than forty percent of this nation's current merchandise trade deficit is related to the automotive industry. Well over a million people work for the Big Three Auto companies alone (General Motors, Ford, and Chrysler), not to mention the myriad related organizations and industries that serve as suppliers to and customers of the automobile companies. Moreover, since 1981 nearly half a million jobs have been affected by downsizing activities in the Big Three firms.

Each of the thirty organizations in the study had engaged in downsizing activities. Some downsized in years prior to the study (pre-1987), almost all downsized during the years of the study, and many were planning to downsize in the immediate future as well. Reductions in the workforce in these firms ranged from +14 percent to –69 percent of white-collar employees and from +69 percent to –49 percent of blue-collar employees. (That is, some organizations increased the white-collar workforce while decreasing the blue-collar workforce, or vice versa.) The smallest of these organizations employed approximately 100 employees; the largest employed over 6000. Interviews were conducted every six to nine months with the head of each organization between 1987 and 1990. This top manager was treated as the key informant to provide ongoing information regarding how downsizing and organizational redesign activities were being implemented. Each manager was interviewed five times over the four-year period, with each interview lasting about two hours. Two separate researchers, one involved in conducting the interviews and one not involved, read the transcripts of the interviews and independently identified the themes, issues, and strategies that characterized each organization. Relationships between organizational effectiveness and implementation processes were especially noted. Agreement between the interview coders for these themes, issues, and strategies was very high.

In addition to the interviews, approximately 2500 questionnaires were collected from white-collar employees in these 30 organizations, asking for perceptions of strategies, corporate culture, leadership, and outcomes of downsizing. Measures of effectiveness were obtained by asking respondents to compare their organization's current performance with its performance in the previous two years, with the performance of its best domestic and global competitors, with stated goals for the current year, and with perceived customer expectations. Table 1 reports the range of organizational effectiveness scores for firms in the study. Statistical analyses of the questionnaire responses uncovered the factors that are most closely associated with organizational effectiveness. These analyses are not reported in detail here,[5] but the findings related to implementation processes are discussed below. It was discovered that the way in which downsizing occurred was more important in accounting for effectiveness than the size of the work force reduction or the cost savings that accrued. The following discussion explains these effective implementation processes.

BEST PRACTICES IN DOWNSIZING ORGANIZATIONS

Analyses of the set of interviews together with the questionnaires revealed that very few of the organizations in the study implemented downsizing in a way that improved their effectiveness. Most deteriorated instead of improving in

Table 1

AVERAGE ORGANIZATIONAL EFFECTIVENESS SCORES
IN 30 FIRMS IN THE U.S. AUTO INDUSTRY

Highly Effective	*Moderately Effective*	*Ineffective*
Effectiveness Scores Above 4.0	(on a 5.0 point scale) Between 3.0 and 4.0	Below 3.0
Presence of the Six Strategies All six present	Some of the six present	Few of the six present
Number of Organizations N = 4 firms	N = 22 firms	N = 4 firms

terms of pre-downsizing levels of quality, productivity, effectiveness, and the "dirty dozen" (e.g., conflict, low morale, loss of trust, rigidity, scapegoating). However, in a few of the firms especially noteworthy practices were associated with improvement in organizational effectiveness over time. Specifically, six general strategies highlight the best practices typical of the firms in the U.S. auto industry that are downsizing effectively. Other less effective firms may have been characterized by some of the processes, but only in the most effective firms were all six present.

1. The most successful downsizing was implemented by command from the top-down, but it was also initiated from the bottom-up.

On the other hand, the best downsizing strategies were, at the same time, recommended and designed by employees, not top managers.

In effective organizations, leaders initiated downsizing. They exhibited aggressive, strong leadership, and they remained visible and interactive with their employees. They had clearly articulated visions of where they wanted the organization to go. Effective downsizing was managed and monitored by top managers; it required hands-on involvement and momentum that originated at the top of the organization.

On the other hand, the best downsizing strategies were, at the same time, recommended and designed by employees, not top managers. Employees analyzed the operations of the organization job-by-job and task-by-task. This sometimes happened in cross-functional teams, sometimes in blue-ribbon committees, sometimes in self-managed task forces. Members identified redundant jobs and partial tasks, determined how employees were spending their time, found ways to eliminate organizational fat and improve efficiency, and planned ways in which the changes could be implemented. External organizations that had previously downsized were studied by these teams and task forces. When employees (1) understood the reasons for downsizing, (2) were assured that their personal employment was guaranteed with the firm for a certain period of time, even if they recommended the elimination of their own jobs, and (3) trusted managers to listen and be fair, downsizing strategies were implemented smoothly and effectively from the bottom-up.

One CEO's process took this form:

We held a meeting for all the salaried people . . . we gave them an overview of the [downsizing] plan. And we spent time talking about that, and then different staff heads talked about their strategy and where they're headed . . . We do that on a quarterly basis now. Once you start doing that you can drive the plan down into the organization. People understand it, they embrace it, they figure out, "Here's what I've got to do at the departmental level and at the group level and at the individual level. Here's how everything ties together. . . ." You can almost pick out the date on the calendar when this stuff started happening because you see the significant improvement.

In one organization, employees were told that if their jobs were eliminated, they would still receive full pay for a year, but in the meantime would be required to create another value-added job inside the firm or find another position outside. Retraining would be paid for, but employees had to justify the expenditure in a proposal. Employees were encouraged to look more broadly than just joining an existing unit; instead, they were urged to find ways to innovate, to initiate new products or services, or to improve current products and processes. Some employees used the time to find jobs outside the firm; others found ways to try out new projects that improved both bottom-line (cost control) and top-line (revenues) results.

Downsizing from the top down provided consistency, vision, and clear direction as well as visible commitment and hands-on involvement. Downsizing from the bottom-up helped foster innovation and improvements that would not have been possible had top management simply mandated headcount reductions. In one firm, for example, an employee analysis resulted in new tooling that reduced 37 different tool sets to just one, in turn, reducing the number of set-up operators significantly along with other costs. Better union-management relations eliminated the need for several "watch-dog" positions. Improvement in paperwork processing and standardized forms (e.g., insurance claims, reporting forms) eliminated a variety of non-value-added positions and $2 million from bottom-line costs. A suggestion system contributed to the elimination of more than $1 million in costs in another firm. The redesign of a door panel in one company, from seven pieces to three pieces, allowed each product to be manufactured with fewer employees and at lower cost. In each case, it took bottom-up analysis to identify the potential for these improvements coupled with top-down motivation, mandate, and monitoring to implement them.

Nonprioritized downsizing, on the other hand, was similar to tossing a grenade into a crowded room. There could be little prediction of who would be eliminated, how many would be gone, or which talents and skills would be lost.

2. The most successful downsizing was short-term and across-the-board, but it was also long-term and selective in emphasis.

In firms that downsized effectively, implementing across-the-board cutbacks was an effective means of capturing employees' attention, mobilizing the energy of all the organization's members, and overcoming resistance to change. It highlighted the seriousness of conditions faced by the firm and woke up the organization to the need for new approaches to day-to-day work. Cutbacks made it clear that the status quo was no longer acceptable. Generalized downsizing also helped avoid charges of favoritism and potential legal or contract issues. Especially, it helped achieve headcount and cost-savings goals quickly and visibly.

Nonprioritized downsizing, on the other hand, was similar to tossing a grenade into a crowded room. There could be little prediction of who would be eliminated, how many would be gone, or which talents and skills would be lost. Companies were continually taken aback, for example, by how many or how few employees accepted early retirement offers. The harm caused by these approaches, therefore, frequently off-set the positive effects of "unfreezing" the organization. One dramatic example occurred in an organization where a 30-year employee in the purchasing department was the primary agent for ordering steel. Over the years, modifications had been made in the types of steel and alloys ordered, but changes in the written specifications had not kept pace. Shortly after this purchasing agent accepted an early retirement option, an order was placed unknowingly for the wrong kind of steel. This produced a $2 million loss for the organization in downtime, rework, and repair. The organizational memory, as well as the expertise needed to do the work, left with the purchasing agent without any chance of replacement or retraining because of the expedient and nonprioritized method used in downsizing. Simply put, when implemented in the absence of other strategies, "grenade" approaches to downsizing were rarely positive and frequently negative in their consequences.

Three types of downsizing strategies characterized the methods used in these organizations. They are summarized in Table 2: workforce reduction strategies, organization redesign strategies, and systemic strategies. Workforce reduction strategies were actions that eliminated individual jobs by, for example, layoffs, attrition, or buyouts and retirement incentives. They were usually implemented on a short-run, across-the-board basis, and they produced immediate decreases in headcount (grenade approaches). These strategies were by far the most commonly used by downsizing firms; in fact, they were used by all the firms in our study. But the most effective firms didn't stop there.

Organization redesign strategies were difficult to implement quickly because some redesign of the organization was required (e.g., eliminating a function, merging two subunits). They were, by and large, medium-term strategies used by firms to eliminate or re-position subunits within the organization or to eliminate work. Sometimes eliminations of a hierarchical level, for example, were accomplished without a redesign of the work, but generally some kind of work redesign accompanied these strategies.

Systemic strategies were aimed at changing the mind-set or culture of the organization. Instead of a single action or program, they involved a change in the way employees interpreted and approached their work. Minds as well as actions became the target of change. These strategies could not be implemented quickly but were part of a long-term change process. Downsizing was redefined as a continuous, never-ending set of opportunities. No size or savings level was set as a target because whatever that level was, it could be improved. The main advantage of systemic strategies was in helping the firm avoid the need for more short-term workforce reductions in the future when another economic downturn or

Table 2

THREE TYPES OF DOWNSIZING STRATEGIES

Type of Strategy	Characteristics	Examples
Workforce Reduction	Aimed at headcount reduction Short-term implementation Fosters a transition	Attrition Transfer & Outplacement Retirement Incentives Buyout packages Layoffs
Organization Redesign	Aimed at organization change Moderate-term implementation Fosters transition and, potentially, transformation	Eliminate functions Merge units Eliminate layers Eliminate products Redesign tasks
Systemic	Aimed at culture change Long-term implementation Fosters transformation	Change responsibility Involve all constituents Foster continuous improvement & innovation Simplification Downsizing: a way of life

crisis occurred. Relatively few firms adopted systemic strategies in their downsizing efforts.

The most successful firms implemented all three types of strategies: workforce reduction, organization redesign, and systemic strategies. That is, they implemented both short-term (workforce reduction) and long-term (redesign and systemic change) strategies as they downsized. They used both across-the-board and targeted downsizing. They focused on the immediate measurable changes that were required as well as unmeasurable changes in the way work was defined and approached.

One firm accomplished this by conducting a "value analysis" of all tasks in the organization before beginning any downsizing. The question addressed was, "What value does this task have to the final product or service for which we are in business?" Conducted by the employees themselves, this analysis resulted in prioritizing the most valuable individuals, tasks, and jobs, which were not only protected but strengthened. Investment increased in some areas at the same time that individuals and jobs in areas adding less value were reassigned, redesigned, or removed. For example,

> We sent out a survey to every employee and asked them . . . to describe exactly what you do, whether your boss knows about it or doesn't. What is it that

you do? We took all 743 of those and we charted those suckers. And it filled up most of the hotel down there in Ann Arbor . . . And then we started sorting out the duplicates . . . and the things that don't fit, that lead to dead ends . . . From where I sit at the top, I couldn't give you four job descriptions, so how would I know about what 743 are doing?

Together with an across-the-board early retirement program, for example, one firm offered certain employees incentives to remain in their jobs while others were given incentives to retire early. At the same time, work was redesigned when the quality control and maintenance functions were eliminated. Those tasks were reassigned so that the remaining employees became responsible for incorporating them into their own jobs. This necessitated a non-trivial investment in the training of all employees. Training focused on implementing a new culture of continuous downsizing and preparing employees for organizational changes that were to occur. Costs increased in the short run, therefore, due to the investment in training. To offset this increase, one employee in this firm proposed changing the work week from five eight-hour days to four ten-hour days to generate savings in maintenance, security, and energy costs.

3. The most successful downsizing involved paying special attention to those employees who lost their jobs. It also involved paying special attention to those who didn't.

Effective firms provided outplacement services, personal and family counseling, relocation expenses, and active sponsoring of employees whose positions were eliminated. Several top managers proudly announced that none of their white-collar employees was without a position someplace else. A wide variety of options was generated for these employees including severance pay, benefit packages, retraining, and employment opportunities. Temporary consulting arrangements were even made available to some terminated employees. In short, the best firms took responsibility for the transitions created by loss of employment.

On the other hand, white-collar employees who remained with the firm were likely to experience what Brockner and his colleagues[6] labelled "survivor guilt." Psychological reactions among survivors of layoffs commonly include increased anxiety about job loss, decreased loyalty to the firm, and guilt feelings regarding displaced co-workers. Survivor guilt occurs when the remaining employees feel guilty about working overtime, for example, or receiving paychecks when their friends and former co-workers may not be working at all. In addition, survivors may feel that the attributes traditionally valued in good employees—loyalty, hard work, and personal competence—no longer count in the firm. Individuals who displayed those traits still lost their jobs. Evidence of survivor guilt was prevalent in the firms in this study.

In addition to this deterioration in morale, practical work problems were even more noteworthy. As a result of downsizing, for example, fewer numbers of employees were left in the firm to do more work and, frequently, to do a more complex set of tasks than before.

A common complaint among top managers was that downsizing created job demands that most remaining managers were not qualified or experienced enough to fulfill. Management survivors were required to manage a larger number of employees, maintain accountability for multiple (often new) functions, and to coordinate among more subunits than before. Many were simply not equipped to handle the increased work demands or the additional knowledge required. Management burn-out was a common complaint.

While outplacement support and attractive incentive packages were provided to those leaving the organization, survivors in most organizations received disincentives such as increased workloads, smaller or no raises, loss of cost-of-living-allowances (COLA), the same or a reduced title, demands to learn new tasks and take on broader responsibilities, and sometimes, an escalation in the "dirty dozen" dynamics. "Survivor envy" as well as survivor guilt was a common outcome.

In firms that downsized successfully, however, special attention was paid to the transition experienced by employees who remained with the organization as well as those who exited. One way this transition was managed was by increasing the amount and frequency of information communicated to these employees. For example, some top managers reported going the extra mile to make certain that all employees knew the rationale and circumstances underlying the downsizing effort. Openness in sharing information with employees at all levels was a priority. One company held regular "forums" where data was shared on both the company's and its major competitors' costs and performance. These included question and answer periods with blue- and white-collar workers. Data that might have been confidential before was posted in several locations throughout the company, so that organization members were included in downsizing planning and implementation. Other firms held special events to signal the end of the degeneration phase and the beginning of the regeneration phase for the company (e.g., "launch lunches," a new company logo, new signs, fresh paint, colors in the production area).

The point was to communicate a different message to employees than had been communicated before. Whereas downsizing has usually created loss of loyalty, morale, and trust, some companies made special efforts to convey a sense of excitement and opportunity in a new phase of the firm's lifecycle. In particular, top managers passed messages that the survivors were survivors because they were highly valued and respected. The need to downsize was not due to their mistakes, but they were the ones who would make (or keep) the firm competitive. Managers often targeted an outside scapegoat as the culprit in unpleasant downsizing actions (e.g., the economy, the Japanese transplants, the rising quality expectations of the public). One highly effective CEO, in a speech to his recently downsized top management group, stated it this way: "Despite all the problems created for us, despite all the obstacles placed in our way, I'm confident that this team has the guts, and the ability, and the talent to see this program through to the end and bring us back to profitability."

But increases in communication went both ways. Survivors were encouraged to put forth their ideas at the front-end of the change process. They were encouraged to pass information upward as well as provide feedback on information passed downward. The point is that increasing information exchange was an important way to give special notice to surviving employees.

Changes in the human resource system were a second way the transition faced by survivors was managed effectively. Training and development opportunities were provided for survivors, and they received incentives for learning new tasks and expanding personal competencies. For example, one manager noted:

> We don't delegate training. We're trying to get every department to say training is our responsibility . . . In other words, we have a person who's in a level 6 job, but he can grow to a level 7 or 8 if he becomes the trainer for three or four locations within the section, in addition to his regular job . . . responsibility for training new people as well as existing people. So the curriculum and materials are really developed by the people, up-dated by the people, and administered by the people.

In organizations that downsized most effectively, changes in the HRM system (i.e., selection, appraisal, reward, development) preceded as well as followed the implementation of downsizing strategies. For example, in one organization training and development activities began a year before the downsizing was implemented, so that white-collar employees were prepared for changes that would occur in the structures and management processes. In another firm every employee, salaried and hourly, attended a forty-hour training workshop on the implementation and implications of downsizing. The appraisal system was also redesigned in advance of downsizing. Managers were held accountable for the extent to which they developed and trained their own subordinates in new jobs and functions. In sum, incentives were put in place to motivate survivors who faced new demands in a downsized organization. Both casualties and survivors were made to feel valued, and both groups had opportunities to make contributions and fulfill their potential.

4. The most successful downsizing was surgical and targeted inside the firm, but it was also generalized and included the firm's external network.

The most effective firms, however, engaged in surgical procedures. That is, they identified precisely where redundancy, excess cost, and inefficiencies existed, and they attacked those areas specifically.

Inefficiencies and redundancies are not always easy to identify in an organization, so it is often difficult to know where to target downsizing activities. One manager highlighted this problem in his organization:

> As long as you've got as many people as we've got buying stuff, you're going to have lots of suppliers. As long as I've got as many people as I do designing and engineering, I'm going to have as many models as I have. I'm going to have all the variation I have. That's job security. If I'm not generating ideas and I'm not designing new widgets, I don't have a job. So, I'm going to drive changes on parts that customers never see, and I'm going to change them every year because I'm a good engineer, or designer, and that's what I'm supposed to do. And we throw away all kinds of money in that regard.

The most effective firms, however, engaged in surgical procedures. That is, they identified precisely where redundancy, excess cost, and inefficiencies existed, and they attacked those areas specifically. Internal data gathering and data monitoring became systematic and precise, so that employees had access to performance and cost data almost instantaneously. For example,

> We have cathode ray tubes . . . about 300 of them, in the plant. And they have all of our performance categories on it, everything from cost of cars to grievances to absenteeism to daily quality to corporate quality. Any one of the 900 pages on this is easily accessible to any hourly-rate employee by just hitting numbers on a keyboard. Not only is it regularly updated, but it's constantly changing to get more and more information out to the hourly people.

Employees of this firm logged several thousand sign-ons daily just checking on performance statistics. Aspects of the work such as container sizes, distance indexes, number of line stations, number of parts per work station, batch sizes, inventory sizes, and so forth, were examined carefully to find areas in which costs could be reduced. The "tight ship" or "lean and mean" metaphors were typical of managers' descriptions.

At the same time, firms that downsized effectively also applied downsizing universally to the entire system of suppliers, customers, and distributors. In planning and implementing downsizing, they reduced the number of outside agents dealt with directly. These outside agents were treated as involved partners as · well as potential targets of the downsizing efforts. For example, several firms reduced multiple, redundant single-item suppliers to a single-source supplier of systems of parts. Instead of twenty-eight separate suppliers for an electrical component system, for example, one organization reduced that number to one supplier who provided the entire system. This, in turn, reduced the number of staff coordinators needed to administer supplier relations, including purchasing, inspection, negotiation, and so on. Redundancy in suppliers had been considered necessary to assure that a labor action or a disruption in one supplier organization did not disrupt production in the customer organization. But this firm selected its single source supplier on the basis of reliability and dependability of service as well as cost and quality of the product. It also involved that supplier in many aspects of design, production, marketing, and service of the final product. (Many former suppliers became "second-tier" suppliers to the single-source, system supplier.)

Similarly, reducing distribution points helped several firms improve on-time delivery and eliminate much of the overhead necessary to schedule, transport, and warehouse products for customers when multiple outlets were being maintained. Identifying targeted customer groups helped pare down marketing and sales activities so that efficiencies could be gained in advertising, sales, and customer follow-up. The successful firms were both systemic and surgical in approach, encouraging generalized system change and implementing specific targeted cutbacks simultaneously. The strategic intent was to consolidate around the company's core competency. To accomplish this, every element within the firm and in its external environment was considered in downsizing planning, analysis, and execution.

5. The most successful downsizing resulted in small, semi-autonomous organizations, but it also resulted in large integrated organizations.

Theoretically, small organizations run more efficiently than large organizations. They are unencumbered by multiple management layers and staff functions, fostering rapid, efficient decision making and innovativeness. Face-to-face communications cuts down on sign-offs and implementation time. On the other hand, large organizations can call upon economies of scale and integration to reap efficiencies not available to small organizations. The availability of abundant resources provides flexibility and responsiveness under conditions of uncertainty. Cross-functional and multi-layered teams bring to issues broadened insight and perspective that are not available in small organizations. In this study, the best downsizing was aimed at producing specialized, flexible, loosely coupled units, while at the same time producing generalized, coordinated, centralized units.

Some analysts have suggested that decentralized organizations (composed of small, autonomous units) are more effective than centralized organizations (composed of large, coordinated units).[7] Yet centralization always engenders decentralization, and vice versa. What appears to be decentralization from the perspective of corporate headquarters (e.g., forming semi-autonomous units and powerful unit heads), is viewed as centralization from the perspective of the unit itself. For example, some firms removed from corporate headquarters functions such as purchasing, accounting, marketing, customer relations, or engineering. These functions were dispersed to separate operating units. From the corporate perspective this was decentralization. From the unit perspective, which now had the resources and authority to operate autonomously, it was centralization. On the other hand, the unit may also decentralize its resources and authority to teams. The teams are provided with discretion and control over the resources required to do their work (e.g., staffing, purchasing, scheduling, appraising). The team, therefore, is centralized but the unit is decentralized. Depending on where one looks, therefore, centralization is really decentralization, and vice versa.

The most effective downsizing strategies produced autonomous or semi-autonomous units within the larger organization as well as strong, centralized functions. Unit leaders were given the responsibility to manage functions previously centralized at headquarters, or they were given profit-center responsibility and could decide for themselves which functions to eliminate, which to purchase from corporate headquarters, and which to contract out.

For example, one large organization divided itself into three semi-autonomous units, each producing a different product. Within each of these units, area heads and team leaders were given control over the resources they needed to manufacture products in the most efficient way. Some decided that certain functions were not needed at the sub-unit level and could be purchased from a central staff unit at the parent company's headquarters (for example, finance and person-nel). They were not required to match headquarters staff functions at the subunit level as they had been previously. Other firms in the study had staff functions at the unit level simply because corporate staff heads wanted a counterpart in the subunits. In those cases, decentralization created inefficiencies. Effective decen-tralization, on the other hand, created unit managers who had the necessary flex-ibility, discretion, and control to improve their own efficiencies and contain their own costs.

At the same time, the effective organizations produced efficiencies by cen-tralizing functions and creating large organizations. The information processing function was removed from geographically dispersed subunits in one organiza-tion to form a large centralized system. Previously diverse data entry and soft-ware systems were standardized and consolidated into a single network. The elimination of duplication and coordination costs resulted in substantial savings. The merger of several related subunits into a single large entity with combined staff functions made it possible for another organization to eliminate two man-agement layers and reassign about half the staff employees. Geographic or prod-uct reorganizations often produced larger, more centralized units within (decentralized) parent companies.

The use of a "clan" control system[8] was a key to the successful formation of simultaneous small and large organizations during downsizing. Of the three types of control systems Ouchi identified, the bureaucratic (relying on rules, audits, and hierarchical relationships) and the market (relying on competition, goals, and exchange relationships) control mechanisms characterized all the firms in the study. But in a few, those with the highest levels of effectiveness, a clan con-trol system was also fostered. The clan relies on common values, shared vision, and a collective perspective. Its advantage, of course, is that employees can be self-regulating because they hold a common set of values and assumptions. Fewer resources are required to monitor and manage their work. Some managers engendered a clan control system through the use of symbolic events and involvement activities.

For example, one organization instituted a "Build With Pride Week" in the initial phases of downsizing. Family members were invited to the firm on one day, customers on another, suppliers on another, local government officials on another. Special events, special refreshments, and special decorations were used through-out the week to signal the beginning of a new era in the firm, particularly of a team-oriented approach to work. Non-management employees served as hosts and guides, and outsiders were permitted to question and observe workers as they performed their jobs. Dramatic improvements in productivity and product quality, and a sense of collective pride and teamwork followed from this event.

Another organization developed a sense of teamwork through employee-designed and administered rewards.

> The latest gimmick is alligator hats . . . they have the plant quality logo sewn into the top of them. People give each other hats for doing something good for quality. The important issue is that it is an on-going process. People are

involved. They make the decisions. It's not something that is tightly managed by a staff group or something. And it's always kind of nice to have your peers trying to find something good about you instead of bad.

Some firms simply made label changes, such as renaming the quality control department "the customer satisfaction department," or generating names and slogans for sub-unit teams (e.g., one product design team became Delta Force—"seek and destroy errors before customers catch them"). The intent was not just to be cute, but to help create a different mindset among employees about the downsizing and redesign efforts. Other firms offered both advance and follow-up employee training, emphasized constant and consistent articulation of a vision by top managers, implemented a congruent reward system, and emphasized cross-functional teamwork. As a result, the decentralized, semi-autonomous units operated harmoniously with the centralized, large units and did not require extra management resources to assure consistency.

   6. The most successful organizations emphasized downsizing as a means to an end, but they also emphasized downsizing as the targeted end.

Downsizing was interpreted in some firms as an admission of failure or weakness. More commonly it was considered a temporary, protective mechanism that would help the firm weather-the-storm until a normal growth orientation could be resumed. For example, a number of substitutes for the term downsizing were used in these firms to avoid negative connotations: resizing, right-sizing, rationalizing, rebuilding, rebalancing, reassigning, reorganizing, reallocating, redeploying, streamlining, slimming, slivering, functionalizing, demassing, downshifting, consolidating, contracting, compressing, ratcheting-down, and even leaning-up. This negative interpretation generally resulted from downsizing being defined as a reactive strategy rather than a proactive strategy.

All the firms in the study implemented downsizing primarily as a reaction to loss of market share or profitability, entrance of a lower-cost competitor, or a parent company mandate. In most of these cases, downsizing took a defensive form. It was associated with exclusive use of workforce reduction strategies (as opposed to redesign and systemic strategies) and mechanistic shifts in organization structure (e.g., rigidity, restricted communication flows, lower levels of employee involvement).

On the other hand, some firms interpreted downsizing as an opportunity for improvement or as part of an aggressive strategy leading to enhanced competitiveness. To illustrate, one of the effective top managers commented:

"We're not getting smaller, we're getting better. This change is necessary for continuous improvement. It just happens that fewer employees is a way to accomplish it." In these firms downsizing was associated with a combination of workforce reduction and redesign downsizing strategies, and, in a few cases, with systemic strategies as well. Higher levels of employee involvement, participation, and flexibility were also typical.

In this study, the most effective firms did both. That is, in the face of an unequivocal need to retrench, the most effective downsizing firms targeted downsizing as a central, critical outcome. "Taking out headcount" and "trimming the fat" were clear and consensual objectives. But these firms also treated downsizing as just one in a cluster of strategies designed to achieve organizational improvement. "Improving productivity" and "enhancing competitiveness" were labels that helped position downsizing as just one strategy to improve firm performance.

In one firm, for example, downsizing was framed in terms of continuous improvement focused on the core mission of the company:

> They've got a crystal clear corporate focus that involves everybody in regard to continuous improvement in meeting the challenges that are upon them. Consistent day in and day out. Everybody knows the score. It's not herky-jerky reorganization, jump to this, jump to that. They have a very clear focus in each piece of their business. They go after it. Everybody just functions that way. Building cars and trucks is absolute uno-priority.

The relationship between effective downsizing and the approach to quality employed in these firms was especially notable. Cost savings associated with improved quality have been publicized recently in the literature, but a particular quality culture emerged here.

Cameron[9] described three approaches to quality that characterize organizations. No organization is characterized by only one approach to quality, but most have a dominant emphasis. For example, when a firm focuses on *error detection,* it emphasizes inspecting and detecting errors after the product or service has been produced. The goal is to reduce waste and to find and fix mistakes. The approach to customers seeks to avoid making them unhappy, meet expectations, and be responsive to their needs and complaints.

An *error prevention* approach emphasizes avoiding errors in the first place. The goal is to produce zero defects by doing work right the first time. This is done by finding root causes of problems (rather than just product defects) and monitoring and adjusting the work processes to eliminate them. The approach to customers involves actively satisfying their preferences (not just needs) and occasionally exceeding expectations.

The third approach, *creative quality coupled with continuous improvement,* emphasizes surprising and delighting customers by delivering products and services that not only exceed but actually create new preferences and expectations. The standard is improvement in the quality of products, not just meeting a goal or target. Small, incremental, continuous improvements are coupled with innovation (large, visible changes) to achieve new levels of quality. To illustrate, when new equipment or technologies were introduced into most firms an assumption was made that this was the best condition the new material would ever be in (i.e., no repair and little maintenance needed). In the firms with a continuous improvement culture, on the other hand, it was assumed that this was the *worst* condition the new material would ever be in (i.e., it had not yet been improved).

Most organizations in this study were dominated by an emphasis on the first approach to quality-error detection. This approach, with its reliance on quality control departments and inspection, was associated with higher costs, more floor space dedicated to rework and touch-up, and higher numbers of personnel than the other two approaches. The most effective firms coupled downsizing with the latter two approaches to quality—error prevention and creative quality. When downsizing was coupled with a focus on process improvement (error prevention), not just produce improvement (error detection), and when a continuous improvement culture operated in the organization (creative quality), downsizing was associated with higher levels of organizational effectiveness as well as lower costs.

In the few organizations where the approach to quality emphasized prevention and creativity more than detection, a subtle shift had occurred from thinking of customers as end-users or recipients of a product or service to defining customers as anyone with whom an employee interacted, inside or outside the firm. Customer expectations were continuously measured and monitored in the effective firms.

For example,

> We've got a great push to work on a more caring attitude toward the customer which is being spread throughout our organization . . . It's really dealing with how do you get out and get the voice of the customer, and then how do you respond to that voice in a manner that makes the customer believe and understand that we are caring about their attitude and their feelings. . . . ?

Several of the most effective top managers indicated that, in their firms, it was assumed that employees would exceed, not just meet, expectations for both inside and outside customers, and for past, present, and future customers. It was especially noteworthy in these firms that improvements in quality were linked to continuous downsizing—employees were encouraged to constantly look for ways to reduce resource requirements and increase response time and efficiency. Questions such as the following were part of job expectations: Can this task be eliminated? Can it be completed in less time? Can it be completed at less cost? Can someone else do it better? Can it be simplified or reduced? The relationship between quality and downsizing—i.e., that each should enhance the achievement of the other—was made explicit. Cost savings attributable to process improvements and increases in quality were highlighted in company newsletters, mini-ceremonies, and one-time bonuses.

In sum, whereas downsizing was clearly the central target of these firms—e.g., reduce headcount, cut costs, and/or consolidate units—the means they used to define and achieve quality facilitated the achievement of that goal. Developing a mature approach to quality helped reduce current costs *and* created a continuous improvement mentality for future downsizing.

CONCLUSION

Almost daily, press accounts announce layoffs or plant closings by firms suffering the effects of an economic recession or foreign competition. Published case histories of layoffs, closings, and bankruptcies are common, yet few accounts have analyzed the most effective ways to implement a downsizing strategy. Almost no studies have been done across multiple organizations to identify "best practices" for managers to follow as they face the need to downsize.

In this study of white-collar downsizing in the U.S. automobile industry, six critical strategies characterized the firms that were downsizing most effectively. These six strategies have at least two important implications for practicing managers. One implication relates to common assumptions about organizational dynamics; the other to strategic contradictions.

Assumptions about Organizations

At the beginning of the 1990s several fundamental assumptions dominated thinking about organization and management. Most managers, as well as most scholars, assumed: (1) that *bigger means better;* that is, having more employees, more products, more plants, or more money is better than having fewer or less;[10] (2) that *unending growth is a natural and desirable process in organizational life cycle development;* that is, forms of nongrowth such as decline or stagnation are undesirable aberrations from a normal life cycle pattern;[11] (3) that *adaptability and flexibility are associated with slack resources, loose coupling, and redundancy;* that is, uncommitted resources facilitate experimentation and the ability to take advantage of new opportunities;[12] and (4) that *consistency and congruence are hallmarks of effective organizations;* that is, strategy, structure, culture, and systems should all fit together synchronously to achieve effectiveness.[13]

However, the characteristics found to typify the most effective downsizing organizations challenge those assumptions. These characteristics highlight a *dual* set of assumptions that require an expansion of past assumptions about common organizational dynamics. These six characteristics point out that, contrary to the way we thought in the past, smaller organizations (not just bigger organizations) may also be better organizations. Downsizing not only can improve productivity and competitiveness in organizations, but it can lead to a more humane and enjoyable working environment. Fewer hierarchical levels and smaller units usually mean better communication, more participation, and stronger feelings of belonging.

Similarly, unending organizational growth, as proposed in most organizational life cycle models, is fiction. Decline and, most certainly, downsizing are likely to be a recurring part of many organizations' life cycle stages in the future. In fact, this study's results suggest that downsizing *should* become a permanent and on-going activity in organizations. Like fine-tuned athletes who constantly try to improve their performance, firms should be constantly looking for ways to improve efficiency through downsizing.

The third assumption, that looseness and redundancy produce flexibility and adaptability, is also dispelled by these findings. The presence of nonredundancy and tight coupling in effective downsizers provide an alternative viewpoint. Firms were effective when their downsizing activities eliminated the slack and duplication that produced longer response times, less flexibility, and an inability to adapt to environmental changes.

Like fine-tuned athletes who constantly try to improve their performance, firms should be constantly looking for ways to improve efficiency through downsizing.

Finally, the congruence-produces-effectiveness assumption is also challenged by these results. The presence of dualities and contradiction in organizational downsizing implies inconsistency and incongruence, and it is precisely this lack of consistency and congruence that is most closely associated with organizational effectiveness in the process of downsizing. While most firms were congruent in their approaches to downsizing, the best organizations (albeit only a few of them) engaged in seemingly contradictory processes. This theme of contradictions, in fact, highlights the second important implication that emerged from the findings.

Apparent Contradictions in Strategy

An analysis of the firms that were downsizing effectively supports the conclusion that most organizations were inclined to downsize in inappropriate or ineffective ways. They engaged in downsizing activities that fostered dysfunctional outcomes (e.g., decreasing morale and commitment, increasing conflict and criticism) rather than improved performance. This is partly because they tried to be consistent in their downsizing approach, and effective downsizing was found to involve contradiction. That is, effectiveness was typified by processes that are often thought to be opposite or incompatible.

This existence of apparent contradiction was the best overall explanation of the difference between effective and ineffective downsizing firms. As explained earlier, top managers in the few effective firms were actively pursuing strategies that included a duality. The top managers in the ineffective firms, on the other hand, attempted to maintain consistency, harmony, and fit. They pursued one side of the strategy alone—for example, a short-term, internal approach without its accompanying long-term, external approach. Managers in effective firms adopted a "both/and" approach to downsizing instead of an "either/or" approach. For most managers in the study, this both/and approach was viewed as incompatible with effective management and inconsistent with traditional approaches to change.

Of course, the apparent contradictions in the downsizing strategies are not inherent. They are contradictions only because the presence of one strategy caused most of the managers interviewed in the study to deny the possibility that the opposite strategy could, and should, also occur in their organizations. In only a few of the most effectively downsizing firms were these processes not defined as contradictory. Thus, when managers were not open to adopting a bifurcated, both/and approach to downsizing, their firms actually deteriorated in performance instead of improved.

In sum, an important lesson emerging from this investigation is that the perspectives of both scholars and managers may need to be expanded. On one hand, the six effective downsizing strategies highlight the need to broaden assumptions of scholars and practitioners about the nature of organizational dynamics. Past assumptions bound too narrowly the research questions being investigated and the change strategies being pursued. On the other hand, effective downsizing processes help illustrate the desirability for managers of considering dualities, apparent contradictions, and a broader approach to managing organizational downsizing. In the foreseeable future, downsizing is likely to remain a major managerial challenge and contradictions will be a hallmark of effectiveness.

Endnotes

[1]It should be noted that some authors such as Richard T. Pascale (*Managing on the Edge*, New York: Simon & Schuster, 1990) and Michael Porter (*The Competitive Advantage of Nations*, New York: Free Press, 1990) argue that the U.S. has *never* been globally competitive. U.S. businesses succeeded in the past precisely because there was virtually no global competition. The argument is that U.S. industries do not need to regain competitiveness but to develop it for the first time.

[2]Most of the following statistics come from the Bureau of Labor Statistics and the Department of Commerce and have been re-published in many popular and academic publications.

[3]See Peter R. Richardson, *Cost Containment*, (New York: Free Press, 1988) for supportive evidence.

[4]Kim S. Cameron, Myung U. Kim, and David A. Whetten, "Organizational Effects of Decline and Turbulence," *Administrative Science Quarterly*, 32, 1987, 222–240.

[5]See Kim S. Cameron, "Organizational downsizing," In George Huber, et al. *Organizational Change and Effectiveness*, (New York: Cambridge University Press, 1992) for a more extensive statistical analysis of the data from this study.

[6]For an analysis of the survivor guilt phenomena see Joel Brockner, Steven Grover, Thomas Reed, Rocki DeWitt, and Michael O'Malley, "Survivors' Reactions to Layoffs: We Get by with a Little Help for our Friends," *Administrative Science Quarterly*, 32(4), 1987, 526–541.

[7]See, for example, a study by G. P. Huber, C. C. Miller, and W. H. Glick, "Developing More Encompassing Theories about Organizations: The Centralization-Effectiveness Relationship as an example," *Organization Science*, 1, 11–40. A theory of centralization and organizational effectiveness is proposed in that article.

[8]An extensive discussion has been published on clan control systems. One of the original, and best, sources for this perspective is in William G. Ouchi, "Markets, Bureaucracies, and Clans," *Administrative Science Quarterly*, 25:130, 1980.

[9]A more extensive discussion of this model of quality is available in Kim S. Cameron, "Quality Culture in Product and Service Organizations." Working paper, University of Michigan Business School, 1990.

[10]See David A. Whetten, "Sources, Responses, and Effects of Organizational Decline," in John R. Kimberly and Robert H. Miles (eds.) *The Organizational Life Cycle*, (San Francisco: Jossey-Bass, 1980). This chapter points out that organizational decline, up until 1980, had been a largely ignored phenomenon.

[11]A review of organizational life cycle models is reported in Kim S. Cameron and David A. Whetten, "Perceptions of Organizational Effectiveness over Organizational Life Cycles," *Administrative Science Quarterly*, 26, 1981, 525–54.

[12]A class book, Karl E. Weick, *The Social Psychology of Organizing* (2nd ed.) (New York: Random House, 1979) introduces assumptions of loose coupling, redundancy, and flexibility.

[13]A discussion of the association between congruence and effectiveness is provided by David Nadler, and Michael Tushman, "A Model for Diagnosing Organizational Behavior," *Organizational Dynamics*, 9(2), 1980, 35–51.

READING 19

MANAGING EMPLOYEE SEPARATIONS WITH THE REWARD SYSTEM

David B. Balkin

Executive Overview

While executives in many companies find it necessary to reduce the size of their work-forces, some are starting to rethink their approach. Instead of forcing certain employees deemed redundant to quit, more participative approaches are now being used to influence certain employees to leave the firm. The pivotal aspect of these voluntary workforce reductions is the reward system which can provide incentives for workers to quit. This article explains how employee separations can be managed through designing and administrating specific pay and benefit policies. It also shows that by using the reward system to make employee separations a participative decision, management can avoid the potential threat of unwanted litigation.

Making decisions that result in layoffs and discharge of employees are among the most painful and difficult ones that an executive will make in his or her career. Yet the restructuring of entire industries, such as banking, and the increased level of global competition is forcing executives to find ways to reduce the size of their workforces and run leaner organizations. The traditional top-down approach of selecting employees for discharge on a *fait accompli* basis is frequently being abandoned. A more participative approach that gives employees more control over their destiny is being used instead. Organizations that adopt this approach to outplacement try to develop policies that encourage the right employees to leave voluntarily instead of enduring the trauma of a discharge.

The reward system is the key driving force that makes this new approach to employee separations work effectively. By designing pay and benefits policies that support the need to manage the outflow of human resources, management can minimize the costs and unpleasantness associated with terminating employees. As additional legal barriers have been established that constrain management from firing a worker the costs associated with separations have increased.

Source: "Managing Employee Separations With the Reward System" by David B. Balkin, *Academy of Management Executive*, 1992, Vol. 6, No. 4, 64–69.

This article seeks to explain how some organizations are designing their reward systems to manage downsizing. First, the legal constraints that are making it more difficult to force employees to quit will be identified. Next, key human resource outflow decisions are examined. Associated with each of these decisions are reward policies that encourage employees to leave voluntarily. Details of the administration of these reward policies are examined and examples of how these policies work are also provided.

LEGAL ENVIRONMENT FOR EMPLOYEE SEPARATIONS

The legal system that governs employee separations is becoming more protective of employee job rights in the United States. The result is that management is bearing more risk when deciding to discharge an employee. A combination of federal and state laws and court cases has weakened management's ability to decide to separate an individual from his or her job. The three cases where employer-initiated separations are being met with increasing legal resistance are retirements, layoffs, and dismissals.

Retirements

The Age Discrimination in Employment Act makes it illegal for an employer to force an employee to retire on the basis of age (only a few job categories, such as top management, are exempt from this law). Research indicates that the median retirement age in the United States is sixty three, and most employees postpone their retirement until they are close to sixty five because they are then entitled to full Social Security and Medicare benefits.[1] Employers who want some workers to retire early, before age sixty five, most likely will have to rely on the voluntary cooperation of the targeted employees.

Layoffs

The Worker Adjustment and Retraining Notification Act (WARN) requires that employers with 100 or more employees give sixty days advance notice to employees who will be involved in a layoff due to a plant closing or mass separation of fifty or more workers.[2] This law, passed in 1988, was enacted to facilitate workers' ability to find new work opportunities. The advance notice requirement, however, could negatively affect the firm's credit rating with bankers and suppliers as well as the perceived value of the stock. This makes layoffs costly.

Using layoffs to trim the workforce may also jeopardize a firm's ability to maintain a culturally diverse workforce and stay in compliance with EEOC regulations since many companies select workers for layoff based on seniority (last hired, first fired). A recent Supreme Court case requires firms that have seniority rules for layoffs to use them even if it reduces the number of women and minorities in that organization.[3] Since virtually all companies with unions have seniority provisions for layoffs, the loss of scarce minority employees could add to the cost of the layoff.

Dismissals

When an employee's behavior is inappropriate management may move to dismiss the employee. Not sustaining an adequate level of performance or some form of misconduct are examples of inappropriate behavior. The discharge is usually the result of several oral and written warnings and other disciplinary actions which failed to correct the employee's behavior. The case of gross misconduct such as theft, or physical assault, for example, is an exception and requires a more serious and immediate response from management.

A recent Supreme Court case requires firms that have seniority rules for layoffs to use them even if it reduces the number of women and minorities in that organization.

Courts and various state laws have made it riskier for an employer to fire an employee without *just* cause. While employees under union contracts and government employees under civil service rules are protected from wrongful discharge, the majority of employees who are outside these jurisdictions, until recently, have had little recourse for wrongful discharge. Courts in forty states have now moved to extend protection of employees' job rights in the case of wrongful discharge.[4] For example, in California, plaintiffs have recently won large settlements for wrongful discharge that routinely exceeded one half million dollars.

Other states besides California are also awarding plaintiffs settlements that include damages as well as lost wages. For example, a plaintiff in Washington prevailed in a 1986 case and was awarded $102,000, of which $88,000 was for emotional distress.[5]

A successful tactic used in wrongful discharge cases is for the plaintiff's attorney to press for a jury trial composed of peers who are sympathetic to the dismissed employee's case. Not surprisingly the corporation's attorney may seek to avoid the trial and negotiate an out-of-court settlement rather than risk a larger award that includes back pay and punitive damages from the jury (not many executives or managers are available for jury duty).

Courts in forty states have now moved to extend protection of employees' job rights in the case of wrongful discharge.

In 1987 Montana passed a state law making it unlawful to fire an employee without just cause. Other state legislatures are considering enacting a law similar to Montana's to protect employees' job rights. This change in the legal environment means that employers who seek to discharge a worker for poor performance or misconduct will need to provide a well-documented case for dismissal that is able to meet the burden of proof test required by courts. In many cases in the current legal environment, management may want to discharge an employee yet hesitate due to a lack of solid evidence or to avoid unwanted litigation. Even if management wins the case, attorney's fees and lost management time due to court appearances and depositions are expensive.

MANAGING EMPLOYEE SEPARATIONS WITH THE REWARD SYSTEM

Legal risks associated with forcing employees to quit an organization have caused managers and executives to search for alternative ways to manage employee separations. Using a reward system is very effective in encouraging the

Exhibit 1

PAY POLICIES THAT FACILITATE EMPLOYEE SEPARATIONS

Separation Decision	Pay Policy
• Early Retirements	• Early Retirement Incentives
	• Health Benefits Extension
• Voluntary Reduction in Workforce	• Voluntary Severance Plans
	• Outplacement Benefits
• Dismissal for Poor Performance	• Strong Emphasis on Performance Contingent Compensation
• Sustain Functional Attrition Rates	• Retirement Plan Design
	• Emphasis on Cash Compensation

"right" employees to leave a firm voluntarily thereby avoiding legal penalties. The reward system consists of the pay and benefits policies that govern how to compensate employees for their contributions. Management can fine tune the system to make it unattractive (in terms of foregone benefits and earnings) for employees to remain with the firm. The employee may rationally respond to the incentive and voluntarily quit the organization.

Exhibit 1 shows how pay policies are linked to specific types of separation decisions. Discussion follows showing how the reward system can be used to facilitate the decision and minimize the risk of litigation.

Early Retirements

Enticing senior employees who are close to retirement age to leave can significantly reduce fixed pay costs. Many times less expensive junior employees can replace higher cost senior workers. Early retirements allow a company to recruit outsiders who bring fresh ideas and new perspectives into the firm. It is illegal to force employees to retire, but an early retirement incentive package can make it financially attractive for senior employees to leave.

Typical retirement incentives may consist of accelerating the age requirement for retirement benefits, increasing years of service used to determine retirement income, and a lump sum of cash derived from a formula that ranges from one to four weeks of salary for each year of service. For example, an early retirement plan may add five years to an employee's age (so that a fifty five-year-old employee may qualify under an age fifty nine requirement for eligibility), five years are added to company service, and the cash equivalent of two weeks of salary for each year of service may be given as a lump sum. Health benefits are usually extended as an additional incentive so that the employee is covered until eligible for Medicare at age sixty five.

IBM announced an early retirement incentive plan to reduce its workforce in 1991. Employees with 30 years of service can qualify for full retirement benefits and receive a lump sum of one year's salary under the plan.[6] Age requirements are relaxed to allow more employees who meet the service requirements to retire early. Service credits are capped at thirty years. Employees who work additional years do not get credit in the calculation of retirement benefits.[7] As is typical of early retirement plans, there is an "open window" of several months when the employee can take advantage of the early retirement incentives.[8]

Early retirement incentives can result in significant workforce reductions. DuPont used early retirement incentives to reduce its workforce by ten percent and EXXON achieved a fifteen percent reduction with these inducements.[9]

Care must be taken when designing the incentive to avoid losing too many employees. Excess resignations may occur since all employees who meet the age and company experience requirements are eligible. Surveys can help predict how a given type of policy will affect senior employees' retirement decisions. If the survey indicates too few early retirements would result from the policy, the benefits may need to be enhanced. In this way the policy can be fine tuned to reach workforce reductions goals.

Sometimes a highly valued employee may take advantage of the early retirement program. The impact of losing a valued employee can be minimized by developing policies that allow the firm to retain the skills of that individual as a temporary consultant until a suitable replacement is hired and trained.

Surveys can help predict how a given type of policy will affect senior employees' retirement decisions.

Ann Howard recently studied AT&T's early retirement program and found that there were no performance differences between those employees who took the early retirement offer and those that did not.[10] This suggests that organizations that use these programs to reduce their workforces lose employees who are just as talented as those who choose to stay. The key difference was that those who left reported lower levels of job satisfaction and greater financial security than those who stayed. This indicates that the financial and psychological costs of retiring were lower for the employees who opted for the early retirement program.

Management needs to administer the early retirement program so that eligible employees do not think that they are being coerced to leave. This may result in litigation. Lower performance ratings for senior employees or circulating a rumor of a major layoff—calculated to encourage senior employees to leave—could be construed as coercive management action. A former employee sued IBM for age discrimination and was awarded $315,000 in compensating damages by a jury because the plaintiff claimed he was pressured to take an early retirement against his will.[11] Evidence that the plaintiff introduced to convince the jury of age discrimination included having his job reclassified after voicing some reservations about taking early retirement and receiving a warning that the next performance evaluation would be unsatisfactory.

To avoid exposure to age discrimination management needs to treat early retirement programs on a voluntary basis both in the letter and the spirit of the policy. This means being sensitive to the needs of senior employees who have vested a significant number of years of their lives in a company and want to leave with a sense of appreciation and conviction that the personal investment was worthwhile.

Voluntary Reduction in Workforce

When business is in decline, large cuts in the workforce may be necessary. Companies in newer and highly volatile industries such as computers and electronics may have few employees close to retirement age. Cost savings from early retirements would be modest. A voluntary reduction in workforce can help avoid the legal problems and psychological pain associated with a layoff. The key to getting employees to quit voluntarily is to provide a voluntary severance pay package as indicated in Exhibit 1.

The voluntary severance plan is sometimes called a *buy-out* and it consists of a lump sum of cash representing several years of earnings provided to employees who voluntarily resign. The plan can be used in conjunction with early retirement incentives to motivate a significant number of a firm's workforce to quit. The buy-out is particularly attractive to a business that provides a "lifelong employment policy" to its employees or one that cares deeply about the psychological contract between the company and its workforce. Recently IBM used a voluntary severance plan to reduce the workforce at its Boca Raton, Florida plant. Employees willing to resign were given the equivalent of two years salary. Using a reward system allowed IBM to avoid a layoff which it has taken pride in for many years.

Herman Miller, an office furniture manufacturer, designed a policy called the "silver parachute" which provides financial security to all employees in the event of a hostile takeover. In most companies this privilege is usually reserved for top executives and called a golden parachute. Under the silver parachute policy at Herman Miller, if within two years of a hostile takeover, an employee's job is terminated, the employee with two years of work experience is entitled to one year's salary as severance pay. Employees with five years of work experience are eligible to receive two and one half years of salary.[12] Employees may also use this benefit if they quit voluntarily due to the hostile takeover. This policy is derived from the overall company philosophy at Herman Miller which tries to foster mutual trust and teamwork between employees and management.

Outplacement benefits complement the voluntary severance plan by providing resources for employees to make the transition into a new job with a different organization. Job location assistance from professional career counselors, office space and clerical support to conduct a job search, and training in job search skills such as interviewing and resume preparation, are a few examples of outplacement services.

Outplacement assistance is expensive. It can average several thousands of dollars per employee. Of course the benefits of outplacement frequently outweigh its management costs which is why there has been a rapid increase in the number of firms that use this service.[13] It is often beneficial to demonstrate social responsibility to the stakeholders, especially to the public and remaining employees. By assisting departing workers with their transition to a new job the firm maintains its image in the community as a good corporate citizen.[14] In addition the remaining employees' anxiety levels are reduced as they view the firm as being a fair employer despite their regrets about the departing employees.

The administration of voluntary severance plans must be performed as carefully as early retirement incentives. Management must construct the program to avoid losing too many employees with critical skills. Restricting eligibility of the buy-out to employees in a specific division or location is one way to do this.

Endnotes

[1]B. Rossen and T. H. Jerdee, "Managing Older Workers' Careers," in K. Rowland and G. Ferris (Eds.), *Research in Personnel and Human Resources Management*, Vol. 6, (Greenwich, CT: JAI Press, 1988).

[2]R. G. Ehrenberg and G. H. Jakubson, "Advance Notification of Plant Closing: Does it Matter?" *Industrial Relations, 28,* 1989, 60–71.

[3]Firefighters Local 1784 v. Stotts, 104 U.S. 2576 (1984).

[4]J. Hoerr, "What Should Unions Do?" *Harvard Business Review,* 69(3), 1991, 30–45.

[5]J. W. Hunt, *The Law of The Workplace* (Washington D.C.: BNA, 1989).

[6]M. Kolbasuk, McGee "Can IBM Retain its Full Employment Policy?" *Management Review,* 80(9), 1991, 22–25.

[7]M. Rowland, "IBM's Cadillac of Retirement Plans," *New York Times,* July 21, 1991, F14.

[8]P. B. Grant, "The Open Window— Special Early Retirement Plans in Transition," *Employee Benefits Journal,* 16(1), 1991, 10–16.

[9]R. Tomasko, "Downsizing: Layoffs and Alternatives to Layoffs," *Compensation and Benefits Review,* 23(4), 1991, 19–32.

[10]A. Howard, "Who Reaches for the Golden Handshake?" *Academy of Management Executive,* 2, 1988, 133–144.

[11]M. Beck, "Old Enough to Get Fired," *Newsweek,* December 9, 1991, 64.

[12]M. Moskowitz, "Companies That Put Perks in Every Pot," *Business and Society Review,* 69, 1989, 26–29.

[13]V. M. Gibson, "The Ins and Outs of Outplacement," *Management Review,* 80(10), 1991, 59–61.

[14]D. H. Sweet, "Outplacement," in W. F. Cascio (Ed.), *Human Resource Planning and Placement* (Washington, DC: Bureau of National Affairs, 1989).

JOB CHOICE AND RECRUITMENT

INTRODUCTION

Demographic studies and statistics from reports like *Workforce 2000* have driven home the point that by the turn of the century the typical new entrant to the labor pool will differ dramatically from that encountered ten years ago. By the year 2000, we expect a labor shortage and a change in the nature of labor in that 59 percent of the entering work force will be nonwhite and nonmale, and companies need to increase their understanding of how to best take advantage of this new labor pool. Indeed, the competitive positions of individual firms, and of the U.S. economy as a whole, depend heavily on increasing the effectiveness of employer recruiting and individual decision making in choosing jobs. The readings selected for this section look at job choice and recruiting.

Our first reading, by Sara Rynes, Robert Bretz, and Barry Gerhart, is entitled "The Importance of Recruitment in Job Choice: A Different Way of Looking." This article reports the results of a study that used longitudinal structured interviews to let job seekers explain in their own terms how they searched for jobs and chose jobs. A key finding in this study was that applicants viewed many aspects of recruiting and the recruiter as symbolic and indicative of broader organizational characteristics. This study provides many direct anecdotes and stories from actual job applicants that dramatically convey how they were affected by different aspects of the recruiting process at different stages in their search. The message conveyed by these people is that specific acts or policies on the part of recruiters (e.g., delays in being contacted) have a greater impact on their decisions than was formerly believed, based on survey research.

In our second reading, "Applicant Attraction Strategies: An Organizational Perspective," Sara Rynes and Alison Barber focus on the impending labor shortage, and they discuss the means by which organizations can more effectively recruit people when the competition for labor becomes more intense. These authors highlight three specific strategies. First, organizations need to improve recruitment practices by more carefully selecting their recruiter and by honing the messages sent in recruitment interviews. Companies also need to improve the nature of inducements offered to prospective employees, trying to get a better fit between the needs and values of those in their labor pool and the pay and benefit package of the organization. Finally, organizations need to explore "nontraditional" sources of applicants such as immigrants, the disabled, working students, part-time employees, and minimally educated workers.

READING 20

THE IMPORTANCE OF RECRUITMENT IN JOB CHOICE
A Different Way of Looking

Sara L. Rynes
Robert D. Bretz, Jr.
Barry Gerhart

Recent literature reviews have called into question the impact of recruitment activities on applicants' job choices. However, most previous findings have been based on cross-sectional ratings obtained immediately after initial screening interviews, thus raising questions about the degree to which prior conclusions are bound to that particular methodology. In contrast, the present study used longitudinal structured interviews to let job seekers explain, in their own words, how they made critical job search and choice decisions. Interview transcripts revealed that recruitment practices played a variety of roles in job seeker decisions. For example, consistent with signaling theory, subjects interpreted a wide variety of recruitment experiences (recruiter competence, sex composition of interview panels, recruitment delays) as symbolic of broader organizational characteristics. In addition, a number of "contingency" variables emerged that seemed to affect the perceived signaling value of recruitment experiences (e.g., prior knowledge of the company, functional area of the recruiter). Also notable were the strongly negative effects of recruitment delays, particularly among male students with higher grade point averages and greater job search success. Finally, our results suggest that certain applicant reactions may be systematically related to sex, work experience, grade point average, and search success. The article concludes with practical and research implications.

Recent research findings have cast doubt on the importance of recruitment in applicants' job choices. For example, a recent meta-analysis concluded that the presentation of "realistic" versus "inflated" recruitment messages has little, if any, effect on applicants' job acceptance rates (Premack & Wanous, 1985). Similarly, it has been argued that recruiters have little effect on job choices, once job characteristics are taken into account (Powell, 1984; Rynes & Barber, 1990; Taylor

Source: "The Importance of Recruitment in Job Choice: A Different Way of Looking" by Sara L. Rynes, Robert D. Bretz, Jr., and Barry Gerhart, *Personnel Psychology*, 1991, Vol. 44, 487–521.

& Bergmann, 1987). Recruitment delays and other administrative aspects have also been reported to have little apparent impact on applicants' decisions (e.g., Rynes & Boudreau, 1986; Taylor & Bergmann, 1987).

However, these recent findings are at odds with earlier research which suggested that recruiters, recruitment timing, and other aspects of the job search process might have substantial effects on the allocation of applicants to vacancies (Rynes, Heneman, & Schwab, 1980). For example, using an interview methodology, Glueck (1973) concluded that "in over a third of the cases, the recruiter was the major reason the applicant chose a particular company" (p. 78). Additionally, on the basis of archival data, Arvey, Gordon, Massengill, and Mussio (1975) found that delays between recruitment phases had substantial effects on the size and composition of the applicant pool. Similarly, Soelberg's (1967) longitudinal tracking of job-seeking business students suggested that recruitment timing (e.g., getting to an applicant before other employers do) might have substantial effects on eventual choices.

The popular press also appears to attach greater importance to recruitment than do recent academic findings. Professional and business journals continue to assert that applicants can be wooed not only through improved job attributes, but also through better-planned and more attentive recruitment procedures (e.g., Bureau of National Affairs, 1989; Marcus, 1982; Stoops, 1984). Recent job acceptees also stress the importance of competent recruitment practices in securing applicants' acceptances (Gerstner, 1966; Luck, 1988).

In sum, although recent academic research has tended to conclude that little variance in applicants' decisions is accounted for by recruitment practices, earlier academic research and the practitioner literature suggest that recruitment experiences can be very important in job choice. Hence, two questions arise: What factors account for these different views? And is one "more correct" than the other?

Neither question, particularly the second, can be answered definitively on the basis of current evidence. However, following an extensive review of the job search and choice literatures, Schwab, Rynes, and Aldag (1987) concluded that "different results were clearly associated with substantial differences in the methodology employed" and that, as a result, "judgments must be made about the likely sources of invalidity of the various approaches" (pp. 153–154).

Accordingly, Schwab et al. (1987) examined likely sources of invalidity for the two most common job choice methodologies: cross-sectional questionnaire rating research (the dominant recent method) and longitudinal interview research. Although strengths and weaknesses were acknowledged for both approaches, Schwab et al. concluded that, on balance, open-ended longitudinal research was likely to give a truer picture of applicants' search and choice processes:

> Although previous studies of sequential search have left some unanswered questions, we nevertheless believe that the methodologies used by these researchers are likely to prove more useful. . . . For one thing, sequential methodologies have traced job seekers' reactions over time. This would seem to be a prerequisite for observing the full range of search and evaluation

behaviors, as well as the great variation in strategies that may be employed by different individuals. . . . Demand characteristics (in questionnaire rating research) may cause subjects to provide expectancy, instrumentality, and valence estimates for multiple attributes, even though they do not actually make their decision on the basis of those attributes (pp. 154–155).

Similar conclusions were reached by Rynes and Barber (1990), who reviewed previous recruitment research from an organizational strategy perspective:

In most cases, existing studies are extremely simplistic when evaluated against real-world attraction complexities. In particular, most studies have examined single strategies and limited dependent variables at single phases of the attraction process. For example, recruiter research has been dominated by applicant impressions at the campus interview . . . with few exceptions, our present knowledge of actual practices is insufficient to provide much guidance . . . as such, we recommend that would-be prescriptive researchers begin by becoming more "informed" by solid descriptive findings (pp. 305–307).

In light of the preceding comments, we felt there was a potentially major contribution to be made by letting job seekers tell us, in their own words, how they made the various decisions leading up to a job choice. One anticipated benefit of this approach was to obtain a better understanding of the underlying "psychology" of job choice and its relationship to organizational recruitment practices. Another was its potential for generating future research questions by getting "closer" to the subjects of investigation:

One finds many instances where closeness to sources of data made key insights possible—Piaget's closeness to his children, Freud's proximity to and empathy with his patients, Darwin's closeness to nature, and even Newton's intimate encounter with an apple. In short, closeness does not make bias and loss of perspective inevitable, and distance is no guarantee of objectivity (Patton, 1990, p. 48).

The present research is based on structured, open-ended interviews conducted at two points in the job search process. According to Patton (1990), interviews are the most basic form of qualitative inquiry in that subjects' responses were constrained by "writing skills of the respondents, the impossibility of probing or extending responses, and the effort required of the person completing the [written] questionnaire." Although findings from this method are "longer, more detailed, and more variable in content" and "analysis is difficult because responses are neither systematic nor standardized," the method is regarded as valuable because it "enables the researcher to understand and capture the points of view of other people without predetermining those points of view through prior selection of questionnaire categories" (Patton, p. 24).

In adopting this methodology, we are moving in a direction consistent with recent developments—both empirical and theoretical—in a wide variety of decision contexts (e.g., capital investment decisions, strategic business decisions, group decision processes). Empirically, for example, there has been a steady

Table 1

SAMPLE CHARACTERISTICS

Variable	M	SD	Range	1	2	3	4
1. Sex[a]	.41	.50	0–1	1.00			
2. Grad status[b]	.46	1.16	0–1	.17	1.00		
3. GPA	3.33	.32	2.7–3.8	.00	.39**	1.00	
4. Intern/Summer (mo.)	6.31	5.25	0–20	–.12	–.25	.09	1.00
5. Experience (mo.)	19.77	29.82	1–120+	.20	.66***	.07	–.49***
6. Extracurriculars	4.49	2.32	0–9	.11	–.09	–.09	–.03
7. Offices	1.44	1.29	0–4	.15	–.02	–.03	.02
8. Think about search[c]	1.05	.91	0–2	–.36**	–.28*	–.10	.19
9. First interview[d]	1.83	.81	0–4	–.09	.21	.31*	–.27
10. Campus interviews	18.03	8.64	2–40	.23	.22	.03	–.01
11. Second interviews	6.63	4.78	1–20	.30*	.25	.21	–.07
12. Offers	3.00	2.85	0–15	.43***	.18	.18	–.02

increase in qualitative, small-sample observational or interview studies that seek to determine how decision makers "construe reality" in particular environmental contexts (e.g., Eisenhardt, 1989a; Gersick, 1989; Isabella, 1990; Saunders & Jones, 1990). Theoretically, researchers have called for methodologies that would lead to a better balance between search and choice, process and outcome, and induction and deduction (e.g., Eisenhardt, 1989b; Lord & Maher, 1990; Tsoukas, 1989; Yin, 1989). The present study represents an attempt to nudge the current balance in job search and recruitment research toward a greater concern for search, process, and contextual fidelity.

METHOD

Subjects

Subjects were 41 graduating students from four colleges (arts and sciences, engineering, industrial relations, and business) of a major northeastern university. Because we wished to identify a wide range of recruitment experiences and reactions, the sample was chosen to be as broadly diversified as possible within size limitations. Sample size was limited by the labor-intensiveness of the data collection process, the time constraints of interviewers and subjects (who were both carrying full academic loads while searching for jobs), and the labor-intensiveness of content coding and analysis procedures.

Diversity was achieved with the help of the four placement directors, each of whom was asked to nominate 10 job seekers (industrial relations nominated

Table 1

continued

5	6	7	8	9	10	11	12
1.00							
−.49***	1.00						
−.03	.36**	1.00					
−.54***	.11	−.18	1.00				
.14	−.09	.10	.16	1.00			
.02	−.02	.20	−.17	−.07	1.00		
.21	−.02	.01	−.36**	−.04	.36**	1.00	
−.02	.17	−.03	−.22	−.11	.16	.64***	1.00

*p < .10; **p < .05; ***p < .01 (two-tailed; N = 41)

[a]Female = 0; Male = 1

[b]Undergrad = 0; Grad = 1

[c]Year prior to graduation = 0; Summer before graduation = 1; Fall of graduation year = 2

[d]Year prior to graduation = 0; September = 1; October = 2; November = 3; December or later = 4

11) who, taken as a set, would maximize variability on factors such as race, sex, academic performance, articulateness, self-insight, and likely employability. Although certain "objective" elements of diversity (e.g., race, sex, grade point) could have been obtained through formal records, these characteristics often show little relationship to applicant reactions (e.g., Harris & Fink, 1987) or job search outcomes (Gerhart & Rynes, 1991; Smith, 1990). Because of their close contact with job-seeking students, placement directors were in the best position to identify less tangible—but perhaps more important (see Rynes & Gerhart, 1990)—determinants of job search experiences, such as interpersonal skills, articulateness, self-confidence, and goal orientation.

The end result of this nomination process was a sample that was, in fact, highly diversified in terms of background characteristics, job search and interviewing patterns, and search success (see Table 1). Moreover, the fact that objective qualifications (i.e., grade point averages, internships, work experience) were uncorrelated with any of the measures of search success (e.g., site visits or job offers) suggests that our strategy to sample students with a wide range of intangible as well as observable characteristics was a wise one. (Job offers *were* correlated with sex, however: men averaged 4.4 offers vs. 1.9 for women; p < .01. Although sex is typically observable, it is not a job-related qualification per se.)

Table 2

SAMPLE CHARACTERISTICS BY COLLEGE

Variable	College			
	Arts and sciences	Engineering	Industrial relations	Business
Male	.30	.40	.36	.60
Graduate students***	.00	.20	.50	1.00
GPA	3.29	3.17	3.42	3.36
Intern/Summer (mo.)	5.88	6.70	8.42	3.44
Experience (mo.)***	.50	8.60	20.50	48.33
Extracurriculars*	5.50	5.50	3.83	3.33
Offices	1.13	1.50	1.50	1.56
Think about search	1.38	1.38	1.73	2.22
Date of first interview	2.00	1.38	1.73	2.22
Campus interviews**	12.30	19.70	17.17	24.38
Site visits	3.80	7.30	7.67	7.67
Job offers	2.44	3.11	3.25	3.13

$*p < .10$; $**p < .05$; $***p < .01$ (Omnibus F-test; $N = 41$)

There also were several statistically significant relationships among subjects' background characteristics. For example, those with full-time experience were less likely to participate in extracurricular activities and internships (Table 1). This makes sense because internships and extracurricular activities are often pursued as substitutes for full-time experience, prior to a first job search. In addition, males and graduate students began thinking about search earlier than did women and undergraduates, while students with higher grade point averages (GPAs) took later interviews.

The colleges sampled were also quite diverse (see Table 2). For example, colleges ranged from undergraduate only (arts and sciences) to mixed graduate-undergraduate (engineering and industrial relations) to graduate only (business). Colleges also differed in terms of the amount of prior work experience of their students ($F = 6.07$), the number of extracurricular activities ($F = 2.47$), and the number of campus interviews ($F = 3.71$).

Procedure

In order to capture decision dynamics, each student was interviewed at two points in the job search process. Initial interviews were conducted in the first few weeks (late January–early February) of the second semester of 1990. At this point, most students had spent somewhere between 1–3 months in the campus interview process. A resume was also collected as part of the interviewing procedure, and was used to generate information about work experience, grade point average, extracurricular activities, and offices held. Two individuals who had initially been nominated as subjects proved unreachable, and were replaced by two new nominees.

The second round of interviews began in late March and continued until early May. The intent was to wait long enough to produce substantial variation in search experiences, but not so long that subjects became unavailable or unwilling to complete second interviews (final exams began in the second week of May). Within this range, attempts were made to schedule second interviews 8–10 weeks after the first, such that those who interviewed earlier in the first round also interviewed earlier in the second. However, scheduling was constrained to some extent by subject availability, given that subjects were still full-time students and traveling to anywhere between 1–20 site visits.

Interviewers were research assistants of the principal investigators and placement directors. All interviewers were given identical training prior to each interviewing round. Prior to finalizing interview content, all interviewers, the principal investigators, and the industrial relations placement director gathered together to discuss the entire interview, question by question. Any ambiguities about question wording or intent were resolved, and a revised interview prepared.

Interviews ranged from 20 minutes to more than an hour. Given that there were substantial differences in length across interviews conducted by the same interviewer, length appeared to be mainly a function of the articulateness and task involvement of the subject. Although longer interviews resulted in more numerous and/or elaborate "critical incidents," there is no evidence that length was systematically correlated with differences in response *content* (e.g., whether particular factors, such as delays or recruiters, were mentioned as being important to a decision).

Interview Questions

The data described in this paper were derived from a broader investigation of recruitment and job search processes. The principal investigators (and two of the placement officials) had long been intrigued by the frequency with which both recruiters and applicants mentioned the importance of "fit" in their decisions, often without being able to articulate precisely what they meant by the term (e.g., Bretz, Ash, & Dreher, 1989; Ricklefs, 1979; Rynes & Gerhart, 1990). Given this interest, a decision was made to investigate how job seekers (and recruiters) assess fit over the course of the job search and recruitment process.

Given our limited understanding of both the fit construct (Rynes & Gerhart, 1990) and job choice processes in general (see Schwab et al., 1987), the use of researcher-generated rating questionnaires seemed premature. Accordingly, a decision was made to use structured, open-ended interview questions based on a "critical incidents" approach (questions are reproduced in the Appendix).

Although our methodology was not precisely identical to the critical incidents technique outlined by Flanagan (1954), both interviews were designed to elicit information about reactions to specific companies and specific decisions made with respect to those companies (e.g., not to accept a site visit). Hence, most of the data reported here do, in fact, refer to "critical" components of judgments and decisions, rather than to abstract impressions about recruiters, fit, or job choice in general. By having subjects focus first on particular organizations, events, or decisions, it was then easy for most of them to recall specific incidents that led to those impressions and decisions.

Within this general framework, the two interviews were segmented to tap different phases of the job search process. The first focused primarily on how applicants form initial impressions of fit with various organizations. This question is of critical importance in filling interview schedules, but has been largely ignored in previous recruitment research (Rynes & Barber, 1990). Questions asked for three specific examples of good (perceived) fit, three examples of poor fit, examples of good fit and bad fit that ran counter to peer opinions, and positive and negative changes in assessments of fit since beginning job search. In each case, named examples were probed to determine the beliefs, incidents, or causes underlying the initial or changed fit assessment.

The second interview focused more on later phases of the search process (e.g., site visits and job choices) and general impressions of recruitment practices per se. These latter questions were added because, although the study had initially been conceived as a "fit" rather than a "recruitment" study, casual inspection of first-round transcripts suggested a large role for recruitment variables in general fit assessments. For this reason, several specific questions about recruitment (questions 12–14 in the Appendix) were added to the second interview.[1]

Analyses

All 82 interviews were tape-recorded and transcribed. Transcripts were read in their entirety by the three principal investigators, who independently designed alternative coding schemes for summarizing the data. After developing a consensus scheme and instructions, actual coding was performed by one of the investigators and a research assistant. The two coders agreed in 93% of the cases; the final 7% were resolved by a different principal investigator. On no question did interrater agreement fall below 85%. To facilitate reader comprehension, the specific coding of each question is discussed concurrently with the results.

Because the main point of this study was to gain insight into the cognitive processes associated with job search, statistical findings were supplemented by a considerable amount of content-based interpretation. That is, after reviewing the descriptive statistics pertaining to a particular question, transcripts were reexamined for insight into the incidents, judgments, and processes underlying the

---

[1]Because of the study's broad objectives, more data were collected than can feasibly be discussed in a single paper. Our decision rules for inclusion in this paper were: (a) to focus only on the applicant's perspective (analogous data from recruiters are not reported); (b) to summarize only the most general questions with fewest demand characteristics (these questions were also placed earliest in the interviews to avoiding priming effects); and (c) to emphasize content analysis of recruitment-related responses to a greater extent than other kinds of responses (e.g., those concerning job characteristics). Additional information about unanalyzed questions and coding schemes is available from the authors upon request.

quantitative results. In most cases, content analysis added substantially to our understanding of the psychology and emotion (Lopes, 1987) of job search and choice decisions. Sample quotations are provided throughout the Results section to illustrate this point.

Additional analyses (e.g., *t*-tests, one-way analyses of variance) were performed to detect potentially important relationships between applicants' personal characteristics and their search and choice behaviors. Although these analyses are clearly exploratory, they are nevertheless conservative in at least three ways. First, some real relationships are likely to go undetected due to our modest statistical power. For example, with a sample size of 41, the power to detect a true correlation of .2 is only .25 at $\alpha = .05$, or .35 at $\alpha = .10$ (two-tailed test; Cohen, 1988). Second, two-tailed significance tests were used throughout, despite the fact that reasonable directional hypotheses could have been offered in some cases (e.g., sex, work experience, search success) but were not due to space limitations. Third, the bulk of our questions were very nondirective, which probably led to underreporting of recruitment incidents by subjects with limited self-insight, articulateness, or motivation to be interviewed.

RESULTS

On average, subjects attended 18.0 campus interviews, 6.6 site visits, and received 3.0 job offers. As such, the results that follow are based on a total of 738 campus interviews and 271 site visits.

First Interview: Assessments of Initial Fit and Early Changes in Fit Assessment

At the beginning of the first interview, subjects were asked to name three companies they thought would provide the best fit to their employment objectives (question 2 in Appendix), as well as three that would produce the worst fit (question 3). In addition, they were asked to name companies for which their personal assessments of good fit and poor fit ran counter to general impressions among their peers (questions 4–5).

Preliminary analyses of these questions revealed that three distinct sets of variables were responsible for early fit perceptions: (a) perceived job and organizational characteristics (hereafter shortened to "job characteristics"), (b) interactions with formal organizational representatives, and (c) contacts with other people (besides recruiters) already in the organization. Six variables were created to reflect these categories (three variables for positive fit responses, three for negative). Responses were coded 1 if the category was mentioned as a reason for inferring fit, and 0 otherwise. Thus, a subject who mentioned both job characteristics and organizational acquaintances as reasons for positive fit assessments, but only recruitment experiences as a reason for negative fit assessments, would be coded 1,0,1,0,1,0.

Analyses revealed that every single subject mentioned job characteristics as important factors in positive assessments of initial fit (Table 3, item 1). Although a

Table 3

RESPONSES TO INTERVIEW QUESTIONS*

First Interview:

1. Reasons for judging companies to be good initial fits and/or good initial fit even though peers are not attracted:

Job characteristics	41
Recruitment/Representatives	12
Friends/Acquaintances	9

2. Reasons for judging companies to be poor initial fits and/or poor initial fit even though peers are attracted:

Job characteristics	39
Recruitment/Representatives	23
Friends/Acquaintances	1
N/A (no poor fits)	1

3. Reasons companies that were once perceived as good fits are now perceived as poor fits:

Job characteristics	23
Recruitment/Representatives	16
N/A (no negative changes)	10

4. Reasons companies not perceived as good fits initially are now perceived as good fits:

Job characteristics	20
Recruitment/Representatives	16
N/A (no positive changes)	13

Second Interview:

5a. Position accepted (or intended to accept) was favorite at beginning of job search:

No (self-report)	23
No (cross-check)	25
Yes (self-report)	18

5b. For initially non-favored positions, what happened to make them favorites?

Job characteristics	19
Recruiters/Representatives	14
N/A (chose a favorite)	18

6a. Number reporting companies that were once attractive, but no longer:

Yes	35
No	2
Missing	4

6b. Reasons companies that were once attractive are no longer attractive:

Job characteristics	20
Recruitment	20
Delays	9

full content analysis of job characteristic responses is beyond the scope of this paper (see Footnote 1), commonly mentioned characteristics included general company reputation, attitude toward the product or industry, perceived status of the subject's particular functional area (e.g., marketing, design, human resources) in the company, perceived training or advancement opportunities, and geographic location. Press coverage appeared to play a considerable role in some subjects' impressions, particularly coverage concerning environmental sensitivity, business ethics, and personnel practices (e.g., laying off senior workers while

Table 3

continued

7a. Turn down any offers for site visits?
     Yes   28
     No   12
     Missing   1

7b. Reasons for turn-downs:
     Job characteristics   15
     Delays/Timing   20
     Characteristics + Timing   6
     Recruiters   3
     N/A   13

8. Extent to which very good, or very bad, recruiters influenced willingness to accept offers:
     Strong influence   19
     Some/It depends   19
     Little/No influence   3

9a. Number experiencing very long delays after first interview:
     Yes   39
     No   2

9b. Assumed reasons for delays:
     Not favorite candidate   28
     Disorganized organization   21
     Both   12
     N/A (no delays)   2

9c. Delays affected willingness to accept offers:
     Yes, definitely   20
     Somewhat/"Depends"   11
     No, not at all   8
     N/A (no delays)   2

10. Extent of agreement that recruitment practices are *not* very important (7 = very strong agreement):
     7 = 1 (recruitment not at all important)
     6 = 5
     5 = 4
     4 = 6
     3 = 9
     2 = 5
     1 = 1 (recruitment very important)

---

*Figures represent number of subjects providing each response (overall $N = 41$). Data are presented in raw (rather than percentage) form because for some questions there are "not applicable" or missing responses.

hiring new ones, failure to give notice regarding impending layoffs). In addition, 12 subjects specifically mentioned that initial contacts with company representatives had been responsible for early impressions of good fit:

> I was really impressed by ———. They interviewed about a hundred people in a day. Then, based on the initial interview, people were asked to re-interview the next day in different divisions. So instead of just putting resumes in

> a pile and having people look at them, they were on the ball. Before we went through this process, they had a nice reception, they talked to us about it and explained how it worked . . . I was really impressed by that (female engineering undergraduate).

> The woman from ———— was top-notch and did a great job of recruiting. She was a real big factor in my decision to do the on-site with them and to follow through (female graduate in industrial relations; ultimately accepted this offer).

Exploratory analyses also revealed two background characteristics associated with the tendency to mention recruitment experiences as a basis for initial assessments of positive fit. Specifically, those who mentioned recruitment had less full-time work experience ($t = 2.01; p < .05$) and began thinking later about job search ($t = 2.38; p < .05$).

Having friends or acquaintances already in the organization was at least partially responsible for positive assessments among 9 subjects. All 9 of these subjects were female, a significant difference at $p < .01$.

Turning to reasons for negative initial assessments of fit, 39 subjects mentioned job characteristics, 23 mentioned recruitment or recruiters, and 1 mentioned a disliked acquaintance. Note that the number forming negative impressions on the basis of recruitment is nearly double the number forming positive impressions on this basis. Consider the following example:

> ———— has a management training program which the recruiter had gone through [*sic*]. She was talking about the great presentational skills that ———— teaches you, and the woman was barely literate. She was embarrassing. If that was the best they could do, I did not want any part of them. Also, ———— and ————'s recruiters appeared to have real attitude problems. I also thought they were chauvinistic (female arts undergraduate).

> One firm I didn't think of talking to initially, but they called me and asked me to talk with them. So I did, and then the recruiter was very, very rude. Yes, *very* rude, and I've run into that a couple of times (female engineering graduate).

On average, those mentioning recruitment as a reason for negative impressions of initial fit had lower GPAs than those who didn't ($t = 2.85; p < .01$).

Following questions about initial impressions, subjects were asked to consider whether they had changed their impressions of specific companies in either a positive or negative direction (questions 6–7 in Appendix). Here, changes fell into two categories: changes due to acquisition of more detailed job information, and those due to recruitment representatives or practices. Again, these categories were not mutually exclusive; a subject could attribute a changed assessment to both reasons (coded 1,1) or only one (1,0 or 0,1).

Ten subjects reported no negative changes in impressions regarding early favorites. Among those who did, 23 cited revised information about job characteristics, while 16 mentioned recruiters or recruitment experiences:

> For example, the ———— companies [specific industry] wouldn't put even one woman on my schedule. That scares me. I would ask to have a woman put on

my schedule and at best, maybe there would be one (female industrial relations graduate).

The guy at the interview made a joke about how nice my nails were and how they were going to ruin them there due to all the tough work (female engineering undergraduate).

There were also some differences in background characteristics among those who reported negative changes in assessment due to recruitment. Those who attributed negative changes to recruitment had lower GPAs ($t = 2.19; p < .05$), more internship experience ($t = 1.90; p < .10$), and were more likely to be female ($t = 2.04; p < .05$).

In terms of positive changes in fit assessments (Table 3, item 4), 20 attributed these changes to improved information about job characteristics, while 16 mentioned recruitment or organizational representatives:

I wasn't sure of the fit at first. But after talking with people there, I feel there is a pretty good fit. I have talked to seven people there and liked all of them. They also hired a lot of people from [this program] last year. I look for sincerity and good follow-up when trying to assess fit (female MBA).

They invited me to a closed schedule, and I wasn't really sure. I didn't know enough about the company to decide whether I liked them or not. But I loved the people who came to interview me. I thought it was a really good sign that the company sent two women recruiters to interview. And then when I went down to my plant visit, probably half the people I saw on my schedule were female managers, and to me that's a big plus for the company (female MBA, ultimately accepted this offer).

There were no discernible differences in background characteristics between those who mentioned recruitment as a reason for revised perceptions of fit in a positive direction, and those who didn't.

Second Interview: Later Changes in Assessments, Site Visits, and Job Choices

The second interview began with general questions about the number of interviews, site visits, and job offers acquired, and whether or not subjects had accepted an offer. These were followed by other questions concerning changes in impressions since the first interview.

One way of assessing changed evaluations was to ask whether the jobs accepted by subjects (or, in the case of the 10 without acceptances, the job they hoped or expected to accept) had been among their initial favorites. More than half our subjects ($n = 23$) said that it was not (Table 3, item 5a). In addition, a cross-check of responses from the earlier interview revealed an additional 2 subjects who, although they said they had chosen an initial favorite, had not mentioned the chosen company as one of their three "best-fitting" companies in the first interview. In short, these findings suggest that more than half our subjects were open to a substantial amount of positive influence during the search and choice process.

Given the large proportion of individuals who took (or expected to take) jobs with companies that were not initially favored, it is instructive to examine the reasons behind the changes (Table 3, item 5b). New information about the job or organization was cited by 19 of the 23 self-reported changers. In addition, 14 explicitly mentioned recruitment and/or the treatment they had received on site visits. Of particular importance were the status of the people met during recruitment, the extent to which applicants felt "specially" treated, the organization's flexibility in scheduling visits, and the professionalism of the site visit (e.g., amount of "down time"). Also, it is interesting to note that although we did not explicitly track all job offers, only 1 subject seemed to have changed favorites involuntarily. The rest all seemed to be genuinely enthusiastic toward their choices, consistent with earlier arguments that by the time job-takers announce their decisions, they have adjusted their attitudes to be cognitively consistent with their decisions (Soelberg, 1967; Vroom, 1966).

In terms of individual differences, those who were positively influenced by recruitment treatment were more likely to be female ($t = 2.93$; $p < .01$), to have interviewed later ($t = 1.95$; $p < .10$) to have taken more site visits ($t = 1.88$; $p < .10$), and to have engaged in fewer extracurricular activities ($t = 2.30$; $p < .05$).

It is also instructive to look at changes in the opposite direction; that is, why subjects lost interest in organizations that were once initial favorites (Table 3, items 6a-b). Of the 35 subjects indicating that they had lost interest in at least one initial favorite, 20 mentioned improved information about job characteristics. However, 20 also mentioned organizational representatives and/or recruitment practices:

> ———— had a set schedule for me which they deviated from regularly. Times overlapped, and one person kept me too long which pushed the whole day back. They almost seemed to be saying that it was my fault that I was late for the next one! I guess a lot of what they did just wasn't very professional. Even at the point when I was done, where most companies would have a cab pick you up, I was in the middle of a snowstorm in Chicago and they said, 'You can get a cab downstairs.' There weren't any cabs. I literally had to walk 12 or 14 blocks with my luggage, trying to find some way to get to the airport. They didn't book me a hotel for the night of the snowstorm so I had to sit in the airport for 8 hours trying to get another flight . . . they wouldn't even reimburse me for the additional plane fare (female industrial relations graduate student).

> I had a very bad campus interview experience . . . the person who came was a last minute fill-in . . . I think he had a couple of "issues" and was very discourteous during the interview. He was one step away from yawning in my face . . . The other thing he did was that he kept making these (nothing illegal, mind you) but he kept making these references to the fact that I had been out of my undergraduate and first graduate programs for more than 10 years now . . . (female MBA with 10 years experience).

Another 9 subjects volunteered that delays caused their loss of interest. On average, those who mentioned delays as a reason for losing interest had more job offers than those who did not ($t = 2.79$; $p < .01$).

A more behaviorally based question pertaining to loss of interest concerned whether (and why) job seekers had turned down any invitations for site visits (Table 3, items 7a-b). At least one visit was turned down by 28 subjects, the most frequent reason being that the invitation came too late in the process (20 cases); 15 refused visits because they perceived the job to be less attractive than their other alternatives; 6 cited a combination of timing and perceived job attractiveness.

On average, experienced workers ($t = 2.19$; $p < .05$) and graduate students ($t = 2.18$; $p < .05$) were less likely to reject site visits due to lateness. These findings suggest greater tolerance for prolonged job search among applicants who have worked before.

Three respondents turned down site visits because of negative experiences with campus recruiters. This is a fairly dramatic response to a poor recruiter, although the numbers involved are quite small. Because negative reactions of one interview party probably "infect" the other party as well (Dipboye, 1982; Eder & Buckley, 1988), it seems likely that many applicants who had negative reactions to particular recruiters did not receive any further invitations to "reject."

Second Interview: Reactions to Recruitment Practices

Up to this point, all reported results were obtained in response to questions that did not ask anything about recruitment practices per se. In the sections that follow, we report on responses to direct questions about recruiters, delays, and general recruitment practices.

Recruiters.   Previous research has suggested that recruiters do not have much impact on job choices, particularly when compared against characteristics of the vacancy itself (e.g., Rynes, 1991; Rynes & Barber, 1990; Wanous & Colella, 1989). However, these findings have typically been obtained with respect to subject ratings of the most recent interview experience. As such, they are likely to underestimate the extent to which "extreme" recruiter behaviors might influence decisions. For this reason, we asked subjects how much their willingness to accept job offers was influenced by either "very good" or "very poor" recruiters (Appendix, question 13).

Open-ended responses to this question fell into three categories: strong influence (coded 2); some or "qualified" influence (e.g., "It depends on whether I have other offers" or "It depends on how much I know about the company," coded 1); and little or no influence (coded 0). As Table 3 indicates (item 8), the vast majority of subjects felt that they were either strongly or somewhat influenced by recruiters. The only background characteristics that differentiated the degree of reported influence was the number of offices held ($r = .27$; $p < .05$).

Content analysis was very revealing in terms of the psychological mechanisms underlying the degree of influence. Generally speaking, influence seemed to depend almost entirely on the extent to which recruiters were seen as reliable signals of what it would be like to work for the company:

> There were a lot of companies that I had little or no information about, other than what they make. I generalize a lot about the company from their

representative. If that person is not very sharp, does not seem to be particularly interested in me, or asks the same questions as every other recruiter, it does not impress me (male undergraduate with four job offers).

It's a real big factor. . . . I guess it's an impression I get of what the entire organization is like, and whether that's right or wrong, it's real. I would assume that the company would want to send the best person they possibly could to represent them. If they're sending a person who is not very good, that tells me something about how they view this whole process—that they're not aware of the impression these people make (female graduate student with three job offers).

Conversely, those who accorded the recruiter less influence did so because they believed recruiters were *not* representative of the organization:

If they are very bad, it just leave me where I was. I just chalk it up; there are always going to be bad apples and that is just a bad apple (female arts undergraduate).

Interviewers aren't necessarily representative of the company at all, so even if I have a bad first interview, if I like the company or the position, I'll take a second interview regardless of whether I liked the person, because I don't necessarily connect them with the company [*sic*] (female MBA).

Some of the responses also included clues as to *why* certain recruiters were regarded as more valid signals than others. For example, signaling influence was greater when subjects knew little about the organization:

If I didn't know much about the company, [the recruiter] probably influenced me a lot. If I did know about it, probably less so (male industrial relations undergraduate).

If they're very good and being very encouraging, then they make me want to work for the company. If they're very bad, it would be just the opposite, unless the company had a really big name. One of my ——— interviews was rotten, but I already knew enough about ——— to know what ——— was like. They have such a huge name [that] I knew this guy was just a jerk (female engineering undergraduate).

On the other hand, signaling influence was lower when the representative was not from the applicant's functional area. As one engineer put it, "I don't really care how personnel people treat me . . . personnel people really don't understand anything about me or my work." Finally, representatives seemed to be scrutinized more closely once applicants began to experience success in the labor market. At that point, recruiters had to work very hard to get their organizations into the applicant's "feasible choice set," while a poor representative often sealed the organization's fate.

Curiously, many subjects who reported being completely unaffected by recruiters volunteered that the people they met on site visits (potential managers, coworkers, and incumbents from different areas) were very important to their choices. Many subjects were highly suspicious about the motives of campus recruiters (but, curiously, almost never about the motives of on-site representatives), while others had misgivings about the extent to which campus recruiters actually understood the vacancy and its requirements.

Another (small) group of applicants seemed to recognize the self- and social desirability elements involved in questions about recruiter impact. These people believed that it was somehow "irrational" to be influenced by recruiters, but worried that they might have been anyway:

> Consciously, the recruiter doesn't matter, but I'm sure that subconsciously it does. If the person makes you feel more comfortable, then you'll feel more comfortable about the job (male engineering undergraduate).

> I usually try not to let it affect me because you can't really let one person represent an entire organization. [However, subject (a male arts undergraduate) goes on to say that two recruiters made him so angry he only completed the interviews so as not to embarrass the placement director].

Finally, consistent with self-fulfilling prophecy arguments by Dipboye (1982), a number of subjects indicated that recruiter behaviors probably had subtle effects on their own interviewing performances:

> If a recruiter is not that good and things don't click, you don't get past that [first interview] stage anyway because you don't make a good impression (female arts undergraduate).

> I don't think it affects the job choice as far as actual offers go, but it affects your first impression and it affects how you go into your second interview, and [that] can really alter how [well] the second interview goes (female MBA).

Recruiting delays.   Previous studies have reported mixed results as to whether or not applicants are adversely affected by delays. For example, using archival data, Arvey et al. (1975) found that delays reduced the size of the available applicant pool, particularly among minorities. In contrast, neither Rynes and Boudreau (1986) nor Taylor and Bergmann (1987) found evidence of an adverse effect on applicants. However, Rynes and Boudreau's results were based on perceptions of recruitment administrators, while Taylor and Bergmann's sample suffered from severe attrition (and, hence, possible selection bias) over the course of the study.

In the present study, 39 of the 41 subjects named at least one organization that was very late (subjectively interpreted) in getting back to them (Table 3, items 9a–c). Presumed causes of late follow-ups fell into two distinct categories: inferences about self, and inferences about the organization.

The largest group ($n = 28$) attributed delays to personal rejection or relegation to second-choice status. These subjects differed from those who did not mention possible rejection by having begun interviewing later in the season ($t = 2.00$; $p < .05$) and having received fewer job offers ($t = 2.10$; $p < .05$). In general, the impression created by subjects inferring rejection was one of lower self-confidence and qualifications:

I assumed I was going to get a ding letter, which is what usually happens when you don't hear from a company within a few weeks. So I started to look at other options and I didn't take that company as a serious option (female arts undergraduate with no honors, no leadership positions, no experience, and no job offers).

Companies who were late, I did not think that the initial interview had been very well [*sic*] (female industrial relations undergraduate with lowest grade point average in the sample).

On the other hand, 21 subjects made organizationally based attributions (rather than, or in addition to, personal ones). Generally speaking, subjects who attributed delays to organizational characteristics appeared to be more highly qualified than those who did not: they had higher GPAs ($t = 1.91$; $p < .10$); started thinking earlier about job search ($t = 4.24$; $p < .01$); and had experienced greater search success ($t = 2.26$ for campus interviews, $p < .05$; $t = 3.15$ for site visits, $p < .01$; $t = 2.19$ for job offers, $p < .05$). They were also more likely to be male ($t = 2.97$; $p < .01$) and graduate students ($t = 1.85$; $p < .10$). The greater tendency of more qualified applicants to attribute delays to organizational characteristics can be seen in the following examples:

Being very confident, and with my background, . . . I felt pretty sure I would be chosen. For me, it was more a sign of [their] not being on the ball, or [being] administratively inept. I didn't look at it as a personal thing, their not getting back to me; I looked at it as a negative on the company (male Hispanic graduate student with 3 years of work experience and eight job offers).

I would think that within 2–3 weeks they should be giving some response; my assumptions were either a disorganized staff, or else they were pulling my chain. In either case, I was not impressed. . . . I had indicated at the beginning that I had a pretty busy schedule, and the fact that they got back to me late meant I had already committed to others. I just eliminated them from my list (male undergraduate with Japanese language skills and six job offers).

If they work [the schedule] with your needs in mind, it can really work to their advantage. But they don't realize that . . . They don't look at it as them competing with 45 other companies for 17 of us [industrial relations graduate students]. They just think, 'Everyone *must* want to work for *us*!' (female graduate student with 4 years experience and four offers).

It should be noted that a few of the subjects who attributed delays to organizational factors made inferences that were less negative than those quoted above. Some said generally forgiving things like, "They're running a business, and a lot of things happen in business that we don't know about," while others had more specific reasons for giving a charitable interpretation (e.g., they had been warned about the delay, the organization had never done college recruiting before). Still, these examples were in the minority, as most delay-related attributions were decidedly negative in tone.

Finally, subjects who had experienced delays were asked to indicate whether those delays had affected their willingness to take jobs. Responses fell into four categories (Table 3, item 9c), with the largest number ($n = 20$) saying either that delays had "definitely" affected their willingness, or offering specific examples of organizations whose follow-up came too late to matter. Relatively speaking, males were more affected by delays ($t = 1.81$; $p < .10$), as were those with higher grade point averages ($r = .34$; $p < .05$).

Content analysis of subjects' responses suggested that even when delays did not have direct effect on job choices, they might have had *indirect* effects, either by triggering more elaborate information processing or by allowing the individual to generate alternative offers in the meantime:

> I think [the delay] caused me to look deeper at certain parts of the company, to look more at the planning, to see if there was something I missed, or if it was something that just happened in my case . . . So it didn't necessarily affect my willingness to take a job with the company, but it did suggest that I *had to look at certain things about the company a little more closely than I might otherwise have done* [italics added] (male industrial relations graduate).

> *Especially after I had an offer, I started judging more* [italics added]. In the beginning, it was just, 'Like me, please like me' (male industrial relations graduate).

Overall recruitment practices.   The final question asked subjects to indicate the extent of their agreement with the following statement: "When it comes right down to it, recruitment practices are not very important because people choose jobs on the basis of things like pay, location, and reputation rather than recruitment" (1 = *strongly disagree*; 7 = *strongly agree*). This was the only question in the entire interview that required an explicit numerical rating. Its negative phrasing was designed to avoid "mom and apple pie" responses (e.g., "Yes, of *course* recruitment is important!").

The mean rating (3.5) indicated that subjects disagreed slightly with this statement; that is, they found recruitment to lean toward being "important." However, the actual distribution was skewed around a modal response of 2 (Table 3, item 10). As such, the "typical" respondent thought recruitment was considerably more important than suggested by the mean rating.

A one-way analysis of variance indicated that there were significant differences in reported importance by college ($p < .05$), with industrial relations students rating it most highly ($\bar{x} = 2.7$), followed by engineering (3.2), business (3.8), and arts (4.2). Two things are potentially interesting about this result. First, most of the industrial relations students were looking for jobs in human resources. As such, one would expect recruitment experiences to have more signaling value for these students than for any others. Second, on average, industrial relations students had the most job offers, while arts students had the least. According to Rynes et al. (1980) and Breaugh (1983), recruitment's importance would be expected to increase in situations where individuals have more freedom of choice.

Interestingly, differences in importance were also significantly related to whether or not subjects had experienced delays in the recruitment process (the average rating of those who did not experience delays was 6.5, as compared with

2.8 for those who did; $p < .01$). This suggests that out-of-the-ordinary recruitment experiences may increase recruitment's salience to applicants. Finally, rated importance was higher for those with more internship experience ($r = -.28$; $p < .10$), but lower for those with more extracurriculars ($r = .26; p < .10$) and higher grade point averages ($r = .29; p < .10$).

Explanations of the more extreme responses to this item (1 or 2, 6 or 7) were very illuminating. As with the question about recruiter impact, the biggest differentiator between high- and low-importance groups was the extent to which they viewed recruitment practices as valid indicators of what it would be like to work for the company. Consider the following examples:

> I think a lot of people look at recruiting practices as reflective of the company, and in many cases that's absolutely accurate. Despite the fact that other factors matter, people do make choices based on how they're treated and how they feel about what's happening. If someone feels they've been treated badly, even it it's just one person who is screwing up all the way, I think that would sway their decision. . . . You don't have a real perspective on the world of work (2 response; female industrial relations graduate student with highest grade point average in the sample).

> Recruiting doesn't really matter at all; only the job itself (6 response, female arts undergraduate).

In addition to revealing a difference in the perceived signaling value of recruitment experiences, content analysis revealed another interesting finding: that most (if not all) of the 6 and 7 responses could arguably be classified as rating errors. This conclusion is based on the fact that these subjects' justifications of their ratings seemed to contradict the rating per se, as indicated in the following examples.

First, several low-importance respondents used an extremely narrow conceptualization of "recruitment practices" in assigning their ratings. In particular, there was a tendency to define recruitment as consisting solely of campus recruiters from personnel departments: "When it comes right down to it, the people who really sell the company are not the human resources people, but rather the people students are actually going to work with" (male arts undergraduate). The engineering undergraduate who said he didn't "pay attention to personnel because personnel don't know the job" also fit into this category, even though he contradicted himself in the very next sentence: "Of course, if the interviewers really give me a bad opinion, then it's totally over."

The rest of the low-importance respondents either restricted their vision to effects on ultimate job choices, ignoring earlier effects on job search, or based their ratings only on "typical" recruitment practices, ignoring the influence of extreme experiences:

> Recruitment is just the means to get that far [to the job choice]. If you go through recruitment and you get a job offer, recruitment doesn't have an impact on the job choice, *but you had to like the recruitment and agree with it to get that far* [italics added] (female arts undergraduate).

Recruiting doesn't really matter at all; only the job itself. [Two sentences later:] I suppose recruitment does play a secondary role in that if the person really ticks me off, *my enthusiasm goes way down and I start wondering what kind of people they have in the company* [italics added] (female arts undergraduate).

Finally, 2 of these respondents seemed to be saying that recruitment "shouldn't" be important, although it might be (to someone else):

It didn't affect me at all, [although it probably does affect] . . . those who are looking shorter term, or those who were not considering taking a job, but were swayed by recruitment (male industrial relations undergraduate).

Recruitment doesn't mean anything . . . it's a game and I think a *lot of people get screwed by it* [italics added] (male arts undergraduate; only 7 rating).

In conclusion, these responses do not seem to support ratings of recruitment as "very unimportant." Rather, they seem to suggest that a number of people think that it either shouldn't be important, or wish that it weren't. In any event, the divergence between the ratings per se and their justifications raises some interesting methodological questions.

DISCUSSION

The primary objective of this research was to generate new insights about recruitment dynamics through use of a less structured, more intensive methodology than has commonly been employed in the job choice area. In this section, we discuss the major areas in which our results shed new light or raise new questions about prior recruitment research.

Timing and delays. One of the major revelations of this research concerns the extent to which timing (particularly delays) was mentioned as an important factor in applicants' impressions and decisions. To recap, our results suggest that: (a) long delays between recruitment phases are not uncommon; (b) negative inferences are usually drawn in response to delays; (c) the inference that something is "wrong" with the organization is more likely to be made by the most marketable job seekers; and (d) regardless of the inferences made, candidates take other offers if delays become too extended.

These results are in conflict with recent findings using other methodologies (Rynes & Boudreau, 1986; Taylor & Bergmann, 1987), but are highly consistent with earlier longitudinal job choice research (e.g., Reynolds, 1951; Soelberg, 1967). Soelberg, for example, argued that job seekers' anxiety and their desire to get the choice "settled" causes them to perceptually distort evaluations in favor of early, rather than late, alternatives. Although it is difficult to determine the extent to which "perceptual distortions" were operating in this study, preferences for quick follow-up and the tendency to tire of extended job search characterized a majority of our subjects as well.

Regardless of the psychological mechanisms, the fact remains that late market entries and delayed follow-ups often cost job acceptances (see also Arvey et al., 1975). This suggests that organizations pay particular attention to getting applicants' attention early, and then keeping it through prompt follow-ups and feedback.

Individual differences.   A second important finding in our study concerns the vast differences in individual search and choice strategies. Subjects varied widely in terms of when they started search, how many interviews they pursued, whether they turned down site visits, the credibility they attached to campus recruiters, the attributions they made concerning delays, and so on. Moreover, at least some of these differences appeared to be systematically related to identifiable background characteristics and to job search success. A summary of observed differences in search and choice behaviors is presented in Table 4.

Turning first to sex differences, women seemed to be more affected than men by their interactions with recruiters and potential coworkers. Women were more likely to mention acquaintances as reasons for initial interest in organizations, and recruitment interactions as reasons for unfavorable changes in fit assessments and for decisions to take jobs in companies that were not initial favorites.

Relatedly, it is interesting to note that many women continue to experience what they regard as "offensive" recruitment interactions. A post hoc content review revealed that fully 50% of our female subjects described at least one negative gender-related experience. This would seem to be a very high figure, considering that no explicit questions were asked about bias. Examples of offensive incidents included inappropriate comments about women's personal appearance, negative comments about other "minority" groups (e.g., elderly workers), being asked to interview in a man's hotel room, and receiving correspondence addressed to "Mr." even after an initial interview. Other negatives for women (though not necessarily offensive) included failing to meet any managerial women on site visits, getting the feeling that things were run according to an "old boys' network," or being explicitly told that women tend not to advance as far as men.

Moreover, research suggests that it may well be "rational" for women to attach credence to such signals. For example, sociological studies have shown that promotion and pay prospects are in fact more favorable for women in organizations that already have larger proportions of women and minorities, particularly at high levels (e.g., Fierman, 1990; Konrad & Pfeffer, in press; Pfeffer & Davis-Blake, 1987). As such, not being able to get an interview with a woman, seeing no women at high levels, being told that the organization is "pretty macho," or feeling that the organization is run like a men's club *is* a cause for concern, on average.

On the other hand, although women were more seriously affected by recruiters and recruitment interactions, men were more greatly affected by delays and more likely to attribute delays to organizational causes. These findings are

Table 4

SIGNIFICANT DIFFERENCES IN BACKGROUND CHARACTERISTICS ASSOCIATED WITH JOB SEARCH BEHAVIORS, IMPRESSIONS, AND DECISIONS

Male vs. Female:

Males began thinking about job search earlier ($p < .05$); Women more likely to mention acquaintances in organization as reason for positive fit assessment ($p < .01$); Women more likely to mention recruitment experiences as reason for negative change in fit assessment ($p < .05$); Women more likely to mention recruitment as reason for taking job with company not initially favored ($p < .01$); Males were more likely than females to make organizational attributions for recruitment delays ($p < .01$); Males were more likely to report being negatively affected by delays ($p < .10$).

Graduate vs. Undergraduate:

Graduates began thinking about search earlier than undergraduates ($p < .10$); Grads were less likely than undergrads to turn down site visits due to timing ($p < .05$); Grads were more likely than undergrads to attribute delays to organizational characteristics ($p < .10$).

Full-time Work Experience:

Less experienced were more likely to mention recruiters as reasons for positive fit assessments ($p < .05$); More experienced were less likely to reject site visits due to timing ($p < .05$).

Summer or Internship Experience:

More internship experience associated with more mentions of recruitment experiences as reasons for negative changes in fit assessment ($p < .10$); Those with more internship experience rated recruitment as more important ($p < .10$).

Extracurriculars and Offices Held:

Those with fewer extracurriculars were more likely to mention recruitment as a reason for taking job with organization not initially favored ($p < .05$); Those holding more offices reported higher importance for recruiters ($p < .05$); Those with more extracurriculars rated recruitment as less important ($p < .10$).

Grade Point Average:

Students with higher GPAs took later first interviews ($p < .10$); Students with lower GPAs were more likely to form negative initial fit assessments on the basis of recruitment ($p < .01$) and more likely to change assessments in a negative direction due to recruitment ($p < .05$); Higher GPAs were more likely to make organizational attributions for recruitment delays ($p < .10$); Those with higher GPAs were more negatively affected by recruitment delays ($p < .05$); Those with higher GPAs rated recruitment as less important ($p < .10$).

Early vs. Late Job Search:

Those who thought about search earlier were less likely to mention recruiters as reasons for positive fit assessment ($p < .05$); Those who interviewed later were more likely to mention recruitment as a reason for taking jobs with organizations not initially favored ($p < .10$); Those who interviewed later were more likely to infer personal rejection from recruitment delays ($p < .05$); Those who thought about search earlier were more likely to attribute delays to organizational characteristics ($p < .01$).

Job Search Success:

Those with more site visits were more likely to mention recruitment as a reason for accepting jobs with organizations not initially favored ($p < .10$); Those with more job offers were more likely to lose interest in initially favored organizations due to delays ($p < .01$); Those with fewer job offers were more likely to infer personal rejection from delays ($p < .05$); Organizational attributions for recruitment delays were more likely to be made by more successful job seekers (those with more campus interviews, $p < .05$; more site visits, $p < .01$; and more job offers, $p < .05$).

consistent with a large body of prior research suggesting that men are less likely than women to attribute negative outcomes to their own shortcomings (e.g., Deaux, 1984; Hansen & O'Leary, 1985; Lenney, 1977). Moreover, because men received significantly more job offers than women in our study, they would have had both less reason to question their own marketability and greater freedom to "write off" late-responding organizations.

A number of differences were also observed with respect to previous work experience. Specifically, more experienced subjects were more likely to pursue all site visits, and less likely to mention campus recruiters as reasons for positive fit assessments. Conversely, subjects with more internship experience (on average, those with less full-time experience; $r = -.49$) were more likely to mention recruitment as a reason for negative changes in perceived fit and to rate overall recruitment practices as more important. Generally speaking, then, experienced subjects appeared to be less affected by recruitment practices and more focused on acquiring information about the job itself. Although this pattern was predicted more than a decade ago (Rynes et al., 1980), it has not previously been detected in ratings-based studies. Of course, additional research is necessary to replicate the present findings.

Additionally, subjects with higher grade point averages seemed to display greater confidence in their search strategies than subjects with lower GPAs. For example, high-GPA subjects took later first interviews, were less likely to be negatively swayed by recruitment experiences, were more likely to attribute delays to organizational causes, had more negative reactions to late-responding organizations, and rated recruitment practices as less important than low-GPA subjects.

Finally, evidence suggests that applicants who were more successful in job search were also more affected by recruitment experiences. For example, students who received more site visit invitations were more likely to mention recruitment as a reason for accepting a job with an initially nonfavored organization; those who had more offers were more likely to lose interest following delays; and those with more interviews, site visits, and job offers were more likely to make negative organizational inferences following delays.

Signaling theory and contingency variables.   It has been proposed that because job choice takes place under imperfect information, recruitment experiences frequently serve as signals of unobservable organizational characteristics (e.g., Rynes et al., 1980 or Rynes & Miller, 1983; following Spence, 1973). Our results not only provide strong support for signaling theory, but also reveal some of the contingency variables associated with variations in signaling strength.

For example, content analyses suggest that recruitment experiences have stronger signaling value when little is known about the organization prior to job search, when organizational representatives are in the same functional area as the applicant, and when experiences occur during the site visit as opposed to the campus interview. If generalizable, these observations have some interesting implications for organizations.

For example, the finding that functional representatives have a bigger impact than staff representatives suggests that it is doubly important to select and train these representatives to create positive impressions. And yet functional-area recruiters, hiring managers, and potential coworkers are probably least likely to receive such training because recruitment is viewed as something they do "alongside" their "real" jobs. Similarly, the fact that site visits transmit stronger signals than campus interviews suggests that improving overall recruitment impressions will be far more difficult (but also more important) than improving campus interviews.

Continued existence of unimpressive recruitment practices. Despite recent concern about dwindling supplies of qualified new entrants to the labor force (e.g., Deutschman, 1990; Johnston, 1987), despite increased awareness of the implications of recruitment and attraction for overall selection utility (e.g., Boudreau & Rynes, 1985; Murphy, 1986), and despite more than 25 years' worth of EEO enforcement (e.g., Scovel, 1991), our study suggests that poor recruitment practices continue to exist, even in Ivy League placement offices. For example, in addition to the quotations presented earlier, campus recruiters in our study were variously described as "rude, boring, obnoxious, full of themselves, incompetent, barely literate, and jerks."

In some cases, negative recruitment experiences were enough to completely eliminate the organization from further consideration. In other cases, recruitment merely raised a "red flag" that caused applicants to apply more scrutiny than they otherwise would have. Recently researchers using an elaboration likelihood framework (Petty & Cacioppo, 1988) have speculated about how to get applicants to process recruitment information in a "core" (i.e., attentive) rather than "peripheral" (superficial) fashion (e.g., Harris, 1989; Powell, 1991). The present research suggests that core processing often sets in when organizations least desire it—that is, after very negative recruitment experiences!

Importance of social factors in job choice. Although social effects have been mentioned only briefly to this point, it is important to indicate that they were evidenced in a variety of ways in this research. For example, nearly a quarter of our sample chose at least one initial favorite on the basis of information from friends or acquaintances already inside the organization. Social effects were also seen in terms of common interviewing and bidding patterns, as well as exchanges of information about what occurred during interviews and site visits. For example, several applicants turned down visits to a particular organization when it became known that an entire day was "wasted" (subjects' words) flying to the organization, providing a urine specimen, and being put through a psychological assessment.

Another common topic of information-sharing concerned whether delays were being experienced by all interviewees, or only by oneself. Finally, networks often revealed that an applicant's recently acquired job offer had already been rejected by someone else (usually a decidedly negative influence on perceived valence).

The prevalence of social exchange networks in campus recruiting has several implications for organizations. For example, organizations cannot count on interview questions or testing procedures remaining unknown over the course of a campus visit (see also Sackett, Burris, & Ryan, 1989). Moreover, information about disliked recruiters or selection procedures is likely to set a negative tone for subsequent applicants.

On the more positive side, building strong recruitment networks through internships and multi-year hiring relationships can have beneficial effects, particularly in terms of enhancing applicant willingness to attend a first interview. More generally, our results support Granovetter's (1974) and Kilduff's (1988) contentions that social considerations merit additional attention in future job choice research.

FUTURE RESEARCH

Although our study has some unique advantages over prior research in terms of data richness and contextual fidelity, the method could usefully be extended in future investigations. For example, one potentially important contribution would be to begin interviewing applicants earlier in the search process and/or to track them through additional time periods. Another would be to keep a complete record of every contacted company (from campus receptions onward) so that applicant impressions and decisions can be more clearly separated from (or interpreted in light of) organizational actions and decisions. Still another improvement would be to track sufficiently large numbers of subjects to permit multivariate analyses. This would be particularly useful because certain characteristics tended to cluster together in our sample (e.g., graduate status, more work experience, and fewer extracurriculars; higher grade point averages and delayed job search; maleness and job offers).

The discrepant responses we observed between ratings and open-ended responses to the overall importance question suggest that additional research be conducted to understand the properties of each method as applied to job choice, as well as the relationships between them. On the basis of present results, we tentatively hypothesize that individuals are less guarded while "telling stories" in interviews than when responding to rating scales. If so, this reduced guardedness may translate into greater variability in responses which, in turn, may result in a greater ability to detect systematic sources of individual variation.

In addition, however, we suspect that some of the frankness of our transcripts was due to the fact that subjects were interviewed by student peers rather than professors or placement directors. We suspect that this arrangement provided benefits in terms of closer interviewer-subject rapport and reduced concerns about naming organizations and relaying negative incidents.

Additional contributions could be made by using methodologies that more closely mirror the way job choices are actually made. Although longitudinal interviews reveal more of job seekers' decision processes than do correlations among rating scales, they nevertheless capture those processes in a very loose way.

More structured methods of longitudinal tracking would almost certainly shed new light on the relationships between recruitment and job choice processes.

It would also be interesting to probe the factors underlying the vast observed differences in such variables as trust in recruiters and enjoyment (vs. dread) of the job search process. Although some underlying factors emerged in this study, others remain a mystery.

Another useful type of research would be studies that seek to determine the cost-effectiveness of programs designed to improve recruitment image and outcomes. For example, field experiments could be used to monitor the improvement in yield rates and/or applicant quality when organizations implement recruiter training or improved systems for tracking follow-up delays. In a sense, this approach argues that the value of recruitment programs is "in the pudding": recruitment is important if greater investments in it pay off in terms of better yields, higher quality, or improved retention. Nevertheless, given that the strongest recruitment signals occur at very decentralized levels among functional-area employees, large organizations in particular would seem to confront major obstacles in trying to improve their recruitment outcomes. Practical research is sorely needed in this area (Rynes & Barber, 1990).

CONCLUSION

To the extent that our findings are even moderately generalizable, they suggest a somewhat different picture of recruitment than has emerged from ratings-based research. Although most researchers are more comfortable with the apparent precision (not to mention the ease and speed) of collecting large-sample ratings data, the present methodology has considerable advantages in terms of contextual fidelity and "feel" for the job seeker's decision task.

Recently, there has been a renewed call for intensive longitudinal research, both in general decision making and in job choice contexts (e.g., Eisenhardt, 1989b; Lord & Maher, 1990; Rynes & Barber, 1990; Schwab, et al., 1987). Again, the objective is to supplement, rather than supplant, conventional quantitative methods. Knowledge of job choice and recruitment processes might be strengthened considerably by adding a more in-depth perspective to the accumulating array of inferential statistics. We hope the present research will inspire others to apply similar methodologies in under-researched areas of recruitment and job choice.

References

Arvey, R. D., Gordon, M., Massengill, D., Mussio, S. (1975). Differential dropout rates of minority and majority job candidates due to time lags between selection procedures. *Personnel Psychology, 38,* 175–180.

Boudreau, J. W., Rynes, S. L. (1985). Role of recruitment in staffing utility analysis. *Journal of Applied Psychology, 70,* 354–366.

Breaugh, J. A. (1983). Realistic job previews: A critical appraisal and future research directions. *Academy of Management Review, 8,* 612–619.

Bretz, R. D., Ash, R. A., Dreher, G. F. (1989). Do people make the place? An examination of the attraction-selection-attrition hypothesis. *Personnel Psychology, 42,* 561–582.

Bureau of National Affairs. (1989). Now hiring: An employer's guide to recruiting in a tight labor market. Washington, DC: Author.

Cohen, J. (1988). *Statistical power analysis for the behavioral sciences* (2nd ed.). Hillsdale, NJ: Lawrence Erlbaum Associates.

Deaux, K. (1984). From individual differences to social categories: Analysis of a decade's research on gender. *American Psychologist, 39,* 105–116.

Deutschman, A. (1990). What 25-year-olds want. *Fortune, 122 (5),* 42–50.

Dipboye, R. L. (1982). Self-fulfilling prophecies in the selection interview. *Academy of Management Review, 7,* 579–586.

Eder, R. W., Buckley, M. R. (1988). The employment interview: An interactionist perspective. In Ferris, G. R., Rowland, K. M. (Eds.), *Research in personnel and human resources management* (Vol. 6, pp. 75–107). Greenwich, CT: JAI Press.

Eisenhardt, K. M. (1989a). Making fast strategic decisions in high-velocity environments. *Academy of Management Journal, 32,* 543–576.

Eisenhardt, K. M. (1989b). Building theories from case study research. *Academy of Management Review, 14,* 532–550.

Fierman, J. (1990). Why women still don't hit the top. *Fortune, 122 (3),* 40–62.

Flanagan, J. C. (1954). The critical incident technique. *Psychological Bulletin, 51,* 327–358.

Gerhart, B., Rynes, S. (1991). Determinants and consequences of salary negotiations by male and female MBA graduates. *Journal of Applied Psychology, 76 (2),* 256–262.

Gersick, C. J. G. (1989). Marking time: Predictable transitions in task groups. *Academy of Management Journal, 32,* 274–310.

Gerstner, L. V. (1966). College recruiting: Why the good ones get away. *Management Review, 55,* 4–12.

Glueck, W. F. (1973). Recruiters and executives: How do they affect job choice? *Journal of College Placement, 34,* 77–78.

Granovetter, M. S. (1974). *Getting a job: A study of contacts and careers.* Cambridge, MA: Harvard University Press.

Hansen, R. D., O'Leary, V. E. (1985). Sex-determined attributions. In O'Leary, V. E., Unger, R. K., Wallston, B. S. (Eds.), *Women, gender and social psychology.* Hillsdale, NJ: Lawrence Erlbaum.

Harris, M. M. (1989, August). The recruitment interview as persuasive communication: Applying the elaboration likelihood model. In Breaugh, J., Harris, M., Taylor, M. S. (Chairs), *Organizational recruitment research: Taking stock and setting future directions.* Symposium conducted at the annual meeting of the Academy of Management, Washington, DC.

Harris, M. M., Fink, L. S. (1987). A field study of employment opportunities: Does the recruiter make a difference? *Personnel Psychology, 40,* 765–784.

Isabella, L. A. (1990). Evolving interpretations as a change unfolds: How managers construe key organizational events. *Academy of Management Journal, 33,* 7–41.

Johnston, W. B. (1987). *Workforce 2000: Work and workers for the 21st century.* Indianapolis: Hudson Institute.

Kilduff, M. J. (1988). *Decision making in context: Social and personality correlates of choices of organizations.* Unpublished doctoral dissertation, Cornell University, Ithaca, NY.

Konrad, A., Pfeffer, J. (in press). Understanding the hiring of women and minorities: How gender and ethnic composition is produced and reproduced in educational organizations. *Sociology of Education.*

Lenney, E. (1977). Women's self-confidence in achievement settings. *Psychological Bulletin,* *84,* 1–13.

Lopes, L. L. (1987). Between hope and fear: The psychology of risk. In Berkowitz, L. (Ed.), *Advances in Experimental Social Psychology* (Vol. 20, pp. 155–295). San Diego: Academic Press.

Lord, R. G., Maher, K. J. (1990). Alternative information-processing models and their implications for theory, research, and practice. *Academy of Management Review, 15,* 9–28.

Luck, R. (1988, September 26). How industrial recruiters sell themselves short. *Wall Street Journal,* p. 26.

Marcus, R. (1982, September 22). The lavish wooing of legal whiz kids. *Washington Post,* pp. C1–C5.

Murphy, K. R. (1986). When your top choice turns you down: Effect of rejected offers on the utility of selection tests. *Psychological Bulletin, 99,* 133–138.

Patton, M. Q. (1990). *Qualitative evaluation and research methods* (2nd ed.). Newbury Park, CA: Sage.

Petty, R. E., Cacioppo, J. T. (1986). The elaboration likelihood model of persuasion. In Berkowitz, L. (Ed.), *Advances in Experimental Social Psychology* (Vol. 19, pp. 123–205). San Diego: Academic Press.

Pfeffer, J., Davis-Blake, A. (1987). The effect of the proportion of women on salaries: The case of college administrators. *Administrative Science Quarterly, 32,* 1–24.

Powell, G. N. (1984). Effect of job attributes and recruiting practices on applicant decisions: A comparison. *Personnel Psychology, 37,* 721–732.

Powell, G. N. (1991). Applicant reactions to the initial employment interview: Exploring theoretical and methodological issues. *Personnel Psychology, 44,* 67–84.

Premack, S. L., Wanous, J. P. (1985). A meta-analysis of realistic job preview experiments. *Journal of Applied Psychology, 70,* 706–719.

Reynolds, L. G. (1951). *The structure of labor markets.* New York: Harper and Row.

Ricklefs, R. (1979, September 19). The hidden hurdle: Executive recruiters say firms tend to hire "our kind of person." *The Wall Street Journal,* pp. 1W, 1E.

Rynes, S. L. (1991). Recruitment, job choice, and post-hire consequences: A call for new research directions. In Dunnette, M. D., Hough, L. (Eds.), *Handbook of Industrial and Organizational Psychology* (2nd ed.). Palo Alto, CA: Consulting Psychologists' Press.

Rynes, S. L., Barber, A. E. (1990). Applicant attraction strategies: An organizational perspective. *Academy of Management Review, 15,* 286–310.

Rynes, S. L., Boudreau, J. W. (1986). College recruiting in large organizations: Practice, evaluation and research implications. *Personnel Psychology, 39,* 729–757.

Rynes, S. L., Gerhart, B. (1990). Interviewer assessments of applicant "fit": An exploratory investigation. *Personnel Psychology, 43,* 13–35.

Rynes, S. L., Heneman, H. G. III, Schwab, D. P. (1980). Individual reactions to organizational recruiting: A review. *Personnel Psychology, 33,* 529–542.

Rynes, S. L., Miller, H. E. (1983). Recruiter and job influences on candidates for employment. *Journal of Applied Psychology, 68,* 147–154.

Sackett, P. R., Burris, L. R., Ryan, A. M. (1989). Coaching and practice effects in personnel selection. In Cooper, C. L., Robertson, I. (Eds.), *International review of industrial and organizational psychology* (pp. 145–183). New York: Wiley.

Saunders, C., Jones, J. W. (1990). Temporal sequences in information acquisition for decision making: A focus on source and medium. *Academy of Management Review, 15,* 29–46.

Schwab, D. P., Rynes, S. L., Aldag, R. J. (1987). Theories and research on job search and choice. In Rowland, K. M., Ferris, G. R. (Eds.), *Research in personnel and human resource management,* (Vol. 5, pp. 129–166). Greenwich, CT: JAI Press.

Scovel, K. (1991). Testers to expose illegal hiring practices. *Human Resource Executive, 5*(3), 10.

Smith, C. L. (1990). *Job search strategies: Their effects on job placement success.* Unpublished master's thesis, Cornell University, Ithaca, NY.

Soelberg, P. O. (1967). Unprogrammed decision making. *Industrial Management Review, 8,* 19–29.

Spence, M. (1973). Job market signaling. *Quarterly Journal of Economics, 87,* 355–374.

Stoops, R. (1984). Reader survey supports market approach to recruitment. *Personnel Journal, 63 (3),* 22–24.

Taylor, M. S., Bergmann, T. J. (1987). Organizational recruitment activities and applicants' reactions at different stages of the recruitment process. *Personnel Psychology, 40,* 261–285.

Tsoukas, H. (1989). The validity of ideographic research explanations. *Academy of Management Review, 14,* 551–561.

Vroom, V. H. (1966). Organizational choice: A study of pre- and post-decision processes. *Organizational Behavior and Human Performance, 1,* 212–225.

Wanous, J. P., Colella, A. (1989). Organizational entry research: Current status and future directions. In Rowland, K. M., Ferris, G. R. (Eds.), *Research in personnel and human resources management* (Vol. 7, pp. 59–120). Greenwich, CT: JAI Press.

Yin, R. K. (1989). *Case study research: Design and methods* (rev. ed.). London: Sage Publications.

Appendix

CONTENT-ANALYZED INTERVIEW QUESTIONS

First Interview:

1. When did you first start thinking about your job search? When was your first interview?

2. What three companies do you feel would provide the best fit with your employment objectives? (Probe for specific reasons, incidents).

3. What three companies do you feel would provide the worst fit with your employment objectives? (Probe).

4. Are there other companies that most students are interested in, but where you do not feel you would fit well? (Probe).

5. Are there other companies that most students are not interested in, but where you feel you would fit well? (Probe).

6. Are there companies where you once thought you would fit well, but now don't think so? (Get names; then probe to find specific reasons why not).

7. Are there companies where you did not think you would fit well, but now do? (Get names, probe for specifics).

Second Interview:

8. To this point, how many on-campus interviews have you participated in? How many on-site visits have you gone on? Did you turn down any offers for site visits? If so, why?

9. Have you received any job offers? If so, how many? Have you accepted one?

10. Think about the position you have accepted. Was it one of your favorite companies at the beginning of your job search? If not, what specific things happened to change your mind? (An alternative form of the question was asked about the current "favorite company" for the 10 subjects who had not accepted offers).

11. Are there any companies that were attractive to you earlier in the search process, but that you no longer find attractive? (Name them). If so, what happened to change your opinion?

12. Have you had any companies that were very late in getting back to you after the first interview? If "yes": What assumptions did you make about why they weren't getting back to you? Did the delay affect your willingness to take a job with them? Explain why/why not.

13. When on-campus recruiters are either very good or very bad, relative to other recruiters, to what extent does it affect your willingness to accept an offer? (Probe as to why it does/doesn't affect willingness).

14. This last question asks you to respond in terms of a 7-point scale, where 1 = *strongly disagree* and 7 = *strongly agree*. Having gone through the job search and choice process for some time now, to what extent do you agree, or disagree, with the following statement?: "When it comes right down to it, recruitment practices are not very important because people choose jobs on the basis of things like pay, location, and reputation rather than recruitment." (Get the number, then probe for explanations).

READING 21

APPLICANT ATTRACTION STRATEGIES
An Organizational Perspective

Sara L. Rynes
Alison E. Barber

Labor shortages, which are predicted to last into the next century, are expected to increase the importance of applicant attraction for organizations. Unfortunately, previous research has provided little unified theory or operational guidance for organizations that are confronted with such difficulties. In part, this is because much research has been framed from the applicant's, rather than the organization's, perspective. In addition, attraction-related theories and research are scattered across a variety of literatures, and often are identified with other topics (e.g., wage, motivation, or discrimination theories). Drawing on multiple literatures, this article develops a model of applicant attraction from the organization's perspective, which (a) outlines three strategies for enhancing applicant attraction, (b) proposes categories of contingency factors that are expected to affect the choice (and potential effectiveness) of alternative strategies, (c) suggests probable interrelationships among the strategies, (d) links applicant attraction strategies to other human resource practices, (e) outlines dimensions of attraction outcomes, and (f) discusses implications for future research.

Organizations have always been concerned with attracting and selecting the right types of employees (e.g., Schneider, 1976, 1987). However, the attention they pay to attracting, versus screening, new employees depends on many factors such as the relative attractiveness of the vacancy and the general state of the labor market (Guion, 1976; Rynes, in press).

In the latter regard, demographic developments such as the baby bust and the leveling off of female labor force participation rates suggest that widespread labor shortages will develop and persist well into the 21st century. Along with these trends, demographers predict an increased emphasis on attracting labor (Johnston & Packer, 1987). Indeed, increased concerns about attracting applicants are already apparent in the popular press (e.g., Bernstein, 1987; Finney, 1989; Hamlet, 1989; Hanigan, 1987; Merrill, 1987).

Source: "Applicant Attraction Strategies: An Organizational Perspective" by Sara L. Rynes and Alison E. Barber, *Academy of Management Review*, 1990, Vol 15, No. 2, 286–310.

To date, the management and organizational behavior literatures have focused on recruitment as the dominant tool for attracting applicants (Rynes, Heneman, & Schwab, 1980; Schwab, 1982; Wanous, 1980). However, prior economic research into the functioning of labor markets suggests that improved recruitment is often an inadequate response to attraction difficulties, particularly when vacancies are unattractive or when labor shortages persist (e.g., Kerr & Fisher, 1950; Malm, 1955; Doeringer & Piore, 1971). In such situations, more aggressive strategies are generally necessary.

In light of these considerations, this article draws from multiple literatures (economics, human resource management, industrial psychology, organizational behavior, and sociology) to develop an interdisciplinary model of applicant attraction. Moreover, unlike most psychological treatments of applicant attraction (e.g., Rynes et al., 1980; Wanous, 1977), this model is developed from the organization's, rather than the applicant's, perspective.

Anticipated benefits of adopting an interdisciplinary organizational perspective include (a) discussion of a broader range of strategies for attracting applicants, (b) delineation of contingency factors affecting strategic choices, (c) consideration of potential interrelationships among alternative strategies, (d) emphasis on increased awareness of potential differences in organizational responses to diverse environmental conditions, (e) description of testable propositions regarding the conditions under which various strategies or combinations of strategies will be employed, (f) discussion of greater awareness of the interrelationships between attraction strategies and other human resource practices, (g) consideration of a broader range of attraction-related outcomes, and (h) suggestions for making future research more relevant to organizational decision makers.

DOMAIN AND BOUNDARIES

At the outset, it is helpful to delineate the boundaries of the present discussion. First, the model focuses primarily on applicant attraction, as distinct from screening or selection. Although attraction and selection are inherently interconnected in the process of filling vacancies (e.g., Boudreau & Rynes, 1985; Schwab, 1982), the focus here is on activities designed either to increase the number or to change the characteristics of individuals who are willing to consider applying for or accepting a job.

Second, the model distinguishes between attraction and recruitment. Although recruitment theories often treat recruitment as synonymous with attraction (e.g., Rynes et al., 1980; Schwab, 1982), this article views recruitment as a *means* of attracting the applicant. Thus, improved recruitment is regarded as one potential strategy for enhancing attraction, but so are decisions to modify employment inducements or to target different kinds of applicants.

Third, the model is concerned primarily with strategic choices in novel or changed situations (e.g., precipitous decline in labor supply, new job creation). Under normal conditions, organizational decision makers follow largely automatic scripts involving little conscious decision making or strategic choice (e.g.,

Klein, 1989; Osterman, 1987). However, when conventional scripts fail to produce satisfactory results, decision makers begin to consciously seek more effective strategies. In short, it is assumed that satisficing (rather than maximizing) decision processes are applied in most attraction situations (e.g., March & Simon, 1958), although the focus here is on nonroutine searches for better solutions (presumably the best solutions, given perceived constraints) when traditional procedures prove unsatisfactory.

Fourth, there are many ways to deal with labor shortages other than through labor attraction strategies. These range from closely related human resource activities (e.g., redesigning jobs, retraining employees for nontraditional jobs) to decisions that go right to the core of the business strategy (e.g., decisions to relocate overseas or decisions to curtail franchise expansion). However, consideration of these broader strategic responses would considerably lengthen and complicate the present discussion; as such, the focus here is restricted to attraction strategies per se. The reader should bear in mind, however, that under extremely adverse conditions (e.g., widespread labor shortages, very low ability to pay), there may be no combination of attraction strategies that, by itself, is capable of bringing about desired results.

Finally, the present discussion is confined to external staffing procedures. Although generic strategic options in any attraction scenario (e.g., improving recruitment, targeting different applicants) are basically the same for both internal and external staffing, there are sufficient differences in the relevant contingency variables affecting strategy formulation to warrant separate study of attraction practices in internal labor markets (e.g., Anderson, Milkovich, & Tsui, 1981).

THE MODEL

The present model outlines three distinct strategies for attracting applicants: (a) altering recruitment practices, (b) targeting nontraditional applicants, and (c) modifying employment inducements (Figure 1). Although psychological research has primarily emphasized recruitment strategies, economic and sociological field research have demonstrated that inducement and applicant-targeting strategies also play an integral role in organizations' attempts to attract more, better, or more cost-effective applicants.

As shown in Figure 1, a number of contingencies are hypothesized to influence the mix of the three strategies. These include labor market conditions (e.g., expected duration of labor shortages), vacancy characteristics (e.g., relative attractiveness), organizational characteristics (e.g., ability to pay), phase of the attraction process (e.g., job application versus job acceptance stage), and legal considerations.

Additionally, the model suggests that when conscious decision processes come into play, alternative strategies usually are considered interactively, rather than independently (e.g., Doeringer & Piore, 1971). Thus, for example, decisions about applicant pools and recruitment messages are based at least in part on decisions about employment inducements.

The model also suggests several ways in which attraction strategies interact with other human resource (HR) practices. More specifically, attraction strategies

Figure 1

MODEL OF THE ATTRACTION PROCESS

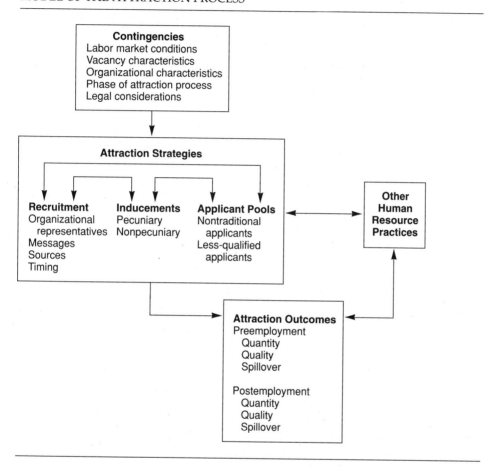

both affect and are affected by HR practices. For example, the adoption of new inducement strategies is frequently constrained by current compensation practices. Conversely, decisions to target new applicant pools often precipitate changes in selection methods (Doeringer & Piore, 1971; Osterman, 1987), as well as posthire practices such as socialization and training (Fisher, 1986; Sutton & Louis, 1987).

The model also emphasizes the multidimensionality of attraction outcomes. For example, there are both short-term (related to attraction per se) and long-term (postjob acceptance) implications of attraction practices. Moreover, there are both quantitative and qualitative dimensions within each time frame (e.g., percent job acceptances and signaled productivity characteristics in the short term, retention rates and revealed productivity in the longer term). Finally, there can be significant spillover effects from attraction activities, both to applicants' decisions other than job choice (e.g., whether to buy the organization's products) and to individuals other than current applicants (e.g., potential applicants, current employees).

With one exception, the model is elaborated in subsequent sections in the order represented by the flow diagram in Figure 1. However, a decision was made to discuss attraction outcomes (i.e., dependent variables) first instead of last, based on the logic that it is difficult to discuss strategic alternatives and factors affecting choices among them without some notion of what one is attempting to achieve.

ATTRACTION OUTCOMES: WHAT IS AT STAKE?

From an organizational perspective, the most fundamental objective of attraction activities is to fill vacancies (e.g., Hanssens & Levien, 1983; Krett & Stright, 1985; Maurer & Howe, 1989; Stoops, 1984). Not surprisingly, then, most prescriptive evaluation models recommend including multiple measures that reflect the *quantity* of applicants (e.g., number of applications received, percent unfilled vacancies) (Cascio, 1987; Rynes & Boudreau, 1986). However, most prescriptions also advocate the importance of assessing *efficiency*, in terms of both time and money. For example, Cascio (1987) recommended such measures as cost-per-hire, acceptance-to-offer ratios, and time elapsed between various attraction stages. In practice, however, managers appear to be far more likely to attend to vacancy rates per se than to more refined measures involving costs, yield ratios, or time lapses (e.g., Laitamaki, 1989; Miner, 1979; Rynes & Boudreau, 1986).

In addition, practicing managers as well as academics agree that the *quality*, as well as quantity, of applicants and job acceptors is a crucial outcome of the attraction process (e.g., Boudreau & Rynes, 1985; Cascio, 1987; Schneider, 1976; Schwab, 1982). Indeed, there are both conceptual and empirical reasons for believing that most vacancies are eventually filled with *someone* (e.g., Laitamaki, 1989; Rynes & Boudreau, 1986; Thurow, 1975). As such, the most interesting questions often involve not the numbers, but the characteristics, of those attracted.

Unfortunately, the true quality or productivity of an applicant cannot be known with certainty during the attraction process. Although some productivity-related characteristics of job applicants are directly observable or testable (e.g., word-processing skills, computer-programming skills), others (e.g., aptitude for future learning, motivation) only can be inferred via imperfect signals (e.g., Spence, 1973; Thurow, 1975). Nevertheless, a variety of applicant characteristics have become accepted, accurately or not, as signals of actual quality or productivity. These include education, experience, predictor scores on selection devices, and demographic characteristics (e.g., Arrow, 1972; Konrad & Pfeffer, in press; Spence, 1973).

Finally, a few models emphasize that the effects of attraction strategies may *spill over* beyond the job choice decisions of current applicants (e.g., Rynes et al., 1980). One example of such spillover is that organization-applicant interactions may influence applicants' subsequent consumption decisions (e.g., "I won't buy anything from a company that asks those kind of questions!"). In addition, the impressions created during the attraction process may be transmitted from current to potential applicants, thus affecting the organization's general image or reputation. However, these spillover effects, although frequently acknowledged anecdotally, have not been incorporated into formal prescriptive or evaluative models (e.g., Boudreau & Rynes, 1985; Cascio, 1987; Wanous, 1980).

The preceding discussion pertains only to attraction per se, that is, to effects that occur either prior to or at the point of job acceptance. However, both theoretical and empirical works have suggested that variations in attraction practices can have important effects on long-term (i.e., postacceptance) outcomes as well. Moreover, similar to prehire effects, posthire outcomes also have quantitative, qualitative, and spillover components.

For example, regarding the quantitative dimension, variations in recruitment practices (choice of recruitment source, presentation of realistic recruitment messages) are sometimes associated with differences in number of retained new hires over various periods of time (e.g., Gannon, 1971; Premack & Wanous, 1985; Ullman, 1966). Similarly, decisions to enhance attraction inducements (e.g., housing assistance, higher starting salaries) have been shown to lead to reduced turnover (e.g., Hamlet, 1989; Lakhani, 1988).

In terms of quality, validation research suggests that decisions to target attraction activities toward different applicant pools (e.g., those with different credentials or higher/lower predictor scores) are likely to be associated with differences in posthire performance evaluations, promotion rates, salaries, and other quality-related indices (e.g., Gaugler, Rosenthal, Thornton, & Bentson, 1987; Howard, 1986; Tenopyr, 1981). Similarly, efficiency wage theory (e.g., Weiss, 1980; Yellen, 1984) suggests that decisions to enhance attraction inducements have a positive impact on the quality, as well as quantity, of those attracted to and retained by organizations.

Finally, psychologists, sociologists, and economists have documented how changes in attraction practices can have spillover effects on current employees. For example, attraction of non-traditional applicants may increase long-term organizational viability by imparting new skills, methods, and viewpoints that are critical to organizational adaptability (e.g., Schneider, 1987; Sutton & Louis, 1987). On the other hand, recruiting new types is frequently resisted by organizational insiders and can result in both negative and positive outcomes, particularly in the shorter term. For example, Granovetter (1986) argued that the hiring of nontraditional applicants sometimes results in the refusal of current employees to engage in the kinds of socialization and training behaviors necessary for new employees to become successful performers. Additionally, the hiring of nontraditional employees can result in reduced solidarity among workers, the emergence of separate enclaves of demographically distinct workers, and the redrawing of conventional career lines and internal labor market patterns (e.g., Gordon, Edwards, & Reich, 1982; Kanter, 1977).

The fact that variations in attraction strategies can have diverse outcomes affecting many individuals over multiple time periods raises the question of how these potentially conflicting outcomes are weighted by organizational decision makers when they choose among alternative attraction strategies. Prescriptively, Cascio (1987) suggested 24 types of cost and quality analyses that "should be performed regularly" so that "critical trade-offs between cost and quality can be made intelligently on the basis of empirical data, not haphazardly on the basis of hunch or intuition" (p. 252). Unfortunately, the reader is left with little guidance as to how to translate such widely varying criteria as cost per hire by source, offer/interview ratios, and analysis of reasons for acceptance and termination into a common metric so that such decisions can truly proceed beyond intuitive processing.

Alternatively, Boudreau and Rynes (1985) proposed a model for evaluating combined recruitment and selection utility according to a monetary metric. However, to date no research has applied this model to actual attraction situations, most likely because of the complexity of the model and the problems (e.g., reliability, validity, credibility) associated with providing the requisite monetary estimates. Moreover, the model does not incorporate all potential outcomes of attraction strategies (e.g., spillover effects).

Turning to descriptive rather than prescriptive research, there is also little hard evidence as to how various potential outcomes are actually weighted in practice. Early institutional studies of local labor markets, based on employers' self-reports of recruitment and selection criteria, suggested that (presumed) applicant quality dominates the choice of attraction strategies (Schwab, 1982). However, other studies suggest that organizations rarely collect evaluative data beyond the number of vacancies filled or, less frequently, costs per hire (e.g., Drake, Kaplan, & Stone, 1973; Miner, 1979; Rynes & Boudreau, 1986). This, in turn, suggests that attraction strategies may be driven more by short-term and cost considerations than managers are willing to admit. (See Tsui and Gomez-Mejia, 1988, for similar evidence concerning HR evaluation in general.) Although evidence concerning formal data-keeping procedures is hardly sufficient to rule out long-term quality considerations as important decision criteria, it does suggest that to the extent such factors figure into strategy formulation, they do so largely on an ad hoc, subjective basis.

GENERAL ATTRACTION STRATEGIES

Under any given set of market conditions, there are at least three distinct strategies for increasing attraction success: (a) improving recruitment practices, (b) altering employment inducements, and (c) targeting nontraditional applicants. Each is discussed in turn.

Recruitment Practices

Of the proposed attraction strategies, recruitment practices have received the most attention in the management and organizational behavior literatures. This article briefly summarizes four dimensions of recruitment that have been hypothesized to influence applicant attraction.

Organizational Representatives. Several characteristics of organizational representatives (e.g., personality, informedness, credibility) have been hypothesized to affect applicants' impressions and decisions about organizations. If, in fact, organizational representatives have important effects on job applicants, it would make sense to train or select recruiters to ensure that they possess the right characteristics for favorably influencing applicants (Rynes & Boudreau, 1986).

Unfortunately, the research on organizational representatives, though voluminous, is of limited usefulness to organizations in several important respects. First, with few exceptions (e.g., Fisher, Ilgen, & Hoyer, 1979; Liden & Parsons, 1986), this research has concentrated almost exclusively on campus recruiters. As such, its results are of questionable generalizability to applicant pools other than graduating college students.

Moreover, even among this highly restricted applicant sample, campus recruiters are less likely to figure significantly in applicants' job-choice decisions than are other organizational representatives (e.g., hiring managers, potential co-workers). For example, potential co-workers are viewed as more credible sources of information than are campus recruiters (Fisher et al., 1979), partly because of their proximity to the vacancy and partly because co-workers are less likely to be seen as professional job sellers.

An additional limitation of this research is that although the fundamental objectives of organizational-attraction activities are behavioral in nature (e.g., job acceptances), research on organizational representatives has focused almost exclusively on attitudes, rather than behaviors. Moreover, this focus has been narrowed still further to attitudes held only at very early stages of the attraction process (i.e., immediately after the initial campus interview). As such, there is almost no empirical evidence concerning the extent to which organizational representatives, particularly those other than the campus recruiter, influence actual job choices. (For an exception, see Taylor and Bergmann, 1987.) Furthermore, the intertemporal reliabilities of many commonly used dependent variables are questionable, due to mismatching between phase of the attraction process (e.g., campus interview) and the applicant judgment required (probability of accepting the job, if offered).

Finally, even the existing evidence on post-campus-interview attitudes (the stage at which recruiters are hypothesized to have the greatest impact) is not very supportive of the hypothesis that campus recruiters are likely to have important effects on ultimate job choices. For example, a recent review of the literature observed that recruiter characteristics explained more variance in attitudes that are far removed from job choice (e.g., impressions of recruiters per se) than in attitudes closer to choice (e.g., likelihood of accepting a job offer) (Rynes, in press). Additionally, recruiter characteristics typically explained less (and, most commonly, nonsignificant) variance in studies that controlled for vacancy characteristics, relative to those that did not. Because the former type of study more closely mirrors actual attraction situations, studies that ignore vacancy characteristics are likely to suffer from serious omitted variable biases (James, Mulaik, & Brett, 1982) that inflate the apparent role of organizational representatives (Rynes, in press; Rynes & Miller, 1983).

Thus, the employer that wishes to attract more or better applicants will not find much support for the notion that improving the performance of organizational representatives enhances job acceptance rates. It should be noted, however, that prior research has not directly tested the potential benefits of more careful selection and training programs for organizational representatives. Rather, recruiters have been studied as naturally occurring phenomena in campus placement offices. Second, the one-shot, cross-sectional designs that typify research on recruiters are incapable of detecting subtle, but potentially important, indirect effects of recruiters on behavioral objectives (e.g., effective recruiter behaviors may cause interviewees to convey positive messages to potential applicants, which may increase the number of individuals who actually apply, which in turn may influence eventual recruitment yields).

Recruitment Messages.   A second recruitment dimension that may affect attraction is the nature of the message transmitted to prospective employees. Although vacancies are ostensibly composed of a given set of characteristics, discretion is possible regarding the ways in which the content, favorability, and details of the vacancies are described. Room for discretion arises from such factors as imperfect information of the job seeker, inherent subjectivity in describing and evaluating vacancy characteristics (e.g., career prospects), and the flexibility built into many job descriptions (Schwab, Rynes, & Aldag, 1987).

To date, the vast majority of research has focused on message favorability (usually called *realism*), rather than on content or level of detail. (For exceptions, see Barber, 1989; Giannantonio, 1989; Rynes & Miller, 1983.) Interest in this problem arose from concerns that employers frequently take advantage of job seekers' uncertainty by overselling vacancies (e.g., Schneider, 1976), perhaps at the expense of subsequent employee satisfaction and turnover.

Empirical evidence is mixed as to whether or not more realistic (i.e., usually less favorable) messages reduce job acceptance rates. For example, a meta-analysis of 10 studies showed no effect (d = .00) until a large "outlier" study containing more than one fourth of the total sample was eliminated from the analysis (Premack & Wanous, 1985). Additionally, considerable work remains to identify the psychological processes involved in the processing of message content, the generalizability of effects across a wide variety of jobs and applicants, and the productivity-related characteristics of acceptors versus rejectors under more (less) favorable messages (Rynes, in press).

Beyond favorability, however, other potentially important message dimensions remain almost completely unstudied. These include (a) the effects of emphasizing certain kinds of content over others, (b) the effects of revealing various kinds of information at early versus late stages of the process, (c) the most effective ways to present credible information about nonverifiable attributes, (d) the extent to which strategies for designing effective recruitment messages generalize across "good" and "bad" jobs (provided that "good" and "bad" jobs can be identified), and (e) whether different kinds of information (e.g., verifiable and nonverifiable) are equally effectively communicated across different media (e.g., recruiters versus company brochures).

Recruitment Sources.   Success in attracting desirable employees also may depend on the source(s) that are used to locate applicants. Presumably, sources differ in the extent to which they provide detailed and accurate information (to applicants and to employers), as well as in the productivity-related characteristics of the applicants reached (e.g., Schwab, 1982; Ullman, 1966).

To date, research on recruitment sources has focused exclusively on selectees, rather than job applicants, and posthire, rather than prehire, outcomes (e.g., Breaugh, 1981; Taylor & Schmidt, 1983). Unfortunately, such research designs inherently confound employer selection, applicant self-selection, and posthire employer-employee interactions as possible explanations for observed source-outcome relationships (Rynes, in press). As such, extant research has little to say about the effects of sources on either the quantity or quality of the initial applicants from which selectees are obtained (and subsequently studied).

Recruitment Timing.   Two hypotheses have been offered as to how recruitment timing might be modified to an employer's advantage. The first suggests that by avoiding delays between recruitment stages, employers can minimize the chances of discouraging applicants, which may lead to their accepting other offers (Rynes et al., 1980). To date, this hypothesis has received little empirical attention and only mixed support (cf. Arvey, Gordon, Massengill, & Mussio, 1975; Taylor & Bergmann, 1987).

The second hypothesis suggests that the employer who extends the first offer to a candidate may have an advantage over those who extend subsequent offers. According to Soelberg (1967), the costs, anxieties, and uncertainties of searching for a job cause many applicants to favor actual offers over uncertain ones, provided they do not contain any minimally unacceptable features (e.g., insufficient salary). If this is true, employers who practice early recruitment may have a competitive advantage in attracting applicants. However, this strategy may work only for employers who are competitively above average because the best applicants may not jump at early offers, unless those who make them are highly desirable employers (e.g., Weiss, 1980; Yellen, 1984).

In sum, despite the fact that the timing of recruitment activities has been hypothesized to affect both the quantity and quality of attracted applicants, no firm conclusions can be drawn about the effects of timing.

Employment Inducements

A second strategy for enhancing applicant attraction is to improve the nature of the inducements offered. For example, employers can raise salaries, improve benefits, implement flextime, provide child- or eldercare, develop internal career paths, or make any number of other improvements in working conditions.

Before discussing previous research in this area, it may be useful to describe what is meant by the term *employment inducements*. Although previous studies (particularly in psychology) typically have used the term *job attributes* in discussing the role of vacancy characteristics in job choice, we use the term *inducements* to convey the notion of deliberately modifying attributes for the explicit purpose of enhancing the attractiveness of a job to potential applicants.

Although virtually all job attributes could be regarded as inducements, in practice, some attributes are more likely to be deliberately used as attraction tools than others. For example, changes in salaries, benefits, and hours of work are more likely to be implemented explicitly for attraction purposes than, say, changes in supervision. This is because supervisors have other, more central roles than that of an applicant attraction device, and also because many supervisory characteristics cannot be known by applicants prior to accepting the job (e.g., Schwab et al., 1987).

However, because previous research has not made these distinctions, it is impossible to separate attribute from inducement effects in prior research. As such, we use the term *inducements* because it better conveys the strategic possibility of viewing a wide range of job and organizational characteristics as potential attraction devices. Occasionally, however, we do distinguish between pecuniary and nonpecuniary inducements.

Turning now to previous research, it is fair to say that most inducement studies, similar to most recruitment research, are of limited usefulness to organizations. For example, the vast number of rating or ranking studies that have examined the relative importance of inducements (e.g., Jurgensen, 1978) share a number of serious flaws that threaten both their internal and external validity (Lawler, 1971; Opsahl & Dunnette, 1966; Rynes, Schwab, & Heneman, 1983). Although policy-capturing experiments address some of these difficulties (e.g., reducing social desirability tendencies and providing a concrete decision context), they introduce limitations of their own. For example, policy-capturing experiments involve hypothetical, rather than real, job choices; they cannot be generalized beyond the inducements and inducement levels presented, and they presume market characteristics that are not realistic for most job seekers (e.g., perfect information, simultaneous alternatives) (Schwab et al., 1987).

Nevertheless, previous research has suggested that inducements are the major determinants of applicants' attitudes and behaviors. For example, in the few psychological studies that have simultaneously examined recruiters and inducements, both laboratory experiments and field surveys have suggested that inducements dominate applicants' attitudes, particularly at later stages of the attraction process. In fact, recruiter effects have typically faded to nonsignificance, once job attributes are taken into account (e.g., Powell, 1984; Rynes & Miller, 1983; Taylor & Bergmann, 1987). (For an exception, see Harris and Fink, 1987.)

Moreover, inducement research occasionally has moved beyond attitudinal surveys or laboratory investigations to field experiments that examine actual applicant behaviors. For example, experimental inducement programs in the Armed Services have suggested that both the quantity and quality (as measured by aptitude test scores) of Army recruits are highly sensitive to changes in extrinsic inducements such as salaries, recruitment and retention bonuses, and educational incentives (e.g., Lakhani, 1988; Tannen, 1987). Similar results were obtained in a cross-sectional examination of Navy enlistment rates by region, where enlistments were modeled as a function of alternative employment opportunities, regional office expenditures on recruitment, and Naval salaries, relative to local wage levels (Hanssens & Levien, 1983).

Unfortunately, a variety of difficulties prohibit firm conclusions as to precisely *which* inducements are most strongly related to applicant attraction (Schwab et al., 1987). For example, it appears that when given the opportunity to directly report the factors influencing their job choices, applicants tend to give self-flattering descriptions of their motivations. In particular, intrinsic outcomes tend to dominate over extrinsic concerns such as pay or job security. However, reversed preference orderings generally are revealed by more subtle methodologies (e.g., policy capturing) that bypass direct self-reporting of relative inducement importance (e.g., Arnold & Feldman, 1981; Rynes et al., 1983).

An additional difficulty is that the relative importance of various inducements appears to be subject to both individual differences (Lawler, 1971; Rynes & Lawler, 1983) and differences in market characteristics (Reynolds, 1951; Rynes et al., 1983). Still, theoretical arguments (e.g., Rottenberg, 1956; Schwab et al., 1987) and limited empirical evidence (e.g., Lakhani, 1988; Rynes et al., 1983; Tannen, 1987) have suggested that verifiable inducements with calculable pecuniary value are likely to be particularly effective motivators of job application and job acceptance decisions.

Applicant Pools

A third way to increase the ability to attract labor is to direct recruitment efforts toward individuals who are, for one reason or another, less marketable than either traditional applicants or the applicants sought by competitors (e.g., Finney, 1989). In general, organizations are assumed to target initial recruitment activities toward the most desirable individuals they think they can attract (e.g., Doeringer & Piore, 1971; Kerr & Fisher, 1950; Malm, 1955). However, if such efforts fail, it is hypothesized that organizations progressively relax their standards until all vacancies are filled (Thurow, 1975).

Considerable empirical evidence supports these assumptions. For example, during World War II, employers sought women and handicapped applicants for jobs formerly filled only by able-bodied men (Kerr & Fisher, 1950). In the 1980s, employers turned to internal, untrained clerical employees to fill entry-level computer-programming jobs when external programmers became scarce or too expensive (Osterman, 1987). Similar substitutions of foreign for native-born applicants have become increasingly common at both ends of the occupational spectrum (e.g., Central Americans at unskilled levels; East Asians in professional jobs).

Although targeting nontraditional applicants might, at first glance, be assumed to lead to lower quality applicants and subsequent lower productivity, it should be noted that some employer preferences (and, hence, factors determining applicant marketability) may not be productivity-related (e.g., Doeringer & Piore, 1971; Thurow, 1975). Low marketability may be the result of various forms of discrimination, rather than true productivity-related differences (Arrow, 1972; Konrad & Pfeffer, in press; Spence, 1973). For example, occupational crowding (i.e., the restriction of applicants with particular demographic characteristics to a narrow range of occupations) may artificially create an excess supply of applicants (and, hence, lower wages) in these occupations.

Thus, it is not clear that all marketability-related characteristics (e.g., age, sex, prior experience, country of origin) are associated with true differences in productivity, length of service, or other determinants of overall utility. Indeed, it is possible that pursuit of nontraditional applicants will sometimes lead to improved cost effectiveness because these individuals may be equally productive, yet will work for lower wages than conventional applicants (Doeringer & Piore, 1971; Konrad & Pfeffer, in press; Major & Konar, 1984). (In subsequent sections, we use the term *nontraditional* applicants when referring to situations in which the productivity effects of changing pools are undocumented and, hence, uncertain. In contrast, we use the term *lower qualified* when discussing shifts to applicants with lower scores on validated selection instruments, for example, dipping lower into a pool based on aptitude or ability test scores.)

In any event, because pursuit of nontraditional applicants appears to be a common organizational adaptation to attraction difficulties, additional research in this area is warranted. Moreover, this strategy is likely to increase in importance, given widespread projections that the vast majority of new entrants to the U.S. labor force over the next decade are likely to be women, minorities, or immigrants (e.g., Fullerton, 1987; Johnston & Packer, 1987; Schwartz, 1989).

CONTINGENCIES AFFECTING CHOICE OF STRATEGY

As mentioned previously, any attraction strategy is likely to have complex and varied outcomes. Therefore, the three attraction strategies discussed in the preceding section are not perfect substitutes for one another. Relatively speaking, for example, changes in recruitment practices are low-cost, low-risk strategies that are likely to have few consequences beyond the attitudes and behaviors of the attracted applicants. However, their impact on attraction may also be limited, particularly in tight labor markets (Doeringer & Piore, 1971). In contrast, changes in applicant pools and inducements can be far more extreme in that they entail either higher costs (e.g., salary spillover to other jobs) or greater risks (greater uncertainty regarding future productivity). However, these strategies are also likely to yield greater improvements in attraction per se (Rynes, in press).

Because alternative strategies are not perfectly interchangeable, it becomes important to understand how attraction strategies are actually chosen under various conditions. Although choices undoubtedly will depend to some extent on an organization's unique situation and idiosyncratic practices, we believe that some general contingencies affecting these choices can be proposed. Five such factors (labor market conditions, vacancy characteristics, organizational characteristics, phase of the attraction process, and legal considerations), intended to be illustrative rather than all-inclusive, are discussed in the following sections.

Before proceeding, it is important to clarify the intent and assumptions behind the propositions that follow. First, the propositions are primarily descriptive, rather than prescriptive, in nature. Although the ultimate objective of our model might be to derive a series of valid prescriptions for organizations confronting diverse situations, extant theory and research are simply too underdeveloped to justify such recommendations at present. However, in many cases there *is* enough empirical evidence, anecdotal evidence, or theoretical speculation to make predictions about what organizations actually *do* under various situations.

Second, although we do not assume that organizations' strategic choices are inherently utility-maximizing, we do assume that attraction strategies are selected on the basis of rational criteria (albeit perhaps *subjectively* rational). Further, as indicated previously, we suspect that in the typical labor-shortage situation, quantitative short-term criteria are weighted more heavily than long-term or qualitative criteria. Our logic is that the former outcomes are (a) more immediate and directly observable (hence, more salient), (b) more easily and reliably measured, and (c) more clearly attributable to prehire strategies than long-term and qualitative outcomes.

Still, relative emphases on long- versus short-term or quantitative versus qualitative outcomes are likely to vary considerably across conditions. For example, long-term quality criteria are probably weighted more heavily for vacancies at higher ends of the occupational spectrum or when labor scarcities are less severe. Although we speculate about such nuances where we feel there is sufficient evidence, in general, we derive our propositions from the assumption that short-term, satisficing objectives—that is, the ability to fill vacancies with at least minimally qualified people at acceptable costs—are the primary determinants of strategic choices among alternatives.

Finally, each of the following propositions should be interpreted in an "all else equal," rather than "under all conditions," sense. As will become apparent in subsequent sections, probable interactions among attraction strategies and between attraction strategies and other HR practices are likely to call into question each of the following propositions under at least some combinations of background circumstances.

Labor Market Conditions

The supply of available workers, relative to demand, determines the severity of an organization's attraction problem. As the magnitude, duration, or anticipated duration of shortages increase, organizations become increasingly willing to employ more costly attraction strategies. For example, evidence suggests that when shortages first develop, organizations typically respond by altering recruitment practices, in particular by using more (and more expensive) recruitment methods and sources (e.g., Doeringer & Piore, 1971; Malm, 1954). However, organizations move on to applicant pool and inducement strategies as shortages deepen or persist (Kerr & Fisher, 1950; Malm, 1955; Osterman, 1987). Thus:

> Proposition 1: All else being equal, in the initial stages of a labor shortage, recruitment strategies will be tried before turning to inducement or applicant-pool strategies.

> Proposition 2: The greater the shortfall between supply versus demand or the longer the expected duration of a labor shortage, the greater the likelihood of employing inducement or non-traditional applicant-pool strategies.

Vacancy Characteristics

Several vacancy characteristics also are likely to have an impact on choice of strategy. For the sake of illustration, five are considered: position level, embeddedness, number of incumbents, attractiveness relative to competitors, and rigidity of skill requirements.

Level.   Vacancies at higher levels are believed to entail greater potential risks to an organization; they also require higher levels of aptitude in response to greater uncertainty, complexity, and rapidly changing environmental conditions. As a result, changes in applicant pools are likely to be more strongly resisted at high levels due to the greater risks involved in hiring individuals with less certain, or lower, productivity-signaling characteristics (e.g., Kanter, 1977; Konrad & Pfeffer, in press).

At the same time, as any basic utility model indicates (e.g., Boudreau & Rynes, 1985), improved attraction outcomes also hold the promise of greater potential payoffs (i.e., service value) where high-level positions are involved. Hence, inducement strategies may be more readily employed, as well as made more lucrative, in these positions due to the greater expected payoffs from attracting and retaining high-quality applicants. Thus:

> Proposition 3: Organizations are less likely to pursue applicants with uncertain or lower productivity-signaling characteristics (i.e., to target alternative applicant pools) for positions at higher organizational levels.

> Proposition 4: Both the use and the magnitude of enhanced inducement strategies increase at higher position levels.

Embeddedness.   Attraction strategies also may depend on the degree to which vacancies are embedded in well-established career progressions. Because positions that are strongly embedded in career ladders are observed with great interest by internal employees, changes either in inducements or in applicant pools would be expected to entail greater potential risk to employers (e.g., salary or productivity spillover to other positions; demotivation of internal candidates) (Doeringer & Piore, 1971; Granovetter, 1986; Lewin, 1987). As such, the embeddedness of a vacancy is expected to lead to conservative attraction strategies. Hence:

> Proposition 5: Because of the potential costs associated with spillover effects, inducement and applicant-pool strategies are less likely to be employed in jobs that are strongly embedded in internal career progressions.

Number of Incumbents.   Additionally, the number of incumbents in a position may affect attraction strategies. For example, inducement strategies are less expensive if they do not have to be extended to a large number of peers. Similarly, the hiring of nontraditional applicants may be more feasible for jobs that have few incumbents because it is less likely that these jobs will be stereotyped by sex, race, and so forth (Kanter, 1977). Therefore, we predict:

Proposition 6: Because of the potential costs associated with spillover effects, organizations will be less likely to use inducement strategies when the number of present incumbents is large.

Proposition 7: All else being equal, large numbers of homogeneous incumbents will decrease the propensity to seek nontraditional applicants due to the greater likelihood of strong stereotyping about "appropriate" applicant characteristics.

Relative Attractiveness. The attractiveness of a vacancy (compared to similar vacancies among competitors) is also likely to have an effect on strategic choices. For example, when vacancies are attractive, there is less need to employ costly or risky attraction strategies. Additionally, the content of recruitment messages may change according to the attractiveness of the vacancy. For example, although many employers appear to avoid realistic recruitment strategies because of anticipated negative effects on attraction (Schneider, 1976; Stoops, 1984), this tendency may be considerably abated when vacancy characteristics compare favorably with competitors'. Thus:

Proposition 8: The more attractive a vacancy is relative to the competition, the less likely are employers to need or use enhanced inducement or nontraditional applicant strategies to fill vacancies.

Proposition 9: The more attractive the vacancy, the more realistic the recruitment message.

Rigidity of Skill Requirements. If the position includes very specific skill requirements, organizations may be constrained from shifting to applicants with unknown (or lower) productivity-signaling characteristics, particularly if the needed skills cannot be acquired on the job during a reasonable time period. In such situations, pursuing nontraditional or less-qualified applicants may not be a viable option. In fact, in times of general labor shortages, a combination of improved recruitment and inducement strategies may be the only feasible alternative for positions with rigid skill requirements. Thus:

Proposition 10: Organizations are less likely to pursue nontraditional applicants when skill requirements are inflexible.

Organizational Characteristics

A variety of organizational characteristics also are likely to influence the choice of attraction strategies. We focus here on four: ability to pay, business strategy, culture and values, and organizational demographics.

Ability to Pay. One important consideration in choosing among attraction strategies is the extent to which an organization is constrained by its ability to pay. Inducement strategies, particularly salary and benefits-related changes, may entail substantial direct costs for employers, especially if there are many vacancies or if enhancements cannot be confined to new hires. As such, pecuniary inducement strategies are less likely to be employed by organizations that have a low ability to pay.

In contrast, alternative inducements that include lower direct costs (e.g., flexible hours, opportunities to work at home) may be used to attract applicants (Rynes, 1987). Additionally, organizations that have a low ability to pay may be more inclined to pursue nontraditional applicants, partly because such applicants are usually willing to work for lower wages (e.g., Konrad & Pfeffer, in press; Lewin, 1987; Major & Konar, 1984; Osterman, 1987). Thus:

> Proposition 11: Organizations that have a low ability to pay are less likely to use pecuniary inducement strategies, but they may be more inclined to modify nonpecuniary inducements.

> Proposition 12: Organizations that have a low ability to pay are more likely to (or may be forced to) seek nontraditional applicants or applicants with lower productivity-signaling characteristics.

Business Strategy.   The strategy literature (e.g., Miles & Snow, 1978; Porter, 1985) posits that there are multiple ways to succeed in any business. However, regardless of the business strategy employed, it is hypothesized that successful implementation depends in part on the compatibility of business strategies and functional strategies such as human resources (e.g., Olian & Rynes, 1984; Snow & Miles, 1986).

One example is provided by Schuler and Jackson (1987), who argued that there are at least three viable business strategies (cost reduction, quality improvement, innovation), each of which has different implications for appropriate HR practices. More specifically, in the case of applicant attraction, each strategy implies certain desirable applicant-pool characteristics. For example, businesses that pursue innovation strategies are characterized by rapidly changing, highly uncertain environments that require workers to be autonomous and flexible. As such:

> Proposition 13: Because of the importance of high aptitude in innovative environments, innovators will be less likely to pursue applicants that have unknown or lower productivity-signaling characteristics. At the same time, they will be more likely to offer high inducements to attract applicants of the necessary caliber.

In contrast, businesses that adopt a cost reduction strategy are characterized by more highly routinized, controlled environments, and they will have concomitantly lower requirements for workers. Thus:

> Proposition 14: Organizations with cost-reduction strategies are more likely to pursue nontraditional applicants. This is because of both the applicants' presumed willingness to work for lower inducements, and the more routine and tightly controlled nature of the work.

Culture and Values.   The nature of an organization's culture and values (e.g., strong versus weak emphasis on product quality or customer service, employee identification with the company) may also influence the choice of attraction strategies. Although the full range of possibilities is too extensive to be addressed here, an illustrative example is provided. Specifically, to the extent that organizational norms emphasize strong internal labor markets, internal pay equity, and long-term organizational careers, one would expect more limited use of nontraditional pool and inducement strategies to attract external candidates. This is due to the greater likelihood of spillover effects to other jobs and incumbents in internally focused environments. Thus:

> Proposition 15: Organizations that have a strong internal labor market focus will be less inclined to use inducement or nontraditional applicant pool strategies to attract external candidates.

Organizational Demographics. In their study of hiring patterns for top administrators in higher education, Konrad and Pfeffer (in press) concluded that "segregation of the past is one of the most pervasive influences on the hiring patterns of the present." More specifically, they found that the higher the proportion of women and minorities in all positions in an organization, the greater the likelihood of finding women and minorities in top positions. Moreover, this effect was not due entirely to enhanced internal promotion opportunities for nontraditional internal candidates; organizations that were not dominated by white males were more likely to hire women or minorities through external channels as well. Additionally, the chances of hiring women or minorities for positions traditionally held by white males (based on national statistics) were also enhanced if the previous organizational incumbent was a woman or a minority. Similar phenomena have been reported by Kanter (1977) and Pfeffer and Davis-Blake (1987). By extension, we propose that:

> Proposition 16: Pursuit of nontraditional applicants, particularly for high-level positions, will be least likely in organizations that are most heavily dominated by white males.

Phase of the Attraction Process

In order to ultimately fill vacancies, organizations must succeed in attracting applicants through a series of stages (e.g., submitting an application, undergoing multiple interviews and other screening procedures, and, sometimes, forgoing alternative offers). A shortage of willing or qualified applicants at any one of these stages creates a potential need to modify attraction practices. Therefore, the appropriate modifications may be a function of the stage in which the shortage occurs.

For example, improved recruitment activities may be effective in encouraging an increase in initial applications. However, evidence suggests that recruitment practices per se become less influential as candidates move closer to making a job choice (Rynes, in press; Taylor & Bergmann, 1987). Therefore, shortfalls occurring at later stages of the process (e.g., low job acceptance ratios) are likely to be ineffectually addressed by recruitment strategies. Thus:

Proposition 17: Attraction difficulties at early stages of the process are most likely to be addressed through enhanced recruitment techniques. In contrast, inducement strategies are (relatively) more likely to be used to address difficulties at later stages.

Legal Considerations

Attraction strategies also are influenced by the legal and political climates in which organizations operate. Two aspects of the legal environment that may be particularly influential are wage and salary regulation and equal employment opportunity (EEO) legislation (Schwab, 1982).

Wage and salary regulations constrain an employer's ability to attract applicants through monetary inducements. In general, such constraints cause employers to turn either to other kinds of inducements or alternative applicant strategies. For example, government-imposed wage controls generally result in benefit enhancements as a means of attracting and retaining desired workers (Rosenbloom & Hallman, 1986). Alternatively, mandated increases in minimum wage requirements may lead to reduced willingness to employ nontraditional applicants (hence, the arguments for a two-tier minimum wage).

EEO legislation can have an impact on all three attraction strategies. For example, equal pay legislation may restrict an employer's ability to take advantage of "protected" applicants' willingness to work for lower wages. Additionally, the threat of legal action may persuade organizations that have segregated work forces to target nontraditional applicants or to broaden recruitment sources beyond employee referrals, which tend to reproduce current demographic patterns.

Historically, however, the extent of EEO influence has varied considerably according to changes in legislative, judicial, and executive administrations. For example, former governmental emphasis on class-action prosecutions increased the vulnerability of large organizations and job categories with large numbers of demographically homogeneous incumbents. However, administrative guidelines and legal rulings made in the late 1980s suggest a trend toward less emphasis on numbers per se and more emphasis on managerial intent (e.g., *Price Waterhouse v. Hopkins*, 1989; *Wards Cove Packing v. Atonio*, 1989). Therefore, although legal considerations undoubtedly affect attraction and selection behaviors (e.g., Leonard, 1985; Tenopyr, 1981), specific propositions related to EEO are not offered here because of the uncertainties created by these court decisions.

INTERRELATIONSHIPS AMONG ALTERNATIVE STRATEGIES

Although various contingencies may lead organizations to focus primarily on one strategy in filing a particular vacancy, organizations are not restricted to using a single approach. In fact, interdependencies between the alternatives make reliance on a single strategy unlikely. A complete discussion of all possible interdependencies is beyond the scope of this paper; however, in the following sections selected situations are discussed in which decisions and outcomes involving one attraction strategy appear to be integrally related to choices concerning other strategies (Schwab, 1982).

Applicant Pools and Inducements

Efficiency wage and segmented market theories suggest that both the quantity and quality of available workers are functions of the level of inducements (e.g., Thurow, 1975; Weiss, 1980; Yellen, 1984). Simply put, better applicants are expected to be attracted to and to remain in better vacancies. Thus, if all else is equal, organizations that seek applicants with higher productivity-signaling characteristics must either enhance inducements or accept lower levels of attraction success. Therefore, we propose that:

> Proposition 18: Applicant pool choices are determined partly by the level of inducements offered. Conversely, the choice of a particular pool may dictate changes in inducements.

Decisions about applicant pools also appear to interact with the *type* of inducements offered. For example, employer-subsidized childcare has been used to attract parents of young children; educational benefits to attract college-oriented youth; language and housing assistance to attract the foreign-born; and part-time or flexible schedules to attract students, parents, and retirees (e.g., Hamlet, 1989; Merrill, 1987; Tannen, 1987). Thus, organizations that wish to target a specific applicant pool may find that tailoring inducements is a cost-effective strategy:

> Proposition 19: Inducement strategies, particularly those involving optional benefits or flexible scheduling, may be designed to complement the characteristics of an applicant pool. Conversely, the choice of an applicant pool is at least partly constrained by the organization's ability or willingness to modify particular inducements.

Applicant Pools and Recruitment

An organization's decision to seek nontraditional applicants may bring about changes in recruitment practices. For example, because different kinds of applicants use different sources (Schwab, 1982; Taylor & Schmidt, 1983), decisions about applicant pools and recruitment sources are closely connected. However, sources are chosen for a variety of reasons other than targeting a particular pool (e.g., cost, pre-screening services), and any given pool usually can be assessed through multiple sources (Olian & Rynes, 1984). Thus, although a decision to target nontraditional applicants does not completely dictate the choice of source(s), it appears that there are considerable interdependencies between the two decisions:

> Proposition 20: Decisions to target nontraditional applicants will be accompanied by shifts in recruitment sources. In particular, walk-ins and employee referrals are less likely to be used because these sources are most likely to produce applicants that are similar to current employees.

The choice of organizational representatives also may be affected by decisions to target nontraditional applicants. Although there is little reason to believe that organizational representatives have much effect on job choices, limited evidence suggests that applicants have more favorable attitudes toward representatives who are demographically similar (although somewhat older and higher in status) to themselves (Rynes, in press). Also, even though the issue has not received explicit research attention, it is possible that because of the importance (and scarcity) of role models for on-the-job success among nontraditional employees (Konrad & Pfeffer, in press), perceived similarity may be more important for attracting nontraditional versus traditional applicants. Thus, we speculate that:

> Proposition 21: Decisions to target nontraditional applicants will be accompanied by increased use of nontraditional organizational representatives.

Finally, decisions to pursue nontraditional applicants may lead to modifications of recruitment messages. For example, focusing on characteristics that are highly salient to applicants will probably have a greater impact (either positive or negative) on attraction than emphasizing less important factors. Although we have only limited information about the salience of various job characteristics for different kinds of applicants, there is some evidence that relative importance is associated with both individual (e.g., age, sex, education) and occupational differences (e.g., Goldthorpe, Lockwood, Bechhofer, & Platt, 1969; Jurgensen, 1978; Rynes et al., 1983). If such differences can be reliably determined, the content of the recruitment message can be tailored to any applicant pool (e.g., Krett & Stright, 1985). Thus, we expect that:

> Proposition 22: Decisions to pursue nontraditional applicants are accompanied by changes in recruitment messages that are designed to reflect the perceived salience of various inducements to the newly targeted audience.

ATTRACTION AND OTHER HUMAN RESOURCE PRACTICES

Attraction strategies do not operate in isolation from other human resource policies and practices. Although a full elaboration of attraction-HR interactions is beyond the scope of this article, we propose that attraction strategies interact with other HR activities in two basic ways.

First, as implied in previous sections, current HR practices act as constraints that influence the relative viability of alternative attraction strategies. For example, changes in monetary inducements may be less feasible in organizations that usually place a strong emphasis on internal equity (Doeringer & Piore, 1971) or in organizations in which the centralization of HR decision making places constraints on local inducement practices. Similarly, shifts to more flexible work hours may be more difficult in organizations in which union contracts or other work rules strictly regulate work scheduling (Pierce, Newstrom, Dunham, & Barber, 1989). Thus:

> Proposition 23: An organization's choice of attraction strategies is determined in part by existing HR practices.

Second, changes in attraction strategies often cannot be operationalized without simultaneous or subsequent changes in other HR practices. For example, shifts to nontraditional applicant pools may be resisted unless accompanied by more rigorous selection and validation procedures to counteract the increased uncertainty of hiring unknowns (e.g., Doeringer & Piore, 1971). Similarly, although nontraditional applicants may be easier or less expensive to attract, additional investments may be necessary for their socialization and training (e.g., Kanter, 1977) or for managing potentially negative spillover effects to other employees (e.g., Schneider, 1987; Sutton & Louis, 1987).

Strategies for attracting nontraditional applicants also may require changes in job design. For example, law firms faced with a shortage of affordable top-tier law graduates have facilitated the shift to second-tier applicants by creating less-challenging, entry-level positions which are segmented from the conventional partnership career path (Lewin, 1987). Conversely, attempts to attract more highly qualified applicant pools may require job enlargement (e.g., Lawler, 1986). Thus:

> Proposition 24: Implementation of changes in attraction strategies often necessitates changes in other HR practices.

IMPLICATIONS FOR FUTURE RESEARCH

Additional research on applicant attraction is needed in many areas. For example, organizations would clearly benefit from further development of both internal- and external-staffing models (Anderson, Milkovich, & Tsui, 1981; Olian & Rynes, 1984). Moreover, much of the previously reviewed applicant-centered research, particularly recruitment research, could be made more useful to organizations with a few basic modifications. Among the most important would be to study applicants longitudinally at multiple phases of the attraction process, to include a wider variety of substantive and control variables in single investigations, and to supplement the vast number of applicant perception studies with either objective or behavioral outcomes (Rynes, in press; Schwab, 1982; Schwab et al., 1987).

Despite these and many other content issues that merit future investigation, we focus here on research that would be most useful in testing, revising, and extending the present model. In so doing, we segment our discussion into two categories: descriptive and prescriptive. Although prescriptive research is likely to benefit organizations most, our basic understanding of what organizations actually do to attract applicants (and why) is not sufficiently developed to justify strong statements about what they *should* be doing. As such, we begin with a discussion of needed descriptive research.

Descriptive Research

According to the large number of recent anecdotal reports about labor shortages, it is clear that organizations are adopting a wide variety of tactics to attract applicants. These include importing foreign workers, relocating workers (even unskilled) to different areas of the country, providing house-finding and rental assistance, integrating part-time work with formal remedial education programs, allowing semiretired employees to earn educational scholarships for their grand-children, tying salary increase programs to increases in the cost of housing, and so on.

What is lacking, however, is *systematic* information about the use of attraction strategies. For example, little is known about (a) how frequently each strategy is pursued, (b) what causes different organizations to pursue different strategies, (c) whether or not strategy adoption follows a consistent pattern across organizations (e.g., recruitment first, inducements as a last resort), (d) whether discussions of particular attraction strategies inevitably involve consideration of certain other strategic alternatives, and (e) whether the practical importance of proposed contingency variables is largely universal, or highly situation-dependent (e.g., are EEO concerns more critical for public than for private organizations?).

Even though some of the most fruitful areas for future research concern the strategic options, contingency variables, and proposed interactions outlined in the preceding model, there are other potentially important content areas that might make a difference to whether a strategy is adopted and whether or not it is successful.

One such topic involves the question of who makes the critical decisions concerning attraction policy. For example, what are the contributions of top managers, low-level managers, line managers, and HR managers to strategy formulation? Following the logic of our model, we would expect considerable variability in locus of decision making across firms, depending on a number of contingencies. For example, we would expect organizations with diversified business units that require substantially different types of employees to place increased decision-making authority at the business-unit level.

According to the same logic, we would expect variability in decision-making practices within organizations, but across job levels. For example, attraction strategies might be formulated at the local level for jobs filled entirely from the surrounding community, but formulated at the corporate level for vacancies filled from regional or national labor markets.

Another content area worthy of investigation concerns the emphasis that various outcomes (e.g., filling vacancies within certain time periods, quality and retention of new hires) have on formulating attraction strategies. Because these objectives frequently work at cross purposes to one another, strategy selection ultimately may be a function of the relative weights assigned to individual outcomes. Thus, research is needed that examines how outcomes are weighted in various situations.

However, in order to be useful, such research must take into consideration the potential biases inherent in alternative methodologies for assessing the importance of specific factors in decision making. This is particularly important because managers' self-reports of attraction priorities (Schwab, 1982) do not correspond with evidence about the outcomes that are most frequently measured and recorded (e.g., Rynes & Boudreau, 1986). (Because many of the relevant methodological issues are highly similar to those encountered when applicants are asked to describe factors that are important to their job choices, the interested reader is encouraged to consult Lawler, 1971, Opsahl and Dunnette, 1966, Rynes et al., 1983, or Schwab et al., 1987.)

As the preceding paragraph implies, would-be descriptive researchers confront a variety of methodological, as well as content, issues. At present, most of the little we know about organizational attraction strategies comes from anecdotal accounts in practitioner journals (e.g., Hamlet, 1989; Hanigan, 1987; Merrill, 1987), qualitative interpretations of small-sample case investigations (e.g., Doeringer & Piore, 1971), or dated institutional economic studies of the operation of local labor markets (e.g., Reynolds, 1951).

In the late 1980s, a few attempts have been made to investigate attraction practices through field surveys (e.g., Finney, 1989; National Association of Manufacturers, 1989). However, these studies typically have examined only a subset of potential attraction strategies, and they have provided limited information (if any) about variables associated with *differential* adoption of various strategies (i.e., contingencies).

Thus, there is a pressing need to apply more diverse methodologies in order to gain a better understanding of what kinds of employers are adopting which attraction strategies, and why. One potentially valuable approach would be to conduct intensive interview-based case studies of strategy formulation across a range of carefully selected organizations (e.g., different levels of the same organization, different business units of the same corporation, or different companies in the same industry that confront different levels of labor shortages or have widely varying abilities to pay). The practice of intense information gathering in organizations that vary widely in terms of one or more hypothesized contingency variables might prove very useful in assessing (a) the completeness of the proposed model in terms of its variables and (b) the accuracy of its contingency propositions.

A second approach for assessing the range of attraction practices and their association with various contingencies is the large-sample field survey. Although field surveys have a tendency to lose some of the richness of the data, they have advantages in terms of sample size, standardization, potential for quantitative assessment of contingency relationships, and likely external generalizability. Again, such research should be conducted on multiple samples (e.g., companies that have different types of shortages, varying abilities to pay, or different demographic compositions).

A third (and dramatically underutilized) methodology for examining contingencies in the formulation of attraction strategies is laboratory experimentation. Of particular use would be policy-capturing or process-tracing studies, whereby individuals responsible for developing attraction strategies are asked what actions they would undertake across a range of background conditions. These methods would complement other research strategies by (a) providing tight controls over theoretically relevant substantive and control variables and (b) permitting examination of multiple judgments of a single decision maker under various conditions, thus controlling for individual differences as well. On the negative side, such methods rely on hypothetical, rather than real, decisions. As such, they raise questions about whether intentions translate into actual behaviors or whether preferred or ideal strategies are applied in real, constrained organizations. (See Olson, Dell'Omo, and Jarley, 1987, for some reassuring evidence on these issues in a different decision context.)

Prescriptive Research

In general, prescriptive attraction research tries to discover what organizations *ought* to be doing to achieve desired outcomes. In this sense, the vast majority of attraction-related research has had a prescriptive, rather than descriptive, orientation. For example, attribute importance studies purport to determine which inducements should be enhanced for the optimal attraction of applicants, just as recruitment source studies attempt to discover which sources should be used to maximally retain them.

However, the proposed model of applicant attraction suggests that evaluation of the effectiveness of attraction strategies is both complex and multidimensional. For example, the impact of any single strategy is hypothesized to depend on both external and internal contingencies, as well as on other attraction strategies and HR practices. Moreover, a complete assessment of effectiveness would require evaluation of a broad range of both prehire and posthire outcomes.

Although there is a great deal of variability in the quality of previous attraction-related research, in most cases existing studies are extremely simplistic when evaluated against real-world attraction complexities. In particular, most studies have examined single strategies and limited dependent variables at single phases of the attraction process. For example, recruiter research has been dominated by applicant impressions at the campus interview stage, while realistic preview research has emphasized posthire selectee retention.

As a result, we know very little about the relative effectiveness of one strategy versus another under various conditions. Worse yet, because of the failure to test for variations in effectiveness across wide ranges of potentially important contingencies, prior research may have produced misleading results—in particular, apparent homogeneity of effects where true contingencies may exist (Breaugh, 1983; Rynes, in press). For example, although the attractiveness of a particular vacancy (relative to the same kind of position in competing organizations) might be expected to affect the results of presenting realistic recruiting information, previous inattention to this variable precludes examination (meta-analytic or otherwise) of prior research on this basis. These types of considerations limit our ability to make prescriptions that are likely to hold up across the wide range of situations encountered in real-world attraction.

Admittedly, the proposed model is sufficiently complex so that no single study can begin to incorporate all relevant factors. However, regardless of the primary content issue or methodology employed, researchers can become more attentive to real-world complexities by (a) including several (versus one) of the *most important* substantive independent and dependent variables and (b) at least discussing (preferably measuring) the levels and likely effects of potentially important contingency variables.

In addition, similar to descriptive research, there is a pressing need to apply multiple methodologies to prescriptive attraction research. Although a wide variety of methods have been applied *across* the three strategies, individual strategies have tended to become heavily associated with only one or two methodologies (e.g., recruiter research with field surveys; RJPs with field experiments; inducement strategies with rating/ranking surveys or policy-capturing experiments).

As such, one of the most useful general directions for future research would be to supplement currently dominant methods in particular strategic areas with nontraditional methodologies. For example, because prior inducement research has been dominated by applicant-oriented rating/ranking surveys and policy-capturing experiments, future inducement research might shift toward organizational field experiments (e.g., Lakhani, 1988; Tannen, 1987) and field surveys of organization-level practices and outcomes (e.g., Hanssens & Levien, 1983). Because statistically significant effects can be obtained for virtually any laboratory investigation if enough alternative explanations are controlled or omitted, supplementation with field research is essential for determining the *practical* significance of prescriptive conclusions based on laboratory results.

Similarly, because information about applicant pool strategies has come primarily from field interviews and case studies, researchers might consider alternative methods such as policy-capturing or process-tracing simulations. Although field experiments are useful in this regard, the typical organization is unlikely to pursue nontraditional applicant strategies "just to see what happens." However, researchers who happen to be in the right place at the right time (e.g., when managers deem that circumstances beyond their control dictate a change in applicant pools) could capitalize on pending changes by attempting to get reasonable before-and-after measures and credible comparison groups.

Analogous recommendations can be made concerning the choice of dependent variables, units of analysis, and the like. For example, because prior research on organizational representatives has assessed applicant perceptions at the individual level of analysis, future research should move toward behavioral outcomes at organizational levels.

Additionally, as researchers move toward a more equitable balance between organizational and applicant attraction perspectives, certain kinds of organizational sampling strategies are likely to produce the most useful results. For example, given the almost overwhelming number of variables that might affect attraction strategies and outcomes, it would seem wise to restrict organizational samples on at least some important contingency variables (e.g., product or labor markets) as a way of narrowing down the potential alternative explanations. For example, the sampling of multiple business units within a single corporation would control for several important contingencies and would add the possible advantage of greater standardization and control over measurement and evaluation procedures.

Finally, although there is certainly a place for prescriptive studies in attraction research, we strongly believe that organizationally oriented research will prove more useful if it is first preceded by careful descriptive research. The complexities of the attraction process dictate that in order to be useful, prescriptive studies must focus primarily on practices that are most frequently adopted by employers, and outcomes that are of the greatest consequence to them. With few exceptions, our present knowledge of actual practices is insufficient to provide much guidance in this area. As such, we recommend that would-be prescriptive researchers begin by becoming more "informed" by solid descriptive findings.

CONCLUSION

Prior research on applicant attraction has been conducted primarily from the applicant's perspective. Moreover, attraction-related research has evolved across a variety of literatures, each of which has developed its own unique perspective of the attraction process. For example, industrial psychologists have focused on recruitment practices and applicant attitudes; economists have studied employment inducements and applicant behaviors; and sociologists have researched the social aspects of recruitment, job search, and early socialization procedures.

An integration of these perspectives is particularly desirable in light of widespread anticipated labor shortages as well as shifts in demographic and productivity-related characteristics of available applicants (Johnston & Packer, 1987). These developments will force more and more organizations to shift from scripted attraction behaviors to conscious strategic deliberation. The present article provides a tentative framework for organizational decision makers who are confronted with attraction challenges and for researchers who wish to increase our understanding of the overall attraction process.

References

Anderson, J. C., Milkovich, G. T., & Tsui, A. (1981) A model of intraorganizational mobility. *Academy of Management Review, 6,* 529–538.

Arrow, K. J. (1972) Models of discrimination. In A. H. Pascal (Ed.), *Racial discrimination in economic life* (pp. 83–102). Lexington, MA: Lexington Books.

Arvey, R., Gordon, M., Massengill, D., & Mussio, S. (1975) Differential dropout rates of minority and majority job candidates due to time lags between selection procedures. *Personnel Psychology, 38,* 175–180.

Barber, A. E. (1989, August) *Pay as a signal in organizational recruiting.* Paper presented at the meeting of the Academy of Management, Washington, DC.

Bernstein, A. E. (1987, October 19) Dispelling the myths about a higher minimum wage. *Business Week,* p. 146.

Boudreau, J. W., & Rynes, S. L. (1985) Role of recruitment in staffing utility analysis. *Journal of Applied Psychology, 70,* 354–366.

Breaugh, J. A. (1981) Relationships between recruiting sources and employee performance, absenteeism, and work attitudes. *Academy of Management Journal, 24,* 142, 147–148.

Breaugh, J. A. (1983) Realistic job previews: A critical appraisal and future research directions. *Academy of Management Review, 8,* 612–619.

Cascio, W. F. (1987) *Applied psychology in personnel management* (3rd ed.). Englewood Cliffs, NJ: Prentice-Hall.

Doeringer, P. B., & Piore, M. (1971) *Internal labor markets and manpower analysis.* Lexington, MA: Lexington Books.

Drake, L. R., Kaplan, H. R., & Stone, R. A. (1973) Organizational performance as a function of recruitment criteria and effectiveness. *Personnel Journal, 52,* 885–891.

Finney, M. I. (1989) The ASPA labor shortage survey. *Personnel Administrator*, 34(2), 35–42.

Fisher, C. D. (1986) Organizational socialization: An integrative review. In K. M. Rowland & G. R. Ferris (Eds.), *Research in personnel and human resources management* (Vol 4, pp. 101–146). Boston: Allyn & Bacon.

Fisher, C. D., Ilgen, D. R., & Hoyer, W. D. (1979) Source credibility, information favorability, and job offer acceptance. *Academy of Management Journal*, 22, 94–103.

Fullerton, H. N. (1987) Labor force projections: 1986 to 2000. *Monthly Labor Review*, 110(9), 19–29.

Gannon, M. J. (1971) Sources of referral and employee turnover. *Journal of Applied Psychology*, 55, 226–228.

Gaugler, B. B., Rosenthal, D. B., Thornton, G. C., & Bentson, C. (1987) Meta-analysis of assessment center validity. *Journal of Applied Psychology*, 72, 493–511.

Giannantonio, C. M. (1989, August) *The role of positive inferences on reactions to the recruitment interview.* Paper presented at the meeting of the Academy of Management, Washington, DC.

Goldthorpe, J. H., Lockwood, D., Bechhofer, F., & Platt, J. (1969) *The affluent worker in the class structure.* Cambridge, England: Cambridge University Press.

Gordon, D. M., Edwards, R., & Reich, M. (1982) *Segmented work, divided workers: The historical transformation of labor in the United States.* Cambridge, England: Cambridge University Press.

Granovetter, M. S. (1986) Labor mobility, internal markets, and job matching: A composition of the sociological and economic approaches. In R. V. Robinson (Ed.), *Research in social stratification and mobility* (Vol. 5, pp. 3–39). Greenwich, CT: JAI Press.

Guion, R. M. (1976) Recruiting, selection, and job placement. In M. D. Dunnette (Ed.), *Handbook of industrial and organizational psychology* (pp. 777–828). Chicago: Rand McNally.

Hamlet, K. B. (1989, August 14) Slowing the service sector's revolving door. *The Wall Street Journal*, p. A-8.

Hanigan, M. (1987) Campus recruiters upgrade their pitch. *Personnel Administrator*, 32(11), 55–58.

Hanssens, D. M., & Levien, H. A. (1983) An econometric study of recruitment marketing in the U.S. Navy. *Management Science*, 29, 1167–1184.

Harris, M. M., & Fink, L. S. (1987) A field study of employment opportunities: Does the recruiter make a difference? *Personnel Psychology*, 40, 765–784.

Howard, A. (1986) College experiences and managerial performance. *Journal of Applied Psychology*, 71, 530–552.

James, L. R., Mulaik, S. A., & Brett, J. M. (1982) *Causal analysis: Assumptions, models, and data.* Beverly Hills, CA: Sage.

Johnston, W. B., & Packer, A. E. (1987) *Workforce 2000: Work and workers for the 21st century.* Indianapolis: Hudson Institute.

Jurgensen, C. E. (1978) Job preferences (What makes a job good or bad?) *Journal of Applied Psychology*, 63, 267–276.

Kanter, R. M. (1977) *Men and women of the corporation.* New York: Basic Books.

Kerr, C., & Fisher, L. H. (1950) Effect of environment and administration on job evaluation. *Harvard Business Review*, 28(3), 77–96.

Klein, J. J. (1989) An integrated control theory model of work motivation. *Academy of Management Review*, 14, 150–172.

Konrad, A. M., & Pfeffer, J. (in press) Understanding the hiring of women and minorities: How gender and ethnic composition is produced and reproduced in educational organizations. *Sociology of Education.*

Krett, K., & Stright, J. F. (1985) Using market research as a recruitment strategy. *Personnel*, 62(11), 32–36.

Laitamaki, S. E. (1989) Relationships between organizational characteristics, college recruiting policies and practices, and recruitment outcomes. Unpublished master's thesis, Cornell University, Ithaca, NY.

Lakhani, H. (1988) The effect of pay and retention bonuses on quit rates in the U.S. Army. *Industrial and Labor Relations Review*, 41, 430–438.

Lawler, E. E., III (1971) *Pay and organizational effectiveness: A psychological view.* New York: McGraw-Hill.

Lawler, E. E., III (1986) *High involvement management.* San Francisco: Jossey-Bass.

Leonard, J. S. (1985) What promises are worth: The impact of affirmative action goals. *Journal of Human Resources*, 20, 1–20.

Lewin, T. (1987, March 11) Law firms add second tier. *New York Times*, sec. 4, p. 1.

Liden, R. C., & Parsons, C. K. (1986) A field study of job applicant interview perceptions, alternative opportunities, and demographic characteristics. *Personnel Psychology*, 39, 109–122.

Major, B., & Konar, E. (1984) An investigation of sex differences in pay expectations and their possible causes. *Academy of Management Journal*, 27, 777–793.

Malm, F. T. (1954) Recruiting patterns and the functioning of labor markets. *Industrial and Labor Relation Review*, 7, 507–525.

Malm, F. T. (1955) Hiring procedures and selection standards in the San Francisco Bay area. *Industrial and Labor Relations Review*, 8, 231–252.

March, J., & Simon, H. (1958) *Organizations.* New York: Wiley.

Maurer, S. D., & Howe, V. (1989, August) *Organizational recruitment as job marketing: A study of the engineering labor market.* Paper presented at the meeting of the Academy of Management, Washington, DC.

Merrill, P. (1987) Sign of the times. *Personnel Administrator*, 32(11), 62–65.

Miles, R. E., & Snow, C. C. (1978) *Organizational strategy, structure, and process.* New York: McGraw-Hill.

Miner, M. G. (1979) *Recruiting policies and practices.* Washington, DC: Bureau of National Affairs.

National Association of Manufacturers. (1989) *The NAM small manufacturers' survey.* Washington, DC: Author.

Olian, J. D., & Rynes, S. L. (1984) Organizational staffing: Integrating practice with strategy. *Industrial Relations*, 23, 170–183.

Olson, C. A., Dell'Omo, G. C., & Jarley, P. (1987) *A comparison of arbitrator decision making in experimental and field settings.* Paper presented at the meeting of the Econometric Society, Chicago.

Opsahl, R. L., & Dunnette, M. D. (1966) The role of financial compensation in industrial motivation. *Psychological Bulletin*, 66, 94–118.

Osterman, P. (1987) Choice of employment systems in internal labor markets. *Industrial Relations, 26,* 46–67.

Pfeffer, J., & Davis-Blake, A. (1987) The effect of the proportion of women on salaries: The case of college administrators. *Administrative Science Quarterly, 32,* 1–24.

Pierce, J. L., Newstrom, J. W., Dunham, R. B., & Barber, A. E. (1989) *Alternative work schedules.* Boston: Allyn & Bacon.

Porter, M. E. (1985) *Competitive advantage: Creating and sustaining superior performance.* New York: Free Press.

Powell, G. N. (1984) Effect of job attributes and recruiting practices on applicant decisions: A comparison. *Personnel Psychology, 37,* 721–732.

Premack, S. L., & Wanous, J. P. (1985) A meta-analysis of realistic job preview experiments. *Journal of Applied Psychology, 70,* 706–719.

Price Waterhouse v. Hopkins, U.S. Supreme Court, Docket 87–1167 (May 1, 1989).

Reynolds, L. G. (1951) *The structure of labor markets.* New York: Harper & Bros.

Rosenbloom, J. S., & Hallman, G. V. (1986) *Employee benefit planning* (2nd ed.). Englewood Cliffs, NJ: Prentice-Hall.

Rottenberg, S. (1956) On choice in labor markets. *Industrial and Labor Relations Review, 9,* 183–199.

Rynes, S. L. (1987) Compensation strategies in recruitment. *Topics in Total Compensation, 2,* 185–196.

Rynes, S. L. (in press) Recruitment, job choice, and post-hire consequences: A call for new research directions. In M. D. Dunnette (Ed.), *Handbook of industrial and organizational psychology* (2nd ed.). Palo Alto: Consulting Psychologists' Press.

Rynes, S. L., & Boudreau, J. W. (1986) College recruiting in large organizations: Practice, evaluation, and research implications. *Personnel Psychology, 39,* 729–758.

Rynes, S. L., Heneman, H. G., III, & Schwab, D. P. (1980) Individual reactions to organizational recruiting: A review. *Personnel Psychology, 33,* 529–542.

Rynes, S. L., & Lawler, J. (1983) A policy-capturing investigation of the role of expectancies in decisions to pursue job alternatives. *Journal of Applied Psychology, 68,* 620–631.

Rynes, S. L., & Miller, H. E. (1983) Recruiter and job influences on candidates for employment. *Journal of Applied Psychology, 68,* 147–154.

Rynes, S. L., Schwab, D. P., & Heneman, H. G., III (1983) The role of pay and market pay variability in job application decisions. *Organizational Behavior and Human Performance, 31,* 353–364.

Schneider, B. (1976) *Staffing organizations.* Santa Monica, CA: Goodyear.

Schneider, B. (1987) The people make the place. *Personnel Psychology, 40,* 437–454.

Schuler, R. S., & Jackson, S. E. (1987) Linking competitive strategies with human resource management practices. *Academy of Management Executive, 1,* 207–220.

Schwab, D. P. (1982) Recruiting and organizational participation. In K. Rowland & G. Ferris (Eds.), *Personnel management* (pp. 103–128). Boston: Allyn & Bacon.

Schwab, D. P., Rynes, S. L., & Aldag, R. J. (1987) Theories and research on job search and choice. In K. Rowland & G. Ferris (Eds.), *Research in personnel and human resource management* (Vol. 5, pp. 129–166). Greenwich, CT: JAI Press.

Schwartz, F. N. (1989) Management women and the facts of life. *Harvard Business Review, 67*(1), 65–76.

Snow, C. C., & Miles, R. E. (1986) Organizational strategy, design, and human resource management. In S. L. Rynes & G. T. Milkovich (Eds.), *Current issues in human resource management* (pp. 60–69). Plano, TX: Business Publications.

Soelberg, P. O. (1967) Unprogrammed decision making. *Industrial Management Review*, 8, 19–29.

Spence, M. (1973) Job market signaling. *Quarterly Journal of Economics*, 87, 355–374.

Stoops, R. (1984) Reader survey supports marketing approach to recruitment. *Personnel Journal*, 63(3), 22–24.

Sutton, R. I., & Louis, M. R. (1987) How selecting and socializing newcomers influences insiders. *Human Resource Management*, 26, 347–361.

Tannen, M. B. (1987) Is the Army college fund meeting its objectives? *Industrial and Labor Relations Review*, 41, 50–62.

Taylor, M.S., & Bergmann, T. J. (1987) Organizational recruitment activities and applicants' reactions at different stages of the recruitment process. *Personnel Psychology*, 40, 261–285.

Taylor, M. S., & Schmidt, D. W. (1983) A process-oriented investigation of recruitment source effectiveness. *Personnel Psychology*, 36, 343–354.

Tenopyr, M. L. (1981) The realities of employment testing. *American Psychologist*, 36, 1120–1127.

Thurow, L. (1975) *Generating inequality.* New York: Basic Books.

Tsui, A. S., & Gomez-Mejia, L. R. (1988) Evaluating human resource effectiveness. In L. D. Dyer (Ed.), *Human resources management: Evolving roles and responsibilities* (pp. 187–219). Washington, DC: Bureau of National Affairs.

Ullman, J. C. (1966) Employee referrals: Prime tool for recruiting workers. *Personnel*, 43(3), 30–35.

Wanous, J. P. (1977) Organizational entry: Newcomers moving outside to inside. *Psychological Bulletin*, 84, 601–618.

Wanous, J. P. (1980) *Organizational entry: Recruitment, selection, and socialization of newcomers.* Reading, MA: Addison-Wesley.

Wards Cove Packing Co. v. Atonio, U.S. Supreme Court, Docket 87–1387 (June 5, 1989).

Weiss, A. (1980) Job queues and layoffs in labor markets with flexible wages. *Journal of Political Economy*, 88, 526–538.

Yellen, J. L. (1984) Efficiency wage models of unemployment. *American Economic Review*, 74, 200–205.

PERSONNEL SELECTION AND PLACEMENT

INTRODUCTION

An organization is only as strong as the people who make it up. Thus, decisions made about whom to select and whom to reject for organizational membership are critical to the company's ability to derive competitive advantage through its human resources. The competitive aspects of selection decisions become even more critical when firms hire from the same labor market. If one firm systematically skims off the best applicants, the remaining firms must make do with what is left. The readings provided in this section explore the process of personnel selection, with an emphasis on meeting the changing demands placed on those who make such decisions.

Our first reading, "Personnel Selection in the Future: The Impact of Changing Demographics and the Nature of Work," by Lynn Offermann and Marilyn Gowing, specifically examines many of the changing demands confronted by those in personnel selection. Some of these changes involve the nature of the labor pool in terms of the age distribution of workers, racial and cultural diversity, and the sexual composition of the work force. Other changes revolve around the evolution of modern organizations that are changing in size and structure. These organizations are also becoming more flexible and increasingly global in scope. Finally, this article focuses on the possible response that organizations can make in light of these developments.

One of the potential responses identified by Offermann and Gowing is to take a broader look at people being hired. This theme is followed up in our second article by David Bowen, Gerald Ledford, and Barry Nathan. These authors echo some of the concerns expressed in Offermann and Gowing's article and then focus specifically on "Hiring for the Organization, Not the Job" as one potential response to these changes. The approach advocated by Bowen et al. looks at individuals in terms of their long-term potential to contribute to the organization, as opposed to a short-term focus on meeting the requirements of one specific job. As such, this system emphasizes the potential employee's personality attributes and his or her match with the organizational culture and deemphasizes traditional measures of knowledge, skills, and abilities.

◣

PERSONNEL SELECTION IN THE FUTURE
The Impact of Changing
Demographics and the Nature of Work

Lynn R. Offermann
and Marilyn K. Gowing

Widespread societal change is radically altering employment in the United States. The nature of work, the workforce, and the workplace have all undergone and will continue to undergo tremendous change, bringing new challenges and opportunities to those interested in personnel selection issues (Offermann & Gowing, 1990). With these changes comes the realization that traditional selection practices will no longer serve the best interests of organizations wishing to be globally competitive. In this chapter, we address the current and future impact of these work changes on personnel selection. We begin by briefly summarizing the major demographic changes affecting organizations today and into the future as well as the changing demands created by the nature of work itself. We then discuss the implications of change for new or modified constructs of job performance, and examine the effects of projected changes on recruitment, selection, and promotion of the new workforce. For many organizations, that "future" is already here, and we present their experiences and solutions as instructive to those concerned about maintaining organizational competitiveness into the next century.

CHANGING WORKERS, CHANGING WORK

Demographic changes in the composition of the workforce as well as changes in the nature and structure of work organizations present an important challenge to those charged with maintaining the effective use of human resources. Some future trends in workforce composition can be foreseen with relative accuracy. For example, over two-thirds of the individuals who will be members of the workforce in the year 2000 are working today. While prognostications about the nature of organizations are more speculative than those about demographic

Source: Lynn R. Offermann and Marilyn K. Gowing, "Personnel Selection in the Future: The Impact of Changing Demographics and the Nature of Work," Neal Schmitt et al., eds. *Personnel Selection in Organizations* (San Francisco: Jossey-Bass Publishers, 1993), 385–412. Copyright 1993 by Jossey-Bass, Inc. Used with permission.

changes in the domestic workforce, several clear trends can still be identified that pose significant challenges for personnel selection.

Changing Demographics

Recently, we attempted to summarize the best prognostications about the nature of the U.S. workforce in coming years (Offermann & Gowing, 1990). We found that most scenarios about future workforce changes included four areas of concern: (1) the age distribution of the workforce, (2) the sexual, cultural, and ethnic composition of the workforce, (3) worker skills, and (4) job attitudes possessed by workers.

Age Distribution of the Workforce. Significantly fewer young people will enter the job market than in the recent past. The so-called baby bust will produce a small pool of entry-level talent, with greater organizational competition for their services. At the same time, the escalating number of middle-aged individuals in the workforce (products of the baby boom) will result in increasingly limited promotion opportunities. A large-scale motivational problem may develop as many workers reach career plateaus. One traditional solution to this problem has been early retirement—a solution based on the assumption of available, recently trained, less expensive, and more motivated young workers. This assumption will become increasingly questionable with the small incoming cohort of new workers. Yet, programs to keep older workers or delay retirement have often not been enthusiastically endorsed by organizations (Towers Perrin, 1990). Older workers still face age bias, despite consistent evidence that age is typically unrelated to job performance for most jobs (for example, McEvoy & Cascio, 1989).

Sexual, Ethnic, and Cultural Composition of the Workforce. The increasing diversification of the workforce will continue unabated. White males will make up only 15 percent of the net increase in the workforce during the next ten years. Increasingly, the U.S. workplace is populated by women, minorities, and immigrants. Organizations that never really mastered affirmative action are now scrambling somehow to "manage diversity." Prior attempts to force diverse groups to meld into a homogeneous organization were never totally successful. The extent of the diversity challenge will be affected by immigration patterns and organizational policies. Reich (1991) and others have charged that rather than training local entry-level talent, many U.S. organizations merely export work abroad. New approaches to training and managing resident individuals from diverse backgrounds will be ever more necessary as we approach the century's end if the United States is to realize both economic productivity and a developed native workforce.

Worker Skills. The skill level of new workers is expected to be far less than desirable. Talk is rampant about a "skills gap" wherein the organizational need for increasing skills in a technologically advanced world far outstrips the skill level of the applicant group. In fact, current concerns about skills often focus on lack of even the basic literacy skills that were assumed to be possessed by previous cohorts of new workers on organizational entry. A recent study at Nynex found that only 4 percent of 57,000 entry-level job seekers passed its rudimentary employment test (Fuchsberg, 1991). Current workers face three to four career changes in their lifetime, making the need for skill retraining and flexibility critical.

Job Attitudes. Job attitudes are also changing. Increased desire for autonomy, self-development, and balance between work and family life is surfacing among many workers (Hall & Richter, 1990). Attracting and keeping employees with these desires will force organizations to consider new programs for worker involvement and motivation, as well as options such as flextime, job sharing, and work at home to allow workers to coordinate the work and nonwork aspects of their lives.

Many organizations are already very concerned about these projected workforce changes, and some have instituted programs to deal with them. In 1990, Towers Perrin reported data from 645 organizations across the United States designed to represent a cross section of both industry and location. Of their respondents, the majority are concerned about the increasing diversity in their workforce, the needs of women employees, and future labor shortages. Currently, 70 percent report difficulty in recruiting technical personnel, 63 percent in hiring professionals, and 55 percent in finding secretarial and clerical staff. Table 1 summarizes some of the key findings about employer concerns as well as actions being taken. It can be seen that the level of action is not keeping up with the level of concern expressed.

Changing Organizations

Just as the people composing the workforce are changing, so too are organizations. Among the more dramatic changes we have noted (Offermann & Gowing, 1990) are (1) changes in organizational size and structure, (2) a shift to a service economy, (3) globalization, (4) increasing importance of work teams, and (5) increasing technology.

Changing Size and Structure. Companies are failing at a substantial rate; many of those surviving are reducing the size of their workforce. It is ironic that well-educated white male workers are being laid off in record numbers at a time when organizations are forecasting their shortage in future supply (Fuchsberg, 1991). Companies are restructuring along flatter, leaner lines, with fewer layers of management and fewer people at upper levels. This is occurring at the same time that large numbers of baby boomers are ready to take their places in those positions. Mergers, acquisitions, and buy-outs are creating new corporate cultures virtually overnight, with great attendant stress.

The Service Economy. The focus of today's organizations has shifted from manufacturing to service. The service sector continues to grow, unaccompanied by comparable gains in productivity. Future concerns about national productivity will inevitably emphasize performance in the service sector. The challenge

Table 1

EMPLOYER RESPONSES TO DEMOGRAPHIC CHANGES

What they are concerned about	Percentage
Managing diversity	74
Needs of women	68
Labor shortage	65
Skills gap	42
Aging workforce	40

What they are currently doing

Managing diversity

Formal harassment policy	81
Supervisory training for women	57
Minority recruiting programs	42
Manager diversity training	29
Specific hiring for women	15
Supervisory training for minorities	12
Minority support groups	11
Immigration assistance	11
Mentor programs—minorities	10
English as a second language	9
Mentor programs—women	8
Women's support groups	8

Work/family issues

Flexible spending accounts	36
Extended maternity leave	32
Sick days for kids	31
Child-care information	27
Paternity leave	20
Gradual return to work	13
On-site day care	8
Sick child care	6

Source: Data compiled from Towers Perrin, 1990.

for employers is to identify those factors contributing to top-quality service, including human, material, and technological resources.

Globalization. The increasing globalization of U.S. businesses is forcing a new consideration of the skills needed for successful performance. The sun now sets on the British Empire, but, as Brown points out, not on IBM, Hitachi, or Volkswagen (Toffler, 1980, p. 320). Becoming truly global means not only understanding one's foreign clients and suppliers, but managing the diverse elements within the company as well. As more companies become global, "what once was 'nice to understand' becomes imperative for survival, let alone success" (Adler, 1991, p. 121).

Work Teams. There is considerable agreement that team structures will play an increasingly key role in organizations in the future (for example, Tuttle, 1988). Some have gone so far as to advocate that all functions be organized into largely self-managing teams (Peters, 1988). As such work teams gain in popularity, new employee skills in performing as a member of a group will be required. Can the demand for selection systems to predict this performance be far behind?

Increasing Technology. Increasing use of technology theoretically allows organizations to maximize performance through the optimal combination of human and automated capabilities. Practically, however, increased technology may require an increasingly skilled workforce to utilize it effectively. It is feared that technology is expanding the skills gap faster than organizations can find ways to span it. Further, although ideally technology should be used in place of workers whom the organization cannot find, in practice advanced technologies currently are replacing those employees available in greatest numbers (Greller, 1990).

CONSTRUCT ISSUES

The changes in the nature of workers and their work detailed above suggest the need to reexamine some of the core constructs used in personnel selection. New methods of job and organizational analysis need to be considered, as well as expanded predictor measures of individual capabilities that go beyond the assessment of knowledge, skills, and abilities to include motivation, attitudes, and values. Criterion measures will also require expansion to broader organizational concerns about commitment, retention, teamwork, and quality service.

What Are We Selecting For?

This new organizational complexity demands new selection methodologies, including revised procedures for occupational analysis to determine present and future work requirements. Molecular job analytic methods are too narrow in their focus, even those designed as multipurpose procedures to provide job data for all human resource (HR) management systems (Bemis, Belenky, & Soder, 1983; Schmidt, Hunter, & Pearlman, 1981).

Occupational Analyses. Job analytic procedures must be undertaken, but at a higher level of abstraction, such as analyses of occupations or occupational groups. Researchers must use these procedures to search for underlying commonalities in the work and for the personal dimensions or constructs contributing to effective performance across occupations. Such procedures will enable organizations to maximize the use of their human resources through skills transferability. Skills transferability helps organizations to adapt to changing environmental conditions and to retrain their employees as necessary to fill openings when they encounter labor shortages. Several studies have successfully identified such generalized work and worker characteristics for use in defining occupational families (O'Leary, Rheinstein, & McCauley, 1989, 1990; Outerbridge, 1981; Pearlman, 1980).

Organizational Analysis.   It is not sufficient for occupational analysis systems to identify generalized work requirements. They must also capture the situational or organizational factors within which the work is carried out. Examples of organizational factors include the nature of the organization's leadership or the support from top management (for example, for the development of quality cultures or environments), the degree of strategic planning conducted by management, the focus on the customer and customer satisfaction, the opportunity for employee training and recognition, the type of information systems and measurement procedures available, the type of quality assurance program, and the emphasis on quality and productivity improvement. These situational factors underlie both the Malcolm Baldrige National Quality Award and its public-sector counterpart, the President's Award for Quality and Productivity Improvement. Recent winners have included Motorola, Federal Express, and the U.S. Air Force (Logistics). There is increasing recognition that many of these factors shape corporate culture and that corporate culture dramatically influences immediate and long-term profitability of organizations (Petrock, 1990).

Future selection procedures will need to identify those persons who can function effectively in such total-quality environments, by using such criteria as pride in one's work, a value for quality, and a commitment to the pursuit of excellence. Selection procedures designed to assess need for achievement and need for self-actualization may have relevance here, and new measures will need to be developed.

Outcome Assessment.   Similarly, the occupational analysis systems of the future must describe individual, team, and organizational outcomes. These outcomes include products and services delivered and indices of productivity, defined as the efficiency of transformation of inputs into outputs (Mahoney, 1988). B. F. Skinner argued forcefully for behavior analysis of individual outcome measures to identify the reinforcement contingencies that would make it possible "to design better environments—personal environments that would solve existing problems and larger environments or cultures in which there would be fewer problems" (1990, p. 1210). However, as Guzzo (1988) points out, individual output is but one component of productivity. Only by analyzing the entire organizational environment (the situational or process factors) and all outputs (outcome variables) will accurate predictions be made regarding the individual attributes required for effective functioning within organizations.

Some new methodologies have already been conceptualized and implemented to capture such occupational information, including MOSAIC (Multipurpose Occupational Systems Analysis Inventory—Closed-End; see U.S. Office of Personnel Management, 1991) and the Air Force's CODAP ASCII. The Department of Labor has appointed an advisory panel for the *Dictionary of Occupational Titles (DOT)* to advise on the appropriateness of such methodologies of occupational analysis for identifying, classifying, defining, and describing jobs in the *DOT*.

Whole-Person Measurement

Numerous reviews (for example, Corts & Gowing, 1992; Fleishman & Quaintance, 1984; Hough, Eaton, Dunnette, Kamp, & McCloy, 1990; Mumford, Fleishman, Levin, Korotkin, & Hein, 1988; Northrop, 1989) suggest that many individual attributes contribute to effective individual performance at the professional, supervisory, managerial, and executive levels. What is needed is emphasis on "whole-person" measurement, whereby motivation, attitudes, values, and interests as well as knowledge, skills, and abilities are assessed. Such evaluation of the whole person can maximize prediction of performance.

For example, in 1990, the U.S. Department of Labor appointed the Secretary's Commission on Achieving Necessary Skills (SCANS) to develop a preliminary list of core proficiencies needed for entry-level work. These include the ability to use resources such as time, money, and staff; interpersonal abilities such as teaching or serving others, working on teams, leading, and working with culturally diverse individuals; the ability to use social, organizational, or technological systems and performance monitoring; and the ability to use technology. Each of these core proficiencies can be viewed as a part of the whole person. Three underlying dimensions to these competencies were also identified: basic skills such as reading, writing, and mathematics; thinking skills such as problem solving and knowing how to learn; and personal qualities such as individual responsibility, self-management, and sociability. These dimensions are another way of viewing whole-person measurement. Future selection systems may be used to develop generic work samples for occupational groups that assess core proficiencies necessary for entry-level work or to focus directly on the assessment of the three foundation skills through objective market tests.

Administrative Careers with America.   A recent example of an attempt at measurement of the whole person is the new Administrative Careers with America examination of the U.S. Office of Personnel Management (OPM). This test battery, which is used to assess applicants for entry-level administrative and professional occupations in the federal government, consists of an ability test and a structured biodata questionnaire. The ability test contains items constructed according to the principle of logic-based measurement (Colberg, Nester, & Trattner, 1985). It is complemented by a biodata instrument, the Individual Achievement Record (IAR), which is supported by evidence of both criterion-related validity (Gandy, Outerbridge, Sharf, & Dye, 1989) and construct validity (Dye, 1990). Preliminary results suggest the IAR is measuring several constructs, including cognitive ability, self-esteem, and motivation or willingness to achieve (Dye, 1990).

Building Composite Batteries.   Literature reviews on the criterion-related validity of alternative selection procedures (for example, Hunter & Hunter, 1984; MacLane, 1988; Reilly & Chao, 1982; Tenopyr, 1981) are useful in identifying possible instruments to augment the validity of composite batteries, as are studies of validity generalization (Pearlman, Schmidt, & Hunter, 1980; Rothstein, Schmidt, Erwin, Owens, & Sparks, 1990). Similarly, research investigations focusing on the construct validity of such alternatives are also useful (for example, Reilly, Henry, & Smither, 1990; Shore, Thornton, & Shore, 1990).

Changing Definitions of Success

Just as definitions of individual attributes are expanding to include new dimensions for selection batteries, so too are definitions of criteria evolving. The measurement focus is shifting from consideration of individual criterion measures to variables including team and organizational performance.

Individual Outcomes

Traditionally, industrial and organizational psychologists have sought criterion measures that included measures of the quality of individual behavior, such as performance appraisal ratings. Although criterion measures have traditionally focused on job performance, the need to maintain competitiveness and service quality may increase the use of other types of criterion measures, such as commitment and organizational citizenship behaviors. Research will be needed to identify and validate such measures. Projected shortages in the workforce have also brought renewed attention to retention and turnover as key outcome variables. If organizations are going to make large investments in their human resources, then they will expect those personnel to stay for a reasonable period of time to maximize their return on investment.

Individual outcome measures of the future will undoubtedly include composite measures of the quality of individual performance on multiple dimensions as well as measures of individual retention. For example, the OPM is currently experimenting with the development of biographical data profiles to select those individuals who will both perform effectively and stay on the job for several years. These profiles are designed for government occupations with traditionally high turnover rates.

Team Outcomes

Organizations are increasingly relying on teams of workers to perform complex work assignments. The restructuring of work into team assignments mandates new evaluation criteria that accurately reflect the group's contribution to meeting organizational objectives and to enhancing organizational productivity. Although research findings indicate that self-managing teams can positively affect productivity, the magnitude of the effect is not well known owing to the scarcity of well-designed evaluations (Goodman, Devadas, & Hughson, 1988).

As noted earlier, the projected popularity of work teams in the future will also require the development of more sophisticated measurement methods to select individuals capable of performing effectively in team environments. Traditional methods of individual performance prediction must be expanded to include skills such as supporting and building on the work of others, getting along with others, and managing conflict. Future selection procedures can replicate work team settings. Simulations similar to leaderless group discussion exercises found in assessment centers can easily be adapted to evaluate potential effectiveness in team environments. As an alternative, biographical questionnaire items designed to assess past success in team activities in school, volunteer work, or prior jobs may well be found to be predictive of team effectiveness in future work situations.

Organizational Outcomes

Traditionally, organizations have viewed financial figures as the foundation for measuring organizational performance (Eccles, 1991). Although other measures, such as quality, market share, and other nonfinancial measures, have been tracked for years, they have only recently been given equal (or even greater) status in determining strategy, promotions, bonuses, and other rewards. Recently, in some companies earnings per share have been placed last on the list when evaluating organizational performance, being preceded by customer satisfaction, cash flow, manufacturing effectiveness, and innovation.

The total quality management (TQM) revolution has certainly contributed to this phenomenon. The *Federal Total Quality Management Handbook* defines quality as "meeting customer's requirements, needs, and expectations, the first time and every time" (Federal Quality Institute, 1990, p. 2). In the last ten years, TQM has caught on very fast in both the public and private sectors. Inspired by the work of Deming and others, TQM has caused measures of productivity improvement, cost reduction, and performance management to be deemphasized in favor of a new commitment to work quality (Hyde, 1990).

We project that future organizational outcome measures will use composites to reflect multiple interests. The composites will include measures of (1) bottom-line productivity, (2) success in meeting customer expectations under a TQM system, and (3) organizational processes (such as strategic planning and employee empowerment) that result in products or the delivery of services.

IMPLICATIONS FOR RECRUITMENT

Elizabeth Dole, former secretary of the U.S. Department of Labor, has predicted that organizations of the future will "need to utilize all possible workers to make up for the shrinking labor pool of the 1990s" (Dole, 1990, p. 17). Although traditional selection practices have focused on the organization (who should we choose from the wide array of available candidates?), those practices are now becoming more focused on the individual (how can we get those we want to accept our offers?). This change in focus places increasing emphasis on good recruitment practices.

Attracting Applicants

Now that employers have been placed in a competitive position for talent, increased attention is being given to examining what will attract members of the future workforce. According to surveys by the University of California, Los Angeles, and the American Council on Education, the percentage of college freshmen who said that it is "important to be well-off financially" rose from 41 percent in 1966 to 76 percent in 1987 (National Commission on the Public Service, 1989). At the same time, average starting salaries are increasing in both the private and the public sectors. The National Commission on the Public Service reported that the average starting salary for careers in private-sector consulting and research rose 15 percent in real terms over the past decade, while pay for careers in banking, finance, and insurance increased 18 percent. Although the future workforce values pay to attain an acceptable standard of living, many future employees also value altruism. The number of college freshmen who see helping others as an essential or very important objective in life has remained steady at almost 60 percent over the past twenty years (National Commission on the Public Service, 1989). Organizations have recognized the need to publicize career opportunities satisfying such values.

Introducing Flexible Human Resources Management Programs. Organizations are also initiating a variety of HR management programs to attract and retain a quality workforce. Some companies are taking steps to accommodate the needs of dual-career couples, especially when both individuals have strong identification with their chosen professions (Quaintance, 1989). Two working partners may have problems arranging both work and family obligations. Such couples affect the organization's ability to move people geographically and often require dual-career management (Schein, 1981).

The increasing number of women in the workforce has led some companies to take a critical look at their family-directed policies. In analyzing the work patterns of nine thousand women, the Census Bureau found that 71 percent of the women with maternity benefits returned to work within six months of childbirth, compared with 43 percent of those without benefits (DeLoux, 1990). General Dynamics has implemented a part-time program for mothers returning from maternity leave, has made unpaid leave available before and after delivery, and is currently addressing the issue of child care (DeLoux, 1990). Apple Computer pays women two-thirds of their full pay during maternity leave, with the remainder made up through accrued sick leave. Apple also gives a $500 bonus to any employee who has a baby or adopts a child, allows unpaid personal leave of up to six months, and provides on-site child care and a resource referral network to help employees find child-care providers. Apple's turnover rate of 5 percent is very low for high-technology companies (DeLoux, 1990), and this may reflect the company's innovative programs.

The care of preschool children of working parents is likely to remain a major issue for the coming decades. Abraham and Bowdidge (1990) note that the issue has similarities to other "revolutions," such as civil rights, occupational safety, and age discrimination, which have since been legislated into public policy. Until legislation is enacted, employers who are voluntarily progressive in establishing policies in this area may well find themselves in a more competitive position for attracting the 56 percent of married couples composed of two working parents.

Numerous organizations are experimenting with programs such as job sharing, alternative work schedules, and flexiplace or telecommuting, in which employees are allowed to work at least part of their workweek at their own homes. LINK Resources Corporation has collected survey data from twenty-five hundred randomly selected households that suggest that a total of 32.8 million Americans currently work at home, compared with 26.8 million a year ago (U.S. Office of Personnel Management, 1990). Companies with telecommuting efforts in the private sector include Pacific Bell, J. C. Penney, Digital Equipment Corporation, Du Pont, Traveler's Insurance, Control Data, IBM, Johnson & Johnson, Blue Cross/Blue Shield, and American Express (Joice, 1989). Public-sector flexiplace initiatives have been undertaken by the states of Washington, Florida, California, and Arizona.

Professionalizing Recruiters.   Renewed emphasis has been placed on the importance of recruiters and interviewers, who serve as the organization's representatives to those in the labor force. We are seeing increased attention and resources dedicated to recruitment efforts (Ingraham, 1990) as well as to enhancing the quality of preemployment interactions with potential employees (Byham, 1990). Recruiters need to become more sensitive to diversity issues in order to attract needed talent to their organizations.

Expanding Traditional and Nontraditional Sources of Recruitment

Some organizations already are facing staff shortages for entry-level positions, with projections indicating more hiring difficulty to come. As a result, organizations have been forced to develop new mechanisms for securing needed staff while reaching out to underrepresented groups. The result has been creative interfaces with the country's educational system at several levels as well as reconsideration of recruiting efforts directed at segments of the population previously hired in more limited numbers.

Partnerships with Colleges and Universities.   Projections of increasing numbers of minorities in the future workforce have led employers to seek new partnerships with colleges and universities having large minority populations. For example, the OPM announced Project Partnership, a memorandum of understanding with the presidents of the Hispanic Association of Colleges and Universities (HACU) and National IMAGE, Inc. The intent of the project is for the combined resources of HACU, IMAGE, and OPM to work with federal agencies to promote the additional use of federal student employment programs as an avenue to increase representation of Hispanics in the federal workforce. Similarly, in 1991 OPM hosted a meeting between federal agencies and the nation's historically black colleges and universities. The meeting established avenues for continuing partnerships to bring the best and brightest students from outstanding black institutions of learning into government service. Private-sector organizations are likewise pursuing relationships with traditionally minority colleges and universities.

Partnerships with Junior and Senior High Schools.   In light of the predicted "skills gap" and the lack of a structured transition from school to the workplace, there have been many partnerships between businesses and schools operating for years at both the junior high and high school levels. American Express led the way with its Academy of Finance, offering a special two-year curriculum for public high school juniors and seniors, on-the-job internships with businesses in the summer, and training for public high school teachers to instruct the academy courses. In 1990, the first Academy of Public Service was begun in Washington, D.C., under the sponsorship of the National Academy Foundation.

Many other such partnerships are under way throughout the country. These are documented by the National Association of Partners in Education, a nonprofit association sponsoring symposia, conferences, and training academies throughout the country. Among the partnerships under way are adopt-a-school programs by 3M, Citibank, and the Travelers Corporation. Such programs vary dramatically. The 3M program encourages young women to pursue careers in the fields of science and engineering. The Citibank branches each adopted a school and created a fund to award cash grants to local educators who devise ways to cut Miami's dropout rate ("Adopt a School," 1990).

Recruiting People with Disabilities.   Shortages in the labor pool are leading employers to be more creative in tapping non-traditional recruitment sources. The recent passage of the Americans with Disabilities Act (ADA) is encouraging employers to reevaluate their hiring practices and to seek qualified workers with disabilities. For example, Kreonite, Inc., a small business based in Kansas that manufactures photographic and graphic arts film, reported that its annual turnover rate was reduced from 32 percent to 10–12 percent after increasing the number of employees with disabilities (Martinez, 1990). These employees are totally integrated into the workforce, holding positions such as machine operator, electronics assembler, and fiberglass trimmer. Recruiting resources for these workers include municipal and state rehabilitation services, Gallaudet University, the Epilepsy Foundation, the Bridges Program funded by Marriott, and the Lighthouse for the Blind. Employer resources to accommodate their workplace to those with disabilities are available from the President's Committee on Employment of People with Disabilities.

Future assessment procedures for persons with disabilities are likely to be power, rather than speeded, tests to ensure the measurement of the individual's full capacity. Depending on the disability, some modifications may have to be made in the media used to assess a given applicant. As with many nontraditional groups, the overall focus needs to be on what individuals *can* do rather than cannot, and matching their abilities with job requirements identified through careful job analysis.

Recruiting Older Workers.   With an aging population, some employers are turning to those who have retired to fill their workforce needs. The American Association of Retired Persons offers a job counseling service to its members attempting to match their skills with organizational job requirements.

Assessment practices appropriate for selecting older workers have been well documented by Hunt and Lindley (1989), and again include the avoidance of speeded tests as well as sensitivity to declines in visual and auditory skills necessary for effective test performance but unnecessary for job performance. Oddly enough, according to the Towers Perrin (1990) survey, only 40 percent of companies expressed concern about aging workers, with 30 percent of companies using retirees on special projects or as consultants. Few companies (3 percent) had gradual retirement programs or retrained older workers. Despite increasing health and longevity, the current trend toward early retirement shows no sign of abating. Given future projections, it is surprising that organizations have not shown more concern about keeping workers on the job longer. A valuable human resource seems to be going untapped.

Although societal pressures and civil rights legislation have attempted to create a workforce representative of the nation's diversity at every level of the organization, this goal has not been fully achieved. The shifting demographics will help ensure that those who have been denied fair and open competition for employment opportunities in the past will now be actively sought after by organizations in the public and private sectors. Research is needed to determine effective recruiting strategies for diverse groups. At present, favorable ratings as an employer of minorities or women as published by popular magazines are touted by Xerox and Hewlett-Packard to prospective applicants from those groups (Dreyfuss, 1990). It may be that the best future recruiting strategy is a reputation for fair, unbiased personnel practices. To accomplish this, effective human resource systems will undoubtedly consider some or all of the selection options discussed below.

FURTHER IMPLICATIONS FOR SELECTION

The changes to recruitment just described present additional challenges for selection procedures. Good recruitment practices are designed to generate a sizable pool of talent from which the organization can make judicious selections. However, the size of the talent pool is already shrinking for many occupations. As fewer new workers enter into the workforce, higher selection ratios for many positions have resulted, with still higher selection ratios likely to exist in years to come. And as selection ratios rise, the utility of traditional selection testing may decrease. For many companies already facing personnel shortages, the idea of selection already seems a fond memory. For them, the traditional selection focus on exclusion has already changed to a recruitment, placement, and retention model.

Broadening Selection.   Despite these changes, selection is hardly a dying field. In fact, as organizations downsize and select fewer applicants, each new selection will have greater potential impact on productive potential (Greller & Nee, 1989). Rather, the field of personnel selection needs to be broadened to emphasize the assessment of individual talents and abilities in relation to organizational needs. We believe that the traditional focus on exclusion on the basis of talents lacked will change to a focus on inclusion on the basis of talents possessed or that could be developed. Testing may be used less as a screen than as a diagnostic for placement and development. The notion of whole-person measurement already discussed is an example of attempts to more completely profile individuals with an eye toward matching individual profiles with occupational responsibilities. Given the rampant changes in organizational needs over time, selection becomes the initial point of measurement in a comprehensive system of evaluation that could be updated regularly to continue matching future jobs with the developing profiles of incumbent workers. General Foods' Professional Development Program (Courtney, 1986) is an example of a successful application of a system that continually updates both employee qualifications and job-performance standards.

Selecting Generalists. The likelihood of organizational change and the need for periodic retraining over the course of a career may increase the demand to hire generalists rather than specialists in order to maximize adaptability. Organizations such as AT&T have already found liberal arts graduates to be as successful or more so in general management positions as business graduates in terms of performance and promotions (Howard, 1986). The capacity to learn, rather than the skills possessed, may become more critical as a selection target under conditions of great change. The projected lack of necessary applicant skills makes this trainability a doubly important selection criterion. In addition, testing for generic skills such as reading, writing, and mathematics will also continue to increase. The demand for team functioning by diverse individuals may increase testing for basic communication skills such as the ability to interact successfully with people of different backgrounds and origins.

Computer-Adaptive Testing. Another possible option to deal with increasingly diverse applicants is the use of computer-adaptive testing. Such individually tailored testing has been shown to have equal or better reliability than conventional tests while providing more accurate estimates of the ability levels of those of high or low ability (Anastasi, 1988). Given the projected differences in worker ability levels and the projected number of low-skilled applicants, these techniques may prove particularly useful. It is also possible that some groups may be differentially sensitive to test length and exposure to many items beyond their ability level. If so, the capability of adaptive tests to estimate ability levels with 50 percent fewer items and with more positive examinee responses (Green, 1991) by routing questions by ability level may limit such sensitivity problems. Some of these tests will increasingly be at the level of basic literacy assessment.

Compensatory and Provisional Selection. Another approach to deal with the projected lack of adequately skilled applicants is the greater use of compensatory models of selection (Steinhaus & Morris, 1990). Such models would need to identify strengths in some areas of performance that offset weaknesses in other areas. Compensatory selection systems may also help to minimize adverse impact and improve prediction (see Chapter Six). Provisional selection may also be used more extensively, where individuals are selected despite some deficit provided they reach minimum training requirements within a given amount of time.

Sensitivity to Diversity. Specific selection techniques will need to be far more sensitive to the increasing diversity of the new workforce. The potential for differential performance may increase along with the diversity of job applicants and needs to be carefully considered. In addition to traditional concerns about the performance of different groups on predictive tests, recent work is addressing the issue of test bias and fairness from the level of the test item. Differential item functioning (DIF) occurs when a test question itself produces group differences rather than reflecting real differences between groups of similar ability taking the test. Early results from research examining federal tests indicate that although few items show potential bias, placement of the item within the test and certain item characteristics such as abstractness or the amount of verbal information may affect the amount of DIF found (Harris, 1989). Because DIF analyses take into account differences in applicant ability, they may prove even more appropriate than traditional assessments of adverse impact in the future. Far more research will be needed to understand group differences in individual item performance.

More work also needs to be done addressing different subgroup characteristics that may affect performance on the predictors used for selection. Some selection techniques may be considered inappropriate or offensive by some groups, thereby driving away potential applicants. In other cases, the process of test-taking itself is unfamiliar to some groups, such as the elderly, for whom test formats and directions may need restructuring. Some cultures consider it unseemly to discuss one's accomplishments, and thus may behave more modestly in interview situations. These possibilities present opportunities for increased error of measurement with diverse applicants, error that could be controlled by greater information about the effects of selection techniques themselves on different subgroups.

What most of these options in selection methodologies have in common is an increasing focus on the individual applicant in selection as opposed to traditional group-oriented strategies. It has long been argued that individual profiles on a variety of measures are most critical when labor is scarce (Dunnette, 1966). As more organizations find themselves in situations of diverse applicants and scarce labor supply, we should not be surprised to see targeted selection strategies increase.

IMPLICATIONS FOR PROMOTION

Changes in workers and their organizations warrant reconsideration not only of the job entry process but also of the way individuals are treated once they have joined the organization. Although progress has been made in getting members of traditionally underrepresented groups into organizations, there is growing concern about their prospects for advancement. Indeed, future opportunities for advancement are likely to be more limited for everyone. While one person in twenty was promoted to a top management position in 1987, that ratio is expected to be one in fifty by the year 2001 (Arnett, 1989). What will be required is a reexamination of career paths and motivating opportunities other than vertical advancement, as well as HR systems that fairly promote individuals of diverse backgrounds.

Career Ladders/Lattices

Traditionally, employees have spent their careers aspiring for vertical progression up the career ladders in their occupations. More recently, organizations have begun to use the term *career lattice* to suggest a variety of paths for individual development across occupations and organizations. Career lattices will become increasingly frequent as organizations streamline their managerial positions, leaving fewer top career opportunities, and struggle to find ways to deal with career plateaus. Ingraham (1990) noted that those organizations offering such diversity of experience to young workers and others who are undecided about long-term career objectives will be more competitive in their recruitment efforts.

The idea of a career lattice allows for lateral career moves. Several organizations, such as IBM, Hartford Insurance Group, Atlantic Richfield, and the Sheraton Hotel chain, have set up separate equivalent career ladders for high-technology nonmanagement employees so that grade levels, pay ranges, recognition, and rewards for these people correspond with positions in the management hierarchy (Goddard, 1990). These positions promote technical and professional excellence. Lombardo and Eichinger (1989) present eighty-eight different assignments that can be used for "development in place," that is, increasing the challenge of one's existing job without promotion.

One of the key provisions of the career lattice is the need for skills transferability. The occupational analysis methodology used to establish the career lattice requires gathering information on the level of difficulty of various knowledge, skills, abilities, and other individual attributes required to perform the occupational responsibilities. In some companies, these skill transferability linkages are made by using the organization's point factor job evaluation system (Wellback, Hall, Morgan & Hamner, 1983). Quaintance (1989) reported that prior to a job transfer in Sears the new position is compared to the individual's current position. The transfer is made if the new position requires at least one additional skill area for effective performance, a 10 percent increase in work demands as evidenced by the total number of job evaluation points, and some assignments in different functional areas.

The advisory panel on the *Dictionary of Occupational Titles* is attempting to use an occupational analysis methodology to study all occupations in the U.S. economy and to address their commonality in terms of skills transferability. Once completed, it will provide an invaluable data base to assist organizations wishing to develop career lattices for their employees.

Advancing Women and Minorities

Advancement and retention of women and minorities is still a problem in many organizations. Although the percentage of minority and women managers has grown, most are still in positions with little authority and relatively low pay (Morrison & Von Glinow, 1990). Organizations maximizing their ability to promote as well as attract and retain diverse individuals will have a competitive advantage in the future. Companies that have already been actively recruiting minorities and women have often been discouraged to find that those hired have not progressed as far in the organization as was hoped. For example, Corning and Digital Equipment both found it easier to attract women and minorities than to keep them (Dreyfuss, 1990). According to Thomas (1990), many companies faced with this pattern blamed selection strategies for failing to bring in the "right" people and proceeded to try again—still searching for women and minorities to bring into the pipeline, only to fail once more. What they fail to realize is that affirmative action alone is not enough to achieve management diversity at all levels. The goal can no longer be assimilation, but management and affirmation of unassimilated diversity.

Persons brought to the organization by competent selection must be provided with environments allowing diverse individuals to thrive. According to Thomas (1990), "So long as racial and gender equality is something we grant to minorities and women, there will be no racial and gender equality. What we must do is create an environment where no one is advantaged or disadvantaged, an environment where 'we' is everyone" (p. 109). Thomas (1990) likens the situation to a car engine designed to run on regular fuel: changing to a mixed fuel does not just require pumping the new gas in, but requires basic changes to the engine itself to allow it to run effectively on the new fuel. Organizations have tried—and often failed—to assimilate different types of people by hiring without changing the basic assumptions and behaviors driving the organization. Small wonder that many persons with different backgrounds found such organizations to be inhospitable places in which to build their career. Future selection practices may play a role in creating more agreeable environments by identifying applicants who, in addition to other credentials, score high on measures of interpersonal sensitivity or who have successfully worked in diverse environments in previous jobs.

Identifying Leaders Who Can Manage Diversity

Successful management of a diverse workforce is now a key issue for organizations. Research suggests that increasing differences in supervisor-subordinate demographics in terms of age, gender, race, education, and job and company tenure are associated with lower supervisor perceptions of subordinate effectiveness, less liking for the subordinate, and greater subordinate role ambiguity (Tsui & O'Reilly, 1989). If diverse employees are to have equal chances of success on the job, the first line of needed action is with supervisors and managers. Although no one expects to eliminate lifelong attitudes over the course of a few days' training, current managers are being sent for training in managing diversity in large numbers as a way of developing awareness. For example, Wang Laboratories has sent more than one thousand managers through their diversity-training program (Braham, 1989), and Mobil has been using such programs since 1986 (Kleeb, 1989). The Towers Perrin (1990) survey reports that about 29 percent of companies are currently doing something to train managers to deal with diversity.

Although typically lacking in clear evaluation data indicating objective measures of program success, the experiences of some companies (for example, Digital Equipment) that have increased retention of minorities since program implementation are encouraging. The number of initiatives being undertaken is enormous, and organizations go about it quite differently and for different reasons. The second Society for Industrial and Organizational Psychology Practice Series book presents in-depth case analyses of different organizational experiences with managing diversity (Jackson, 1992). These cases demonstrate that the strategies proposed to manage diversity are as diverse as the workforce itself.

Future challenges for managerial selection and promotion will include the identification of individuals capable of working with diverse individuals rather than solely training existing managers. As with the selection of workers at all levels, skills and abilities related to interpersonal sensitivity, cultural awareness, and acceptance of differences may take on new prominence. Further research in selection is critically needed, first to identify the requisite skills for working with diversity and then to develop appropriate selection strategies to assess it. Given the present and projected demographic changes, such research should be a high priority in personnel selection.

CONCLUSION

The changes in workers and work itself pose numerous challenges for organizations. Some organizations are already facing staffing shortages and are devising new solutions to their selection problems. Other organizations have chosen not to respond to the changes predicted, perhaps in the hope of riding out the current trends until conditions similar to those of the past are restored. Those organizations should recognize that in terms of demographics, it was the baby boom that was the anomaly (Greller, 1990). The present so-called bust is actually a reestablishment of more typical birth patterns. A return to past conditions of wide choices within a limited demographic group is considered very unlikely. The organizations that make changes now will be the ones that will have the resilience to accommodate workers of many backgrounds, use their diverse talents, and make themselves strong market forces.

As the costs of recruitment and selection escalate, retraining trained employees becomes ever more critical. As selection prospects are found lacking in basic skills, placement models combined with organizational training will gain in prominence. The increased importance of training and retraining does not substitute for good selection, but rather supplements it. The best HR management systems will integrate the traditional personnel functions of recruitment, selection, placement, and training into a coordinated total effort. It will not be enough to select people for the skills they currently possess, but rather for their potential to learn and adapt through training as conditions change. It will not be enough to recruit and select diverse individuals, but rather consideration must be given to changing organizational culture, procedures, and practices to use effectively the skills provided by this diversity. This indicates a need for training not only for those entering the organization but also for present employees.

The trends described in this chapter indicate that those of us working with organizations on selection issues will see many changes in the years ahead. Although the projections described in this chapter provide a reasonable future scenario, changes in economic, social, and organizational conditions can all affect the future reality. Changes made by organizations today can have tremendous impact on the choices made by current and potential workers. In keeping with the change in the U.S. economy from products to services, Bowen and Greiner (1986) suggest that it is we ourselves who need a change from the traditional selection "product orientation" of stamping persons as qualified or unqualified to a greater "service orientation" whereby we provide individuals matched to different client needs. That service orientation should continue once individuals are selected and placed to permit them an environment in which they can thrive and contribute. Only then will we have achieved the dual objectives of fully using the nation's diverse human resources and improving organizational performance.

References

Abraham, Y. T., & Bowdidge, J. S. (1990). Work-place child care act: A prototypical portrayal of potential public policies. *Public Personnel Management, 19,* 411–418.

Adler, N. J. (1991). *International dimensions of organizational behavior* (2nd ed.). Boston: PWS-Kent.

Adopt a school. (1990, September). *The Atlantic,* p. 23.

Anastasi, A. (1988). *Psychological testing* (6th ed.). New York: Macmillan.

Arnett, E. C. (1989, July 20). Futurists gaze into business's crystal ball. *Washington Post,* pp. F1–F2.

Bemis, S. E., Belenky, A. H., & Soder, D. A. (1983). *Job analysis: An effective management tool.* Washington, DC: Bureau of National Affairs.

Bowen, D. E., & Greiner, L. E. (1986). Moving from production to service in human resources management. *Organizational Dynamics, 15,* 34–53.

Braham, J. (1989). No, you don't manage everyone the same. *Industry Week, 238,* 28–35.

Byham, W. C. (1990). Keep job candidates from becoming lost hires. *HR Magazine, 35*(12), 52–54.

Colberg, M., Nester, M. A., & Trattner, M. H. (1985). Convergence of the inductive and deductive models in the measurement of reasoning abilities. *Journal of Applied Psychology, 70,* 681–694.

Corts, D. B., & Gowing, M. K. (1992). *Dimensions of effective behavior: Executives, managers, and supervisors* (PRD-92-05). Washington, DC: U.S. Office of Personnel Management.

Courtney, R. S. (1986). A human resources program that helps management and employees prepare for the future. *Personnel, 65,* 32–40.

DeLoux, G. (1990). Is your maternity policy ready for the 90's? *HR Magazine, 35*(11), 61–62.

Dole, E. (1990). Four by four: "Ready, set, work," says labor secretary. *Training & Development Journal, 44,* 17–22.

Dreyfuss, J. (1990). Get ready for the new work force. *Fortune, 121,* 165–181.

Dunnette, M. D. (1966). *Personnel selection and placement.* Belmont, CA: Wadsworth.

Dye, D. A. (1990). An explication of a model for assessing the quality of the federal work force. Washington, DC: U.S. Office of Personnel Management.

Eccles, R. (1991, January–February). The performance measurement manifesto. *Harvard Business Review, 69*, 131–137.

Federal Quality Institute. (1990). *Federal total quality management handbook: How to get started.* Washington, DC: Author.

Fleishman, E. A., & Quaintance, M. K. (1984). *Taxonomies of human performance: The description of human tasks.* San Diego, CA: Academic Press.

Fuchsberg, G. (1991, January 22). Despite layoffs, firms find some jobs hard to fill. *The Wall Street Journal*, pp. B1, B3.

Gandy, J. A., Outerbridge, A. N., Sharf, J. C., & Dye, D. A. (1989). *Development and initial validation of the individual achievement record (IAR).* Washington, DC: U.S. Office of Personnel Management.

Goddard, R. (1990). Lateral moves enhance careers. *HR Magazine, 35*(12), 69–70.

Goodman, P. S., Devadas, R., & Hughson, T.L.G. (1988). Groups and productivity: Analyzing the effectiveness of self-managing teams. In J. P. Campbell, R. J. Campbell, & Associates, *Productivity in organizations: New perspectives from industrial and organizational psychology* (pp. 295–327). San Francisco: Jossey-Bass.

Green, B. F. (1991). Guidelines for computer testing. In T. B. Gutkin & S. L. Wise (Eds.), *The computer and the decisionmaking process.* Hillsdale, NJ: Erlbaum.

Greller, M. M. (1990). The changing work force and organization effectiveness: An agenda for change. *Journal of Organizational Change Management, 3*, 4–15.

Greller, M. M., & Nee, D. M. (1989). *From baby boom to baby bust: How business can meet the demographic challenge.* Reading, MA: Addison-Wesley.

Guzzo, R. A. (1988). Productivity research: Reviewing psychological and economic perspectives. In J. P. Campbell, R. J. Campbell, & Associates, *Productivity in organizations: New perspectives from industrial and organizational psychology* (pp. 63–81). San Francisco: Jossey-Bass.

Hall, D. T., & Richter, J. (1990). Career gridlock: Baby boomers hit the wall. *Academy of Management Executive, 4*, 7–22.

Harris, P. A. (1989). *A summary report on differential item functioning on a written ability test: An application of the Mantel-Haentzel procedure.* Unpublished manuscript, U.S. Office of Personnel Management, Washington, DC.

Hough, L. M., Eaton, N. K., Dunnette, M. D., Kamp, J. D., & McCloy, R. A. (1990). Criterion-related validities of personality constructs and the effect of response distortion on those validities. *Journal of Applied Psychology, 75*, 581–595.

Howard, A. (1986). College experiences and managerial performance. *Journal of Applied Psychology, 71*, 530–552.

Hunt, T., & Lindley, C. (1989). *Testing older adults: A reference guide to geropsychological assessments.* Austin, TX: Pro Ed.

Hunter, J. E., & Hunter, R. S. (1984). The validity and utility of alternative predictors of job performance. *Psychological Bulletin, 95*, 72–98.

Hyde, A. C. (1990). Quality measurement and TQM. *The Bureaucrat, 19*(4), 16–20.

Ingraham, P. W. (1990). Federal recruitment revisited. *The Bureaucrat, 19*(3), 13–17.

Jackson, S. E. (1992). *Diversity in the workplace: Human resource initiatives.* New York: Guilford Publications.

Joice, W. (1989). Home based employment: A consideration for public personnel management. *Public Personnel Management, 20,* 49–60.

Kleeb, R. (1989). Mobil drills holes through the color barrier. *Business & Society Review, 70,* 55–57.

Lombardo, M. M., & Eichinger, R. W. (1989). *Eighty-eight assignments for development in place: Enhancing the developmental challenge of existing jobs.* Greensboro, NC: Center for Creative Leadership.

MacLane, C. N. (1988, May). *After the PACE: A summary of alternatives research under the Luevano consent decree* (OED Report No. 88-16). Washington, DC: U.S. Office of Personnel Management.

Mahoney, T. A. (1988). Productivity defined: The relativity of efficiency, effectiveness, and change. In J. P. Campbell, R. J. Campbell, & Associates, *Productivity in organizations: New perspectives from industrial and organizational psychology.* (pp. 13–39). San Francisco: Jossey-Bass.

Martinez, M. (1990). Creative ways to employ people with disabilities. *HR Magazine, 35*(11), 40–44, 101.

McEvoy, G. M., & Cascio, W. F. (1989). Cumulative evidence of the relationship between employee age and job performance. *Journal of Applied Psychology, 74,* 11–17.

Morrison, A. M., & Von Glinow, M. A. (1990). Women and minorities in management. *American Psychologist, 45,* 200–208.

Mumford, M. D., Fleishman, E. A., Levin, K. Y., Korotkin, A., & Hein, M. B. (1988). *Taxonomic efforts in the description of leadership behavior: A synthesis and cognitive interpretation.* Unpublished manuscript, George Mason University, Fairfax, VA.

National Commission of the Public Service. (1989). Leadership for America: Rebuilding the public service. Washington, DC: Author.

Northrop, L. C. (1989). *The psychometric history of selected ability constructs.* Washington, DC: U.S. Office of Personnel Management.

Offermann, L. R., & Gowing, M. K. (1990). Organizations of the future: Changes and challenges. *American Psychologist, 45,* 95–108.

O'Leary, B. S., Rheinstein, J., & McCauley, D. E., Jr. (1989, November). *Developing a taxonomy of generalized work behaviors.* Paper presented at the annual conference of the Military Testing Association, San Antonio, TX.

O'Leary, B. S., Rheinstein, J., & McCauley, D. E., Jr. (1990, November). *Developing job families using generalized work behaviors.* Paper presented at the annual conference of the Military Testing Association, Orange Beach, AL.

Outerbridge, A. N. (1981). *The development of generalizable work behavior categories for a synthetic validity model* (Report No. PRR-81-1). Washington, DC: U.S. Office of Personnel Management.

Pearlman, K. (1980). Job families: A review and discussion of their implications for personnel selection. *Psychological Bulletin, 87,* 1–27.

Pearlman, K., Schmidt, F. L., & Hunter, J. E. (1980). Validity generalization results for tests used to predict job proficiency and training success in clerical occupations. *Journal of Applied Psychology, 65,* 373–406.

Peters, T. J. (1988). *Thriving on chaos.* New York: Knopf.

Petrock, F. (1990). Corporate culture enhances profits. *HR Magazine, 35*(11), 64–66.

Quaintance, M. K. (1989). Internal placement and career management. In W. F. Cascio & D. H. Sweet (Eds.), *Human resource planning employment and placement.* Washington, DC: Bureau of National Affairs.

Reich, R. B. (1991). *The work of nations: Preparing ourselves for 21st century capitalism.* New York: Knopf.

Reilly, R. R., & Chao, G. T. (1982). Validity and fairness of some alternative employee selection procedures. *Personnel Psychology, 35,* 1–62.

Reilly, R. R., Henry, S., & Smither, J. W. (1990). An examination of the effects of using behavior checklists on the construct validity of assessment center dimensions. *Personnel Psychology, 43,* 71–84.

Rothstein, H. R., Schmidt, F. L., Erwin, F. W., Owens, W. A., & Sparks, C. P. (1990). Biographical data in employment selection: Can validities be made generalizable? *Journal of Applied Psychology, 75,* 175–184.

Schein, E. H. (1981). Increasing organizational effectiveness through better human resource planning and development. In D. E. Klinger (Ed.), *Public personnel management: Readings in context and strategies.* Palo Alto, CA: Mayfield.

Schmidt, F. L., Hunter, J. E., & Pearlman, K. (1981). Task differences as moderators of aptitude test validity in selection: A red herring. *Journal of Applied Psychology, 66,* 166–185.

Shore, T. H., Thornton, G. C., III, & Shore, L. M. (1990). Construct validity of two categories of assessment center dimension ratings. *Personnel Psychology, 43,* 105–116.

Skinner, B. F. (1990). Can psychology be a science of mind? *American Psychologist, 45,* 1206–1210.

Steinhaus, S. D., & Morris, G. W. (1990). Human resource evaluation for the 1990s and the workforce 2000. *Journal of Organization Change Management, 3,* 80–94.

Tenopyr, M. L. (1981). The realities of employment testing. *American Psychologist, 36,* 1120–1127.

Thomas, R. R., Jr. (1990, March–April). From affirmative action to affirming diversity. *Howard Business Review,* 107–117.

Toffler, A. (1980). The third wave. New York: Morrow.

Towers Perrin. (1990). *Work force 2000: Competing in a seller's market.* New York: Author.

Tsui, A. S., & O'Reilly, C. A., III (1989). Beyond simple demographic effects: The importance of relational demography in superior-subordinate dyads. *Academy of Management Journal, 32,* 402–423.

Tuttle, T. C. (1988). Technology, organizations of the future, and non-management roles. In J. Huge (Ed.), *Futures of organizations* (pp. 163–180). Lexington, MA: Lexington Books.

U.S. Office of Personnel Management. (1990, September). Survey indicates 22% increase in working at home. *Flexiplace Focus, 4.*

U.S. Office of Personnel Management. (1991). A proposal for multipurpose occupational systems analysis inventory—closed-end (MOSAIC). Washington, DC: Author.

Wellback, H. C., Hall, D. T., Morgan, M. A., & Hamner, W. C. (1983). Planning job progression for effective career development and human resources management. In K. M. Rowland, G. R. Ferris, & J. L. Sherman (Eds.), *Current issues in personnel management* (2nd ed.). Needham Heights, MA: Allyn & Bacon.

HIRING FOR THE
ORGANIZATION, NOT THE JOB

David E. Bowen,
Gerald E. Ledford, Jr.,
and Barry R. Nathan

Executive Overview

This article examines a new approach to selection in which employees are hired to fit the characteristics of an organization, not just the requirements of a particular job. Diverse firms—high and low-tech, U.S. and Japanese-owned—are using the approach to build cultures that rely heavily on self-motivated, committed people for corporate success. New, often expensive, hiring practices are changing the traditional selection model. An organizational analysis supplements a job analysis, and personality attributes are screened in addition to skills, knowledge, and abilities. We outline the basic steps of the new selection model and present a case description of a manufacturing company that used the model in hiring employees to work in its high-involvement organization. The new model works to its fullest advantage in organizations that allow employees enough freedom to use their unique attributes to influence job performance.

Conventional selection practices are geared toward hiring employees whose knowledge, skills, and abilities (KSAs) provide the greatest fit with clearly defined requirements of specific jobs. Traditional selection techniques rarely consider characteristics of the organization in which the jobs reside. Traditional techniques also ignore characteristics of the person that are irrelevant to immediate job requirements. In common management parlance, the organization hires new "hands" or new "heads"—that is, parts of people.

A new model of selection is emerging, however, that is geared toward hiring a "whole" person who will fit well into the specific organization's culture. It reflects a fundamental reorientation of the selection process toward hiring "people," not just KSAs, for "organizations," not just jobs. This leads to hiring practices that seem peculiar, and needlessly extravagant, from a traditional

Source: "Hiring For the Organization Not the Job" by David E. Bowen, Gerald E. Ledford, Jr., and Barry R. Nathan, *Academy of Management Executive*, 1991, Vol. 5, No. 4, 35–51.

human resource standpoint. Consider the hiring practices of three different organizations.

- AFG Industries builds two new float glass plants. The plants use practices such as work teams, extensive training, and skill-based pay that create a high level of employee involvement. The hiring process for factory workers includes screening formal resumes (not job applications), personality testing, pre-employment training that simulates some plant jobs, interviews with panels of managers and/or employees, and a medical exam.

- Sun Microsystems is the fastest-growing U.S. company in the past five years, with annual growth averaging more than 100 percent.[1] Filling open jobs is critical to Sun's effectiveness, phenomenal growth, and profitability. Yet, the hiring process is extremely time-consuming and labor-intensive. Potential hires at all levels are brought into the organization from four to seven times for interviews with up to twenty interviewers. The process is full of ambiguity, lacks formal rules, and demands that all employees engage in problem solving to get themselves hired.

- Toyota (USA) screens 50,000 applications for 3,000 factory jobs in the initial staffing of its plant in Georgetown, Kentucky.[2] Each employee hired invests at least eighteen hours in a selection process that includes a general knowledge exam, a test of attitudes toward work, an interpersonal skills assessment center, a manufacturing exercise designed to provide a realistic job preview of assembly work, an extensive personal interview, and a physical exam.

As we shall see, these organizations adopt unusual hiring practices to find employees who fit the organization and to encourage those who do not fit to seek employment elsewhere. Although potential hires with skills that meet the demands of specific jobs are not ignored, these companies maintain that the person-job fit needs to be supported and enriched by person-organization fit. These companies are willing to invest substantial resources in rigorously assessing this fit. Why and how organizations approach hiring in this way are explored in this article.

How Important are Hiring Decisions, Really? The Person-Situation Controversy Revisited

Is individual behavior, such as job performance, a function of the person (attributes of an employee), the situation (characteristics of the work setting), or the interaction of the person and situation? This question is age-old. Proponents of employee selection as a key to human resource effectiveness answer that individual behavior is largely a function of the person. Selection techniques attempt to capitalize on enduring differences between individuals by choosing those individuals who are best suited to the job. Conversely, advocates of socialization and training practices that attempt to mold employees after they are hired assume that the situation is the principal determinant of individual behavior.[3] The majority of researchers and managers subscribe to some form of the interactionist perspective. They assume that both the person and the situation matter, and that the combination of the two determines individual performance and other behaviors.

A basic assumption of bureaucratic organizations is that individuals cannot be trusted to manage their own behavior. Thus, management designs the organization to control employee behavior as tightly as possible, through the managerial hierarchy, impersonal rules and procedures, close supervision, and extensive socialization and training.

We argue that both researchers and managers have overemphasized the situation and have paid only lip service to the individual in recent years. In research on organizational behavior, people variables (for example, needs) usually are treated as secondary to situational variables (for example, job designs) and researchers generally are skeptical about the ability of personality variables to predict job performance.[4] Managerial interest in individual testing appears to have dropped sharply after several 1970 court decisions held that unvalidated and discriminatory selection procedures were illegal.

An overemphasis on the importance of the situation fits the managerial ideology dominant among American corporations. A basic assumption of bureaucratic organizations is that individuals cannot be trusted to manage their own behavior. Thus, management designs the organization to control employee behavior as tightly as possible, through the managerial hierarchy, impersonal rules and procedures, close supervision, and extensive socialization and training. This curtails the expression of individual differences in behavior. As a result, the organization is designed to be what researchers have called a "strong situation," one in which the intensity of the situation suppresses variation in behavior that is attributable to the person.[5] Thus, managers create a self-fulfilling prophesy. The belief that the situation is the most important predictor of behavior leads to the organizational design which suppresses individual differences. This self-fulfilling pattern is further reinforced by basing hiring decisions on a single, brief interview, which has proved to be unreliable and of poor validity.[6] It is not surprising, then, that managers often conclude that the selection system is not a key success factor.

Yet, some organizations are designed as "weak situations," allowing a range of employee responses to work requirements.[7] These organizations have less control over individuals and the effects of person variables are greater. In such organizations, it is more important than in traditional organizations to do a good job of hiring the right people.

Consider the three organizations we described at the beginning of this article. They are more different than similar. They include high-tech and moderately low-tech, manufacturing-driven and engineering-driven, white collar and blue collar, and U.S.-owned and Japanese-owned firms. Yet these organizations share a set of management assumptions about organizational success. Each is attempting to build a distinctive culture that is intentionally "fragile," meaning that management relies heavily on self-motivated, committed people for system effectiveness.[8] While all three organizations have a management hierarchy, organizational policies, and other tools of external control, all rely to an unusual degree on employees to make the system work effectively. And they use sophisticated selection systems to hire the whole person whose skills and personality fit the type of organization, not just a job.

THE NEW SELECTION MODEL: HIRING FOR PERSON-ORGANIZATION FIT

Exhibit 1 presents the new selection model for hiring for person-organization fit. As we shall see, it differs from the traditional selection model in several important

Exhibit 1

A HIRING PROCESS FOR PERSON-ORGANIZATION FIT

1. ASSESS THE OVERALL WORK ENVIRONMENT
   – Job analysis
   – Organizational analysis

2. INFER THE TYPE OF PERSON REQUIRED
   – Technical knowledge, skills and abilities
   – Social skills
   – Personal needs, values, and interests
   – Personality traits

3. DESIGN "RITES OF PASSAGE" FOR ORGANIZATION ENTRY THAT ALLOW BOTH THE ORGANIZATION AND THE APPLICANT TO ASSESS THEIR FIT
   – Tests of cognitive, motor, and interpersonal abilities
   – Interviews by potential co-workers and others
   – Personality tests
   – Realistic job previews, including work samples

4. REINFORCE PERSON-ORGANIZATION FIT AT WORK
   – Reinforce skills and knowledge through task design and training
   – Reinforce personal orientation through organization design

ways.[9] Our model represents a synthesis of the steps taken by the organizations mentioned in our opening case examples as well as by other progressive firms. Although any one firm may not fully implement every step, all of these steps together offer the best guarantee of person-organization fit.

We will describe the steps in the model and then present a case description of a firm where hiring practices are a close match to the ideal. First, however, we clarify the meaning of "person-organization fit."

Person-Organization Fit

The model in Exhibit 1 places the selection process in the context of a rich interaction between the person and the organization, both of which are more broadly defined and assessed than in the traditional selection model.

Person-organization fit requires that two types of fit be achieved in the hiring process: (1) between the KSAs of the individual and the task demands or critical requirements for the job; and (2) between the overall personality of the individual (e.g. needs, interests, and values) and the climate or culture of the organization.

The traditional selection model focuses almost exclusively on the first type of fit (KSAs—job) while tending to ignore, or assessing far less rigorously, the second types (personality—climate/culture).[10] The narrow focus of the traditional selection model reflects several factors. One is that managers tend to think of individual job performance as the key outcome of the hiring process and they believe that job performance is a function of the fit between KSAs and task demands. Additionally, the traditional selection model is more concerned with finding new employees than with retaining them. There is less attention to whether the whole person finds the organization's culture satisfying enough to stay. Organizations have also been constrained by the unavailability of proven selection technologies for producing the fit between personality and climate/culture. This situation can be improved, we believe, by following the steps for hiring that are described next.

Step One: Assess the Work Environment

The job analysis of the traditional model of selection is also conducted in the new model. It remains instrumental in achieving the fit between individual KSAs and task demands. Alternative job analysis techniques include the position analysis questionnaire, task inventories, and critical incident techniques.[11]

While many job analyses include evaluations of the work context, the person-organization fit model explicitly recognizes that successful employees have knowledge, skills, abilities, and other personal characteristics that match both the content and the context of the job.

The purpose of an organizational analysis is to define and assess the work environment in terms of the characteristics of the organization, rather than just in terms of the characteristics of a specific job. It identifies the behaviors and responsibilities that lead to organizational effectiveness, and implies the personal characteristics most likely to be associated with such behaviors and responsibilities. Organizational analysis also is important because job analysis data may quickly become outdated as rapidly changing products and technologies reshape employees' jobs. The organization's overall philosophy and values are likely to be more stable and consequently, the more important long-term focus for fit.

Techniques for organizational analysis are not well-established, largely because there is little research that systematically associates the characteristics of organizations and individual behavior patterns. Managers need to identify the important dimensions of the organization and their implications for the kinds of employees who would best fit those situations. Although organizational analysis techniques are not nearly as well-developed as job analysis techniques, a variety of methods are available. For example, the training field offers guidelines for conducting an organizational analysis as one component of a training needs analysis. Organization characteristics assessed include short- and long-term goals, staffing needs, properties of the environment (for example, stability), and employee perceptions of organization climate. Organizational culture audits have emerged in the last decade that offer both qualitative and quantitative methods for describing an organization's norms and values.[12] Quite promising is a sophisticated Q-sort methodology that assesses the content, integrity, and crystallization of organizational values and matches them with an assessment of individual values.[13] Finally, there is a long-standing approach to diagnosing the characteristics of an organization's four subsystems (individuals, tasks, organizational arrangements, informal organization) that can yield organizational analysis data.[14]

Organization analysis does not replace job analysis. Rather it ensures that important components of the work context as well as its content are identified and evaluated for their importance to job success. While many job analyses include evaluations of the work context, the person-organization fit model explicitly recognizes that successful employees have knowledge, skills, abilities, and other personal characteristics that match both the *content* and the *context* of the job.

Step Two: Infer the Type of Person Required

In step two, managers deal with applicants in terms of who they are, not just what they can do. It is still necessary to infer from the job analysis the KSAs that employees need to be technically competent. However, step two also requires inferring, from the organizational analysis, the needs, values and interests—that is, the personality—an employee must possess to be an effective member of the organization. For example, if the organizational analysis reveals that teamwork is a key norm or value in the setting, then selection tools must be used to find people who are team players. Furthermore, social and interpersonal skills will be necessary, in addition to the cognitive and motor abilities that are the dominant skills-focus of the traditional selection model.

The move by some organizations toward hiring the total person coincides with a renewed interest by researchers in personality as a predictor of job attitudes and behaviors. These researchers believe that studies in which personality measures fail to predict job performance often have been plagued by problems such as focusing on personality aspects of questionable relevance to the job, poor research methods, and so on.[15] These problems have given personality a bad name and fostered the impression that the situation matters much more than the person in influencing job attitudes and performance. In contrast, more recent research has yielded such interesting findings that individual personality attributes can predict job satisfaction later—more than fifty years and even for different jobs. The research implies that job satisfaction may be associated with a stable, enduring personality attribute rather than a function of the situation.[16] This indicates that the types of people hired is very important.

Organizations also must pay attention to technical skills needed by the organization. Often applicants with the most appropriate personalities and social skills are not those with the right technical skills. If the organization faces the need to upgrade technical skills quickly, it may be forced to make tradeoffs. Organizations in this situation often place greater weight on personality and social skills, on the grounds that it is easier to train technical skills than change personalities or develop social skills. This can lead to increased short-term training costs and temporary overstaffing. However, if the work technology is complex and training times are long, management may be forced to hire some employees who better fit the organization's technical requirements than its cultural requirements. Douglas Bray, noted pioneer of the AT&T Management Progress Study, considers this tradeoff and suggests that selection decisions about needs, values, and interests may be more critical than those for skills.[17] For example, a desire to learn new jobs is an attribute that cannot be taught easily to employees, as job skills can. You either hire people who have this attribute, or do without.

Step Three: Design "Rites of Passage" That Allow the Organization and the Individual to Assess Fit

The battery of screens used in the new approach to hiring may seem designed to discourage individuals from taking the job.[18] Yet, these screens have several

First, the use of multiple screening methods, raters, and criteria has long been recommended by researchers as the best approach to hiring.[19] Yet most organizations still hire employees using a single interview with a single interviewer.

purposes. First, the use of multiple screening methods, raters, and criteria has long been recommended by researchers as the best approach to hiring.[19] Yet most organizations still hire employees using a single interview with a single interviewer. More sophisticated techniques, if used, typically are reserved for executives and sometimes sales people. Second, multiple screenings not only allow the organization to select employees, but also provides applicants with sufficient realistic information about the work environment so that they can make an informed choice about whether they even want the job. Third, the people who join the organization feel special. They have survived the elaborate rites of passage necessary to join the organization. They experience the sense of accomplishment associated with completing boot camp when entering military service.

A recent *Fortune* article described these fresh approaches as "The New Art of Hiring Smart."[20] One ingredient has been increased use of job simulation exercises for assembly workers. These simulations, or work sample tests, help both the person and the organization assess fit. The applicant receives a realistic job preview of the work. The organization has an opportunity to assess applicants' technical skills and, when group interaction is required in an exercise, their interpersonal skills as well. Intelligence tests also seem to be on the rebound.

Sun Microsystems offers a good example of the use of rites of passage to allow mutual assessment of fit. This fast-growing Silicon Valley firm, like many high-technology companies, is constantly changing in response to rapidly developing markets, evolving technologies, and the pace of internal growth. Employees who prefer clear job descriptions, stability, a leisurely pace, and predictability would be unhappy at Sun. The hiring process is such a challenge, and so full of ambiguity, that unsuitable applicants tend to give up before the process is completed. Those hired have survived multiple interviews with many different possible co-workers. A joke at Sun is, "after seven sets of interviews, we put applicants on the payroll whether they've been hired or not." The hiring process thus introduces prospective employees to the culture of the organization.

Personality tests are another way to assess mutual fit. It appears that "personality tests are back."[21] For example, the Meyers-Briggs Type Indicator is used by companies such as Allied Signal, Apple, AT&T, Citicorp, Exxon, G.E., Honeywell, and 3M. These tests are used primarily in management development programs. However, personality tests are used increasingly as selection tests, particularly for assembly worker positions.

There is renewed interest in personality tests even though past efforts to validate them have been largely unsuccessful.[22] However, there is a growing belief that personality tests can be validated under the proper conditions.[23] These include:

1. Using personality measures that are tailored to the work setting. Major personality tests were not developed for work settings, so their poor track record in validation studies is not surprising.

2. Using personality measures to predict global criteria. That is, multi-faceted measures of job attitudes and behaviors, rather than one specific criterion such as quarterly sales.

3. Using measures of personality dimensions that are logically or theoretically associated with the work in the organization. This contrasts with screening for personality attributes that are not job related but hold some particular interest to managers.

Whereas personality tests provide organizations with information about applicants, realistic job previews (RJPs) provide applicants with information about organizations. Examples of RJPs are the Toyota USA job simulations/work sample tests that show applicants the repetitive nature of manufacturing work and the requirements for teamwork. Applicants can then make informed choices about whether they would be satisfied there. "Turned-off" applicants may drop out of the hiring process. Those hired are more likely to join the organization with a sense of commitment and realistic expectations. Fundamentally, an RJP helps individuals decide if they want to join an organization, based on their own assessment of their personality and how it might fit with a particular type of organization.[24]

Step Four: Reinforce Person-Organization Fit at Work

Selection is clearly the first and, arguably, the most important step in implementing a fragile system philosophy. However, the hiring process must be integrated with, and supported by, the firm's other human resource management practices. Japanese-owned plants in the U.S. and high involvement organizations illustrate this point.

Japanese automobile manufacturers operating in the United States provide examples of how to accomplish this. The Japanese "Auto Alley" in the U.S. provided more than 6,000 assembly jobs in 1989. Key operations include Nissan in Smyrna, Tennessee; Toyota in Georgetown, Kentucky; Honda in Marysville, Ohio; Mazda in Flat Rock, Michigan; and Diamond-Star Motors Corporation in Normal, Illinois.[25] The Japanese have attempted to create a certain type of organization, characterized by now-familiar values of teamwork, consensual decision-making, peer control, egalitarianism, and non-specialized career paths. Broad job classifications encourage employee flexibility, rather than identification with specific jobs. Extensive on-the-job training and job rotation further increase flexibility. Group activities encourage employees to contribute ideas for organizational improvement and promote teamwork. Employment stability helps the organization realize a return on its training and other investments in human resources, and increases employee loyalty to the organization. Thus, a selection system in such organizations typically screens for interest in work variety, social needs and skills, and organization commitment.

High involvement organizations (HIOs) are another class of organization that uses multiple systems to support hiring for person-organization fit. HIOs are a relatively new organizational form; there are perhaps a few hundred examples now existing in the U.S.[26] HIO's have two key characteristics.[27] First, the organization is designed to create very high levels of employee involvement. Power, information, skills, and rewards for performance are pushed down to the lowest levels of the organization. Self-managed teams or other structures enable employees to share decision-making power. Extensive training in technical, social, and business skills provides team members with the skills needed for effective self-management. Information systems communicate the performance data that teams need to manage themselves. Reward systems such as skill-based pay and gainsharing motivate needed behaviors, such as learning and problem solving. For obvious reasons, hiring practices in HIOs typically attempt to select employees who prefer working in groups and who have high needs for personal growth and development. Thus, the hiring process is one design element of many that must fit with the overall design.

The following case description of the hiring process in a new HIO illustrates all four steps of the new selection model.

Hiring for Person-Organization Fit: The Case of a Start-up High Involvement Organization

The research reported here was conducted as part of an action research project at a new float glass plant in the western United States.[28] The plant is a classic new HIO. Research on the selection system described here is part of a larger, on-going action research effort. Management was interested in developing selection procedures and tools for hiring employees with the necessary job skills, needs, and aspirations to fit the organization design. Researchers helped design the hiring process, conducted extensive research on the initial hiring process at the plant, and explored the validity of personality measures as possible future selection tools. The overall effort essentially followed the four steps previously discussed for hiring for person-organization fit.

Step One: Assess the Work Environment

Since the plant was a start-up operation, there were no existing jobs to analyze in this initial step. There were individual jobs with comparable content at other organizational sites, but management was committed to designing the new plant as the first high involvement organization in the company. Thus, analyzing the work environment of the existing plants would have been of limited use in designing a hiring process to match the new HIO. Instead, top management and two of the researcher/consultants (the second author and Tom Cummings of the University of Southern California) conducted an organizational analysis to assess key desired organizational characteristics, norms, and values. This analysis followed standard sociotechnical systems procedures, and specifically considered requirements for the level of employee growth and social needs. This led to the development of the management philosophy and practices that would define the new organization. A customized version of the HIO concept, tailored to the needs of the organization, emerged from this work.

Glass-making lent itself to an HIO design for several reasons. First, there was a great deal of task interdependence which required worker cooperation and teamwork. Second, technical uncertainty was high. Workers were responsible for making immediate decisions about the glass-making process from the procurement to furnace melting of raw materials and various stages of cooling, inspecting, cutting, packing, and storing. The plant's profitability is directly related to production efficiency and glass quality. Quality is directly dependent on workers' ability to maintain a continual, steady flow of glass, by constantly monitoring and regulating the temperature and speed of flow of the product through the system. Deviations from desired parameters must be corrected as soon as possible after detection. Internal control by employees is more responsive to system fluctuations than external control through supervision, rules, and procedures.

This work environment led management to adopt a work design that encouraged high levels of employee teamwork and decision making. Employees were organized into self-regulating work teams at each sequential stage of production. Management saw this job design as most appropriate for the relatively high task interdependence and task uncertainty of the plant technology. Management expected that as team members developed technical and social skills, they would make joint decisions about work methods and assignments and solve production problems on the line.

Step Two: Infer the Type of Person Required

Since work in the high involvement glass plant required understanding and becoming involved in the entire production process, selecting on the basis of technical skills was not enough. Basic KSAs, such as motor and arithmetic skills, while necessary, would not be sufficient for organizational success. Workers also had to feel a sense of commitment to working in this type of organization. Furthermore, the jobs were to be dynamic. Over time, employees were expected to learn different skills within their team and in other teams, and to take on an increasing share of decision making. Top management expected that the number of supervisors and layers of management would be reduced as the teams matured. A fit between applicant characteristics and the work requirements of a high involvement organization as a whole was required.

In addition to the necessary technical skills, two personality characteristics were especially important to the organization. One was growth need strength. The HIO design placed many demands on employees for continuous learning, decision making, and assuming responsibility for organizational structuring, functioning, and performance. For example, employees were required to train each other, give feedback to follow team members on their performance, and help design organizational changes. Applicants who desired little challenge or learning opportunity and those who prefer narrowly defined jobs would have been misfits with this organization. Conversely, those who valued or had strong needs for personal growth, accomplishment, and personal development would be more committed to working in the new plant.

A second relevant personality characteristic was social needs. This was obvious because self-regulating teams demand cooperation and teamwork. In addition, management planned to make heavy use of special problem-solving groups, committees, and task forces. Those who saw working with others as a burden would have been misfits in such a setting, while people with high social needs were expected to prefer group forms of work and group activities.

Step Three: Design "Rites of Passage" That Allow the Organization and the Individual to Assess Fit

Participants were given a realistic portrayal of what it would be like to work in a team-based, high involvement structure, including the kinds of work behaviors that would be expected.

The hiring process consisted of several stages that involved multiple methods, raters, and criteria. A state agency conducted an initial screen of approximately 1000 candidates responding to local advertisements about job openings at the plant, which was then under construction. At this stage applicants received scores for their education and experience, such as a high school degree or GED, manufacturing or related experience, and ability to understand process instrumentation and complete a time card. In addition, tests using potential predictors based on personality and other survey questions also were administered at this time. Personality characteristics were assessed using the Personality Research Form— Form E, or PRF, a highly regarded personality assessment instrument.[29] The PRF measure of affiliation needs is very similar to social needs as described previously. Three PRF measures were relevant to growth needs: achievement, endurance, and dominance. (The dominance items measure desire to influence others or social achievement, not oppressiveness.) These two personality dimensions, affiliation and growth needs, were logically associated with the nature of work in an HIO and the PRF measures were moderately tailored to better fit the work setting. Of the 540 applicants who passed the initial screening and were invited to a pre-employment assessment and training program (described below), approximately 500 candidates responded.

Performance was assessed in four half-day sessions of a pre-employment assessment and training program, designed to capture characteristics of work in a high involvement float glass factory. The company used this program both as a selection tool and as a realistic job preview. As an RJP, the program showed how a high involvement organization is designed to operate, technical and social requirements, what it would be like to handle glass (for example, lacerations are common and special protective clothing is used to minimize the likelihood of injury), and various tasks employees would be expected to perform.

The program was divided into two approximately equal segments. One part involved work simulations consisting of handling and packing glass and operating hand tools and equipment required for glass making. Participants were given instructions about work methods, rules, and safety procedures, and engaged in glass making and packing tasks as a team. The second part of the training program involved classroom learning and experiential exercises aimed at group decision making. Almost half of the classroom time was used to present information about glass making and the design features of the high involvement plant, including self-regulating groups, participative leadership, egalitarian human-resource practices, skill-based pay, and gainsharing. Participants were given a realistic portrayal of what it would be like to work in a team-based, high involvement structure, including the kinds of work behaviors that would be expected. They also were tested on basic math and measurement skills needed to perform glass making and packaging tasks, as well as given homework covering basic processes and terminology used in making glass as well as the nature of one's work and responsibility in a high involvement organization.

For more than half of the classroom time, participants engaged in exercises designed to simulate the kind of group interaction and decision-making occurring in self-regulating groups. One exercise, for example, involved reaching a group consensus about the ranking of items needed to survive in the rugged outdoors. Another exercise involved role playing a group decision about which department should receive a new piece of equipment. These exercises were followed by extensive debriefing about members' behaviors and interactions and how the learning applies to the work of teams in the plant.

The scoring procedure evaluated applicants from a holistic perspective, that is how well each applicant fit in a high involvement setting rather than how he or she performed on individual job-related tasks. Applicants were evaluated by managers and supervisors who had received training on how to avoid common rater errors. Classroom activities, group exercises, and work simulations were scored. Applicants were evaluated on the quality and thoroughness of homework assignments and were required to attain minimum passing scores on arithmetic and tape measure reading tests. Group exercises were scored on the degree applicants exhibited participating, negotiating, gatekeeping, and probing behaviors. Finally, work simulations were scored on four factors: absence and tardiness over the four days; safety behavior; responsibility, meaning following instructions and not exhibiting disruptive or distracting behavior; and general behavior, meaning exhibiting team skills, paying attention to instructors, and not breaking plant rules or abusing equipment. Thus, the work simulations were not scored on task performance per se. Instead, they were scored on behaviors relevant to the overall success of the organization. This focus on behaviors ensured that the selection process could be defended legally, if necessary, on the basis of content validity.

The pre-employment assessment and training program met two important goals. First, it was consistent with technical and professional standards for employment selection. As in assessment centers, job behaviors were sampled systematically across different situations. Multiple and diverse activities and assessment methods afforded evaluators an opportunity to assess how well applicants would fit into an HIO generally, rather than just on how well applicants could perform specific tasks. The use of global criteria satisfied another condition for successfully validating a personality test as selection tools. Second, the program gave applicants a realistic job preview of what working in a high involvement glass plant would be like. The task activities provided applicants with a preview of the physical and potentially dangerous nature of the work. (One of the authors was present when a piece of tempered glass was mishandled and literally exploded in an applicant's hands.) The classroom activities prepared applicants for the organization's emphasis on working together and taking responsibility for action.

Those who passed this program were invited to a final selection interview with a panel of managers. This structured interview consisted of questions regarding manufacturing experience, education, understanding the high involvement and autonomous work group design, past experience and interest in group activities, and other performance skills and creative experiences. Finally, applicants were required to pass a physical examination including a drug screen. Ultimately, 250 applicants of the original 1000 applicants successfully completed these phases and the physical examination.

We subsequently validated the PRF personality test. Specifically, scores on the PRF were significantly correlated with performance in the pre-employment training program and with applicants anticipated satisfaction with work in the organization.[30] This means that it would be appropriate and legal for the company to use measures of social and growth needs from this test in future hiring decisions. Since the analysis was completed long after most employees had been hired at the site, however, the company did not use the test in hiring decisions.

Step Four: Reinforce Person-Organization Fit at Work

The objectives of the hiring process were reinforced by various organization design features that emphasized high involvement and team functioning. For example, extensive training was provided, both in technical skills and in social skills such as group decision making. A skill-based pay system gave employees increases in base pay for learning new jobs within their team. This in turn reinforced employees' interest in receiving training, which enabled them to earn pay increases. The plant adopted a gainsharing plan from the beginning that provided generous plant-wide monetary bonuses when plant performance met specific objectives. This reinforced the need for teamwork, since no individual could win a bonus at the expense of another. The gainsharing plan also provided incentives for exemplary performance and for developing improvements in the production process that could result in greater payouts. Extensive business information was routinely shared with employees, in part to make the gainsharing plan work more effectively. Employees were also involved as needed in task forces of various kinds to solve business, personnel, and other problems. In short, there was extensive reinforcement for the behaviors and characteristics that management sought during the hiring process.

The results of the hiring process have been positive. A survey of employees after startup indicated that employee quality of work life, according to various measures of satisfaction, organization commitment, and so on, was very high— a likely indication of person-organization fit. After an initial period of high turnover, turnover has dropped below national norms. On most key performance measures, the plant is one of the most effective in the company. Its main rival is

Extensive business information was routinely shared with employees, in part to make the gainsharing plan work more effectively. Employees were also involved as needed in task forces of various kinds to solve business, personnel, and other problems.

Exhibit 2

POTENTIAL BENEFITS AND PROBLEMS WITH
HIRING FOR PERSON-ORGANIZATION FIT

POTENTIAL BENEFITS
  1. More favorable employee attitudes (such as greater job satisfaction, organization commitment, and team spirit)
  2. More desirable individual behaviors (such as better job performance and lower absenteeism and turnover)
  3. Reinforcement of organizational design (such as support for work design and desired organizational culture)

POTENTIAL PROBLEMS
  1. Greater investment of resources in the hiring process
  2. Relatively undeveloped and unproven supporting selection technology
  3. Individual stress
  4. May be difficult to use the full model where payoffs are greatest
  5. Lack of organizational adaptation

---

another new high involvement plant that opened shortly after startup of the plant described here; it was developed on the same HIO model and used a similar hiring process. On the whole, it appears that the plant has been a very effective organization and that hiring for the organization, not just the job, has contributed to that effectiveness.

BENEFITS AND PROBLEMS FROM HIRING FOR PERSON-ORGANIZATION FIT

Clearly, the new approach to hiring for person-organization fit requires more resources than the traditional selection model. Is it worth the cost? Consider the potential benefits (see Exhibit 2).

(1) Employee Attitudes. Researchers have long proposed that a fit between individual needs and organizational climates and cultures would result in greater job satisfaction and organization commitment.[31] There is ample data documenting that the realistic job previews typically used in the new selection model are associated with higher on-the-job satisfaction.[32] Greater team spirit also is likely when new employees have shared the experience of moving successfully through the demanding rites of passage that lead to organizational entry.

Surveys of applicants in our case example indicated that these favorable attitudes were associated with the hiring process. For example, the majority of applicants felt the pre-employment training program accurately measured how well they could do the job and get along with others, and was a help in subsequent performance on the job and interacting with co-workers. Applicants also felt it provided a realistic preview of working at the plant. An overwhelming seventy seven percent reported that after going through pre-employment training, the work seemed more satisfying than when they first applied for the job. Only two percent thought it would be less satisfying.

(2) Employee Behaviors. Studies indicate that high involvement organizations, which typically use the new selection model, have low rates of absenteeism, turnover, and grievances.[33] The data are even clearer that using realistic job previews in Step 3 is associated with lower turnover.[34] We also have presented a strong case that person-organization fit will result in employees displaying more of what have been labelled "organizational citizenship behaviors." These are behaviors that employees perform above and beyond explicit job requirements. The thinking here is that fitted employees see themselves as really belonging to the organization and willing to invest their own resources in its on-going maintenance.[35]

(3) Reinforcement of Organization Design. The effectiveness of Japanese transplants that hire according to this model is common knowledge. HIOs often are very high performers. For example, a study of a large sample of high involvement organizations found that HIOs outperformed their industry on return on sales by an average of 532 percent and outperformed their industry on return on investment by an average of 388 percent.[36] Researchers often argue that the power of such an organization derives from the mutual reinforcement of its parts, including the selection process. The hiring process in HIOs helps select employees who are interested in challenging, responsible, varied jobs and pay systems that reward needed behaviors and performance.

Potential Problems

Hiring for person-organization fit may also have its disadvantages (see Exhibit 2):

(1) Greater Investment in Hiring. This model requires a much greater investment of resources in the hiring process. For example, Mazda in Flat Rock, Michigan spends about $13,000 per employee to staff its plant.[37] It appears that organizations hiring within this model are spending the same time and money on hiring an assembly worker as they do in conducting an executive search.

The costs of making revisions in the hiring process also are different in the new model. A traditional hiring process needs to be revised whenever the requirements of the job change significantly. A hiring process for person-organization fit needs to be changed whenever the business, technological, or cultural requirements of the organization change significantly. This means that changes in hiring practices for person-organization fit are likely to be less frequent but much greater in scope than changes in traditional hiring processes. A change in hiring practices for person-organization fit may well involve a change in how every new employee is hired.

(2) Undeveloped Selection Technology. The supporting selection technology is still relatively undeveloped and unproven. One problem is the still-thin track record of successfully validating personality tests against job performance. However, the present authors' study in which measures of growth needs and social needs predicted candidates' performance in a pre-employment simulation of high-involvement work demonstrates that personality measures, carefully chosen and developed, can be validated. Yet until personality tests acquire a deeper inventory of successful validation studies, organizations will doubt their usefulness.

In the context of person-organization fit, techniques for assessing people are more developed than those for assessing work environments. Even on the people side, though, the field is not nearly as sophisticated in measuring work-related personality facets as it is in assessing KSAs. Moreover, there is a great need for techniques of organizational analysis that are as sophisticated as those for job analysis (e.g., the PAQ). Overall, the challenge in organizational analysis is to: (a) identify relevant underlying dimensions of settings and how they can be measured, (b) determine the major impact on individual attitudes and behaviors, and organizational effectiveness, and (c) determine how such impacts differ depending upon individuals' personality.[38]

Managers may be concerned about the legality of these developing tools. More broadly, managers may be concerned about whether selecting for organization fit is legal. This concern is groundless, in our view. The legal standards for person-organization fit are no different than those for person-job fit. In general, selection procedures that do not result in adverse impact on protected minorities and women are not illegal. If the selection system does result in adverse impact, then evidence of job-relatedness must be presented. Job-relatedness is based on the content, construct, and criterion-related validity of the selection procedures. The procedures we have described establish job-relatedness.

In fact, there may be less adverse impact as a result of hiring for organization fit than in traditional hiring systems.

In fact, there may be less adverse impact as a result of hiring for organization fit than in traditional hiring systems. Traditional systems rely mostly on tests of abilities to predict job performance. Intellectual ability tests typically result in adverse impact against minorities, and physical ability tests often result in adverse impact against women. Organization fit, in contrast, is based largely on values, needs, and motives that may be more evenly distributed in the population.

(3) Employee Stress. Individuals fitted to "fragile systems" may find their organizational lives to be more stressful. The firms in the Japanese Auto Alley, high-involvement organizations, firms in the Silicon Valley, and so on, which rely on carefully selected people for system effectiveness are also laying substantial claims to those people's lives. This higher level of involvement at work may be associated with experiencing more stress on the job. These workers have reported that they now take work problems home with them and feel the strains more typically associated with managerial roles.[39]

(4) Difficult to Use the Full Model Where the Benefits are Greatest. A new hiring model may offer the greatest potential benefits to new organizations, such as new plants and startup companies. This is because hiring the right kinds of employees can help establish the desired culture of the organization from the very beginning. In existing organizations that are attempting to change their culture, there may be a long period in which the proportion of employees with unwanted attributes drops through attrition, while the proportion of employees with desired attributes gradually increases due to an improved hiring process.

Most of the hiring model we have described can be used in new organizations. However, one component of the model, specifically formal selection testing, often cannot be used appropriately or legally early in the life of the organization because the tests have not yet been validated. By the time the validation studies have been conducted, most of the workforce will have been hired. In some circumstances, it may be possible to avoid this problem by validating the tests before hiring in the new organization. For example, many companies that develop one high involvement organization (or other unusual culture) go on to develop others. It may be possible to validate the tests in an existing location if the culture of the existing organization and that desired of the new location are similar. AFG Industries, for example, could use the PRF test to hire employees in other plants that are designed as high involvement organizations.

Another way to avoid this problem is taken by Development Dimensions International, a consulting firm that designed the hiring system for Toyota's Kentucky plant as well as other hiring systems aimed at person-organization fit.[40] DDI identifies the desired characteristics of new hires through a diagnosis conducted with senior managers of the organization. Potential hires explicitly are told about the desired characteristics during the orientation process. Then, the new hires complete a Job Fit Inventory, which includes items relevant to the desired qualities of employees in the organization. The instrument intentionally is very "transparent" and fakeable. Thus, it does not serve the same purposes as personality tests. Rather, it is used to screen out the bottom five to fifteen percent of applicants—those who admit they lack the attributes that they are told explicitly that the company is seeking.

(5) Lack of Organizational Adaptation.   A problem could arise in hiring for the organization if it led to a workforce in which everyone had the same personality profile. The organization might become stagnant because everyone would share the same values, strengths, weaknesses, and blindspots. (Obviously, the issue is the same whether employees all tend to have the same point of view because of the selection system or because of training and socialization.) There has been considerable debate about whether a powerful organizational culture, whatever its source, leads to success or leads to dry rot and lack of innovativeness. There is some evidence, for example, indicating that organizations with little internal variability in employee perspectives perform better in the short run but worse in the long run, presumably as a result of inferior adaptation.[41]

However, we expect that significant internal variability will co-exist with person-organization fit. Even the best selection system is still imperfect; we do not succeed in hiring only the "right types." More fundamentally, the hiring process still results in variability on the desired characteristics. Even though all those hired may meet minimum standards, some will be higher than others on the desired characteristics. Finally, employees are not clones of one another just because they are similar on some personality dimensions. We would expect considerable variation on demographic, cultural, and personality dimensions that were not the basis for selection.

THE FUTURE OF HIRING FOR PERSON-ORGANIZATION FIT

What does the future hold for this more sophisticated and elaborate approach to employee selection? Will it be adopted by an increasingly large share of corporations?

We believe that hiring for the organization, not the job, will become the only effective selection model for the typical business environment. The defining attributes of this business environment—such as shortened product life cycles, increasingly sophisticated technologies, growing globalization of markets, shifting customer demands—make for very transitory requirements in specific employee jobs. Organizational success in this environment requires hiring employees who fit the overall organization, not those who fit a fixed set of task demands. Employee personalities must fit the management philosophy and values that help define the organization's uniqueness and its fitness for the future.

We also believe that senior managers must become more "person-oriented" in their own implicit resolution of the person-situation controversy if hiring for person-organization fit is to become a more common approach to selection. Again, generally speaking, managers tend to believe that tightly controlled situations are more effective in shaping employee performance than less-structured situations that allow the expression of individual differences. Managers who believe this are more inclined to spend resources on creating strong situations via job descriptions, close supervision, and so on than on sophisticated selection procedures.

Finally, we offer an important caveat to "person-oriented" managers who are committed to hiring for person-organization fit. They must manage a paradox. They must build strong organizational cultures yet, at the same time, design work situations that are weak enough to allow the unique qualities of individual employees to impact work performance. The key ingredient in balancing this paradox is to create a strong organizational culture with values that empower employees to apply their individual potentials to the conduct of their work. In this way, fragile systems release the employee energy necessary to compete in today's business environment.

Endnotes

[1] See William E. Sheeline, "Avoiding Growth's Perils," *Fortune*, August 13, 1990, 55.

[2] "Japan's Gung-Ho U.S. Car Plants," *Fortune*, January 30, 1989, 78–85.

[3] For a review of the person-situation controversy, see Larry James and Terrence Mitchell (Eds) of several articles in a special forum, "Situational versus Dispositional Factors: Competing Explanations of Behavior," *Academy of Management Review*, 1989, 14. In particular, see Jennifer Chatman, "Improving Interactional Organizational Research" in that issue for implications of the controversy for selection and training.

[4] See, for example, Terrence Mitchell, "Organizational Behavior" in M. R. Rosenzweig and L. W. Porter, (Eds) *Annual Review of Psychology, Vol 30* (Palo Alto, CA: Annual Reviews 1979); Howard Weiss and Seymour Adler, "Personality and Organizational Behavior" in Barry Staw and Larry Cummings (Eds), *Research in Organizational Behavior, Vol 6* (Greenwich, CT: JAI Press, 1984).

[5]See, for example, Chatman, op cit., Weiss and Adler, op cit.

[6]A number of research reviews have documented the low validity of the employment interview. For example, see R. D. Arvey and J. E. Campion, "The Employment Interview: A Summary and Review of Recent Research," *Personnel Psychology*, 1982, 35, 281–322. For an overview of higher validity coefficients reported for appropriately designed, or structured, interviews, see Neal Schmitt and I. Robertson, "Personnel Selection," in M. R. Rosenzweig and L. W. Porter (Eds), *Annual Review of Psychology, Vol 41* (Palo Alto, CA: Annual Reviews Inc., 1990).

[7]See, for example, Chatman, op cit.; Weiss and Adler, op cit.

[8]John P. MacDuffie, "The Japanese Auto Transplants: Challenges to Conventional Wisdom," *ILR Report*, Fall, 1988, 26(1), 12–18; Huaro Shimada and John Paul MacDuffie, "Industrial Relations and 'Humanware,' Japanese Investments in Auto Manufacturing in the United States," Working Paper, Sloan School of Management, MIT, 1987.

[9]For an overview of the steps in the classic selection model, see Benjamin Schneider and Neal Schmitt, *Staffing Organizations*, Second Edition (USA: Scott Foresman and Company, 1986). The goal of the traditional selection model is to produce a fit between the critical requirements of a particular job and the job-relevant KSAs of job applicants. This approach consists of three steps. First, a job analysis is conducted to determine the critical requirements of a particular job. Second, on the basis of the job analysis the analyst infers the knowledge, skills, and abilities that are needed for the job. Finally, selection tests are chosen or developed that are intended to indicate the degree to which job applicants possess the KSAs needed on the job. The tests are administered to all applicants. The tests are validated by collecting data on criteria measures, such as job performance, and then examining the correlation between applicant test scores and criteria measures. A statistically significant and reasonably high correlation indicates that the test is capable of discriminating appropriately between employees who do well and those who do poorly on the criteria measures.

[10]See John P. Wanous, *Organizational Entry: Recruitment Selection, and Socialization of Newcomers,* (Reading, Mass: Addison-Wesley Publishing Company, 1980) for a more complete discussion of these two types of fit and how both the organization and individual approach them.

[11]For more detail on job analysis techniques, see Schneider and Schmitt, op cit.

[12]Caren Siehl and Joanne Martin, "Measuring Organizational Culture: Mixing Qualitative and Quantitative Methods," in M. O. Jones et al. (Eds), *Inside Organizations* (Beverly Hills: Sage, 1988).

[13]Chatman, op cit.

[14]Michael Tushman and David Nadler, "A Diagnostic Model of Organizational Behavior."

[15]As examples of this thinking, see Barry M. Staw, Nancy E. Bell, and John A. Clausen, "The Dispositional Approach to Job Attitudes: A Lifetime Longitudinal Test," *Administrative Science Quarterly*, 1986, 31, 56–77; Weiss and Adler, op cit.

[16]Staw, et al., op cit.

[17]"Doug Bray: You're Got to Pick Your Winners," *Training*, February, 1988, 79–81.

[18]Richard Pascale, "Fitting New Employees into the Company Culture," *Fortune*, May 28, 1984, 28–42.

[19]For an overview of this issue, see Schneider and Schmitt, op cit.

[20]Brian Dumaine, "The New Art of Hiring Smart," *Fortune*, August 17, 1987, 78–81.

[21]Wilton Woods, "Personality Tests Are Back," *Fortune*, March 30, 1987, 74–82.

[22]For a review of the track record of validation studies of personality tests as selection tools, versus other measures, see R. M. Guion and R. F. Gottier, "Validity of

Personality Measures in Personnel Selection," *Personnel Psychology*, 1965, 18, 49–65; R. M. Guion, "Changing Views for Personnel Selection Research," *Personnel Psychology*, 1987, 40, 199–213; Schmitt and Robertson, op cit., and N. Schmitt, R. Gooding, R. Noe, and M. Kirsch, "Meta-Analysis of Validity Studies Published Between 1964 and 1982 and the Investigation of Study Characteristics," *Personnel Psychology*, 1984, 37, 407–422.

[23]Schneider and Schmitt, op cit., 353.

[24]See Wanous, op cit.

[25]"Japan's Gung-Ho U.S. Car Plants," op cit.

[26]Richard E. Walton, "From Control to Commitment in the Workplace," *Harvard Business Review*, March-April 1985, 76–84.

[27]Edward E. Lawler III, *High-Involvement Management*, (San Francisco: Jossey-Bass, 1986); S. Mohrman, G. Ledford, Jr., E. E. Lawler III, and A. M. Mohrman, "Quality of Work-Life and Employment Involvement," in C. L. Cooper and I. Robertson (Eds), *International Review of Industrial and Organizational Psychology*, (New York: John Wiley & Sons, 1986).

[28]The case description is an illustrative overview of the steps and some techniques associated with hiring for the organization, not the job. Readers may contact the authors if they are interested in more details about the hiring process, such as assessment methods, validation strategies, scoring of simulations, and so on.

[29]D. N. Jackson, *Personality Research Form Manual*, 3rd ed., (Port Huron, MI: Research Psychologists Press, 1984). For a review of the PRF, see J. S. Wiggins, *Personality and Prediction: Principles of Personality and Assessment*, (Reading, MA: Addison-Wesley, 1973).

[30]The significant correlation between scores in the composite growth needs scale and performance in the pre-employment training program was a 0.22 (and it was 0.27 after correction for unreliability in the criterion). This compares favorably to the average validity of 0.15 found in a recent review of research using personality measures (N. Schmitt, R. Z. Gooding, R. A. Noe, & M. Kirsch, "Meta-Analysis of Validity Studies Published between 1964 and 1982 and the investigation of study characteristics," *Personnel Psychology*, 1984, 37, 407–422). In addition, scores on the social needs measure were significantly correlated (.16) with anticipated satisfaction.

[31]See Wanous, op cit. for a discussion of this proposition.

[32]For a review of the research findings, see S. C. Premack and J. P. Wanous, "A Meta-Analysis of Realistic Job Preview Experiments," *Journal of Applied Psychology*, 1985, 70, 706–719.

[33]R. A. Guzzo, R. D. Jette, & R. A. Katzell, "The Effects of Psychologically Based Intervention Programs on Worker Productivity: A Meta-Analysis," *Personnel Psychology*, 1985, 38, 275–291; G. E. Ledford, Jr., T. G. Cummings and R. W. Wright, "The Structure and Effectiveness of High Involvement Organizations," Working Paper, Center for Effective Organizations, University of Southern California, 1991.

[34]Premack and Wanous, op cit.

[35]See Chatman, op cit.

[36]Ledford et al.

[37]William J. Hampton, "How Does Japan Inc. Pick Its American Workers?" *Business Week*, October 3, 1988, 84–88.

[38]For a discussion of these issues, see J. L. Holland, "Some Speculation About the Investigation of Person-Environment Transactions," *Journal of Vocational Behavior*, 1987, 31, 337–340; R. H. Moos, "Person-Environment Congruence in Work, School and Health-Care Settings," *Journal of Vocational Behavior*, 1987, 31, 231–247; and J. B. Rounds, R. V. Dawis, and L. H. Lofquist, "Measurement of Person-Environment Fit and Prediction of Satisfaction in the Theory of Work Adjustment," *Journal of Vocational Behavior*, 1987, 31, 297–318.

[39]E. E. Lawler III, "Achieving Competitiveness by Creating New Organizational

Cultures and Structures" in D. B. Fishman and C. Cherniss (Eds), *The Human Side of Corporate Competitiveness* (Newbury Park: Sage Publications), 69–101.

[40]*Assessment Strategies for Selection* (Pittsburgh, PA: Development Dimensions International, 1990).

[41]D. R. Denison, *Corporate Culture and Organizational Effectiveness* (New York: Wiley, 1990).

PART IV

DEVELOPING HUMAN RESOURCES

TRAINING

INTRODUCTION

Training may be the most important human resource management practice for preparing the company to deal with its competitive challenges. To deal with technological, global, social, and quality challenges, employees must have a well-developed base of interpersonal and technical skills. For example, the quality challenge requires that employees be trained to use statistical process control techniques to monitor manufacturing process and service quality. To produce high-quality products and services, provide employees with the opportunity to perform interesting work, and capitalize on employees' skills, many companies are beginning to form work teams. For teams to be successful, employees must have high levels of interpersonal skills such as communication and conflict resolution. Employees must also be able to understand and work with other employees who have different cultural backgrounds (a diversity training issue).

Reading 24, "Training System Issues in the Year 2000," by Goldstein and Gilliam, emphasizes the training system that companies should use to maximize the return on their training investment. Such a training system includes several steps. The first step, needs assessment, involves determining whether a training need exists, whether the company has the financial and technical resources available to meet the training need, and which employees need training. The second step of the process, development of instructional objectives, involves identifying what the company hopes to achieve from training in specific, measurable terms. Simultaneous with the development of instructional objectives, the company needs to develop criteria to evaluate whether the instructional objectives have been reached. The third step of the process is choosing a training program to meet the instructional objectives. In addition, the training environment should be developed to maximize trainees' learning. Also, employees' managers and peers need to be prepared to help employees use what they have learned in training on-the-job. The last step of the design of a training system is evaluation. Managers need to evaluate whether the instructional objectives were achieved and the degree to which trainees apply training content to their jobs. This information is valuable for determining the return on a training investment, as well as suggesting possible modifications in the training system to make it more effective. Goldstein and Gilliam also discuss how labor force characteristics, technology, and legal issues are influencing training systems.

"One Size Does Not Fit All" (Reading 25) by Newstrom and Lengnick-Hall discusses the factors that affect the extent to which employees learn in training. The basic principles of adult learning are emphasized. Adult learning emphasizes that for learning to occur, trainees must feel the need to learn, be actively involved in learning, be able to share experiences with other trainees, and believe that the content of training is meaningful to them. Newstrom and Lengnick-Hall also discuss the trainee characteristics that influence learning and what managers can do to ensure trainees have a high level of motivation. For example, managers need to ensure that trainees understand the purpose of training, believe they can learn course content, and understand the types of rewards they can receive from participating in training and using skills on the job.

READING 24

TRAINING SYSTEM ISSUES IN THE YEAR 2000

Irwin L. Goldstein
and Patrice Gilliam

Abstract

This article discusses the influence of future changes in the demographics of working populations and the characteristics of the workplace on research, development, and policy for training systems. Analyses of these changes indicate that there will be more expectations that training programs will serve as a positive hope to maximize the potential of each person. This will result in increased emphasis on research to identify abilities required to perform more cognitively complex jobs. Also, research on basic skill and support programs to permit unskilled youth to enter the world of work will be required. In addition, there will be a need for research on training necessary to help future managers and leaders work with members of a more diverse work force. Finally, the implications of these changes suggest that we need policies that consider research and development on retraining as a national need to help all individuals maximize their individual talents.

Training represents a positive hope for persons first entering the world of work or for individuals changing their work environment. When training is designed well, it gives individuals opportunities to enter the job market with needed skills, to perform new functions, and to be promoted into new situations. Therefore, it is not surprising that labor unions have included training opportunities as an item in contract bargaining negotiations or that large companies such as General

Source: Irwin L. Goldstein and Patrice Gilliam, Training Issues in the Year 2000, © *American Psychologist*, February 1990, vol. 45, no. 2, 134–142. Reprinted by permission.

We thank Ben Schneider, Katherine Klein, and the graduate students of the industrial/organizational psychology program at the University of Maryland at College Park for their helpful comments. We also wish to extend our appreciation to Lynn Offermann and Marilyn Gowing both for their comments and for their patience in working with us on this article. We also wish to thank Brooks/Cole Publishing Company for their permission to reprint the figure in the text and for their permission to use some concepts originally developed in Irwin L. Goldstein's text on training.

Patrice Gilliam is now employed at the Drug Enforcement Agency, Department of Justice.

Correspondence concerning this article should be addressed to Irwin L. Goldstein, Department of Psychology, University of Maryland, College Park, MD 20742.

Electric have designed multimillion dollar facilities to train thousands of crafts persons annually in new technological innovations ("For Your Information," 1980).

This article examines training issues that will need to be considered as the year 2000 approaches. First, a training systems model is presented to provide the reader with a context for training issues. Next, the article focuses on future work force issues that are particularly relevant to training. Finally, on the basis of these future work place issues, the article discusses specific training concerns.

When learning events are planned in a systematic fashion and are focused on the work environment, they are called training programs. From this point of view, the training process is defined as the systematic acquisition of skills, rules, concepts, or attitudes that result in improved performance in the work environment. Thus, training programs can result in a more considerate supervisor or a more consistent technician. In some cases, such as on-the-job training, the instructional environment is almost identical to the actual job environment. In other instances, such as a classroom lecture on electronics theory for technicians, the learning environment is far removed from the job situation. In both situations, effective training stems from a systematically designed learning atmosphere based on a careful evaluation or analysis of job requirements and the capabilities of the trainees. The simplicity of these statements hides a very complex systems interaction involving persons, jobs, and organizations. For example, federal government decisions to provide financial incentives for retraining individuals displaced by technological change can stimulate organizations to make a policy decision to design new training programs. Similarly, organizational decisions to compete in international markets affect policy concerning the types of training necessary for their employees.

TRAINING SYSTEMS

A useful model in conceptualizing training systems is an instructional technology model (see Figure 1) that emphasizes careful needs assessment, precisely controlled learning experiences designed to achieve instructional objectives, use of performance criteria, and the collection of evaluation information to provide feedback about the system's effects. This viewpoint considers training intervention as just one component within a larger set of interacting organizational and societal systems. This article presents only a limited description of this model for the purpose of providing a framework for the reader (see Goldstein, 1986, for a full description).

The first set of components shown in the model refers to the needs assessment process that is used to provide critical information necessary to design both the training program and the evaluation model. There are a number of different steps in the needs assessment process. One part is *organizational analysis,* which focuses on a macro level analysis of the role of training and includes an examination of the system-wide components of the organization that interact with a training program's design, development, and effectiveness. This phase includes an examination of the organizational goals, climate for training, and the internal and

Figure 1

AN INSTRUCTIONAL SYSTEM

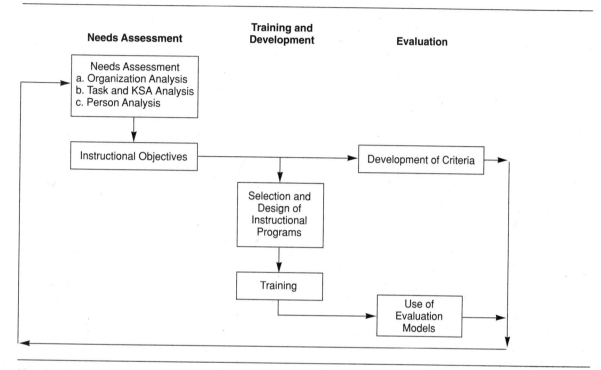

Note: From *Training in Organizations: Needs Assessment, Development, and Evaluation* Third Edition (p. 21) by Irwin L. Goldstein. Copyright © 1993, 1986, 1974 by Wadsworth, Inc. Reprinted by permission of Brooks/Cole Publishing Company, Pacific Grove, California, 93950.

external constraints present in the organizational environment. In this stage, it is determined whether training is the appropriate strategy to use in resolving the human resources issues facing the organization. In addition, information is provided to determine whether there are organizational system constraints that might prevent training programs from being successful. An example of such constraints might be the behavior of supervisors who do not support the training systems being employed or who might require that the job be performed differently than as taught in training, either of which constraints would make it difficult for what is learned in training to be successfully transferred to the job.

As presented in the model, another phase of the needs assessment is the determination of which tasks are required on the job and which knowledge, skills, and abilities (KSAs) are critical in learning to perform those tasks, that is, *task and KSA analysis.* This is a complex process that involves asking questions such as which KSAs should be learned in training, acquired before training, or acquired in the job environment after training. During the last decade, a number of researchers (e.g., Goldstein, 1986; Prien, Goldstein, & Macey, 1987) have contributed information concerning the design of needs assessment systems relevant to training issues.

Another component of the needs assessment is *person analysis,* which involves a determination of the trainees' capabilities. This involves an assessment of the skills of the individuals who will be trained and can include as a target population persons already in the organization or individuals who are not yet part of the organization. By determining the capabilities of these target populations in relation to the required KSAs for the job, it becomes possible to focus the training program on critical KSAs that are not in the repertoire of the target population.

From the information obtained in the various phases of the needs assessment process, a blueprint emerges that describes the KSAs that should be achieved as a result of participation in the training program. This provides input for the design of the training program as well as for the measures of success (criteria) that will be used to judge the program's outcomes.

Campbell (1988) noted the importance of these issues by stating that the most important question to be resolved by designers, users, and investigators of training is, "What is to be learned?" Campbell pointed to a largely unnoticed article by Gagné (1962) in the *American Psychologist* entitled "Military Training and Principles of Learning." Campbell presented the following critical argument:

> For Gagné, the question of what is to be learned also takes precedence over the traditional questions addressed by research in learning, such as whether massed versus distributed practice is more effective. Unfortunately, answering this primary question is a difficult and painstaking task. It does not deal in high-tech bells and whistles and has little glamour associated with it. In the marketplace, it is a thankless task to argue that beating one's head against this question is far more important than using computerized instruction, having well appointed training facilities, or stocking a library with the latest videotapes. (p. 188)

The next step is *designing the training environment.* This is a delicate process that requires a blend of instructional learning principles and media selection. The analysis of job tasks and required KSAs and the design of a matching training environment are important research issues (e.g., Gagné, 1984) with many questions remaining to be resolved.

Another aspect of the design of instructional environments is the consideration of learning principles to support the acquisition and transfer of the learned behavior. A definitive list of learning principles that could be adapted to the training setting has not been completely specified for adult learners in work environments. However, cognitive and instructional theorists have progressed to a stage of development in which information is emerging concerning the choice of the proper instructional variable and level of that variable (e.g., Campbell, 1988; Howell & Cooke, 1989). An example of such a system is the use of advanced organizers, which are essentially verbal, quantitative, graphic, or conceptual cues that afford the learner a means of classifying and incorporating the to-be-learned material into his or her present knowledge base.

The design of training environments is a complicated process, and in some cases, there is evidence that even when training performance is positive, improved performance on the job may not result (Rouillier, 1989). Thus, it is necessary to treat training programs as interventions that require the collection of data in order to provide feedback that can be used to modify the program. The third column in the model refers to *evaluation components,* which are used to develop feedback information.

The evaluation process centers around two procedures: (a) establishing measures of success (criteria), and (b) using evaluation research designs to determine what changes have occurred during the training and transfer process, that is, the back-to-work environment. Criteria must be established for both the evaluation of trainees at the conclusion of the training program and the evaluation of on-the-job performance. Serious research issues pertain to the integration of the large number of criteria often needed to evaluate a program and to the difficulties associated with the collection of relevant criterion information.

In addition to criterion development, the evaluation phase involves the specification of evaluation designs needed to assess the training program. Depending on the information required, different evaluation models or at the very least different forms of the same evaluation model are needed. As most readers know, Cook and Campbell (1979) described a number of creative designs to control for the different types of internal and external threats to validity that might occur in field settings. Recently, Arvey and Cole (1989) analyzed a variety of experimental designs and specified sample size requirements necessary to detect change as well as the impact of unreliable measures on the assessment of change.

In addition to experimental designs, there are other approaches to evaluation that provide varying degrees of information, such as content validity models that help determine whether the critical KSAs determined in the needs assessment are appropriately emphasized in the training program (e.g., Ford & Wroten, 1984; Goldstein, Schneider, Katzmen, & Braverman, 1989).

Finally, the model stresses the idea that a training program should be a *closed-loop system,* in which the evaluation process provides for continual modification of the program. The information may become available at many different stages in the evaluation process. For example, an effective process evaluation might indicate that the training program is not being implemented as originally planned. In other instances, different conclusions might be supported by comparing data obtained from the training evaluation or transfer evaluation. Even in those instances in which the training program achieves its stated objectives, there are continual developments that can affect the program, including any changes in the characteristics of trainees on the job. In this sense the development of training programs must be viewed as a continually evolving process.

The foregoing discussion has presented an overview of training issues. For a more comprehensive treatment of the research agenda concerning training system issues, the interested reader is referred to Campbell (1988), Goldstein (1986, 1989), Latham (1988), and Wexley and Latham (1981). In addition, it is important to note that although this article focuses on training issues, there are many other important human resource systems (e.g., fair compensation systems and concern with job promotion and advanced opportunities) that help determine whether work organizations will function successfully. In the next section of this article, we will focus briefly on specific developments in work-related issues that are likely to affect the future agenda for training research and implementation. A more comprehensive treatment of these issues can be found in Offermann and Gowing's article (this issue, pp. 95–108).

THE FUTURE WORKPLACE

Changes in Demographics of Entry-Level Persons in the Work Force

Since individuals who will enter the labor force in the year 2000 have been born, it is possible to project, with relative accuracy, future trends in labor force participation (Fullerton, 1985). Projections clearly indicate that the work force is changing (Fullerton, 1985) and thus will impact human resources management in ways not experienced before (Cascio & Zammuto, 1987).

What these projections suggest is that the work force will grow more slowly in the upcoming decades, and new entrants or those primarily between the ages of 16 and 24 will decrease substantially. In addition, the proportion of White members of this entry-level work force will decline, and the proportion of minority populations will increase significantly (Cascio & Zammuto, 1987; Fullerton, 1985). The composition of the work force will also change to include more older workers and more women. Data indicate that individuals between the ages of 45 and 64 years will increase 25% or more (Fullerton, 1985; Odiorne, 1986). For women, factors such as career aspirations, enhanced opportunities, and supportive services such as child care facilities and flex time have contributed to participation in the labor force. The female work force, as a whole, is expected to steadily increase in the coming decade (Vaydanoff, 1987). However, the inclusion of older workers and women in the work force still will not change the fact that growth of the total work force will be lower than experienced in the past. The number of individuals usually comprising the entry pool and serving as selectees for industry will be dismal at best (Cascio & Zammuto, 1987).

Increased Technology in the World of Work

There is a clear trend toward more highly technologically sophisticated systems in work environments (Turnage, this issue, pp. 171–178). Researchers (e.g., Cascio & Zammuto, 1987), believe that technology will result in increased productivity and product quality and as a result will permit the United States to regain a competitive edge in global market competition. Klein and Hall (1988) pointed to technological developments such as programmable automation, which includes the use of robots that are reprogrammable, multifunctional machines that will manipulate materials, and various forms of computer-assisted design and computer-assisted manufacturing. These authors believe that programmable automation will have its greatest impact on semiskilled and unskilled jobs, sectors of the work force in which job loss is likely to be significant. In any case, increases in technology require a highly trained work force to design and operate the systems, and demographic predictions indicate that there will be relatively fewer such persons entering the work force in the years 2000 and beyond.

Shifts from Manufacturing to Service Jobs

There also is a shift in the economy from a manufacturing to a service orientation. In the period from 1984 to 1995, it is expected that nearly nine out of ten new jobs will be in the service-producing industries (Personick, 1985). These jobs are characterized by an increase in the importance of "people work," that is, working with customers and clients rather than interacting primarily with co-workers and things (Klein & Hall, 1988). Entry level service-oriented jobs are also characterized by lower pay levels than those in the manufacturing sector. Displaced manufacturing sector workers have discovered that they are expected to learn new interpersonal skills for service-oriented jobs but that the pay levels for their performance of these jobs are below what they have previously earned. Interestingly, advances in technology are also having an impact on service-oriented jobs (for example, witness the use of automated banking services).

Increased Influence of International Markets

An examination of future trends makes it increasingly obvious that in order for organizations to survive, they will need to operate in an international environment. Many novel strategies are being explored. For example, Klein and Hall (1988) noted that some firms are exploring projects in which data entry functions are performed in foreign countries because the advantages of low wages and surplus workers outweigh the disadvantages of long-distance electronic data transmission. Most consumers now realize that it is not unusual for a manufacturer to produce a product (e.g., an automobile) that is partially manufactured in the United States and partially manufactured in a foreign country. Sometimes these efforts involve arrangements between liaison teams that direct efforts involving different employees in different organizations in different countries, all contributing to the production of a single final product.

IMPLICATIONS OF THE FUTURE WORKPLACE FOR TRAINING SYSTEMS

There are a number of important training implications for the world of work in the year 2000 that stem from the analyses presented earlier. One concern relates to the fact that a large number of skilled persons will be needed for entry-level jobs, but the available pool of young persons will be composed of large numbers of unskilled and undereducated individuals. Another difficulty is the increasing sophistication of technological systems and the greater training requirements those jobs will require. There are also issues concerning maximizing worker potential by addressing the present underutilization of minorities, women, and older workers. Finally, there are training issues concerning work organizations as they become an even greater part of a competitive international work environment, notably a need for greater focus on management training. The following sections consider these issues.

The Problem of Unskilled Youth

The analyses of demographic information about persons entering the work force require the consideration of some harsh realities. First, there will be fewer persons available to enter the work force. Yet the analyses indicate that demand for workers will remain high especially given the development of service sector jobs. Demographics also indicate that a large number of individuals who will be available for entry into the work force will be undereducated youth (Cascio & Zammuto, 1987; Fullerton, 1985). Significant numbers of these individuals will be members of culturally diverse groups that society has not completely integrated into the work force (Goldstein, 1986). Although many members of minority groups have successfully entered professional and technical careers, it is also true, as indicated later, that many of the hard-core unemployed are minorities. This section will focus on the problems of undereducated youth. It is a fact that society will, in the future, need their talent in the workplace.

An analysis of unemployed youth contained in a Ford Foundation report entitled "Not Working: Unskilled Youth and Displaced Adults" (Berlin, 1983) has troubling implications. Figures concerning youth indicated that in 1982, when the U.S. unemployment rate was unusually high (10.8%), the comparable rates for teenagers who were high school graduates were 17.1% for Whites, 53.5% for Blacks, and 28% for Hispanics. For high school dropouts, the rates rose to 29%, 71%, and 35%. When unemployment rates improved nationally to only 5.4% in 1985, the rates for teenage youth were 16% for Whites, 42% for Blacks, and 23% for Hispanics.

These data reflect a problem that remains unsolved even through programs such as the War on Poverty, which was launched by President Lyndon Johnson in 1964. One proposed solution has been the development of training programs for the hard-core unemployed (HCU). For the purposes of entry into most of these programs, the HCU are defined as individuals who have not been regular members of the work force and in many cases have not been employed for the previous six-month period. Most HCU are young, members of a minority group, and lacking a high school education (Goldstein, 1986).

Research on training of the hard-core unemployed provides data on important concerns that will face future researchers and policy planners concerned with integrating unskilled youth into the work force. First, there are serious research issues concerning the design of needs assessment systems (see Figure 1) that provide the information requirements for the design of training programs. Thus, the question of which skills and how they are to be taught has been a long-standing research issue underlying the design of these programs. As long ago as 1967, research by Miller and Zeller found that large percentages of HCU trainees who graduated from a program for highway construction machinists were unemployed. These researchers were able to document many inadequacies including poor program design and limited task practice. Similar problems are still being described ("How Not to Retrain Workers," 1983) in which programs are designed to have a level of technical detail well beyond the capabilities of the trainees chosen for the program. It is clear that the design of needs assessment techniques required to specify properly the required knowledge, skills, and abilities for job performance (Goldstein, 1986; Wexley & Latham, 1981) has become increasingly important, especially in situations in which the skill levels of the trainees are a critical factor.

Although not many efforts have been successful in integrating the HCU into the work force, the few that exist have resulted in a number of important research findings. For example, a number of studies have noted that many HCU individuals are lacking basic literacy skills. A study of a successful military program known as Project 100,000 (Sticht, Armstrong, Hickey & Caylor, 1987) reached the conclusion that reading, writing, and arithmetic were best learned by having the practice material coordinated with relevant information from the intended job field. Sticht et al. also noted that teaching basic literacy and job skills together shortened training time because it reduced the time needed for providing basic literacy training separately and then adding job-relevant training skills. In addition, these studies demonstrated the positive effect of other training support schemes, including the revision of training materials to match trainee aptitudes.

Additional programs are being emphasized in the private sector. Polaroid Corporation has recently spent $700,000 to provide a basic course in English and math for 1,000 employees ("The Literacy Gap," 1988). Domino's Pizza, using a $150,000 grant from the U.S. Department of Labor, is teaching the basic reading and math needed for dough making at the same time the trainee is being taught to actually make the dough for the pizza ("Literacy on the Job," 1988). One important conclusion from this research is that when instructional approaches focus on important knowledge, skills, and abilities identified by solid needs assessment procedures, powerful interventions can result. The results of other less positive programs have been devastating (e.g., "How Not to Retrain Workers," 1983).

Another important factor in training programs for the HCU has been issues related to non-specific work skills. Research studies (Gilliam, 1988) continue to provide evidence that factors such as information on how to complete an application blank and how to search and interview for a job, job placement services, and counseling are critical to the programs' success. It appears that without these skills, many potential job applicants are lost to the employment market. Gilliam (1988) designed a training program involving an unusual HCU group in that they were all college graduates. Gilliam found that it was possible to teach a variety of skills including resume development, networking, and interviewing and that persons attending the training program secured jobs more frequently than persons who attended a traditional training program that did not include those opportunities. It is interesting that programs that have provided training for displaced workers have not typically emphasized these services.

Another important issue is the degree to which the organization itself is making a commitment rather than assuming that all of the necessary change must come from the trainee. Thus, supportive behavior by the supervisor (Friedlander & Greenberg, 1971) relates to effective HCU performance. As noted by these authors but unfortunately not yet learned well by most organizations, "programs geared primarily toward adapting the HCUs' work attitudes to the predominant social structure in the organization are far less potent than those that also incorporate the adaptation of the organizational climate" (p. 287). This means that organizations that are likely to be successful in integrating persons from diverse cultural groups will need to provide training for individuals already in their organization as well as for the entry-level trainee. This is also a salient issue in integrating older workers and women into the work force. Obviously, there will be many young persons entering the world of work who cannot, in any sense, be classified as unskilled. Many of the issues discussed earlier, such as the need for careful matching of the KSAs required to the capabilities of the individual, will be equally important for skilled workers. In addition, there are likely to be many other changes in the world of work that will impact on training for all members of the work population.

Training for Jobs With Increasing Cognitive Complexity

Almost all descriptions of future work organizations describe them as requiring more complex cognitive skills. This is clear from a description by executives at a new Mazda plant in Michigan of their expectations of their workers.

> They want their new employees to be able to work in teams, to rotate through various jobs, to understand how their tasks fit into the entire process, to spot problems in production, to trouble shoot, articulate the problems to others, suggest improvements and write detail charts and memos that serve as a road map in the assembly of the car. (in Vobejda, 1987, p. A14)

Paradoxically, changes in technology and machine responsibility increase the demands on the human. As noted by Howell and Cooke (1989), smart machines increase the cognitive complexity of the tasks performed by the human being. Instead of simple procedural and predictable tasks, the human becomes responsible for inferences, diagnoses, judgment, and decision making, often under severe time pressure.

Adding to the complexity of these issues is the rapid technical obsolescence of individuals who previously had very advanced training. Thus, estimates are that the engineer's education has a half life of five years, meaning that half of what is learned in school is obsolete five years after graduation (Kaufman, 1978). Unfortunately, not much is known about training and retraining issues. London and Bassman (1989) indicated that there are a number of factors involved in mid-career shifts that make it even more likely that there will be increasing changes in job requirements in the future. First, jobs will be changing in response to technological shifts. In addition, there are health and economic factors beyond an individual's control that result in job and career shifts. Also, as people live longer, individuals are likely to discover that 40 years is a long time to devote to one career. At the very least, these issues add another dimension to the question of what needs to be learned.

It will now be even more important to understand how to build on previously learned behavior in order to transfer learning to the performance of new tasks. Fleishman and Mumford (1989) have begun exploring how different abilities are acquired at varying points in the training process. If job requirements will be shifting quickly, it may become necessary, as argued by Schneider and Konz (1989), to figure out how to determine training requirements for jobs that do not yet exist. At the system level, there may also be a need for training to sensitize people to opportunities and career paths in which already gained skills are useful.

Concern for Maximizing Individual Worker Potential

One of the implications of the decreasing size of the work force is that it will become increasingly necessary to maximize the potential of each individual worker. This means that the future of work organizations will become more dependent on their ability to utilize effectively all members of society, often by providing training to maximize each person's potential. In considering this point, it is important to note the history of groups that have been under-employed in the past. In spite of evidence that indicates the importance of work in the lives of most individuals, there have been a number of harsh realities within the world of work. Many researchers have concluded that a contributing factor, which has resulted in lost opportunities, is the cycle of discrimination plaguing minorities, women, and older workers (Cross, 1986; Rhodes, 1983). As noted earlier, minorities often have been found to be locked out from full access to the work opportunity structure and thus are overrepresented in menial positions that are characterized as dull, routine, unrewarding, and stagnant (Cross, 1986; Wilson, 1978). Considering total representation in the work force, data from recent years indicate some improvement in the representation of minorities in the work force. However, research continues to show a two-to-one ratio of minority to White unemployment and slow progress for minority individuals in ranks beyond middle management in corporate and professional occupations (Cross, 1986; Morrison & Von Glinow, this issue, pp. 200–208; Westcott, 1982).

Research on women indicates that they have also been limited in attaining a proportionate share of the nation's income, wealth, and positions of power (Blau & Ferber, 1987). Women historically have been concentrated in the administrative support and service occupations, whereas men have been heavily represented in executive and managerial positions. Recent data reveal gains by women in the work force (Blau & Ferber, 1987; Chusmir, 1986). However, women represent a distinct minority in management, particularly at the higher levels, and there are still signs that employers continue to use misconceptions about differences between the sexes to select women out of certain types of work (Dipboye, 1987; Morrison & Von Glinow, this issue).

Most of the discussions regarding training issues and women have been focused on their entry into nontraditional career fields such as management.

Before discussing that issue, it is important to note that the preceding material concerning undereducated youth involves women as well as men, and certainly issues involving older workers, as discussed later, equally affect women and men. It is perhaps significant that there appear to be few empirical or theoretical discussions distinguishing between men and women within the work force sectors of undereducated youth and older workers. As we approach the year 2000, that issue needs further study. For example, it is clear that all individuals are living longer, but that is even more true for women. The implications of that fact for a workplace that will need all future workers in order to remain competitive deserve attention.

There are some excellent articles (e.g., White, Crino, & DeSanctis, 1981) that describe the problems of barriers to women entering nontraditional fields. One implication of the existence of these barriers is that training issues are more complex than can be addressed by simply asking what training the individual requires. Rather, the organization needs to provide the training necessary for helping individuals at work to accept persons first entering the organization. In the case of women entering new careers, that point cannot be emphasized enough. The issue is the same for minorities. There is no evidence that the task requirements for the job of a manager for a female or minority male are any different than for a White male. Also, there is no evidence from person analysis that females need special training on particular KSAs that is not required by males. Thus, it is not presently possible to support the need for special training programs for women. However, that has not prevented the development of thousands of such specialized training programs for women, even though data supporting accomplishments of these programs is virtually nonexistent. Another important conclusion is a point that is not stated often enough. It is not true that all forms of training are worth either the effort for the individual or the cost to the organization. However, it is clear that individuals already in the organization often need training on how to provide a supportive climate for individuals just entering the workplace. This is especially true when individuals entering the workplace are from populations that have in the past been nontraditional in that work setting.

Older people are another group that has been required to contend with discrimination or what is specifically referred to as "ageism" (Sheppard, 1978). Research suggests that this situation stems from stereotypes that impact many of the personnel decisions made pertaining to older workers (Meltzer, 1981). When skilled workers are displaced, older persons have the most difficulty finding reemployment. One study indicated that all the younger skilled workers of a displaced group obtained jobs, whereas 38% of the older workers stayed unemployed (Sheppard, 1978). In addition, older workers who found jobs were usually paid less than they had previously earned. In this study, the older worker was defined as anyone over age 38! Perceptions about older workers are that they are more difficult to train (Britton & Thomas, 1973) and are more resistant to change (Rosen & Jerdee, 1978).

It is important to note that these stereotypes persist in spite of research that does not provide support for such beliefs. A meta analysis (McEvoy & Cascio,

1989) of 96 studies published in the last 22 years found that age and performance were generally unrelated across all types of performance measures. It was only for very young employees that age and performance were related in a modestly positive direction. In previous analyses (Rhodes, 1983), in those few instances in which relations between age and performance were found, they tended to be in jobs in which there were high demands for speed and accuracy of movement, with older individuals performing less well than younger persons. As expected, there were few jobs extreme enough in physical demands to show even those differences. Also, of course, in many jobs in which physical demands were extremely high, it is probable that the older workers who remained on the jobs were those who could still perform those activities. This points to a problem with most research studies included in these analyses in that they are nearly all cross-sectional rather than longitudinal designs. It is also clear that organizations will need to reconsider their views concerning the desirability of training older workers in order to make use of the potential resource pool of individuals that will exist in the future.

At the present time, even data that show a relation between age and performance must be interpreted carefully. As noted by Rosen and Jerdee (1978), older workers are less likely to receive support for retaining. When considering the obsolescence process, Fossum and his colleagues (Fossum, Arvey, Paradise, & Robbins, 1986) noted that when there is a relation between age and performance, it may result from employers withholding developmental resources from older employees.

In this regard, Sterns and Doverspike's (1989) review of the training and retraining literature led them to note that there are factors being identified in research programs that can help older employees in training programs. They suggest the following:

1. Training should be organized so that the material is job relevant, gives positive feedback, and encourages self-confidence.

2. Training must ensure that trainees gain complete task mastery of previous components before they move on to the next step.

3. Where possible, training should build on elements that are familiar to the trainees from past learning and jobs.

4. Systems should be designed to organize information systems so that memory requirements are limited.

5. Paced or time-pressured situations should be eliminated.

Of course, most of these training principles would be beneficial in any training effort. However, Sterns and Doverspike believed that they were particularly pertinent to older workers who are highly motivated to learn, but who may fear failure in competition with more recently educated trainees. Thus, the principles are designed to assure successful completion of each component, thereby contributing to the trainee's self-efficacy (Bandura, 1977).

Training and Fair Employment Practices

Many training issues concerning minorities, women and older populations result in litigation. Thus, any consideration of training in the year 2000 must also examine these concerns. The Federal *Uniform Guidelines on Employee Selection Procedures* (1978) and court decisions have made it clear that employment discrimination can refer to any technique used in making a decision about employees. In recent years, there has been increased litigation focusing on decisions involving training opportunities and their availability to the work force, especially as they relate to use as a hurdle or criterion for promotional opportunities. This is consistent with individuals viewing training as instrumental in helping them achieve advanced opportunities.

The future history of litigation in the year 2000 concerning training programs and fair employment practices is somewhat ambiguous. It is likely that in the immediate future there will be increased litigation as more members of protected groups use the courts to seek training opportunities as a path toward advancement in work organizations. In the future there will be more advanced job opportunities because there will not be enough persons available for the many jobs that need to be performed. If members of protected classes are given opportunities to seek those advanced positions, there will probably be less court litigation. It is hoped that organizations will focus more on providing training opportunities and thereby have less need to respond to lawsuits. We suspect, from a utility point of view, that even the cost of providing outstanding training opportunities is cheaper than litigating court actions. Certainly, providing training has more positive long range implications for organizations than spending resources in court.

Managerial Training Implications of a Competitive Environment

It seems appropriate to conclude by suggesting that the material presented in this article strongly indicates important management training implications for organizations. First, it is obvious that future managers will need to be very skilled individuals. They will have to be able to provide on-the-job training to integrate unskilled youth in the work force, while also working with job incumbents and other managers who may not be a traditional part of their work force. Supervisors will need to perform these activities at a time when jobs become increasingly complex and national and international competition increasingly intense. In addition, the increase in service sector jobs will require managers to work more with other persons than objects and things from the assembly line. All of this will make training in areas such as interpersonal skills even more important in the future workplace.

As so often happens in disciplines such as industrial/organizational psychology, these concerns have fueled theoretical and empirical interest in the area of managerial and leadership learning and training. Thus, as described by Latham (1988, 1989), there are a number of important developments in leadership training, including research on intervening variables such as self-efficacy as well as training techniques such as behavioral role modeling. There is also thoughtful work (Ronen, 1989) describing the training issues for both individuals and organizations resulting from a more international environment. For example, Ronen asked whether managers educated in one culture are equipped to make attributions about emotional, cognitive, and value sets that may affect a host-country manager's behavior. In discussing the enormous training implications, Ronen noted that the manager given an assignment in a foreign country must possess the "patience of a diplomat, the zeal of a missionary, and the linguistic skill of a U.N. interpreter" (p. 418).

In addition to these developments, the competitive environment will require decision makers to have more information about the outcomes of training. Thus, there will be increasing emphasis on evaluation models to provide information on the effectiveness of training. Cascio (1989) has recently developed utility models that permit the researcher to be able to specify gains from training programs in different metrics such as dollars and percentage increase in output. His analyses include considerations of various assumptions such as situations in which training effects remain strong over a number of years as compared with those in which effects decline over time. Also, Arvey and Cole (1989) have reexamined evaluation models to help determine the impact of sample size requirements and reliability of measures.

CONCLUSION

In summary, we would like to restate our view that training can be a positive force for both the individual and the organization. When training succeeds, it permits individuals to both enter and earn increased responsibility and makes it more likely that work organizations will be successful. For this to occur, there needs to be research and development in a number of areas described in this article.

In a number of instances, researchers have produced information about some of these issues, but that knowledge is not always being successfully translated into policy decisions. Also, whereas there are isolated comments concerning future training needs, there does not yet appear to be a comprehensive federal government policy regarding retraining as a national need. As noted by London and Bassman (1989), it is likely that in the near future national leaders will find it necessary to address this issue. A public policy that stresses maximizing the talent of all persons will have positive benefits for both the work organization and the individual.

References

Arvey, R. D., & Cole, D. (1989). Evaluating change due to training. In I. L. Goldstein (Ed.), *Training and development in work organizations: Frontiers of industrial and organizational psychology* (pp. 89–118). San Francisco, CA: Jossey-Bass.

Bandura, A. (1977). *Social learning theory.* Englewood Cliffs, NJ: Prentice-Hall.

Berlin, G. B. (1983). *Not working: Unskilled youth and displaced adults.* New York: Ford Foundation.

Blau, F. D., & Ferber, M. A. (1987). Occupations and earnings of women workers. In K. S. Koziara, M. H. Moskow, & L. D. Tanner (Eds.), *Working women: Past, present, future* (pp. 37–68). Washington, DC: Bureau of National Affairs.

Britton, J. O., & Thomas, K. R. (1973). Age and sex as employment variables: Views of employment service interviewers. *Journal of Employment Counseling, 10,* 180–186.

Campbell, J. P. (1988). Training design for performance improvement. In J. P. Campbell & R. J. Campbell (Eds.), *Productivity in organizations: Frontiers of industrial and organizational psychology* (pp. 177–216). San Francisco, CA: Jossey-Bass.

Cascio, W. F. (1989). The use of utility approaches as an evaluation model. In I. L. Goldstein (Ed.), *Training and development in work organizations: Frontiers of industrial and organizational psychology* (pp. 63–88). San Francisco, CA: Jossey-Bass.

Cascio, W. F., & Zammuto, R. F. (1987). *Societal trends and staffing policies.* Denver: University of Colorado.

Chusmir, L. H. (1986). Increasing women's job commitment: Some practical answers. *Personnel, 63,* 41–44.

Cook, T. D., & Campbell, D. T. (1979). *Quasi-experimentation: Design and analysis issues for field settings.* Chicago: Rand McNally.

Cross, T. (1986). *The black power imperative: Racial inequality and the politics of nonviolence.* New York: Faulkner Books.

Dipboye, R. L. (1987). Problems and progress of women in management. In K. S. Koziara, M. H. Moskow, & L. D. Tanner (Eds.), *Working women: Past, present, future* (pp. 118–153). Washington, DC: Bureau of National Affairs.

Fleishman, E. A., & Mumford, M. D. (1989). Individual attributes and training performance: Applications of ability taxonomies in instructional systems design. In I. L. Goldstein (Ed.), *Training and development in work organizations: Frontiers of industrial and organizational psychology* (pp. 183–255). San Francisco, CA: Jossey-Bass.

For your information. (September, 1980). *Training and Development Journal, 30,* 8–9.

Ford, J. K., & Wroten, S. P. (1984). Introducing new methods for conducting training evaluation and for linking training evaluation to program design. *Personnel Psychology, 37,* 651–655.

Fossum, J. A., Arvey, R. D., Paradise, C. A., & Robbins, N. E. (1986). Modeling the skills obsolescence process. *Academy of Management Review, 11,* 362–374.

Friedlander, R., & Greenberg, S. (1971). Effect of job attitudes, training and organizational climate on performance of the hard-core unemployed. *Journal of Applied Psychology, 55,* 287–295.

Fullerton, H. N., Jr. (1985). The 1995 labor force: BLS' latest projections. *Monthly Labor Review, 117,* 17–25.

Gagné, R. M. (1962). Military training and principles of learning. *American Psychologist, 17,* 83–91.

Gagné, R. M. (1984). Learning outcomes and their effects: Useful categories of human performance. *American Psychologist, 39,* 377–385.

Gilliam, P. (1988). *The effects of a job acquisition training program on the attitudes, behaviors, and knowledge of educated black adults.* Unpublished doctoral dissertation, University of Maryland, College Park.

Goldstein, I. L. (1986). *Training in organizations: Needs assessment, development and evaluation.* Pacific Grove, CA: Brooks-Cole.

Goldstein, I. L. (1989). A perspective on training issues: Past, present and future. In I. L. Goldstein (Ed.), *Training and career development in work organizations: Frontiers of industrial and organizational psychology* (pp. 1–22). San Francisco, CA: Jossey-Bass.

Goldstein, I. L., Schneider, B., Katzmen, L., & Braverman, E. (1989). *Content validity in training program evaluation.* Unpublished manuscript, University of Maryland, College Park.

How not to retrain workers. (1983, November 12). *Washington Post,* p. A18.

Howell, W. C., & Cooke, N. J. (1989). Training the human information processor: A look at cognitive models. In I. L. Goldstein (Ed.), *Training and development in work organizations: Frontiers of industrial and organizational psychology* (pp. 121–182). San Francisco, CA: Jossey-Bass.

Kaufman, H. G. (1978). Continuing education and job performance: A longitudinal study. *Journal of Applied Psychology, 63,* 248–251.

Klein, K. J., & Hall, R. J. (1988). Innovations in human resource management: Strategies for the future. In J. Hage (Ed.), *Future of organizations.* Lexington, MA: Lexington.

Latham, G. P. (1988). *Human resource training and development.* In *Annual Review of Psychology* (pp. 545–582). Palo Alto, CA: Annual Reviews.

Latham, G. P. (1989). Behavioral approaches to the training and learning process in organizations. In I. L. Goldstein (Ed.), *Training and development in work organizations, Frontiers of industrial and organizational psychology* (pp. 256–296). San Francisco, CA: Jossey-Bass.

The literacy gap. (1989, December 19). *Time,* p. 56.

Literacy on the job. (December 27, 1988). *USA Today,* p. 6B.

London, M., & Bassman, E. (1989). Training and retraining: Contributions to career growth, continuous learning and organizational strategies. In I. L. Goldstein (Ed.), *Training and Development in Work Organizations: Frontiers of industrial and organizational psychology* (pp. 333–375). San Francisco, CA: Jossey-Bass.

McEvoy, G. M., & Cascio, W. F. (1989). Cumulative evidence of the relationship between employee age and job performance. *Journal of Applied Psychology, 74,* 1–5.

Meltzer, H. (1981). Aging realities in managing organizations. In H. Meltzer and W. R. Nord (Eds.), *Making organizations human and productive: A handbook for practitioners.* New York: John Wiley & Sons, Inc.

Miller, R. W., & Zeller, F. A. (1967). *Social psychological factors associated with responses to retraining.* Final report, Research Grant No. 91-52-66-56. Washington, DC: U.S. Department of Labor.

Morrison, A. M., & Von Glinow, M. A. (1990). Women and minorities in management. *American Psychologist, 45,* 200–208.

Odiorne, G. S. (1986). The crystal ball of HR strategy. *Personnel Administrator, 31,* 104.

Offermann, L. R., & Gowing, M. K. (1990). Organizations of the future: Changes and challenges. *American Psychologist, 45,* 95–108.

Personick, V. A. (1985, November). A second look at industry output and employment trends through 1995. *Monthly Labor Review,* pp. 26–41.

Prien, E. P., Goldstein, I. L., & Macey, W. H. (1987). Multidomain job analysis: Procedures and applications. *Training and Development Journal, 41,* 68–72.

Rhodes, S. R. (1983). Age-related differences in work attitudes and behavior: A review and conceptual analysis. *Psychological Bulletin, 93,* 328–367.

Ronen, S. (1989). Training the international assignee. In I. L. Goldstein (Ed.). *Training and career development in work organizations: Frontiers of industrial and organizational psychology* (pp. 417–454). San Francisco, CA: Jossey-Bass.

Rosen, B., & Jerdee, T. H. (1978). The influence of age stereotypes on managerial decisions. *Journal of Applied Psychology, 63,* 573–578.

Rouillier, J. (1989). *The effects of organizational climate on the transfer of training and job performance.* Unpublished doctoral dissertation, University of Maryland, College Park.

Schneider, B., & Konz, A. (1989). Strategic job analysis. *Human Resource Management, 28,* 51–63.

Sheppard, H. L. (1978). *Research and development strategy on employee related problems of older workers.* Washington, DC: Department of Labor, Manpower Administration.

Sterns, H. L., & Doverspike, D. (1989). Aging and the training and learning process in organizations. In I. L. Goldstein (Ed.). *Training and Development in Work Organizations: Frontiers of industrial and organizational psychology* (pp. 299–332). San Francisco, CA: Jossey-Bass.

Sticht, T. G., Armstrong, W. B., Hickey, D. T., & Caylor, J. S. (1987). *Cast off youth.* New York: Praeger.

Turnage, J. J. (1990). The challenge of new workplace technology for psychology. *American Psychologist, 45,* 171–178.

Uniform guidelines on employee selection procedures. (1978, August 25). *Federal Register, 45* (166).

Vaydanoff, P. (1987). Women's work, family, and health. In K. S. Koziara, M. H. Moskow, & L. D. Tanner (Eds.), *Working women: Past, present, future.* Washington, DC: Bureau of National Affairs.

Vobejda, B. (1987, April 14). The new cutting edge in factories. *The Washington Post,* p. A14.

Westcott, D. N. (1982). Blacks in the 1970's: Did they scale the job ladder? *Monthly Labor Review, 105,* 29–37.

Wexley, K. N., & Latham, G. P. (1981). *Development and training human resources in organizations.* Glenview, IL: Scott, Foresman.

White, M. C., Crino, M. D., & Desanctis, G. L. (1981). A critical review of female performance, performance training, and organizational initiatives designed to aid women in the work-role environment. *Personnel Psychology, 34,* 227–248.

Wilson, W. J. (1978). *The declining significance of race.* Chicago, IL: University of Chicago Press.

READING 25

ONE SIZE DOES NOT FIT ALL

John W. Newstrom
Mark L. Lengnick-Hall

No doubt, HRD professionals want to provide programs that will help trainees learn and master the skills necessary to perform efficiently in their jobs. But, despite careful planning and good intentions, sometimes trainees come away from training sessions with little or nothing gained. One culprit is typically overlooked: trainers' perceptions of the learning process.

Every HRD professional holds a set of beliefs and assumptions about how people learn. We might call these belief sets learning paradigms. These paradigms serve as an operating framework that guides a trainer's actions and choices about the most appropriate and effective methods for different groups.

Whenever these paradigms remain implicit or are not regularly and rigorously tested, trainers may become afflicted with "paradigm paralysis," the belief that an existing explanation or learning framework is the best one available and should not be changed. When this happens, trainers may refuse to question their paradigms or resist modifying their assumptions, even in the face of conflicting evidence. In the end, the trainee loses out when that particular paradigm does not meet his or her needs.

One particular paradigm that is rarely questioned is the andragogical model for adult learning. This model has been widely popular and influential in the past two decades, but has not received the level of careful examination needed to justify its unquestioned acceptance.

The andragogical model for adult learning is rarely questioned.

While widely used, the andragogical approach is not the most effective method for training. Instead, a method called the contingency approach might be more suitable to meet the needs of trainees in the nineties.

To help clarify this contention, let's look at two models—the pedagogical and andragogical—that we feel have shortcomings in the learning process. Then we'll look at why the contingency approach to adult learning is a viable and effective alternative.

Source: John W. Newstrom and Mark L. Lengnick-Hall, "One Size Does Not Fit All," reprinted from *Training & Development,* copyright June 1991, the American Society for Training and Development. Vol. 45, no. 6, 43–47. Reprinted with permission. All rights reserved.

THE PEDAGOGICAL PARADIGM

Under a pedagogical model, trainees are viewed as passive recipients of knowledge.

For years, trainers held a relatively stable and widely accepted (though possibly implicit) paradigm regarding the nature of their trainees. Many new trainers had made career transitions from elementary and secondary schools to the world of corporate training. They retained a mental portrait of the learning process (and the typical trainee) that was based on pedagogical assumptions. In other words, they explicitly or implicitly presumed that the nature and characteristics of trainees are those of young and somewhat immature persons.

Under a traditional and extreme pedagogical model, trainees are viewed as passive recipients of knowledge and skills; they are vessels into which new information can be poured. The trainees react when necessary, but they do not take much initiative to control their learning. They have relatively dependent personalities, feeling most comfortable when the trainer is in control of the learning process. In fact, this paradigm views trainees as preferring and enjoying a clearly dependent relationship.

Pedagogically based trainers also assume that trainees have relatively little experience that relates to the training. Under this model, most trainees are blank slates—uncluttered by prior learning—on which trainers can write. They are also viewed as subject-centered in their orientation—interested primarily in the content to be learned and basically motivated by external pressures, goals, and the promise of extrinsic rewards.

Once they are embraced, many paradigms logically lead to behaviors that are highly compatible with them. This fulfills the natural drive toward self-consistency between how people view themselves and others, and how they act as a consequence of those views. Therefore, some trainers unfold a relatively simple repertoire of training methodologies that are natural outgrowths of the pedagogical paradigm.

Pedagogical trainers might hold these viewpoints:

- The trainer's dominant role is that of lecturer.
- Trainees are basically a homogeneous group. Therefore, training practices should be applied equally and consistently across all trainees—one size fits all.
- Success of a training program is a function of the quantity of material that can be transmitted into receptive trainees within fixed time limits.
- The trainer should always be visibly in control of the training process so as to fulfill trainee expectations of the desire superior/subordinate relationship.
- Use of the training content back on the job can best be induced by application of simple rewards, such as certificates, diplomas, or an entry in a personnel record signifying course completion.

In retrospect, the pedagogical paradigm had the merit of being quite simple; unfortunately, it was never widely articulated. That is, some trainers may have acquired and implicitly embraced the pedagogical approach without consciously examining and debating its underlying assumptions. This led to its unquestioned acceptance by other trainers and, even more unfortunately, to its never being refined or improved. The pedagogical model stagnated because its original scope was limited, and because its implicit nature deprived it of the opportunity for further development.

THE ANDRAGOGICAL PARADIGM

Malcolm Knowles achieved considerable fame by recognizing and attacking the limitations of the traditional (pedagogical) learning model. He appropriately pointed out its inherent restrictions and the constraints it placed on the behavior of trainers and trainees.

In its place, he proposed the new term *andragogy,* which he defined as the art and science of teaching adults. The andragogical paradigm, he suggested, contained an alternative set of assumptions that trainers could make about adult learners that would have powerful implications for the instructional process.

These andragogical assumptions are an interconnected set of beliefs about learners that are deeply rooted in humanistic psychology:

- Adult learners have a deep and powerful drive to be self-directing—to be in charge of their developmental destinies and to take control of their learning processes.
- Adults have accumulated a substantial reservoir of quality experiences. These not only represent a rich resource for the individual to build upon and relate new material to, but also can be shared with colleagues.
- Adults recognize their own need to learn as a function of their developmental stage in life and the pressures they feel to avoid technological obsolescence. In short, adults will learn best when they feel the need.
- Adults are basically problem/task-oriented—they want to learn things that will be applicable to work-related challenges they have experienced or expect to encounter in the near future.
- Adults are life-centered. Many want to know how the training fits in with their long-term career objectives.
- Adults are largely intrinsically motivated; the dominant unsatisfied needs in their lives are for self-esteem, achievement, competence, self-confidence, and self-actualization.

The same andragogically based trainers who use well-established "classic" learning principles such as repetition, practice, careful sequencing, and reinforcement also believe it is important to create a positive psychological climate to support learning. Such a climate would be characterized by mutual respect (between trainer and trainee, as well as among trainees), collaboration, freedom to participate, mutual trust, openness, opportunities to share, authenticity, humanness, and pleasure.

These trainers involve learners in diagnosing the participants' own learning needs, translating needs into training objectives, mutually planning the course of the training process (such as through the use of learning contracts), designing and managing a pattern of learning experiences that will support individual learning plans, and involving learners in the evaluation of their own learning effectiveness.

CRITICAL CONCERNS ABOUT ANDRAGOGY

The benefit of more than two decades of experience with andragogy makes it possible, timely, and desirable to assess its limitations. This is necessary because even the most recent publications about andragogy and its originator are uncritical. The problems and weaknesses identified here fall into five major areas.

Face Validity.   The andragogical paradigm has substantial face validity or surface believability. This may be due to the persuasive arguments articulated by Malcolm Knowles, its chief proponent. The close identification of the model with a respected and influential figure has created a dedicated following among trainers. That makes it difficult to criticize the model without implicitly offending its creator and a wide array of its advocates.

More significant, however, is the fact that the model describes adult learners as most of us would like to be seen—self-directing, experienced, capable of judging our own need to learn, task-oriented, life-centered, and intrinsically motivated. Because the model describes our idealized selves, we tend to attribute to it a high degree of face validity. Unfortunately, that validity has made constructive criticism or debate of the model less likely.

Paradigm Rigidity.   Trainers want to believe that the andragogical assumptions are true about themselves. Simultaneously, they embrace a democratic norm of equality for others. That subtly compels them to project those assumptions onto their trainees.

Whether the assumptions would actually hold up under scrutiny is not the issue. What is apparent is that the andragogical model is implicit and has not been closely explored by its users. Consequently, it basically is unchanged from its original form.

Good paradigms need to be tested, modified, and re-tested so that they can become better. Because it is a model with strong value connotations, the andragogical paradigm has not enjoyed the benefits of continual examination and refinement that could have helped it keep pace with the emerging workforce.

Operationality.   A key feature of the original presentation of the pedagogy/andragogy distinction revolved around the identification of characteristics of a child for the former, and an adult for the latter. An adult was defined as "one who has achieved a self-concept of being in charge of his or her own life, of being responsible for making his or her own decisions, and of living with the consequences."

This conceptual description is difficult to put into practice, however, and raises several key definitional and operational questions:

- Are all three of these characteristics necessary before a trainee is identified as an adult?

- Who makes that assessment—the trainer, the trainee, or some other party?

- If a person doesn't qualify as an adult, is "child" the only viable alternative, or is human development actually a continuous process with many intermediate levels?

In addition to these definitional problems, how can the measurement of adulthood be operationalized? For example, is chronological age an adequate proxy for locating a person on the hypothetical continuum from childhood to adulthood? If so, at what age does a trainee qualify as an adult? These and other penetrating questions suggest that andragogy currently lacks the capacity to be a practical tool for the HRD professional.

Role Flexibility.   This is the idea that trainees possibly do not behave consistently in either childlike or adult-like manners. Instead, they demonstrate either set of dominant behaviors depending on the situations and contexts in which they find themselves.

In other words, an employee could take on the role of an adult in one situation and that of a child in another, contradicting a trainer's predictions based on application of a single learning model.

For example, an adult-like employee may, because of learned responses to early socialization experiences, unconsciously respond to the classroom-like setting during a workshop and assume a childlike behavior mode, with childlike expectations, needs, and responses. Here, at least in the short term, a pedagogical approach would be most congruent with that trainee's nature.

Within-Group Differences.   There are many important differences within groups of adult trainees that are unaccounted for by the andragogical model of the adult learner.

For example, among a group of 15 to 20 trainees ranging in age from 35 to 45, there are likely to be important individual differences that would influence the effectiveness of a training program. Some of the trainees may bring more cognitive ability and some may have more highly developed specific skills, while others may arrive with limited educational backgrounds.

These and many other individual differences among adult learners should be considered in the design and delivery of training and development programs.

A CONTINGENCY APPROACH

Trainers need a new learning paradigm that provides an alternative perspective on contemporary employees. This paradigm should retain the elements of simplicity and practicality, be updated to incorporate current portraits of the emerging and diverse workforce, and overcome some of the limitations currently associated with pedagogy and andragogy. Specifically, trainers need to adopt a contingency approach to adult learning.

The goal of the revised model is to stimulate human resource professionals to reflect on their own guiding paradigms and improve them when appropriate. Our contingency model, based on a review of the prevailing research literature, also reflects our own range of experiences with a variety of training groups.

This model suggests moving away from characterizing trainees as homologous adult learners who require a uniform and singular approach to training and development. Instead, adult learners are a heterogeneous group requiring different approaches to training and development depending on individual differences across important characteristics. This model offers a more complex view of individual trainees and the process of designing and delivering training programs, but it provides a more comprehensive and realistic perspective than many popular views.

The central assumption of the contingency model is that trainees differ from each other on many important dimensions. Trainees can be assessed on those dimensions and programs can be designed and delivered to better fit their characteristics.

Instead of considering trainees late in the design process and assuming that they are more adaptable than training programs, the process should be reversed. In other words, the characteristics of a training program should be adapted to conform to the characteristics of the trainees.

Research supports that assumption. A recent review of research by Fleishman and Mumford suggests that training strategies that emphasize the independent acquisition of information improve learning for trainees in high-ability samples. On the other hand, more detailed, concrete training strategies that focus on basic principles can facilitate learning for those in low-ability samples.

They suggest that in the early stages of skills acquisition, trainees will be more likely to profit from learning activities that are compatible with their more general abilities. Rather than focusing on generalized adult characteristics (andragogy) and a single approach to training adults, it is necessary to adapt training programs to the different needs among adults. Apparently, one size does not fit all.

The contingency approach may be effective, but some practitioners view it as a costly and impractical approach to training and development. Clearly, tailoring training programs to each individual in a diverse group could be prohibitively expensive.

However, the construction of group-specific training programs can be cost effective if trainers group trainees according to common profiles. Selection of trainees for training programs requires identification of important trainee characteristics and the search for common trainee profiles. So, in addition to the traditional needs analysis used for identifying training content, it is also necessary to assess trainee characteristics in order to determine how training programs can be effectively designed and delivered.

What trainee characteristics should you assess?

Exhibit 1

DIMENSIONS FOR ASSESSING THE TRAINEE

1. **Instrumentality**
   Degree to which the trainee is concerned with the immediate applicability of the concepts and skills being taught.

2. **Skepticism**
   Degree to which the trainee exhibits a questioning attitude and demands logic, evidence, and examples.

3. **Resistance to change**
   Degree to which the trainee fears the process of moving to the unknown, or the personal effects of that process.

4. **Attention span**
   Length of time the trainees can focus attention before substantial attentiveness is diminished.

5. **Expectation level**
   Level of quality (process) and quantity (content) that the trainee requires from the trainer or the training.

6. **Dominant needs**
   Range of intrinsic and extrinsic individual needs that currently drive the trainee.

7. **Absorption level**
   Pace at which the trainee expects and can accept new information.

8. **Topical interest**
   Degree to which the trainee can be expected to have personal (job-relevant) interest in the topic.

9. **Self-confidence**
   Degree to which the trainee independently and positively views him- or herself and thus requires high or low levels of feedback, reinforcement, and success experiences.

10. **Locus of control**
    Degree to which trainee perceives that she or he can implement the training successfully back on the job with or without organizational support.

Differences in ability among trainees were discussed earlier. Other individual differences are also important to consider. The foundation for the contingency approach identifies ten major factors on which trainees often vary: instrumentality, skepticism, resistance to change, attention span, expectation level, dominant needs, motivational level, topical interest, self-confidence, and locus of control for learning and application (see Exhibit 1).

The real value of this process lies in stimulating each trainer to assess carefully the composition of each trainee group encountered. The approach makes no prior assumptions about the character of a trainee group, nor does it make value judgments about which characteristics are best—it simply recommends that we identify the actual characteristics and then respond to them.

ASSESSING GROUPS

Groups of prospective trainees can be assessed in many ways. For example, trainees could be surveyed using criteria similar to those in the exhibit, with

Allow trainees to revel in their own progress. Provide rewards for individual and group accomplishments.

response options arrayed on 7-point Likert scales. Or, if the groups are homogeneous in nature and are drawn from the same work area, the trainees' manager could be carefully interviewed to create a composite picture. Either approach should cost little in terms of time and money.

For example, assume that a careful assessment of a group of trainees results in a common profile in which the mean scores on the ten dimensions are rated as follows: relatively high on items 1, 2, 3, 5, and 6, and relatively low on items 4, 7, 8, 9, and 10. The broad implications for the trainer might then include the following pragmatic recommendations:

- Highly instrumental. Minimize theory; maximize practice sessions; ensure that opportunities exist for early application on the job (transfer of training).

- Highly skeptical. Provide substantial evidence, examples, data, testimonials from previous users, and individual models who can be identified as applying the material.

- Highly resistant to change. Allow expression of reservations without counterattack. Use force-field analysis to identify pros and cons. Involve the trainees in the design and implementation process.

- Short attention span. Use a wide variety of instructional methods, media, exercises, and classroom seating arrangements.

- High expectations. Focus as much on the presentational process as on the content. Practice and critique all presentations. Explain limitations so that trainees can adjust their expectation levels.

- Wide range of needs. Allow opportunity for trainees to revel in their own progress and achievements. Encourage mutual stroking from within the group. Provide extrinsic rewards for individual and group accomplishments.

- Low absorption level. Break the sessions into brief modules and highlight the key items most worthy of retention. Provide multiple forms of job aids; use repetition heavily.

- Low topical interest. Recognize and accept that some trainees may not want to be there, or don't understand why they were sent. Establish a need for the topic and identify their problems that relate to the content. Use dramatic examples. Provide brief explanations of underlying theory.

- Low self-confidence. Don't overwhelm trainees with content, pace, or theory. Instead, provide early success experiences (such as easy progress tests or simple skill challenges); give constructive and supportive feedback.

- External locus of control. These trainees claim they would like to change, but their environment constrains them. The trainer should encourage them to reassess their own potential role in the process and work with their supervisors to solicit on-the-job support and reinforcement. It also will help to provide examples of "success stories" of others' achievements.

Unless the survey/interview approach reveals an unusually homogeneous group, problems may still remain. Rather than arbitrarily adapting the entire program to fit the group mean, here are several options a trainer can use to incorporate a contingency approach.

- Attempt to construct homogeneous sub-groups based on the data obtained, and achieve the training objectives in different fashions for the different sub-groups. This may be readily feasible in large organizations that plan to have large numbers of employees go through a training program, but less viable for small firms.
- Handle individual exceptions to the norm of trainee characteristics in either of two ways: explain the differences between the few trainees involved and the majority and ask them to adapt as best they can to the program's inherent structure, or work with specific trainees to create individualized learning plans that most effectively build on their unique styles of learning.
- Accept the heterogeneity within the group by incorporating a variety of instructional methods and explaining at the outset that some modules and some approaches will fit individual learners better than others, but that every trainee can still benefit in some way from each approach.

BENEFITS OF THE CONTINGENCY APPROACH

Tested against the five criteria used earlier to criticize the andragogical paradigm, the contingency approach represents a significant improvement.

Face validity is of less concern, since the contingency paradigm does not construct an ideal portrait of trainees, but recommends an actual assessment of them. Paradigm rigidity is defined away, since the contingency model represents a flexible approach and not a static image of trainees. Operationality is always a concern with any model; here we have a practical format for assessing individual trainees or groups of trainees on 10 key dimensions.

Role flexibility could remain a problem; trainees can always choose to vary their behavior outside of their own norm. But the assessment built into the contingency approach does attempt to capture their typical behaviors. Within-group differences would appear to have been resolved through three alternatives offered earlier for handling diverse groups.

Overall, the contingency approach holds substantial promise by being analytical, relatively simple, inexpensive, and practical.

The contingency approach is highly compatible with several contemporary trends in human resource development. These include individual training "contracts," self-paced instruction (either computer-based or in printed form), the formation of cooperative learning groups that have homogeneous needs and interests, and the use of learning resource centers that are adaptable to trainee characteristics.

Congruence, or fit, between the nature of today's trainees and the learning approach used is more important than ever for achieving the required payoff from investments in human resource development. Such a fit can only occur through systematic assessment of the nature of trainees, conscious construction of guiding paradigms that describe the characteristics of trainees, and the design and use of appropriately matching methods, media, content, and delivery.

EMPLOYEE DEVELOPMENT

INTRODUCTION

Development refers to the acquisition of knowledge, skills, and behaviors that improve employees' ability to meet changes in job requirements and internal or external customer demands. Development involves learning that may not be related to the employees' current job. Employee development is a key component of companies' strategy to meet the competitive challenges. Increased globalization of product markets makes it necessary for employees to understand cultures and customs that affect business practices. The roles of executives, managers, and employees have changed due to technology that makes it easier to share information in companies. Also, work is increasingly being performed in teams. Teams increase the likelihood that employees will be innovative, creative, and able to quickly react to changing market needs and customer preferences for products and services. Employees are performing many roles traditionally reserved for managers (e.g., hiring, work scheduling, conflict resolution). Legislation, labor market forces, and social responsibility dictate that companies create work environments to allow all employees, regardless of gender, culture, religion or sexual preference, to be productive, innovative, and grow personally. The readings in this chapter discuss how various aspects of development—creating a multicultural organization, managing a global work force, creating successful work teams, and using feedback from employees—can help companies create a competitive advantage.

Reading 26, "Work Teams That Work," by Montebello and Buzzotta, discusses the different approaches companies use to design and organize work teams. Teams can be formed based on combining tasks, establishing relationships with people who use products and services, or giving employees the capability not only to perform work but to schedule and control the work process. The authors note that teams are not automatically productive. Teams go through a series of development stages involving building relationships between team members and learning how to perform the job.

Reading 27, "The Multicultural Organization," by Cox, discusses the characteristics of a multicultural organization. Some of the characteristics of a multicultural organization include an absence of discrimination and prejudice,

454

women and minorities having complete access to formal and informal information networks, and a work force profile in which women and minorities have equal representation in management positions. Reading 27 also describes how education, career development, and reward systems can be used to create a multicultural organization.

READING 26

WORK TEAMS THAT WORK

Anthony R. Montebello
Victor R. Buzzotta

Here's how to get teams up and running quickly and producing more efficient and effective results.

A new and fundamentally different way of managing people is taking shape in U.S. business. Teamwork is replacing the outmoded, adversarial approach that has grown between management and labor and that now threatens the competitiveness of many corporations around the world.

Teamwork can be more productive, can produce higher quality, and is more cost-efficient than solo efforts. Teamwork also tends to improve job satisfaction, motivation, and employee morale.

Companies that are willing to rethink old ways and develop teams can profit by increasing quality and productivity. And they can develop a workforce that is motivated and committed.

An American Society for Training and Development HRD Executive Survey received responses from 230 HRD executives about teamwork results. The survey found that

- Productivity improved in 77 percent of the respondents' companies.
- Quality improvements due to teamwork were reported in 72 percent of the companies.
- Waste was reduced in 55 percent of the firms.
- Job satisfaction improved in 65 percent of the respondents' firms.
- Customer satisfaction improved in 57 percent.

Additional benefits cited by respondents included more efficient production scheduling, improved production goal setting, and increased ability of team members to resolve their own disputes.

Source: Anthony R. Montebello and Victor R. Buzzotta, "Work Teams that Work," reprinted from *Training & Development*, copyright March 1993, the American Society for Training and Development. Vol. 47, no. 3, 59–64. Reprinted with permission. All rights reserved.

Executives surveyed in 1990 in an *Industry Week* poll were also positive about the benefits of teams. When respondents were asked to name the top benefits, improved quality (reported by 30 percent of respondents) headed the list, followed by improved productivity (24 percent). The surveyed executives also cited increased morale and fewer layers of management as significant benefits.

Reports and statistics published by individual companies support the ASTD survey findings. *Fortune* reports that productivity is as much as 40 percent higher at General Mills plants that use teams than at those that don't. A division of 3M that formed a network of cross-functional teams to develop new products is one of the company's most innovative and fastest-growing divisions. Teams at one of Ingersoll-Rand's manufacturing plants have reduced scrap in one operation from 15 percent to 3 percent.

Success stories are common, and statistical and case studies also support the idea that teamwork works. Tom Peters, management guru and long-time advocate of teams, says in his book *Thriving on Chaos: Handbook for a Management Revolution*, "I observe that the power of the team is so great that it is often wise to violate common sense and force a team structure on almost anything."

Companies that do, he reasons, will achieve greater focus, stronger task orientation, more innovation, and enhanced individual commitment.

WHY TEAMWORK WORKS

Examine manufacturing and service processes in most organizations and you'll find compartmentalized functions, fragmented tasks, and sequential, simplified activities that reflect the old Henry Ford assembly-line design.

But in the 1990s, most modern work processes are more complex. They are nonlinear and can't be (or shouldn't be) simplified into strings of quick, sequential tasks. The productivity and quality that companies want often require a high degree of collaboration among people, departments, and functions.

Many thinking executives have concluded that, given today's productivity and quality objectives, traditional job designs oversimplify the work process. They've found that changing the traditional structure, in which employees perform specialized job functions, to a team structure, in which team members share a core of functions, improves efficiency and effectiveness.

Here's a case in point. GE Chairman and CEO John F. Welch, Jr., wondered why other U.S. firms were getting higher productivity growth than GE. He found that the companies with the highest sustained productivity growth focus less on how their individual departments perform and more on how the departments work together as products move between them.

We have found that when the tasks that produce an end result are simplified and fragmented, they rob the people who perform the work of self-esteem, a sense of accomplishment, and pride in their work. As many people in the United States have become better educated, they have also become less likely to do oversimplified, mechanical jobs.

In an April 1990 *Fortune* article, Richard Wilkinson, a supervising engineer at Kodak, says that Kodak production teams do nearly the same amount of work in one shift as they previously did in three, mainly because they are more effective in using the skills and brainpower of their workforce. "We realized that there was a tremendous resource that was not being tapped," says Wilkinson.

Many workers—from the manufacturing plant to the customer-service office—can and want to perform more complex and sophisticated jobs. Companies such as Heinz used to have simple processes to package food products. Now, as Heinz CEO Anthony J. F. O'Reilly points out in the 1990 *Fortune* article, they use statistical process control and computerized photo-imaging.

Since the implementation of clerical teams at Federal Express, employees buzz about kaizen—the Japanese concept of continuous improvement—and plot on Pareto charts their teams' solutions to complex business problems.

HOW TO DESIGN AND ORGANIZE TEAMS

Teamwork is successful partly because of the focus it places on people. A 1989 article on teamwork in *Business Week* concludes, "American companies are now discovering what the Japanese learned long ago: that people—not technology alone or marketing ploys—are the keys to success in global competition."

The Hackman-Oldham model of job enrichment in the book *Organization Behavior* is perhaps a useful guide to designing teams, enriching work, and organizing tasks to achieve important business objectives.

It identifies five characteristics inherent, to some extent, in any job:

- skill variety—various job activities that call for different skills and talents
- task identity—the extent to which a job is handled from beginning to end, producing an identifiable and complete outcome
- task significance—the extent to which the work has an effect on others or on society in general
- autonomy—freedom and discretion in planning, organizing, scheduling, and performing the work
- feedback—clear and direct information about performance and effectiveness.

Research has shown that jobs with high degrees of those five characteristics tend to motivate workers, which can have a significant effect on important business results. Teamwork designed with the five elements in mind can organize simplified tasks into a unit that focuses on an important business objective, such as quality or customer service.

In companies in which the five characteristics are present, team members are challenged by worthwhile and important job results, rather than limited to performing simple activities that are carefully monitored. Workers have autonomy over their work; they are not bound by rigid policies and procedures. They are able to determine, on some regular basis, whether their performance is satisfactory. As a result, they are more committed to and more involved in their jobs, they are motivated to perform them better, and they are more capable of achieving important business objectives.

Tom Peters suggests three common approaches to forming teams:

- combining tasks
- establishing internal and external client relationships
- vertical loading.

COMBINING TASKS

This principle suggests that, whenever possible, organizations should combine smaller tasks to form new and larger modules of work. The larger, more meaningful work is then assigned to a team of workers, who are given the autonomy to achieve important business objectives. Team members focus on business results to be achieved and, through cross-training, learn all of the component tasks.

The lease-processing function at AT&T Credit Corporation is a good example. It appeared to be a fairly straightforward operation: Receive and review an application, check the applicant's credit standing, notify the applicant of his or her acceptance or rejection, produce a written contract, and collect payments. But several years ago, President Thomas C. Wajnert discerned a problem: "The employees had no sense of how their jobs contributed to the final solution for the customer."

Wajnert combined related tasks and formed teams that collaborated to perform all functions. The result? Applicants receive approval or disapproval days sooner than before, and the teams process twice as many applications each day.

Under the old system, workers described their jobs in terms of activities—they received, reviewed, checked, and notified. Now the team takes pride in making meaningful and significant contributions to the organization—by extending credit to qualified customers.

ESTABLISHING CLIENT RELATIONSHIPS

Many workers in traditional, linear work structures have little or no contact with the people who use their products or services. Teams who have the opportunity to deal directly with the people who use their work—internal and external customers—see immediate increases in skill variety, autonomy, and feedback.

People who work on some teams—particularly those that involve all team members in customer service—tend to have a greater variety of skills than solo workers have, because all team members need to develop interpersonal skills to maintain client relationships. Teams have some autonomy in deciding how to manage those relationships. Finally, many times team members receive specific feedback on their work directly from their customers. All this results in higher productivity, increased quality, and greater efficiency.

Ingersoll-Rand provides an example of improved productivity through interdepartmental teams. Charged with improving customer responsiveness, a five-member employee team within the Construction Equipment Group formalized a natural link between parts and service personnel. One of the team's accomplishments was a new system for ordering parts that saves mechanics at least four hours a day.

When companies empower teams to accomplish a meaningful business result (better customer service), workers gain greater influence over the work process and are motivated to contribute to organizational goals.

VERTICAL LOADING

Traditional organization structures call for a vertical split between doing, planning, and controlling work. In vertical loading, responsibilities and controls that formerly were reserved for high-level managers are added to a team's job. This can begin with simple decision-making activities; as a team develops, responsibilities can be expanded to hiring decisions and inventory management.

Kodak assembled teams and gave them the responsibility and authority for scheduling their own work hours, inspecting their own work, and repairing their own equipment. Employees who used to operate punch presses now coach fellow team members, meet with suppliers, interview candidates, and manage just-in-time inventory. More effective use of the workers' skills and brainpower has enabled the unit to virtually triple its efficiency.

Scores of tasks can be transferred from supervisors to workers to increase the autonomy of teams. Some of those tasks could include the following:

- assign work activities
- make equipment design changes
- make procedure changes
- select and dismiss workers
- prepare labor and materials budgets
- make quality inspections
- appraise team and member performance
- determine pay rates
- train new team members.

These tasks can and should be delegated to teams as they develop their potential to assume more responsibility.

ACCELERATING TEAMWORK DEVELOPMENT

Trainers and HRD professionals can accelerate the often slow and cumbersome process of developing teamwork. Over the past several decades the teamwork literature has presented many different models documenting the developmental stages through which teams must progress if they are to become truly effective.

Beginning with the pioneering work of B. W. Tuckman and progressing through more recent descriptions of the team-development process, the models are amazingly uniform. They all define a similar developmental progression:

- cautious affiliation
- competitiveness

- harmonious cohesiveness
- collaborative teamwork.

The implication in all the models is that groups must develop through this predetermined sequence if they are to mature into fully effective teams. It also means that teams sometimes go through prolonged and often painful trial-and-error processes as they attempt to achieve their task objectives. And they have to do it while working through relationship issues that inevitably arise when people attempt to work together.

Following are details on the four stages of a typical team-development process.

Stage 1—Cautious affiliation. Stage 1 is an exploration period. In this early stage, members' attachment to the team is tentative. Most employees are anxious about what the team and they, as individual members, are supposed to do. They're concerned about their collective and individual ability to accomplish the tasks ahead.

Team members assess other team members' abilities and attitudes and try to determine how and where they fit into the group. They're worried about the team's ability to cope with group problems and conflicts.

Little is accomplished during this stage. Productivity is low. Working relationships are guarded, cautious, and noncommittal.

Stage 2—Competitiveness. Members grow impatient with the team's lack of progress and become overly zealous. Finally, they realize that the team's job is different and more difficult than they had initially imagined. The gap between expectations and reality leads to frustration and anger.

Consequently, there's a lot of blaming, defensiveness, destructive disagreement, and test confrontations—especially with the team leader or those vying for dominant positions. Subgroups may form, with factions competing for influence.

Feverishly hitting on the issues of mission, goals, tasks, roles, and responsibilities, the group makes some progress toward accomplishing its objectives. But along the way, working relationships take a beating.

Stage 3—Harmonious cohesiveness. By the end of this stage, members have discovered that they, in fact, like the team as an entity, the members as individuals, their social encounters, and the sense of belonging they are beginning to feel.

With the urgent Stage 2 questions of mission, goals, tasks, roles, and standards at least partially resolved, members become less dissatisfied. Animosity toward the leader and each other decreases significantly. Previously warring factions mellow into normal, healthy, interpersonal patterns. Competitive relationships become cooperative, close, and mutually supportive. Communication channels open and feelings of mutual trust deepen. During this developmental stage, individuals discover that they're proud to be associated with the team.

As individual and communal skills develop, the quantity and quality of work slowly increase. But the zeal for tangible results that characterized Stage 2 is gone and members bask in the honeymoon-like happiness of their new, harmonious team relationships.

Stage 4—Collaborative teamwork.   During this stage, a group of individuals becomes a truly collaborative team. Structured processes and procedures emerge to allocate resources, resolve personal conflicts, deal with the larger organization, give warranted positive feedback, and discipline members for unacceptable behavior. Members begin to define high standards for evaluating team and individual performance.

The team makes decisions about task and process, diagnosing and solving (or anticipating and preventing) problems, and choosing and implementing actions and changes. Members freely share and pool viewpoints and information to make sound decisions.

During Stage 4, team members are motivated by pride in their accomplishments and a sense of ownership and belonging. Individual and coordinated task expertise leads to peak performance levels.

THE REAL WORLD OF TEAM DEVELOPMENT

Occasionally, through trial and error, a team eventually evolves to the productive, efficient, and effective state of affairs described in Stage 4 of the commonly accepted team-development models. Such teams objectively satisfy the definition of true teamwork that Robert Legton and V. R. Buzzotta give in *Improving Productivity Through People:* "managed, planned, systematic coordination of effort to achieve common goals in the most productive manner."

Many so-called teams in the real world never achieve optimal performance. Some stall and lose their way. Others regress to earlier stages of team development. In fact, some groups that call themselves teams are little more than loose collections of individuals with nothing more in common than working for the same company or having their names on a team roster.

Of the few teams that do reach Stage 4—collaborative teamwork—many do so only after many painful months or years of hit-or-miss struggle and fluctuation between attending to business at the expense of relationships and focusing on relationships while compromising production.

Psychological Associates made some telling discoveries in a two-year survey of the teamwork patterns that were displayed by 32 teams of top-level executives from *Fortune* 500 companies.

Team members discussed specific examples of effective and ineffective team behavior and reached a numerical consensus on how each team was operating. The 32 teams described only 39 percent of their behavior as typifying Stage 4 of the team-development model.

Roughly 19 percent of the behavior displayed by the teams was characteristic of Stage 1—cautious affiliation. Nearly 33 percent of the team behavior described by survey participants was entrenched in Stage 2—competitive—and some teams seemed unlikely to move past it. One participant explained: "Our

Figure 1

DIMENSIONAL MODEL OF TEAMWORK PATTERNS

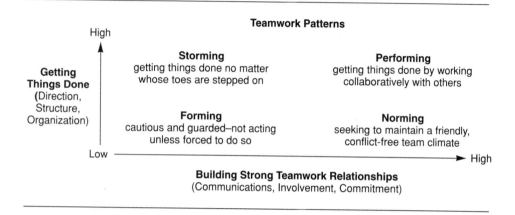

problem is we don't want to resolve our conflicts. We enjoy them too much. We thrive on them. It may be counterproductive, but conflict's a way of life with us."

Implicit in most of the Stage 2 behavior was the fact that the struggle for dominance (assuming there had been one) was clearly settled. A team member participating in the survey said, "With us, decision making is a one-person show. The boss makes the decisions, period. We endorse them. It's a very neat division of labor."

The remaining team behavior (9 percent) described by survey participants was clearly Stage 3—harmonious cohesiveness, typified by this response: "It's been years since I last attended a brisk, businesslike meeting. When we meet, we spin our wheels on small talk, war stories, and inside gossip. It's fun—but what do we accomplish?"

A NEW BEHAVIORAL MODEL

Based on that research, Psychological Associates has developed a behavioral model consisting of two dimensions—getting things done and building strong relationships. This model reflects the two general categories of behaviors commonly exhibited by teams:

- Teams set direction, plan, organize, and structure their activities to get things done.

- Teams work to build strong relationships by fostering open communication— and by getting involvement and commitment—whether they're making decisions, conducting meetings, or resolving conflicts.

The new model—"Dimensional Model of Teamwork Patterns"—is shown in Figure 1. It defines four distinct patterns of teamwork that correspond to four stages of team development: authoritarian (storming), reactive (forming), casual (norming), and true teamwork (performing).

Figure 2 describes the characteristics of the four stages, sorted into quadrants. Each quadrant includes the representative behaviors of the corresponding developmental stage: Quadrant 1, Authoritarian (corresponds to Stage 2 in the old model); Quadrant 2, Reactive (the old model's Stage 1); Quadrant 3, Casual (the old model's Stage 3); and Quadrant 4, True Teamwork (the old model's Stage 4).

Every team behavior described by teams in the Psychological Associates study fell neatly into one of the four patterns, based on its position along the two behavioral dimensions.

Moreover, the fact that these four teamwork patterns correspond to the four stages of team development defined by B. W. Tuckman and others further supports the validity of the new model.

Without guidance or direction, a naturally evolving team would zigzag among the four quadrants before ever reaching Stage 4 and the true teamwork pattern.

A direct pathway to true teamwork is possible. Such a path respects the natural evolutionary inclination of most teams by first addressing issues related to task accomplishment—setting direction, providing structure, and organizing to get results. But there is a critical difference between free-form team development and a guided developmental process. In a guided process, teams address purely task-oriented issues and simultaneously develop communication, involvement, and commitment.

When team members get things done while building strong relationships (for instance, when they make decisions while confronting conflict during meetings), they merge Stage 2 and Stage 3 lessons—and reach Stage 4 more efficiently.

A MICRO VIEW

Does a team ever fully develop to Stage 4, displaying true teamwork patterns in every aspect of its functioning? What happens after a team does reach Stage 4?

Based on the model of teamwork patterns, Psychological Associates developed an assessment process to measure team patterns. The process relates to important operations such as decision making, goal setting, and resolving conflict.

Data from Psychological Associates' study of 32 top-level teams make it clear that teams do not move predictably through the stages of development and the patterns defined by the model. If that were the case, there would be substantially less variation of behavior reported among the stages and much more consistency of behavior across team functions. Rather, teams display behavior that represents vestiges of each pattern, and the patterns vary from activity to activity.

By pigeonholing a team into a specific stage or teamwork pattern, we treat the true complexity of team behavior and dynamics in an overly simplistic way.

The Psychological Associates data also suggest that team development is not a one-shot proposition. It must be ongoing. True teamwork needs to be

Figure 2

RELATIONSHIP BETWEEN TEAM-DEVELOPMENT
BEHAVIOR AND THE FOUR-STAGE MODEL

QUADRANT 1—Authoritarian (Stage 2)
- high structure and direction—low involvement
- gets things done without regard for the needs of team members
- dominated by one or two team members
- overstructured, with tight control
- impatient with lack of progress
- overly competitive and confrontative
- self-serving—"look out for yourself"
- one-way communication
- people become testy, blameful, and overzealous
- frustration, anger, and resistance to goals
- defensiveness, competition, and choosing sides
- subgroup polarization and infighting

QUADRANT 2—Reactive (Stage 1)
- low structure—low involvement
- doesn't act unless forced to
- impersonal, watchful, guarded, and cautious
- tentative attachment to the team
- members cautiously explore boundaries of acceptable individual and team behavior
- tendency to avoid others—to be "loners"
- very little real communication
- tentative attachment to the team
- suspicion, fear, and anxiety about the task ahead
- some anxiety about why they are there, why others are there, who'll lead the group, and what they'll do

QUADRANT 3—Casual (Stage 3)
- low structure—high involvement
- seeks to build a friendly and social team climate
- high concern for the needs of team members
- unfocused, irrelevant, overly friendly communications
- informal information exchanges and social encounters
- feelings of mutual trust, respect, and harmony
- avoidance of conflict
- focus on harmony and conformity
- competitive relationships become cooperative
- sense of team cohesion and close attachment to the team

QUADRANT 4—True Teamwork (Stage 4)
- high structure and direction—high involvement
- gets things done by working collaboratively with each other
- agreement on who they are, what they're doing, and where they are going
- team has clarified relationships and performance expectations
- participation by all team members in achieving challenging goals
- cooperative and productive climate
- open, direct, relevant, and businesslike communications
- ability to prevent or work through team issues

defined in clear behavior standards: teams must use an ongoing process of diagnosis, team critique, and appraisal—supplemented by proper training—to improve on strengths and shore up weak spots. Only then will they approximate and sustain the behaviors we define as the Stage 4 true-teamwork pattern.

Companies that are willing to rethink old ways and follow new behavioral models for organizing teams and developing teamwork will find that the business returns are indeed significant. They'll achieve the twin goals of increasing quality and productivity while developing workforces that are motivated and committed.

READING 27

THE MULTICULTURAL ORGANIZATION

Taylor Cox, Jr.

Executive Overview

Organizations are becoming increasingly diverse in terms of gender, race, ethnicity, and nationality. This diversity brings substantial potential benefits such as better decision making, greater creativity and innovation, and more successful marketing to different types of customers. But, increased cultural differences within a workforce also bring potential costs in higher turnover, interpersonal conflict, and communication break-downs.

To capitalize on the benefits of diversity while minimizing the potential costs, leaders are being advised to oversee change processes toward creating "multicultural" organizations. What are the characteristics of such an organization, and how do they differ from those of the past? What mechanisms are available to facilitate such a change?

This article addresses these questions. It also describes a model for understanding the required features of a multicultural organization and reviews tools that pioneering companies have found useful in changing organizations toward the multicultural model.

As we begin the 1990s, a combination of workforce demographic trends and increasing globalization of business has placed the management of cultural differences on the agenda of most corporate leaders. Organizations' workforces will be increasingly heterogeneous on dimensions such as gender, race, ethnicity and nationality. Potential benefits of this diversity include better decision making, higher creativity and innovation, greater success in marketing to foreign and ethnic minority communities, and a better distribution of economic opportunity. Conversely, cultural differences can also increase costs through higher turnover rates, interpersonal conflict, and communication breakdowns.

To capitalize on the benefits and minimize the costs of worker diversity, organizations of the '90s must be quite different from the typical organization of the past. Specifically, consultants have advised organizations to become "multicultural."[1] The term refers

Source: "The Multicultural Organization" by Taylor Cox, Jr., *Academy of Management Executive*, 1991, Vol. 5, No. 2, 34–47.

to the degree to which an organization values cultural diversity and is willing to utilize and encourage it.[2]

Leaders are being charged to create the multicultural organization, but what does such an organization look like, and what are the specific ways in which it differs from the traditional organization? Further, what tools and techniques are available to assist organizations in making the transition from the old to the new?

This article addresses these questions. I have used an adaptation of the societal-integration model developed by Milton Gordon, as well as available information on the early experience of American organizations with managing diversity initiatives, to construct a model of the multicultural organization.

CONCEPTUAL FRAMEWORK

In his classic work on assimilation in the United States, Milton Gordon argued that there are seven dimensions along which the integration of persons from different ethnic backgrounds into a host society should be analyzed.[3] I use "integration" to mean the coming together and mixing of people from different cultural identity groups in one organization. A cultural identity group is a group of people who (on average) share certain values and norms distinct from those of other groups. Although the boundaries of these groups may be defined along many dimensions, I am primarily concerned with gender, race, ethnicity, and national origin. Gordon's seven dimensions are:

1. Form of acculturation
2. Degree of structural assimilation
3. Degree of intergroup marriage
4. Degree of prejudice
5. Degree of discrimination
6. Degree of identification with the dominant group of the host society
7. Degree of intergroup conflict (especially over the balance of power)

Although Gordon's interest was in societal-level integration, I believe his model can be easily and usefully adapted for analysis of cultural integration for organizations. Therefore, an adaptation of his seven-point framework is used here as a basis for describing organizational models for integrating culturally divergent groups. Exhibit 1 shows my proposed six-dimensional adaptation of the Gordon framework along with definitions of each term.

Acculturation is the method by which cultural differences between the dominant (host) culture and any minority culture groups are resolved or treated. There are several alternatives, the most prominent being: (1) a unilateral process by which minority culture members adopt the norms and values of the dominant group in the organization (*assimilation*); (2) a process by which both minority and majority culture members adopt some norms of the other group (*pluralism*); and

Exhibit 1

CONCEPTUAL FRAMEWORK FOR ANALYSIS OF ORGANIZATIONAL CAPABILITY
FOR EFFECTIVE INTEGRATION OF CULTURALLY DIVERSE PERSONNEL

Dimension	Definition
1. Acculturation	Modes by which two groups adapt to each other and resolve cultural differences
2. Structural Integration	Cultural profiles of organization members including hiring, job-placement, and job status profiles
3. Informal Integration	Inclusion of minority-culture members in informal networks and activities outside of normal working hours
4. Cultural Bias	Prejudice and discrimination
5. Organizational Identification	Feelings of belonging, loyalty and commitment to the organization
6. Inter-group Conflict	Friction, tension and power struggles between cultural groups

(3) a situation where there is little adaptation on either side (*cultural separatism*).[4]
Pluralism also means that minority culture members are encouraged to enact
behaviors from their alternative culture as well as from the majority culture. They
are therefore able to retain a sense of identity with their minority-culture group.
Acculturation is concerned with the cultural (norms of behavior) aspect of integration of diverse groups, as opposed to simply their physical presence in the
same location.

Structural integration refers to the presence of persons from different cultural
groups in a single organization. Workforce profile data have typically been monitored under traditional equal opportunity and affirmative action guidelines.
However, to get a proper understanding of structural integration it is important
to look beyond organization-wide profile data, and examine cultural mix by function, level, and individual work group. This is because it is commonplace in
American companies for gaps of fifteen to thirty percentage points to exist
between the proportion of minority members in the overall labor force of a firm,
and their proportion at middle and higher levels of management.[5]

Even within levels of an organization, individual work groups may still be
highly segregated. For example, a senior human resource manager for a Fortune
500 firm who is often cited as a leader in managing diversity efforts, recently told
me that there are still many "white-male bastions" in his company. As an assistant vice-president with responsibility for equal opportunity, he indicated that
breaking down this kind of segregation was a focal point of his current job.

The *informal integration* dimension recognizes that important work-related
contacts are often made outside of normal working hours and in various social
activities and organizations. This item looks at levels of inclusion of minority-
culture members in lunch and dinner meetings, golf and other athletic outings,

It is commonplace in American companies for gaps of fifteen to thirty percentage points to exist between the proportion of minority members in the overall labor force of a firm, and their proportion at middle and higher levels of management.

and social clubs frequented by organization leaders. It also addresses mentoring and other informal developmental relationships in organizations.

Cultural bias has two components. Prejudice refers to negative attitudes toward an organization member based on his/her culture group identity, and discrimination refers to observable adverse behavior for the same reason. Discrimination, in turn, may be either personal or institutional. The latter refers to ways that organizational culture and management practices may inadvertently disadvantage members of minority groups. An example is the adverse effect that emphasizing aggressiveness and self promotion has on many Asians. Many managers that I have talked to are sensitive to the fact that prejudice is a cognitive phenomenon and therefore much more difficult than discrimination for organization managers to change. Nevertheless, most acknowledge the importance of reducing prejudice for long range, sustained change.

Prejudice may occur among minority-culture members as well as among dominant-culture members. Putting the debate over whether rates of prejudice differ for different groups aside, it must be emphasized that the practical impact of prejudice by majority-culture members is far greater than that of minority-culture members because of their far greater decision-making power (except under extraordinary conditions, such as those of South Africa).

Organizational identification refers to the extent to which a person personally identifies with, and tends to define himself or herself as a member in the employing organization. Levels of organizational identification have historically been lower in the United States than in other countries (notably Japan). Indications are that recent changes in organizational design (downsizing and de-layering) have reduced organizational identification even further. Although levels of organizational identification may be low in general in the U.S. workforce, we are concerned here with comparative levels of identification for members of different cultural identity groups.

Finally, *inter-group conflict* refers to levels of culture-group-based tension and interpersonal friction. Research on demographic heterogeneity among group members suggests that communication and cohesiveness may decline as members of groups become dissimilar.[6] Also, in the specific context of integrating minority-group members into organizations, concerns have been raised about backlash from white males who may feel threatened by these developments. It is therefore important to examine levels of inter-group conflict in diverse workgroups.

TYPES OF ORGANIZATIONS

This six-factor framework will now be employed to characterize organizations in terms of stages of development on cultural diversity.[7] Three organization types will be discussed: the monolithic organization, the plural organization and the multicultural organization. The application of the six-factor conceptual framework to describe the three organization types appears in Exhibit 2.

Exhibit 2

ORGANIZATIONAL TYPES

Dimension of Integration	Monolithic	Plural	Multicultural
Form of Acculturation	Assimilation	Assimilation	Pluralism
Degree of Structural Integration	Minimal	Partial	Full
Integration into Informal Org.	Virtually none	Limited	Full
Degree of Cultural Bias	Both prejudice and discrimination against minority culture groups is prevalent	Progress on both prejudice & discrimination but both continue to exist especially institutional discrimination	Both prejudice and discrimination are eliminated
Levels of Organizational Identification*	Large majority-minority gap	Medium to large majority-minority gap	No majority-minority gap
Degree of Intergroup Conflict	Low	High	Low

*Defined as difference between organizational identification levels between minorities and majorities.

Monolithic Organization

The most important single fact about the monolithic organization is that the amount of structural integration is minimal. The organization is highly homogeneous. In the United States, this commonly represents an organization characterized by substantial white male majorities in the overall employee population with few women and minority men in management jobs. In addition, these organizations feature extremely high levels of occupational segregation with women and racioethnic minority men (racially and/or culturally different from the majority) concentrated in low-status jobs such as secretary and maintenance. Thus, the distribution of persons from minority-cultural backgrounds is highly skewed on all three components of function, level, and workgroup.

To a large extent, the specifications on the frameworks' other five dimensions follow from the structural exclusion of people from different cultural backgrounds. Women, racioethnic minority men, and foreign nationals who do enter the organization must adopt the existing organizational norms, framed by the white male majority, as a matter of organizational survival.

Ethnocentrism and other prejudices cause little, if any, adoption of minority-culture norms by majority group members. Thus, a unilateral acculturation process prevails. The exclusionary practices of the dominant culture also apply to informal activities. The severe limitations on career opportunities for minority-culture members creates alienation, and thus the extent to which they identify with the organization can be expected to be low compared to the more fully enfranchised majority group.

One positive note is that intergroup conflict based on culture-group identity is minimized by the relative homogeneity of the workforce. Finally, because this organization type places little importance on the integration of cultural minority group members, discrimination, as well as prejudice, are prevalent.

While the white-male dominated organization is clearly the prototypical one for the monolithic organization, at least some of its characteristics are likely to occur in organizations where another identity group is dominant. Examples include minority-owned businesses, predominantly Black and predominantly Hispanic colleges, and foreign companies operating in the United States.

Aside from the rather obvious downside implications of the monolithic model in terms of under-utilization of human resources and social equality, the monolithic organization is not a realistic option for most large employers in the 1990s. To a significant degree, large U.S. organizations made a transition away from this model during the '60s and '70s. This transition was spurred by a number of societal forces, most notably the civil-rights and feminist movements, and the beginnings of changes in workforce demographics, especially in the incidence of career-oriented women. Many organizations responded to these forces by creating the plural organization.

Plural Organization

The plural organization differs from the monolithic organization in several important respects. In general, it has a more heterogeneous membership than the monolithic organization and takes steps to be more inclusive of persons from cultural backgrounds that differ from the dominant group. These steps include hiring and promotion policies that sometimes give preference to persons from minority-culture groups, manager training on equal opportunity issues (such as civil rights law, sexual harassment, and reducing prejudice), and audits of compensation systems to ensure against discrimination against minority group members. As a result, the plural organization achieves a much higher level of structural integration than the monolithic organization.

The problem of skewed integration across functions, levels, and work groups, typical in the monolithic organization, is also present in the plural organization. For example, in many large U.S. organizations racioethnic minorities now make up twenty percent or more of the total workforce. Examples include General Motors, Chrysler, Stroh Brewery, Phillip Morris, Coca-Cola, and Anheuser-Busch. However, the representations of non-whites in management in these same companies averages less than twelve percent.[8] A similar picture exists in workgroups. For example, while more than twenty percent of the clerical and office staffs at General Motors are minorities, they represent only about twelve percent of technicians and thirteen percent of sales workers. Thus, the plural organization features partial structural integration.

Because of the greater structural integration and the efforts (cited previously) which brought it about, the plural organization is also characterized by some integration of minority-group members into the informal network, substantial reductions in discrimination, and some moderation of prejudicial attitudes. The improvement in employment opportunities should also create greater identification with the organization among minority-group members.

The plural organization represents a marked improvement over the monolithic organization in effective management of employees of different racioethnic, gender, and nationality backgrounds. The plural organization form has been prevalent in the U.S. since the late 1960s, and in my judgment, represents the typical large firm as we enter the 1990s. These organizations emphasize an affirmative action approach to managing diversity. During the 1980s increased evidence of resentment toward this approach among white males began to surface. They argue that such policies, in effect, discriminate against white males and therefore perpetuate the practice of suing racioethnicity, nationality, or gender as a basis for making personnel decisions. In addition, they believe that it is not fair that contemporary whites be disadvantaged to compensate for management errors made in the past. This backlash effect, coupled with the increased number of minorities in the organization, often creates greater inter-group conflict in the plural organization than was present in the monolithic organization.

While the plural organization achieves a measure of structural integration, it continues the assimilation approach to acculturation which is characteristic of the monolithic organization. The failure to address cultural aspects of integration is a major shortcoming of the plural organization form, and is a major point distinguishing it from the multicultural organization.

The Multicultural Organization

In discussing cultural integration aspects of mergers and acquisitions, Sales and Mirvis argued that an organization which simply contains many different cultural groups is a plural organization, but considered to be multicultural only if the organization *values* this diversity.[9] The same labels and definitional distinction is applied here. The meaning of the distinction between *containing* diversity and *valuing* it follows from an understanding of the shortcomings of the plural organization as outlined previously. The multicultural organization has overcome these shortcomings. Referring again to Exhibit 2, we see that the multicultural organization is characterized by:

1. Pluralism
2. Full structural integration
3. Full integration of the informal networks
4. An absence of prejudice and discrimination
5. No gap in organizational identification based on cultural identity group
6. Low levels of intergroup conflict

The plural organization represents a marked improvement over the monolithic organization in effective management of employees of different racioethnic, gender, and nationality backgrounds.

I submit that while few, if any, organizations have achieved these features, it should be the model for organizations in the 1990s and beyond.

CREATING THE MULTICULTURAL ORGANIZATION

As I have discussed issues of managing diversity with senior managers from various industries during the past year, I have observed that their philosophical viewpoints cover all three of the organizational models of Exhibit 2. The few who are holding on to the monolithic model often cite geographic or size factors as isolating their organizations from the pressures of change.

Some even maintain that because American white males will continue to be the single largest gender/race identity group in the U.S. workforce for many years, the monolithic organization is still viable today. I think this view is misguided. By understanding the generic implications of managing diversity (that is, skill at managing work groups which include members who are culturally distinct from the organization's dominant group), it becomes clear that virtually all organizations need to improve capabilities to manage diverse workforces.

Further, focusing too much attention on external pressures as impetus for change, misses the fact that gross under-utilization of human resources and failure to capitalize on the opportunities of workforce diversity, represent unaffordable economic costs.

Fortunately, the monolithic defenders, at least among middle and senior managers seem to represent a minority view. Based on my observations, the majority of managers today are in plural organizations, and many are already convinced that the multicultural model is the way of the future. What these managers want to know is how to transform the plural organization into the multicultural organization. Although progress on such transformations is at an early stage, information on the tools that have been successfully used by pioneering American organizations to make this transformation is beginning to accumulate.

Exhibit 3 provides a list of tools that organizations have used to promote organization change toward a multicultural organization. The exhibit is organized to illustrate my analysis of which tools are most helpful for each of the six dimensions specified in Exhibit 1.

Creating Pluralism

Exhibit 3 identifies seven specific tools for changing organizational acculturation from a unilateral process to a reciprocal one in which both minority-culture and majority-culture members are influential in creating the behavioral norms, values, and policies of the organization. Examples of each tool are given below.

Training and Orientation Programs.   The most widely used tool among leading organizations is managing or valuing cultural diversity training. Two types of training are most popular: awareness and skill-building. The former intro-

Exhibit 3

CREATING THE MULTICULTURAL ORGANIZATION:
TOOLS FOR ORGANIZATION CHANGE

Model Dimension	*Tools*
I. Pluralism *Objective/s:* –create a two-way socialization process –ensure influence of minority-culture perspectives on core organization norms and values	1. Managing/valuing diversity (MVD) training 2. New member orientation programs 3. Language training 4. Diversity in key committees 5. Explicit treatment of diversity in mission statements 6. Advisory groups to senior management 7. Create flexibility in norm systems
II. Full Structural Integration *Objective/s:* –no correlation between culture-group identity and job status	1. Education programs 2. Affirmative action programs 3. Targeted career development programs 4. Changes in manager performance appraisal and reward systems 5. HR policy and benefit changes
III. Integration in Informal Networks *Objective/s:* –eliminate barriers to entry and participation	1. Mentoring programs 2. Company sponsored social events
IV. Cultural Bias *Objective/s:* –eliminate discrimination –eliminate prejudice	1. Equal opportunity seminars 2. Focus groups 3. Bias reduction training 4. Research 5. Task forces
V. Organizational Identification –no correlation between identity group and levels of organization identification	1. All items from the other five dimensions apply here
VI. Intergroup Conflict *Objective/s:* –minimize interpersonal conflict based on group-identity –minimize backlash by dominant-group members	1. Survey feedback 2. Conflict management training 3. MVD training 4. Focus groups

duces the topic of managing diversity and generally includes information on workforce demographics, the meaning of diversity, and exercises to get participants thinking about relevant issues and raising their own self-awareness. The skill-building training provides more specific information on cultural norms of different groups and how they may affect work behavior. Often, these two types of training are combined. Such training promotes reciprocal learning and acceptance between groups by improving understanding of the cultural mix in the organization.

Among the many companies who have made extensive use of such training are McDonnell Douglas, Hewlett Packard, and Ortho Pharmaceuticals. McDonnell Douglas has a program ("Woman-Wise and Business Savvy") focusing on gender differences in work-related behaviors. It uses same-gender group meetings and mixed-gender role-plays. At its manufacturing plant in San Diego, Hewlett Packard conducted training on cultural differences between American-Anglos and Mexican, Indochinese, and Filipinos. Much of the content focused on cultural differences in communication styles. In one of the most thorough training efforts to date, Ortho Pharmaceuticals started its three-day training with small groups (ten to twelve) of senior managers and eventually trained managers at every level of the company.

In addition, anecdotal evidence from managers of many companies indicates that valuing and managing diversity training represents a crucial first step for organization change efforts.

Specific data on the effectiveness of these training efforts is hard to collect, but a study of seventy-five Canadian consultants found that people exposed to even the most rudimentary form of training on cultural diversity are significantly more likely to recognize the impact of cultural diversity on work behavior and to identify the potential advantages of cultural heterogeneity in organizations.[10]

In addition, anecdotal evidence from managers of many companies indicates that valuing and managing diversity training represents a crucial first step for organization change efforts.

New member orientation programs are basic in the hiring processes of many organizations. Some companies are developing special orientations as part of its managing diversity initiatives. Proctor and Gamble's "On Boarding" program, which features special components for women and minority hires and their managers, is one example.

Language training is important for companies hiring American Asians, Hispanics, and foreign nationals. To promote pluralism, it is helpful to offer second language training to Anglos as well as the minority-culture employees, and take other steps to communicate that languages other than English are valued. Leaders in this area include Esprit De Corp, Economy Color Card, and Pace Foods. For many years, the women's clothier Esprit De Corp has offered courses in Italian and Japanese. At Economy Color Card, work rules are printed in both Spanish and English. Pace Foods, where thirty-five percent of employees are Hispanic, goes a step farther by printing company policies and also conducting staff meetings in Spanish and English. Motorola is a leader in the more traditional training for English as a second language where classes are conducted at company expense and on company time.

Insuring Minority-Group Input and Acceptance.   The most direct and effective way to promote influence of minority-culture norms on organizational decision making is to achieve cultural diversity at all organization levels. However, an important supplemental method is through ensuring diversity on key committees. An example is the insistence of *USA Today* President Nancy Woodhull on having gender, racioethnic, educational, and geographic diversity represented in all daily news meetings. She attributes much of the company's success to this action.

Another technique is explicitly mentioning the importance of diversity to the organization in statements of mission and strategy. By doing this, organizations foster the mindset that increased diversity is an opportunity and not a problem. Examples of organizations that have done this are The University of Michigan and the Careers Division of the National Academy of Management. The latter group has fostered research addressing the impact of diversity on organizations by explicitly citing this as part of its interest.

Another way to increase the influence of minority-group members on organizational culture and policy is by providing specially composed minority advisory groups direct access to the most senior executives of the company. Organizations which have done this include Avon, Equitable Life Assurance, Intel, and U.S. West. At Equitable, committees of women, Blacks and Hispanics (called "Business Resource Groups") meet with the CEO to discuss important group issues and make recommendations on how the organizational environment might be improved. CEO John Carver often assigns a senior manager to be accountable for following up on the recommendations. U.S. West has a thirty-three member "Pluralism Council" which advises senior management on plans for improving the company's response to increased workforce diversity.

Finally, a more complex, but I believe potentially powerful, tool for promoting change toward pluralism is the development of flexible, highly tolerant climates that encourage diverse approaches to problems among all employees. Such an environment is useful to workers regardless of group identity, but is especially beneficial to people from nontraditional cultural backgrounds because their approaches to problems are more likely to be different from past norms. A company often cited for such a work environment is Hewlett Packard. Among the operating norms of the company which should promote pluralism are: (1) Encouragement of informality and unstructured work; (2) Flexible work schedules and loose supervision; (3) Setting objectives in broad terms with lots of individual employee discretion over how they are achieved; (4) A policy that researchers should spend at least ten percent of company time exploring personal ideas. I would suggest that item 4 be extended to all management and professional employees.

The most direct and effective way to promote influence of minority-culture norms on organizational decision making is to achieve cultural diversity at all organization levels.

Creating Full Structural Integration

Education Efforts. The objective of creating an organization where there is no correlation between one's culture-identity group and one's job status implies that minority-group members are well represented at all levels, in all functions, and in all work groups. Achievement of this goal requires that skill and education levels be evenly distributed. Education statistics indicate that the most serious problems occur with Blacks and Hispanics.[11]

A number of organizations have become more actively involved in various kinds of education programs. The Aetna Life Insurance Company is a leader. It has initiated a number of programs including jobs in exchange for customized education taught by community agencies and private schools, and its own in-house basic education programs. The company has created an Institute for Corporate Education with a full-time director. Other companies participating in various new education initiatives include PrimAmerica, Quaker Oats, Chase Manhattan Bank, Eastman Kodak, and Digital Equipment. In Minnesota, a project headed by Cray Research and General Mills allows businesses to create schools of its own design. I believe that business community involvement in joint efforts with educational institutions and community leaders to promote equal achievement in education is critical to the future competitiveness of U.S. business. Business leaders should insist that economic support be tied to substantive programs which are jointly planned and evaluated by corporate representatives and educators.

Affirmative Action.   In my opinion, the mainstay of efforts to create full structural integration in the foreseeable future, will continue to be affirmative action programs. While most large organizations have some kind of program already, the efforts of Xerox and Pepsico are among the standouts.

The Xerox effort, called "The Balanced Workforce Strategy," is noteworthy for several reasons including: an especially fast timetable for moving minorities up; tracking representation by function and operating unit as well as by level; and national networks for minority-group members (supported by the company) to provide various types of career support. Recently published data indicating that Xerox is well ahead of both national and industry averages in moving minorities into management and professional jobs, suggests that these efforts have paid off (The Wall Street Journal, November 5, 1989).

Two features of Pepsico's efforts which are somewhat unusual are the use of a "Black Managers Association" as a supplemental source of nominees for promotion to management jobs, and the practice of hiring qualified minorities directly into managerial and professional jobs.

Career Development.   A number of companies including Mobil Oil, IBM, and McDonald's have also initiated special career development efforts for minority personnel. IBM's long standing "Executive Resource System" is designed to identify and develop minority talent for senior management positions. McDonald's "Black Career Development Program" provides career enhancement advice, and fast-track career paths for minorities. Company officials have stated that the program potentially cuts a fifteen year career path to regional manager by fifty percent.

Revamping Reward Systems.   An absolutely essential tool for creating structural integration is to ensure that the organization's performance appraisal and reward systems reinforce the importance of effective diversity management. Companies that have taken steps in this direction include The Federal National Mortgage Association (Fannie Mae), Baxter Health Care, Amtrak, Exxon, Coca-

Cola, and Merck. Fannie Mae, Baxter, Coca-Cola, and Merck all tie compensation to manager performance on diversity management efforts. At Amtrak, manager promotion and compensation are tied to performance on affirmative action objectives, and at Exxon, evaluations of division managers must include a review of career development plans for at least ten women and minority men employees.

For this tool to be effective, it needs to go beyond simply including effective management of diversity among the evaluation and reward criteria. Attention must also be given to the amount of weight given to this criterion compared to other dimensions of job performance. How performance is measured is also important. For example, in addition to work-group profile statistics, subordinate evaluations of managers might be useful. When coded by cultural group, differences in perceptions based on group identity can be noted and used in forming performance ratings on this dimension.

Benefits and Work Schedules.   Structural integration of women, Hispanics, and Blacks is facilitated by changes in human resource policies and benefit plans that make it easier for employees to balance work and family role demands. Many companies have made such changes in areas like child care, work schedules, and parental leave. North Carolina National Bank, Arthur Anderson, Levi Strauss, and IBM are examples of companies that have gone farther than most. NCNB's "select time" project allows even officers and professionals in the company to work part-time for several years and still be considered for advancement. Arthur Anderson has taken a similar step by allowing part-time accountants to stay "on-track" for partnership promotions. Levi Strauss has one of the most comprehensive work-family programs in the country covering everything from paternity leave to part-time work with preservation of benefits. These companies are leaders in this area because attention is paid to the impact on advancement opportunities and fringe-benefits when employees take advantage of scheduling flexibility and longer leaves of absence. This kind of accommodation will make it easier to hire and retain both men and women in the '90s as parents struggle to balance work and home time demands. It is especially important for women, Hispanics, and Blacks because cultural traditions put great emphasis on family responsibilities. Organization change in this area will promote full structural integration by keeping more racioethnic minorities and white women in the pipeline.

Creating Integration in Informal Networks

Mentoring and Social Events.   One tool for including minorities in the informal networks of organizations is company-initiated mentoring programs that target minorities. A recent research project in which a colleague and I surveyed 800 MBAs indicated that racioethnic minorities report significantly less access to mentors than whites. If company-specific research shows a similar pattern, this data can be used to justify and bolster support among majority-group employees for targeted mentoring programs. Examples of companies which have established such targeted mentoring programs are Chemical Bank and General Foods.

A second technique for facilitating informal network integration is company-sponsored social events. In planning such events, multiculturalism is fostered by selecting both activities and locations with a sensitivity to the diversity of the workforce.

Support Groups.   In many companies, minority groups have formed their own professional associations and organizations to promote information exchange and social support. There is little question that these groups have provided emotional and career support for members who traditionally have not been welcomed in the majority's informal groups. A somewhat controversial issue is whether these groups hinder the objective of informal-network integration. Many believe that they harm integration by fostering a "we-versus-they" mentality and reducing incentives for minorities to seek inclusion in informal activities of majority-group members. Others deny these effects. I am not aware of any hard evidence on this point. There is a dilemma here in that integration in the informal networks is at best a long-term process and there is widespread skepticism among minorities as to its eventual achievement. Even if abolishing the minority-group associations would eventually promote full integration, the absence of a support network of any kind in the interim could be a devastating loss to minority-group members. Therefore, my conclusion is that these groups are more helpful than harmful to the overall multiculturalism effort.

Creating a Bias-Free Organization

Equal opportunity seminars, focus groups, bias-reduction training, research, and task forces are methods that organizations have found useful in reducing culture-group bias and discrimination. Unlike prejudice, discrimination is a behavior and therefore more amenable to direct control or influence by the organization. At the same time, the underlying cause of discrimination is prejudice. Ideally, efforts should have at least indirect effects on the thought processes and attitudes of organization members. All of the tools listed, with the possible exception of task forces, should reduce prejudice as well as discrimination.

Most plural organizations have used equal opportunity seminars for many years. These include sexual harassment workshops, training on civil rights legislation, and workshops on sexism and racism.

Focus Groups.   More recently, organizations like Digital Equipment have used "focus groups" as an in-house, on-going mechanism to explicitly examine attitudes, beliefs, and feelings about culture-group differences and their effects on behavior at work. At Digital, the center piece of its "valuing differences" effort is the use of small groups (called Core Groups) to discuss four major objectives: (1) stripping away stereotypes; (2) examining underlying assumptions about outgroups; (3) building significant relationships with people one regards as different; (4) raising levels of personal empowerment. Digital's experience suggests that a breakthrough for many organizations will be achieved by the simple mechanism of bringing discussion about group differences out in the open. Progress is made as people become more comfortable directly dealing with the issues.

Bias-Reduction Training.   Another technique for reducing bias is through training specifically designed to create attitude change. An example is Northern Telecom's 16-hour program designed to help employees identify and begin to modify negative attitudes toward people from different cultural backgrounds. Eastman Kodak's training conference for its recruiters is designed to eliminate racism and sexism from the hiring process. This type of training often features exercises that expose stereotypes of various groups which are prevalent but rarely made explicit and may be subconscious. Many academics and consultants have also developed bias-reduction training. An example is the "Race Relations Competence Workshop," a program developed by Clay Alderfer and Robert Tucker of Yale University. They have found that participants completing the workshop have more positive attitudes toward Blacks and inter-race relations.

A very powerful tool for reducing discrimination and (to a smaller extent) prejudice, is to conduct and act on internal research on employment experience by cultural group.

Leveraging Internal Research.   A very powerful tool for reducing discrimination and (to a smaller extent) prejudice, is to conduct and act on internal research on employment experience by cultural group. Time Inc. conducts an annual evaluation of men and women in the same jobs to ensure comparable pay and equal treatment. A second example comes from a large utility company which discovered that minority managers were consistently under-represented in lists submitted by line managers for bonus recommendations. As a result of the research, the company put pressure on the managers to increase the inclusion of minority managers. When that failed, the vice president of human resources announced that he would no longer approve the recommendations unless minorities were adequately represented. The keys to the organization change were, first obtaining the data identifying the problem and then acting on it. My experience suggests that this type of research-based approach is underutilized by organizations.

Task Forces.   A final tool for creating bias-free organizations is to form task forces that monitor organizational policy and practices for evidence of unfairness. An example of what I consider to be a well-designed committee is the affirmative action committee used by Phillip Morris which is composed of senior managers and minority employees. This composition combines the power of senior executives with the insight into needed changes that the minority representatives can provide. Of course, minority culture-group members who are also senior managers are ideal but, unfortunately, such individuals are rare in most organizations.

Minimizing Intergroup Conflict

Experts on conflict management have noted that a certain amount of interpersonal conflict is inevitable and perhaps even healthy in organizations.[12] However, conflict becomes destructive when it is excessive, not well managed, or rooted in struggles for power rather than the differentiation of ideas. We are concerned here with these more destructive forms of conflict which may be present with diverse workforces due to language barriers, cultural clash, or resentment by majority-group members of what they may perceive as preferential and unwarranted treatment of minority-group members.

Survey Feedback.   Probably the most effective tool for avoiding intergroup conflict (especially the backlash form that often accompanies new initiatives targeting minority-groups of the organization) is the use of survey feedback. I will give three examples. As one of the most aggressive affirmative action companies of the past decade, Xerox has found that being very open with all employees about the specific features of the initiative as well as the reasons for it, was helpful in diffusing backlash by whites. This strategy is exemplified by the high profile which Chairman David Kearns has taken on the company's diversity efforts.

A second example is Proctor and Gamble's use of data on the average time needed for new hires of various culture groups to become fully integrated into the organization. They found that "join-up" time varied by race and gender with white males becoming acclimated most quickly, and black females taking the longest of any group. This research led to the development of their "on-boarding program" referred to earlier.

A final example is Corning Glass Works' strategy of fighting white-male resistance to change with data showing that promotion rates of their group was indeed much higher than that of other groups. This strategy has also been used by U.S. West which recently reported on a 1987 study showing that promotion rates for white men were seven times higher than white women and sixteen times higher than non-white women.

The beauty of this tool is that it provides the double benefit of a knowledge base for planning change, and leverage to win employee commitment to implement the needed changes.

Conflict-Resolution Training.   A second tool for minimizing intergroup conflict is management training in conflict resolution techniques. Conflict management experts can assist managers in learning and developing skill in applying alternative conflict management techniques such as mediation and superordinate goals. This is a general management skill which is made more crucial by the greater diversity of workforces in the '90s.

Finally, the managing and valuing diversity training and focus group tools discussed previously are also applicable here. AT&T is among the organizations which have explicitly identified stress and conflict reduction as central objectives of its training and focus group efforts.

CONCLUSION

Increased diversity presents challenges to business leaders who must maximize the opportunities that it presents while minimizing its costs. To accomplish this, organizations must be transformed from monolithic or plural organizations to a multicultural model. The multicultural organization is characterized by pluralism, full integration of minority-culture members both formally and informally, an absence of prejudice and discrimination, and low levels of inter-group conflict; all of which should reduce alienation and build organizational identity among minority group members. The organization that achieves these conditions will create an environment in which all members can contribute to their maximum potential, and in which the "value in diversity" can be fully realized.

Endnotes

[1]See, for example, Lennie Copeland, "Valuing Workplace Diversity," *Personnel Administrator*, November 1988; Badi Foster et al. "Workforce Diversity and Business," *Training And Development Journal*, April 1988, 38–42; and R. Roosevelt Thomas, "From Affirmative Action to Affirming Diversity," *Harvard Business Review*, Vol. 2, 1990, 107–117.

[2]This definition has been suggested by Afsavch Nahavandi and Ali Malekzadeh, "Acculturation in Mergers and Acquisitions," *Academy of Management Review*, Vol. 13, 83.

[3]In his book, *Assimilation in American Life* (New York: Oxford Press, 1964) Gordon uses the term assimilation rather than integration. However, because the term assimilation has been defined in so many different ways, and has come to have very unfavorable connotations in recent years for many minorities, I will employ the term integration here.

[4]These definitions are loosely based on J. W. Berry, 1983. "Acculturation: A Comparative Analysis of Alternative Forms," in R. J. Samuda and S. L. Woods: *Perspectives in Immigrant and Minority Education*, 1983, 66–77.

[5]This conclusion is based on data from nearly 100 large organizations as cited in "Best Places for Blacks to Work," *Black Enterprise*, February 1986 and February 1989 and in Zeitz and Dusky, *Best Companies for Women*, 1988.

[6]Examples of this research include, Harry Triandis, "Some Determinants of Interpersonal Communication," *Human Relations*, Vol. 13, 1960, 279–287 and J. R. Lincoln and J. Miller, "Work and Friendship Ties in Organizations," *Administrative Science Quarterly*, Vol. 24, 1979, 181–199.

[7]The concept of stages of development toward the multicultural organization has been suggested in an unpublished paper titled "Toward the Multicultural Organization" written by Dan Reigle and Jarrow Merenivitch of the Proctor and Gamble Company. I credit them with helping me to recognize the evolutionary nature of organizational responses to workforce diversity.

[8]See note 5.

[9]A. L. Sales and P. H. Mirvis, "When Cultures Collide: Issues of Acquisitions," in J. R. Kimberly and R. E. Quinn, *Managing Organizational Transition*, 1984, 107–133.

[10]For details on this study, see Nancy J. Adler, *International Dimensions of Organizational Behavior*, (Kent Publishing Co., 1986), 77–83.

[11]For example, see the book by William Julius Wilson which reviews data on educational achievement by Blacks and Hispanics in Chicago, *The Truly Disadvantaged: Inner City, the Underclass and Public Policy* (The University of Chicago Press, 1987). Among the facts cited is that less than half of all Blacks and Hispanics in inner city schools graduate within four years of high school enrollment and only four in ten of those who do graduate read at the eleventh grade level or above.

[12]For example, see *Organization Behavior: Conflict in Organizations*, by Gregory Northcraft and Margaret Neale, (The Dryden Press, 1990), 221.

CAREER MANAGEMENT

INTRODUCTION

Companies' career management policies and employees' beliefs regarding their career will have to be changed to successfully meet competitive challenges. For example, increased involvement of dual-career and single-parent families in the work force suggests that companies will have to become more sensitive about the potential conflicts between employees' work and nonwork roles. Changes in employees' values suggest that many employees may be less interested in promotions or status, traditional indicators of career success, and more interested in employment that is congruent with their personal values. For employees, the trend toward flatter organizational structures means that career success can no longer be defined in terms of promotions—fewer will be available. This has resulted in changes in the psychological contract between company and employees; that is, the expectations that employees and employers have for each other. Companies must help employees understand that other types of career moves, such as job rotation and lateral moves, are signs of career success, not failure. Employees have to realize that job security is not possible. They must increase their value to their current employer (and increase their employment opportunities) by taking responsibility for career planning.

Reading 28, "Career Gridlock: Baby Boomers Hit the Wall," by Douglas Hall and Judith Richter, emphasizes that to be successful companies need to be aware of employees' needs and values and develop career management policies that are congruent with values and needs. The article discusses how companies are being affected by employees born between 1946 and 1964 ("baby boomers"). Baby boomers' values include a concern for basic values, self-focus, need for autonomy, and concern for work/home balance. Hall and Richter argue that to successfully capitalize on the strengths of the baby boomers, companies need to develop career management policies that meet their needs. These policies include more flexible career paths and policies that help employees balance work and nonwork lives such as career assistance for employed spouses and flexible benefits to help meet family needs.

Reading 29, "Managing the Effects of Layoffs on Survivors," by Brockner, discusses how eliminating jobs, positions, and employees may not result in anticipated economic gains or benefits to the organization. Although downsizing reduces labor costs, it may also contribute to increased product costs due to reduced employee motivation, loss of expertise, and difficulty of employees who have survived the downsizing in absorbing the work load of employees whose jobs have been eliminated. Based on his extensive research on the impact of lay-offs on "survivors," Brockner provides suggestions for how managers can reduce the impact of layoffs on employee morale, motivation, and productivity.

READING 28

CAREER GRIDLOCK
Baby Boomers Hit the Wall

Douglas T. Hall
and Judith Richter

Executive Overview

This article examines ways in which work organizations have been affected by people born between 1946 and 1964. The baby boomers' values, behaviors, and family orientations are significantly impacting industry. Over the next ten years, this group faces the likelihood of serious career plateauing. The difference in career orientation and advancement prospects equates to a growing value and opportunity gap in management. While the number of ways of achieving promotional success is finite (and shrinking), we believe that the number of ways of achieving psychological success is infinite. In addition, many people in this age group have a good sense of where they want to head with their protean or self-directed careers. They key is to discourage long-term career planning and instead to facilitate managers and employees in self-assessment, empowering them to take advantage of opportunities for psychological success, as they arise. The challenge for organizations is to match human resource practices with these new career values.

It would appear that the baby boomers have finally arrived. After enduring overcrowded public schools in the '50s and '60s, competing for admission and surviving mass education "megaversities" and the turmoil of war in the '60s and '70s, and then competing for jobs in recessions in the '70s and '80s, most are now in their 30s and comfortably established in careers. Now it's the employers' turn to adapt to the baby boom, as this group composes almost 55 percent of the United States labor force.[1] Indeed, in 1988, a well-publicized member of the baby boom generation was elected Vice President of the United States.

Have the baby boomers really "made it"? They happen to have "arrived" during a period of unprecedented restructuring of American industry, with widespread workforce reductions, streamlining, and reorganizations, all aimed at gen-

Source: "Career Gridlock: Baby Boomers Hit the Wall" by Douglas T. Hall and Judith Richter, *Academy of Management Executive*, 1990, Vol. 4, No. 3, 7–22.

erating greater output from fewer people. Where have all the opportunities gone? How should top management respond to the concerns of this large cluster of new arrivals at midcareer?

Consider the case of Mary Jackson (not her real name, as will be the case with the other baby boomers' names used). After competing with a large number of other bright college graduates 15 years ago, she was accepted into a training program at AT&T. She did outstanding technical work and struggled to get on the managerial track. Finally, after being turned down for a long-hoped-for promotion, she consulted a senior person for advice. He pointed out that the competition for management slots was becoming severe (the result of multiple workforce reductions at AT&T), that being turned down did not mean that she would never make it into management, and that she should be patient and wait for the next round of promotions.

Reconsidering her chances in light of the large number of candidates for the next round of promotions, Mary decided to step out of the race. She is now successfully running her own consulting firm. She also found that the exit from corporate life provides greater balance for marriage and family.

Unfortunately, the effort to stand out leads most baby boomers to feel that their work is taking up too much of their lives. A recent *Fortune* article called this group "the workaholic generation."[2] Work-family balance, which has been a visible management issue lately, is a major problem for members of the baby boom generation. Their attempts to restore balance, either by dropping out, cutting back to "mommy track" or "daddy track" involvement, or simply by continuing to operate at a higher level of conflict and stress, have become a major management "story" of the 1990s.

THE MISSING VIEW: IMPACT OF THE BABY BOOM ON MANAGERIAL CAREERS

Mary Jackson, Fred Revitch, and Brett Johnson are all members of the post-World War II baby boom generation, and they are dealing with issues of how to achieve fulfillment both at work and at home.

Significant media attention has been placed on the baby boom in recent years, even before the 1988 election campaign. *Time* announced in a cover story, "The Baby Boomers Turn 40" (May 19, 1986). The *Boston Globe* wondered about "Middle Managers With No Place To Go" (February 9, 1988). A movie was titled "Baby Boom," and then it became a television series. Several other series were targeted at baby boomers such as "thirtysomething" and "L. A. Law." As *The Wall Street Journal* put it in 1989, "Marketers have been in love with the baby boom for years now."[3]

Do the baby boomers look as distinctive in the workplace as they do in the marketplace? Should organizational career paths be redefined? This article examines these questions and attempts to determine the implications of the baby boom for the management of organizations.

A PROFILE OF THE BABY BOOMERS AT WORK

What are the distinctive values and concerns which characterize people like Mary Jackson and the other baby boom employees? Based upon our own interviews, and other studies, we have identified the following profile of the baby boom:

1. A strong concern for basic values

Not only are there particular values which baby boomers tend to hold, but the issue of values *per se* is important to baby boomers. Whereas older generations may have been more concerned with achievements, success, status, or power for their own sake, baby boomers are more likely to question *why* they are seeking success and what the *personal meaning* of success is to them.

2. A sense of freedom to act on values

Now we see a genera-tion of professional and managerial employees who, with-out making loud corporate protests, are more likely than their predecessors to behave in ways that are congruent with their values.

Baby boomers have a greater sense of freedom to act out their values than previous age groups. In a sense, this is the corporate extension of the 1960's campus rallying cry, "Do it." Now we see a generation of professional and managerial employees who, without making loud corporate protests, are more likely than their predecessors to behave in ways that are congruent with their values.

This quality of independence manifests itself in various ways: a computer specialist who would not even interview in one company because it did a lot of military contract work, the manager who turned down a promotion because it would require four days' travel each week and keep him away from his year-old son, and countless "whistle blowers" who report corporate fraud, at the expense of their careers. For example, Walker Williams, former head of human resources of Westin Hotels, estimates that when the telephone rings, and an employee is told, "We need you in Atlanta in 15 minutes, no questions, just go," half of the people will not go. He estimated that in a few years, 90 percent will say no.

Channeling humanistic values into a professional career is exemplified in the work of Susan McCrea. After completing her undergraduate degree, she wanted to "make health care more accessible to all people in the world." She wanted to influence domestic health care policy, so she took a job with the State of Minnesota as a state health planner. However, she left the public sector after concluding that health care policy didn't necessarily influence health care delivery systems. She went first to an HMO (health maintenance organization), and then became an independent marketing consultant to HMOs and nonprofit health organizations. She later earned an MBA in health care to increase her earning potential and to improve her professional credentials. She is now assistant to the president of a major Boston medical center, responsible for marketing and planning. She feels satisfied that she is able to influence organizational policies and practices in a way that is consistent with her social values.

3. A focus on self

Concern for values and consistency between values and behavior is related to a strong sense of self-awareness. Dr. Phyllis Horner, an internal personnel consultant at Ford Motor Company, reports that this group's definition of professionalism includes one's own determination of the source of one's self-concept. Finding one's work in life, then, becomes a way to find and express one's self identity. Dr. Horner refers to this focus on self as a "health narcissism."

4. Need for autonomy and questioning authority

Implementing a self concept and living out one's values require a certain level of freedom. Indeed, the need for freedom and the impatience with formal hierarchical authority is probably the most distinctive single feature of the baby boom group. Donald Kanter and Philip Mirvis, using a national probability sample of United States workers, found that only 22 percent reported trust in management, even though 70 percent are generally satisfied with their jobs, and 55 percent are satisfied with their job rewards (pay, promotion prospects, benefits, etc.). Although these data include workers of all ages, the authors cited the baby boomers' disillusionment as a major influence on workforce morale. When they sorted their data by age, they found a "relatively high level" of cynicism reported by the baby boomers. Kanter and Mirvis describe the importance of workers' age in this low trust of management:

> These data suggest to us that a central problem in human resource management in 1985 is workers' response to authority in general. A young, hostile, cynical workforce that holds high opinions of itself . . . is not easy to manage, efficient, loyal, or (probably) very receptive to change.[4]

To be more positive, what qualities would baby boomers value in a leader? In a creative research design, William G. Dyer and Jeffrey H. Dyer conducted a survey of what they called the "M*A*S*H Generation," (1,000 people born in the late 1950s and early 1960s). The purpose was to identify the kinds of organizational processes and conditions that people associated with the hospital organization in the TV show M*A*S*H, which was extremely popular among baby-boomers. Dyer and Dyer concluded that the show's Colonel Sherman Potter most clearly fits baby boomers' image of the effective boss:

> He is the only one they identify as having the trait of leadership. Specifically, they want to work under a superior who treats subordinates with respect and is concerned about their welfare and tries to understand them. They list the important personal characteristics of the leader as being broadmindedness, competence, maturity, and fairness.[5]

5. Less concern with advancement

Related to the baby-boomers' questioning of authority is a weaker desire to become part of it. There appears to be less of a driving passion to move up the hierarchy among this group. For example, Ann Howard and James A. Wilson compared motivation profiles for two groups of AT&T managers, one hired in the 1950s and the other in the 1970s (baby boomers). In terms of intrinsic motivation to achieve and perform well on the job, there were no significant differences between the two groups. The big difference came in their desires for upward

Indeed, the need for freedom and the impatience with formal hierarchical authority is probably the most distinctive single feature of the baby boom group.

mobility, expressed in a variety of measures (e.g., a questionnaire measuring desires for upward mobility, needs for dominance, expectations for a higher position in the next five years). Although both groups wanted a challenging job and a middle manager's salary in the following five years, 54 percent of the 1950s sample indicated a desire to advance to a middle management position while only 34 percent of the 1970s cohort chose that outcome. Howard and Wilson concluded that, "By and large, the [1970s] recruits were inclined neither to push their way up the organization hierarchy nor to lead others. In short, the new managers weren't motivated to act like managers." Based on this AT&T research and his own interviews, Walter Kiechel concludes,

> *They don't like telling others what to do any more than they like being told. No respecters of hierarchy, they don't want to get to the top just because it's the top.*[6]

These conclusions are supported by Miner and Smith's finding that the motivation to manage has declined among college students between 1960 and 1980.[7] Similarly, Driver reports a drop in what he calls "linear" (i.e., advancement) career motives for college students in the 1960s and early 1970s (although Driver finds that this trend has now reversed for the post-baby boom group).[8] Although challenging work and financial rewards are still very important to baby boomers, they may be less willing than other groups to assume higher-level managerial responsibilities to attain these rewards. (This may help explain the appeal to baby boomers of investment banking, real estate development, and entrepreneurship, activities in which financial rewards are high but organizational management responsibilities are relatively low.)

6. Crafting: In-place career development

Perhaps related to this lower need for advancement is the baby boomer's orientation to high quality in the current job. In this highly educated, highly principled group, utilizing one's potential (i.e., self-actualization) is not only an important need but a basic value. To perform poorly produces dissatisfaction and guilt.

In this highly educated, highly principled group, utilizing one's potential (i.e., self-actualization) is not only an important need but a basic value.

An Opinion Research Corporation study found that by the late 1970s, concerns for self-fulfillment and personal growth had become pervasive in the work force as a result of the addition of the baby boomers.[9] As one person described his need for growth, "How do I keep myself growing even if my company isn't interested in that?" Walter Kiechel, who called boomers the workaholic generation, asks, "Why do they work so hard? Because they love it, they say, often using the words 'fun,' 'creative,' and 'stimulating' to describe the experience . . . Work is also where they perform, as an athlete performs, winning the applause of the crowd."[10]

This concern for craft in one's work shows up in the baby boomers' preference for professional work, as identified by Raelin (see Endnote 15). The critical motivation is the intrinsic reward which comes from crafting one's work, and doing a high-quality job in the service of a useful purpose.

7. Entrepreneurship

If the baby boomer values achievement and autonomy but does not want to submit to authority or exercise it, what career and organization design options are left open? One option is to become an entrepreneur. A study of 9,000 graduates of the Harvard Business School found that the peak age for entrepreneurship is in the early 30s (30 percent of the entrepreneurs studied start at this age). People in their early 30s represent the peak of the baby boom cohort.

Howard Stevenson of the Harvard Business School's entrepreneurship project, sees entrepreneurship as a way of expressing the counter culture values of the 1960s and 1970s.[11] Warren Bennis views it as an expression of selfhood which is a major legacy of the 1960s, and he predicts a major growth in self-employment over the next 10 years (10 percent of the United States working population is now self-employed). Bennis refers to this phenomenon as the "Big Chill" factor (named after the movie): if there is a hero, he or she is played by an entrepreneur.[12]

8. Concern for work/family balance: the total life perspective

The baby boom group is getting into parenting in a big way. Part of the concern for the self is an awareness of one's personal and family life. Even though work is important, as we have just said, there is a sense among baby boomers that "I work to live; I don't live to work."

The baby boom group has done well occupationally, despite the dire forecasts referred to earlier, and this work success may spill over into private life. Louise Russell found that, although crowded, the baby boom cohort has not suffered educationally because of its size. More of its members were educated than any previous generation, and more money was spent on education per student than ever before. Furthermore, despite the negative effects of their numbers, Russell concluded that baby boomers are still earning real income as high as, or higher than, any previous generation.[13]

Further evidence of the occupational success of this group is found in Joseph Raelin's analysis of what he calls "the 60's generation." Raelin uses census data to show that an unusually high proportion of the 60's generation's members are in professions. Similar findings were reported by Werner and Stillman and by Mills.[14]

There is a sense of costs and benefits of various life and career options (e.g., "Can I really have a truly satisfying career and a truly satisfactory parenting experience?"). There is an ability to make tradeoffs and establish balance between work and family concerns.

The fact that the baby boomer manager/professional cohort has a large proportion of women is a significant factor in this concern for family. We refer to this balanced, autonomous work life, in which the employee takes major responsibility, as the protean career. In the remaining sections, we consider how organizations can cope with these growing numbers of protean baby boomers.

GUIDELINES: TOWARD MORE EFFECTIVE UTILIZATION OF BABY BOOM POTENTIAL

There seems to be great potential in the "problems" represented by the baby boom. They are exceptionally well-educated, value-driven, independent, and quality-oriented. In response to these qualities, what steps might management take to tap this potential? Let us detail some recommendations about how an organization might yield the maximum benefit from its baby boom managers and employees.

1. Concern for Values: Replace the "Promotion Culture" with a "Psychological Success" Culture

Since values are so important to the baby boomer, corporate cultures must be changed to accommodate these new career orientations. As Dave Cornett, a human resources consultant at DuPont said, "The continuous upward mobile employee is a thing of the past. The key for DuPont is to make the current position as rewarding and exciting as possible." In our work with organizations, we have repeatedly heard comments such as, "I personally would like to make a lateral move, but everyone else around here would see that as a mark of failure." Every organization has a career culture which acts as a powerful source of resistance to the changes we just recommended. How might these career cultures be modified to produce an organizational transformation?

Strategic human resource development has been advocated as a way to implement changes in how an organization nurtures its talent.[15] The culture of an organization is reinforced by forces at three levels: the top strategic level is translated into design through managerial systems and programs (the middle level), and put into action at the implementation (bottom) level.

Human resource policies that affect employees' personal growth (e.g., policies of promotion from within, cross-training and cross-functional moves, using key management jobs for developmental purposes, holding managers accountable for subordinate development, and a strong internal succession planning process) are key to human resource development.

We believe that the corporate career culture is changed by promoting dialogue and establishing clear policies, endorsed and acted upon by top management, which promote more diverse and flexible forms of career growth. Time and energy should be directed at these basic development policies before work is put into managerial-level activities (such as training managers in new forms of career management) or implementation level changes (such as career workshops). When the latter activities are worthwhile, their effects are multiplied if supportive human resource policies are in place first.

More organizations are engaging in these new practices all the time. Companies such as DuPont, IBM, and Johnson and Johnson, have committees or task forces on work/family issues, that raise awareness and create significant change in career management practices. DuPont's task force on career and family issues was made up of a cross-section of levels and job functions so that the total work force was represented. The task force met with groups of employees, identified key issues, commissioned a major employee survey, and recommended explicit policies and implementation strategies, that are currently being adopted. Conscious use of organizational development values and processes were important in the success of this process, according to Faith Wohl, co-chair of the task force.

2. Freedom To Act on Values: Support More Protean or Self-Directed Careers

Organizational careers must be reframed to reflect the notion that "up is not the only way," to use the words of author Beverly Kaye.[16] Career paths are becoming more differentiated and self-directed—i.e., more protean. As another part of the culture change process, these protean career paths should be more widely communicated and valued. Employees need to have the option of periodically changing direction, so they are not locked into one single, long-term, career plan. As Will Cookta, personnel director for Beringer Ingelheim Pharmaceuticals, puts it,

> We want our company to look at multiple options, not just up-or-out or up-or-you're-a-jerk. We need to crack the culture.

To tap the great diversity of the baby boom group in a leaner organization, there must be a range of career paths from which to choose: functional specialist (growth within a discipline), consultant, local generalist (rotational, lateral movement, while remaining in one location), fast-track or slow-track into management, project management, permanent part-timer, job specialist (career development within a specific job position), and multipath option (the freedom to move from one of the paths to another). These different career forms are already available in many organizations. However, they are often used on a case-by-case basis, without the realization that they represent the career preferences of large numbers of baby boomers and the needs of contemporary organizations. They need to be legitimized (or "blessed") by the culture as valued and respected careers.

How might we move toward these differentiated career paths to provide opportunities for more protean careers? The following approaches are being taken in some organizations:

To tap the great diversity of the baby boom group in a leaner organization, there must be a range of career paths from which to choose.

- Articulate a policy that the career is the individual's responsibility. This is a radical departure for many organizations that take a more paternalistic approach to career development ("Trust us"). Ford Motor Company has made this change, and employees are assisted through training workshops in asserting more personal control over their careers.[17] It may mean supporting the employee in saying "no" to the company at times. The end result in giving the employee more self control, however, is often better choices and greater employee commitment to their own decisions.

- Encourage the manager's self-assessment. To crack the upward-mobility career culture, managers and executives require special attention. Managers need to become more self-aware and self-directed. A realistic self-assessment is important to a manager's self-directed career choices. Even in an era of widespread career planning, this self-assessment is still a relatively new activity in company-run management education programs. (It is more often done for lower-level employees.) Each person needs to take a good honest look at his or her own skills, interests, and values, compared to those required of fast-trackers. DuPont's Individual Career Management program (ICM), for example, helps employees assess their values, skills, and interests and then develop an action plan for work directions that express these personal preferences.

- Promote early rotational (lateral) moves. To give an employee a sense of the wide range of available career paths, there should be opportunities for lateral, cross-functional, moves early in the career. This prevents people from becoming stuck in a dead-end career path and makes rotational moves a realistic option later in the career. Periodic rotation creates a wide range of skills which can be used for general management or to produce a well-rounded specialist.

According to Goodyear career counselor Laura Bettinger, Goodyear employees submit applications for lateral moves, stating their skills, experience, and the position sought. Managers submit lists of openings and the human resource department serves as an internal placement broker. This lateral pool program has a positive reputation, and many people apply, creating competition for open slots.

- Discourage career planning; stress "work planning." While we have stressed the need for activities like self-assessment, we have not specifically recommended career planning. Organizations should not encourage long-term career planning.

In view of the volatile nature of today's organizational environments, it is difficult for both organizations and individuals to do effective long-term planning. What may be more realistic is to encourage people to assess their own values, interests, skills, and lifestyle needs in relation to various work options that are available.

The focus is on identifying the type of work the person would like to do over the next few years, without trying to worry about the rest of his or her career.

Self-assessment is different than setting a long-term plan for a career with a complete set of specific goals and stepping stones. Given the turbulence in the environments of today's organizations, the latter is unrealistic. Using solid, realistic self-understanding and skills the individual is empowered to recognize and use career opportunities as they arise. Shorter-term work plans, combined with a longer-term sense of personal direction, is required.

Indeed, a shorter-term focus fits well with that of most employers. As Joe Robinson, budget manager for First Union Corporation, said, "I've noticed in job interviews that nobody asks what you plan to be doing five to ten years from now. They only talk about one-year plans."

- Define career growth as the development and use of new skills and abilities. One concrete way to reinforce the notions of work planning and up-is-not-the-only-way is to communicate the idea that growth in the career is the development and use of new skills and abilities. For most people, and in particular for intrinsically-motivated, growth-oriented baby boom managers, the important experience in the career is learning and growing, not necessarily ascending the hierarchy, as mentioned earlier. However, top management must legitimize this concept and set a policy facilitating career-long growth. For example, Chrysler encourages employees to establish stretch goals for their current positions, an activity that is supported by a pay-for-performance program. These practices are combined with development of new learning through periodic job changes (e.g., rotational moves, in-place changes in responsibility).

3. Focus On the Self: Self-Development and Lifelong Learning in the Work Itself

Almost 30 years ago, Chris Argyris raised the issue of whether the needs of psychologically healthy individuals could be congruent with the goals of the employing organization.[18] Today, it seems clear that the answer is, yes, the *effective* organization can find ways to make human need satisfaction and organizational goal attainment compatible. The move to participative and team leadership practices in today's downsized and delayered organization is probably the most important change in management circles today, and it certainly fits well with the self-directed, authority-questioning values of the baby boom cohort.[19] This is the "silver lining" which can be seen in the wake of severe corporate cutbacks and restructuring.

John Morley, personal manager at Kodak, described an example of this delayering, in which a vice president of operations moved up to replace an executive vice president who retired. However, there was no replacement for the vice president. This one move impacted ten levels in the company. While these changes do produce frustrations, they also result in greater spans of control and responsibility for lower level managers and employees. To support this increased responsibility, managers are trained to coach and develop their employees. These in-place development activities are supported by a pay-for-performance program.

Creating small, autonomous work units, such as the small project team that developed IBM's personal computer has great potential. Autonomous work teams, described in Tracy Kidder's *The Soul of a New Machine*, created a new computer at Data General. Project engineers and managers (in their 20s and 30s, primarily) often would work late into the night and through the weekend, motivated by the "pinball theory": if you win the game, you get to play it again (i.e., you get another project, with greater significance and more resources). The rewards came from learning and solving complex problems, so that good performance demanded the development of new knowledge and skills.[20]

The autonomy and intrinsic challenges associated with these new leadership styles provides the employee with a greater opportunity for self-development. Another way to think of this is as in-place career development. The smart manager attempts to give employees freedom to generate their own solutions to work

The move to participative and team leadership practices in today's downsized and delayered organization is probably the most important change in management circles today, and it certainly fits well with the self-directed, authority-questioning values of the baby boom cohort.

problems and to implement them in their own ways. Not only does this auton-omy provide a way to tap employees' creativity and motivation most effectively, but it is often virtually demanded by the wider spans of control resulting from eliminating layers of management. Managers who try to supervise too closely soon realize that they are overworked to the point of burnout. Permitting greater employee freedom is congruent with the high-autonomy and self-related values of the baby-boom manager. More stress on life-long learning is a natural by-product of restructured leaner organizations.

4. Concern for Autonomy: More Flexibility and Diversity

As organizations face the need for more flexible human resource policies, flexibil-ity in employee work arrangements needs to be extended. This is especially important for women. A growing number of women and men in their mid-to-late-thirties are beginning to conclude that they cannot have it all (career, mar-riage, and family) and are opting for marriage and family. For women, this often happens after an attempt to resume working after the first baby is born. The real-ization comes that (1) they have already proven to themselves that they can be successful in the career, (2) life is short, and (3) at this time in their life they would rather be home raising the family. At this point, many women are opting out of organizational careers. Our hunch is that in five to ten years, they will be back at a different form of work. For women to continue rising in the ranks of manage-ment, organizations are going to have to find even more flexible arrangements to accommodate them.[21]

How might this greater flexibility be attained? One method is to use more permanent part-time jobs. As organizations are forced to make part-time work available to recruit and retain qualified employees (especially working mothers), part-time work is becoming more common in professional and managerial posi-tions. It has always been an option for hourly and clerical employees. Parental leaves, with a phased re-entry period, are becoming longer and more flexible. Flextime is also widespread and a boon to working parents. Similarly, "flexplace" (working in the home) is becoming more available thanks to computer technol-ogy and a more liberal corporate culture. Baby boomers who are well established in their careers and are now part of management have more leverage to negotiate work arrangements. Given the choice of being flexible or losing a valued manager or professional, many organizations have opted for flexibility. This was the work/family balance track that Felice Schwartz recommended in her widely-quoted *Harvard Business Review* article, "Management, Women and the New Facts of Life."[22] However, if the organization has not been confronted by baby boom managers with this choice, this flexibility is not freely offered.

Baby boomers who are well established in their careers and are now part of man-agement have more leverage to negotiate work arrangements.

Moving to part-time work has to be done carefully and on a job-by-job basis, as not all jobs are conducive to part-time schedules. One organizational induce-ment, however, is that part-time managers and professionals usually contribute full-time involvement.

Corporate timetables must be adjusted to let part-timers rise at a more grad-ual rate. In the Westin Hotel organization, for example, employees' needs and career preferences are included as part of the potential assessment process. The company uses different development strategies for employees who report they are geographically mobile and for those who are not. "When we know what they want to do, we won't try to sell the person on a move they don't want. In the past, managers could staff a position with exactly who they wanted. Now we will have to change the company's expectations," reported Walker Williams, former head of Westin's human resources.

5. Less Concern for Advancement: More Diversity in Career Paths

In contrast to earlier eras when people had to conform to the structure of the work place, the structure of assignments can be more responsive to people's needs. As industries become more competitive and new technologies widely available, the competitive edge is often obtained through the flexible use and development of people.

For example, a construction firm founded by two baby-boom Harvard graduates is rapidly acquiring a reputation for building individualized, high-quality, bright, airy, aesthetic, energy-efficient townhouses in the Cambridge area. (These townhouses are in great demand by their fellow baby boomers.) How do they maintain the quality of their work as the number of projects expands? They use fairly simple designs and simple, high-quality materials that are easy to install and are not labor-intensive. Since the Boston work force is so unpredictable, they adjust the structure of their designs to fit the capabilities of the available workforce resulting in a high level of quality.

Consulting is another way to retain a valued professional or manager in a more autonomous role. An employee who needs large blocks of time off can be hired on a retainer basis, and used for specific projects and problems. This keeps the employee involved and up to date so re-entering the organization on a basis if his or her personal situation changes is made easier.

Organization structures are also being made more flexible by *differentiated career paths*. Not everyone aspires to be president of the company. There are, of course, high potential young people who have senior executive aspirations, and they need to be moved across a variety of specialties, to learn the complete business. However, many other talented people aspire to be the best within their particular specialty:

> Not everyone needs to be a high potential achiever. For many people, being the food and beverage director at the Plaza Hotel would be a lifelong fulfillment. We need to establish different disciplines (e.g., personnel, front office, maintenance) as *career objectives* and create specialized career paths within them. (Walker Williams, Westin Corporation)

Monsanto found that the focus on more specialized career paths fits well in a leaner organization with slower overall corporate growth. There is a need to invest more creativity and energy in specific businesses and plant locations. According to Charles Arnold:

With less corporate mobility, there is a need to emphasize the employees' identification with their own unit or location. This does not mean that some employees will not be asked to move around the corporation, but it does mean that broad corporate career programs are being de-emphasized, and specialization is OK.

Local identification is a way to provide more freedom, and to nurture creativity and innovation with less bureaucracy, but within the context of a worldwide organization. It also places more stress on development within the current assignment.

Greater differentiation in career development paths means that development is being encouraged in the following directions:

- within the present job (in-place development)
- within the present function (or specialty or discipline)
- within the present geographic location (which could include cross-functional rotational moves within that location)
- across functions and locations (i.e., corporate mobility for high-potential employees)

6. Crafting: Reward Quality of Performance, Not Potential

In the management and professional ranks in most organizations, there is a tendency to pay for potential rather than performance. For example, if two people are both performing at the same level, and if one person is a 25 year old "high potential" manager and the other is 40 years old and seen as plateaued, the younger "hi-po" person usually gets larger salary increases, and the older manager feels unrewarded for his or her performance. The organization suffers a tremendous loss in motivation by linking pay to future promotions.

Many organizations, such as Eli Lilly, are now seeking ways to identify and reward performance excellence, regardless of the person's age or career stage. One-time cash awards can be given for outstanding achievements (and in some cases they can simply be honorific awards and still be effective). In addition to helping de-couple promotion and rewards, such excellence awards fit nicely with the baby boomer's appreciation of quality and craftsmanship.

7. Entrepreneurship: Encourage It in the Organization's Interest

We recommend two strategies for using baby boomers' entrepreneurial potential. The first, and preferable, route is to harness energy in the service of organizational change. When baby boom managers or professionals become restless and start thinking about starting up their own venture, find a "start up" activity for them in your own organization. This could be a project assignment (either full-time or part of the current job) to explore the creation of a new product, service, or process. The person would be responsible for gathering resources, forming coalitions with key supporters, and championing the idea. In Rosabeth Kanter's terms, he or she would be expected to be a "change master."

News columnist Ellen Goodman has commented on how much corporate vitality and renewal is lost when baby boom entrepreneurs (whom she calls "corporate misfits, blue-jeaned [people] in three-piece corporations") leave to start up their own ventures.

> The new breed are among the liveliest most exciting business people I meet. I don't want to read failure into their personal success, but few are starting the next IBM. Few will become the employers of hundreds of thousands.
>
> And as they leave larger companies, those workplaces are diminished. They lose another agent for change. More to the point, as these entrepreneurs walk out the door, one by one, American corporations lose another source of ideas, of innovation, of energy.
>
> And sometimes, after I have heard these success stories, I wonder how many of their old colleagues and bosses ever realize the gap left by another "misfit" who dropped a pair of old floppy wing tips beside the exit door.[23]

As newly restructured organizations attempt to tap the commitment and involvement of all employees to produce "high-performance systems," the entrepreneurial spirit of baby boom employees is a perfect resource to tap more systematically.

A second strategy is to support baby boomers in exploring entrepreneurial activities outside the organization. Often, helping the individual gather realistic information on starting up one's own business, leads to a decision that the cost and risks are too high. For example, a computer professional in her early 30s was interested in starting a company to make and sell high-quality hand-sewn craft items. Her company, through a career exploration seminar, supported her in interviewing people who had started similar businesses. She also interviewed people in various parts of her own firm to get more realistic information about future career opportunities there. She concluded that even the most successful entrepreneurs in her area of interest were putting in longer hours than she was currently and making less money. At the same time, she found an opportunity to start up a new line of products in her current firm. (In a similar case, a 30 year old software manager who initially wanted to get into real estate development talked it over with his senior management, and they agreed to let him redesign his current job to include new venture activity, with a sizeable incentive compensation arrangement.)

But what if exploration had led these managers to leave rather than stay? We argue that it is in the company's interest to support a person in a decision to leave, if that would be the best fit for her or him. If managers feel coerced to stay, eventually their performance suffers, and they eventually have to leave anyway.

We also recommend that a company keep its door open to allow baby boomers to return if they ever become dissatisfied with working on their own. Many firms, however, have a policy of not hiring ex-employees. To us, this seems self-punitive for the firm, since this strong performer would just go to work for the competition, if she were barred from rejoining her old employer.

We argue that it is in the company's interest to support a person in a decision to leave, if that would be the best fit for her or him.

Thus, our message is, fan this entrepreneurial spirit. Use it to help restructure and vitalize the organization, and support individuals in finding a good fit for their own form of entrepreneurship, either inside or outside the firm. Chances are, a good thorough search will lead them to stay and to use this energy on the organization's behalf.

8. Concern for Balance: More Organizational Sensitivity to the Employee's Home Life

While many organizations recognize that a manager's personal and family life affect work and career decisions, there is reluctance to do anything to assist with strains between work and family life. This arises out of a sincere desire not to intrude in the manager's personal life.

However, sometimes the organization already is intruding on the person's private life to a considerable extent (i.e., through disruptive relocations, demanding work schedules, job stress). There are ways to assist the manager in dealing with work-home conflicts in ways which maintain privacy and enhance autonomy and coping skills. A few possibilities are listed below:[24]

- Establishing corporate dialogue on work-family balance. The critical step is to make this a "discussable" topic in the organization and to establish mechanisms to work on it. The experiences of firms like DuPont and Stride Rite have shown that a representative task force or committee is effective in creating this dialogue.
- Management training sessions in managing the work-home interaction. One pharmaceutical company does this in a three hour seminar, using company cases and a sharing of managers' learnings about how best to deal with work-home conflicts. In this extremely popular seminar, managers consider both what they can do for themselves and to help subordinates.
- After-hours workshops for managers and spouses to share problems and solutions in specific family topics (e.g., coping with a move, the first child, adolescents).
- Including the spouse in discussions about an impending relocation.
- Job search assistance to a career spouse during a relocation. This is often done through informal personnel networks in the new location or by making the firm's outplacement consultants available to the spouse. What is critical is expanding the organization's sphere of perceived responsibility to include the spouse and family, as well as the employee.
- Including spouses in more social events or conferences to share the benefits of corporate life.

There are numerous ways the manager's private life could be insulated more from the stresses of the job. Older managers accept the intrusion of work into family life: baby boom managers do not.

Exhibit 1

SUMMARY OF BABY BOOM CHARACTERISTICS AND
RECOMMENDED ORGANIZATIONAL ACTIONS

Profile of Baby Boom Characteristics	*Recommended Organizational Action*
1. Concern for basic values	1. a. Replace promotion culture with psychological success culture b. Examine, change corporate career criteria c. Focus on corporate ethics
2. Freedom to act on values	2. a. Support protean career paths b. More lateral mobility c. De-couple rewards and the linear career path
3. Focus on self	3. Build on-going development into the job through: • Self-development • Life-long learning
4. Need for autonomy	4. More flexible careers
5. Less concern with advancement	5. More diversity in career paths. More change: • within present job • within present function • within present location • across function and locations
6. Crafting	6. Reward quality performance, not potential
7. Entrepreneurship	7. a. Create internal entrepreneurial assignments b. Encourage employee career exploration (internally and externally)
8. Concern for work/home balance	8. a. More organizational sensitivity to home life b. Training for managing the work-home interface c. Inclusion of spouse in career discussions d. Career assistance for employed spouse e. Flexible benefits to help meet family needs (e.g., child care, elder care, care for sick children) f. More flexible work arrangements

Exhibit 1 summarizes these profile characteristics and provides recommendations. The need to provide support and opportunities for greater self-awareness and empowerment is the common thread running through the recommendations.

CONCLUSION

The basic career and personal values of the baby boom manager are congruent with today's changing management practices and philosophy—as long as we can recognize and be comfortable with the paradoxical idea that the more self-control the manager has over his or her career, the more control (in the form of information and predictability) the organization has as well. The dark side of the baby boom and the downsized organizations is that there are too many good people available for too few management slots. But the bright side is that a lot of good baby boomers have their own sense of where they want to head with their protean careers. While the number of ways of achieving promotional (vertical) success is finite (and shrinking), the number of ways of achieving psychological success is infinite. The more an organization can match its human resource management practices to this new protean career orientation, the more effective it will be in tapping the potential of the baby boom.

Study Methodology

We define career as a series of work-related experiences (events and the person's reactions to those events) which occur over the span of the person's work life. Note that this definition says nothing about advancement to a certain level, nothing about success as defined by salary or other external measures. In fact, surveys of work values in the contemporary work force indicate that the most important kind of success to most people is what we call psychological success: the achievement of those goals which the individual values most. To some people, psychological success might be measured in terms of professional competence, to others, family rewards, and to still others, fame and public recognition. To understand the career situation as it is perceived by members of the baby boom group in today's leaner organization, we need to consider their values, as well as career strategies.

Our information comes from three sources. One source was research literature on the baby boom.[25] A second source is the numerous seminars and workshops, both for MBA students and corporate managers, on self-assessment and career planning which we have offered over the last 15 years. The participants in these seminars have been predominantly members of the baby boom cohort, and many of the issues raised have been related to career stage concerns of this group. Finally, although we did not intend for this to be an empirical article, we did interview 20 managers in the baby boom group and 25 human resource executives in companies noted for progressive human resource practices (e.g., Monsanto, DuPont, Westin, Kodak, Florida Power and Light, AT&T, Corning Glass) to obtain more in-depth examples of how individuals and organizations are being affected by this demographic phenomenon. While somewhat limited, our own data are useful for illustrative purposes, and they are consistent with trends in the research literature.

Endnotes

[1]See Walter Kiechel III, "The Workaholic Generation," *Fortune*, April 10, 1989, 50–62.

[2]*Ibid.*

[3]David Wessel, "One Sure Fact: Baby Boomers are Aging," *The Wall Street Journal,* January 3, 1989, B1.

[4]Donald L. Kanter and Philip H. Mirvis, "Managing Jaundiced Workers," Working Paper, Boston University School of Management, 1985, 12. This work is also reported in D. L. Kanter and P. H. Mirvis,

The Cynical Americans, (San Francisco: Jossey-Bass, 1989).

[5]William G. Dyer and Jeffrey H. Dyer, "The M*A*S*H Generation: Implications for Future Organizational Values," *Organizational Dynamics,* Summer 1984, *13,* 78.

[6]This research is reported in Ann Howard and James A. Wilson, "Leadership in a Declining Work Ethic," *California Management Review,* Summer 1982, Vol. XXIV, *4,* 33. See also Kiechel, *op. cit.,* 50.

[7]See J. Miner and N. Smith, "Decline and Stabilization of Managerial Motivation over a 20-year Period," *Journal of Applied Psychology,* 1982, *67,* 297–305. More data on the lower levels of advancement motivation among baby boomers, compared to the previous generation, are reported in an excellent longitudinal AT&T study. Ann Howard and Douglas W. Bray, *Managerial Lives in Transition,* (New York, Guilford, 1988).

[8]See Michael J. Driver, "Careers: A Review of Personal and Organizational Research," in C. L. Cooper and I. Robertson (Eds.), *International Review of Industrial Psychology 1988,* (London: John Wiley & Sons, Ltd., 1988), 245–277.

[9]See M. R. Cooper, B. S. Morgan, P. M. Foley, and L. B. Kaplan, "Changing Employee Values: Deepening Discontent," *Harvard Business Review,* 1979, *57,* 117–125.

[10]See Kiechel, *op. cit.,* 51–52.

[11]Howard Stevenson, "Entrepreneurship," presentation at Academy of Management Meeting, Boston, 1984.

[12]Warren G. Bennis, "Leadership," presentation at Academy of Management, Boston, 1984. These ideas are elaborated in Bennis's book *Leaders* (co-authored with Burt Nanus), (New York: Harper & Row, 1985).

[13]See Louise B. Russell, *The Baby Boom Generation and the Economy,* (Washington, DC: The Brookings Institute, 1982) 1. Another excellent source is Landon Jones, *Great Expectations: America and the Baby Boom Generation,* (New York: Ballantine Books, 1980).

[14]See Joseph A. Raelin, "The '60s Kids in the Corporation: More than Just 'Daydream Believers,'" *The Academy of Management Executive,* February 1987, 21–30. The Mills survey is reported in D. Quinn Mills, *Not Like Our Parents,* (New York: William Morrow and Company, 1987). See also Rex Werner and Deanne Stillman, *The Woodstock Census* (New York: Viking Press, 1979).

[15]See, for example, D. T. Hall, "Human Resource Development and Organizational Effectiveness," in C. J. Fombrun, N. M. Tichy, and M. A. Devanna, *Strategic Human Resource Development* (New York: John Wiley & Sons, 1984), 159–181; D. T. Hall, "Dilemmas in Linking Succession Planning to Individual Executive Learning," *Human Resource Planning,* 1986, *25,* 235–265; and D. T. Hall, and J. G. Goodale, *Human Resource Management: Strategy, Design, and Implementation* (Glenview, IL: Scott, Foresman, 1986).

[16]See Beverly Kaye, *Up is Not the Only Way,* (Englewood Cliffs, NJ: Prentice-Hall, 1982).

[17]This work was reported in Phyllis C. Horner, "Career Development in Traditional Manufacturing Organizations," Career Division Workshop presentation, Academy of Management Meetings, Boston, August 11, 1984.

[18]This idea was originally reported in Chris Argyris, *Personality and Organization,* (New York: Harper, 1957). It is now showing up in practice as a trend in organizational career programs. See, for example, Manuel London and Steven A. Stumpf, "Individual and Organizational Career Development in Changing Times," in Douglas T. Hall and Associates, *Career Development in Organizations,* (San Francisco: Jossey-Bass, 1985), 21–49, for more discussion of this guideline and the others which follow.

[19]For more discussion on how cutting-edge organizations are designing their career systems to better match individual and corporate career needs, see Thomas Gutteridge, "Organizational Career De-

velopment Systems: The State of the Practice," in Douglas T. Hall and Associates, *op cit.*, 50–94.

[20]See Tracy Kidder, *The Soul of a New Machine* (Boston: Little, Brown and Company, 1981).

[21]See Felice N. Schwartz, "Management Women and the New Facts of Life," *Harvard Business Review*, 1989, *67*, 65–82; Douglas T. Hall and Judith Richter, "Balancing Work Life and Home Life: What can Organizations do to Help?" *Academy of Management Executive*, 1988, *2*, 213–223; and Douglas T. Hall, "Promoting work/family balance: An organization change approach," *Organizational Dynamics*, Winter, 1990, 18, 5–18.

[22]See Schwartz, *op. cit.*

[23]Ellen Goodman, "Corporate Misfits," *Boston Globe*, November 1, 1988, 13.

[24]For more discussion on work-home balance, see Hall and Richter, *op. cit.*, and Hall, "Promoting work/family balance," *op. cit.*

[25]See, for example, the work of Raelin, Jones, Russell, Mills, and Werner & Stillman referred to in Notes 13 and 14. See also the work on student values in the 1960s reported in Douglas T. Hall, "Potential for Career Growth," *Personnel Administration*, May-June, 1971, 18–30; Douglas T. Hall, "Humanizing Organi-

zations: The Potential Impact of New People and Emerging Values Upon Organizations," in H. Meltzer and F. R. Wickert (eds.), *Humanizing Organizational Behavior* (Springfield, IL: Charles C. Thomas, 1976), 158–174; S. E. Seashore and T. Barnowe, "Collar color doesn't Count," *Psychology Today*, August 1972, 53–54, 80–82; L. D. Johnston, J. G. Backman, and P. M. O'Malley, "Monitoring the Future: Questionnaire Responses from the Nation's High School Seniors, 1979" (Ann Arbor, MI: Institute for Social Research, University of Michigan, 1979); D. Yankelovich, "Putting the New Work Ethic to Work," (New York: The Public Agenda Foundation, September 1983); P. Renwick, and E. E. Lawler III, "What You Really Want from Your Job," *Psychology Today*, May 1978, 53–58, 60, 65, 118; R. A. Easterlin, *Birth and Fortune: The Impact of Numbers on Human Welfare* (New York: Basic Books, 1980); "Americans change," *Business Week*, February 20, 1978, 65–66; D. Quinn Mills, *Not Like Our Parents: A New Look at How the Baby Boom Generation is Changing America,* (New York: William Morrow and Company, 1987); and Martin M. Greller and David M. Nee, *From Baby Boom to Baby Bust,* (Reading, MA: Addison-Wesley, 1989).

READING 29

MANAGING THE EFFECTS OF
LAYOFFS ON SURVIVORS

Joel Brockner

Consider the following reactions of two middle-level managers who had recently survived layoffs in their respective organizations:

> You give years of your life to this place, and what do you get for it? I used to think that my job was secure as long as I put in a good day's work. Well, you can forget about that. Plus, the way that they handled the layoff was really unfair. I used to be real gung-ho about working here, but if that's the way they're going to treat people, then they shouldn't expect to get much out of me.

> This is something that the company should have done a long time ago. I feel bad that some people had to be let go, but frankly, they, like the organization, will probably be better off for it over the longer haul. This place is much more ready to tackle the challenge of the 90s; we may have more work to do as a result of the cutbacks, but it's much more interesting than before.

Layoffs were a pervasive workforce reduction strategy in corporate America in the 1980s, and there is every indication that this trend will continue for the foreseeable future. According to a survey of managers attending the American Management Association's (AMA) annual convention in 1989, more than half of the companies represented had experienced downsizing within the past four years; an even greater percentage anticipated that their companies would downsize within the next few years.[1] According to *The New York Times*, many major American companies in numerous industries announced significant job cuts for 1991, including Sears, General Dynamics, General Motors, Citicorp, Pan Am, Digital Equipment, Hills Department Stores, and Aetna Life & Casualty. The specter of layoffs is omnipresent in the public sector as well.[2] As this article was being prepared, many state and local governments were facing massive layoffs.

Most of the research on layoffs has studied their underlying causes, or their effects on the individuals who lost their jobs. Overlooked was the highly practical matter of how both the productivity and morale of the individuals who did not

Source: Copyright 1992 by The Regents of the University of California. Reprinted from the California Management Review, vol. 34, no. 2. By permission of The Regents.

lose their jobs were affected by the layoffs.[3] After all, it is the reactions of the employees who remain—hereafter referred to as the survivors—that will dictate the organization's effectiveness.

The opening quotations suggest that there is no simple or single answer to the question "What effects do layoffs have on survivors?" As exemplified by the first quotation, some managers report that the layoffs have a decidedly negative effect on their subordinates' productivity, morale, and overall commitment to the organization. Reactions similar to those described in the second quotation, while less frequent, also have been reported. Adding to this apparent confusion, some managers report that their subordinates respond very differently even within the same organization or work group.

If the factors that influence survivors' reactions can be identified, then managers will be able to make more informed decisions about how to handle layoffs. Many of the determinants of survivors' reactions are factors that managers can influence. If the layoffs are mismanaged, thereby hampering survivors' productivity and morale, then the organization stands to lose a sizeable portion of the savings it hoped to achieve by introducing layoffs. Consequently, it is incumbent upon executives of a downsizing organization to plan and implement layoffs with special attention devoted to their impact on those who remain.

FACTORS AFFECTING SURVIVORS' REACTIONS

The Role of Perceived Fairness. Survivors' perceptions of the fairness of the layoff are determined by their beliefs about *why* the layoff occurred as well as *how* the layoff was implemented. The general finding emerging from numerous studies is that survivors react more favorably to the extent that they believe that the layoff is fair. While the previous statement should come as no surprise, far less obvious is the fact that survivors' fairness judgments are influenced by a wide range of issues. Some of the fairness-related questions survivors ask include:

- *Is the layoff justified?* Survivors need to believe that the layoff is truly necessary rather than, for example, caused by managerial greed or incompetence. If other firms within the organization's reference groups also are downsizing, then survivors are more likely to believe that the layoff is justified. In addition, if top management clearly considered alternative cost-cutting measures (e.g., attrition, hiring and wage freezes) before deciding upon layoffs, then the layoffs are likely to be received as more justified. One former CEO of a major supermarket chain tried whenever possible to reduce non-personnel costs before resorting to layoffs. One virtue of this cost-cutting strategy is that when layoffs were introduced in this organization, survivors were more likely to view them as justified.

- *Is the layoff congruent with corporate culture?* IBM has adopted a policy of full employment, in which every attempt is made to retrain and redeploy employees whose jobs are eliminated. Moreover, when the workforce at IBM needs to be reduced—IBM announced that it planned to cut 14,000 jobs in 1991 to bring its workforce to 359,000, down nearly 12% from its employment peak of 406,000 in 1986—IBM chooses attrition, early retirement, and other voluntary resignation incentives. At other companies, employment security is an integral part of their informal organization or corporate culture. When these companies choose to implement layoffs—as many so-called paternalistic organizations did in the 1980s (e.g., Kodak, AT&T) and now in the 1990s (e.g., Digital Equipment)—they violate employees' beliefs about the nature of the corporate culture. Layoffs perceived to be inconsistent with corporate culture break the "psychological contract" between employer and employee, and therefore they are more likely to be seen as unfair.[4]

- *Did the organization provide ample advanced notice?* If people are going to lose their jobs due to layoffs, it would seem only fair that they receive adequate advanced notice. In fact, proponents of the federally enacted plant closing law—which requires employers to give at least 60 days advanced notice in the case of plant closings or large-scale layoffs—argued their case in the name of justice. As Senator Howard Metzenbaum (D-Ohio), the bill's chief sponsor, put it: "[60 days notice] should be the law of the land. It's the fair and humane thing to do." In announcing in 1991 that it would close one of its assembly plants in 1993, General Motors said that the long lead time was to allow the laid-off workers to have "the fullest opportunity for planning for their future."

  Of course, what constitutes "ample" advanced notice is likely to vary considerably from one situation to the next. Furthermore, top management will have to weigh the need to provide enough advanced notice against the sometimes justified concern that they may pay the price for providing *too much* advanced notice (in the form of employee slowdown or sabotage). Consider this, however: prior to the passage of the plant closing law, the *average* amount of advanced notification provided to employees that they were about to lose their jobs was one week! It seems likely that in many of these instances laid-off workers could have been given greater advanced notice (i.e., they could have been treated more fairly) with little or no additional cost to the organization.

- *In implementing the layoff, how well did the organization attend to the details?* It would seem that survivors would be highly concerned with the fact that a layoff occurred, and not so interested in the nitty-gritty details of how the news was delivered. However, research has shown that survivors' reactions do depend to a significant extent on the apparently trivial details of implementation.[5] One example of how *not* to communicate the layoff was provided by a petroleum company in which employees were brought together for a meeting. Each employee was given an envelope with the letter A or B on it. The A's were told to stay put, while the B's were ushered into an adjacent room. Then, en masse, the B's were told that they were being laid off. Another example of how *not* to do it was the experience of employees at a communications company, in which the word of layoffs was leaked to the press *before* the people to be laid off were told. As a result, some people learned that they were about to lose their jobs over the radio while driving home from work.

These implementation details affect survivors largely because of their symbolic meaning. People need to be treated with dignity and respect, especially during a painful procedure such as downsizing. The way in which the organization implements the layoff may seem trivial, but the message conveyed in their actions is anything but trivial. Thus, the organization that "sweats the details" of implementation is communicating (to both layoff victims and survivors) that it respects the personhood of its employees; as a result, the layoff will be perceived as more fair.[6]

- *Did management provide a clear and adequate explanation of the reasons for the layoffs?* When the organization takes the time to provide adequate reasons for the layoffs, survivors will judge the process as more fair. The content of the explanation may include valid arguments for the necessity of the layoffs which previously uninformed survivors may not have thought about before. Also, the mere fact that the organization took the time and effort to explain—independent of the content of the explanation—itself symbolizes to survivors that they are being treated in a dignified and respectful way.[7]

- *Were cutbacks shared at higher managerial levels?* A theme emerging thus far is that survivors' fairness judgments depend upon both the substance and style of how the layoff is handled. It is important to do the right thing (substance), and to do things right (style). If the organization is downsizing, then it is especially important for higher levels of management to become cost-conscious, too. For example, when International Harvester was undergoing severe downsizing in 1981, the company forgave loans of its president and chief executive officer (worth more than $2 million). Even though these arrangements were part of the executives' compensation package when they were hired years earlier, somehow it just seemed unfair for top managers to benefit greatly at the same time that the corporation was undergoing severe downsizing. Said one survivor: "Morale is zero. We see Lee Iacocca working for a dollar a year and the general feeling is that our top guys are lapping up the gravy." Another commented that "the company could not be in such trouble if it paid top executives millions of dollars a year."[8] To avoid such reactions, turnaround specialist John Whitney advocates that senior management take pay cuts before (or while) the rank and file are being laid off.

- *What decision rule was used to determine which employees would be laid off versus chosen to remain?* Some of the typical decision rules include merit, seniority, or function. No one decision rule is inherently more fair than the other. Depending upon the corporation's strategy, history, and culture, each may be viewed as most legitimate, at least some of the time. For example, if the post-layoff strategy is to specialize in areas emphasizing certain functional units rather than others, then the decision about who goes or stays is likely to be determined by function. If seniority has historically been the basis for making resource allocations in the organization, and the organization does not wish to buck that tradition, then the decision about who goes or stays may be determined appropriately by seniority.

Perhaps just as important as the content of the decision rule is the way that it is implemented. Consistency and accuracy are two hallmarks of a fairly implemented decision rule.[9] Thus, if merit is the basis for one, then it should be the basis for all. Exceptions may be allowed, but if so it is incumbent to explain why. Moreover, if merit is the chosen basis, then it is crucial that the procedure used be a valid representation of merit. For example, one organization intended to downsize on the basis of merit; performance appraisal ratings were used to distinguish the good from the not-so-good performers. However, the accuracy of the performance appraisal system in this particular organization was viewed as dubious by many, both layoff victims and survivors alike. As a result, the well-intentioned decision to downsize on the basis of merit was viewed as unfair.

- *Did the organization provide tangible caretaking services to help soften the blow for those laid off?* Tangible signs of caretaking include severance pay, outplacement counseling and other forms of helping those laid off find comparable employment elsewhere, and continuation of health insurance and other benefits beyond the date of severance. It is no secret that certain individuals receive more caretaking than others; layoff victims with high status in the organization usually are provided more than their lower-status counterparts. Furthermore, certain organizations do more for their layoff victims than others. For example, when the Defense Department canceled the Navy's A-12 program in January 1991, many subcontractors laid off workers. Subcontractor A did relatively little to take care of the layoff victims; although the company held "two job fairs and contacted possible employers."[10] In sharp contrast, Subcontractor B "ran a hot line, took out full-page newspaper ads inviting prospective employers to call, and set up a resource center with word processors, fax machines, and other facilities for job hunting."[11] In addition, Subcontractor B reportedly provided greater severance pay than Subcontractor A. Although it is possible for a downsizing organization to be too generous in its caretaking of layoff victims—as in the case of a financial services institution who provided so much to the layoff victims that some survivors felt envious!—in general, survivors are more likely to view the layoff as fair if they see concrete evidence of the organization providing for those laid off.

- *Did the organization involve its employees in the layoff decision process?* For some of the many decisions associated with layoffs, employees should participate in the process. For example, prior to downsizing, certain organizations actually seek input from their workforces on how to cut costs. This practice has two benefits. First, employees may have creative solutions on how to do more with less without necessarily having to resort to layoffs. Second, if the employees do opt for layoffs, they are more likely to view them as fair (than if the very same layoffs were autocratically imposed upon them).

In sum, these questions describe some of the fairness-related issues of concern to survivors. In general, survivors' productivity and morale will be greater to the extent that they view the layoffs as fair. Furthermore, perceived fairness is especially likely to affect survivors' reactions under certain specific conditions, such as:

- *When survivors are close to the layoff victims.* Prior to the layoffs, survivors may have developed close professional or personal relationships with the layoff victims. For instance, survivors may have worked interdependently with them for a long period of time. They may live in the same community, and therefore spend time socializing either on or off the job. Survivors may have been laid off in the past themselves, further promoting feelings of identification with the layoff victims. In several studies we found that survivors who were close to those laid off felt that the layoff was more unfair, worked less hard, and became less committed to the organization, relative to survivors who had more distant relationships with the layoff victims.[12] Therefore, when survivors feel attached to the layoff victims (e.g., as in a tightly knit, cohesive group), it is especially important that the layoffs be handled fairly.

- *When survivors are committed to the organization.* In a recent address to the Wall Street Human Resources Conference, James Jones, the CEO of the American Stock Exchange, pointed out that people need to feel that they are part of and contributing to a larger collective. One outgrowth of peoples' need for group membership is that they expect and want to be treated fairly by the collectives to which they belong. Consider the situation of survivors who felt very loyal to the organization prior to the layoff. If they believed that the layoff was handled fairly, their commitment to the organization should be confirmed. However, our research suggests that if these same persons believed that the layoff was unfair, then their loyalty dropped sharply, even more so than survivors who were less committed at the outset and viewed the layoff as unfair.[13] Put differently, the higher they are (in their prior loyalty to the organization), the harder they fall (if they believe the layoff was unfair). Thus, layoff managers who handle the process unfairly may run the risk of alienating the survivors they least wish to alienate: those who were very loyal to the organization at the outset.

The Role of Changed Working Conditions.   Survivors are influenced not only by the perceived fairness of the layoff, but also by changes in their work setting which often accompany layoffs. Some of these changes represent perceived sources of threat, others perceived sources of opportunity. The general finding emerging from research, not surprisingly, is that survivors' productivity and morale decline more if the changes are believed to represent threats rather than opportunities. Some of the more specific concerns survivors have about changes in the workplace include:

- *How much should I worry about the possibility of further layoffs?* Survivors' job insecurity generally increases after layoffs. This is understandable, since many organizations downsize in waves rather than on a one-shot basis. The threat of additional layoffs by itself, however, does not lead to job insecurity. Insecurity is experienced when survivors also believe that if additional layoffs were to occur, there would be little they could do to counteract the negative effects of

Figure 1

THE EFFECT OF JOB INSECURITY ON WORK PERFORMANCE

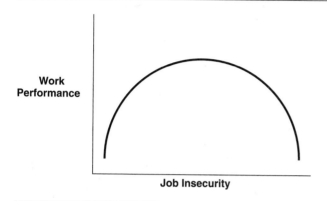

Work Performance

Job Insecurity

job loss.[14] For example, individuals who expect to lose their jobs during the anticipated next round of layoffs will not necessarily feel insecure if they know that they will be able to find a comparable job elsewhere.

High levels of job insecurity lead to negative effects on survivors' productivity and morale. However, there is some evidence that a moderate amount of job insecurity actually leads to greater productivity (but not morale), relative to that caused by low levels of job insecurity. In fact, in one downsizing organization the relationship between job insecurity and work performance took the form of an inverted-U, as shown in Figure 1.[15] The results in Figure 1 raise some interesting and important questions for layoff managers. Is it better for survivors to feel moderate rather than low levels of job insecurity? Figure 1 suggests that moderate job insecurity leads to greater work performance than does low job insecurity. However, it is possible that the organization would pay the price (of moderate job insecurity) in some other way. For example, in that very same sample it was found—but not reported in Figure 1—that survivors' loyalty to the organization was lower when their job insecurity was at a moderate rather than low level.

- *How does my job compare to the one that I had before the layoffs?* Many survivors are likely to find that their job has changed. First, the sheer volume of their workload often increases. With fewer people to do the work, the remaining employees may find that they have more to do. This tendency was observed in a sample of middle managers from a wide variety of downsizing organizations. When asked to describe how their jobs had changed over the years, surviving middle managers reported a sharp increase in the size of their workload; they reported working longer hours and taking fewer vacation days. These results were hinted at in a more recent and larger scale survey conducted by the Wyatt Company, which polled 1,005 corporations employing more than four million people. Nearly all of them (86%) had downsized within the past five years, but less than half (42%) had eliminated the amount of work that their employees had to do.

Second, the nature of the work that survivors perform invariably changes. The same group of middle managers who reported an increase in the quantity of their work also reported that the job had become *more* intrinsically enjoyable. They experienced greater *autonomy* than before, and they also felt that there was more *variety* in their jobs, two attributes that have been shown to increase the intrinsic enjoyability of work. Thus, this group of middle managers experienced both negative and positive changes in their work: the quantity of the work increased (representing a source of threat), but so did its intrinsic quality (representing a source of opportunity).

- *What is my future here?* Layoffs often have the effect of making unclear survivors' future prospects within the organization. For example, consider the plight of first-level supervisors in a downsizing organization who had hoped to be promoted to the ranks of middle management within the next few years. The organization had eliminated many middle management positions during its most recent layoffs, leaving survivors uncertain about their future opportunities within the organization. In other situations, survivors may believe that new career options exist as a result of their organization's recent downsizing. In short, survivors' reactions will depend upon their beliefs about how their career prospects—either within the organization or outside of it—have changed, relative to what they were before the layoff.

- *What are the reactions of my fellow survivors?* In times of stress or uncertainty, people often take cues from their co-workers to help them determine what they should be thinking and doing. Not only are survivors keenly attentive to *objective* changes in their work environment (i.e., whether their workload has increased, or whether their career opportunities have diminished), but they are acutely aware of their fellow survivors' *reactions to* the new work environment. For example, they monitor whether their fellow survivors seem more or less withdrawn from the organization. Their own reactions along these dimensions are determined to a significant extent by those of fellow survivors, particularly those in their immediate work group.[16]

PRACTICAL IMPLICATIONS: THE EFFECTIVE MANAGEMENT OF LAYOFFS

To elicit the most positive reactions among survivors, managers need to: conduct the layoff fairly; help survivors cope with the negative changes (i.e., threats) in the workplace; and encourage survivors to focus on the positive changes (i.e., opportunities) in the work setting. Appropriate managerial action steps can be meaningfully divided into three categories: those taken before, during, and after the layoff.

Before the Layoff

- *Evaluate the relationship between the layoff and corporate strategy and culture.* As dramatic as their effects may be, layoffs are only one of the many factors that will affect the short- and long-term health of the organization. Top managers need to determine the relationship between layoffs and these other factors, most notably corporate strategy and culture. Layoffs generally reflect the organization's strategy of improved productivity through (labor) cost containment. Whereas cost containment may be an appropriate strategy at least some of the time, it may not be optional all of the time. For example, J. H. Heinz enacted a cost cutting strategy (e.g., layoffs, plant closings) throughout the 1980s with considerable financial success. However, its surviving workforce was becoming increasingly alienated, product quality was slipping, and waste was high. Three years ago, Heinz changed the emphasis in its strategy from cost containment to total quality management (TQM). This strategic shift led Heinz to *increase* its workforce in certain instances. Under the cost containment strategy:

> Heinz had cut the workforce at its StarKist tuna canning factories. . . . But the fish cleaners were so overworked that they were leaving literally tons of meat on the bone every day. . . . StarKist managers slowed down the production lines, hired 400 hourly workers and 15 supervisors, and retrained the entire workforce. . . . All told, StarKist increased labor costs by $5 million but cut out $15 million in wastage. Net saving: $10 million annually.[17]

In short, layoffs should be a logical consequence of corporate strategy. If that strategy is poorly defined prior to the adoption of layoffs, then the latter are less likely to be the answer to the firm's short- or long-term problems. Layoffs are a means to an end; corporate strategy helps to define that end. Furthermore, if the strategy suggests that downsizing is warranted, the organization would do well to consider other cost-saving options (e.g., attrition, hiring or wage freezes, or early retirement) instead of, or in addition to, layoffs. These alternatives to layoffs generally are less drastic and therefore may be less likely to send shock waves throughout the organization.[18]

The intricate relationship between layoffs and corporate culture also needs to be thought through prior to the adoption of layoffs. Given the existing culture of the firm, top managers need to evaluate whether layoffs should be implemented, and if so, how they should be implemented. Some managers may decide that the culture of the organization is so strong that it precludes the possibility of involuntary layoffs (e.g., IBM). This is not to say that the decisions regarding whether to lay off or how to implement layoffs *always* need to be consistent with the corporate culture. Indeed, sometimes layoffs are undertaken in order to change the existing culture. For example, some organizations with previously paternalistic cultures have taken the unusual step of laying off workers *precisely because* they wanted to change the culture to be more hard-driving and aggressive. However, if the decision to lay off (or the ways in which the layoffs are implemented) are seen as incongruent with the existing corporate culture, they are more likely to be experienced by survivors as unfair. Of course, management may be able to counteract such perceptions by handling smoothly the other fairness-related issues (e.g., advanced notice, clear explanation of the reasons for the layoff, adequate caretaking of the layoff victims).

- *Provide ample advanced notice.* By providing ample advanced notice, the organization stands to benefit because: the victims of the layoff should exit more gracefully, making them less likely to file wrongful discharge lawsuits (favorable victim reactions should also enhance the organization's reputation and future recruiting efforts); and the survivors of the layoff will be more appreciative, leading to better productivity or morale.

- *Identify key people and solicit their commitment to the new organization.* Key people come in several varieties. First, there are the "star" performers whom the organization will wish to retain for obvious reasons. Second, there are the "opinion leaders" whose viewpoints have reverberating effects on those around them. Given that survivors take their cues from one another about how they should respond, it is especially important for the opinion leaders to have relatively upbeat reactions to the layoff.

  Several action steps may help solicit the commitment of key people to the new organization. For example, they need to be told exactly what their role will be and how important that role is to the success of the downsizing effort. In addition, they can participate in the organizational restructuring decisions or serve on task forces.

- *Prepare supervisors and managers for the layoffs.* Those who implement the often difficult layoff process need to be prepared, both for what to expect and how to behave. They should expect their surviving subordinates to feel a wide range of emotions, including anxiety, anger, relief, guilt, and envy. Many people will feel two or more of these emotions simultaneously. Furthermore, some of these emotions may not seem to make sense. Consider the case of "survivor guilt." People usually feel guilty when they believe that they have done something wrong. Survivors may say to themselves, "Well, I haven't done anything wrong. Why, then, do I feel guilty?" The mere fact that survivors fared better than those laid off can produce guilt feelings, particularly when survivors believe that they, rather than the layoff victims, just as easily could have been the ones who were laid off. It is important for managers and supervisors not to be surprised when and if survivors express emotional pain, even feelings that seem irrational. Survivors' painful emotional states are more likely to become destructive (to themselves and the organization) when they are invalidated, i.e., denied or derogated as not making sense. Therefore, layoff managers who anticipate their subordinates' emotional pain are more likely to give them the room they need to have their feelings, and thereby keep such emotions from having harmful effects.

  Further complicating matters is that those responsible for implementing the layoffs often do a notoriously poor job. First, most implementers do not *want* to face the painful task of telling people that they are about to lose their jobs. People generally do not like to be the bearers of bad news, and layoff managers are no exception. Indeed, managers often say that the most difficult part of their job is telling people that they are being terminated, especially when those being let go have performed reasonably well in the past. As a result of their discomfort, implementers could mishandle the process. For example, they may be evasive, and thereby accused of being unfair for not "being straight" with their subordinates. Other implementers react to their discomfort by coming on too strong, thereby running the risk of being seen as unfair for not treating people with dignity and respect.

Second, most implementers lack the *ability* to handle layoffs smoothly. Whereas some are naturally talented at handling the process, others will only become proficient through experience. However, layoffs are relatively rare events *within* organizations, occurring perhaps yearly or less often. Consequently, implementers often do not reap the benefit of the learning that goes along with doing something repeatedly.

Preparing supervisors and managers for what they need to do is no small matter. Given their unwillingness or inability to implement the layoffs well, they need to be trained in how to behave. Perhaps committees could be established whose mandate it is to develop an appropriate plan of action. As in the case of most behaviors, practice makes perfect; therefore managers and supervisors may benefit from rehearsing or role-playing what they plan to do as they implement the layoffs.

During the Layoff

- *Give full information.* Once the workforce has learned that layoffs will occur, they will be hungry for information. Some of their questions pertain to events in the immediate future, including: Who will be laid off? When will the layoffs occur? Why are they happening? Will they happen again? How will the organization decide who goes and who stays? What does the organization plan to do to soften the blow for those laid off? Other questions refer to events that are likely to unfold over time, such as: What will life be like here after the layoffs? Can management be trusted? One school of managerial thought is that employees should be told as little as possible, i.e., that if management provided information then they would only be putting counterproductive ideas in the minds of the workforce. However, during stressful times such as layoffs, the workforce *already* is likely to have counterproductive fantasies about what is taking place. By not providing information, management allows these fantasies to feed on themselves. First, within survivors' minds they are likely to fill in the blanks with beliefs damaging to the organization. Trust in the organization often is reduced during layoffs, causing survivors to believe that management is guilty until proven innocent. Second, survivors take cues from each other, thus, the grapevine provides another mechanism through which survivors' beliefs can spin out of control, unless they are counteracted by accurate information.

  Clearly, there are certain things that managers may be unwilling or unable to discuss with the surviving workforce. Even here, however, survivors are likely to feel that they were treated more fairly if management acknowledged those issues about which it could not provide information: this would be especially true if managers provided a clear and adequate explanation of why they were unwilling or unable to disclose the information. In short, all of the uncertainties brought on by the layoffs will cause survivors to try to make sense of what is happening, both in the short and long term. People need to know both concrete details about the immediate future, as well as information that symbolizes what they can expect from the organization over time. For these reasons, management needs to be especially attentive to both the substance and style of its communications.

- *Overcommunicate.* Layoff managers need to make the information sought by survivors as vivid as possible. Managers could feel frustrated because they know that they communicated information to survivors, only to discover that their message was not heard. The distracting nature of the post-layoff work environment makes it necessary for management to overcommunicate pertinent information. For example, wherever possible important information should be communicated in a face-to-face manner. Furthermore, information deemed to be important should be communicated more than once, and in different ways. To reinforce its communications, some organizations make use of an in-house TV network (as Ford Motor Company does), or utilize an electronic newsletter (as Bethlehem Steel does) so that people working at computer terminals can receive information in a timely manner. The key assumption that managers need to make in order to overcommunicate is the following: just because information was *sent* to the surviving workforce does not ensure that said information was *heard* by the workforce. Moreover, if the intended message is not heard, the grapevine is likely to become the primary source of information—information that is erroneous or damaging to the organization more often than not.

- *Provide assistance.* Layoffs directly threaten the economic well-being of those laid off, and indirectly threaten that of the survivors (who may be wondering whether they are the next to go). Therefore, it is important for the organization to provide concrete assistance to help ease the pain. Severance pay and outplacement counseling are obvious examples of tangible help. Some downsizing organizations temporarily beef up their Employee Assistance Programs, in order to handle the increased demand on that function that layoffs often produce. The direct costs of these and other tangible caretaking provisions can be considerable to the downsizing organization. However, these costs may be offset to some extent by the positive effects they have on the survivors (as well as the victims) of job loss.

  It is also crucial for management to communicate (again, overcommunicate) to survivors what is being done concretely to help the layoff victims. A major consumer products company that I know of actually provided considerable tangible resources to the layoff victims, only to discover that the surviving workforce still reacted rather negatively. When questioned about what they communicated to the survivors about the assistance provided to the layoff victims, management responded that they had said nothing at all. In not communicating with the survivors about this issue, management missed an opportunity to show its commitment to its employees, even as it was in the process of separating some of them from the organization. This is not to say that survivors need to know every detail about such things as the layoff victims' severance package or outplacement counseling. Moreover, if the organization were overly generous to the layoff victims, then survivors could feel resentful that they were not laid off themselves. Still, survivors need to be reassured that the victims are being provided for, and management needs to be sure to communicate that.

- *Treat victims and survivors with dignity and respect.* One way to treat victims respectfully is by providing tangible forms of assistance, such as severance pay and outplacement counseling. However, the seemingly inconsequential details of *what* was told to victims and survivors, *how* things were said to them, *when* they were told, and *where* they were when they received the news also determine whether the workforce feels that it has been treated with dignity. Furthermore, the direct costs to the organization of handling these apparently trivial details are far less than those associated with the more concrete forms of caretaking such as severance pay and outplacement counseling.

One question that downsizing organizations often face is how to combine the tangible forms of caretaking (such as severance pay) with the intangible forms of caretaking (such as treating the victims and survivors in a humane, dignified way). Obviously, the more that the organization can provide on both of these dimensions, the more favorably survivors will respond to the layoff. Perhaps the most interesting and managerially useful finding to emerge from several studies is that: if survivors felt that the *procedures* used to implement the layoff were fair—that is, ample advanced notice was given, clear explanations of the reasons for the layoff were provided, and the news was delivered in a respectful way—then the impact of the more costly forms of caretaking (such as severance pay) on survivors' reactions was greatly reduced. In other words, survivors generally reacted much more favorably if they felt that the organization was generous rather than stingy in the concrete provisions (e.g., severance pay) it offered to the layoff victims. Such a finding should come as no surprise. However, if the layoff was implemented in a procedurally fair manner, then survivors' reactions did not depend *nearly as much* on the amount of concrete, tangible assistance that the organization provided to the layoff victims. Only when survivors believed that the procedures used to implement the layoff were unfair did their reactions depend greatly upon the amount of concrete assistance offered to those laid off.[19]

This is not to say that downsizing organizations need not concern themselves with providing concrete assistance to the layoff victims. Indeed, if the organization concentrated its efforts solely on the fairness of its downsizing procedures and offered little or nothing in the way of concrete assistance to those laid off, then survivors are likely to react quite negatively. However, once a certain threshold level of concrete assistance has been provided, then the layoff may be handled in a more *cost effective* way not by providing additional concrete assistance to the layoff victims, but rather by ensuring that the procedures used to implement the layoffs were perceived by survivors to be fair.

- *Increase managerial accessibility.* In stressful times such as layoffs, survivors feel confused and upset. A frequent managerial response to the turmoil caused by layoffs is to become more withdrawn from the surviving workforce. In some ways, the withdrawal of managers is understandable. After all, they may feel more self-preoccupied because of their own worries and fears. Furthermore, most of us would just as soon not be involved in communicating bad news to the people with whom we work. However, management at all levels needs to increase rather than decrease its accessibility to the surviving workforce. Information goes a long way toward helping many people cope with stressful circumstances. At one downsizing organization, top level managers increased their frequency of MBWA—management by walking around. Another one instituted a special hotline number that survivors could call to have their questions immediately addressed. A third organization went to extra efforts to publicize its already-existing open-door policy.

- *Use ceremony to facilitate the transition.* Sociologists have noted that important changes in peoples' lives are accompanied by a formal ceremony recognizing the transition. It is somehow easier to accept transitions when people take the time to recognize that their world has changed and to acknowledge their feelings associated with that change, such as grief, anxiety, and guilt. Ceremonies provide people with an opportunity to acknowledge change and their reactions to it. Ceremonies in the survivor setting can take any of a number of forms. For example, small groups of survivors can go out to lunch with the understanding that the purpose of the meeting is to discuss the impending change in the workplace. Or, the organization may hold special meetings *on company time* during which the changes associated with the layoff are acknowledged, and survivors are encouraged to share their reactions to the changes. Of course, these meetings must be organized and led by people with a good deal of interpersonal sensitivity and skill.

  One potential drawback to the latter idea is that if the ceremony is done on company time on a large scale basis—as it probably should—it may at first appear to cost the organization a considerable amount of person-hours. However, survivors already are highly distracted from their daily tasks at this point in the layoff process. Hence, the opportunity cost of having them participate in the ceremony is greatly reduced, and should be more than recouped in the form of more favorable survivor reactions.

After the Layoff.   After the layoffs the surviving workforce will need to regroup. A number of action steps may facilitate this process. Although these steps represent generally sound management practice, the layoff setting represents a specific situation in which it is important to follow these recommendations. Although these steps should be *implemented* after the layoffs, their *planning* needs to occur prior to the implementation of the layoffs.

- *Soliciting employee input.* As soon as management believes that the acute trauma of the layoff has subsided somewhat, survivors should be given every opportunity to play an active role in shaping the post-layoff work environment. Some organizations (e.g., General Electric's "Workout" program) have cultivated participatory processes in which survivors are encouraged to make suggestions on how the organization can do more (work) with less (workers). One organization went so far as to set aside money saved from the downsizing to reward survivors who made useful suggestions on how to work more efficiently. Employee input becomes especially crucial after stressful events such as layoffs. After all, the survivors have just witnessed an event that threatens their sense of control. Perceived control may be restored at least somewhat if survivors are actively involved in decisions that will affect them in the aftermath of the layoff.

- *Rightsizing.* A common complaint among survivors is that they not only have to do their own jobs, but significant portions of the work previously performed by those laid off. Just as the organization needs to think through its strategy to decide whether layoffs are appropriate, so too must it evaluate whether the tasks undertaken by survivors are appropriate to the strategy. Some downsizing organizations (in the minority, to be sure) recently have taken a hard look at eliminating low value work. They compared the work that they *should* concentrate on (based upon their strategy) with the tasks that survivors *actually* were doing. Not surprisingly, the latter often were very different from the former. The next step was to do away with those aspects of the workload that were no longer seen as necessary. For example, Oryx, an oil and gas producer based in Dallas, "junked 25% of all internal reports, reduced from 20 to four the number of signatures required on requests for capital expenditures, and compressed from seven months to six weeks the time it took to produce the annual budget."[20] After undergoing layoffs, the group at Colgate-Palmolive discovered that "instead of concentrating on how to make teeth whiter or clothes brighter, scientists were expending too much energy on supervising and reporting. Researchers at different locations were duplicating one another's efforts. They also were preoccupied with designing new factories, a task that had little to do with the tech group's responsibility for inventing and improving products."[21] Colgate-Palmolive took the necessary steps to ensure that surviving scientists were concentrating their efforts on the work that needed to be done. This was achieved in part by eliminating some of the work that they were doing prior to the layoff that was no longer viewed as useful.

  Habitual behavior is hard to change. Nevertheless, more and more downsizing organizations are learning that "because that's the way we have always done things around here" is not ample justification for having certain tasks included in survivors' job descriptions. By eliminating low value work, the organization benefits in numerous ways, not the least of which is that survivors are less likely to feel overwhelmed by a workload that includes all of their previous responsibilities plus that of some of their recently departed co-workers.

- *Job enrichment.* Survivors' reactions depend not only on the change in the volume or quantity of their workload relative to before the layoffs, but also on the change in the quality or enjoyability of their jobs. If their work has become more intrinsically interesting, then their productivity and morale should increase.[22] Kodak, for example, involves employees in decision making, has them work in teams (which leads to greater variety and reduced isolation), and teaches them how to check their own work (so that they receive feedback on a more regular basis). The post-layoff environment provides especially fertile ground for redesigning the work survivors do so as to make it more psychologically interesting—a process known as job enrichment. Just as the organization needs to examine *what* work its employees are doing as it attempts to rightsize, so too should it look at *how* the work is being done, which may lead to creative ways to make the work more interesting. When survivors' jobs have been altered (to make them more interesting), the organization may have to incur the additional expense of training survivors to handle their new responsibilities. For example, five years ago an employee at Kodak, Daniel Cardinale, "did nothing but operate a punch press eight hours a day. Now he coaches fellow team members in statistical process control, meets with suppliers, interviews prospective recruits, and helps manage just-in-time inventory."[23] The cost of training Cardinale and his colleagues has paid for itself handsomely; it now takes one shift to accomplish the same work that used to be done in three shifts.

- *Make certain that survivors recognize new opportunities.* If done correctly, layoffs represent only part of a larger scale organizational change. Therefore, the opportunities for success that accompanied the old ways of doing things may no longer be present. Unfortunately, many survivors falsely conclude that "there just aren't *any* opportunities around here anymore," a perception that spurs their productivity and morale. In reality, the organization may provide many opportunities (or positive sources of change) in the aftermath of the layoff, but these opportunities may be quite *different* from those that existed previously. Therefore, the organization's responsibility is to make explicit to survivors: the opportunities present in the post-layoff environment, which may range from new ways to work more successfully and happily on a day-in, day-out basis, to methods to enhance one's career prospects (either within the organization or beyond) over the longer haul; and what survivors need to do to capitalize on these potential opportunities. To highlight the opportunities present (and ways to achieve them), managers may do any of the following:

  - Have survivors work at "achievable" goals and tasks. The upset caused by layoffs makes most survivors hungry for a success experience. One way to increase survivors' chances for success is by assigning goals and tasks that they are likely to achieve. On the assumption that numerous tasks could be undertaken in the post-layoff environment, it is important that at least some of them provide survivors with the opportunity for a win, however small. With their self-confidence somewhat renewed, they should be better equipped to tackle some of the more difficult challenges that the post-layoff environment inevitably will pose.

· Publicize the rewards provided to survivors for the new behavior you wish to encourage. People learn a lot simply by watching the outcome of others' behaviors. If survivors know that others have been rewarded for taking the steps necessary to help the organization adapt to the layoffs, they should be more likely to do so themselves. Publicly announced rewards are especially needed to encourage survivors to undertake new behaviors. Recall the earlier example of the downsizing organization that financially rewarded survivors who made useful suggestions on how to improve productivity. Not only were people rewarded for their creative ideas, but also the accolades they received were made visible throughout the organization. This publicity campaign had the effect of showing survivors what was in it for them to work toward furthering the organization's goals.

· Make new career paths explicit. Most of us are motivated by the psychology of hope: the expectation and wish that our future work situation will be better than (or at least as good as) the present one. However, the massive restructurings that often accompany layoffs could leave survivors uncertain about their longer term prospects within the organization. Therefore, it is important to make clear to survivors—especially the star performers—the new sources of rewards in the organization, as well as the ways to achieve those rewards. Some downsizing organizations even provide career counseling to survivors, which focuses less on highlighting the opportunities within the organization and more on encouraging individuals to clarify their personal values and hone their self-marketing skills. At first blush, this practice seems unwise in that it may encourage talented survivors to find a better position in a different organization. However, as William Bridges, a noted change management consultant, commented, even if this service "does give a few people what they need to leave, that is a small cost to pay for the empowerment and revitalization of the great mass of the survivors who will remain. These are the people the organization is depending on, and nothing less than their all-out effort on the organization's behalf will suffice."

CONCLUDING COMMENTS

The managerial prescriptions presented here are general; they will apply to the majority of downsizing organizations most of the time. Each situation has its idiosyncrasies, so the architects of the layoffs will need to evaluate carefully the appropriateness of the various recommendations to their particular circumstances. Managers should be forewarned of the long recovery period that survivors invariably need to adapt to layoffs. *There is no quick fix.* Even if the recommendations offered are implemented properly, layoff managers should prepare themselves for an adjustment period measured more appropriately in terms of years than in months or weeks. For all of their potential turmoil, however, downsizing and layoffs represent *opportunities* for the organization to dramatically improve its health over the long haul. Contributing to this optimistic outlook is the fact that many determinants of survivors' reactions are factors that managers can control. Therefore, as they undertake this arduous but critical change management process, executives need to remember that what they do will have a significant effect on survivors' productivity and morale, and ultimately on the effectiveness and vitality of the organization.

References

[1] Right Associates, "Managing Change in the 90s," *The Right Research* (1990).

[2] *The New York Times*, April 15, 1991.

[3] Joel Brockner, "The Effects of Work Layoffs on Survivors: Research, Theory, and Practice," in Barry M. Staw and Larry L. Cummings, eds., *Research in Organizational Behavior*, Vol. 10 (Greenwich, CT: JAI Press, 1988), pp. 213–255; Joel Brockner and Jerald Greenberg, "The Impact of Layoffs on Survivors: An Organizational Justice Perspective," in John S. Carroll, ed., *Applied Social Psychology and Organizational Settings* (Hillsdale, NJ: Erlbaum, 1990), pp. 45–75; Joel Brockner and Batia M. Wiesenfeld, "Living on the Edge (of Social and Organizational Psychology): The Effects of Job Layoffs on Those Who Remain," in J. Keith Murnighan, ed., *Social Psychology in Organizations: Advances in Theory and Research* (Englewood, NJ: Prentice-Hall, 1992).

[4] Denise M. Rousseau, "Psychological and Implied Contracts in Organizations," *Employee Rights and Responsibilities*, 2 (1989): 121–139.

[5] Joel Brockner, Mary Konovsky, Rochelle Cooper-Schneider, and Robert Folger, "The Interactive Effects of Procedural Justice and Outcome Negativity on the Victims and Survivors of Job Loss," manuscript under review, 1992.

[6] Tom R. Tyler and Robert J. Bies, "Beyond Formal Procedures: The Interpersonal Context of Procedural Justice," in John S. Carroll, ed., op. cit.

[7] Robert J. Bies, "The Predicament of Injustice: The Management of Moral Outrage," in Larry L. Cummings and Barry M. Staw, *Research in Organizational Behavior*, Vol. 9 (Greenwich, CT: JAI Press, 1988), pp. 289–319.

[8] Todd Jick, "Navistar: Managing Change," Harvard Business School Case N9-490-003, 1989.

[9] Gerald S. Leventhal, "The Distribution of Rewards and Resources in Groups and Organizations," in Leonard Berkowitz and Elaine Walster, eds., *Advances in Experimental Social Psychology*, Vol. 9 (New York, NY: Academic Press, 1976), pp. 91–131.

[10] *The Washington Post*, February 17, 1991.

[11] Ibid.

[12] Joel Brockner, Steven Grover, Thomas Reed, Rocki Lee DeWitt, and Michael O'Malley, "Survivors' Reactions to Job Layoffs: We Get By With a Little Help for Our Friends," *Administrative Science Quarterly*, 32 (1987): 526–541.

[13] Joel Brockner, Tom R. Tyler, and Rochelle Cooper-Schneider, "The Effects of Prior Commitment to an Institution on Reactions to Perceived Unfairness: The Higher They Are, The Harder They Fall," manuscript under review, 1992.

[14]Leonard Greenhalgh and Zev Rosenblatt, "Job Insecurity: Toward Conceptual Clarity," *Academy of Management Review,* 9 (1984): 438–448.

[15]Joel Brockner, Steven Grover, Thomas Reed, and Rocki Lee DeWitt, "Layoffs, Job Insecurity and Survivors' Work Effort: Evidence of an Inverted-U Relationship," *Academy of Management Journal,* in press.

[16]Gerald R. Salancik and Jeffrey Pfeffer, "A Social Information Processing Approach to Job Attitudes and Task Design," *Administrative Science Quarterly,* 23 (1978): 224–253.

[17]*Business Week,* April 9, 1990.

[18]Leonard Greenhalgh, Anne T. Lawrence, and Robert I. Sutton, "Determinants of Workforce Reduction Strategies in Declining Organizations," *Academy of Management Review,* 13 (1988): 241–254.

[19]Brockner, Konovsky, Cooper-Schneider, and Folger, op. cit.

[20]*Fortune,* April 9, 1990, p. 43.

[21]Ibid.

[22]J. Richard Hackman and Greg R. Oldham, *Work Redesign* (Reading, MA: Addison-Wesley, 1980).

[23]*Fortune,* April 9, 1990, p. 48.

PART V

COMPENSATING HUMAN RESOURCES

PAY STRUCTURE DECISIONS

INTRODUCTION

Pay decisions are at the heart of the employment relationship, and they have important implications for both employees and employers. Pay has a major impact on employees' standards of living and communicates to them the degree to which their contributions are valued by the employer. Because of its importance to employees, pay is an important tool for employers in influencing employee attitudes, such as perceptions of fairness, and employee behaviors, including whether an employee is attracted to and remains with the employer and how effectively they use their time at work.

The readings in this section focus on pay structure decisions and their consequences. Developing and maintaining a pay structure requires consideration of two general types of information. First, how much are jobs paid relative to other jobs within the organization (internal comparisons)? Pay differentials between jobs influence employee perceptions of equity and behaviors such as interest in promotion and willingness to accept transfers between jobs. Second, how much do other organizations pay for similar types of jobs (external comparisons)? Paying too little relative to competitors may make it difficult to attract and retain a quality work force. Paying too much may hinder the organization's ability to sell its product at a competitive price.

The following readings speak to both internal and external comparisons, with somewhat more focus on the latter. Organizations have been under great pressure to control costs, and they have often done so by reducing employment levels (in many cases by relying on pay programs such as early retirement incentives) and, somewhat less frequently, by reducing pay levels. Another challenge has been how to design pay structures that work well in global organizations that operate in many countries. This is the focus of the second reading.

Jerald Greenberg, in "Employee Theft as a Reaction to Underpayment Inequity: The Hidden Costs of Pay Cuts," describes a field experiment that examined employee reactions to pay cuts with differing communications and explanations to employees. Greenberg found that the pay cuts were seen as significantly less fair when management did not adequately explain the rationale for the cuts. Moreover, an inadequate explanation also contributed to higher levels of employee theft. The study suggests the importance of effective communication to employees regarding changes in the compensation system.

Luis Gomez-Mejia and Theresa Welbourne note that the globalization of business and employment is proceeding rapidly and that this change raises new challenges for organizations' compensation strategies. In particular, they argue that a crucial question concerns "the degree to which reward systems must be customized to cope with diverse cultural contingencies." They argue that the challenge from the point of view of compensation is no longer to take advantage of low labor costs but rather "to design compensation systems that are most appropriate for specific cultural conditions." Gomez-Mejia and Welbourne build on the work of G. Hofstede, who has categorized cultures along four dimensions: (1) power distance, (2) individualism, (3) uncertainty avoidance, and (4) masculinity/femininity. Gomez-Mejia and Welbourne use this classification to develop hypotheses about which types of compensation strategies are most likely to fit different cultures.

READING 30

EMPLOYEE THEFT AS A REACTION TO UNDERPAYMENT INEQUITY
The Hidden Cost of Pay Cuts

Jerald Greenberg

Employee theft rates were measured in manufacturing plants during a period in which pay was temporarily reduced by 15%. Compared with pre- or postreduction pay periods (or with control groups whose pay was unchanged), groups whose pay was reduced had significantly higher theft rates. When the basis for the pay cuts was thoroughly and sensitively explained to employees, feelings of inequity were lessened, and the theft rate was reduced as well. The data support equity theory's predictions regarding likely responses to underpayment and extend recently accumulated evidence demonstrating the mitigating effects of adequate explanations on feelings of inequity.

Employee theft constitutes one of the most pervasive and serious problems in the field of human resource management. Although exact figures are difficult to come by, the American Management Association (1977) has estimated that employee theft cost American businesses from $5 billion to $10 billion in 1975, representing the single most expensive form of nonviolent crime against businesses.

Traditionally, social scientists have considered several plausible explanations for employee theft. Among the most popular are theories postulating that theft is the result of attempts to ease financial pressure (Merton, 1938), moral laxity among a younger workforce (Merriam, 1977), available opportunities (Astor,

Source: Jerald Greenberg, "Employee Theft as a Reaction to Underpayment Inequity: The Hidden Cost of Pay Cuts." *Journal of Applied Psychology*, 1990, vol. 75, no. 5, 561–568. © 1990 by the American Psychological Association, Inc. Reprinted by permission.

A preliminary report of the research reported in this article was presented at the annual meeting of the Academy of Management, San Francisco, August 1990.

I gratefully acknowledge the helpful comments of Robert J. Bies and three anonymous reviewers on an earlier draft of this article.

Correspondence concerning this article should be addressed to Jerald Greenberg, Faculty of Management and Human Resources, Ohio State University, 1775 College Road, Columbus, Ohio 43210-1399.

1972), expressions of job dissatisfaction (Mangione & Quinn, 1975), and the existence of norms tolerating theft (Horning, 1970). More recently, Hollinger and Clark (1983) conducted a large-scale survey and interview study designed to explore these and other explanations of employee theft. Interestingly, they found that the best predictor was employee attitudes: "When employees felt exploited by the company . . . these workers were more involved in acts against the organizations as a mechanism to correct perceptions of inequity or injustice" (Hollinger & Clark, 1983, p. 142).

Hollinger and Clark's (1983) suggestion that employee theft is related to feelings of injustice is consistent with several schools of sociological and anthropological thought. For example, in studies of hotel dining room employees (Mars, 1973) and maritime dock workers (Mars, 1974), Mars found that employees viewed theft *not* as inappropriate but "as a morally justified addition to wages; indeed, as an entitlement due from exploiting employers" (Mars, 1974, p. 224). Similarly, Kemper (1966) argued that employee theft may be the result of "reciprocal deviance," that is, employees' perceptions that their employers defaulted on their obligations to them, thereby encouraging them to respond with similar acts of deviance. Fisher and Baron (1982) made a similar argument in presenting their equity-control model of vandalism. They claimed that vandalism is a form of inequity reduction in that an individual vandal's breaking the rules regarding property rights follows from his or her feelings of mistreatment by authorities. Recent evidence in support of this idea is found in a study by DeMore, Fisher, and Baron (1988). In that study, university students claimed to engage in more vandalism the less fairly they felt they had been treated by their university and the less control they believed they had over such treatment.

Such conceptualizations are in keeping with current theoretical positions in the field of organizational justice (Greenberg, 1987). These formulations allow more precise hypotheses to be developed regarding when employee theft is likely to occur. For example, consider equity theory's (Adams, 1965) claim that workers who feel inequitably underpaid (i.e., those who believe that the rewards they are receiving relative to the contributions they are making are less than they should be) may respond by attempting to raise their outcomes (i.e., raise the level of rewards received). Although research has supported this claim (for a review, see Greenberg, 1982), studies have been limited to situations in which persons paid on a piece-work basis produce more goods of poorer quality to raise their outcomes without effectively raising their inputs. Given earlier conceptual claims and supporting evidence associating student vandalism with inequitable treatment (DeMore et al., 1988), it may be reasoned analogously that employee theft is a specific reaction to underpayment inequity and constitutes an attempt to bring outcomes into line with prevailing standards of fair pay.

Recent research in the area of procedural justice (Lind & Tyler, 1988) has shown that perceptions of fair treatment and outcomes depend not only on the relative level of one's outcomes but also on the explanations given for those outcomes (for a review, see Folger & Bies, 1989). For example, researchers have found that decision outcomes and procedures were better accepted when (a) people were assured that higher authorities were sensitive to their viewpoints (Tyler, 1988), (b) the decision was made without bias (Lind & Lissak, 1985), (c) the decision was applied consistently (Greenberg, 1986), (d) the decision was carefully justified on the basis of adequate information (Shapiro & Buttner, 1988), (e) the decisionmakers communicated their ideas honestly (Bies, 1986), and (f) persons influenced by the decision were treated in a courteous and civil manner (Bies & Moag, 1986). Such findings suggest that interpersonal treatment is an important determinant of reactions to potentially unfair situations (Tyler & Bies, 1990).

It is an interesting idea that perceptions of inequity (and corresponding attempts to redress inequities) may be reduced when explanations meeting the criteria presented in the preceding paragraph are offered to account for inequitable states. This notion was tested in the present study by capitalizing on a naturalistic manipulation—a temporary pay reduction for employees of selected manufacturing plants. Data were available for 30 consecutive weeks: 10 weeks before a pay reduction occurred, 10 weeks during the pay-reduction period, and 10 weeks after normal pay was reinstated. Following from equity theory, it was hypothesized that ratings of payment fairness would be lower during the pay-reduction period than during periods of normal payment (i.e., before and after the pay reduction). It was similarly hypothesized that rates of employee theft would be higher during the reduced-pay period than during periods of normal payment. Such actions would be consistent with equity theory's claim that one likely way of responding to underpayment inequity is by attempting to raise the level of rewards received. Although not previously studied in this connection, employee theft is a plausible mechanism for redressing states of inequity (Hollinger & Clark, 1983).

Additional hypotheses were derived from recent research (e.g., Cropanzano & Folger, 1989; Folger & Martin, 1986; Shapiro & Buttner, 1988; Weiner, Amirkham, Folkes, & Varette, 1987) showing that explanations for negative outcomes mitigate people's reactions to those outcomes (for a review, see Folger & Bies, 1989; Tyler & Bies, 1990). Generally speaking, in these studies the use of adequate explanations (i.e., ones that relied on complete, accurate information presented in a socially sensitive manner) tended to reduce the negative reactions that resulted from such outcomes and facilitated acceptance of the outcomes. From the perspective of Folger's (1986) referent cognitions theory, adequate explanations help victimized parties place their undercompensation in perspective by getting them to understand that things could have been worse. As such, adequate explanations were expected in the present study to lessen the feelings of inequity that accompanied the pay cut. Thus, it was reasoned that employees' feelings of payment inequity, and attempts to reduce that inequity (such as by pilfering), would be reduced when adequate explanations were given to account for the pay reduction. Specifically, it was hypothesized that the magnitude of the expressed inequity—and the rate of employee theft—would be lower when pay reductions were adequately explained than when they were inadequately explained.

Table 1

DISTRIBUTION OF ATTRITION AND TURNOVER ACROSS CONDITIONS

			Resignations			
Condition	Starting *n*	Missing data	Before pay cut	During pay cut	After pay cut	Final *n*
Adequate explanation (Plant A)	64	6	1	1	1	55
Inadequate explanation (Plant B)	53	8	1	12	2	30
Control (Plant C)	66	5	1	0	2	58

METHOD

Participants

Participants in the study were nonunion employees working for 30 consecutive weeks in three manufacturing plants owned by the same parent company. The plants were located in different sections of the midwestern United States and manufactured small mechanical parts mostly for the aerospace and automotive industries. The employees' average age (M = 28.5 years), level of education (M = 11.2 years), and tenure with the company (M = 3.2 years) did not significantly differ among the three plants, $F < 1.00$, in all cases. The local unemployment rates in the communities surrounding the three plants were not significantly different from each other (overall M = 6.4%), $F < 1.00$. It is important to establish this equivalence of characteristics across research sites because the assignment of individuals to conditions was not random across sites, thereby precluding the assumption of equivalence afforded by random assignment (Cook & Campbell, 1976).

As the study began, Plant A employed 64 workers in the following jobs: 5 salaried low-level managerial employees (4 men, 1 woman); 47 hourly-wage semiskilled and unskilled production workers (38 men, 9 women): and 12 hourly-wage clerical workers (all women). Almost identical proportions with respect to job type (and sex of employees within job type) existed in Plant B (n = 53) and Plant C (n = 66). Because some employees failed to complete questionnaires during some weeks, and because some employees voluntarily left their jobs during the study period, complete sets of questionnaires were available from 55 employees of Plant A, 30 employees of Plant B, and 58 employees of Plant C. This constituted a total sample of 143 employees, distributed to conditions as summarized in Table 1. The demographic characteristics of the 40 workers who were not included in the study did not differ significantly from the characteristics of the

143 who remained in the study (in all cases, $F < 2.00$), minimizing the possibility that those who remained in the study were a select group.

Procedure

Because of the loss of two large manufacturing contracts, the host company was forced to reduce its payroll by temporarily cutting wages by 15% across the board in two of its manufacturing plants (Plants A and B). This was done in lieu of laying off any employees. After this decision was made, I was asked to help assess the impact of the wage cuts in several key areas, including employee theft. Each of the payment-group manipulations was carried out in a separate plant. The assignment of Plant A to one experimental condition and Plant B to another experimental condition was determined at random. Assignment to the control group was determined by the host company's decision that pay cuts were not necessary in Plant C.[1]

The *adequate explanation* condition was created in Plant A. To effect this, a meeting (lasting approximately 90 min) was called at the end of a work week. At that meeting, all employees were told by the company president that their pay was going to be reduced by 15%, effective the following week, for a period expected to last 10 weeks. During this meeting several types of explanations were provided. On the basis of recent research (Folger & Bies, 1989; Tyler & Bies, 1990), I hypothesized that these explanations would mitigate reactions to the pay cut. The workers were told that company management seriously regretted having to reduce their pay but that doing so would preclude the need for any layoffs. They were further assured that all plant employees would share in the pay cuts and that no favoritism would be shown.[2] A relevant verbatim passage follows:

---

[1]Admittedly, conducting the study in this manner meant that the two randomly assigned groups may have been nonequivalent with respect to some unknown variables that might have otherwise affected the results (Cook & Campbell, 1976). However, some reassurance of between-group similarity is provided by the demonstrated equivalence between worker characteristics, economic conditions, and job duties for both plants. Moreover, the deliberate assignment of Plant C to the control condition raises the possibility that something besides the lack of manipulation may have been responsible for the results (Cook & Campbell, 1976). However, informal postexperiment interviews with plant officials and employees confirmed that no unusual "local history" events occurred during the study period. Further assurance that this was not a problem comes from the fact that, before and after the pay cut, the control group's responses were identical to the other groups' responses for all measures used in the study.

[2]Before the meetings scheduled in each plant, the individuals involved (i.e., company president in Plant A and a vice president in Plant B) met with me to develop outlines of their presentations. Several carefully crafted sentences conveying salient aspects of the manipulation were prepared for inclusion in the speaker's notes. Because local company norms dictated using informal meetings instead of formal presentations, complete scripts for the entire sessions could not be prepared in advance. As a result, it was necessary to establish that key differences in the manipulated variables were actually communicated in the meetings. With this in mind, each session was videotaped, and the videotapes were played back to a group of 112 undergraduate students after all identifying information was deleted. The students were asked to indicate in which of the two tapes (Tape A for Plant A; Tape B for Plant B) the speaker (a) presented more information about the pay cuts and (b)

Something we hate to do here at [company name] is lay off any of our employees. But, as you probably know, we've lost our key contracts with [company names], which will make things pretty lean around here for a little while. As a result, we need to cut somewhere, and we've come up with a plan that will get us through these tough times. I've been working on it with [name of person] in accounting, and we're sure it will work. The plan is simple: Starting Monday, we will each get a 15% cut in pay. This applies to you, to me, to everyone who works here at [name of plant]. If we do it this way, there'll be no cut in benefits and no layoffs—just a 15% pay reduction. So, either your hourly wages or your salary will be reduced by 15%. Will it hurt? Of course! But, it will hurt us all alike. We're all in it together. Let me just add that it really hurts me to do this, and the decision didn't come easily. We considered all possible avenues, but nothing was feasible. I think of you all as family, and it hurts me to take away what you've worked so hard for. But, for the next 10 weeks, we'll just have to tough it out.

In addition to these remarks, the basis for the decision was clearly explained and justified by presenting charts and graphs detailing the temporary effects of the lost contracts on cash-flow revenues. Projections verified that the cash-flow problem dictating the need for the pay cuts was only temporary, and this was clearly explained. All employees were assured that the pay cut was designed to last only 10 weeks.[3] Specifically, the employees were told the following:

The reason I'm sharing all this information with you is that I want you to understand what is happening here. It's just a temporary problem we're facing, and one that I hope will never happen again. At least the best course of action from our accounting department is clear: The pay cuts will work, and they will not have to last longer than 10 weeks. The new jobs we'll be picking up from [name of company] will really help get us back on our feet. Hopefully, by then we'll be stronger than ever. Of course, I know we're no stronger than our people, and I personally thank each and every one of you for your strength.

The tone of the presentation was such that a great deal of respect was shown for the workers, and all questions were answered with sensitivity. Approximately 1 hour was spent answering all questions. Each response brought an expression of remorse at having to take such action (e.g., "Again, I really wish this weren't necessary."). The good intent of this message was reinforced by the fact that the president issued the message in person.

---

expressed greater remorse about the pay cuts. The order of presentation of the tapes was randomized. Virtually all of the students agreed that the speaker on Tape A presented more information and expressed greater remorse. Taken together with my in-person confirmation that the manipulations were conducted as desired, these findings suggest that differentially adequate explanations were given to the two groups. Unfortunately, it was not possible to conduct further analyses on these tapes because the host company insisted that they be destroyed to prevent the unwanted dissemination of sensitive company information.

[3]Because of the sensitive and privileged nature of the internal accounting information, I was not permitted to divulge these data. Indeed, although I helped company officials present this information in understandable form, these charts and graphs were never made part of my file.

Plant B was the site of the *inadequate explanation* condition. Here, a meeting lasting approximately 15 min was called at the end of a work week. All employees were told by a company vice president that their pay was going to be reduced by 15%, effective the following week, for a period expected to last 10 weeks. The only additional information that was provided indicated that the lost contracts dictated the need for the pay cut. No expressions of apology or remorse were shared, and the basis for the decision was not clearly described. The following verbatim remarks characterize this condition:

> It is inevitable in a business like ours that cost-cutting measures are often necessary to make ends meet. Unfortunately, the time has come for us to take such measures here at [company name]. I know it won't be easy on anyone, but [name of company president] has decided that a 15% across-the-board pay cut will be instituted effective Monday. This is largely the result of the fact that we've lost our contracts with [name of companies]. However, soon we'll be picking up jobs with [name of company], so we're sure the pay cuts will last only 10 weeks. I realize this isn't easy, but such reductions are an unfortunate fact of life in the manufacturing business. On behalf of [company president's name] and myself, we thank you for bearing with us over these rough times. I'll answer one or two questions, but then I have to catch a plane for another meeting.

Finally, because the parts manufactured at Plant C were unaffected by the lost contracts, no pay cuts were mandated there. Plant C constituted the *control* condition for the study.

Measures

Two categories of dependent measures were used: actuarial data on employee theft, and self-report measures tapping some of the processes assumed to be underlying the theft behavior.

Employee theft rates. The measure of employee theft used for this study was the company accounting department's standard formula for computing "shrinkage." The formula yielded the percentage of inventory (e.g., tools, supplies, etc.) unaccounted for by known waste, sales, use in the conduct of business, or normal depreciation. (For a discussion of the difficulties attendant to deriving such measures, see Hollinger & Clark, 1983.) These measures were obtained unobtrusively (during nonwork hours) by representatives of the company's headquarters on a weekly basis during the study period. The persons taking inventory were aware of any legitimate factors that contributed to accounted-for changes in inventory levels (such as shipments received, supplies used during projects, etc.) but were blind to the experimental hypotheses.[4]

---

[4]Although the theft-rate figures (i.e., percentage of inventory loss unaccounted for) were used internally to compute dollar-loss figures, data substantiating a specific dollar-loss amount caused by the thefts were not made available to me. Again, this decision was prompted by the company's desire to avoid potential embarrassment.

Because no single standard for computing shrinkage is uniformly used (Hollinger & Clark, 1983), it was not possible to compare the base rates of employee theft in the present sample to any industry-wide average. However, evidence that the employee theft rate studied here was not atypical was provided by showing that the mean theft rate for the 10-week period before the pay cut was not significantly different from the overall theft rate for all three plants for the prior year, $F < 1.00$. These data are important in that they provide some assurance that the changes in theft rates observed were not simply deviations from unusual patterns that later merely regressed to the mean.[5]

Questionnaire measures.   Two types of questionnaire measures were needed to establish the validity of the study and to facilitate interpretation of the theft data—one group of questions to verify differences in familiarity with the basis for establishing pay (the manipulation check), and another group of questions to establish differences in perceived payment equity. The questionnaires were administered biweekly (during odd-numbered weeks in the study period) at the plant sites during nonworking hours. Because a larger, unrelated study had been going on for several months, the workers were used to completing questionnaires, making it unlikely that any suspicions were aroused by the questions inserted for this study. Participants were assured of the anonymity of their responses.

The "pay basis" measure was designed to provide a check on the validity of the payment-group variable. Participants answered four items on a 5-point scale ranging from *not at all* (1), to *slightly* (2), to *moderately* (3), to *highly* (4), to *extremely* (5). The questions were (a) "How adequate was your employer's explanation regarding the basis of your current pay?" (b) "How familiar are you with the way your employer determines your pay?" (c) "How thoroughly did your employer communicate the basis for your current pay to you?" and (d) "How much concern did your employer show about your feelings when communicating your pay?" A high degree of internal consistency was found for these items (coefficient alpha = .89).

The "pay equity" measure consisted of four items, three of which were anchored with the same scale points as the pay basis items. Specifically, participants responded to the following items: (a) "To what extent do you believe your current pay reflects your actual contributions to the job?" (b) "How fairly paid do you feel you currently are on your job?" and (c) "How satisfied are you with your current overall pay level?" The fourth item asked, "Relative to what you feel you should be paid, do you believe your current pay is:——much too low,——a little too low,——about right,——a little too high,——much too high?" Because only the first 3 points of this bidirectional scale were actually used, responses to this

[5]Unfortunately, week-by-week theft-rate data were not available prior to the study period. As a result, it was impossible to compare the weekly theft rates during the study to earlier weekly theft rates. Thus, it was not possible to rule out the possibility raised by one reviewer that the results may reflect some seasonal fluctuations in theft that coincided with the manipulation period.

3-point scale were combined with the 5-point unidirectional scales for the other items. Coefficient alpha was high (.84), justifying combining the individual items. The option of using existing standardized scales tapping reactions to pay (e.g., the Pay Satisfaction Questionnaire; Heneman & Schwab, 1985) was rejected in favor of ad hoc measures because these were judged to be much more sensitive to the measurement objectives of the present study (cf. Heneman, 1985).

RESULTS

Preliminary Analyses

Prior to the principal data analyses, preliminary analyses were conducted to determine whether to separate the 15 biweekly questionnaire responses into three equal groups, reflecting responses before, during, and after the pay cut. The five 2-week response periods were treated as a repeated measure in mixed-design analyses of variance (ANOVAS) in which the payment group was the between-subjects factor (adequate explanation, inadequate explanation, no pay cut). Separate analyses were conducted for each of the three groups. Because no significant main effects or interactions involving the response periods were obtained in analyses for either questionnaire measure (all $Fs < 1.00$), the decision was made to combine the observations into three groups composed of more reliable observations (before, during, or after the pay cut).

Because only one employee-theft-rate figure was reported for each week (the figure was aggregate, as opposed to individual, data), it was not possible to conduct a parallel set of ANOVAS for this measure. However, separate tests were performed within each payment group to compare each week's theft rate to the mean for all 10 weeks. This process was repeated separately for each of the three response periods (i.e., before, during, and after the pay cut). Because no significant effects emerged in any of these analyses (all values of $t < .50$, $df = 9$), the decision was made (paralleling that for the questionnaire measures) to group the weekly scores into three 10-week response periods.

Employee Theft Rate

Analyses of theft rates were based on a 3×3 mixed-design ANOVA in which payment group was the between-subjects variable, response period was the within-subjects variable, and the 10 weekly theft rates within each cell constituted the data. A significant Payment Period × Response Period interaction was found, $F(4, 56) = 9.66$, $p < .001$. Figure 1 summarizes the means contributing to this interaction.

For each payment group, simple effects tests were performed to determine whether the means differed significantly across response periods. Any significant effects were followed up with the Tukey honestly significant difference (HSD) procedure (with alpha set at .05). In addition, tests for quadratic trend components were performed using orthogonal polynomials (Hays, 1963). This analysis was performed to note trends in the data over time in a situation in which the number of available data points was too small to use time series analyses (Zuwaylif, 1970).

Figure 1

MEAN PERCENTAGE OF EMPLOYEE THEFT AS A
FUNCTION OF TIME RELATIVE TO PAY CUT

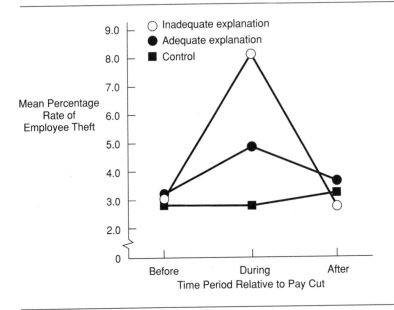

A simple effects test within the inadequate-explanation condition was significant, $F(2, 27) = 9.15, p < .001$. Post hoc tests revealed that significantly higher levels of theft were observed during the pay reduction than before or after the pay reduction. Consistent with this configuration, the quadratic trend was highly significant, $F(1, 27) = 12.18. p < .001$.

Within the adequate-explanation condition, the overall simple effects test was weaker but still significant, $F(2, 52) = 3.76, p < .05$. This effect was the result of a similar, though less pronounced, pattern of means showing theft to be higher during the pay cut than either before or after the pay cut. Tests for a quadratic trend component failed to reach conventional levels of significance, $F(2, 52) = 2.10, p < .15$.

Finally, within the control group, simple effects tests revealed that the means did not differ from each other significantly across the three response periods, $F(2, 55) < 1.00$.

To establish pre- and postmanipulation equivalence, it was useful to compare means between payment groups (adequate explanation, inadequate explanation, no pay cut) within response periods. Simple effects tests showed no significant simple main effects of payment group before or after the pay cut, $F < 1.00$ in both cases. However, the effect of payment group was highly significant during the pay cut, $F(2, 27) = 10.71, p < .001$. Tukey HSD tests revealed that the

Table 2

DATA SUMMARIES FOR QUESTIONNAIRE MEASURES

		Response period					
		Before		*During*		*After*	
Measure/payment group	*n*	*M*	*SD*	*M*	*SD*	*M*	*SD*
Pay basis[a]							
Inadequate explanation	30	40.70$_a$	4.38	42.39$_a$	3.40	43.74$_a$	4.93
Adequate explanation	55	43.22$_a$	5.58	76.10$_b$	6.48	73.73$_b$	5.70
Control	58	42.36$_a$	6.49	40.72$_a$	3.83	41.90$_a$	4.46
Pay equity[b]							
Inadequate explanation	30	56.87$_a$	5.54	40.20$_b$	7.56	57.43$_a$	6.70
Adequate explanation	55	61.22$_a$	9.57	59.56$_a$	9.52	56.03$_a$	9.37
Control	58	61.29$_a$	8.67	60.98$_a$	9.18	58.02$_a$	8.57

Note. Within each row and each column, means not sharing a common subscript are significantly different from each other beyond the .05 level on the basis of the Tukey honestly significant difference technique corrected for confounded comparisons with the Cicchetti (1972) approximation.

[a]Mean scores for the pay basis measure could range from 20 to 100. Higher scores reflect greater degrees of familiarity with the basis for establishing pay. [b]Mean scores for the pay equity measure could range from 20 to 90. Higher scores reflect greater degrees of perceived payment equity.

three means were significantly different from each other. In other words, within the pay-reduction period, the theft rate in the inadequate-explanation condition ($M = 8.9$) was significantly higher than that in the adequate-explanation condition ($M = 5.7$), which was in turn higher than that in the control condition ($M = 3.7$).

Questionnaire Responses

Responses to the pay basis and pay equity questionnaires were analyzed with ANOVA designs identical to that used for the employee-theft measure. For these dependent variables, however, the data consisted of individual responses to the summed items constituting each questionnaire within each cell. The two questionnaire measures were not significantly correlated, $r = .07$.

For the pay basis measure, a significant Payment Group × Response Period interaction was obtained, $F(4, 280) = 256.10$, $p < .0001$. The corresponding means and standard deviations are summarized at the top of Table 2. As shown, post hoc tests revealed that employees in the adequate-explanation condition demonstrated greater understanding of the basis for pay determination than employees in the other two conditions once the explanation occurred (i.e., during and after the pay cut). The adequate-explanation manipulation successfully enhanced employees' understanding of the basis for pay determination.

A significant interaction effect also was obtained for the pay equity measure, $F(4, 280) = 29.05$, $p < .001$. The corresponding means and standard deviations are summarized at the bottom of Table 2. As shown, post hoc tests revealed that during the pay cut, employees in the inadequate-explanation condition expressed the greatest perceptions of pay inequity. Workers whose pay reductions were adequately explained to them did not express heightened payment inequity while their pay was reduced.

Turnover

A summary of missing data and data lost because of voluntary turnover appears in Table 1. Not surprisingly, the majority of the turnover occurred among employees experiencing inadequately explained pay reductions (12 of the 52 workers, or 23.1% of those still on the job at that time). Resignations in other conditions were uniformly 5% or less. Consistent with this, the distribution of resignations over conditions during the pay-cut period was highly significant, x^2 (2, N = 13) = 20.48, p < .001—a result of the fact that 12 of the 13 resignations occurred in the inadequate-explanation group. By contrast, the distribution of resignations across conditions was equal before the pay cut, $x^2(2, N = 3)$ < 0.5, and after the pay cut, $x^2(2, N = 5)$ < 0.5.

DISCUSSION

The data support the hypothesis derived from equity theory (Adams, 1965) that workers experiencing underpayment inequity would attempt to redress that inequity by raising their inputs—in the present case, by pilfering from their employer. Indeed, while workers experienced a 15% pay reduction, they reported feeling underpaid and stole over twice as much as they did when they felt equitably paid. Two distinct interpretations of these theft data may be offered, both of which are consistent with equity theory (Adams, 1965). First, it is possible that the pay reduction led to feelings of frustration and resentment, which motivated the aggressive acts of theft. This possibility is in keeping with recent research findings demonstrating that pay cuts are associated with negative affective reactions to organizational authorities (Greenberg, 1989) and that increases in vandalism correlate positively with perceptions of mistreatment by authorities (DeMore et al., 1988). Such an interpretation follows from a reciprocal deviance orientation to inequity reduction, which suggests that employees' acts of deviance are encouraged by their beliefs that their employers defaulted on their obligations to them by reducing their pay (Kemper, 1966). From this perspective, acts of theft may be understood as a manifestation of feelings of mistreatment.

It is also possible to interpret the thefts as direct attempts to correct underpayment inequity by adjusting the balance of valued resources between the worker and the specific source of that inequity. As such, acts of theft may be interpreted as unofficial transfers of outcomes from the employer to the employee. Because no direct evidence is available suggesting that the stolen items had any positive valence to the employees, it is impossible to claim unambiguously that the theft rates represented employees' attempts to increase their own outcomes. Although such an interpretation is consistent with a considerable amount of evidence on the distribution of rewards and resources (for reviews, see Freedman & Montanari, 1980; Leventhal, 1976), it is also possible that disgruntled employees may have been content to reduce the valued resources available to the agent of their discontent. That is, they may have been motivated to reduce the employer's worth whether or not doing so directly benefited themselves. Unfortunately, the questionnaire items that would have been necessary to provide more refined interpretations of the present data might also have aroused subjects' suspiciousness that theft was being studied, thereby creating the potential for subject reactance (Webb, Campbell, Schwartz, Sechrest, & Grove, 1981). As a result, no such self-report data were collected. Nevertheless, the results are clearly in keeping with equity theory.

The present data also reveal a critical moderator of the tendency to pilfer to restore equity with one's employer—namely, the use of an adequate explanation for the pay cut. Pay cuts that were explained in an honest and caring manner were not seen by employees as being as unfair as pay cuts that were not explained carefully. Accordingly, reactions to carefully explained underpayment also were less severe (i.e., the pilferage rates were lower). These findings add to a recently developing body of research showing that the use of adequately reasoned explanations offered with interpersonal sensitivity tends to mitigate the negative effects associated with the information itself (for reviews, see Folger & Bies, 1989; Tyler & Bies, 1990). The explanations used in the present study were obviously quite successful in reducing costs, both to employees (in terms of inequity distress) and employers (in terms of pilferage and turnover).

An interesting and important aspect of the present study is that a sizeable portion of the participants in the inadequate-explanation condition voluntarily left their jobs during the pay-reduction period; in fact, a much larger proportion resigned than did so in any other condition (or within the same condition at other times). It is tempting to take this finding as support for the idea that quitting one's job is an extreme form of reaction to underpayment inequity (Finn & Lee, 1972) and that the voluntary turnover found here was another form of reaction to inequity. However, because of the nonrandom design of the study, it is not possible to rule out factors other than the experimental manipulation—a difficulty common to quasi-experimental studies (Cook & Campbell, 1976). Despite this problem, several facts lend support to the inequity interpretation. First, the finding that the theft rate immediately before the manipulations did not differ significantly from the previous year's theft rate suggests that nothing out of the ordinary was happening that may have been responsible for the results. Second, because the theft rate was highest precisely under the only conditions in which feelings of inequity were high (i.e., during the pay-cut period following an inadequate explanation), feelings of inequity and theft rate probably are related, both resulting from the manipulated variable exactly as predicted by equity theory (Adams, 1965) and referent cognitions theory (Folger, 1986). Because this interpretation is theoretically supported, its position is strengthened relative to alternatives that may be raised in the absence of random assignment.

Generalizing from the present findings, it appears that adequately explaining inequitable conditions may be an effective means of reducing potentially costly reactions to feelings of underpayment inequity. To be effective, however, such explanations must be perceived as honest, genuine, and not manipulative (Tyler, 1988). Still, to the extent that underpayment conditions are acknowledged and justified by employers (as opposed to ignored or minimized by them), it appears that both workers and their organizations may stand to benefit. Given the high costs of employee theft (American Management Association, 1977), it appears that explaining the basis for inequities may be a very effective (and totally free) mechanism for reducing the costs of employee theft.

Practical implications notwithstanding, the present findings raise some important questions for equity theory (Adams, 1965) about the use of various modes of inequity reduction. Whereas the focus of this study was on pilferage, turnover was another type of response that occurred. Unfortunately, the nature of the present data makes it impossible to determine the trade-offs between various modes of inequity reduction. Did some employees resign in response to under-payment while others (perhaps those with fewer options for alternative employment) stayed on and expressed their negative feelings by stealing? Or was it that the most aggrieved employees stole company property before leaving, while others simply lowered their inputs? Because the theft rates were aggregate, actuarial data and could not be traced to particular employees, and because performance data were not collected, it was not possible to determine when and how different forms of inequity-reduction behavior are likely to occur. As a result, serious questions remain regarding how different inequity-resolution tactics may be used in conjunction with each other.

Confidence in interpretations of the present findings is limited because actuarial-level dependent measures (theft and turnover) were collected in conjunction with an individual-level variable (perceived payment equity), thereby making it impossible to conduct mediational analyses of the results. Exacerbating this problem is the fact that the use of a quasi-experimental design does not allow the discounting of alternative explanations (as noted earlier). Thus, although it is plausible that inequity leads to stealing unless mitigated by an adequate explanation, it is impossible to statistically discount the alternative possibility that unknown preexisting differences between the plants constituting the payment groups (e.g., different norms against stealing or differential acceptance of management's promise that the pay cut would be temporary) may have been responsible for the results. However, in support of the present findings, it is important to note that such limitations are inherent to some degree in all quasi-experimental research designs (Cook & Campbell, 1976).

Although nonrandom assignment precludes the discounting of alternative explanations, support for the present interpretation of the data may be derived from converging sources of theoretically based data. In this case, several lines of analogous research converge with my claim that adequate explanations enhanced the acceptance of undesired outcomes. For example, Folger and his associates (e.g., Folger & Martin, 1986; Folger, Rosenfield, & Robinson, 1983) measured laboratory subjects' feelings of discontent in reaction to procedural changes that created unfavorable conditions for them. Consistent with referent cognitions theory

(Folger, 1986), Folger and his colleagues found that these feelings of discontent were reduced only when the need to make procedural changes was adequately explained. Similarly, in another line of investigation, Weiner et al. (1987) found that persons victimized by another's harmdoing expressed less anger toward the harmdoer when claims of mitigating circumstances were offered for the harmdoer's actions. Both lines of investigation show that negative affective reactions are reduced by the presentation of adequate explanatory information. As such, they provide good convergent evidence for the claim that adequately explained pay cuts mitigated feelings of inequity and reactions to underpayment inequity.

Finally, an important question may be raised about the compound nature of the explanation manipulation used in the present study. Because the adequate-explanation condition and the inadequate-explanation condition differed along several dimensions (postulated a priori to contribute to mitigation of the effects of the inequity), it was not possible to determine the individual effects of the various contributing factors. Specifically, the explanations differed in terms of several factors. Some of these, such as the quality of the information and the interpersonal sincerity of its presentation, have been recognized as mitigating reactions to undesirable outcomes (Shapiro & Buttner, 1988). Other differences between conditions, such as possible differences in the credibility of the source (the president versus the vice president) have not yet been studied. Clearly, the unique effects of these factors are prime candidates for future research efforts.

To conclude, the results of the present study shed new light on employee theft—one of the most important problems in the field of human-resource management. The evidence confirms that employee theft is a predictable response to underpayment inequity and reveals that such reactions can be substantially reduced by the inexpensive tactic of explaining the basis for the inequity in clear, honest, and sensitive terms.

References

Adams, J.S. (1965). Inequity in social exchange. In L. Berkowitz (Ed.), *Advances in experimental social psychology* (Vol. 2, pp. 267–299). San Diego, CA: Academic Press.

American Management Association. (1977, March). *Summary overview of the "state of the art" regarding information gathering techniques and level of knowledge in three areas concerning crimes against business: Draft report.* Washington, DC: National Institute of Law Enforcement and Criminal Justice, Law Enforcement Assistance Administration.

Astor, S. D. (1972, March). Twenty steps to preventing theft in business. *Management Review, 61*(3), 34–35.

Bies, R. J. (1986, August). *Identifying principles of interactional justice: The case of corporate recruiting.* Symposium conducted at the annual meeting of the Academy of Management, Chicago, IL.

Bies, R. J., & Moag, J. S. (1986). Interactional justice: Communication criteria of fairness. In R. J. Lewicki, B. H. Sheppard, & B. H. Bazerman (Eds.), *Research on negotiation in organizations* (Vol. 1, pp. 43–55). Greenwich, CT: JAI Press.

Cicchetti, D. V. (1972). Extension of multiple-range tests to interaction tables in the analysis of variance: A rapid approximate solution. *Psychological Bulletin, 77*, 405–408.

Cook, T. D., & Campbell, D. T. (1976). The design and conduct of quasi-experiments and true experiments in field settings. In M. D. Dunnette (Ed.), *Handbook of industrial and organizational psychology* (pp. 223–326). Chicago: Rand McNally.

Cropanzano, R., & Folger, R. (1979). Referent cognitions and task decision autonomy: Beyond equity theory. *Journal of Applied Psychology, 74*, 293–299.

DeMore, S. W., Fisher, J. D., & Baron, R. M. (1988). The equity-control model as a predictor of vandalism among college students. *Journal of Applied Social Psychology, 18*, 80–91.

Finn, R. H., & Lee, S. M. (1972). Salary equity: Its determination, analysis and correlates. *Journal of Applied Psychology, 56*, 283–292.

Fisher, J. D., & Baron, R. M. (1982). An equity-based model of vandalism. *Population and Environment, 5*, 182–200.

Folger, R. (1986). Rethinking equity theory: A referent cognitions model. In H. W. Bierhoff, R. L. Cohen, & J. Greenberg (Eds.), *Justice in social relations* (pp. 145–162). New York: Plenum Press.

Folger, R., & Bies, R. J. (1989). Managerial responsibilities and procedural justice. *Employee Responsibilities and Rights Journal, 2*, 79–90.

Folger, R., & Martin, C. (1986). Relative deprivation and referent cognitions: Distributive and procedural justice effects. *Journal of Applied Psychology, 22*, 531–546.

Folger, R., Rosenfield, D., & Robinson, T. (1983). Relative deprivation and procedural justification. *Journal of Personality and Social Psychology, 45*, 268–273.

Freedman, S. M., & Montanari, J. R. (1980). An integrative model of managerial reward allocation. *Academy of Management Review, 5*, 381–390.

Greenberg, J. (1982). Approaching equity and avoiding inequity in groups and organizations. In J. Greenberg & R. L. Cohen (Eds.), *Equity and justice in social behavior* (pp. 389–435). San Diego, CA: Academic Press.

Greenberg, J. (1986). Determinants of perceived fairness of performance evaluations. *Journal of Applied Psychology, 71*, 340–342.

Greenberg, J. (1987). A taxonomy of organizational justice theories. *Academy of Management Review, 12*, 9–22.

Greenberg, J. (1989). Cognitive re-evaluation of outcomes in response to underpayment inequity. *Academy of Management Journal, 32*, 174–184.

Hays, W. L. (1963). *Statistics.* New York: Holt, Rinehart, & Winston.

Heneman, H. G., III. (1985). Pay satisfaction. In K. Rowland & G. Ferris (Eds.), *Research in personnel and human resources management* (Vol. 3, pp. 115–139). Greenwich, CT: JAI Press.

Heneman, H. G., III, & Schwab, D. P. (1985). Pay satisfaction: Its multidimensional nature and measurement. *International Journal of Psychology, 20*, 129–141.

Hollinger, R. D., & Clark, J. P. (1983). *Theft by employees.* Lexington, MA: Lexington Books.

Horning, D. (1970). Blue collar theft: Conceptions of property, attitudes toward pilfering, and work group norms in a modern industrial plant. In E. O. Smigel & H. L. Ross (Eds.), *Crimes against bureaucracy* (pp. 46–64). New York: Van Nostrand Reinhold.

Kemper, T. D. (1966). Representative roles and the legitimization of deviance. *Social Problems, 13*, 288–298.

Leventhal, G. S. (1976). The distribution of rewards and resources in groups and organizations. In L. Berkowitz & E. Walster (Eds.), *Advances in experimental social psychology* (Vol. 9, pp. 91–131). San Diego, CA: Academic Press.

Lind, E. A., & Lissak, R. (1985). Apparent impropriety and procedural fairness judgments. *Journal of Experimental Social Psychology, 21,* 19–29.

Lind, E. A., & Tyler, T. (1988). *The social psychology of procedural justice.* New York: Plenum Press.

Mangione, T. W., & Quinn, R. P. (1975). Job satisfaction, counter-productive behavior, and drug use at work. *Journal of Applied Psychology, 11,* 114–116.

Mars, G. (1973). Chance, punters, and the fiddle: Institutionalized pilferage in a hotel dining room. In M. Warner (Ed.), *The sociology of the workplace* (pp. 200–210). New York: Halsted Press.

Mars, G. (1974). Dock pilferage: A case study in occupational theft. In P. Rock & M. McIntosh (Eds.), *Deviance and social control* (pp. 209–228). London: Tavistock Institute.

Merriam, D. (1977). Employee theft. *Criminal Justice Abstracts, 9,* 380–386.

Merton, R. T. (1938). Social structure and anomie. *American Sociological Review, 3,* 672–682.

Shapiro, D. L., & Buttner, E. H. (1988, August). *Adequate explanations: What are they, and do they enhance procedural justice under severe outcome circumstances?* Paper presented at the annual meeting of the Academy of Management, Anaheim, CA.

Tyler, T. R. (1988). What is procedural justice? *Law and Society Review, 22,* 301–335.

Tyler, T. R., & Bies, R. J. (1990). Beyond formal procedures: The interpersonal context of procedural justice. In J. Carroll (Ed.), *Applied social psychology and organizational settings* (pp. 77–98). Hillsdale, NJ: Erlbaum.

Webb, E. J., Campbell, D. T., Schwartz, R. D., Sechrest, L., & Grove, J. B. (1981). *Nonreactive measures in the social sciences* (2nd ed.). Boston: Houghton Mifflin.

Weiner, B., Amirkhan, J., Folkes, V. S., & Varette, J. A. (1987). An attributional analysis of excuse giving: Studies of a naive theory of emotion. *Journal of Personality and Social Psychology, 52,* 316–324.

Zuwaylif, F. H. (1970). *General applied statistics.* Reading, MA: Addison-Wesley.

READING 31

▲

COMPENSATION STRATEGIES
IN A GLOBAL CONTEXT

Luis R. Gomez-Mejia
Theresa Welbourne

Executive Summary

The authors argue that multinational companies should take culture into account when designing compensation strategies. In particular, they illustrate how the cultural dimensions developed by Hofstede (1980) (power distance, individualism, uncertainty avoidance, and masculinity/femininity) can play a role in developing pay systems.

The internationalization of business and employment is reaching dramatic proportions as we enter the 21st century. Investments overseas by U.S. multinational corporations (MNCs) have increased tenfold during the past decade; during the same period, foreign firms have increased ownership of domestic (U.S.) companies by 300 percent (Gomez-Mejia and Balkin, 1991). Approximately 90 percent of the average international management payroll of MNCs is comprised of compensation for local nationals, presenting a major challenge to these firms in managing local employees within diverse countries. The primary reason for reliance on local nationals is that the cost of maintaining an expatriate overseas exceeds $250,000 a year. In the late 1980s, over 320,000 U.S. citizens were employed by firms owned outside the U.S. The Japanese are investing heavily in U.S. operations. At present they employ 250,000 U.S. citizens, and it is anticipated that number might increase to over 1 million by the turn of the century. Michael Blumenthal, Chief Executive Officer of Unisys, noted that more and more European, American, and Japanese giants are willing to move large business units "around the world without particular reference to national borders" (*Business Week*, 1990). A recent cover story in *Business Week* argued that an ever-increasing wave of international mergers, acquisitions, and cross-national strategic alliances is creating a world of "stateless corporations" staffed by a cadre of managers, professionals, and workers of very diverse cultural backgrounds. These firms "are trying to become local companies in many countries" (*Business Week*, 1990).

Source: Luis R. Gomez-Mejia and Theresa Welbourne, "Compensation Strategies in a Global Context," *Human Resource Planning*, vol. 14, no. 1, 29–41. Used by permission.

A crucial question that arises as a result of this global trend is the degree to which reward systems must be customized to cope with diverse cultural contingencies, or the extent to which the effectiveness of particular compensation strategies varies from one country to another. The old days, when lower labor costs were a primary reason for a firm relocating overseas, are gone. Closeness to markets, competitive advantages, and strategic flexibility now are at the fore. The emerging challenge from a compensation perspective for MNCs is not to take advantage of low-wage opportunities, but to design compensation strategies that are most appropriate for specific cultural conditions. This requires a more complex and sophisticated approach to compensation administration on a worldwide basis than that of a traditional multinational (which would shift production around the world to minimize its proportion of labor costs to total costs). The central thesis of this paper is that MNCs that are able to use national culture to their advantage when designing compensation strategies will achieve greater success in managing diverse work forces around the world.

GLOBAL TRENDS IN PAY SYSTEMS

Ironically, internationalization appears to be creating greater consistency in compensation strategies for MNCs, when we would expect just the opposite as these firms face a more heterogeneous cultural milieu. Gomez-Mejia and Balkin (1991) noted that practices are beginning to "look alike" around the world. A study by Towers, Perrin, and Crosby reported that the number of British firms with American-style pay-for-performance schemes increased fivefold from 1978 to 1984 (Mesdag, 1984). Mesdag also indicated that similar pay-for-performance systems are rapidly being introduced in other European countries. Japanese management techniques are viewed as magic wands by many executives and academics in the U.S. (At least 30 "how to" books have been published since the early 1980s on implementing Japanese management techniques in the U.S.) At the same time, the Japanese unexpectedly are beginning to incorporate "American-like" compensation practices—such as providing individual bonuses, pirating mid-career managers from their competitors, and utilizing layoffs (rather than variable pay) to control labor costs. M. Ono, a Japanese personnel officer, noted "my impression is that they'll all [nations] develop [pay policies] in the most neutral, global way possible" (Whenmouth, 1988).

In other words, much imitation in pay practices is taking place around the world. Among several reasons for this trend are: the old adage, "it is always greener on the other side of the fence"; more and more companies exposed to management practices in different countries; compensation consulting firms capitalizing on an expanding and lucrative overseas market for their services; and the growth of compensation as an academic subfield with an emphasis on prescriptive, universal practices. However, we know very little about how effective "exported" compensation practices are in different national settings. To what extent do cultural factors moderate the success of different compensation strategies? Are some compensation strategies universally effective while others must be customized to meet the idiosyncratic nature of national culture? Answers to these questions are becoming increasingly important in an organizational environment that transcends national boundaries.

COMPENSATION STRATEGY AT AN INTERNATIONAL LEVEL

Mahoney (1989) noted, "because of its social as well as economic significance, compensation also exemplifies and reinforces social norms." An international corporation must consider which social norms are being emphasized when devising its compensation philosophy. Rather than merely transferring strategies based on the home country's social and cultural standards, thought should be given to the link between local cultural norms, methods of rewarding employees, and the resulting effect on individual, group, and corporate performance.

A large literature on compensation strategy suggests that the pay system is an essential integrating mechanism through which the efforts of individuals are directed toward the accomplishment of an organization's strategic objectives; when properly designed, it can be a key contributor to firm performance (Gomez-Mejia and Balkin, 1991). Several recent studies show that closer linkage between compensation and corporate strategies leads to improved organization performance. In other words, firms that are able to mold compensation strategies to their business strategies and to the unique contingencies facing the firm tend to be more successful.

Unfortunately, compensation strategy research conducted to date has been parochial in nature, focusing almost exclusively on the U.S. Developing links among corporate and compensation strategies becomes complicated once the corporation's global environment is considered. Organizations do not exist in a vacuum, as suggested by business policy researchers who have argued cogently that corporate strategies can be successful only if they are attuned to the external environment (Fombrun & Shanley, 1990). Studies on compensation strategy conducted within the U.S. have held part of the environment, namely national culture, constant. When moving into the international arena, this variable changes. If pay strategies need to be consistent with organizational strategies, then we would expect that the former also should be adjusted to meet the unique cultural contingencies of employees within the new environment.

RELATIONSHIP BETWEEN NATIONAL CULTURE AND COMPENSATION STRATEGY

Hofstede (1980), in the most ambitious project of its kind using a database with survey responses of 116,000 employees across 50 countries, concluded that national cultures can be categorized along four dimensions. He labeled these: (1) power distance, (2) individualism, (3) uncertainty avoidance, and (4) masculinity/femininity. He then employed his data to score participating countries on each of the four dimensions. Characteristics of cultures attaining extreme high or low scores on each of these dimensions are sketched.

For analytical purposes, we use these four dimensions to examine compensation strategy at an international level. They provide clues as to the compensation strategy configuration most likely to mesh with the value system apparent within a given culture. According to current paradigms and themes in compensation strategy research, firms that experience a better fit between inherent values or characteristics of those national populations from which they draw their work force and compensation strategies should be more successful than firms in which these two sets of factors are not linked. A mismatch between compensation strategies and cultural characteristics is likely to result in a number of dysfunctional consequences including difficulty in attracting and retaining workers, higher labor costs, labor relations problems, violation of personal norms leading to resentment and perhaps destructive employee behaviors, inability to achieve strategic objectives, lower morale, and a negative public image.

We now discuss those compensation strategies that should be most appropriate given a nation's standing on each cultural dimension. Because Japan represents the major U.S. competitor in world markets, and because its multinationals are expanding very rapidly, both Japan and the U.S. will be discussed in some detail to illustrate the effect of cultural elements on compensation strategies. In Exhibits 1–4, several countries that exemplify the extremes of each dimension are shown. Japan and the U.S. do not appear in each exhibit because for some of the dimensions they may not best illustrate the end poles.

Power Distance

This refers to the extent to which citizens readily accept a hierarchical system or power structure in organizations. The greater the power distance, the more status differences between subordinates and superiors are emphasized. Individuals living in a country characterized by low power distance are less likely to tolerate significant inequities between the ranks or job levels, while countries with a high power distance expect large differentials between levels as a part of life.

High Power Distance and Compensation Strategies. The dominant values of countries that tolerate high power distance include top-down communications, class divisions, ascribed status, authoritarianism, dependence on superiors, attraction to power symbols, and disdain of blue-collar work. These countries tend to utilize taller organization structures which reflect greater status differentials between jobs within the corporation. In addition, a greater amount of centralization of functions is used as a control mechanism. This structural orientation should be consistent with compensation policies that are hierarchical in nature. We would expect visible rewards that serve as testimony to the success of those at the top of the corporate pyramid to work best, evidenced by large differences between the base compensation and benefits of those at the top contrasted with that of those at lower echelons. The rewards that come with attaining power would be conspicuous to all employees within the firm. Countries that score at the high extreme on this dimension include Malaysia, Philippines, Mexico, several Arab nations, Venezuela, and Spain (see Exhibit 1).

Exhibit 1

POWER DISTANCE, ORGANIZATIONAL
CHARACTERISTICS, AND COMPENSATION STRATEGIES

POWER DISTANCE		*Dominant Values*	*Corporate Features*	*Compensation Strategies*	*Sample Countries*
	HIGH	• top-down communications • class divisions as natural • ascribed status • authoritarianism • dependence on superiors • power symbols • white-collar jobs valued more than blue-collar jobs	• centralization and tall organization structures • traditional line of command	• hierarchical compensation system • differences in pay and benefits reflect job and status differences; large differential between upper and lower echelons • visible rewards that project power	• Malaysia • Philippines • Mexico • Arab nations • Venezuela • Spain
	LOW	• egalitarianism • populist beliefs • achieved status • joint decision making • high value on participation • inner directed with low dependence on superiors • disdain for power symbols • hard work valued even if manual in nature	• flatter organizational structures • decentralized control • greater reliance on matrix-type networks • great degree of worker involvement	• egalitarian-based compensation systems • small differences in pay and benefits between higher- and lower-level jobs • participatory pay strategies such as gainsharing more prevalent	• Netherlands • Australia • Switzerland • Sweden

Low Power Distance and Compensation Strategies.   The dominant values of countries with low tolerance for power distance include egalitarianism, populist beliefs, achieved status, joint decision making, high value on participation, inner direction with low dependence on superiors, disdain for power symbols, and belief that hard work is honorable even if manual in nature. These countries tend to rely on flatter organization pyramids in an effort to engender a more egalitarian atmosphere. Functions also tend to be less centralized in an attempt to distribute power to divisions or subsidiaries. There is greater reliance on matrix-type networks. Compensation strategies most likely to successfully complement these structures deemphasize differences between lower and higher ranks. The ratio of top executive pay to lower-level workers' compensation should not be as great as in countries where power distance is high. Privileges for those reaching management and executive positions should be kept to a minimum and not widely flaunted. Differences between the ranks should be subdued. Compensation programs requiring extensive employee involvement (such as gain sharing) are more likely to be successful in this type of culture. Countries low in power distance include Netherlands, Australia, Switzerland, and Sweden (see Exhibit 1).

Power Distance and Compensation Strategies: Japan and the U.S. In Hofstede's study, Japan and the U.S. scored somewhat close to one another on the power distance criteria: Japan ranked 33 out of 50 countries; the U.S. ranked 38. As noted above, power distance is evidenced within corporations by their approach to organizational structure. Both Japan and the U.S. generally utilize hierarchical structures, where centralization is common and large differences are apparent between blue-collar positions and professional or management jobs. In both countries, those at the top of the hierarchy make substantially more money than those at the bottom. Power symbols and perquisites are generously provided as individuals move up the pyramid, and upward promotion through a career ladder is an important mechanism to increase income and status. However—and this is consistent with their relative ranks on this dimension—the ratio of the highest paid to lowest paid workers in a firm is significantly higher in the U.S. Also, Japanese firms typically have fewer grade levels than American companies of comparable size.

Individualism

Individualism reflects the degree to which people in a given society value independence versus group membership. Countries high on the individualism dimension place extreme value on personal goals, autonomy, and privacy. Alternatively, high collectivism (or low individualism) is present in countries whose values center on groups, such as families or clans. Loyalty to the group, commitment to its norms, involvement in its activities, social cohesiveness, and intense socialization are typical of these cultures.

High Individualism and Compensation Strategies. Employees in high individualism countries tend to value personal accomplishment, selfishness, independence, individual attribution, internal locus of control, and control over their own destiny. Involvement with an organization is based on a contract-type relationship rather than a moral commitment. The corporation is not expected to care for its workers beyond the scope of the employment relationship. Explicit systems of control are necessary to ensure compliance. Managerial practices tend to promote individual accomplishment. Pay strategies most suitable for this type of culture should emphasize performance-based plans that reward individual, rather than group, outcomes. Firms should make heavy use of extrinsic rewards to recognize employee success. External equity also becomes very important. Because employees associate personal success with financial status, they compare their success to others in monetary units—thus the need to strive for external equity so that an organization's compensation plan is at parity with those of comparable firms. Since individual performance, rather than position, is viewed

Exhibit 2

INDIVIDUALISM, ORGANIZATIONAL CHARACTERISTICS, AND COMPENSATION STRATEGIES

	Dominant Values	*Corporate Features*	*Compensation Strategies*	*Sample Countries*
INDIVIDUALISM — HIGH	• personal accomplishment • selfishness • independence • individual attributions • internal locus of control • belief in creating one's own destiny • utilitarian relationship with employee	• organizations not compelled to care for employees' total well-being • employees look after their individual interests • explicit systems of control necessary to ensure compliance and prevent wide deviation from organizational norms	• performance-based pay • individual achievement rewarded • external equity emphasized • extrinsic rewards are important indicators of personal success • attempts made to isolate individual contributions (i.e., who did what) • emphasis on short-term objectives	• United States • Great Britain • Canada • New Zealand
LOW	• team accomplishment • sacrifice for others • dependence on social unit • group attributions • external locus of control • belief in the hand of fate • moral relationship	• organizations committed to a high level of involvement in workers' personal lives • loyalty to the firm is critical • normative, rather than formal, systems of control to ensure compliance	• group-based performance is important criteria • seniority-based pay utilized • intrinsic rewards essential • internal equity is key in guiding pay policies • personal need (e.g., number of children) affects pay received	• Singapore • South Korea • Indonesia • Japan • Taiwan

as most important, internal job evaluation procedures are less likely to be perceived as valuable; attempts should be made to isolate and recognize individual contributions. The focus on individual accomplishment and rewards also leads to pay policies that emphasize short-term objectives. Bonus plans, for example, would tend to focus more heavily on short-term goals so that individuals can receive immediate feedback about their performance. Given the utilitarian relationship between individuals and the firm, inter-firm mobility is high; employees prefer short-term pay offs and resent compensation schemes that tie them to the organization. Countries that score high on individualism include the U.S., Great Britain, Canada, and New Zealand (see Exhibit 2).

Low Individualism and Compensation Strategies.   Countries that score low on the individualism criteria emphasize team accomplishment, sacrifice for others, dependence on the social unit, group attributions, external locus of control, belief in the role of fate, and moral commitment. Employees anticipate long-term employment relationships and expect the organization to care for their well-being, including their family's, throughout their lifetime. Corporate policies often are based on loyalty to the business, and promotion is based on seniority and conformity. The control system tends to be normative rather than formal in nature. Compensation programs based on group performance support this orientation, with all employees rewarded when the group accomplishes its goal. The use of individual-based criteria tends to neutralize the group atmosphere these companies prefer. Seniority-based rewards are important because they promote long-term relationships with the organization and reinforce loyalty to the firm. Intrinsic rewards should be employed more often than extrinsic rewards, because these tend to promote less competition in the work force. Internal equity thus is seen as an essential goal for the reward program because it maintains the harmony desired by employers who are attempting to build group cohesiveness. Personal need (e.g., number of children) often affects the pay received. Countries scoring low on individualism include Singapore, South Korea, Indonesia, Japan, and Taiwan (see Exhibit 2).

Individualism and Compensation Strategy: Japan and the U.S.   In Hofstede's study, the U.S. scored 91 on this dimension—by far the highest in his sample. This should not surprise us since the U.S. prides itself on supporting every individual's right to freedom and success based on his or her own efforts. Japan scored 44 (or less than half of the U.S. score) on this dimension, reflecting the group orientation that is rampant within Japanese society which emphasizes family relations, belonging, and social commitment.

Employees in group-oriented countries are characterized as having moral relationships with the organization; employees in high individualism countries believe in a more calculative relationship with their employers. This is apparent in Japanese and U.S. orientations toward work: Japanese view their careers as life-long ventures with one employer; U.S. employees generally have no such anticipation.

The focus on long-term careers with one firm requires organizations to place more emphasis on internal equity considerations because employees will tend to compare their compensation packages with those of other workers *within* the firm rather than outside it. This is consistent with Japan's focus on pay-for-seniority: internal equity is addressed by rewarding loyalty and tenure—unambiguous criteria that workers understand and that enhance the values espoused by the organization. An additional outcome is seen in Japanese firms' involvement with their employees' personal and family lives. Intrinsic rewards tend to be emphasized; this creates an atmosphere for employees where personal and business life often intermingle, making it difficult to view the individual as distinct from the firm where he or she works.

Countries with low individualism promote cooperative group behavior. One mechanism for signaling the importance of teamwork and group outcomes is to tie rewards to group objectives. This is a common approach for the Japanese, who are extremely concerned about harming team spirit by imposing individual incentives.

High individualism countries believe the individual is more important than the group; therefore, we expect individual performance measures to be more significant than seniority. Each person is expected to care for him or herself; the business does not assume responsibility for the long-term care of employees. Pay policies within the U.S. tend to follow this pattern: individual-based pay-for-performance programs are the norm. Personal success is recognized, and external equity is emphasized in order to provide star employees with the symbols that signify they are high achievers. Reward programs that consider external equity issues are the norm in the U.S.; salary and benefits surveys abound as indicators of market trends. Inter-firm mobility is expected as a way for employees to improve their situations, and companies attempt to maintain competitive salaries in the marketplace. For most employees, no given firm is an integral part of their identity throughout their lives. An employee's loyalty is primarily to his or her own well-being and to that of his or her family, with minimal affective attachment to employers.

Uncertainty Avoidance

The third dimension, uncertainty avoidance, is concerned with the method by which a society deals with risk and instability for its members. A low score on uncertainty avoidance (or high acceptance of ambiguity) is exhibited by tolerance of risk and the unknown—resulting in lower levels of stress on people with that culture. A high score on uncertainty avoidance is found in countries where citizens constantly try to grapple with uncertainty and control it; this results in tension, stress, and efforts to maintain security for individuals within the society.

High Uncertainty Avoidance and Compensation Strategies.   Countries that score high on the uncertainty avoidance dimension are characterized by: fear of random events and the unknown; high value placed on stability and routine; low tolerance for ambiguity; low risk propensity; and comfort in security, lack of tension, and lack of contradictions. Mechanistic organizational structures are common and result in an emphasis on written rules and procedures and extensive dependence on specialists to clarify routines. Management avoids making risky decisions. Managers' jobs tend to focus on details, with time spent trying to make consistent decisions and develop routines to structure jobs, departments, and the organization. We expect this orientation to result in compensation policies that are clearly specified and bureaucratic. Reward systems should be centralized to assure consistency in administration across all employees. Base pay, or that part of the compensation package that is fixed, should play a more important role than any type of variable pay. Little discretion should be given to supervisors in dispensing pay. Countries scoring high on uncertainty avoidance include Greece, Portugal, Yugoslavia, and Italy (see Exhibit 3).

Low Uncertainty Avoidance and Compensation Strategies.   These countries are characterized by high value placed on challenge, disdain of stability and routine, opportunity seeking, high risk propensity, and use of tensions and contradictions to span innovation, discovery, and a mastery of change. Business in

Exhibit 3

UNCERTAINTY AVOIDANCE, ORGANIZATIONAL
CHARACTERISTICS, AND COMPENSATION STRATEGIES

		Dominant Values	*Corporate Features*	*Compensation Strategies*	*Sample Countries*
UNCERTAINTY AVOIDANCE	HIGH	• fear of random events and the unknown • high value placed on stability and routine • low tolerance for ambiguity • low risk propensity • comfort in security, lack of tension, and lack of contradictions	• mechanistic structures • written rules and policies guide the firm • organizations strive to be predictable • management avoids making risky decisions • careful delineation of responsibilities and work flows	• bureaucratic pay policies utilized • compensation programs tend to be centralized • fixed pay more important than variable pay • little discretion given to supervisor in dispensing pay	• Greece • Portugal • Yugoslavia • Italy
	LOW	• unexpected viewed as challenging and exciting • stability and routine seen as boring • ambiguity seen as providing opportunities • high risk propensity • tensions and contradictions span innovation, discovery, and mastery of change	• organic structure • less-structured activities • fewer written rules to cope with changing environmental forces • managers are more adaptable and tend to make riskier decisions	• variable pay a key component in pay programs • external equity emphasized • decentralized pay program is norm • much discretion given to supervisors and business units in pay allocation	• Singapore • Denmark • Sweden • Hong Kong

these countries strives for a more organic organization style, less-structured activities, and few written policies and procedures. They make greater use of generalists who have freedom to cross boundaries and perform unanticipated tasks. Managers feel free to take more risks and to get involved in strategic decisions. Employees actually may thrive on the unexpected, resulting in higher labor turnover because workers are willing to risk leaving current employers to explore opportunities elsewhere. Compensation programs designed for this type of culture should emphasize risk sharing and provision of matching "blue-book value" counter offers to employees who secure external job offers. External equity would be a key concern for these businesses; they must deal with higher attrition and attempt to match competitors' offers to key employees. Pay policies should be decentralized to meet the specific needs of subgroups within the organization; this allows management within divisions the discretion to design pay programs that meet specific employee needs and particular strategic objectives. Corporations should be willing to accept the problem of inequity across divisions in order to benefit from the positive consequences of allowing diversity. Countries scoring low on uncertainty avoidance include Singapore, Denmark, Sweden, and Hong Kong (see Exhibit 3).

Uncertainty Avoidance and Compensation Strategies: Japan and the U.S.   Japan scored 92 on uncertainty avoidance—one of the top 7 out of Hofstede's 50-country sample. Japan's high score contrasts with the U.S.'s low score of 46 and accompanying rank of 43. As noted above, high uncertainty avoidance evidences itself within an organization through the predominance of formalized organizational routines and the presence of many rules and procedures. This is seen in Japanese firms that maintain strict control over decision-making processes. Compensation programs based on seniority within Japan also might stem from the need for objective criteria with which to make decisions; any other type of performance measurement would be difficult to document and to develop rules and procedures for—as evidenced by the relative lack of success seen with traditional performance-appraisal programs.

High uncertainty avoidance also indicates that organization members will avoid the opportunity to make risky decisions. This is consistent with Japanese disinterest in making frequent judgments of personnel performance, deferring instead to the use of seniority for granting wage increases and promotions. The concept of group harmony, strongly promoted by Japanese firms, aims to avoid conflict within the organization and to create predictability in pay allocations. A typical Japanese worker can forecast with a high degree of reliability what his or her base pay will be, for example, ten years from today.

U.S. corporations tend to have fewer written procedures and less-structured activities. This allows for flexibility in establishing decentralized reward programs. American workers generally accept more risks. This is evidenced by high turnover rates; individuals are willing to move from one firm to another in exchange for possible benefits. High turnover has resulted in a heavy emphasis on external equity in the U.S. where, in many fields, wage compression is a resulting problem. Interestingly, most U.S. workers do not have the level of tolerance for fluctuations in their income attributable to variable pay that typical Japanese employees do. Variable pay reaches 20 percent or more of base pay in Japan. The Japanese use this variable component as a mechanism to absorb shocks to the system when product demand drops, without resorting to layoffs to cut back on costs. Thus, in a sense, the Japanese reduce uncertainty (of being thrown on the street and losing all income) by increasing the amount of pay at risk. American workers are more comfortable assuming the risks of layoffs and of having to seek employment elsewhere than in contending with potential ups and downs in yearly income resulting from variable compensation tied to firm profitability. Lack of loyalty to any given firm reinforces this tendency in the U.S. It should be noted, however, that practically all variable pay in Japan is pegged to corporatewide aggregate indicators (such as business profits) and not to individual or group-based performance. This is consistent with the country's low individualism orientation.

Masculinity/Femininity

The masculinity/femininity dimension characterizes the degree to which assertive or characteristically "masculine" behavior is promoted by society, and the rigidity of stereotyped roles played by men and women. A country that scores high on this dimension accepts the philosophy that men or "masculine" values are dominant within both business and society. It also admires acquisition of material possessions; aggressive attempts to acquire additional wealth or income are viewed positively. A "feminine" society (or country that scores low on the masculinity dimension) encourages caring and nurturing behavior. It values quality of life rather than the acquisition of numerous possessions. In addition, women's roles are less predetermined and broader in scope.

High Masculinity and Compensation Strategies.   These countries are characterized by greater emphasis on material possessions, men accorded higher power and status, rigidity of gender stereotypes, and gender inequities accepted as a given. Men and women tend to have predetermined career roles and segregation of occupations by gender is common. Fewer women are found in high-level management or executive positions. For men, careers are emphasized, and failure within a specific career results in significant stress. This cultural orientation produces compensation programs that incorporate the inequities imposed by the societal structure. Tradition is an acceptable basis for determining pay rates, and thus bureaucratic pay programs that do not factor in tradition cannot be used by businesses.

Among men, those exhibiting more "masculine" traits (e.g., aggressiveness) tend to be rewarded with promotions and other favorable personnel decisions. A patronizing attitude toward women as the "weaker sex" produces a number of special benefits for women such as restricted hours of work, longer breaks, and paid maternity leave, individuals are viewed as getting paid what they deserve, and this is seen as a function of strengths and weaknesses as judged by superiors. Countries scoring high on masculinity include Austria, Germany, Mexico, and the U.S. (see Exhibit 4).

Low Masculinity and Compensation Strategies.   In these countries, quality of life is valued more than material gain, men are not believed to be inherently superior, gender stereotypes are minimal, and a strong belief in equal pay for jobs of equal value regardless of gender is present. Men and women have more career choices. Both sexes can choose whether or not to pursue professional or managerial careers, and acceptable options are available for those who decide to follow alternative paths. More women can be found in higher level jobs within these countries. Compensation programs assure equity between the sexes, and result in carefully spelled-out bureaucratic policies and procedures. Tradition plays a minor role in pay decisions, with work content and performance becoming the prime criteria for establishing pay levels. "Masculine" traits have no inherent advantage where promotions and other personnel decisions that affect pay are concerned. Women enjoy few special benefits based solely on gender. Countries scoring low on masculinity include the Netherlands, Norway, Sweden, Finland, and Denmark (see Exhibit 4).

Exhibit 4

MASCULINITY/FEMININITY, ORGANIZATIONAL CHARACTERISTICS, AND COMPENSATION STRATEGIES

	Dominant Values	Corporate Features	Compensation Strategies	Sample Countries
MASCULINITY — HIGH	• material possessions important • men given higher power and status • rigidity of gender stereotypes • gender inequities in pay accepted as a given	• some occupations labeled as "male" while others are "female" • fewer women in higher-level positions	• differential pay policies that allow for inequities by gender • tradition an acceptable basis for pay decisions • "male" traits rewarded in promotions and other personnel decisions • paternalistic benefits for women in the form of paid maternity leave, day care, hours of work etc.	• Austria • Mexico • Germany • United States
LOW	• quality of life valued more than material gain • men not believed to be inherently superior • minimal gender stereotyping • strong belief in equal pay for jobs of equal value, regardless of gender composition	• more flexibility in career choice for men and women • more women in higher-level jobs	• jobs evaluated regardless of gender composition • focus on work content rather than tradition to assess value of different jobs • well-developed "equity goals" for pay determination • "masculine" traits carry no special value for promotions and other personnel decisions • few perks based on gender membership	• Netherlands • Norway • Sweden • Finland • Denmark

Masculinity and Compensation Strategies: Japan and the U.S.   Although the U.S. and Japan both scored high on this dimension, Japan ranked highest (1) with a score of 95 out of 95; the U.S. ranked 15 with a score of 62 out of 95. A high score indicates that men in these countries place considerable emphasis on career success. The role that women play in high masculine cultures is quite different from their role in low masculine countries. For example, women in countries that score high on the masculinity dimension seldom would be found in high-level executive positions; therefore, corporate pay and benefits would tend to be less for women than for men. This is evidenced by low numbers of women in management in Japan, and few women receiving benefits such as lifetime employment. Although the U.S. is making strides toward moving women into higher-level positions, women continue to dominate many traditionally lower-paid professions such as clerical, secretarial, and nursing—thus receiving lower pay than men in general. "Feminine" traits generally are viewed as synonymous with emotionalism, weakness, low ability to supervise others, and low achievement orientation—any of which results in lower pay and segregation into "women's jobs" with limited growth opportunities.

IMPLICATIONS FOR MULTINATIONAL BUSINESSES

This paper suggests that national culture can play a significant part in the evolution of pay systems and the effectiveness of compensation strategies. Business policy researchers have long studied the relationship between the environment and corporate strategy. They have concluded that organizations able to successfully acquire information about the environment—and more appropriately to react to that data—can have a competitive advantage in their markets. Scanning the environment for information on national culture for compensation purposes should then be considered an extension of this effort. Data on national culture is particularly applicable to reward systems because of these systems' pivotal role in organizations.

More specifically, as businesses move out of their home countries and employ individuals with potentially very different cultural values, it will be essential for corporations to consider the inevitable interface between their compensation strategy and the national culture. Japan is an interesting case in point. The Japanese have been hailed by many as innovators of management practices capable of performing wonders in improving productivity. Why, then, are the Japanese experiencing difficulty exporting their style of human resource management (including compensation policies) overseas? Neghandhi (1987) noted that Japanese multinationals have not been able, to date, to easily transfer their practices to the foreign countries in which they manufacture.

Japanese human resource management practices in general—and compensation strategies in particular—have performed laudably in Japan. But *should* Japanese manufacturers expect their methods of rewarding and motivating employees to be equally effective in countries such as the U.S., where strategies have developed to encourage the performance of employees with values quite different from those of Japanese workers?

Sethi, Namiki, and Swansom (1987) commented, "some scholars, notably Japanese scholars, have suggested that Japanese management practices are culture-unique and therefore are not easily transferable." They also suggested that some Americans have come to view Japanese management methods as associated with "loss of individual freedom that may border on involuntary servitude." In particular, Japanese compensation strategies—with their emphasis on job security, heavy reliance on aggregate variable pay as a shock absorber against demand shifts, high predictability of base pay based on longevity in firm, and inclusion of personal factors (e.g. family size) as criteria for pay decisions—are culture specific and have proven to be very difficult to transport successfully elsewhere.

CAVEATS

While this paper has argued that compensation strategies must be attuned to the value systems of national cultures to be effective, some caveats are in order.

Caveat 1:

"National culture" is an abstract, general concept. In practice, intra-cultural differences may be huge, particularly in large heterogeneous countries. While, at an aggregate level, cultural differences are well documented—and, following the congruency paradigm, we might expect that "fit" or "match" among pay strategies, organizational strategies, and the larger cultural milieu should enhance firm performance—simplistic assumptions based on crude stereotypes can be dangerous and may lead to poor decisions. For instance, Gomez-Mejia (1984) found across 16 countries that an individual's occupation is a more important predictor of work values than cultural variables such as language, religion, or ethnicity. This would indicate that when designing and implementing compensation strategies, a holistic approach that incorporates multiple factors (of which culture is only one) is best. Other factors might include the organization's internal climate, the occupational distribution of the work force, and the nature of the task at hand (Gomez-Mejia and Balkin, 1991). In other words, strategic thinking, almost by definition, is multivariate in nature; obsessive concern with cultural differences when formulating global compensation strategies is likely to produce disappointing results. A few examples based on the authors' experience follow to illustrate this point.

A. One multinational company with a plant in Korea built extensive family facilities for its workers, including playgrounds, a gym, a social hall, and a dining room. It made these expensive investments based on the assumption that family life in Korea is important and these facilities would be seen as an important fringe benefit by employees. To management's surprise, the facilities were hardly used. Most employees in the plant were educated, white-collar workers engaged in the development of software programs. They viewed such facilities as appropriate for common laborers, but below their status.

B. An American pharmaceutical company operating in a Latin country instituted a dual wage scale for men and women. Most of the work force consisted of college educated individuals. Management thought such a wage scale would save on labor costs. They expected no problems, given the stereotype of the culture as "macho." The scale produced mass protests and widespread negative media coverage against the firm. While "machismo" is an important force in most Latin societies, women actually represent a greater proportion of the professional work force than in the U.S. and will resent discriminatory practices by employers, particularly foreign firms.

C. West German firms hiring East German workers frequently found that the latter reacted negatively to incentive systems that had been used successfully with West German counterparts—in spite of sharing the same language, ethnicity, and cultural background. The East Germans distrusted the use of such incentive schemes, reported they felt manipulated by management, and shunned those workers who out-produced others.

Caveat 2:

It is important to resist the temptation to blame cultural differences too quickly for failures of compensation plans overseas. We have found that, quite often, these failures are traced to poor management practices and not to any inherent values in the work force that block the success of these compensation programs. For instance:

A. Some firms rely heavily on piece-rate systems overseas (particularly in third-world countries), and quality assurance becomes a nightmare. But similar problems have been amply demonstrated in the U.S. when piece-rate incentives are introduced.

B. A U.S. firm with multi-plant operations in Italy instituted a profit-sharing plan for employees based on the profits of each unit. This resulted in open conflict and discontent, because all the units were highly interdependent among themselves and with corporate headquarters. Workers and management in each of the units felt they had limited control over the performance of their unit and should not be held accountable for it. Corporate headquarters blamed these problems on the Italian culture—which they felt was prone to squabbles, negativism, and divisiveness. However, similar problems with the use of plant incentives when there is high interdependence across business units are well documented in the U.S., and have little to do with culture per se.

C. A U.S. company introduced individual incentives for R & D employees in its English subsidiary. This created intense conflict, lack of cooperation, and declining performance. Top management blamed the strong role of labor unions in England for these disappointing results. In fact, a large amount of evidence indicates that individual-based incentives are counter-productive when the nature of the task requires extensive team work (as is the case in R & D) and this has nothing to do with cultural elements.

Caveat 3:

Be aware that the amount of empirical research on the interaction between compensation strategies and national culture, and their combined effect on firm performance, is practically nil. This means that those responsible for formulating and implementing transnational compensation strategies must rely on clinical judgment, gut feeling, heuristics, and perceptual data. This demands a great deal of cultural sensitivity, open mindedness, and systemic (rather than specialized) thinking from a technical and functional perspective.

Caveat 4:

Ethics play a major role in most compensation decisions. In an international context, ethical concerns become even more controversial because difficult choices must be made on a country-by-country basis, with each country having different notions of right and wrong. This means that even when cultural elements tolerate or welcome certain compensation strategies, corporate headquarters may have to impose its own value system across multiple nations with conflicting value structures. This suggests that an international code of ethics covering compensation practices may be necessary. A multinational company should be prepared to make decisions on issues such as the following:

1. A conscious policy of discriminating against women and blacks in pay may be legally accepted or even mandated in some countries, yet corporate headquarters may have to refuse to do so, based on ethical standards and cultural norms widely held in the home country that find such practices repugnant.

2. A company may hire workers at abysmal wages in countries with high unemployment and low levels of industrial development. While such practices are legal and allow production at lower costs, the company may decide on humanitarian grounds to pay livable wages to employees and still realize a reasonable profit.

3. In some Asian and African countries child labor is pervasive. Multinational firms may be confronted with the ethical dilemma of whether to hire children at low wages (and therefore save money) or avoid such practices on ethical grounds, even if to do so may result in higher labor costs.

References

Business Week, "The Stateless Corporation," May 14, 1990, pp. 98–105.

Fombrun, C. and Shanley, M. "What's in a Name? Reputation Building and Corporate Strategy," *Academy of Management Journal,* 1990, 33(2), 233–259.

Gomez-Mejia, L. R. (1984). "Effect of occupation on task related contextual, and job involvement orientation: A cross-cultural perspective," *Academy of Management Journal,* 27(4), 706–720.

Gomez-Mejia, L. R. and Balkin, D. B. *Compensation Strategies, Business Policy, and Firm Performance.* (Cincinnati: South-Western, 1991).

Hofstede, G. *Culture's Consequences.* Newbury Park, CA: Sage, 1980.

Mahoney, T. A. "Employment Compensation Planning and Strategy." In L. R. Gomez-Mejia (ed.), *Compensation and Benefits.* Washington, D.C.: Bureau of National Affairs 1989.

Mesdag, L. M. "Are You Overpaid?" *Fortune,* March 19, 1984, 109(6), pp. 20–24.

Negandhi, A. R. *International Management.* Newton, MA: Allyn & Bacon, 1987.

Sethi, S. P., Namiki, N. and Swanson, C. C. *The False Promise of the Japanese Miracle.* Marshfield, MA: Pitman, 1984. pp. 179 and 48.

Whenmouth, A. "Is Japan's Corporate Culture Changing?" *Industry Week,* 1988, 237(7), pp. 33–35.

RECOGNIZING INDIVIDUAL CONTRIBUTIONS

INTRODUCTION

In the preceding section, we focused on setting pay for jobs. However, in most cases, different employees within the same jobs are not paid the same. Thus, although pay is linked to the type of job, pay programs also seek to recognize and reward employees for their contributions to the organization's success.

Organizations have a large degree of discretion in recognizing individual contributions because money can be distributed in many different ways using many different criteria. Individual performance ratings, team productivity, profits, and changes in stock value are examples of criteria that can be used in determining each employee's paycheck. The decision to emphasize one criterion over another can lead to very different employee attitudes and behaviors. For example, pay linked to individual performance may motivate different types of attitudes and behaviors than a pay program that links pay to team or organization performance. As a result, organizations with different goals may take different approaches, and within organizations, different approaches may be used for different types of employees.

The readings that follow illustrate the ways different organizations are recognizing individual employee contributions and provide suggestions on how to do so more effectively.

In "The New Variable Pay Programs: How Some Succeed, Why Some Don't," Steven Gross and Jeffrey Bacher describe the basic features of variable pay plans at a number of organizations, including Nucor Steel, Sutter Health System, and Du Pont Fibers. They develop a list of "plan dos and don'ts" that should be useful for those making decisions about such plans in the future. They emphasize the importance of management and employee support, as well as a design that incorporates several features, including broad participation, understandable and relevant goals, frequent payouts, and careful management of employee pay risk.

George Paulin and Frederic Cook address the controversial issue of executive pay. Paulin and Cook consider criticisms such as the weak relationship between executive pay and organization performance, the contention that U.S.

executives are overpaid relative to foreign counterparts, and the free distribution of stock options by compensation committees. Although Paulin and Cook suggest that each of these criticisms needs to be taken with a grain of salt, they provide a list of 10 recommendations that companies should follow to help restore public and shareholder confidence in the executive pay process.

READING 32

THE NEW VARIABLE PAY PROGRAMS
How Some Succeed, Why Some Don't

Steven E. Gross
Jeffrey P. Bacher

The experiences of a handful of major companies show that certain business conditions make success with variable pay much more likely.

In the United States, the first eight recipients of the coveted Malcolm Baldrige Award for Quality Management, including giants like IBM, Xerox, and Westinghouse, have all implemented some sort of innovative variable compensation program for their employees. One could expect that these organizations would serve as an example, and other firms would follow suit and explore the value of variable pay.

Yet some organizations remain steadfast in their belief that variable pay should not be made available to nontraditional participants—that is, those who are not executives or managers. It is not easy to measure most workers' efforts, say detractors, and the impact of most individuals' work on overall company results is often difficult to gauge. As further proof of the fallibility of variable pay, they point to unsuccessful programs, such as the cash profit-sharing plan abandoned by the Fibers Department of the Du Pont Company only two years after its widely publicized introduction.

The idea of variable pay applies to a wide variety of specifically designed compensation plans. A working definition might be this:

> Any compensation plan that emphasizes a shared focus on organizational success, broadens the opportunity for incentives to nontraditional groups, and operates outside the merit (base pay) increase system.

Is variable pay the currency that can buy struggling firms a one-way ticket to renewed competitiveness? Or is it as initially enticing but ultimately useless as well-crafted counterfeit bills? The answer, as might be expected, lies somewhere in the middle.

Source: Reprinted by permission of publisher, from *Compensation and Benefits Review*, January–February copyright 1993, vol. 25, no. 1, 51–56. American Management Association, New York. All rights reserved.

At the very least, variable pay programs can help companies control compensation costs. But if this is the only purpose companies have for variable pay, they aren't reaping its full benefits. When properly designed and implemented, variable pay vehicles can hold out the very real potential of shaking up any type of organization—whether industrial, financial, health care, or even service. Incentive pay can pull a company out of the doldrums of complacency and create a new, vibrant operating environment in which all truly espouse the concept of "shared destiny" and believe that every individual can make a difference. But without careful and constant attention to every aspect, both philosophical and operational, variable pay plans can instead become self-defeating, creating an even greater sense of frustration than traditional, fixed-pay structures usually generate.

A SLOW CONVERSION

Based on the available statistics, variable compensation seems very much in the experimental stage. Among the organizations surveyed at the 1991 Hay Compensation Conferences held throughout the country, the percentage of companies either currently using or considering using various types of variable plans (gainsharing, cash profit-sharing, group- and individual-incentive, and key-contributor programs) was still under 50% in most cases. Among the firms that were using these types of plans, significantly high percentages reported that as yet they could not tell if their plans had helped improve company performance.

Many organizations persist in viewing—and rejecting—incentives as reminiscent of 1920s-style piecework pay. But year by year, the list of major firms that have at least attempted to implement a variable program continues to lengthen. A closer look at several plans that are in various stages of completion—and that represent varying levels of success—reveals important lessons about why variable pay is or is not taking hold.

NUCOR AND SUTTER HEALTH: PROVEN SUCCESS

Among organizations in which variable pay plans have clearly made a positive contribution to overall performance, two are particularly noteworthy: Nucor Steel, for the sheer endurance of its 25-year-old gainsharing plan and for the way the plan has been linked from the start to the company's operating philosophy and growth strategy; and Sutter Health System, for its ability to disprove the myth that variable pay may not be appropriate in a service environment.

Nucor's unique road to success has been well documented. It was "paved" by the determination of the dynamic chief executive officer, Ken Iverson, who sought to turn the struggling company around through an egalitarian, production-oriented approach, which he instituted when he assumed command in the mid-1960s. Now a "no frills" philosophy permeates every aspect of Nucor's current operations, from its unimposing rented headquarters to its disdain for executive perks to its lean and flat organizational structure (consider that this $1 billion enterprise has just a 17-person corporate staff).

Exhibit 1

WHAT HAPPENED AT NUCOR STEEL

Basic Elements of Plan

Management commitment to the process

"Line of sight" to employee activities

Integration with organizational culture
  —Flat management structure
  —High levels of employee involvement
  —Genuine partnership

Willingness to let the plan succeed

Results

Continuous low-cost production

High employee involvement

Awards equal to 80%–150% of base salary

But perhaps the most well-known part of the Nucor picture—certainly in human resources circles—is its unyielding emphasis on variable pay. For more than two decades, all Nucor employees have drawn a significant portion of their pay from one of four incentive compensation plans. While the plans were originally intended to provide workers with an additional 15% to 20% of their lower-than-average base salaries, actual bonus payouts have been as high as 80% to 150% of base. Nevertheless, Nucor management has kept the program intact—and is quite willing to let these bonuses get even higher. Exhibit 1 gives an overview of the factors that have contributed to Nucor's success with variable pay.

The story of variable pay at Sutter Health may not be as well known as Nucor's; but here, too, Sutter's emphasis on creating and maintaining an all-for-one atmosphere led to its adoption of gainsharing as the appropriate reward vehicle for the organization.

The Sutter plan, called SutterShare, is designed for all 2,200 employees of the hospital and health-care network (with the exception of administrators, directors, and vice-presidents, who have their own plan linked to the same performance measures). Performance is gauged according to measurable hospitalwide and departmental productivity and quality indicators. Sutter measures performance on a quarterly basis, providing timely and repeated feedback. Awards can amount to as much as 20% of an employee's earnings.

First instituted in 1986, SutterShare is now in its second design phase. Executives report that the plan has been well received by employees, yielding significant gains in productivity and cost reductions. Management is now looking at it as a vehicle to strengthen the organization's Total Quality Management initiatives and to address other cultural issues. Exhibit 2 gives an overview of the factors that have led to Sutter's success with gainsharing.

E x h i b i t 2

WHAT HAPPENED AT SUTTER HEALTH

Basic Elements of Plan

Plan integration with other pay, quality, and human resources programs

Flexibility from hospital management

Consistency with organizational culture

Results

Significant gains in productivity and cost improvement

Strong reception from employees

Evolution of program to include Total Quality Management concepts and culture issues

RHÔNE POULENC AND AT&T UNIVERSAL CARD SERVICES: TRYING IT OUT

For two other major organizations, it is still too early to assess the impact of variable pay plans, since they have been implemented only within the past year or so. Already, however, in the case of the agricultural giant Rhône Poulenc, significant differences have surfaced between two locations that were selected to launch a pilot program simultaneously. At AT&T Universal Card Services, the telecommunications firm's new consumer credit card subsidiary, the group incentive plan is so closely tied to the fortunes of the organization that the evaluation, when rendered on the basis of the first year's results, is unmistakably positive.

Rhône Poulenc looked to gainsharing as a way to reinforce its quality programs and ongoing belief in continuous improvement. Two locations were selected as test sites, where all employees except the plant managers were to participate. (As with Sutter Health, Rhône Poulenc's managers had a separate plan, which used different but comparable performance measures, but the two types of plans were linked.)

The performance measure for the Rhône Poulenc employee plans at the two different locations was the same (improvement in the cost of unit production), as was the measurement period (quarterly). The plan provided for a 50/50 distribution between company and employees on any gains realized. The goal of the plan was to exceed the results of the previous year.

While the plan has generated significant improvement at the location where it was actually put into operation, its implementation has been put off at the second site because of "concerns over the timing of its introduction." But the real difference between the two locations seems to be a difference in the "cultural readiness" of the two locations. At the plant where the plan was suspended, there has been significant concern over expected business downturns and the potential for layoffs. The prevailing atmosphere has been one of anxiety and unwillingness to take risks with the pay system. By contrast, at the site where the plan has been

Exhibit 3

WHAT HAPPENED AT RHÔNE POULENC

	Results	
Location A *(Project Suspended)*		*Location B* *(Project Implemented)*
Concerns over timing of introduction		Significant improvement potential
Potential business slowdown		Introduction of new product
"Culture" not ready		Plan consistent with "culture"
—Relatively low trust		—High level of trust
—Struggling team effort		
—Ongoing layoff potential		

successfully implemented, there has been a much higher level of trust and a clear "go for it" mentality. Exhibit 3 compares the experiences of the two sites.

At AT&T Universal Card Services, variable pay has been used to help introduce not only a new product, but a new company. The subsidiary was built up from 300 to 3,000 employees in just 12 months, with a heavy reliance from the outset on quality, customer orientation, and productivity to distinguish the new card from others in the crowded consumer credit market.

If the Universal Card's group incentive plan—and, indeed, the company itself—fail in their efforts, it will not be because of inadequate or imprecise performance measurement. No less than 81 different individual and group measures are reported on *daily*, giving employees in the company's operations center immediate feedback on performance in such key areas as responsiveness to customers and speed and accuracy of information processing. When performance on any given day falls below the goals agreed upon by employees and management, managers are informed the following morning. They are expected to file a report by noon detailing the causes of—and solutions for—the problem. Quarterly summaries reinforce the process.

In the first year of the group incentive plan, which offered a target of 12% of base pay to operations and customer service employees, 75% of the established objectives were reached, yielding 80% payouts of target. The AT&T Universal Card Services is still in for very tough competition; however, management feels it has made significant strides in building the proper culture and developing a "line of sight" to the specific employee activities most critical to the new venture's success (see Exhibit 4).

DU PONT: UNDERLINING THE RISKS

On the flip side of the variable pay ledger, there are several examples of companies whose plans have failed to produce the desired payoffs for the organization

Exhibit 4

WHAT HAPPENED AT AT&T UNIVERSAL CARD SERVICES

Basic Elements of Plan

Collaborative effort in performance measurement/goals

Line of sight to employee activities

Program built on vision of organizational culture

Effective mix of individual/group measures

1990 Results

75% of objectives realized

80% of target awarded

or its employees. Of these, Du Pont, which recently abandoned its Fibers Department Achievement Sharing Plan, has received the most attention.

The Fibers Department's incentive plan was designed for 20,000 workers in this $6 billion division. Employees received bonus payouts of 3.6% of salary for 1988 performance in exchange for giving up 2% of future merit increases for each of the following three years for a total of 6% of base pay after three years. The plan offered employees the potential to receive three times their pay at risk; thus, when fully implemented, up to 18% of their salary could be earned as an award. The plan's goal was to achieve departmental budgeted earnings.

During the fall of 1990, the plan was discontinued. Performance had fallen because of adverse business conditions in the industry, so workers in the Fibers Department faced the prospect of a low bonus payout for that year—or none at all. Although Du Pont had attempted, through a massive education and communications effort, to help employees fully appreciate the downside risk of the plan, the amount of risk remained an issue with workers. Later, it also became apparent that tying pay to departmental business results was no longer consistent with the company's more centralized corporate strategy and culture. Beginning in 1991, Du Pont restored the salaries, eliminating any pay at risk.

The key lessons that can be learned here are that stronger consideration should be given to letting employees select the amount of risk—and reward—they will incur. In addition, employees and managers alike must believe that their efforts can really influence plan results. The experience, however, has not deterred Du Pont from looking for ways to link pay with performance. The company recently adopted a worldwide stock option program for all employees to reinforce the concept of identity with Du Pont worldwide.

PLAN DOS AND DON'TS

What differentiates the successes from the disappointments in these organizations' efforts to implement incentive pay plans? Several common characteristics need to be present if the plan is to have a fighting chance.

Exhibit 5

PLAN DESIGN

	Tends to Work	*Tends Not to Work*
Participation	Broad involvement	Selected groups
	Team orientation	Individual orientation
Measurement	Quantitative	Qualitative
	Line of sight	Minimal linkage
	Simple	Complicated
Baselines	Collaborative	Engineered
Measurement Periods	Shorter	Longer
Risk	Low risk	High risk
Size of Awards	???	???

Management Support

Both executives and line managers must be committed to the program's goals and concepts—even to the point of staying with it when payouts far exceed expectations, as was the case with Nucor. Staying power is also needed when early results are not achieved.

Employee Acceptance

Employees have to believe that the plan is not just another fad, but a fair program, and that its goals are practical and achievable. One potential stumbling block for the Rhône Poulenc plan, even in the plant where it has been culturally accepted, is employees' potential backlash against the constantly rising performance targets. Payouts are tied to beating last year's results. But the continuous ratcheting up of goals (at Rhône Poulenc and many other companies) can eventually lead to employee frustration—and the perception among workers that targets will become unrealistic. One possible way around this sort of "continual compounding" is to create a split in how incentives are gauged within the organization. Below-standard operating units can be motivated through incentives to improve continually, and above-standard units can be rewarded on the basis of their performance relative to the norm (that is, they can receive one level of reward for maintenance above the standard and a higher level for continued improvement).

Supportive Culture

As the circumstances surrounding the success of the two pilot plans at Rhône Poulenc illustrate, teamwork, trust, and involvement at all levels are critical to a plan's ultimate fate.

Effective Design

Plans should be structured around clear goals, unambiguous measurements, and line-of-sight linkage to employee efforts. As the AT&T Universal Card situation demonstrates, attention to details is crucial. Collectively, the case examples illustrate the following aspects of plan design that should be factored in (see Exhibit 5):

- *Participation* that is as broad as possible and that encourages team efforts, rather than singling out selected groups or individuals.
- *Measurement* that is quantitative, simple, and structured to permit a line of sight to the desired work outcome (customer service, quality production, and the like), as opposed to qualitative, overly complex measures based on isolated work flows.
- *Baselines* that are determined through a collaborative effort, with as many viewpoints considered as possible, rather than engineered and imposed by an unseen or unchallenged source.
- *Timing* of measurements and payouts that is shorter rather than longer (so that desired outcomes are constantly reinforced).
- *Employee risk* that is lower rather than higher, and that is balanced with employees' understanding of the need for extended and sustained effort.
- *Awards* that are large enough to make a real difference to employees. (The actual size does not appear to be a critical factor in plan success and can vary from 5% to 100% of base salary. One month's pay is an award size typical of successful plans.)

In terms of future base pay increases, the plan should provide an opportunity for employees to earn additional rewards without increasing base pay above competitive practices. For example, it may be difficult to justify the cost of an "add-on" incentive plan to already high base pay levels. Likewise, the plan should not be perceived as a way to make up for a significantly below-average base pay system.

Timing

While economic swings are often hard to anticipate, it's best to launch a plan at a time when there is minimal risk of downturns that can jeopardize payouts, and when the business climate generally can support the achievement of plan objectives. While plans should not be "sugar coated" or "seeded" to ensure quick payouts artificially, a realistic chance of payout in return for solid effort is important. If a plan does not pay out under "normal" conditions in its first two or three years, it will not be perceived as real.

Effective Implementation

For the amount of effort that goes into plan design, at least three times that amount should be devoted to making the design a reality. Employee education, communication, and training are critical to the likelihood of success.

Exhibit 6

MEASURES OF SUCCESS

Did the plan gain employee acceptance?

Was the plan well implemented and integrated?

Did employee behavior change?

Did the plan achieve operational improvements?

Plan Evaluation

Once all of these issues have been addressed and the plan has run its course for some time, the final step is assessing its long-term success. Some key questions that can guide that assessment are listed in Exhibit 6. If any one of them cannot be answered affirmatively, major adjustments are probably needed.

Remember that the payouts themselves will not necessarily be an indication of plan success (or failure). Even when a plan has not paid out, the effort can still be considered a success as long as employees now view their employer—and their work—in a manner that is more in line with the organization's goals.

READING 33

WHAT SHOULD BE DONE ABOUT EXECUTIVE COMPENSATION?

George B. Paulin
and Frederic W. Cook

Seldom, until recently, did executive compensation receive much attention outside corporate board rooms. Any broader curiosity regarding the subject was more than satisfied by annual articles in business magazines following the release of spring proxy statements. But times have changed. Executive compensation is now prominent on the political agenda, it is an international trade issue (as the CEOs who accompanied President Bush to Japan in early 1992 are keenly aware), and it is a focal point of shareholder activists. It has even been featured on television news shows such as *60 Minutes* and *Nightline*.

Conventional wisdom is that executive pay has increased unfairly while thousands of American workers have been laid off and once-proud major American companies have struggled to compete globally in industries they built and formerly dominated. CEOs of these major companies are at the center of the criticism. The popular view is that they are overpaid relative to average U.S. workers and compared to their counterparts in other industrialized nations. Furthermore, their high pay is viewed as not related to their performance, nor balanced by commensurate risk. Instead, it is seen as being set by boards and consultants who are co-opted by self-interest. This article recommends ways to restore public confidence in executive compensation and the process through which it is determined.

The importance of finding solutions cannot be stressed enough. The issue is critical to America's future productivity and competitiveness. It is not simply a matter of morality involving executive greed and 1980s-style excesses. Likewise, it is not just a matter of corporate accountability and misallocation of corporate assets. The issues are more fundamental: leadership by example, economic fairness and equity in the workplace, and whether the behavior stimulated by financial incentives supports the broader goals of the American economic system.

The Securities and Exchange Commission (SEC) recently acted to give shareholders the ability to initiate executive-compensation proposals in company proxy statements. While such votes would not be binding on company boards, many regard the move as an initial step to *legislate* greater board accountability to shareholders for executive compensation decisions. Other legislation, still in proposed form at the time this article was written, would require additional pay disclosure in proxy statements and additional accounting costs for granting stock options. There are also proposals that would limit the amount of an executive's pay that a company could deduct for taxes. One proposes a limit of 25 times the pay of the company's lowest-paid full-time employee, and another proposes a limit of $1 million a year.

The *real* solutions, however, will come from *within* companies, not from Congress or the SEC. American business leaders are not so out of touch or so arrogant as to disregard the collective voices of Washington, institutional shareholders, foreign trading partners, their employees and in many cases even their own families. There is encouraging evidence that the system already is acting to correct itself. Companies are adopting reforms faster than outside observers appreciate. Public scrutiny and debate are having positive effects.

"A very few top executives in a very few, very big companies have truly enormous earnings ... Economically these few large company executives are quite unimportant. Socially they do enormous damage. They are highly visible and highly publicized. And they are therefore taken as typical rather than as the extreme exceptions that they are."
—Peter F. Drucker, 1977

DIFFERENT PERSPECTIVES OF THE PROBLEM

More than anyone, Graef ("Bud") Crystal is responsible for bringing executive compensation out from the boardroom closet. His views, which he supports with extensive research and years of experience as an executive compensation consultant before turning to academia, are set forth in his 1991 book *In Search of Excess*. At the risk of oversimplification, he believes that CEOs receive excessive pay because of greed and an unbalanced corporate governance process that essentially allows them to set their own pay.

While Crystal frames the problem in terms of executive pay *levels*, others argue quite articulately that the *structure* of executive pay (i.e., program design) is the real problem. The original spokesmen for this perspective were professors Michael Jensen and Kevin Murphy in a 1990 *Harvard Business Review* article titled "It's Not How Much Executives Are Paid, But How." Ira Kay, a compensation consultant, recently sided with them in his 1992 book *Value at the Top*. Kay's thesis, again simplified, is that executive compensation relates to company performance and does motivate executives. While an effective executive labor market exists, stock options, without an ownership intent, cause executives to pursue high-risk strategies that are not in the long-term best interests of shareholders, according to Kay.

The two sides do share some common ground. They appear to agree that the corporate governance process has been weak, that lax proxy reporting rules have allowed easy obfuscation of total pay levels, that there has been undisciplined granting of stock options and that the primary interest of pay consultants often has been to retain their CEO clients.

The following analysis examines the issues and data that are at the core of the executive compensation debate and whether they are related primarily to pay levels or pay structures.

Executive Pay Levels

Crystal argues that CEO pay is too high, with the 1990 average among large companies at approximately $2.8 million, including the annualized present value of stock options and other long-term incentive grants (Crystal 1991, *In Search of Excess*). Adding benefits and perquisites, he estimates average CEO pay levels at perhaps $4 million (Crystal 1991, Senate statement). He points out that these pay levels are excessive in relation to the pay of average employees, and that such ratios have climbed dramatically and unreasonably in the past 20 years (Crystal 1991, *In Search of Excess*).

Kay, on the other hand, argues that CEO pay levels are *not* high relative to performance and that high pay is commensurate with the risk and responsibility of the position. He says CEO pay is modest relative to athletes and entertainers who have far less impact on the economy and that the value society places on CEOs is not out of line with other occupations. The rapid increase in CEO pay over the past decade can be mainly explained by the threefold increase in the stock market, which has produced prodigious stock-option gains, according to Kay. He added that executive pay is a small fraction of company revenues and profits, and that the extreme examples of high executive pay often are associated with exceptionally strong company performance and stock-market gains. While there are high-paid executives in low-performance companies, Kay believes they are exceptions and that their boards should take action to modify their plans (Kay 1992).

Are *average* executive pay levels too high, even after excluding the "outliers"? Crystal would say yes; Kay would say no. In reality, the bull market of the past decade has contributed significantly to rising total compensation levels for executives, primarily through stock options and other stock-based long-term incentives. It is also clear that executive salary and bonus levels have escalated rapidly—more so than for other employee groups. This may be a function of economic forces which, as Kay suggests, have placed an increasingly higher value on executive talent, as measured by pay surveys (Kay 1992). But there is a widespread belief in the business community that surveys have contributed to the rise in executive pay beyond levels otherwise justified by performance. If true, then the surveys influence the market rather than merely measure it.

The escalation of executive-pay levels during the past decade beyond economic justification can be seen most clearly from Figure 1, which shows average 10-year salary and bonus levels (excluding stock options and other long-term incentives) for the CEO of a company whose revenues are held constant at $1 billion. Thus, *both* pay levels and revenues are stated in real terms. The pay levels (both salary and bonus) almost doubled while revenues remained constant. If this same pay-to-revenue ratio holds true for other key employee positions (as pay surveys and reported proxy pay levels indicate to be the case), then aggregate compensation spent to manage a business of constant size has taken up an increasing proportion of revenues during that period. This means less money is available for other expenses, investments, profits and dividends. This does not mean that revenues should be the major determinant of executive pay levels; it

Figure 1

COMPANY AT CONSTANT $1 BILLION REVENUES

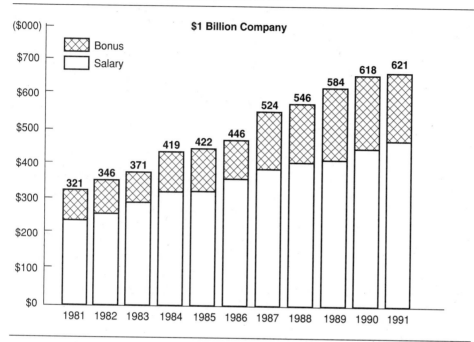

Source: Wyatt Data Services, ECS Top Management Reports; includes bonus and nonbonus, nondurable goods companies.

only serves to make clear that all expenditures, including executive pay, need to be managed in relation to the total resources of the firm.

Executive Pay and Company Performance

Crystal argues that high levels of CEO compensation do not reflect company performance. He bases this conclusion on an analysis of the 1,000 largest U.S. public-company CEOs. Total compensation is defined as including salary and bonus earned for 1991, the estimated present value of stock option *grants* (not actual option profits realized) with no annualization of multi-year or "jumbo" grants, the value of restricted shares at the time of grant, and actual performance-share and performance-unit payments (Crystal 1991, *Executive Compensation in Corporate America 1991*).

After compiling pay levels as described here, Crystal used a regression model to "predict" what each company's pay "should be" by redistributing total CEO compensation among companies using factors of company *size* (based on market capitalization, sales volume, invested capital and total work force) and company *performance* (defined as total market return to shareholders, counting both stock price appreciation and dividends). He found that only about 4 percent of the variation in indicated pay could be explained by performance. Another 30 percent was explained by size. The rest was unexplained by the factors in his model, leading him to conclude there was little rationale or logic to the levels of CEO pay.

Crystal looks at actual pay plus the present value of option grants for each company, and he compares horizontally between companies based on their respective size and total return to shareholders. His method shows very little correlation between CEO pay and performance as he defines both terms. But why would he expect that there would be such a correlation? Adding annual pay earned for a single year to the present value of options granted in the same year, and comparing that total to stock-market returns for 1,000 companies, suggests that is how CEO compensation *should* be administered. There are three problems with this. First, salary and bonus income are not typically administered in relation to changes in a company's stock price (even though some investors think they should be). Second, stock options are granted as an incentive for future market performance, not as a reward for the past. Consequently, Crystal has mismatched pay/performance variables and time periods. Third, Crystal has the benefit of horizontal hindsight. When the compensation committees of the 1,000 companies meet to set their CEOs' pay and to grant stock options, they do not know what the other 999 companies are doing. Thus, there is little reason to expect high correlations among their actions. If the correlations were high, it might be primafacie evidence of collusion.

Kay reached the opposite conclusion in his analyses. He only counted annual pay and related it to the company's financial performance, not to changes in its stock price and returns to shareholders. Also, he looked *longitudinally* within the same companies, not *horizontally* between companies. While Crystal looked at pay for performance among different companies at a point in time, Kay looked at changes in pay and performance within the same companies over a period of time. Kay's method shows that within companies there are fairly substantial swings in annual pay based on changes in traditional financial-performance measures such as accounting profits (Kay 1992).

Kay presents a case for pay for performance by looking within a company and analyzing the relationship between *changes* in CEO annual pay (primarily changes in bonus) and changes in company profit performance. Even here, the correlation between pay and performance is not likely to be high because many companies consider factors other than just changes in company profits in determining bonuses for executives.

Who is right? Given the differences in methods, it is not surprising that Crystal and Kay arrive at different conclusions. It is valid, as Kay suggests, to look within a company over time to see if changes in executive pay relate to changes in company performance. This is what shareholders and employees would look for in assessing the fairness of executive pay changes. It also is valid, as Crystal suggests, to look horizontally across companies in assessing whether absolute pay levels are proper in relation to size and performance. If it were not, then astute

CEOs certainly would accept pay-for-performance strategies so long as they could start from a very high base amount.

U.S. Pay Ratios Versus Other Countries

Crystal argues that U.S. CEO pay ratios are out of line with those found in other industrial nations. He cites an average ratio of total compensation for a large-company CEO at almost 160 times (160x) that of the average U.S. worker (135x if statistical outliers are removed), versus a ratio of less than 20x in Japan and 35x in England. At $2.4 million average total compensation (1990 U.S. average large-company CEO pay, excluding outliers), the average CEO earns seven times as much as his or her Japanese counterpart (Crystal 1991, *In Search of Excess*).

Kay refutes Crystal's argument that U.S. CEO pay ratios are out of line. To make his case, he argues that CEO pay, unlike lower-level employee pay, relates to the size of a company. Because the average U.S. large company is much larger than the average Japanese large company, it is logical for the U.S. ratios to be higher, Kay notes. He also uses only annual pay when computing ratios (disregarding stock option grant values or gains), and he compares CEO pay to average entry-level professionals rather than blue-collar workers. Computed this way, and holding company size constant at $500 million, he finds U.S. pay ratios to be very similar (at 13.6x) to those in Japan, Germany, England, Italy and France (Kay 1992).

Both analyses presumably are accurate based on the data they used, although Crystal recently acknowledged that if he had computed *median* CEO pay instead of average CEO pay, his ratio of 160x actually would be 108x (Crystal 1992). Crystal's data still result in far different conclusions about U.S. pay ratios. Kay's model (same-sized companies and ratio of CEO to entry-level professional) reflects good logic. But his focus on $500 million companies probably is too narrow because the public debate is really about large-company CEO pay. Also, his exclusion of stock-option values is questionable because they are a common part of CEO compensation in the United States.

Informed observers generally would *expect* that U.S. CEOs would be paid more than their counterparts around the world, especially if option values are considered as part of total pay. American culture puts a high value on individual leadership, and it relies heavily on financial incentives to motivate behavior and measure success. Outside the U.S., stock options and long-term incentives rarely are found, but non-U.S. CEOs may have perquisites such as company-provided housing or substantial company expense accounts (as is often contended to be the case in Japan). The point is that comparisons between countries are imprecise at best. Also, the U.S. is unique in requiring extensive executive-pay disclosure, while what is known about practices in other countries is largely word of mouth.

Reward and Risk

Most observers agree that there is insufficient risk in executive compensation to warrant the high pay levels and upside reward opportunities. For example, Crystal

Crystal argues that U.S. CEO pay ratios are out of line with those found in other industrial nations. He cites an average ratio of total compensation for a large-company CEO at almost 160 times that of the average U.S. worker . . . versus a ratio of less than 20x in Japan and 35x in England.

Because the average U.S. large company is much larger than the average Japanese large company, it is logical for the U.S. ratios to be higher, Kay notes . . . Computed [Kay's] way, and holding company size constant at $500 million, he finds U.S. pay ratios to be very similar (at 13.6x) to those in Japan, Germany, England, Italy and France.

believes that the downside impact of poor performance on executive bonuses is not as great as the upside potential for good performance (Crystal 1991, *In Search of Excess*). Kay also believes there is insufficient risk in executive compensation, but he thinks the problem is with stock options, not bonus administration. The problem with options, in Kay's view, is that they represent an opportunity to share in gains without the risk of loss if the stock price drops. He believes this motivates executives to undertake risky strategies such as bad acquisitions. He favors a symmetry of risk profiles between executives and owners so executives will make prudent, optimal long-term investments (Kay 1992).

Executives have been insulated from financial risk in many other ways. There are employment contracts that guarantee continued employment and pay regardless of performance, restricted stock grants to provide capital accumulation even if stock price declines, golden parachutes for takeover protection and supplemental executive pensions for retirement. All of these practices proliferated during the 1980s.

Now, however, there are some encouraging signs of a correction. As evidence, General Motors did not pay bonuses to its North American executives in 1990 and 1991. The year 1990 was a very bad one for the major banks, and at least five of the largest 10 paid no bonuses to their top officers. Those that did pay bonuses, such as BankAmerica and J.P. Morgan, had very good performance in an adverse climate. Many companies that experienced lower profits in 1991 also paid lower or no bonuses to their top executives. (Examples include Alcoa, Caterpillar, Cummins Engine, Ford Motor, General Motors, IBM, Texas Instruments, USG, Union Carbide and Westinghouse). BankAmerica and Baxter Healthcare, meanwhile, are two examples of major companies that have eliminated their golden parachute plans. Furthermore, a number of companies actively have begun to encourage more ownership of company stock by executives through ownership guidelines, incentives and penalties. Chrysler and General Mills are two examples.

Stock-Option Usage

A key element of the executive compensation debate is stock options. They are the real engine of executive wealth creation. In practically every instance where a particular executive's actual total compensation is in the $5 million range and above, it is because valuable options have been exercised. To illustrate, Figure 2 looks at the highest-paid CEOs reported by *Business Week* during the past five years. In aggregate, their total direct compensation totaled approximately $214 million. Of this amount, $198 million (92.5 percent) is attributable to option profits, and the remaining $16 million (7.5 percent) is from salaries, bonuses and other long-term incentives combined. Some regard huge option profits as an appropriate result of the shareholder value created in the bull market that began in 1982, and they adhere to the traditional view that options effectively marry executives' and shareholders' interests. Others, who are increasing in number, believe that option profits are often excessive and underserved, and that they result primarily from market timing and the size of grants instead of long-term value creation.

Figure 2

BUSINESS WEEK HIGHEST-PAID CEOs FOR PAST FIVE YEARS

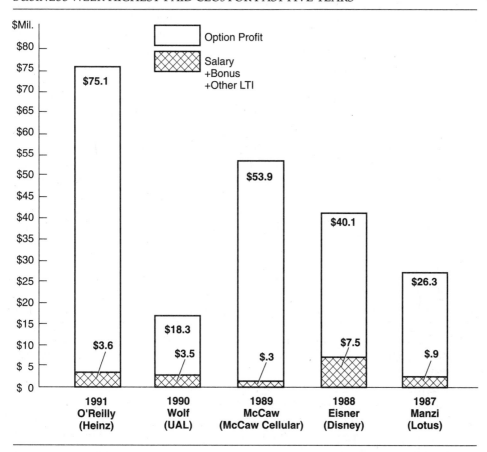

Source: *Business Week,* John A. Byrne, et al., May 2, 1988; May 1, 1989; May 2, 1990; May 6, 1992; and May 4, 1992.

Crystal contends that the size of option grants is out of control, especially those "jumbos" or "megagrants" such as the four million shares that H. J. Heinz granted to its CEO in 1990. Crystal attributes excesses in option-granting practices to the fact that neither the economic value that executives receive at the time of grant nor the actual profits that they receive at the time of exercise are charged as an expense to company earnings, and also to the fact that there is poor proxy disclosure (Crystal 1991, *In Search of Excess*). Kay also believes that favorable accounting treatment for stock options may be a factor in their popularity but does not go much further with the point (Kay 1992). To Crystal, however, a major initiative for the future would be to change the present accounting for stock options, to require companies to reduce their reported earnings to reflect the "value" of options grants (Crystal 1991, *In Search of Excess*).

The general perception is that outside directors, and particularly those who serve on compensation committees, are not truly independent representatives of the shareholders' interests. This situation is attributed partly to their being part of the "club" and partly to the impression that they have been co-beneficiaries of the executive pay spiral in their own companies . . .

Those who argue that there should be a chargeable expense for options against company earnings believe that, because options currently have no direct expense charges, they are "free." In turn, they believe that companies have been overly generous in granting options to senior executives, thereby fueling the rise in executive compensation. They also believe that if options had a cost in terms of lower earnings, and if such cost were expensed on the books (and possibly disclosed in proxy statements), boards and compensation committees would be less inclined to make generous grants to senior executives.

There is a historic basis for arguing that these beliefs may not be correct. Before the SEC recently changed its rules on insider trading, many companies granted stock appreciation rights (SARs) in tandem with regular stock options to their executive officers. *SARs require any appreciation in the underlying shares prior to exercise to be expensed against company earnings.* Despite this onerous accounting, SARs were common practice, and the size of such grants to senior executives increased during the past decade. Adverse accounting had no material effect. Moreover, since the SEC changed its rules on insider transactions, many companies have stopped granting SARs, and there is no evidence that the size of option grants to senior executives has increased as a result. Correspondingly, it is unlikely that the size of senior executives' option grants would be reduced if an earnings charge were imposed on options.

The effect of an earnings charge on stock options would most likely be borne not by the top executives who formerly received SARs, but rather by middle managers and lower-level employees who now receive stock options but never received SARs because they were "too expensive." If an earnings charge were imposed on options, it is likely that the recent favorable trends toward including larger numbers of employees in option grants would be reversed. This would separate the interests of employees in a growing stock price from those of executives, and it would hamper employee-relations initiatives of total quality management, alignment, empowerment and sharing.

Towers Perrin recently conducted a survey on behalf of IBM of about 3,000 senior executives, human resource heads, academicians and consultants from 12 countries (Towers Perrin 1992). The purpose of the survey was to define human resource initiatives and priorities for competitive advantage for the year 2000. There were many important findings. One that touches on stock options was the finding that U.S. respondents placed a high priority on "promoting employee empowerment through ownership." It appears that sharing the gains from ownership with employees will be a continuing initiative that will distinguish American economic efforts from others in future years and, hopefully, enhance those efforts.

Accountability to Shareholders

The primary remaining points of the debate can be grouped under this heading. They include the role of board compensation committees and compensation consultants, disclosure of pay information, and shareholder voting rights, among other issues. In this area, there is actually more agreement than dissent among the experts.

The general perception is that outside directors, and particularly those who serve on compensation committees, are not truly independent representatives of the shareholders' interests. This situation is attributed partly to their being part of the "club" and partly to the impression that they have been co-beneficiaries of the executive pay spiral in their own companies—not to mention their board compensation, which now commonly includes stock grants and pensions, along with higher retainers and fees. Anyone with first-hand knowledge of how board compensation committees operate might have a different view. Generally, there is *no* lack of independence. Also, these committees have a sincere interest in doing what is right for shareholders. The problem is that the committees have no staffs to do their work, as well as limited expertise and time. They want black-and-white answers in an area where most things are gray. In focusing on their fiduciary roles, they concentrate too much on pay surveys (i.e., what other companies are doing) and what has worked at their own companies instead of on more complex, company-specific design issues. Executive compensation program design and administration too often ends up being more competitively driven than business-strategy and performance driven.

On the role of consultants, the criticism is that they typically are hired by management and are therefore beholden to advocate management's interests in increasing pay levels. Another mark against consultants is that they are the source of the competitive surveys that have been used to ratchet up executive pay regardless of market factors. Any defense against these assertions by this article would not be credible for obvious reasons. However, it should be noted that a consultant's appropriate role is not to serve as an advocate for one side versus another, like a lawyer representing the prosecution or the defense, but to provide objective advice. A consultant who can overcome the natural suspicions and earn the trust and confidence of the board could be a great help to the compensation committee in fulfilling its duties.

Lastly, regarding proxy disclosure and voting rights, shareholders need relevant, clear and uniform information to exercise their judgment and to make informed investment decisions. No one should argue with this basic point. Proxy reform has the general support of the Business Roundtable and the American Compensation Association. Hopefully, one important change that will be made when the SEC's current proposals are finalized is in the current requirement to report option profits in the year of exercise. This aggregation of gains from options (which may represent many years of grants lumped into one year of exercise) and combination with annual pay have contributed mightily to public perceptions of executive pay levels being too high and not related to performance.

Shareholders also should have the ability to make their views on executive compensation known to boards. If expanding their voting rights to executive compensation on an advisory basis leads to better, market-oriented solutions, then this is the direction that the SEC should take. If it leads to filling proxy statements with frivolous or vindictive proposals, then the SEC should be quick to go back to the old way.

TEN RECOMMENDATIONS TO RESTORE CONFIDENCE

A consensus on executive compensation should not be expected. Even the experts arrive at different conclusions depending on what companies they look at, when they look, and the statistical methods and assumptions that they apply. However, there is widespread criticism of the current system from the public, employees and shareholders. They see it as inherently unfair, and they have lost confidence that it contributes to the competitiveness of American business. A number of important themes run through the debate such as paying for *results*, balancing rewards and risks, and increasing accountability to shareholders. These themes are embodied in the following recommendations for a 10-part program to address the criticisms and issues related to executive pay. The recommendations follow from the main points being made in the debate, and reflect the authors' experiences and opinions.

1. The independence and accountability of the board of directors and its compensation committee should be strengthened on executive compensation matters. This can be done by adopting a mission or charter for the compensation committee, to ensure its independence and objectivity. Compensation committees should be composed of truly independent directors, should have a knowledgeable and forceful chairperson, and should have a periodic rotation of members. Provision should be made for direct staff or consultant support to the committee, if desired. There should be no interlocking directorships with respect to compensation committees. Furthermore, the compensation committees should meet directly with those who render advice on executive pay or provide competitive survey information. Such face-to-face interchanges will help ensure that these providers understand that their responsibility and accountability is to the board and shareholders, not just to management.

The initiative for recommending the CEO's compensation should be removed from the CEO and assumed directly by the compensation committee, with staff or consulting support as needed. The adoption of employment and serverance contracts for the CEO and other employee directors should be approved by the full board in executive session and *not* delegated to compensation committees. Finally, the compensation committee (or some other committee or senior director) should take responsibility for evaluating the performance of the CEO and other senior executives against strategic objectives and financial performance, reporting the results of those evaluations to the full board in executive session once a year, and making sure that compensation actions are consistent with such evaluations.

2. Companies should voluntarily choose between two different and mutually exclusive executive compensation strategies.   The choice would be between a security-focused compensation program and a performance-focused program, but not the best of both. If the choice is for a security-focused program, then the logical implications and directions would be to increase salaries and decrease performance-based pay in total compensation. Also, there would be below-competitive stock option and other long-term incentive grant strategies, offset by higher pensions. Long-term ownership of company stock would not be stressed or encouraged by a company pursuing a security-focused compensation strategy.

If the choice is for a performance-focused program, then the implications and directions would be to increase performance-based pay and decrease fixed pay (salaries) in total compensation. There would be above-competitive stock option and other long-term incentive grant strategies, offset by retirement benefits based on salary only. Long-term stock ownership by executives should be encouraged by a performance-focused company to reinforce and support long-term company interests in increasing stock price and to build in high leverage and risk. Specifically, shares earned through performance or stock-price increases should be expected to be held for the long term, net of any sales necessary to satisfy the option price and/or taxes due. Stock in a company pursuing this type of program would be an important part of the continuing risk and reward mechanism and is not meant to be considered as part of an executive's trading account to be managed for maximum gain. Lower pensions would be a trade-off for higher long-term incentives and stock options, which would provide the basis for long-term wealth accumulation for retirement.

A few decades ago, the argument could have been made that U.S. executive-compensation practices were different and distinguished from other industrialized nations because they were more entrepreneurial and incentive-oriented, particularly in the use of stock options and longer-term equity-building arrangements. This was balanced by an absence of lucrative special benefits and supplemental retirement arrangements that seemed to be more characteristic of the practices among large European companies. There was a tradeoff, and this system seemed fair. Companies could select between the U.S. model, which was more incentive-oriented, or the European model, which was more benefits-oriented.

Many U.S. companies, however, for a variety of reasons, have now adopted the class-driven benefit system of Europe while retaining the more entrepreneurial U.S. incentives that contributed to American success. This does not seem right. Companies and their executives should not have it both ways. The systems do not work well together because the combination is perceived as unfair by lower-level employees and the public, and the high guaranteed benefits provide a safety net that dulls and undercuts the power of the incentives.

3. Executive compensation strategies and actions should look beyond a singular focus on shareholder value creation. A major purpose of executive compensation clearly should be to align the interests of executives in large public companies, who typically are not major shareholders, with the interests of shareholders who are financial investors and not directly involved with management. But is this the only purpose? Can executive compensation be tilted too far in the direction of shareholder interests? Are the claims of shareholders so much greater than the claims of employees, customers, communities and the economy at large that they should dominate the debate and executive-pay programs of the

TEN RECOMMENDATIONS TO RESTORE CONFIDENCE

1. The independence and accountability of the board of directors and its compensation committee should be strengthened on executive compensation matters.

2. Companies should voluntarily choose between two different and mutually exclusive executive compensation strategies.

3. Executive compensation strategies and actions should look beyond a singular focus on shareholder value creation.

4. Executive compensation strategies and actions should be aligned with important employee-relations initiatives.

5. Instead of adopting the executive pay levels and practices of foreign countries and cultures, U.S. corporations should affirm the positive principles of pay for performance and sharing in the rewards of ownership, and they should extend those principles to lower levels.

6. Changes in annual compensation (salary and bonus income) for top executives should be aligned with changes in absolute annual financial performance.

7. Special benefits and executive perquisites should be re-examined for continued relevance and business need.

8. Compensation surveys should be de-emphasized as determinants and drivers of executive pay actions.

9. The business community should accept and support increased dialogue with shareholders on executive pay matters.

10. The business community should support the continuation of current stock-option accounting rules that encourage the sharing of equity ownership with executives and employees.

future? An opposing view says that executives are not working for the shareholders but for the economic entity that is the company, and that their job is to maximize the long-term viability, profitability and growth of the company. This is accomplished by balancing the need for current profits with the need to invest for the future.

Who cares more about the long-term viability, profitability and growth of the company than its executives and employees who devote their lives to advancing its interests? To the shareholder, companies are often mere holdings in a portfolio that is managed for maximum return. Many shareholders are not interested per se in the success or growth of the company, only in the growth of their share value. And is it not true that employees themselves in many companies, through their employee benefit and retirement funds, are significant shareowners in their own right? Are they interested in the company's market value being managed for maximum return at any point in time? Who is speaking for their interests? If boards and compensation committees reorient executive compensation totally to serve the interests of financial investors, are the interests of employee investors and other shareholders in the company being fairly considered?

U.S. corporations are chartered by states and encouraged and protected by a legal and government system because of the benefits they provide to the economy and society at large. Traditionally, they have been very successful in providing expanded employment opportunities to a growing and diverse workforce, as well as products, services and wealth that enhance the standard of living. The U.S. economy and society, therefore, have a strong interest in the well-being of corporations, including the demise and reallocation of assets of companies that are inefficient or have out-lived their usefulness. Are shareholders as interested in the well-being of corporations? The answer for many is no. What shareholders are interested in is a rising market value *per share*. If executives focused solely on their stock options and other stock-based equity incentives, they too would be interested not in aggregate growth in market value but in value growth per share. In such cases, they might prefer to use excess cash to buy back shares, thereby concentrating profitability and share value over a smaller number of shares. They might not invest that cash in expansion of productive capacity, new products and markets.

Executives with a natural balance of motivations probably would prefer that their corporations grow rather than shrink. Certainly, growth for growth's sake should not be rewarded, nor should size alone be a major determinant of executive pay levels. But the financial incentives of executives should not be so far altered in the other direction that they are driven solely or predominantly by the imperative of increasing the value *per share* of their companies' stock. While it is clear this would benefit financial investors, it is not equally clear that this would be to the benefit of the economy, society and free-enterprise system.

The debate about executive compensation is about many things: pay levels; pay practices; ratios to other employees; relationship to performance, both short- and long-term; and what factors should drive executive motivation and compensation. Institutional investors wish to have corporate executives more beholden to their interests, and they are using the concept of corporate governance, the proxy process, the federal government and the SEC to advance their aims. There is definitely a role for aligning executive compensation to shareholder interests, and it is an important role. But it should not dominate executive compensation considerations. Maximization of shareholder value is not the only goal of corporations in U.S. society or of executives who manage those corporations.

4. Executive compensation strategies and actions should be aligned with important employee-relations initiatives.   Related closely to the preceding point, if companies wish to be successful in increasing employee involvement and productivity, and in reducing costs and improving quality, then employees must support the organization's mission and values. Employees may not give their full support if they believe only the executives and shareholders are benefiting from employee sacrifices and good performance. Furthermore, employees may withhold their support if they believe executives are rewarding themselves while cutting back on other employees' compensation or laying off fellow workers. Kay is wrong to say that shareholders should be willing to reward executives for laying off employees and undertaking other unpleasant tasks that benefit shareholders (Kay 1992). It is a blatant bribe that will drive a wedge between executives and employees, to the long-term detriment of the company. It also violates fundamental principles of fairness and equality of sacrifice in hard times. If executives are not willing to reduce their compensation when restructuring the company to improve future performance, then why should they participate in the rewards that improved future performance will bring?

Executive compensation strategies, plans and actions should be examined to see whether they support or undercut important employee-relations initiatives to improve quality, productivity and competitiveness. If companies go so far in aligning the interests of executives to shareholder value that executives are seen as the enemy of employees, then these initiatives have a high probability of failure, and American business will suffer.

5. Instead of adopting the executive pay levels and practices of foreign countries and cultures, U.S. corporations should affirm the positive principles of pay for performance and sharing in the rewards of ownership, and they should extend those principles to lower levels.   Rather than creating class distinctions between employees and executives, companies should consider "seamless" compensation programs such as those at AT&T, Corning, DuPont and 3M, where large numbers of salaried employees are compensated on the same performance measures and rewarded proportionately to the CEO for their contributions to success. Broad-based stock plans, including ESOPs and the recent all-employee stock option grants at companies such as DuPont, Merck and PepsiCo, are also worthwhile if companies believe it is beneficial and motivational for large numbers of employees—not just top executives—to have a financial interest in a rising stock price. Rather than abandoning executive compensation principles in the face of external criticism, leading companies are extending them to a broader range of employees as part of programs for employee involvement and sharing. This is not corporate altruism. It is in the self-interest of executives and shareholders to include large numbers of employees in executive-type incentives if those employees are critical to future success.

6. Changes in annual compensation (salary and bonus income) for top executives should be aligned with changes in absolute annual financial performance.   The result would be visible increases in executive pay when performance improves and decreases when performance deteriorates. It may strike some as unfair to administer executive bonuses based on changes in accounting profits when so many other performance indices—such as cash flow, customer service, cost reductions, strategic issues and affirmative action—are vying for executive attention. But, for the CEO and other proxy-visible executives, a direct connection between reported pay changes and absolute results is important to the credibility of executive compensation practices to shareholders, employees and the public at large. Let these other performance factors affect lower-level bonuses if appropriate.

At the senior levels, executives should believe that if their bonuses are based on profits and growth, they will be well-rewarded in the long run because good "strategic" performance in a poor-profit year eventually will be rewarded when those strategic actions lead to higher profits (i.e., give up something now and potentially get back more in the future). This is far different from many of today's bonus plans that reward for profit performance relative to budgets or internal projections. In these plans, for example, the budget is lower in years when planned (i.e., previously foreseen) investments are being made. This protects current bonuses. But budgets are higher in years when the investments are harvested, so there is no future reward for success. Obviously, under budget-driven plans, there would be a disincentive to make opportunistic, unbudgeted investments because these would hurt current bonuses, with no chance for future recovery of what was lost.

7. Special benefits and executive perquisites should be re-examined for continued relevance and business need.   A high level of special benefits, supplemental executive retirement plans (SERPs) and perquisites is not consistent with high pay and a strong long-term incentive and ownership orientation. Special benefits have not been part of the public debate, but they should be. They create class distinctions between employee groups and therefore hinder teamwork, cohesiveness and productivity. At a time when management is trying to bring benefit costs under control, it seems inconsistent to impose sacrifices on employees while protecting the benefits and prerogatives of management. Many companies recognize this, and some recently have moved to rescind golden parachutes, abandon company-car programs, eliminate tax gross-ups on financial counseling and personal use of company facilities, and cut back on SERPs. More should do so, or at least re-examine the continued relevance and business justification of such items. Elitism, entitlement and privilege are not themes companies are embracing for the 1990s.

8. Compensation surveys should be de-emphasized as determinants and drivers of executive pay actions.   Surveys often are used by low-paying and low-performing firms that wish to emulate their better-paying and better-performing peers in pay but cannot justify it by performance. Reliance on surveys to support pay actions not otherwise justifiable by performance has a ratchet effect on executive-pay levels. Surveys have a role in monitoring where a company stands in relation to its peers and in developing an overall competitive framework. Within that framework, however, companies should administer their pay programs based on internal dynamics of group performance, individual contribution and equitable ratios to other employee levels—not merely by the need to be competitive in the marketplace.

9. The business community should accept and support increased dialogue with shareholders on executive pay matters.   This can include:

- Proxy initiatives on executive pay by qualified shareholders who want a voice in important matters of executive-compensation policy.
- Ratification of executive stock plans by shareholders (including material amendments).
- Possible ratification by shareholders of senior executive employment and severance contracts.

- Summary statements by the compensation committee chairman in the proxy statement or in annual meetings as to important actions taken during the previous year.

- Direct meetings or communications arranged through management between the compensation committee (representing the board) and representative shareholders who have important executive compensation issues or problems to express.

10. The business community should support the continuation of current stock-option accounting rules that encourage the sharing of equity ownership with executives and employees. The costs of a stock option are costs borne by the shareholder—not by the corporation itself—in terms of dilution of earnings and equity values. The reasons are fairly simple and relate to the fact that the grant or exercise of a typical stock option, unlike other forms of compensation, normally results in no use of cash or other assets of the company. Also, the current accounting for stock options is similar to that of other equity securities issued to investors that have similar characteristics, such as warrants, rights offering and debentures or preferred stock convertible into common stock at a fixed price.

If the Financial Accounting Standards Board (FASB) determines there should be a charge to earnings for the value of stock options granted to employees, despite the fact that there is little or no cost to the corporations granting them, then it should do so based upon strict application of logical accounting principles. But if it is pressured into a political solution based upon objectives not likely to be reached because the assumptions are invalid, then a major U.S. human-resource initiative for gaining competitive advantage in global competition by the year 2000—and a unique characteristic of U.S. compensation programs—will be lost.

The Continuing Debate

There is no doubt that executive compensation abuses will continue because a free-enterprise system without the potential for abuses would not be free. It is important that executive compensation actions deemed to be abusive of public trust and accountability continue to be publicized, isolated and condemned for what they are—tacky behavior on the part of greedy management, compliant boards and consultants who put executive interests and personal considerations ahead of the company as a whole. It is equally important to acknowledge what is right with executive compensation and to publicize and support behavior and trends that are in the long-term best interests of the company.

Executive compensation is not an abstract subject to be addressed from a moralistic perspective. The motivation and reward systems for executives and key employees of our public corporations affect corporate performance. The matter is too important to the nation's future prosperity to run the risk of damage by the blunt hand of government regulation or fiscal engineering.

There are problems with executive compensation, and it is good to debate them. The public, employee and shareholder perceptions of executive compensation are not good, and these perceptions need to be changed if public corporations are to be allowed to retain the freedom to compensate executives under a free-enterprise system. The danger is not in isolated examples of abuse that are acknowledged for what they are—exceptions to an otherwise healthy system. The danger is when abuse is perceived as pervasive. Then, government intervention and other actions of a more revolutionary than evolutionary nature may be expected. The situation is near that point now. Those who believe existing executive compensation systems are effective and evolving in the right direction should say so. Likewise, those who think the business community should consider changes to address public concerns also should say so.

References

Crystal, Graef S. *Executive Compensation in Corporate America 1991.* Washington, D.C.: United Shareholders Association. 1991.

Crystal, Graef S. *In Search of Excess: The Overcompensation of American Executives.* New York and London: W. W. Norton & Company. 1991.

Crystal, Graef S. "Medians Versus Averages." *The Crystal Report.* January-February 1992. 8.

Crystal, Graef S. *The SEC and the Runaway Executive Pay Issue.* Statement made before the U.S. Senate Subcommittee on Oversight of Government Management. 102nd Congress, 1st session, May 15, 1991.

Drucker, Peter F. "Is Executive Pay Excessive?" *The Wall Street Journal,* May 23, 1977. A20.

Jensen, Michael C., and Kevin J. Murphy. "It's Not How Much Executives Are Paid, But How." *Harvard Business Review.* May-June 1990. 138–53.

Kay, Ira T. *Value at the Top: Solutions to the Executive Compensation Crisis.* New York: Harper Collins. 1992.

Towers Perrin. *Priorities for Competitive Advantage.* New York: 1992. 57, 100–101.

EMPLOYEE BENEFITS

INTRODUCTION

Some of the most pressing challenges of the day for employers are in the area of employee benefits. The readings in this section focus on two such challenges. First, one way to increase the return on investment in employee benefits has been the growth in cafeteria, or flexible, benefits plans, in which employers give employees the opportunity to design a benefits package that meets their needs and, in the process, may also help employees understand the value of their benefits package. Second, the growth in the number of women in the labor force has contributed to greater concern among employers and employees regarding how to balance work and family responsibilities. The final reading proposes some options to be considered.

The fact that employees may underestimate the value of their benefits, combined with the fact that benefits make up a growing share of compensation costs, demands that organizations design their benefits packages in ways that help control further cost increases while obtaining as great an impact on employee attitudes and behaviors as possible with the money already being spent. One solution is to allow employees to choose among a variety of benefits and benefits levels in cafeteria-style or flexible benefits plans, the focus of the study by Alison Barber, Randall Dunham, and Roger Formisano. The idea is that by having employees make such choices, they will better understand the value of their benefits and also have a benefits package that is better matched to their particular needs. These, in turn, should contribute to increased satisfaction with benefits and the job in general. Indeed, this is what Barber and her colleagues found when a flexible benefits plan was implemented in the company they studied.

In "Management Women and the New Facts of Life," Felice N. Schwartz points out that "women in the corporation are about to move from a buyer's to a seller's market" because women will account for much of the growth in the labor force. Therefore, employers will need to be better positioned to effectively manage the careers of their women employees. Schwartz suggests that there are two career tracks for women. First, there are what she calls "career-primary" women. These women "make a career decision to put in extra hours, to make sacrifices in their personal lives, to make the most of every opportunity for professional development. For women, of course, this decision also requires that they remain single or childless or, if they do have children, that they be satisfied to have others raise them." However, Schwartz argues that most women are "career-and-family women." She describes these women as a "precious resource that has yet to be mined" and describes most of them as "willing to trade some career growth and compensation for freedom from the constant pressure to work long hours and weekends." This career track has been referred to by some as the "mommy track," and Schwartz has been criticized for her suggestion that women with families need to be on a different career track. In any case, Schwartz suggests that the cost of employing these women is greater than that of employing most men or the career-primary women. Still, she suggests that it is in employers' best interests to take greater advantage of this pool of talent by providing more flexible career paths and by providing benefits such as family leave, job sharing, part-time work, and so forth that help provide the flexibility in their jobs that will permit women (and men) to succeed in both their careers and their family lives. The recent enactment of the Family and Medical Leave Act is consistent with this point of view.

READING 34

THE IMPACT OF FLEXIBLE BENEFITS ON EMPLOYEE SATISFACTION
A Field Study

Alison E. Barber
Randall B. Dunham,
Roger A. Formisano

This study examines the attitudes of 110 employees of a financial service organization before and after the introduction of a flexible benefit plan. A large, statistically significant increase in benefit satisfaction was observed following implementation, as was a smaller significant increase in overall satisfaction. Employee understanding of the benefit package also increased significantly. No significant relationships were found between demographic characteristics and responses to the flexible plan. Potential confounds due to the complexity of the intervention are discussed. Future research is called for to examine the processes through which flexible benefits impact worker reactions and to examine the impact of flexible benefits on behavioral responses such as attraction and retention.

Employee benefits accounted for 19% of payroll in the United States in 1950 (Bloom & Trahan, 1986). By 1986, they accounted for 39% of payroll (Bureau of National Affairs, 1988). Part of this increase is attributable to the rising costs of specific benefits (e.g., medical care coverage). However, the scope of benefit coverage has also expanded. Whereas most early benefit plans provided little more than basic health and retirement coverage, today's plans often offer profit-sharing and stock ownership benefits, legal, educational, and child-care assistance, dental and vision insurance, and life insurance for employees and their dependents. Because the United States provides little in the way of nationalized benefit plans (Alpert, 1989), pressure on U.S. employers to provide and manage this broad spectrum of benefits is particularly intense.

The wide variety of potential benefits raises an important issue for plan design: which of the many available benefits should an organization include in its plan? Traditionally, this decision has been made unilaterally by professional

Source: "The Impact of Flexible Benefits on Employee Satisfaction: A Field Study" by Alison E. Barber, Randall B. Dunham, and Roger A. Formisano, *Personnel Psychology*, 1992, Vol. 45, 55–75.

benefits managers in consultation with top-level management. An increasingly popular option today is the "cafeteria" or "flexible" benefit plan, in which employees may choose among a variety of benefits, or choose among varying levels of benefits. Typically, employers establish limits for total plan costs and, within certain limits, allow employees to determine how the total benefit dollars are spent. The amount of choice permitted by these plans can vary considerably.

Flexible benefit plans were first explored in the late 1970s. The growth in adoption of these programs since 1980, primarily in the United States, has been great. A Hewitt Associates report indicates that, while only eight major employers had federally qualified flexible benefit plans in 1980, over 800 offered them in 1988 ("Section 125 Flexible Benefit Programs," 1988). This trend is likely to continue, particularly given that flexible programs are most prevalent in the service sector ("Demographics," 1989), the fastest growing employment sector in the U.S. economy (Haugen, 1989).

Flexible programs were initially explored in response to changing demographics. During the decade of the 1960s, family and workforce patterns changed dramatically. Increased divorce rates, lowered childbirth rates, and increased female employment led to a more heterogeneous workforce. It was argued that traditional benefit plans geared to the needs of the formerly preponderant nuclear family (i.e., an employed male head of household, nonworking spouse, and children) failed to accommodate the interests of the new workforce ("Demographics," 1989).

By the 1980s, exploding costs of health insurance and other employee benefits, combined with significant general inflation, brought a broader interest in flexible benefit plans as a cost containment tool. Cost savings can be realized by (a) limiting the total cost of benefits by allowing employees to choose personally valued benefits within a cost constraint and, (b) improving efficiency of benefit use through increased awareness of benefit costs. A recent survey ("Changing Work Force," 1988) indicated that cost containment is particularly effective for medical benefits, with medical cost increases for flexible plans averaging about 70% of the cost increases of traditional (nonflexible) plans. To some extent, however, the cost containment effect of flexible benefits could be offset by increased administrative costs (associated with processing individual benefit choices) and by adverse selection (where only heavy users of a particular benefit opt for that benefit).

Flexible benefit plans may also result in positive employee relations outcomes. Advocates of flexible plans claim that they can increase satisfaction with benefits per se, enhance job satisfaction in general, produce higher levels of motivation and productivity, and increase attraction and retention of employees (e.g., Beam & McFadden, 1988; Employee Benefits Research Institute, 1982; Rosenbloom & Hallman, 1986). These claims, however, are based on anecdotal evidence, since no available reports of empirical studies have addressed either the attitudinal or the behavioral impact of flexible benefit plans.

An important first step in evaluating flexible benefit plans would be to document the impact of flexible benefit plans on employee benefit satisfaction.

Job satisfaction is frequently viewed as the sum of satisfaction with a number of independent job elements, such as pay, promotions, and working conditions (Locke, 1976). More recently, researchers have argued that pay satisfaction can be subdivided into independent elements such as satisfaction with benefits, pay level, pay administration, and pay structure (Heneman & Schwab, 1985.) Empirical research has consistently supported the existence of the benefit satisfaction dimension (Scarpello, Huber, & Vandenberg, 1988). Furthermore, attitudes toward benefits have been found to be significant determinants of pay satisfaction (Berger, 1984; Dreher, 1981) and pay satisfaction has been shown to be related to behavioral outcomes such as absenteeism and turnover (Motowidlo, 1983; Weiner, 1980).

If flexible benefits (or other benefit innovations) influence employee behaviors, they likely do so through their impact on benefit satisfaction. Thus enhanced benefit satisfaction may be a prerequisite for other outcomes. (For a general review of the effects of pay satisfaction on employee outcomes, see Heneman, 1985.)

Several reasons for the assumed linkages between flexible benefits and benefit satisfaction have been proposed. First higher satisfaction might result if flexible benefits produce a better match between the benefits individual employees want and the benefits they receive (Rosenbloom & Hallman, 1986). This need-satisfaction argument is consistent with Locke's (1969, 1976) discrepancy definition of job satisfaction. Locke posits that job satisfaction is "a function of the perceived relationship between what one wants from one's job and what one perceives it as offering or entailing" (Locke, 1969, p. 316). If the benefits desired by the growing number of nontraditional employees (e.g., single employees, dual career couples) are not provided by conventional benefit plans, flexible benefit plans may provide a mechanism to reduce this discrepancy and hence increase their benefit satisfaction.

Flexible benefits may also enhance benefit satisfaction by making employees more aware of the nature and value of their benefits (Beam & McFadden, 1988). Employees are often unfamiliar with the value of their benefit packages, either in absolute (dollar) terms (Wilson, Northcraft, & Neale, 1985) or relative to the benefits received by others (Dreher, Ash, & Bretz, 1988). Research also indicates that employees frequently undervalue their benefits (Wilson et al., 1985). It is frequently argued that participating in the process of designing and/or selecting benefits under an individualized (flexible) plan will lead to better understanding and appreciation of benefit value on the part of employees (e.g., Miceli & Lane, in press; Rosenbloom & Hallman, 1986). If the information acquired leads employees to view their benefits in a more positive light, benefit satisfaction should increase.

Despite the fact that there are several sound reasons why implementing a flexible benefit plan could increase employee benefit satisfaction (and subsequently behavioral outcomes), there has yet to be an empirical evaluation of this effect. The primary purpose of the present study is to empirically evaluate, in a field setting, the impact of the implementation of a flexible benefit plan on employee benefit satisfaction. Thus:

Hypothesis 1: Implementation of a flexible benefit plan will lead to an increase in satisfaction with benefits.

The anecdotal literature also suggests that flexible benefit plans will lead to increases in general job satisfaction. This suggestion is based on a view of overall job satisfaction as the sum of evaluations of individual job elements (Locke, 1969). Because benefit satisfaction is an element of overall satisfaction, an increase in the former should yield an increase in the latter. However, given the variety of elements that have been shown to be components of overall job satisfaction (e.g., Smith, Kendall, & Hulin, 1969; Weiss, Dawis, England, & Lofquist, 1967), the contribution of a single element to overall job satisfaction is likely to be small. Thus, we hypothesized that:

Hypothesis 2: Implementation of a flexible benefit plan will lead to an increase in job satisfaction. However, this increase will be smaller in magnitude than the increase in benefit satisfaction.

Several additional research questions were formulated to provide a preliminary examination of the mechanisms by which flexibility influences benefit satisfaction. First, we investigated whether flexible benefits might reduce discrepancies between the benefits employees want and the benefits they receive. Many advocates of flexible benefits argue that benefit preferences are determined by demographic characteristics, and that the benefit preferences of nontraditional workers are not well met by traditional plans. Therefore, we assessed the extent to which subjects in the present study differed from the "traditional" (i.e., married male head of household) demographic profile, and whether divergence from the traditional profile was related to benefit satisfaction either before or after implementation of the flexible benefit plan. We expected a negative relationship between benefit satisfaction and nontraditional status under the original (i.e., nonflexible) benefit plan, as a result of the anticipated discrepancy between the needs of nontraditional employees and the benefits offered by a traditional benefit plan. This negative correlation should be reduced by flexible plans because individuals can choose benefits to minimize any discrepancies.

The arguments of flexible benefits advocates notwithstanding, prior research has provided only mixed support for the relationship between demographics and benefit preferences (Milkovich & Newman, 1990). Many other factors can influence individual benefit preferences (e.g., risk aversion, individual demand for leisure; Miceli & Lane, in press). Therefore, a more general test of the discrepancy argument was needed. Presumably, employees experiencing severe discrepancies between benefits desired and benefits received under the traditional plan will make substantial changes to their benefit plan when given the opportunity to do so, regardless of how their preferences are determined. Once these changes are made, however, discrepancies should diminish. Therefore, we anticipated a negative relationship between the extent of changes made under the flexible plan and benefit satisfaction prior to implementation of the flexible plan. Again, this negative correlation should be diminished under the flexible plan, as individuals design plans to minimize discrepancies.

METHOD

Sample

Primary data for this study were collected between 1985 and 1987 from a professional management organization serving associated financial institutions. Approximately 475 professional, technical, and administrative workers were employed by the organization at the beginning of the study. All employees were included in the flexible benefit plan. A pretest survey was voluntarily completed by 314 employees (response rate of 66%), and a posttest survey was completed by 270 (response rate of 57%). This shrinkage was in part due to employee failure to attend meetings where the surveys were distributed, and in part to employees choosing not to complete the survey. These samples are referred to as the full pretest and full posttest samples.

Employees were asked to include their names on each survey, to allow matching of pretest and posttest questionnaires. This self-identification was strictly voluntary. A total of 110 employees responded to and identified themselves on both surveys. The substantive hypotheses of this study are tested using this subset of subjects (referred to as the matched sample.)

Subjects in the matched sample were predominately (75%) under the age of 40. Two thirds were female, two thirds were married, half had children living at home, and over half had spouses who worked outside of the home. Half were members of a clerical union. Approximately 20% were professional employees, 25% held supervisory or managerial positions, and the rest worked at technical or administrative jobs. Average tenure with the company was relatively low: 40% of the subjects had less than three years of organizational service; only 25% had more than 8 years of service.

Because of substantial shrinkage from the full pretest and posttest samples to the matched sample, numerous tests were conducted to identify differences between those who self-identified on both surveys (and therefore could be matched) and those who did not. Chi-square and *t*-tests comparing the demographic characteristics of the matched sample to those of the full pretest and full posttest samples identified no significant differences. In addition, no differences in tenure or in gender were observed between survey respondents and the organizational population. No other demographic variables were available for the population.

A comparison of satisfaction levels of those who self-identified on both surveys (i.e., the matched sample) and those who did not (i.e., the full pretest and full posttest samples) indicated no statistically significant differences in mean levels of benefit satisfaction or in distribution of benefit satisfaction scores at either the pretest or the posttest. Average overall satisfaction was slightly higher for those who self-identified at the time of the pretest (3.70 vs. 3.58, $p < .05$), but was not significantly different on the posttest. No significant differences were observed in understanding of the benefit plan at either pretest or posttest. Finally, no significant differences in benefits selected under the flexible plan were found.

Table 1

BENEFIT SATISFACTION ITEMS

Respondents were asked to indicate their agreement/disagreement with the following six items using a 5-point scale, where 1 = strongly disagree, 2 = disagree, 3 = neither agree nor disagree, 4 = agree, 5 = strongly agree.

1. The benefits I receive from (xxx) provide me (and my family) with a sense of security.
2. My needs are not satisfied by the benefits I receive from (xxx).
3. My overall attitude toward my job is favorably influenced by the benefits I receive from (xxx).
4. I wish the benefits I receive from (xxx) would be changed.
5. Considering what services cost in this area, the benefits I receive from (xxx) are adequate.
6. I am satisfied with the (xxx) benefit plan.

An independent sample of 165 subjects from another organization was also used to assess convergence of our benefits satisfaction measure with the benefits satisfaction subscale of the Pay Satisfaction Questionnaire (Heneman & Schwab, 1985), an instrument that became the subject of considerable research following the initial design of our study. Information on this sample, and on the results of this analysis, are provided in the appendix.

Measures

Two surveys (pretest and posttest) were administered. Both surveys contained six benefit satisfaction items from an instrument created for this study (see Table 1). To develop the benefit items, one of the authors met with two small groups of employees (a total of eleven) to discuss the domain of benefit satisfaction. (Although it cannot be known for sure, it is probable that several of these small group members were included in the 110 person matched sample.) After a general discussion, the groups drafted items which would address benefit satisfaction. Following these meetings, the authors wrote a variety of items which were revised after review by the group participants. These items were written in a format consistent with the other survey items.

Both surveys also contained eight items from a shortened version of the Index of Organizational Reactions (IOR; Dunham & Pierce, 1977; Dunham, Smith, & Blackburn, 1977; Smith, 1976) to measure satisfaction with work, pay, coworkers, supervision, amount of work, physical working conditions, and the company itself. These eight items were combined with unit weighting to form a measure of overall job satisfaction. Note that while this scale included two general pay satisfaction items, there were no items that referred specifically to employee benefits. A subset of these items, consisting only of items not expected to be influenced by implementation of the flexible benefits plan (satisfaction with kind of work, amount of work, coworkers, supervision, and physical working conditions), was used to create a scale representing noncompensation satisfaction.

In addition, two 5-point Likert items were used to measure employees' understanding of the benefit plan ("I understand the benefit plan quite well," and "I would like more information about the benefit plan"). The pretest survey also included a number of items used to aid in the design of the new benefit plan.

A scale was formed to indicate the extent to which individual subjects differed from the traditional employee demographic profile. Information on demographics was obtained from the pretest survey. Measures of gender, marital status, whether one's spouse worked, whether one had children, and two levels of job tenure were dummy-coded, with the traditional categories (long-tenure, married males with children and nonworking spouses) coded as zero. These variables were then summed to create a demographic profile index with values ranging from 0–6, with higher index numbers representing a greater divergence from the traditional profile.

Finally, an index of the extent to which subjects actually changed their benefit plans (relative to the existing plan) after flexible benefits were implemented was created using data from the company's payroll records. Variables indicating whether subjects made changes in six major benefit categories (health insurance, life insurance, retirement, vacation, long-term disability, prepaid spending account) were each coded "0" if no change was made and "1" if a change was made. In addition, a variable indicating whether employees chose to receive cash in lieu of a portion of their benefit coverage was coded "0" if no cash was received and "1" if cash was received. These variables were then summed to generate an index of extent of change, with higher index numbers representing greater change.

Procedure

Pretest.   Participants were assembled in groups of 20–50 in an on-site conference room during working hours. They were shown a videotape in which one of the authors and the organization's vice president of human resources explained the purpose of the study. The pretest survey was then administered by and returned to the researchers.

After the pretest, participants were given a packet of materials that described and asked for reactions to all existing benefits and a number of alternative benefits. These reactions consisted of valuation (on a scale from 0–10) of each element of the current benefit plan and each of a variety of alternatives under consideration for inclusion in the new plan. In addition, employees were asked to choose benefits under a simulated flexible benefit plan which was very similar to the plan later implemented. Some design changes were made based on the value attached to each benefit element and the frequency of choice alternatives.

Plan implementation.   The flexible benefit plan implemented as part of this research was designed, in large part, based on input solicited during the pretest phase. The plan, implemented 14 months after the study began, included a core comprised of basic health, life, and long-term disability benefits. A number of new benefit options (e.g., more or less life insurance, more or less vacation time, and more or less long-term disability coverage) were made available. Several health insurance options were offered, as were opportunities to receive cash in lieu of some noncash benefits. The option of retaining the exact same coverage as had been provided by the "old" benefit plan was also offered. The flexible plan was designed so that the dollar value of benefits provided would be equal to the dollar value of benefits offered under the old plan.

Introduction of the flexible plan was accompanied by several informational items describing the nature and administration of the new plan. In addition, up to 2 hours of group training were provided to help employees use the plan. Virtually all employees participated in these group sessions, which were conducted by the organization's human resources group. At the sessions, written materials describing the plan were distributed and discussed, as was the process to be used for selecting benefits.

Posttest.   Four months after the introduction of the flexible benefit plan, a second survey was administered on-site by a member of the research team. Responses were returned directly to the researchers. Participants were assured confidentiality, but they were asked to identify themselves by name on each survey to allow matching of pretest and posttest responses. This self-identification was entirely voluntary.

Data collected from organizational records at the time of the posttest indicated that over 90% of study participants opted for the flexible plan. Most of these took advantage of the substantial flexibility the new plan offered. For example, over 85% replaced the core health care option and over 80% enhanced their disability coverage.

Summary of design.   It is important to note that a number of events occurred as part of this complex organizational intervention. All have been noted above. However, to summarize, the intervention included (a) discussions with 11 employees to develop survey items, (b) the pretest survey, (c) training and communication regarding the flexible plan, (d) implementation of the flexible plan, and (e) the posttest survey.

Analyses

Principal component factor analysis with varimax rotation and coefficient alpha reliability analyses were used to assess reliability and validity for the benefit satisfaction measure. Pretest and posttest data from the matched sample were used for this analysis. (See appendix for convergence of this measure with the benefits subscale of the Pay Satisfaction Questionnaire.) Coefficient alpha internal consistency estimates were also obtained for the other scales.

A nonequivalent dependent variables design (Cook & Campbell, 1979) was used to test the hypotheses of this study. One-tailed, paired-sample t tests were used to test for increases from pre- to post-intervention means for benefit satisfaction and overall job satisfaction. We also tested for differences in facets of satisfaction that were *not* expected to change following implementation of the flexible plan: satisfaction with physical working conditions, coworkers, supervision, kind of work, and amount of work. These items were combined into a 5-item scale representing noncompensation satisfaction. There were two purposes for combining these items. The first was to allow assessment of measurement reliability, an indicator of whether true changes would have been registered had they occurred (Cook & Campbell, 1979). The second was to minimize the number of hypothesis tests performed, thereby reducing the probability of finding significant results by chance. However, results for individual facets of satisfaction were also reported.

A one-tailed *t* test was used to test for increased understanding of the benefit plan. Correlations between demographic profiles and pre-and posttest benefit satisfaction were used to assess whether (a) there was a negative relationship between nontraditional demographic characteristics and benefit satisfaction at the pretest stage, and (b) whether this relationship was diminished following implementation of the flexible plan. In addition, correlations between the index of actual benefit changes and pre- and posttest benefit satisfaction were examined in order to assess more directly whether discrepancies between benefits desired and benefits received under the original plan might be associated with lower benefit satisfaction at the pretest stage, and whether this relationship was reduced under the flexible plan. This analysis is based on the assumption that those who felt the largest discrepancies under the original plan would make more substantial changes in their benefits than would those who experienced small discrepancies.

RESULTS

Measures

Principal component factor analyses of the six-item benefit satisfaction measure suggested a two-factor solution for the pretest (using the criterion that eigenvalues for retained factors should exceed 1.0). This solution explained 63.9% of the variance. After varimax rotation, the first factor was defined by items 1, 2, 4, 5, and 6, with the second factor defined solely by Item 3. Results for the posttest suggested a single factor defined by all six items and explaining 42.8% of the variance. However, the loading for Item 3 was low. Examination of the content of Item 3 ("My overall attitude toward my job is favorably influenced by the benefits I receive") suggests that this item may measure both benefit satisfaction and the amount of spillover that occurs between benefit satisfaction and overall satisfaction. Therefore, we omitted Item 3 from the benefit satisfaction scale. Factor analysis of the remaining five items yielded single factors explaining 53.5% of the variance for the pretest, and 49.3% for the posttest. Coefficient alpha for the five-item scale was .78 for the pretest and .73 for the posttest.[1]

---

[1]Factor analysis using the full posttest sample (*n* = 270) and the sample used to test convergence between our scale and the PSQ (*n* = 149; see appendix) also suggested a five-item scale, with Item 3 excluded. However, factor analysis using the full pretest sample (*n* = 314) suggested a two-factor structure, with Items 1 and 3 loaded on the second factor.

Table 2

MEANS AND CORRELATIONS

Variable	Mean	SD	1	2	3	4	5	6	7	8	9	10
1. Pretest benefit satisfaction	3.61	.54	1.00									
2. Posttest benefit satisfaction	4.21	.47	.21	1.00								
3. Pretest overall satisfaction	3.70	.48	.19	−.03	1.00							
4. Posttest overall satisfaction	3.82	.51	.00	.34**	.38**	1.00						
5. Pretest noncompensation satisfaction	3.72	.58	.10	−.07	.90**	.42**	1.00					
6. Posttest noncompensation satisfaction	3.78	.57	−.02	.30*	.27*	.91**	.40**	1.00				
7. Pretest benefits understanding	2.85	.78	.15	.05	.02	.10	.03	.10	1.00			
8. Posttest benefits understanding	3.66	.65	.18	.21	.14	.19	.11	.18	.28*	1.00		
9. Demographic profile	2.44	1.03	.11	−.04	−.15	−.14	−.17	−.14	−.33**	−.27*	1.00	
10. Changes in benefits	2.35	1.00	.07	−.11	.02	−.09	.03	−.15	−.24	−.04	.12	1.00

$n = 95$; $*p < .01$; $**p < .001$

Internal consistency estimates for the overall job satisfaction scale were .67 for the pretest and .72 for the posttest. Internal consistency estimates for the noncompensation satisfaction scale were .64 for the pretest and .63 for the posttest. For the understanding of benefits scale, both pretest and posttest estimates were .67.

Substantive Issues

Table 2 provides means and correlations for scales used in the study. Satisfaction and understanding of benefits were 5-point scales. The demographic profile index had a potential range from 0 (perfectly fits traditional profile) to 6. The changes in benefits index had a potential range from 0 (no changes made) to 6.

Table 3 presents results of paired t tests for changes in satisfaction following implementation of the new benefit plan. Hypothesis 1 of this study was confirmed by the statistically significant ($p < .001$) increase in benefit satisfaction following introduction of the flexible plan. The mean level of benefit satisfaction rose from 3.61 to 4.21, an increase of more than one standard deviation.

Hypothesis 2 was also confirmed. As Table 3 indicates, overall job satisfaction increased significantly following introduction of the flexible plan ($p < .05$),

Table 3

PRETEST/POSTTEST DIFFERENCES IN BENEFIT SATISFACTION,
OVERALL JOB SATISFACTION, AND UNDERSTANDING OF BENEFITS
(STANDARD DEVIATIONS IN PARENTHESES)

Variable	Pretest	Posttest	Standardized difference	T-value
Benefit satisfaction	3.61 (.54)	4.21 (.47)	1.11	10.00**
Overall job satisfaction	3.70 (.48)	3.82 (.51)	0.25	2.53*
Noncompensation satisfaction	3.71 (.58)	3.78 (.57)	0.14	1.11
Individual satisfaction dimensions:				
Physical working conditions	3.67 (1.05)	3.65 (1.05)	−0.02	0.18
Coworkers	3.90 (.72)	4.07 (.68)	0.24	2.45*
Kind of work	4.11 (.74)	4.22 (.76)	0.15	1.40
Amount of work	3.43 (.94)	3.33 (1.02)	−0.11	−.93
Supervision	3.50 (1.06)	3.62 (.93)	0.11	.97
Understanding of benefits	2.85 (.78)	3.66 (.65)	1.04	9.74**

Note: Tests are one-tailed. Adjustment of alpha levels to account for the multiple significance tests being conducted reduces the results for overall satisfaction and satisfaction with coworkers to nonsignificance.

*$p < .05$; **$p < .01$

thus supporting Hypothesis 2. However, the magnitude of the increase in job satisfaction was small (3.70 to 3.82) relative to the increase in benefit satisfaction. Furthermore, adjustment of alpha levels to account for the multiple significance tests conducted in this study (using the Bonferroni procedure; Huberty & Morris, 1989) reduces this effect to nonsignificance.

As expected, no statistically significant change in noncompensation satisfaction was observed. Analysis of individual items indicated no significant changes in satisfaction with physical working conditions, kind of work, supervision, or amount of work. A slight, but significant, increase in satisfaction with coworkers was observed (from 3.90 to 4.07). However, after adjustment of alpha levels, this change became nonsignificant. Power to detect a moderate change in these items exceeded .95 (estimated using procedures outlined in Cohen, 1970.)

Table 3 also shows that there were significant increases in the degree to which employees understood their benefit plan (2.85 to 3.66). While it was anticipated that pretest benefit satisfaction would be negatively related to nontraditional profiles (i.e., high profile scores) and to changes in benefits, neither of these correlations were statistically significant (see Table 2).[2]

DISCUSSION

The results of this study support the hypothesis that the implementation of a flexible benefit plan would be followed by increases in employee satisfaction with benefits. The increase observed in this sample was both statistically significant and of considerable magnitude. In addition, overall job satisfaction increased somewhat. Thus, the present research provides much needed empirical confirmation of anecdotal reports of increased satisfaction following the implementation of a flexible plan.

This study also provides evidence on the role of needs discrepancies and communication in increasing benefit satisfaction. Although it has often been argued that changes in workplace demographics lead to a mismatch between benefits desired and benefits received, the nonsignificant correlations between nontraditional demographic profiles and satisfaction with the original (pretest) benefit plan fail to support this point of view. Other studies attempting to use demographics as predictors of benefit preferences have also failed to provide convincing support for the demographics argument (Milkovich & Newman, 1990).

Of course, the determination of benefit preferences may not be a simple function of demographics. For example, preferences may be determined by other individual difference factors such as risk aversion or demand for leisure (Miceli & Lane, in press). However, the lack of a significant relationship between the extent to which our subjects changed their benefits and their benefit satisfaction at either the pretest or the posttest level makes any discrepancy argument hard to support.

On the other hand, our results are consistent with the argument that increased understanding of benefits following implementation of a flexible benefit plan generates increased satisfaction. Self-assessed understanding of the benefit plan increased considerably after implementation of the new plan. This should not be surprising, given the extensive communication and training that was part of that implementation. This communication could have led employees to a more favorable view of their benefits package. However, communication is a vital and integral part of the implementation of flexible benefit plans, as employers wish to avoid misinformed choices on the part of employees. Furthermore, the fact that employees must make decisions based on this information may make them more likely to attend to it than if it were presented with no action required. Therefore, we believe communication and training should be viewed as an inherent (and, as this study suggests, important) part of the process by which flexible benefits increase satisfaction.

The results of this study should be interpreted with caution for at least four reasons: the lack of a control group, the high initial benefit satisfaction level, the single posttest assessment, and the response rate.

---

[2]Furthermore, no significant correlations were observed between pretest or posttest benefit satisfaction and individual demographic variables or changes in individual benefit items.

As often happens in field research, we were unable to obtain a control group for this study. Control groups are extremely valuable as means of assessing whether observed effects are due to the treatment of interest or to other events (history factors) that might have occurred between the pretest and the posttest (Cook & Campbell, 1979). Presumably, if history factors other than the benefit plan caused the observed increase in benefit satisfaction, dimensions of satisfaction unrelated to compensation would have been affected as well. Thus, it is important to note that no changes were observed in the noncompensation satisfaction scale or in satisfaction with working conditions, kind or amount of work, or supervision. There was a small but significant increase in satisfaction with coworkers. Reasons for this increase are unknown.

Extensive interviews conducted with members of the organization's management failed to identify factors other than the implementation of flexible benefits (e.g., union contract negotiations, changes in wage or salary levels, staff reorganizations) that might have affected benefit satisfaction. Turnover during this period was neither particularly high nor low, and overall employment levels were constant. Nonetheless, a study incorporating a control group would represent an improvement over the design used for this study.

A second reason to exercise caution in interpreting the results of this study concerns the issue of generalizability. The original benefit plan of the organization studied was generous compared to plans found elsewhere in the community, and initial satisfaction levels were fairly high (3.6 on a 5-point scale). Furthermore, the generosity of the plan was maintained when the flexible plan was implemented (i.e., the employer did not reduce its benefits expenditures). Generalization to organizations with less generous plans may be risky. Organizations offering inferior plans may have room for greater increases in satisfaction than were possible here. On the other hand, if an employer has not traditionally been generous with benefits, the introduction of a flexible plan might be viewed with suspicion by employees (e.g., as an attempt to disguise reductions in benefits). This could result in decreased benefit satisfaction. Thus, to explore the boundary conditions of our findings, there is a need to investigate the impact of flexible benefits in a variety of organizational contexts.

Third, this study included only a single assessment of postimplementation satisfaction. This measure was taken only a few months after the plan was implemented. Thus, we do not know whether the observed increase in satisfaction persisted over time. Assessment of the long-term effects a flexible plan might have on benefit satisfaction is warranted.

Finally, it should be noted that a substantial number of employees chose not to self-identify on both pretest and posttest measures, and therefore were not part of the final sample used in this study. While our analyses failed to uncover systematic differences between those who were and those who were not included in the final sample, it would nonetheless have been desirable to have had less shrinkage in the sample.

Caveats notwithstanding, the present study suggests that substantial increases in benefit satisfaction may be observed following implementation of a flexible benefits plan, particularly where communication is high. This lends some credence to the host of anecdotal reports on flexible benefits, and suggests that further research on the consequences of flexible benefits is merited.

However, in attempting to generalize from these results, it is important to note that the organizational intervention evaluated in this research was complex in nature, consisting of a package of related interventions. The first component consisted of discussions with 11 employees during which the nature of employee benefit plans was discussed, the concept of flexible plans was explored, and potential survey items were considered. The second component consisted of the pretest, at which time the nature of both fixed and flexible benefit plans were discussed and the first survey was administered. The third aspect of the intervention included the distribution of materials about the new plan and training sessions during which the nature and administration of the upcoming flexible benefit plan were explored. The introduction and use of the flexible plan completed the intervention package. Although the complexity of this change is not unusual for organizational interventions, the design of the present study is not capable of separating the impact of the intervention's various components. Separation of some of these factors might best be accomplished in a simulation setting as opposed to the field setting where our research was conducted. It would be difficult in the field, for example, to introduce a flexible plan without providing information describing the plan and training in its use.

Suggestions for Future Research

At least two additional lines of research would complement the research reported in this paper. First, further research on the processes by which flexible benefits influence benefit satisfaction is in order. Two possible processes were described earlier: reduction in discrepancies between benefits desired and benefits received, and increased (favorable) information about benefits. This study suggests that increased understanding of benefits was a key factor in enhancing benefit satisfaction, and that discrepancies between benefits received and benefits desired were relatively unimportant. Further research on both of these issues is in order. First, regarding understanding of benefits, this study used a self-report measure of perceived understanding, rather than an objective test aimed at measuring actual knowledge of the plan. Further studies might attempt to differentiate between *feelings* of understanding versus *actual* understanding as contributors to benefits satisfaction, perhaps by including both measures in a single design. In addition, it would be desirable to control for the quantity and content of information received about the benefit plan. As noted earlier, it is assumed that the additional information received under flexible plans increases the employees' evaluation of the plan. If the information received is not positive (e.g., if the plan does not provide coverage the employees assumed they had), satisfaction would be expected to decrease, not increase.

While we found no evidence to support the argument that flexible benefits enhance benefit satisfaction by reducing discrepancies between benefits desired and benefits received, this issue must be tested in other organizational contexts. The original benefit plan provided by this organization was generous. Therefore, it may be that few employees experienced any sizable discrepancies, and that changes to benefit plans represented little more than "fine tuning" of an already satisfactory plan. Discrepancies may well play a role in organizations with less generous plans.

While we have focused on two of the most commonly discussed mechanisms by which flexible benefits may influence satisfaction, other mechanisms should also be explored. In particular, it has been argued that employees may react positively to the increased involvement that flexible benefit plans allow. The degree of involvement permitted by flexible plans can vary, from merely choosing one's own benefits (a form of delegation) to actual participation in plan design. Miceli and Lane (in press) argue that involvement in flexible benefit plans may enhance benefit satisfaction in two ways. First, self-efficacy may be enhanced; employees who feel they have more control over their work environment tend to be more satisfied. Second, employees who participate in the structuring of a benefit plan may have greater commitment to its final design. It is important to note that the implementation reported in this paper involved both choice of benefits and extensive participation in plan design, and that plans providing for less involvement may yield smaller increases in satisfaction.

Comparison of benefit satisfaction across firms whose flexible benefit plans permit different amounts or different forms of employee involvement would add to our understanding of the role of participation and/or delegation. Alternatively, within-firm comparisons may be possible where the extent of involvement varies across employees (for example, where some subset of organization members are selected to represent all employees in plan design.)

It is particularly likely that the involvement provided by flexible plans will affect satisfaction with benefit plan administration. The measure of benefit satisfaction used in this paper focuses primarily on the content of the benefit package, rather than on the way benefits are administered. It has been argued, however, that benefit satisfaction is itself multidimensional (Miceli & Lane, in press). Future research on flexible benefits should attempt to assess both dimensions of benefit satisfaction, and to identify processes affecting each.

A second line of research encouraged by the findings of this study involves the behavioral consequences of flexible benefit plans. Anecdotal evidence suggests that flexible plans lead to improvements in attraction and retention, but this has yet to be empirically investigated. It may be that benefits (and employee reactions to benefits) are such a small part of the total work experience that they lack the power to influence employee behaviors. On the other hand, they may have considerable influence *at the margin*. For example, if employees are choosing among jobs that differ on a number of characteristics, benefits may play a small role in attraction and retention. However, if the labor market for applicants and employees consists of a number of apparently similar jobs, offering a flexible benefit plan may significantly improve an organization's ability to attract and retain. The importance of job attribute variability has been documented (e.g., Rynes, Schwab, & Heneman, 1983) and represents an important boundary condition for studies of the impact of flexible benefits on employee behaviors.

Surprisingly little empirical research has been conducted on flexible benefit programs, or, for that matter, on the topic of employee benefits in general. This is unfortunate in that benefits constitute a large (and increasing) portion of the total compensation package, particularly for firms operating in the United States. Although much remains to be learned, the present study provides a first step in demonstrating that benefit innovations can influence employee reactions.

References

Alpert, R. N. (1989). Mandating health care benefits in an environment of escalating costs. *Proceedings of the 41st Annual Meeting of the Industrial Relations Research Association,* 102–109. Madison, WI: Industrial Relations Research Association.

Ash, R. A., Dreher, G. F. (1990, August). Revision of the Henemen and Schwab Pay Satisfaction Questionnaire. Presented at 1990 annual meeting of the Academy of Management, San Francisco.

Beam, B., McFadden, J. (1988). *Employee benefits* (2nd ed.). Homewood, IL: Richard D. Irwin.

Berger, C. J. (1984). *The effects of pay level, pay values and employee benefits on pay satisfaction.* Unpublished manuscript, Krannert School, Purdue University.

Bloom, D. E., Trahan, J. T. (1986). *Flexible benefits and employee choice.* New York: Pergamon Press.

Bureau of National Affairs. (1988). *BNA policy and practice series: Compensation.* Washington, DC: Author.

Changing work force, acquisitions, mergers fuel growth of Sec. 125 cafeteria plans. (1988, April). *Employee Benefit Plan Review, 10,* 14–17.

Cohen, J. (1970). Approximate power and sample size determinations for common one-sample and two-sample hypothesis tests. *Educational and Psychological Measurement, 30,* 811–831.

Cook, T., Campbell, D. T. (1979). *Quasi-experimentation: Design and analysis issues for field settings.* Boston: Houghton Mifflin.

Demographics: Driving force behind flexible plans. (1989, April). *Employee Benefit Plan Review, 10,* 14–16.

Dreher, G. F. (1981). Predicting the salary satisfaction of exempt employees. *Personnel Psychology, 34,* 579–589.

Dreher, G. F., Ash, R. A., Bretz, R. D. (1988). Benefit coverage and employee cost: Critical factors in explaining compensation satisfaction. *Personnel Psychology, 41,* 237–254.

Dunham, R. B., Pierce, J. L. (1986). Attitudes toward work schedules: Construct definition, instrument development, and validation. *Academy of Management Journal, 29,* 170–182.

Dunham, R. B., Smith, F. J., Blackburn, R. S. (1977). Validation of the index of organizational reactions with the JDI, the MSQ, and the faces scales. *Academy of Management Journal, 20,* 420–432.

Employee Benefits Research Institute. (1982). *America in transition: Implications for employee benefits.* Washington, DC: Author.

Haugen, S. E. (1989, August). Employment gains slow in the first half of 1989. *Monthly Labor Review, 112,* 3–9.

Heneman, H. G. III. (1985). Pay satisfaction. In Rowland, K., Ferris, G. (Eds.), *Research in personnel and human resource management: Vol 3.* (pp. 115–139). Greenwich, CT: JAI Press.

Heneman, H. G. III, Schwab, D. P. (1985). Pay satisfaction: Its multidimensional nature and measurement. *International Journal of Psychology, 20,* 129–141.

Huberty, C. J., Morris, J. D. (1989). Multivariate analysis versus multiple univariate analyses. *Psychological Bulletin, 105,* 302–308.

Locke, E. A. (1969). What is job satisfaction? *Organizational Behavior and Human Performance, 4,* 309–336.

Locke, E. A. (1976). The nature and causes of job satisfaction. In Dunnette M.D. (Ed.), *Handbook of industrial and organizational psychology* (pp. 1297–1349). Chicago: Rand McNally.

Miceli, M. P., Lane, M. C. (in press). Antecedents of pay satisfaction: A review and extension. In Rowland, K., Ferris, G. (Eds.), *Research in personnel and human resource management* (Vol. 9). Greenwich, CT: JAI Press.

Milkovich, G., Newman, J. (1990). *Compensation* (3rd ed.). Homewood, IL: Richard D. Irwin.

Motowidlow, S. J. (1983). Predicting sales turnover from pay satisfaction and expectation. *Journal of Applied Psychology, 68,* 484–489.

Rosenbloom, J. S., Hallman, G. V. (1986). *Employee benefit planning* (2nd ed.). Englewood Cliffs, NJ: Prentice-Hall.

Rynes, S. L., Schwab, D. P., Heneman, H. G. III. (1983). The role of pay and market pay variability in job application decisions. *Organizational Behavior and Human Performance, 31,* 353–364.

Scarpello, V., Huber, V., Vandenberg, R. J. (1988). Compensation satisfaction: its measurement and dimensionality. *Journal of Applied Psychology, 73,* 163–171.

Section 125 flexible benefit programs gain both employers' and employees' support. (1988, April). *Employee Benefit Plan Review, 10,* 24–28, 120.

Smith, F. J. (1976). The index of organization reactions (IOR). *JSAS Catalog of Selected Documents in Psychology, 6,* Ms. no. 1265.

Smith, P. C., Kendall, L. M., Hulin, C. L. (1969). *The measurement of satisfaction in work and retirement.* Chicago: Rand McNally.

Weiner, N. (1980). Determinants and behavioral consequences of pay satisfaction: A comparison of two models. *Personnel Psychology, 33,* 741–757.

Weiss, D. J., Dawis, R. V., England, G. W., Loftquist, L. H. (1967). *Manual for the Minnesota Satisfaction Questionnaire.* Minnesota Studies in Vocational Rehabilitation: XXII, Minneapolis, University of Minnesota Industrial Relations Center Work Adjustment Project.

Wilson, M., Northcraft, G. B., Neale, M. A. (1985). The perceived value of fringe benefits. *Personnel Psychology, 38,* 309–320.

APPENDIX

After our original data collection, the benefits subscale of the Pay Satisfaction Questionnaire (PSQ; Heneman & Schwab, 1985) became the focus of substantial research (e.g., Ash & Dreher, 1990; Scarpello, Huber, & Vandenberg, 1988). Therefore, we collected additional data in 1989 to test the convergence of our benefits satisfaction measure with the PSQ subscale. Subjects for this analysis worked in a single office of a large midwestern insurance company. This unit was selected because it represented a cross-section of jobs similar to those held by subjects in the substantive phase of our research. All 165 administrative and professional employees in this office were asked to participate. The voluntary response rate was greater than 90%.

Questionnaires containing all 10 benefit items (six items from our scale, plus the four items from the PSQ benefits subscale) were distributed to participants by the organization's vice president of corporate research via company mail. Confidential responses were returned directly to her and then forwarded to the researchers.

Principal component factor analysis verified the dimensionality of the new scale. As with the posttest sample, this analysis suggested a single-factor solution, in this case explaining 65.3% of the variance. The loading of Item 3, however, was again low. Item 3 was dropped from the scale.

Principal component factor analysis was then used to determine whether the refined five-item benefit satisfaction measure and the PSQ scale tapped a single dimension. This analysis yielded a single factor explaining 68% of the variance. All items loaded strongly on this factor, suggesting that the two sets of items measure the same construct.

The convergence of our five-item benefit satisfaction instrument with the PSQ benefits subscale was further assessed by correlating the two scale scores. The correlation between the two scales was .85, indicating a high degree of convergence. Internal consistency reliability estimates were similar for the two scales. Coefficient alpha for the new five-item scale was .91; for the PSQ subscale, .89.

READING 35

MANAGEMENT WOMEN
AND THE NEW FACTS OF LIFE

Felice N. Schwartz

The cost of employing women in management is greater than the cost of employing men. This is a jarring statement, partly because it is true, but mostly because it is something people are reluctant to talk about. A new study by one multinational corporation shows that the rate of turnover in management positions is 2½ times higher among top-performing women than it is among men. A large producer of consumer goods reports that one half of the women who take maternity leave return to their jobs late or not at all. And we know that women also have a greater tendency to plateau or to interrupt their careers in ways that limit their growth and development. But we have become so sensitive to charges of sexism and so afraid of confrontation, even litigation, that we rarely say what we know to be true. Unfortunately, our bottled-up awareness leaks out in misleading metaphors ("glass ceiling" is one notable example), veiled hostility, lowered expectations, distrust, and reluctant adherence to Equal Employment Opportunity requirements.

Two facts matter to business; only women have babies and only men make rules.

Career interruptions, plateauing, and turnover are expensive. The money corporations invest in recruitment, training, and development is less likely to produce top executives among women than among men, and the invaluable company experience that developing executives acquire at every level as they move up through management ranks is more often lost.

The studies just mentioned are only the first of many, I'm quite sure. Demographic realities are going to force corporations all across the country to analyze the cost of employing women in managerial positions, and what they will discover is that women cost more.

But here is another startling truth: The greater cost of employing women is not a function of inescapable gender differences. Women *are* different from men, but what increases their cost to the corporation is principally the clash of their perceptions, attitudes, and behavior with those of men, which is to say, with the policies and practices of male-led corporations.

It is terribly important that employers draw the right conclusions from the studies now being done. The studies will be useless—or worse, harmful—if all they teach us is that women are expensive to employ. What we need to learn is how to reduce that expense, how to stop throwing away the investments we make in talented women, how to become more responsive to the needs of the women that corporations *must* employ if they are to have the best and the brightest of all those now entering the work force.

The gender differences relevant to business fall into two categories: those related to maternity and those related to the differing traditions and expectations of the sexes. Maternity is biological rather than cultural. We can't alter it, but we can dramatically reduce its impact on the workplace and in many cases eliminate its negative effect on employee development. We can accomplish this by addressing the second set of differences, those between male and female socialization. Today, these differences exaggerate the real costs of maternity and can turn a relatively slight disruption in work schedule into a serious business problem and a career derailment for individual women. If we are to overcome the cost differential between male and female employees, we need to address the issues that arise when female socialization meets the male corporate culture and masculine rules of career development—issues of behavior and style, of expectation, of stereotypes and preconceptions, of sexual tension and harassment, of female mentoring, lateral mobility, relocation, compensation, and early identification of top performers.

The one immutable, enduring difference between men and women is maternity. Maternity is not simply childbirth but a continuum that begins with an awareness of the ticking of the biological clock, proceeds to the anticipation of motherhood, includes pregnancy, childbirth, physical recuperation, psychological adjustment, and continues on to nursing, bonding, and child rearing. Not all women choose to become mothers, of course, and among those who do, the process varies from case to case depending on the health of the mother and baby, the values of the parents, and the availability, cost, and quality of child care.

In past centuries, the biological fact of maternity shaped the traditional roles of the sexes. Women performed the home-centered functions that related to the bearing and nurturing of children. Men did the work that required great physical strength. Over time, however, family size contracted, the community assumed greater responsibility for the care and education of children, packaged foods and household technology reduced the work load in the home, and technology eliminated much of the need for muscle power at the workplace. Today, in the developed world, the only role still uniquely gender related is childbearing. Yet men and women are still socialized to perform their traditional roles.

Men and women may or may not have some innate psychological disposition toward these traditional roles—men to be aggressive, competitive, self-reliant, risk taking; women to be supportive, nurturing, intuitive, sensitive, communicative—but certainly both men and women are capable of the full range of behavior. Indeed, the male and female roles have already begun to expand and merge. In the decades ahead, as the socialization of boys and girls and the experience and expectations of young men and women grow steadily more

Women who compete like men are considered unfeminine. Women who emphasize family are considered uncommitted.

androgynous, the differences in workplace behavior will continue to fade. At the moment, however, we are still plagued by disparities in perception and behavior that make the integration of men and women in the workplace unnecessarily difficult and expensive.

Let me illustrate with a few broadbrush generalizations. Of course, these are only stereotypes, but I think they help to exemplify the kinds of preconceptions that can muddy the corporate waters.

Men continue to perceive women as the rearers of their children, so they find it understandable, indeed appropriate, that women should renounce their careers to raise families. Edmund Pratt, CEO of Pfizer, once asked me in all sincerity, "Why would any woman choose to be a chief financial officer rather than a full-time mother?" By condoning and taking pleasure in women's traditional behavior, men reinforce it. Not only do they see parenting as fundamentally female, they see a career as fundamentally male—either an unbroken series of promotions and advancements toward CEOdom or stagnation and disappointment. This attitude serves to legitimize a woman's choice to extend maternity leave and even, for those who can afford it, to leave employment altogether for several years. By the same token, men who might want to take a leave after the birth of a child know that management will see such behavior as a lack of career commitment, even when company policy permits parental leave for men.

Women also bring counterproductive expectations and perceptions to the workplace. Ironically, although the feminist movement was an expression of women's quest for freedom from their home-based lives, most women were remarkably free already. They had many responsibilities, but they were autonomous and could be entrepreneurial in how and when they carried them out. And once their children grew up and left home, they were essentially free to do what they wanted with their lives. Women's traditional role also included freedom from responsibility for the financial support of their families. Many of us were socialized from girlhood to expect our husbands to take care of us, while our brothers were socialized from an equally early age to complete their educations, pursue careers, climb the ladder of success, and provide dependable financial support for their families. To the extent that this tradition of freedom lingers subliminally, women tend to bring to their employment a sense that they can choose to change jobs or careers at will, take time off, or reduce their hours.

Finally, women's traditional role encouraged particular attention to the quality and substance of what they did, specifically to the physical, psychological, and intellectual development of their children. This traditional focus may explain women's continuing tendency to search for more than monetary reward—intrinsic significance, social importance, meaning—in what they do. This too makes them more likely than men to leave the corporation in search of other values.

The misleading metaphor of the glass ceiling suggests an invisible barrier constructed by corporate leaders to impede the upward mobility of women beyond the middle levels. A more appropriate metaphor, I believe, is the kind of cross-sectional diagram used in geology. The barriers to women's leadership occur when potentially counterproductive layers of influence on women—maternity, tradition, socialization—meet management strata pervaded by the largely unconscious preconceptions, stereotypes, and expectations of men. Such interfaces do not exist for men and tend to be impermeable for women.

One result of these gender differences has been to convince some executives that women are simply not suited to top management. Other executives feel helpless. If they see even a few of their valued female employees fail to return to work from maternity leave on schedule or see one of their most promising women plateau in her career after the birth of a child, they begin to fear there is nothing they can do to infuse women with new energy and enthusiasm and persuade them to stay. At the same time, they know there is nothing they can do to stem the tide of women into management ranks.

With too few men to go around, women have moved from a buyer's to a seller's market.

Another result is to place every working woman on a continuum that runs from total dedication to career at one end to a balance between career and family at the other. What women discover is that the male corporate culture sees both extremes as unacceptable. Women who want the flexibility to balance their families and their careers are not adequately committed to the organization. Women who perform as aggressively and competitively as men are abrasive and unfeminine. But the fact is, business needs all the talented women it can get. Moreover, as I will explain, the women I call career-primary and those I call career-and-family each have particular value to the corporation.

Women in the corporation are about to move from a buyer's to a seller's market. The sudden, startling recognition that 80% of new entrants in the work force over the next decade will be women, minorities, and immigrants has stimulated a mushrooming incentive to "value diversity."

Women are no longer simply an enticing pool of occasional creative talent, a thorn in the side of the EEO officer, or a source of frustration to corporate leaders truly puzzled by the slowness of their upward trickle into executive positions. A real demographic change is taking place. The era of sudden population growth of the 1950s and 1960s is over. The birth rate has dropped about 40%, from a high of 25.3 live births per 1,000 population in 1957, at the peak of the baby boom, to a stable low of a little more than 15 per 1,000 over the last 16 years, and there is no indication of a return to a higher rate. The tidal wave of baby boomers that swelled the recruitment pool to overflowing seems to have been a one-time phenomenon. For 20 years, employers had the pick of a very large crop and were able to choose males almost exclusively for the executive track. But if future population remains fairly stable while the economy continues to expand, and if the new information society simultaneously creates a greater need for creative, educated managers, then the gap between supply and demand will grow dramatically and, with it, the competition for managerial talent.

The decrease in numbers has even greater implications if we look at the traditional source of corporate recruitment for leadership positions—white males from the top 10% of the country's best universities. Over the past decade, the increase in the number of women graduating from leading universities has been much greater than the increase in the total number of graduates, and these women are well represented in the top 10% of their classes.

The trend extends into business and professional programs as well. In the old days, virtually all MBAs were male. I remember addressing a meeting at the Harvard Business School as recently as the mid-1970s and looking out at a sea of exclusively male faces. Today, about 25% of that audience would be women. The pool of male MBAs from which corporations have traditionally drawn their leaders has shrunk significantly.

Of course, this reduction does not have to mean a shortage of talent. The top 10% is at least as smart as it always was—smarter, probably, since it's now drawn from a broader segment of the population. But it now consists increasingly of women. Companies that are determined to recruit the same number of men as before will have to dig much deeper into the male pool, while their competitors will have the opportunity to pick the best people from both the male and female graduates.

Under these circumstances, there is no question that the management ranks of business will include increasing numbers of women. There remains, however, the question of how these women will succeed—how long they will stay, how high they will climb, how completely they will fulfill their promise and potential, and what kind of return the corporation will realize on its investment in their training and development.

There is ample business reason for finding ways to make sure that as many of these women as possible will succeed. The first step in this process is to recognize that women are not all alike. Like men, they are individuals with differing talents, priorities, and motivations. For the sake of simplicity, let me focus on the two women I referred to earlier, on what I call the career-primary woman and the career-and-family woman.

Like many men, some women put their careers first. They are ready to make the same trade-offs traditionally made by the men who seek leadership positions. They make a career decision to put in extra hours, to make sacrifices in their personal lives, to make the most of every opportunity for professional development. For women, of course, this decision also requires that they remain single or at least childless or, if they do have children, that they be satisfied to have others raise them. Some 90% of executive men but only 35% of executive women have children by the age of 40. The *automatic* association of all women with babies is clearly unjustified.

The secret to dealing with such women is to recognize them early, accept them, and clear artificial barriers from their path to the top. After all, the best of these women are among the best managerial talent you will ever see. And career-primary women have another important value to the company that men and other women lack. They can act as role models and mentors to younger women who put their careers first. Since upwardly mobile career-primary women still have few role models to motivate and inspire them, a company with women in its top echelon has a significant advantage in the competition for executive talent.

Men at the top of the organization—most of them over 55, with wives who tend to be traditional—often find career women "masculine" and difficult to accept as colleagues. Such men miss the point, which is not that these women are just like men but that they are just like the *best* men in the organization. And there is such a shortage of the best people that gender cannot be allowed to matter. It is clearly counterproductive to disparage in a woman with executive talent the very qualities that are most critical to the business and that might carry a man to the CEO's office.

Clearing a path to the top for career-primary women has four requirements:

1. Identify them early.
2. Give them the same opportunity you give to talented men to grow and develop and contribute to company profitability. Give them client and customer responsibility. Expect them to travel and relocate, to make the same commitment to the company as men aspiring to leadership positions.
3. Accept them as valued members of your management team. Include them in every kind of communication. Listen to them.
4. Recognize that the business environment is more difficult and stressful for them than for their male peers. They are always a minority, often the only woman. The male perception of talented, ambitious women is at best ambivalent, a mixture of admiration, resentment, confusion, competitiveness, attraction, skepticism, anxiety, pride, and animosity. Women can never feel secure about how they should dress and act, whether they should speak out or grin and bear it when they encounter discrimination, stereotyping, sexual harassment, and paternalism. Social interaction and travel with male colleagues and with male clients can be charged. As they move up, the normal increase in pressure and responsibility is compounded for women because they are women.

Stereotypical language and sexist day-to-day behavior do take their toll on women's career development. Few male executives realize how common it is to call women by their first names while men in the same group are greeted with surnames, how frequently female executives are assumed by men to be secretaries, how often women are excluded from all-male social events where business is being transacted. With notable exceptions, men are still generally more comfortable with other men, and as a result women miss many of the career and business opportunities that arise over lunch, on the golf course, or in the locker room.

The majority of women, however, are what I call career-and-family women, women who want to pursue serious careers while participating actively in the rearing of children. These women are a precious resource that has yet to be mined. Many of them are talented and creative. Most of them are willing to trade some career growth and compensation for freedom from the constant pressure to work long hours and weekends.

Most companies today are ambivalent at best about the career-and-family women in their management ranks. They would prefer that all employees were willing to give their all to the company. They believe it is in their best interests for all managers to compete for the top positions so the company will have the largest possible pool from which to draw its leaders.

A policy that forces women to choose between family and career cuts hugely into profits and competitive advantage.

"If you have both talent and motivation," many employers seem to say, "we want to move you up. If you haven't got that motivation, if you want less pressure and greater flexibility, then you can leave and make room for a new generation." These companies lose on two counts. First, they fail to amortize the investment they made in the early training and experience of management women who find themselves committed to family as well as to career. Second, they fail to recognize what these women could do for their middle management.

The ranks of middle managers are filled with people on their way up and people who have stalled. Many of them have simply reached their limits, achieved career growth commensurate with or exceeding their capabilities, and they cause problems because their performance is mediocre but they still want to move ahead. The career-and-family woman is willing to trade off the pressures and demands that go with promotion for the freedom to spend more time with her children. She's very smart, she's talented, she's committed to her career, and she's satisfied to stay at the middle level, at least during the early child-rearing years. Compare her with some of the people you have there now.

Consider a typical example, a woman who decides in college on a business career and enters management at age 22. For nine years, the company invests in her career as she gains experience and skills and steadily improves her performance. But at 31, just as the investment begins to pay off in earnest, she decides to have a baby. Can the company afford to let her go home, take another job, or go into business for herself? The common perception now is yes, the corporation can afford to lose her unless, after six or eight weeks or even three months of disability and maternity leave, she returns to work on a full-time schedule with the same vigor, commitment, and ambition that she showed before.

But what if she doesn't? What if she wants or needs to go on leave for six months or a year or, heaven forbid, five years? In this worst-case scenario, she works full-time from age 22 to 31 and from 36 to 65—a total of 38 years as opposed to the typical male's 43 years. That's not a huge difference. Moreover, my typical example is willing to work part-time while her children are young, if only her employer will give her the opportunity. There are two rewards for companies responsive to this need: higher retention of their best people and greatly improved performance and satisfaction in their middle management.

The high-performing career-and-family woman can be a major player in your company. She can give you a significant business advantage as the competition for able people escalates. Sometimes too, if you can hold on to her, she will switch gears in mid-life and re-enter the competition for the top. The price you must pay to retain these women is threefold: you must plan for and manage maternity, you must provide the flexibility that will allow them to be maximally productive, and you must take an active role in helping to make family supports and high-quality, affordable child care available to all women.

The key to managing maternity is to recognize the value of high-performing women and the urgent need to retain them and keep them productive. The first step must be a genuine partnership between the woman and her boss. I know this partnership can seem difficult to forge. One of my own senior executives came to me recently to discuss plans for her maternity leave and subsequent return to work. She knew she wanted to come back. I wanted to make certain that she would. Still, we had a somewhat awkward conversation, because I knew that no woman can predict with certainty when she will be able to return to work or under what conditions. Physical problems can lengthen her leave. So can a demanding infant, a difficult family or personal adjustment, or problems with child care.

I still don't know when this valuable executive will be back on the job full-time, and her absence creates some genuine problems for our organization. But I do know that I can't simply replace her years of experience with a new recruit. Since our conversation, I also know that she wants to come back, and that she *will* come back—part-time at first—unless I make it impossible for her by, for example, setting an arbitrary date for her full-time return or resignation. In turn, she knows that the organization wants and needs her and, more to the point, that it will be responsive to her needs in terms of working hours and child-care arrangements.

In having this kind of conversation it's important to ask concrete questions that will help to move the discussion from uncertainty and anxiety to some level of predictability. Questions can touch on everything from family income and energy level to child care arrangements and career commitment. Of course you want your star manager to return to work as soon as possible, but you want her to return permanently and productively. Her downtime on the job is a drain on her energies and a waste of your money.

For all the women who want to combine career and family—the women who want to participate actively in the rearing of their children and who also want to pursue their careers seriously—the key to retention is to provide the flexibility and family supports they need in order to function effectively.

Time spent in the office increases productivity if it is time well spent, but the fact that most women continue to take the primary responsibility for child care is a cause of distraction, diversion, anxiety, and absenteeism—to say nothing of the persistent guilt experienced by all working mothers. A great many women, perhaps most of all women who have always performed at the highest levels, are also frustrated by a sense that while their children are babies they cannot function at their best either at home or at work.

In its simplest form, flexibility is the freedom to take time off—a couple of hours, a day, a week—or to do some work at home and some at the office, an arrangement that communication technology makes increasingly feasible. At the complex end of the spectrum are alternative work schedules that permit the woman to work less than full-time and her employer to reap the benefits of her experience and, with careful planning, the top level of her abilities.

Part-time employment is the single greatest inducement to getting women back on the job expeditiously and the provision women themselves most desire. A part-time return to work enables them to maintain responsibility for critical aspects of their jobs, keeps them in touch with the changes constantly occurring at the workplace and in the job itself, reduces stress and fatigue, often eliminates the need for paid maternity leave by permitting a return to the office as soon as disability leave is over, and, not least, can greatly enhance company loyalty. The part-time solution works particularly well when a work load can be reduced for one individual in a department or when a full-time job can be broken down by skill levels and apportioned to two individuals at different levels of skill and pay.

I believe, however, that shared employment is the most promising and will be the most widespread form of flexible scheduling in the future. It is feasible at every level of the corporation except at the pinnacle, for both the short and the long term. It involves two people taking responsibility for one job.

Two red lights flash on as soon as most executives hear the words "job sharing": continuity and client-customer contact. The answer to the continuity question is to place responsibility entirely on the two individuals sharing the job to discuss everything that transpires—thoroughly, daily, and on their own time. The answer to the problem of client-customer contact is yes, job sharing requires re-education and a period of adjustment. But as both client and supervisor will quickly come to appreciate, two contacts means that the customer has continuous access to the company's representative, without interruptions for vacation, travel, or sick leave. The two people holding the job can simply cover for each other, and the uninterrupted, full-time coverage they provide together can be a stipulation of their arrangement.

Flexibility is costly in numerous ways. It requires more supervisory time to coordinate and manage, more office space, and somewhat greater benefits costs (though these can be contained with flexible benefits plans, prorated benefits, and, in two-paycheck families, elimination of duplicate benefits). But the advantages of reduced turnover and the greater productivity that results from higher energy levels and greater focus can outweigh the costs.

A few hints:

- Provide flexibility selectively. I'm not suggesting private arrangements subject to the suspicion of favoritism but rather a policy that makes flexible work schedules available only to high performers.

- Make it clear that in most instances (but not all) the rates of advancement and pay will be appropriately lower for those who take time off or who work part-time than for those who work full-time. Most career-and-family women are entirely willing to make that trade-off.

- Discuss costs as well as benefits. Be willing to risk accusations of bias. Insist, for example, that half time is half of whatever time it takes to do the job, not merely half of 35 or 40 hours.

The woman who is eager to get home to her child has a powerful incentive to use her time effectively at the office and to carry with her reading and other work that can be done at home. The talented professional who wants to have it all can be a high performer by carefully ordering her priorities and by focusing on objectives rather than on the legendary 15-hour day. By the time professional women have their first babies—at an average age of 31—they have already had nine years to work long hours at a desk, to travel, and to relocate. In the case of high performers, the need for flexibility coincides with what has gradually become the goal-oriented nature of responsibility.

Family supports—in addition to maternity leave and flexibility—include the provision of parental leave for men, support for two-career and single-parent families during relocation, and flexible benefits. But the primary ingredient is child care. The capacity of working mothers to function effectively and without interruption depends on the availability of good, affordable child care. Now that women make up almost half the work force and the growing percentage of managers, the decision to become involved in the personal lives of employees is no longer a philosophical question but a practical one. To make matters worse, the quality of child care has almost no relation to technology, inventiveness, or profitability but is more or less a pure function of the quality of child care personnel and the ratio of adults to children. These costs are irreducible. Only by joining hands with government and the public sector can corporations hope to create the vast quantity and variety of child care that their employees need.

Until quite recently, the response of corporations to women has been largely symbolic and cosmetic, motivated in large part by the will to avoid litigation and legal penalties. In some cases, companies were also moved by a genuine sense of fairness and a vague discomfort and frustration at the absence of women above the middle of the corporate pyramid. The actions they took were mostly quick, easy, and highly visible—child care information services, a three-month parental leave available to men as well as women, a woman appointed to the board of directors.

Incredibly, very few companies have ever studied the costs and statistics of maternity leave.

When I first began to discuss these issues 26 years ago, I was sometimes able to get an appointment with the assistant to the assistant in personnel, but it was only a courtesy. Over the past decade, I have met with the CEOs of many large corporations, and I've watched them become involved with ideas they had never previously thought much about. Until recently, however, the shelf life of that enhanced awareness was always short. Given pressing, short-term concerns, women were not a front-burner issue. In the past few months, I have seen yet another change. Some CEOs and top management groups now take the initiative. They call and ask us to show them how to shift gears from a responsive to a proactive approach to recruiting, developing, and retaining women.

I think this change is more probably a response to business needs—to concern for the quality of future profits and managerial talent—than to uneasiness about legal requirements, sympathy with the demands of women and minorities, or the desire to do what is right and fair. The nature of such business motivation varies. Some companies want to move women to higher positions as role models for those below them and as beacons for talented young recruits. Some want to achieve a favorable image with employees, customers, clients, and stockholders. These are all legitimate motives. But I think the companies that stand to gain most are motivated as well by a desire to capture competitive advantage in an era when talent and competence will be in increasingly short supply. These companies are now ready to stop being defensive about their experience with women and to ask incisive questions without preconceptions.

Even so, incredibly, I don't know of more than one or two companies that have looked into their own records to study the absolutely critical issue of maternity leave—how many women took it, when and whether they returned, and how this behavior correlated with their rank, tenure, age, and performance. The unique drawback to the employment of women is the physical reality of maternity and the particular socializing influence maternity has had. Yet to make women equal to men in the workplace we have chosen on the whole not to discuss this single most significant difference between them. Unless we do, we cannot evaluate the cost of recruiting, developing, and moving women up.

Now that interest is replacing indifference, there are four steps every company can take to examine its own experience with women:

Wouldn't we all be better off with men in the office and women in the home? The answer is emphatically no.

1. Gather quantitative data on the company's experience with management-level women regarding turnover rates, occurrence of and return from maternity leave, and organizational level attained in relation to tenure and performance.

2. Correlate this data with factors such as age, marital status, and presence and age of children, and attempt to identify and analyze why women respond the way they do.

3. Gather qualitative data on the experience of women in your company and on how women are perceived by both sexes.

4. Conduct a cost-benefit analysis of the return on your investment in high-performing women. Factor in the cost to the company of women's negative reactions to negative experience, as well as the probable cost of corrective measures and policies. If women's value to your company is greater than the cost to recruit, train, and develop them—and of course I believe it will be—then you will want to do everything you can to retain them.

We have come a tremendous distance since the days when the prevailing male wisdom saw women as lacking the kind of intelligence that would allow them to succeed in business. For decades, even women themselves have harbored an unspoken belief that they couldn't make it because they couldn't be just like men, and nothing else would do. But now that women have shown themselves the equal of men in every area of organizational activity, now that they have demonstrated that they can be stars in every field of endeavor, now we can all venture to examine the fact that women and men are different.

On balance, employing women is more costly than employing men. Women can acknowledge this fact today because they know that their value to employers exceeds the additional cost and because they know that changing attitudes can reduce the additional cost dramatically. Women in management are no longer an idiosyncrasy of the arts and education. They have always matched men in natural ability. Within a very few years, they will equal men in numbers as well in every area of economic activity.

The demographic motivation to recruit and develop women is compelling. But an older question remains: Is society better for the change? Women's exit from the home and entry into the work force has certainly created problems—an urgent need for good, affordable child care; troubling questions about the kind of parenting children need; the costs and difficulties of diversity in the workplace; the stress and fatigue of combining work and family responsibilities. Wouldn't we all be happier if we could turn back the clock to an age when men were in the workplace and women in the home, when male and female roles were clearly differentiated and complementary?

Nostalgia, anxiety, and discouragement will urge many to say yes, but my answer is emphatically no. Two fundamental benefits that were unattainable in the past are now within our reach. For the individual, freedom of choice—in this case the freedom to choose career, family, or a combination of the two. For the corporation, access to the most gifted individuals in the country. These benefits are neither self-indulgent nor insubstantial. Freedom of choice and self-realization are too deeply American to be cast aside for some wistful vision of the past. And access to our most talented human resources is not a luxury in this age of explosive international competition but rather the barest minimum that prudence and national self-preservation require.

PART VI

SPECIAL TOPICS IN HUMAN RESOURCE MANAGEMENT

LABOR AND MANAGEMENT RELATIONS

INTRODUCTION

Although the percentage of employees represented by unions, 16 percent of all employees and 12 percent of private sector employees, is at a 30-year low, unions continue to exert an important influence in the U.S. economy, in part because of their continued influence in key industries (e.g., automobiles). The readings in this section describe the evidence of union influence on productivity, profits, and employee rights. In addition, they provide insight into how union-management relations can be structured to more effectively help both parties achieve their goals.

In "A New Portrait of U.S. Unionism," Freeman and Medoff describe "the two faces of trade unionism." The monopoly face describes unions as having a detrimental effect on economic efficiency, making the distribution of national income more unequal and contributing to discrimination, corruption, and narrow political interests. In contrast, the collective voice/institutional response face paints a much more positive picture, with trade unions seen as increasing economic efficiency, contributing to a more equal distribution of income, and providing for industrial democracy by representing workers' interests.

Paul S. Adler's article provides an in-depth examination of the successful turnaround at an automotive plant in Fremont, California. The plant went from being a General Motors plant to being a joint venture between General Motors and Toyota, called New United Motor Manufacturing Inc. (NUMMI). General Motors was to be responsible for marketing and sales, while Toyota would be in charge of product design, engineering, and daily operations (including human resource management). Before the changeover in management, GM-Fremont had been described as "the worst plant in the world," with productivity, quality, and labor relations being among the worst in all of GM. After the changeover, however, it became the best GM plant in terms of both quality and productivity, and labor relations was markedly improved. Although there were probably multiple reasons for the dramatic turnaround, one critical element, according to Adler, was the change in how management approached its relationship with its employees. Management has sought to build an atmosphere of trust and common purpose and to communicate that the company is the property of both management and employees. Perhaps most important, management has not only given employees the responsibility for plant success, it has also empowered them to make suggestions for improvement and solve problems to improve plant performance. Management's role has changed from directing and supervising to coaching and providing expertise.

READING 36

A NEW PORTRAIT OF U.S. UNIONISM

*R. B. Freeman
and J. L. Medoff*

Trade unions are the principal institution of workers in modern capitalistic societies. For over 200 years, since the days of Adam Smith, economists and other social scientists, labor unionists, and businessmen and women have debated the social effects of unionism. Despite the long debate, however, no agreed-upon answer has emerged to the question: What do unions do?

On the one side, many economists view unions largely as monopolies in the labor market whose primary economic impact is to raise members' wages at the expense of unorganized labor and of the efficient functioning of the economy. These analysts stress the adverse effects of union work rules on productivity, the loss of employment in the organized sector due to union wage effects, and the consequent crowding of the nonunion sector with displaced workers. Consistent with this view, managers frequently complain about inflexible operations and work disruptions due to unions, while many social critics paint unions as socially unresponsive, elitist, non-democratic, and crime-riddled institutions.[1]

On the other side are those who believe unions have beneficial economic and political effects. Industrial relations experts have long stressed the ways in which collective bargaining can induce better management and higher productivity. These specialists note that unions can increase the development and retention of skills, provide information about what occurs on the shop floor, improve morale, and pressure management to be more efficient in its operations.[2] Unionists point out that in addition to increasing wages, unions provide workers both with protection against arbitrary management decisions and with a voice at the work place and in the political arena. Even the managements of some organized companies have cited positive impacts of unions on their business. Consider, for example, this statement by Thomas Murphy, then Chairman of General Motors, on the fiftieth anniversary of the "Battle of the Running Bulls," one of the turning points in the struggle to organize the company by the United Auto Workers:

Source: R. B. Freeman and J. L. Medoff, "A New Portrait of U.S. Unionism," *What Do Unions Do?* (New York: Basic Books, 1984). Based on R. B. Freeman and J. L. Medoff, "The Two Faces of Unionism," *The Public Interest*, vol. 57, 1–25.

> The UAW may have introduced the sit-down strike to America, but in its relationship with GM management it has also helped introduce . . . mutually beneficial cooperation. . . . What comes to my mind is the progress we have made, by working together, in such directions as providing greater safety and health protection, in decreasing alcoholism and drug addiction, in improving the quality of work life.[3]

During the past twenty-five years, however, the negative view of trade unions has become increasingly dominant. While there are notable exceptions, many on both the right and left now doubt the social relevance and value of America's organized labor movement.[4] The widespread, one might say textbook, picture of U.S. unions today is of institutions adept at advancing their own interests at the public's expense. Economists concerned with quantifying the economic effects of collective bargaining have focused almost exclusively on the monopoly wage impact of unions, developing a large and valuable literature on the differences in wages paid to organized and unorganized labor.[5] Because monopolistic wage increases are socially harmful—in that they can be expected to induce both inefficiency and inequality—most economic studies, implicitly or explicitly, have judged unions as being a negative force in society.

When the research for this book was begun ten years ago, there was very little quantitative evidence concerning the impact of U.S. unionism on outcomes other than wages. Whereas adherents to the monopoly view of unions could cite numerous quantitative studies of union wage effects, those stressing the nonwage impact of unions were limited to citing specific cases and personal observation.

It was this shortage of statistical evidence concerning what unions do beyond raising wages that set the stage for our research. The recent availability of computerized data files, which contain vast amounts of information on thousands of individuals, establishments, and companies, offers the opportunity for quantitative analyses of many of the nonwage effects of trade unions to parallel the analyses of the wage effects of unions, and thus for broadening the forum of the debate on unionism. Our quantitative analyses of those of our colleagues elsewhere in the social sciences have, indeed, yielded new findings that, taken in conjunction with case-study evidence and the observations of industrial relations experts, provide a new picture of the impact of unions on the economy and on the broader society.[6]

This newly emergent picture of what unions do has important implications for the assessment of unions by labor and management and by the general public. The average unionized worker will see that unions generally "deliver the goods," by providing higher wages and benefits as well as a voice at the bargaining table and on the shop floor, but that some of "the goods" have a social cost. Many nonunion workers will recognize that, because of the threat of unionization, their wages and working conditions are better than they might have been, although generally not as good as they would be under collective bargaining, while others will find that their economic position is worse as a result of unionism. Employers of unionized workers will see that while unionism is associated with a lower rate of return on capital and less managerial flexibility, the extent to which a union is a liability or an asset depends crucially on how management responds to it. Nonunion employers will learn that while the benefits of being union-free generally exceed the costs of union avoidance, the former are often overstated and the latter are often understated. Finally, the general public will see that in the economic sphere, unions reduce wage inequality, increase industrial democracy, and often raise productivity, while in the political sphere, unions are an important voice for some of our society's weakest and most vulnerable groups, as well as for their own members.

THE "TWO FACES" DEBATE

The meaning of the results of our study of U.S. trade unionism can best be understood by recognizing that unions have two faces, each of which leads to a different view of the institution: a *monopoly* face, associated with their monopolistic power to raise wages; and a *collective voice/institutional response* face, associated with their representation of organized workers within enterprises.

The Monopoly Face

Most, if not all, unions have monopoly power, which they can use to raise wages above competitive levels. Assuming that the competitive system works perfectly, these wage increases have harmful economic effects, reducing the national output and distorting the distribution of income. The analysis of unions as monopolies focuses on the magnitude of the union markup of wages and traces the ways in which this markup causes firms to lower employment and output, thereby harming economic efficiency and altering the distribution of income.

Despite the attention economists give to the monopoly face of unionism, analysis of union monopoly behavior is much less fully developed than is the analysis of monopolistic enterprises. The principal reason is that unions are not the simple monopolies of economics textbooks but rather collective organizations of workers with diverse interests. Unlike the monopoly firm that sets prices to maximize profits, unions rarely set wages; they bargain over wages with employers. Unless one believes that the process of collective bargaining is a sham, the wages obtained by unions must be viewed as the joint responsibility of management and labor: the stronger management resistance to union wage goals is, the smaller union wage gains will be. Moreover, unions' ability to raise wages is limited by the fact that, all else the same, higher union wages will induce employers to reduce employment. Some members gain when wages are very high; others lose. Despite decades in which unions have been part of the economic scene, economists lack an accepted maximizing theory of union behavior that would predict the results of bargaining within the union over wage goals. Under some circumstances a union may seek a high wage at the cost of employment; under others, it may be more moderate in its wage demands to preserve jobs. This union concern is quite distinct from the worries of a monopolist, whose sole goal is to maximize profits, regardless of what happens to the number of units sold.[7]

Analysis of the monopoly face of unionism must confront the important issue of the source of union monopoly power. If unions operated in perfectly competitive markets, and if *all* they did were to raise wages above competitive levels, unions would have a very difficult time surviving, for organized firms would necessarily have higher costs of production than other firms. One way unions could survive in such markets would be by organizing the entire industry or sector. If production costs are higher for all establishments in a sector, output and employment will be lower than they would be in the absence of unionism, but the sector will survive. Alternatively, if unions operate in markets where firms have different cost structures (for reasons unassociated with unionism), unions could survive by organizing firms with the lowest costs of production, raising wages at the expense of above-normal profits or "rent."[8] Perhaps most importantly, union monopoly power is likely to be closely related to the market power of the sector it organizes. When unions organize noncompetitive firms, they are able to raise wages without endangering the life of the firm. In sum, from the monopoly perspective, unions are likely to exist in industries where new firms have difficulty entering and/or where some enterprises have cost advantages over their competitors.

The fact that union monopoly power is likely to be important only when unionized firms either completely dominate a market or operate in a non-competitive market has created an interesting, intellectual anomaly. Some economists of a strong free-enterprise bent, who one might expect to be strongly opposed to unions, are in fact rather indifferent. They believe that markets are competitive enough to give unions little or no power to extract monopoly wage gains.

The Collective Voice/Institutional Response Face

As Hirschman pointed out in his important book *Exit, Voice, and Loyalty*, societies have two basic mechanisms for dealing with social or economic problems.[9] The first is the classic market mechanism of exit-and-entry, in which individuals respond to a divergence between desired and actual social conditions by exercising freedom of choice or mobility: the dissatisfied consumer switches products; the diner whose soup is too salty seeks another restaurant; the unhappy couple divorces. In the labor market, exit is synonymous with quitting, while entry consists of new hires by the firm. By leaving less desirable for more desirable jobs, or by refusing bad jobs, individuals penalize the bad employer and reward the good, leading to an overall improvement in the efficiency of the economic system. The basic theorem of neoclassical economics is that, under well-specified conditions, the exit and entry of persons (the hallmark of the free-market system) produces a situation in which no individual can be made better off without making someone worse off. Much economic analysis can be viewed as a detailed study of the implications of this kind of adjustment and of the extent to which it works out in real economies. As long as the exit-entry market mechanism is viewed as the *only* adjustment mechanism, institutions like unions are invariably seen as impediments to the optimal operation of the economy.

The second mode of adjustment is the political mechanism that Hirschman termed "voice." "Voice" refers to the use of direct communication to bring actual and desired conditions closer together. It means talking about problems: complaining to the store about a poor product rather than taking business elsewhere; telling the chef that the soup had too much salt; discussing marital problems rather than going directly to the divorce court. In a political context, "voice" refers to participation in the democratic process, through voting, discussion, bargaining, and the like.

The distinction between the two mechanisms is best illustrated by a specific situation—for instance, concern about the quality of schools in a given locality. The exit solution to poor schools would be to move to a different community or to enroll one's children in a private school, thereby "taking one's business elsewhere." The voice solution would involve political action to improve the school system through schoolboard elections, Parent Teacher Association meetings, and other channels of communication.

In the job market, voice means discussing with an employer conditions that ought to be changed, rather than quitting the job. In modern industrial economies, and particularly in large enterprises, a trade union is the vehicle for collective voice—that is, for providing workers as a group with a means of communicating with management.

Collective rather than individual bargaining with an employer is necessary for effective voice at the workplace for two reasons. First, many important aspects of an industrial setting are "public goods," that is, goods which will affect the well-being (negatively or positively) of every employee in such a way that one individual's partaking of the good does not preclude someone else from doing so. Safety conditions, lighting, heating, the speed of the production line, the firm's formal grievance procedure, pension plan, and policies on matters such as lay-offs, work-sharing, cyclical wage adjustment, and promotion all obviously affect the entire workforce in the same way that defense, sanitation, and fire protection affect the community at large. One of the most important economic theorems is that competitive markets will not provide enough of such goods; some form of collective decision making is needed. Without a collective organization, the incentive for the individual to take into account the effects of his or her actions on others, or to express his or her preferences, or to invest time and money in changing conditions, is likely to be too small to spur action. Why not "let Harry do it" and enjoy the benefits at no cost? This classic "free-rider" problem lies at the heart of the so-called "union-security" versus "right-to-work" debate.

A second reason why collective action is necessary is that workers who are tied to a firm are unlikely to reveal their true preferences to an employer, for fear the employer may fire them. In a world in which workers could find employment at the same wages immediately, the market would offer adequate protection for the individual, but that is not the world we live in. The danger of job loss makes expression of voice by an individual risky. Collective voice, by contrast, is protected both by the support of all workers and by the country's labor law: "It shall be an unfair labor practice for an employer by discrimination in regard to hire or tenure or employment or any term or condition of employment to encourage or discourage membership in any labor organization" (National Labor Relations Act, Section 7a of the 1935 law). Court interpretation of U.S. labor law makes a sharp distinction between collective and individual actions at the workplace: even nonunion workers acting in a concerted fashion are protected from managerial retaliation.[10] However, the nonunion protester acting alone and not seeking a union is "terminable at will" and must speak very carefully.

The collective nature of trade unionism fundamentally alters the operation of a labor market and, hence, the nature of the labor contract. In a nonunion setting, where exit-and-entry is the predominant form of adjustment, the signals and incentives to firms depend on the preferences of the "marginal" worker, the one who might leave because of (or be attracted by) small changes in the conditions of employment. The firm responds primarily to the needs of this marginal worker, who is generally young and marketable; the firm can to a considerable extent ignore the preferences of typically older, less marketable workers, who—for reasons of skill, knowledge, rights that cannot be readily transferred to other enterprises, as well as because of other costs associated with changing firms—are effectively immobile. In a unionized setting, by contrast, the union takes account of *all* workers in determining its demands at the bargaining table, so that the desires of workers who are highly unlikely to leave the enterprise are also represented. With respect to public goods at the workplace, the union can add up members' preferences in much the same manner as a government can add up voters' preferences for defense, police protection, and the like to determine social demand for them. In sum, because unions are political institutions with elected leaders, they are likely to respond to a different set of preferences from those that prevail in a competitive labor market.

In a modern economy, where workers tend to be attached to firms for many years, younger and older workers are likely to have different preferences (for instance, regarding pension or health insurance plans versus take-home pay, or layoffs ordered inversely to seniority versus cuts in wage growth or work sharing). The change from an approach that focuses only on workers at the coming-or-going margin to one that considers all employees is likely to lead to a very different labor contract. Under some conditions, the union contract—by taking account of all workers and by appropriately considering the sum of preferences for work conditions that are common to all workers—can be economically more efficient than the contract that would result in the absence of unions.

Finally, as a collective voice unions also fundamentally alter the social relations of the workplace. The essence of the employment relationship under capitalism—as stressed by such diverse analysts as Karl Marx, Herbert Simon, and Ronald Coase—is the payment of money by the employer to the employee in return for the employer's control over a certain amount of the employee's time. The employer seeks to use his employee's time in a way that maximizes the profitability of the enterprise. Even in the case of piece rates, employers monitor employee activity to assure the quality of output, prevent the wastage of materials, and protect the stock of capital. As a result, the way in which the time purchased is utilized must be determined by some interaction between workers and their employer. In the absence of unionism, the worker has limited responses to orders that he feels are unfair: the worker can quit, or he can perhaps engage in quiet sabotage or shirking, neither of which is likely to alter the employer's actions. In the union setting, by contrast, the union constitutes a source of worker power, diluting managerial authority and offering members protection through both the "industrial jurisprudence" system, under which many workplace decisions are based on rules (such as seniority) instead of supervisory judgment or whim, and the grievance and arbitration system, under which disputes over proper managerial decision making on work issues can be resolved. As a result, management power within enterprises is curtailed by unionism, so that workers' rights are likely to be better enforced. Consider, for example, a firm that decides to fire senior workers immediately before they become eligible for pension rights. In the nonunion setting, a firm may be able to get away with such a maneuver; in the union setting, it is unlikely to have such power. Economic theorists of all persuasions have increasingly recognized that unions' ability to enforce labor agreements, particularly those with deferred claims, creates the possibility for improved labor contracts and arrangements and higher economic efficiency.[11]

MANAGEMENT'S ROLE IN WHAT UNIONS DO

The two views of unionism lead to fundamentally different analyses of what management does in response to the existence of a union. In the most basic monopoly analysis, in which unions can simply raise wages, management's responses are limited. It can reduce employment, substitute capital for labor, or hire more skilled workers to raise labor's productivity. Since management is assumed to be doing everything just right in the absence of unions, these adjustments are socially harmful.

By contrast, the voice/response face directs attention to the possibility that, because of incomplete information, lack of coordination in an enterprise, and organizational slack, management can respond to unionism in more creative ways, which may be socially beneficial. This view is consistent with modern theories of the firm, in which management is taken to be not a simple all-knowing profit-maximizer, but rather a mediator of the interests of relatively permanent employees, stockholders, and consumers.[12] The greater the imperfection of markets, and the further real-world management is from a computer programmed by the Invisible Hand, the greater are the possibilities for management's response to unions to improve the operation of the economy, and thus the greater the validity of voice/response insights into what unions (and unionized managements) do.

If management uses the collective bargaining process to learn about and improve the operation of the workplace and the production process, unionism can be a significant plus to enterprise efficiency. On the other hand, if management responds negatively to collective bargaining (or is prevented by unions from reacting positively), unionism can significantly harm the performance of the firm. If management acquiesces to exorbitant union wage demands, the organized sector may suffer serious economic decline. If it reaches sensible agreements with labor, all parties may benefit. At the worst, if management cooperates with racketeers who suppress union democracy and offer "sweetheart" contracts, the organized sector will be a sorry place indeed.[13] The important point is that just as there are two sides to all markets, demand and supply, there are also two sides to all collective bargaining arrangements, management and unions. Industrial relations practices and economic outcomes depend on the policies and actions of both management and labor. The reader who believes that the industrial relations and personnel policies of management can affect the outcome of the economic system will find our results more believable than the reader who believes that all enterprises are *always* operating with perfect information in a way that makes profits as large as possible.

THE ISSUES IN QUESTION

Table 1–1 provides a capsule summary of the differences in how the monopoly and voice/response faces of unionism affect three major economic outcomes: the level and composition of national output (efficiency); the distribution of income; and the extent of economic equality and political freedom. On each of the issues, the monopoly face implies social losses while the voice/response face offers potential social gains. And on each of the issues, as illustrated in the quotations that follow, there has been considerable debate over which face is dominant.

Efficiency

> . . . their activities necessarily reduce the productivity of labor all around and therefore also the general level of real wages; because, if union action succeeds in reducing the number of workers in the highly-paid jobs and in increasing the number of those who have to stay in the less remunerative ones, the result may be that the over-all average will be lower. It is, in fact, more than likely that, in countries where unions are very strong, the general level of real wages is lower than it would otherwise be. This is certainly true . . . where union policy is strengthened by the general use of restrictive practices of a 'make-work' character.[14]

> . . . a strong union, guided by farseeing men who have a grave sense of responsibility, is found to enable a few minutes' quiet conversation to settle innumerable petty disputes that in old times would have caused much delay and worry and loss of mutual feeling. . . . In such trades we may conclude confidently that Trade Unions on the whole facilitate business.[15]

As monopoly institutions, unions reduce society's output in three ways. First, union-won wage increases cause a misallocation of resources by inducing organized firms to hire fewer workers, to use more capital per worker, and to hire workers of higher quality than is socially optimal. Second, strikes called to force management to accept union demands reduce gross national product. Third, union contract provisions—such as limits on the loads that can be handled by

Table 1-1

THE TWO FACES OF TRADE UNIONISM

	Union Effects on Economic Efficiency	Union Effects on Distributions of Income	Social Nature of Union Organization
Monopoly Face	Unions raise wages above competitive levels, leading to too little labor relative to capital in unionized firms. Union work rules decrease productivity.	Unions increase income inequality by raising the wages of highly skilled workers. Unions create horizontal inequities by creating differentials among comparable workers.	Unions discriminate in rationing positions. Unions (individually or collectively) fight for their own interests in the political arena. Union monopoly power breeds corrupt and nondemocratic elements.
Collective Voice/Institutional Response Face	Unions have some positive effects on productivity—reducing quit rates, inducing management to alter methods of production and adopt more efficient policies, and improving morale and cooperation among workers. Unions collect information about the preferences of all workers, leading the firm to choose a better mix of employee compensation and a better set of personnel policies.	Unions' standard-rate policies reduce inequality among organized workers in a given industry. Union rules limit the scope for arbitrary actions in the promotion, layoff, and recall of individuals. Unionism fundamentally alters the distribution of power between marginal (generally junior) and more permanent (generally senior) employees, causing union firms to select different compensation packages and personnel practices from those of nonunion firms.	Unions are political institutions that represent the will of their members. Unions represent the political interests of lower-income and disadvantaged persons.

Source: Based on R. B. Freeman and J. L. Medoff, "The Two Faces of Unionism," *The Public Interest* 57 (Fall 1979): 75.

workers, restrictions on tasks performed, and featherbedding—lower the productivity of labor and capital.

By contrast, the voice/response face of unionism suggests important ways in which unionism can raise productivity. First of all, voice at a workplace should reduce the rate of quitting. Since lower quit rates imply lower hiring and training costs and less disruption in the functioning of work groups, they should raise productivity. In addition, the likelihood that workers and firms will remain together for long periods of time should increase the incentive for investment in skills specific to an enterprise, which also raises productivity.

The fact that senior workers are likely to be relatively more powerful in unionized firms points to another way in which unions can raise productivity. Under unionism, promotions and other rewards tend to depend less on individual performance and more on length of service. As a result, feelings of rivalry among individuals are likely to be less pronounced in union plants than in nonunion plants, and the amount of informal training and assistance that workers are willing to provide one another is greater. On the other hand, however, a greater reliance on seniority in determining who gets jobs can reduce productivity by placing individuals in jobs for which they are less qualified than other workers. Which of these effects dominates is an empirical question.

Unionism can also improve efficiency by putting pressure on management to tighten job-production standards and accountability in order to preserve profits in the face of higher wages. Because unionized management can be challenged by the union, moreover, it will tend to discard vague paternalistic, authoritarian personnel policies in favor of practices in which explicit rules govern behavior. After making comprehensive case studies of management in over one hundred unionized firms, Slichter, Healy, and Livernash concluded: "The challenge that unions presented to management has, if viewed broadly, created superior and better-balanced management, even though some exceptions must be recognized."[16] Management's ability to do a better job can be greatly helped by the union, which can perform helpful roles, such as explaining changes in day-to-day routine.

Finally, through the voice/response mechanism, the collective bargaining apparatus opens an important communications channel between workers and management, one likely to increase the flow of information between the two and possibly improve the productivity of the enterprise. As Reynolds (Yale) has observed, "Unions can do valuable work by pointing out improvements that perhaps should have been obvious to management but were not, and that, once discovered, can be installed with a net gain to the company as well as the workers."[17] Union impacts on the composition of compensation packages—on the balance between working conditions or fringes and wages, for example—have often been cited as reflecting, at least in part, the greater flow of information about worker desires. If, for a given dollar of labor cost, workers are better off because the division of the dollar between wages, fringes, and work conditions is more nearly optimal, social productivity, broadly defined, is higher as a result of union activity.

Distribution of Income

If unions raise wage rates in a particular occupation or industry, they necessarily make the amount of employment available in the occupation or industry less than it would otherwise be—just as any higher price cuts down the amount purchased. The effect is an increased number of persons seeking other jobs, which forces down wages in other occupations. Since unions have generally been strongest among groups that would have been high-paid anyway, their effect has been to make high-paid workers higher paid at the expense of lower-paid workers. Unions have therefore not only harmed the public at large and workers as a whole by distorting the use of labor; they have also made the incomes of the working class more unequal by reducing the opportunities available to the most disadvantaged workers.[18]

Summing up these diverse consequences of collective bargaining, one can make a strong case that unionism has at any rate not worsened the wage structure. We are inclined to be even more venturesome than this, and to say that its net effect has been beneficial.[19]

One of the most striking implications of the analysis of the monopoly face of unions, greatly stressed by opponents of unionism, is that union wage gains increase inequality in the labor market. According to the monopoly argument, the workers displaced from unionized firms as a result of union wage gains raise the supply of labor to nonunion firms, which can therefore be expected to reduce wages. Thus, unionized workers are likely to be made better off at the expense of nonunion workers. The fact that organized blue-collar workers who are more skilled would be higher paid than other blue-collar workers even in the absence of unionism implies further than unionism benefits "labor's elite" at the expense of those with less skill and earning power. Since many people have supported unions in the belief that they reduce economic inequality, evidence that unions have the opposite effect would be a strong argument against the union movement.

The voice/response face suggests very different effects. Given that union decisions are based on a political process in which the majority rules, and given that the majority of workers are likely to have earnings below average in any workplace, unions can be expected to seek to reduce wage inequality within firms. Furthermore, union members are also likely to favor a less-dispersed distribution of earnings for reasons of ideology and organizational solidarity. Finally, to reduce managerial discretion in the wage-setting process, unions seek equal pay for workers in the same job rather than pay according to the manager's perception of individual merit.

Social Organization

> I do hold that large and powerful labor unions are integral elements in a total institutional complex whose development is everywhere antithetical to economic freedom, to political liberty, and to world peace.[20]

> In the last analysis the major thrust of labor's activities has been to increase the political participation of poorer segments of society and to provide a coordinated and coherent political voice to workers who would otherwise be largely disorganized. Whatever one may think of the political platform that results from this activity, it is hard to deny the value of these endeavors in a democratic society. It is precisely because issues of policy are so often controversial that the nation has based its system of government on the vote of all interested members. Under these circumstances, one can hardly disapprove of the efforts of any organization to broaden the participation of all interested groups in the political process.[21]

The monopoly critique of unions as social organizations is harsh. It holds that much of union monopoly power arises from the coercive and potentially violent acts of union activists to disrupt production through strikes and related activity. Some claim that the essence of union monopoly power is the power of forcefully preventing nonunion workers from obtaining jobs at organized plants and of coercing workers to join in strikes.[22] Monopoly power is also said to foster corruption and undemocratic behavior and to lead to high dues or entry fees, so that the dominant faction in the union reaps the rewards of the union's market power. In addition, it is believed that unions use their control over the supply of labor to extort funds from firms—especially small, weak ones. The archetypical union in this view is a gangster-ridden Teamsters local. In the political sphere, unions reveal their monopoly face through efforts to obtain special-interest legislation that strengthens union power to extract monopoly gains. The prime lobbying activity of unions, often in alliance with business, is to obtain governmental regulations that restrict competition and raise prices and wages for the sector, at the expense of consumers.

The voice/response view is that unions are democratic institutions operating on behalf of their members and that their political activities are part-and-parcel of modern democratic states. Unions are expected to be democratic because they require the approval of a majority of workers, who elect the leadership and determine policy through conventions, referenda, or change of leadership. In the United States, both union constitutions and the law, particularly the Landrum-Griffin Act (1959), require unions to operate under democratic rules. The union is often said to represent its "median" member, since in a political organization the views of the median person will, under some circumstances, dominate. Within the political sphere, unions are viewed as representing the general working population, devoting much political muscle to promoting legislation that would be of no more material gain to unionized workers than to other workers. For instance, organized labor was active in pushing for the passage of the Public Accommodation Act of 1964, the Voting Rights Act of 1965, equal-employment-opportunity legislation, anti-poverty legislation, and the Occupational Safety and Health Act of 1971. It is argued that though unions fight for self-interest legislation—as do other groups in our pluralistic society—they have scored their greatest political victories on more general social legislation and thus are more effective as a voice of the whole working population and the disadvantaged than as a vehicle for increasing the power of a monopoly institution.

The Debate

Social analysts who focus on only one of unionism's two faces have strikingly different pictures of the institution. According to those who see only the monopoly face, unions are desirable impediments to the social good; according to those who see only the voice/response face, unions make many valuable contributions to the functioning of the economy. Those in the first camp hail the decline, from the 1950s through the 1980s, in the percentage of wage and salary workers unionized in the private sector in the United States as a desirable development that will increase productivity and reduce inequality. Those in the second camp view the dwindling of private-sector unionization as an undesirable development with serious negative economic and social consequences.

Since, in fact, unions have both a monopoly and a voice/response face, the key questions for understanding the impact of private-sector unionism in the United States relate to the relative importance of each. Are unions primarily monopolistic institutions, or are they primarily voice institutions that induce socially beneficial responses? What emphasis should be given to these two disparate faces to obtain a realistic portrait of the role trade unionism plays in society?

THE STUDY AND ITS FINDINGS

To answer these questions, we have studied a wide variety of data that distinguish between union and nonunion establishments and between union and nonunion workers, and we have interviewed representatives of management, labor officials, and industrial-relations experts. Although additional study will certainly alter some of the specifics, we believe that the results of our analysis provide a reasonably clear and accurate picture of what unions do—a picture that stands in sharp contrast to the negative view that unions do little more than win monopoly wage gains for their members.

Our most far-reaching conclusion is that, in addition to well-advertised effects on wages, unions alter nearly every other measurable aspect of the operation of workplaces and enterprises, from turnover to productivity to profitability to the composition of pay packages. The behavior of workers and firms and the outcomes of their interactions differ substantially between the organized and unorganized sectors. On balance, unionization appears to improve rather than to harm the social and economic system. In terms of the three outcomes in Table 1–1, our analysis shows that unions are associated with greater efficiency in most settings, reduce overall earnings inequality, and contribute to, rather than detract from, economic and political freedom. This is not to deny the negative monopoly effects of unions. They exist. They are undesirable. But they are not the only ways in which unions affect the society. Our analysis indicates that, in fact, focusing on them leads to an exceedingly inaccurate representation of what unions do. In the United States in the period we have studied, the voice/response face of unions dominates the monopoly face, though we stress that an accurate portrait must show both faces.

Following is a capsule summary of the more specific findings that underlie this broad conclusion:

1. On the wage side, unions have a substantial monopoly wage impact, but there is no single union/nonunion wage differential. The union wage effect is greater for less educated than more educated workers, for younger than for prime-age workers, and for junior than for senior workers, and it is greater in heavily organized industries and in regulated industries than in others. It increased in the 1970s as unionized workers won wage gains exceeding those of their nonunion peers. Most importantly, the social costs of the monopoly wage gains of unionism appear to be relatively modest, on the order of .3 percent of gross national product, or less.

2. In addition to raising wages, unions alter the entire package of compensation, substantially increasing the proportion of compensation allotted to fringe benefits, particularly to deferred benefits such as pensions and life,

accident and health insurance, which are favored by older workers. These changes are, on balance, to be viewed as a social plus.

3. The claim that unions increase wage inequality is not true. It is true that unions raise the wages of organized blue-collar workers relative to the wages of unorganized blue-collar workers, and thus increase that aspect of inequality. But they also raise blue-collar earnings relative to the higher white-collar earnings, thus reducing inequality between those groups. Moreover, by adopting pay policies that limit managerial discretion in wage-setting, they reduce inequality among workers in the same establishments and among different establishments. Quantitatively, the inequality-reducing effects of unionism outweigh the inequality-increasing effects, so that on balance unions are a force for equality in the distribution of wages among individual workers.

4. By providing workers with a voice in determining rules and conditions of work, by instituting grievance and arbitration procedures for appealing supervisors' decisions, and by negotiating seniority clauses desired by workers, unionism greatly reduces the probability that workers will quit their jobs. As a result, unionized work forces are more stable than nonunion workforces paid the same compensation.

5. Unionism alters the way in which firms respond to swings in the economy. In cyclical downturns, unionized firms make more use of temporary layoffs and less use of cuts in wage growth than do nonunion firms, while in cyclical upturns, unionized firms recall relatively more workers and nonunion firms tend to hire new employees. In a decline that threatens the jobs of senior employees, unions negotiate wage and work-rule concessions of substantial magnitudes.

6. Union workplaces operate under rules that are both different from and more explicit than nonunion workplaces. Seniority is more important in union settings, with unionized senior workers obtaining relatively greater protection against job loss and relatively greater chance of promotion than nonunion senior workers. In addition, management in union companies generally operates more "by the book," with less subjectivity and also less flexibility, than does management in nonunion companies, and in more professional, less paternalistic or authoritarian ways.

7. Some nonunion workers, namely those in large nonunion firms that are trying to avoid unions through "positive labor relations," obtain higher wages and better working conditions as a result of the existence of trade unions. The average employed nonunion blue-collar worker may enjoy a slight increase in well-being because the threat of unionism forces his or her firm to offer better wages and work conditions, but the average white-collar worker appears essentially unaffected by the existence of blue-collar unionization. Some workers, however, may suffer from greater joblessness as a result of higher union wages in their city or their industry.

8. Paradoxically, while unionized workers are less willing to leave their employers than nonunion workers, unionized workers often report themselves less satisfied with their jobs than nonunion workers. Unionists are especially dissatisfied with their work conditions and their relations with supervisors. One explanation is that unions galvanize worker discontent in order to make a strong case in negotiations with management. To be effective, voice must be heard.

9. The view of unions as a major deterrent to productivity is erroneous. In many sectors, unionized establishments are more productive than nonunion establishments, while in only a few are they less productive. The higher productivity is due in part to the lower rate of turnover under unionism, improved managerial performance in response to the union challenge, and generally cooperative labor-management relations at the plant level. When labor-management relations are bad, so too is productivity in organized plants.

10. Unionized employers tend to earn a lower rate of return per dollar of capital than do nonunion employers. The return is lower under unionism because the increase in wages and the greater amount of capital used per worker are not compensated for by the higher productivity of labor associated with unionism. The reduction in profitability, however, is centered in highly concentrated and otherwise historically highly profitable sectors of the economy.

11. Unions have had mixed success in the political arena. Legislators representing highly unionized districts or receiving considerable union campaign support tend to support unions' political goals in the Congress, but legislators representing less unionized districts or receiving more support from business and other interest groups often oppose union political goals. In the important area of major labor legislation, bills opposed by unions have been enacted while bills favored by unions have been voted down. In general unions have managed to *preserve* laws augmenting monopoly powers in specific sectors but have not been able to use the law to *expand* their monopoly power. Most union political successes have come in the areas of general labor and social goals that benefit workers as a whole rather than unionists alone.

12. The picture of unions as nondemocratic institutions run by corrupt labor bosses is a myth. Most unions are highly democratic, with members having access to union decision-making machinery, especially at the local level. While corruption exists in some unions, its occurrence seems to be highly concentrated in a few industries.

13. The percentage of the U.S. private-sector work force that is in trade unions has declined precipitously since the mid 1950s. The decline is due largely to a dramatic increase in the amount and sophistication of both legal and illegal company actions designed to forestall the organization of workers, and reduced union organizing activity per nonunion worker.

Some of our findings are controversial. They challenge the prevailing negative assessment of the economic and political impact of unions. Not surprisingly, they have engendered considerable critical comment. It is therefore important to understand the strengths and weaknesses of the evidence on which they are based.

The distinctive feature of the evidence presented in this book is that it is derived largely from quantitative analyses of data from many sources. Some of this information is from samples of thousands of individuals or establishments, some from companies, and some from industries.[23] While labor economists have been using similar data for over a decade to estimate the effect of unions on wages, it is only in the past few years that we and others have used this sort of information to examine the effects of unions on the nonwage outcomes central to the voice/response face of unionism.

Quantitative analysis of computer data files of the type we have undertaken has the advantage of providing numerical estimates of the magnitude of union effects and of covering a sufficiently large number of workers and firms to permit generalizations about overall economic effects. Analysis of this sort also has problems, however, and we believe the problems should not be concealed by the quantity of the output.

The chief difficulty with our (and other social scientists') quantitative analysis is that the data we study are not generated by an "ideal" experiment in which we have altered one factor while holding all else of relevance fixed. (In the case of unionism, such an ideal experiment would involve unionizing a randomly chosen individual, establishment, or industry while allowing no other relevant changes to occur, and observing the resultant outcomes.) Rather than coming from such a controlled experiment, our data are based on either comparisons of union/nonunion individuals or firms at a moment in time (cross-sectional analyses) or comparisons of the persons or firms as they change union status over time (before/after, or longitudinal, analyses). Both comparisons are imperfect, for several reasons. First, despite our statistical efforts not *all* other relevant factors are held fixed. Second, our variables invariably suffer from measurement error because of faulty responses, coding mistakes, key punch mistakes, and the like. And third, individuals or firms with similar measured characteristics are unlikely to be unionized on a random basis. If individual or firm X gets organized and individual or firm Y does not, there is probably some difference between them that explains their different unionization history. This uncaptured "pre-union difference" may explain part of the outcome difference that we attribute to unionism.

The problem of controlling for all relevant factors except the one under investigation is particularly severe when we try to estimate the voice/response effects of unionism, because these effects are presumed to operate on top of, or in addition to, the monopoly effects. When the two effects operate in the same direction, failure to control adequately for the monopoly impact of unionism can lead to an erroneous conclusion that union-nonunion differences are due to voice/response rather than to monopoly behavior. For instance, we expect the higher wages that unions win for workers to reduce quits, and we also expect the greater voice that unions win for workers to reduce quits. To isolate the reduction in quits due to voice/response, we must accurately measure the reduction in quits due to monopoly wage gains. If we do not, estimates of the union voice-induced reduction in quits may be illusory, the result of poor statistical experiments rather than the reflection of true behavior.

How did we deal with these problems?

First, we based our conclusions on comparisons of persons or establishments that are as similar as possible. We did this by performing multivariate statistical analyses in which we controlled for a wide variety of other factors ranging from the demographic characteristics of workers to the industry-occupation-regional locus of jobs. In particular, when studying voice/response effects, we always tried to control for the union wage effect and all reactions to it.

Second, we used as many different data sets and types of data as possible. If one survey lacked a certain control, we sought others which contained it. While we could not replicate experiments as natural scientists do, we could perform the same basic analysis on several different data sets, obtained from different samples, by different sampling procedures, and with different survey instruments.

Third, we performed various statistical checks on our findings, which allowed us to estimate how much results might vary if some variables were, say, better measured, or if one had information on factors not available in a particular data set.

Fourth, we conducted special small surveys designed to obtain answers to specific questions which could not be addressed with existing information.

Finally, we discussed our results with labor, management, and neutral participants in industrial relations and compared our statistical findings with their perceptions and with the findings of case studies.

These efforts to prune our statistical results of potential biases do not, of course, guarantee that all our findings are correct: some certainly are, while others unfortunately may not be. The most we hope is that our overall assessment of unionism as an institution with important voice/response as well as monopoly wage effects is close to the mark.

In the remainder of this book, after briefly setting out in Chapter 2 the institutional background of the American industrial relations system, we present the detailed results of our new empirical analysis of unions. Chapters 3–5 focus on what unions do to the level, composition, and distribution of compensation. Chapters 6–10 turn to what unions do to various nonwage outcomes: labor turnover and the attachment of workers to firms, cyclical work force adjustments, work rules, and job satisfaction, and examines the potential spillover of union gains to nonunion workers. Chapters 11–14 analyze what unions do to the "bottom line" economic outcomes of productivity and profitability, and to the "bottom line" social outcomes of internal union affairs and national economic legislation. Chapter 15 examines the ongoing decline in unionism in the United States. Finally, chapter 16 seeks to construct a whole from the preceding parts. It contrasts the voice/response and monopoly effects of unionism to reach an overall quantitative assessment of the benefits and costs of what unions do.

Endnotes

¹For examples of economics with generally negative views of labor unions, see Henry C. Simons, *Economic Policy for a Free Society* (Chicago: University of Chicago Press, 1948); Gottfried Haberler, "Wage Policy and Inflation," in P. D. Bradley, ed., *The Public Stake in Union Power* (Charlottesville, Va.: University of Virginia Press, 1959), 63–85; Milton Friedman and Rose Friedman, *Capitalism and Freedom* (Chicago: University of Chicago Press, 1962), 123–25, and *Free to Choose* (New York: Harcourt Brace Jovanovich, 1980), 228–47; W. H. Hutt, *The Theory of Collective Bargaining* (London: P. S. King, 1930); Fritz Machlup, *The Political Economy of Monopoly* (Baltimore: Johns Hopkins University Press, 1952).

²For examples of economists with generally positive outlooks on labor unions, see Lloyd G. Reynolds and Cynthia H. Taft, *The Evolution of Wage Structure* (New Haven: Yale University Press, 1956); Sumner H. Slichter, James J. Healy, and E. Robert Livernash, *The Impact of Collective Bargaining on Management* (Washington, D.C.: The Brookings Institution, 1960); and Derek C. Bok and John T. Dunlop, *Labor and the American Community* (New York: Simon and Schuster, 1970).

³Mr. Murphy's statement was made at the GM-UAW Contract Anniversary Dinner, in Detroit, Michigan, on February 11, 1977. The text of his comments was provided by the General Motors Corporation Public Relations Library.

⁴The results of a recent Gallup poll illustrate the growing ambivalence about unions. In August, 1978, only 59 percent of people polled approved of unions. By contrast, in January, 1957, 76 percent of people polled approved of unions. See *The Gallup Index*, August 1978, Report Number 157.

⁵This work has been reviewed in several places. See H. Gregg Lewis, *Unionism and Relative Wages in the United States*, (Chicago: University of Chicago Press,

1963) for a discussion of pre-1960s studies. See George E. Johnson, "Economic Analysis of Trade Unionism," *American Economic Review*, 65 (May 1975): 23–38, for a brief description of many post-1960s studies. H. Gregg Lewis, *Union Relative Wage Effects: A Survey* (Forthcoming) and R. B. Freeman and J. L. Medoff, "The Impact of Collective Bargaining: Illusion or Reality?" in J. Steiber, R. B. McKersie and D. Q. Mills, *U.S. Industrial Relations 1950–1980: A Critical Assessment* (Madison, Wis.: Industrial Relations Research Association, 1981), 47–97, also provide summaries of recent work.

⁶The empirical investigations referred to are summarized in R. B. Freeman and J. L. Medoff, "The Impact of Collective Bargaining: Can the New Facts be Explained by Monopoly Unionism?" in Joseph D. Reid, Jr., ed., *Research in Labor Economics: New Approaches to Labor Unions*, supp. 2 (Greenwich, Conn.: JAI Press, 1983).

⁷For a discussion of possible union maximands see John T. Dunlop, *Wage Determination Under Trade Unionism* (New York: Augustus M. Kelley, 1950), 28–44; and Wallace N. Atherton, *The Theory of Union Bargaining Goals* (Princeton, N.J.: Princeton University Press, 1973).

⁸The concept of economic rent refers to the returns to a relatively fixed factor. A union can raise wages and therefore lower returns of a firm with economic rent without putting the enterprise out of business.

⁹See Albert O. Hirschman, *Exit, Voice, and Loyalty* (Cambridge, Mass.: Harvard University Press, 1971).

¹⁰Protection for collective action without union status is found in section 7 as well, which guarantees "the right to engage in other concerted activities for the purpose of collective bargaining or other mutual aid or protection. . . ." Individuals acting alone are not protected by law. For a more detailed discussion, see Archibald Cox and Derek Bok, *Labor Law Cases and*

Materials (Mineola, N.Y.: The Foundation Press, 1969), 858–904. A text of the NLRA is contained in A. Cox and D. C. Bok, *1966 Statutory Supplement, Labor Law Cases and Materials* (Brooklyn, N.Y.: The Foundation Press, 1966), 38–59.

[11]Among the studies that make this point are Peter Kuhn, "Malfeasance in Long Term Employment Contracts: A New General Model With An Application to Unionism" (National Bureau of Economic Research Working Paper No. 1045, December 1982); Edward P. Lazear, "Why Is There Mandatory Retirement," *Journal of Political Economy* 87 (December 1979); 1261–84; Benjamin Eden, "Competitive Price Setting, Labor Contracts and Trade Unions" (University of Iowa, mimeographed 1983); James M. Malcomson, "Trade Unions and Economic Efficiency," *Economic Journal,* supp. (March 1983); 51–65; Melvin W. Reder, "Unionism, Wages and Contract Enforcement," in Joseph D. Reid, Jr., ed., *Research in Labor Economics: New Approaches to Labor Unions,* supp. 2 (Greenwich, Conn.: JAI Press, 1983).

[12]The idea that human resources management involves the mediation between various groups within the firm is central in the literature of organizational behavior. See, for example, Michael Beer, Paul R. Lawrence, D. Quinn Mills, and Richard Walton, *Human Resources Management* (Free Press, forthcoming). This point is also important in the work of a number of economists who focus on the internal operations of firms. See, for example, Harvey Leibenstein, *Beyond Economic Man* (Cambridge, Mass.: Harvard University Press, 1976); Oliver E. Williamson, "Efficient Labor Organization," University of Pennsylvania Discussion Paper No. 123 (Revised) (Philadelphia: Center for the Study of Organizational Innovation, April 1982), 21–22; and Herbert Simon, "Rational Decision Making in Business Organizations," *American Economic Review* 69 (September 1979): 493–513.

[13]The response of management is a decisive determinant of whether unions have positive or negative effects on the operation of enterprises, a point most strongly stressed by Harvard's Slichter, Healy, and Livernash in their classic study, *The Impact of Collective Bargaining on Management.* On the potential role of any form of external pressure on management, see H. Leibenstein, "Allocative vs. X-Efficiency," *American Economic Review* 56 (June 1966): 392–415.

[14]F. A. Hayek, *A Tiger by the Tail* (London: Institute of Economic Affairs, 1972), 72.

[15]Alfred T. Marshall, *Elements of Economics,* 3rd ed. (London: Macmillan, 1899), 381–82.

[16]Slichter, Healy, and Livernash, *Impact of Collective Bargaining,* 951.

[17]Lloyd G. Reynolds, *Labor Economics and Labor Relations,* 8th ed., (Englewood Cliffs, N.J.: Prentice-Hall, 1982), 474.

[18]Friedman and Friedman, *Capitalism and Freedom,* 124.

[19]Reynolds and Taft, *Evolution of Wage Structure,* 194.

[20]Henry C. Simons, "Some Reflections on Syndicalism," *Journal of Political Economy* 52 (March 1944): 23.

[21]Bok and Dunlop, *Labor and the American Community,* 425–26.

[22]The view of unions as coercive forces was expressed at an early date. See Henry George, *The Condition of Labor: An Open Letter to Pope Leo XIII* (New York: United States Book Co., 1891), 86. For a later version of this opinion, see Mancur Olson, *The Logic of Collective Action* (Cambridge, Mass.; Harvard University Press, 1971), 71.

[23]For a description of the data sets, see appendix.

READING 37

TIME-AND-MOTION REGAINED

Paul S. Adler

With workers defining their own job standards, quality and productivity at the Fremnot plant went from worst to best.

Standardization is the death of creativity.

Time-and-motion regimentation prevents continuous improvement.

Hierarchy suffocates learning.

U.S. manufacturing is in the throes of revolution, and assumptions like these are becoming the new conventional wisdom about work. This new gospel sets up Frederick Winslow Taylor and his time-and-motion studies as the villain. It asserts that quality, productivity, and learning depend on management's ability to free workers from the coercive constraints of bureaucracy. It insists that detailed standards, implemented with great discipline in a hierarchical organization, will inevitably alienate employees, poison labor relations, stifle initiative and innovation, and hobble an organization's capacity to change and to learn.

But what if, as I believe, this new creed is wrong? What if bureaucracy can actually be designed to encourage innovation and commitment? What if standardization, properly understood and practiced, should prove itself a wellspring of continuous learning and motivation?

In Fremont, California, a GM-Toyota joint venture called New United Motor Manufacturing, Inc., NUMMI, for short, has succeeded in employing an innovative form of Taylor's time-and-motion regimentation on the factory floor not only to create world-class productivity and quality but also to increase worker motivation and satisfaction. What's more, NUMMI's intensely Taylorist procedures appear to encourage rather than discourage organizational learning and, therefore, continuous improvement.

This outcome seems surprising because for decades our attitudes toward work have been shaped by a chain of reasoning that has led us to expect (and guaranteed that we would get) a vicious circle of escalating managerial coercion and employee recalcitrance. The reasoning runs something like this:

Source: Reprinted by permission of *Harvard Business Review*. "Time-and-Motion Regained," Paul S. Adler, January–February 1993. Copyright © 1993 by the President and Fellows of Harvard College; all rights reserved.

- When tasks are routine and repetitive, efficiency and quality require standardized work procedures.
- High levels of standardization rob jobs of their intrinsic interest, reducing motivation and creativity.
- Demotivating work leads to dysfunctional employee behavior such as absenteeism, high turnover, poor attention to quality, strikes, even sabotage.
- Counterproductive behavior by the work force requires more authoritarian management, more hierarchical layers, and even higher levels of standardization.

In short, Taylorism leads inevitably to workforce discontent and union belligerence, which in turn leads inevitably to higher levels of bureaucratic excess. The organization of work comes to build on the dehumanizing logic of coercion and reluctant compliance. Meanwhile, quality, profits, and job satisfaction all suffer.

NUMMI's experience flies directly in the face of this thinking. That's because the second step in this chain of reasoning is false. Formal work standards developed by industrial engineers and imposed on workers *are* alienating. But procedures that are designed by the workers themselves in a continuous, successful effort to improve productivity, quality, skills, and understanding can humanize even the most disciplined forms of bureaucracy. Moreover, NUMMI shows that hierarchy can provide support and expertise instead of a mere command structure.

What the NUMMI experiment shows is that hierarchy and standardization, with all their known advantages for efficiency, need not build on the logic of coercion. They can build instead on the logic of learning, a logic that motivates workers and taps their potential contribution to continuous improvement.

In practice, NUMMI's "learning bureaucracy" achieves three ends. First, it serves management by improving overall quality and productivity. Second, it serves workers by involving them in the design and control of their own work, increasing their motivation and job satisfaction, and altering the balance of power between labor and management. Third, it serves the interests of the entire organization—management and the work force—by creating a formal system to encourage learning, to capture and communicate innovation, and to institutionalize continuous improvement.

THE WORST PLANT IN THE WORLD

NUMMI is housed in what was once the General Motors assembly plant in Fremont, California, 35 miles southeast of San Francisco, which opened in 1963 and manufactured GM trucks and the Chevy Malibu and Century. At the old GM-Fremont plant, work was organized along traditional Taylorist lines, with more than 80 industrial engineers establishing assembly-line norms that management then did its best to impose on the work force, with the predictable results.

Over the years, GM-Fremont came to be what one manager called "the worst plant in the world." Productivity was among the lowest of any GM plant, quality was abysmal, and drug and alcohol abuse were rampant both on and off the job. Absenteeism was so high that the plant employed 20% more workers than it needed just to ensure an adequate labor force on any given day. The United Auto Workers local earned a national reputation for militancy; from 1963 to 1982, wildcat strikes and sickouts closed the plant four times. The backlog of unresolved grievances often exceeded 5,000.

GM-Fremont reached its peak employment of 6,800 hourly workers in 1978. Numbers then declined steadily to a little over 3,000 when GM finally closed the plant in February 1982.

Discussions between GM and Toyota about a possible joint venture began that same year. In February 1983, the two companies reached an agreement in principle to produce a version of the Toyota Corolla, renamed the Nova, at the Fremont plant, using Toyota's production system. GM would be responsible for marketing and sales; Toyota would take on product design, engineering, and daily operations. The new entity, NUMMI, would manufacture and assemble the car. Beginning in 1986, the plant also made Corolla FXs. In 1988, both the Nova and the FX were phased out, and Fremont began building Corollas, Geo Prizms, and, as of late 1991, Toyota trucks.

The two companies' objectives were complementary. GM wanted to learn about Toyota's production system. It also obtained a high-quality subcompact for its Chevrolet division at a time when GM's market share was rapidly eroding. Toyota wanted to help defuse the trade issue by building cars in the United States. To do this, it needed to learn about U.S. suppliers.

Toyota later claimed it had also wanted "to gain experience with American union labor," but at first Toyota wanted nothing to do with UAW. As it happened, there was no alternative. GM offered them no other facility, and the UAW had de facto control of Fremont. Moreover, GM was afraid of a union backlash at other plants if it tried to set up the joint venture as a nonunion shop.

In September 1983, NUMMI and the union signed a letter of intent recognizing the UAW as sole bargaining agent for the NUMMI labor force, specifying prevailing auto-industry wages and benefits, and stipulating that a majority of the work force would be hired from among the workers laid off from GM-Fremont. In return, the UAW agreed to support the implementation of a new production system and to negotiate a new contract.

NUMMI was formally organized in February 1984. Toyota contributed $100 million in capital, and GM supplied the Fremont plant. Hiring began in May. Every applicant went through three days of production simulations, written examinations, discussions, and interviews. Managers and union officials jointly evaluated applicants for the hourly jobs: team leader and team member. The union also played a role in selecting managers, except for the 16 who came directly from GM and a group of about 30 Toyota managers and production coordinators who came from Japan. The CEO, Tatsuo Toyoda, brought with him the prestige of the company's founding family.

Over the following 20 months, NUMMI hired 2,200 hourly workers—85% from the old GM-Fremont plant, among them the old union hierarchy. (Almost none of GM-Fremont's salaried employees was rehired. In any case, many had long since moved to other GM plants.) Since GM-Fremont had done little hiring for several years before it closed, the average age of the new work force was 41. Most had high school·educations. About 26% were Hispanic, 20% black, and 15% female.

The first group of 450 team leaders and the entire NUMMI management team attended a three-week training program at the Toyota plant in Japan— Takaoka—on which NUMMI was modeled. These people then helped to set up the new plant and train workers.

The NUMMI production system required people to work harder than they had at GM-Fremont. Jobs at the old plant occupied an experienced worker about 45 seconds out of 60. NUMMI's norm is closer to 57 seconds out of 60. And because workers have to meet much higher quality and efficiency standards, they have to work not only harder but smarter as well.

By the end of 1986, NUMMI's productivity was higher than that of any other GM facility and more than twice that of its predecessor, GM-Fremont. In fact, NUMMI's productivity was nearly as high as Takaoka's, even though its workers were, on the average, ten years older and much less experienced with the Toyota production system. Quality, as rated by internal GM audits, customer surveys, and *Consumer Reports* was much higher than at any other GM plant and, again, almost as high as Takaoka's.

Equally important, absenteeism has dropped from between 20% and 25% at the old GM-Fremont plant to a steady 3% to 4% at NUMMI; substance abuse is a minimal problem; and participation in the suggestion program has risen steadily from 26% in 1986 to 92% in 1991. When GM-Fremont closed its doors, it had more than 2,000 grievances outstanding. As of the end of 1991, some 700 grievances had been filed at NUMMI altogether over the course of eight years. The overall proportion of employees describing themselves as "satisfied" or "very satisfied" has risen progressively to more than 90%.

In 1990, Toyota announced that it would invest $350 million in an additional assembly line to build a Toyota truck for the U.S. market. So NUMMI hired 650 hourly workers on top of the 3,100—plus 400 salaried personnel—already employed. The first trucks rolled off the line in August 1991.

FEAR, SELECTION, SOCIALIZATION

NUMMI's remarkable turnaround poses an obvious question: How is it possible to convert a plant from worst to best quality and from dismal to superlative productivity over the course of a few months? The most obvious answers are not entirely satisfying.

For example, fear. The GM-Fremont plant closed in 1982, and the people rehired by NUMMI didn't go back to work until 1984. Two years of unemployment can produce a great deal of cooperation. In fact, some NUMMI workers believe management makes deliberate use of the specter of another plant closure as a veiled threat to keep people in line. But the chairman of the union bargaining committee points out that while the old plant's closure obviously made workers

The NUMMI production system not only made people work harder, it made them work smarter as well.

VOICES FROM THE FACTORY FLOOR: EXCERPTS FROM INTERVIEWS
WITH MANAGERS, WORKERS, AND UNION OFFICIALS

Team Leader

I'll never forget when I was first hired by GM many years ago. The personnel manager who hired us got the . . . workers who were starting that day into a room and explained: "You new employees have been hired in the same way we requisition sandpaper. We'll put you back on the street whenever you aren't needed any more." How in the hell can you expect to foster a loyal and productive work force when you start out hearing stuff like that? At NUMMI, the message when we came aboard was "Welcome to the family."

Team Leader

Once you start working as a real team, you're not just work acquaintances anymore. When you really have confidence in your co-workers, you trust them, you're proud of what you can do together, then you become loyal to them. That's what keeps the absenteeism rate so low here. When I wake up in the morning, I know there's no one out there to replace me if I'm feeling sick or hung over or whatever. . . . At NUMMI, I know my team needs me.

Team Leader

The average worker is definitely busier at NUMMI than he was at Fremont. That's the point of the NUMMI production system and the way it ties together standardized work, no inventories, and no quality defects. The work teams at NUMMI aren't like the autonomous teams you read about in other plants. Here we're not autonomous, because we're all tied together really tightly. But it's not like we're just getting squeezed to work harder, because it's the workers who are making the whole thing work—we're the ones that make the standardized work and the *kaizen* suggestions. We run the plant—and if it's not running right, we stop it. At GM-Fremont, we ran only our own little jobs.

We'd work really fast to build up a stock cushion so we could take a break for a few minutes to smoke a cigarette or chat with a buddy. That kind of "hurry up and wait" game made work really tiring. There was material and finished parts all over the place, and half of it was defective anyway. Being consistently busy without being hassled and without being overworked takes a lot of the pain out of the job. You work harder at NUMMI, but I swear it, you go home at the end of the day feeling less tired—and feeling a hell of a lot better about yourself.

Team Member

In our standardized work training, our teachers told us we should approach our fellow team members and suggest ways to improve their jobs. Hell, do you see me trying that with a team member who's six-foot-four and weighs 250 pounds? You'd be picking me up off the floor if I tried that. . . . Standardized work is a joke as far as I can see. We're supposed to go to management and tell them when we have extra seconds to spare. Why would I do that when all that will happen is that they'll take my spare seconds away and work me even harder than before? I'd rather just do the job the way I'm already comfortable with. I'm no fool.

Department Manager

Our assumption at NUMMI is that people come to work to do a fair day's work. There are exceptions, and you would be foolish to ignore them. But 90% of people, if you give them a chance to work smarter and improve their jobs, and if they find that by doing that they have created free time for themselves, will spontaneously look for new things to do. I've got hundreds of examples. I don't think that people work harder at NUMMI than in other plants. Not physically anyway. But the mental challenge is much greater.

VOICES FROM THE FACTORY FLOOR: EXCERPTS FROM INTERVIEWS WITH MANAGERS, WORKERS, AND UNION OFFICIALS

Team Leader

I don't think industrial engineers are dumb. They're just ignorant. Anyone can watch someone else doing a job and come up with improvement suggestions that sound good. . . . And it's even easier to come up with the ideal procedure if you don't even bother to watch the worker at work, but just do it from your office, on paper. Almost anything can look good that way. Even when we do our own analysis in our teams, some of the silliest ideas can slip through before we actually try them out.

There's a lot of things that enter into a good job design. . . . The person actually doing the job is the only one who can see all factors. And in the United States, engineers have never had to work on the floor—not like in Japan. So they don't know what they don't know. . . . Today *we* drive the process, and if we need help, the engineer is there the next day to work on it with us.

UAW Official

One thing I really like about the Toyota style is that they'll put in a machine to save you from bending down. The Toyota philosophy is that the worker should use the machine and not vice versa . . . It would be fine if the robots worked perfectly—and the engineers always seem to imagine that they will. But they don't, so the worker ends up being used by the machine. At NUMMI, we just put in a robot for installing the spare tire—that really helps the worker, because it was always a hell of a tiring job. It took awhile, and we had to raise it in the safety meetings and argue about it. And they came through. That would never happen at GM-Fremont—you never saw automation simply to help the worker.

UAW Official

In the future we're going to need union leaders with more technical and management knowledge. We're much more involved now in deciding how the plant operates. That stretches our capabilities. Management is coming to us asking for our input. . . . The old approach was much simpler—"You make the damned decision, and I'll grieve it if I want." Now we need to understand how the production system works, to take the time to analyze things, to formulate much more detailed proposals. This system really allows us to take as much power as we know what to do with.

UAW Official

Now when I try to explain [NUMMI] to old UAW buddies from other plants . . . they figure that I'm forced to say all this stuff because they shut our plant down and I had no choice. They figure going along with the team concept and all the rest was just the price we had to pay to get our jobs back. I explain to them that the plant is cleaner, it's safer, we've got more say on important issues, and we have a real opportunity to build our strength as a union. I explain to them that our members can broaden their understanding of the manufacturing system and build their self-esteem, and that the training we've gotten in manufacturing problem solving, quality, and so on can help them reach their full potential and get more out of their lives. I explain to them that in a system like this, workers have got a chance to make a real contribution to society—we don't have to let managers do all the thinking. But these guys just don't see it. Maybe it's because they haven't personally experienced the way NUMMI works. Whatever the reason, they just see it all as weakening the union. Someone like Irving Bluestone probably understands what we're doing. He had the idea a long time ago: if the worker has the right to vote for the president of the United States, he ought to have the right to participate in decisions on the shop floor.

continued

VOICES FROM THE FACTORY FLOOR: EXCERPTS FROM INTERVIEWS
WITH MANAGERS, WORKERS, AND UNION OFFICIALS (*continued*)

Team Member

In the old days, we had to worry about management playing its games, and the union was there to defend us. But now, with the union taking on its new role, it's not as simple as before, and we have to worry about both the management games and the union games. I don't want the type of union muscle we used to have. You could get away with almost anything in the old plant, because the union would get you off the hook. It was really crazy. But it wasn't productive.

Team Leader

There are people here who will tell you they hate this place. All I say is: actions speak louder than words. If people were disgruntled, there's no way that we'd be building the highest quality vehicle. You wouldn't have a plant that's this clean. You would still have the drug problems we had before. You would still have all the yelling and screaming. You can't force all that. And try this: go into any of the bathrooms, and you'll see there's no graffiti. If people have a problem with their manager, they don't have to tell him on the bathroom wall. They can tell him to his face. And the boss's first words will be: "Why?" Something's happened here at NUMMI. When I was at GM, I remember a few years ago I got an award from my foreman for coming to work for a full 40 hours in one week. A certificate! At NUMMI, I've had perfect attendance for two years.

more receptive to NUMMI's new approach, a return to old coercive management methods would have produced a rapid return to old antagonistic work-force behavior patterns.

A second possibility is that management weeded out troublemakers in the rehiring process. But in fact NUMMI rehired the entire union hierarchy and many well-known militants. In general, very few applicants were screened out. The union even won a second chance for some who failed drug tests the first time around.

A third answer is that NUMMI made use of a comprehensive socialization process during hiring to instill a new set of values in the new work force. Certainly, NUMMI did its best to shape and alter the attitudes of both workers and managers. For example, the company tried to undercut the customary we-they divisions between workers and management by eliminating special parking and eating facilities for managers and by introducing an identical dress code—uniforms—for everyone. Management also devoted a great deal of attention to each individual hire and welcomed each personally to the company that was going to build "the finest vehicles in America."

However much these three factors—fear of unemployment, selection, and socialization—may have contributed to the final outcome, they do not adequately explain NUMMI's continuing success or its ability to let workers draw improved motivation and greater satisfaction from a system that places them in a more regimented and bureaucratic environment and makes them work harder and faster. The most critical piece of that explanation lies in the production system itself and in the policies and practices that buttress it.

THE NUMMI PRODUCTION SYSTEM

The idea of a production *system* is itself something of a novelty in many U.S. manufacturing plants. All factories have production techniques, procedures, and policies, but these usually comprise not so much a system as an ad hoc accumulation of responses to changing and often contradictory business and design demands. NUMMI's production system is a finely tuned, superbly integrated whole, refined by Toyota over decades of manufacturing experience.

The basic techniques are familiar at least in name. The assembly line is a just-in-time operation that does away with work-in-progress and makes quality assurance the responsibility of each work station. The application of *kaizen*, or continuous improvement, includes an extraordinarily active suggestion program, constant refinement of procedures, and the designation of special kaizen teams to study individual suggestions or carry out specific improvement projects. Every machine and process is designed to detect malfunctions, missing parts, and improper assemblies automatically. Every job is carefully analyzed to achieve maximum efficiency and quality. Job rotation is standard; workers are crosstrained in all team assignments and then allowed to shift from one task to another. Planned production leveling eliminates variation in daily and weekly schedules.

This system is essentially the same one Toyota uses in Japan, the same one many American manufacturers are now beginning to adopt. But NUMMI's approach is distinctive in two respects; first, its strong commitment to the social context in which work is performed, and, second, its intense focus on standardized work.

The NUMMI approach has two distinctive features: a commitment to the social context of work and a focus on standardization.

In terms of social context, NUMMI seeks to build an atmosphere of trust and common purpose. NUMMI maintains exceptional consistency in its strategies and principles, it carefully builds consensus around important decisions, and it has programs ensuring adequate communication of results and other essential information.

The basic structural unit is the production team, of which NUMMI has approximately 350, each consisting of five to seven people and a leader. The idea is that small teams encourage participative decision making and team bonding. Four teams comprise a group, led by a group leader who represents the first layer of management.

Above and beyond the production teams, the bigger team is everyone—all the workers, team leaders, managers, engineers, and staff in the plant as well as NUMMI's suppliers. Toyota leadership wants workers to understand that the company is not the property of management but of everyone together. In NUMMI's view, the primary purpose and responsibility of the management hierarchy is to support the production teams with problem-solving expertise.

The most substantive expression of this big-team strategy is the no-layoff policy spelled out in NUMMI's collective-bargaining agreement with the union. Recognizing that "job security is essential to an employee's well being," NUMMI agrees "that it will not lay off employees unless compelled to do so by severe economic conditions that threaten the long-term viability of the Company." NUMMI agrees to take such drastic measures as reducing management salaries and assigning previously subcontracted work to bargaining unit employees before resorting to layoffs.

Management sees the no-layoff policy as a critical support for its overall production strategy not only because it reinforces the team culture, but also because it eliminates workers' fear that they are jeopardizing jobs every time they come up with an idea to improve efficiency.

Workers came to trust this no-layoff commitment when in 1988 poor sales of the Nova brought capacity utilization down to around 60%. Workers no longer needed on the assembly line were not laid off but instead assigned to kaizen teams and sent to training classes.

Another important support for NUMMI's team concept is its radically simplified job classification system. Where GM-Fremont had 18 skilled trades classifications, NUMMI has two. Where GM-Fremont had 80 hourly pay rates, at NUMMI all production workers get the same hourly rate—currently $17.85—regardless of their jobs, except that team leaders get an extra 60 cents. There are no seniority-, performance-, or merit-based bonuses. Important as money is, equity is more important still in reducing tensions and resentments.

The second distinctive feature of NUMMI's system is standardization. Typically, American companies approach team empowerment by allowing teams considerable autonomy in how they accomplish tasks. NUMMI, in contrast, is obsessive about standardized work procedures. It sees what one NUMMI manager has called "the intelligent interpretation and application of Taylor's time-and-motion studies" as the principal key to its success. The reference to Taylor may be jarring, but it fits.

STANDARDIZED WORK

At GM-Fremont, industrial engineers did all time-and-motion analysis and formal job design, and workers tended to view them with resentment or contempt. The problem, as one union official described it, was that management assumed a "divine right" to design jobs however it saw fit. Industrial engineers with no direct experience of the work beyond capsule observation would shut themselves in a room, ponder various potentials of the human body, time the result, and promulgate a task design. Or so it seemed to workers, whom no one ever consulted despite their intimate familiarity with the specific difficulties of the work in question.

Normally, when an industrial engineer presented one of these pedantically designed jobs to a supervisor, the supervisor would politely accept it, then promptly discard it in favor of the more traditional kick-ass-and-take-names technique. The worker, in turn, usually ignored both engineer and foreman and did the job however he or she was able—except, of course, when one of them was looking. If an industrial engineer was actually "observing"—stop-watch and clipboard in hand—standard practice was to slow down and make the work look harder. The entire charade was part of an ongoing game of coercion and avoidance. Multiply this scenario by two shifts and thousands of workers, and the result is anything *but* the rational production of a high-quality car.

At NUMMI, in radical contrast to GM-Fremont, team members themselves hold the stopwatch. They learn the techniques of work analysis, description, and improvement. This change in the design and implementation of standardized work has far-reaching implications for worker motivation and self-esteem, for the balance of power between workers and management, and for the capacity of the company to innovate, learn, and remember.

The job design process itself is relatively simple. Team members begin by timing one another with stopwatches, looking for the safest, most efficient way to do each task at a sustainable pace. They pick the best performance, break it down into its fundamental parts, then explore ways of improving each element. The team then takes the resulting analyses, compares them with those of the other shift at the same work station, and writes the detailed specifications that become the standard work definition for everyone on both teams.

Taking part in the group's analytical and descriptive work involves every team member in a commitment to perform each task identically. In one sense, therefore, standardized work is simply a means of reducing variability in task performance, which may seem a relatively trivial achievement. In fact, however, reduced variability leads to a whole series of interconnected improvements:

- Safety improves and injuries decline because workers get a chance to examine all the possible sources of strain and danger systematically.

- Quality standards rise because workers have identified the most effective procedure for each job.

- Inventory control grows easier, and inventory carrying costs go down because the process flows more smoothly.

- Job rotation becomes much more efficient and equitable, which makes absences less troublesome.

- Flexibility improves because all workers are now industrial engineers and can work in parallel to respond rapidly to changing demands. For example, NUMMI can convert to a new line speed in four to six weeks, a process that might easily have taken six months to a year at GM-Fremont, with its engineers frantically recalculating thousands of tasks and trying to force the new standards on workers. In fact, GM-Fremont never even attempted anything as demanding as a line-speed change. If orders declined, GM-Fremont had to lay off an entire shift. NUMMI's new capacity to alter line speed means, among other things, that the plant can accommodate a drop in orders by slowing production.

If orders decline, NUMMI can slow the production line to produce fewer cars. In the same situation, GM-Fremont had to lay off an entire shift.

- Standardized work also has the overall benefit of giving control of each job to the people who know it best. It empowers the work force. Not surprisingly, NUMMI discovered that workers bought into the process quite readily. As one manager put it, "They understood the technique because it had been done to them for years, and they liked the idea because now they had a chance to do it for themselves."

. . . AND CONTINUOUS IMPROVEMENT

Yet, by far the most striking advantage of standardized work is that it gives continuous improvement a specific base to build on. As one manager put it, "You can't improve a process you don't understand." In this sense, standardization is the essential precondition for learning.

Indeed, standardization is not only a vehicle and a precondition for improvement but also a direct stimulus. Once workers have studied and refined their work procedures, problems with materials and equipment quickly rise to the surface. Moreover, since each worker is now an expert, each work station is now an inspection station—and a center of innovation.

At GM-Fremont, worker suggestions were apt to meet a brick wall of indifference. At NUMMI, engineers and managers are meant to function as a support system rather than an authority system. When a team can't solve a problem on its own, it can seek and get help. When a worker proposes complex innovation, engineers are available to help assess the suggestion and design its implementation.

The difference between traditional Taylorism and the learning-oriented NUMMI version resembles the difference between computer software designed to be "idiot-proof" and the kinds of computer systems that are meant to leverage and enhance their users' capabilities. The first "de-skills" the operator's task to an extent that virtually eliminates the possibility of error, but it also eliminates the operator's ability to respond to unpredictable events, to use the system in novel ways or adapt it to new applications. The idiot-proof system may be easy to use, but it is also static and boring. Leveraging systems make demands on the operator. They take time to learn and require thought and skill to use, but they are immensely flexible, responsive, and satisfying once mastered.

The difference goes deeper yet. At GM-Fremont—where work procedures were designed to be idiot-proof—the relationship between production system and worker was adversarial. Standards and hierarchy were there to coerce effort from reluctant workers. If the system functioned as expected and the operator was sufficiently tractable and unimaginative, the two together could turn out a fair product. There was little the operator could improve on, however, and the role of the system was utterly rigid until it broke down, whereupon everything stopped until a specialist arrived.

At NUMMI, the relationship of workers to the production system is cooperative and dynamic. Instead of circumventing user intelligence and initiative, the production system is designed to realize as much as possible of the latent collaborative potential between the workers and the system.

Suggestion programs illustrate the two approaches to organizational technology design. At many companies, suggestion programs are idiot-proof and opaque. They are designed primarily to screen out dumb ideas, and the basic review criteria, the identity of the judges, the status of proposals, and the reasons for rejection are all a black box as far as the workers are concerned. Predictably, a lot of these programs sputter along or die out altogether.

At NUMMI, the program is designed to encourage a growing flow of suggestions and to help workers see and understand criteria, evaluators, process, status, and results. Like a computer system designed to leverage rather than de-skill, the program helps employees form a mental model of the program's inner workings. Not surprisingly, workers made more than 10,000 suggestions in 1991, of which more than 80% were implemented.

In systems that de-skill and idiot-proof, technology controls, indeed dominates, workers. In systems designed for what experts call usability, the operator both learns from and "teaches" the technology. Using learned analytical tools, their own experience, and the expertise of leaders and engineers, workers create a consensual standard that they teach to the system by writing job descriptions. The system then teaches these standards back to workers, who, then, by further analysis, consultation, and consensus, make additional improvements. Continual reiteration of this disciplined process of analysis, standardization, re-analysis, refinement, and restandardization creates an intensely structured system of continuous improvement. And the salient characteristic of this bureaucracy is learning, not coercion.

This learning orientation captures the imagination. People no one had ever asked to solve a problem, workers who never finished high school, men and women who had spent 20 years or more in the auto industry without a single day of off-the-job training found themselves suddenly caught up in the statistical analysis of equipment downtime, putting together Pareto charts. One worker reported that he did literally a hundred graphs before he got one right.

A woman on the safety committee in the body shop described how she applied kaizen techniques to her kitchen at home after a fire on her stove. She analyzed the kitchen layout, installed a fire extinguisher, and relocated her pot tops so she could use them to smother flames. In short, she subjected herself and her home work space to the formal problem-solving procedures she had learned at the NUMMI plant.

The paradoxical feature such stories have in common is their enthusiasm for a form of disciplined behavior that both theory and past practice seem to rule out. This paradox grows from our failure to distinguish between what Taylorist, bureaucratic production systems *can* be and what, regrettably, they have usually been.

THE PSYCHOLOGY OF WORK

The chain of reasoning by which disciplined standardization leads inescapably to coercion, resentment, resistance, and further coercion seems to turn Taylorism and bureaucracy into what sociologist Max Weber called an iron cage. Taylorism and bureaucracy may have a devastating effect on innovation and motivation, the reasoning goes, but their technical efficiency and their power to enforce compliance seem to be the perfect tools for dealing with employees assumed to be recalcitrant. Taylor himself at least occasionally endorsed this coercive view of work. Italics bristling, he once wrote, "It is only through the *enforced* standardization of methods, *enforced* adoption of the best implements and working conditions, and *enforced* cooperation that this faster work can be assured. And the duty of enforcing the adoption of standards and of enforcing this cooperation rests with the *management* alone."

Against this background, it is hardly surprising that most managers and academics, at least in the West, have come to believe that Taylorism and bureaucracy will inevitably alienate workers and squander their human potential. But the psychological assumption underlying this expectation is that workers are incapable of delayed gratification. Managers seem to believe that performance will improve only as work comes more and more to resemble free play—our model of an intrinsically motivating activity. Indeed, it is an elementary axiom of economics that work is something that workers will always avoid.

NUMMI demonstrates the error of imputing infantile psychology to workers. Interviews with NUMMI team members suggest, in fact, that this whole historical accumulation of assumptions obscures three sources of adult motivation that the NUMMI production system successfully taps into:

First, the desire for excellence.

Second, a mature sense of realism.

Third, the positive response to respect and trust.

The first of these—the desire to do a good job, the instinct for workmanship—comes up again and again in conversations with workers. The NUMMI production system and the training that went with it increased both the real competence of workers and their feelings of competence. Workers talk a lot about expertise, pride, and self-esteem. One UAW official named "building a quality product" as one of the strategic goals that the union found most compelling at NUMMI. Perhaps the most striking story about pride in all the interviews came from a team leader:

> Before, when I saw a Chevy truck, I'd chuckle to myself and think,"You deserve that piece of crap if you were stupid enough to buy one." I was ashamed to say that I worked at the Fremont plant. But when I was down at the Monterey Aquarium a few weekends ago, I left my business card—on the windshield of a parked Nova with a note that said, "I helped build this one." I never felt pride in my job before.

The second element of motivation is a mature sense of realism—in this case, the understanding that unless NUMMI constantly improves its performance, competitors will take its market and its workers' jobs. A useful psychological theory cannot assume that workers are so captive to the pleasure principle that their only source of motivation is the immediate pleasure of intrinsically meaningful work. The evidence suggests that at least some of the workers at NUMMI are powerfully motivated by the simple recognition that international competition now forces them to "earn their money the old-fashioned way."

Some workers take powerful motivation from the knowledge that they have to "earn their money the old-fashioned way."

Other things being equal, work that is intrinsically motivating—as opposed to mundane and routine—is better than work that isn't. But workers at NUMMI recognize that other things are *not* equal, and they are realistic in their recognition of having had an unlucky draw in terms of education and opportunity. They see automobile assembly as work that can never have much intrinsic value, but they understand that their own motivation levels can nevertheless vary from strongly negative, at GM-Fremont, to strongly positive, at NUMMI.

"What we have here is not some workers' utopia," said one NUMMI worker. "Working on an assembly line in an automobile factory is still a lousy job. . . . We want to continue to minimize the negative parts of the job by utilizing the new system." Even though this work lacks the kind of intrinsic interest that would bring a worker in on a free Sunday, for example, the difference between the levels of motivation at NUMMI and at GM-Fremont spells the difference between world-class and worst-in-class.

The third explanation of increased motivation is the respect and trust that management shows workers in NUMMI's ongoing operations. For example, when the plant first began operations, the new NUMMI managers responded quickly to requests from workers and union representatives for items like new gloves and floor mats, which surprised workers used to seeing requests like these turn into battles over management prerogative.

After a few months of getting everything they asked for, workers and union representatives started trying to think of ways to reciprocate. Eventually, they decided that chrome water fountains were unnecessary and told management they'd found some plastic ones for half the price. A few weeks later, management upped the ante one more time by giving work teams their own accounts so they could order supplies for team members without prior approval from management. This kind of behavior led workers to conclude that they did indeed share common goals with management.

POWER AND EMPOWERMENT

The NUMMI production system confronts us with a set of formalized procedures that seem designed not primarily as instruments of domination but as elements of productive technique that all participants recognize as tools in their own collective interest. Management *and* labor support the NUMMI system. In fact, the first and overwhelming fact to emerge from interviews is that no one at NUMMI wants to go back to the old GM-Fremont days. Whatever their criticisms and whatever their positions, everyone feels that NUMMI is a far superior work environment.

NUMMI's no-layoff policy, management efforts to build an atmosphere of trust and respect, the NUMMI production system—especially the stimulus of its learning orientation—all help to explain this attitude. Beyond these formal policies, however, there are two more factors that help explain NUMMI's success with workers. The first of these, as we've seen, is the psychology of work. The final piece of the puzzle has to do with power.

There are two kinds of power to consider: hierarchical power within the organization and the power balance between labor and management. NUMMI takes a distinctive approach to both.

In terms of hierarchical layers, NUMMI is a fairly typical U.S. manufacturing plant, and in this sense, as well as in work-flow procedures, it is a very bureaucratic organization. NUMMI's structure is not flat. It has several well-populated layers of middle management. But consistent with the idea of turning the technologies of coercion into tools for learning, the function of hierarchy at NUMMI is not control but support.

Decisions at NUMMI are made by broad vertical and horizontal consensus. At first glance, decision making appears to be somewhat *more* centralized than at most U.S. factories, but this is because consensus-based decision making draws higher and lower layers into a dialogue, not because higher levels wield greater unilateral control. Both ends of the hierarchical spectrum are drawn into more decision-making discussions than either would experience in a conventional organization.

The contrast with the popular approaches to empowerment is striking. At one U.S. telecommunications company, the model organization today is a plant of 90 workers in self-managed teams, all reporting to a single plant manager. The company's old model included a heavy layer of middle management whose key function was to command and control, so it is easy to understand the inspiring effect of the new approach. But at NUMMI, middle management layers are layers of expertise, not of rights to command, and if middle managers have authority, it is the authority of experience, mastery, and the capacity to coach.

As for the second aspect of power, many observers have assumed that the intense discipline of Toyota-style operations requires complete management control over workers and elimination of independent work-force and union power. But at NUMMI, the power of workers and the union local is still considerable. In some ways, their power has actually increased. In fact, it may be that the NUMMI model has succeeded only *because* of this high level of worker and union power.

What makes the NUMMI production system so enormously effective is its ability to make production problems immediately visible and to mobilize the power of teamwork. Implemented with trust and respect, both these features of the system create real empowerment. Wielded autocratically, they would have the opposite effect. Visible control could easily turn into ubiquitous surveillance. Teamwork could become a means of mobilizing peer pressure. A healthy level of challenge could degenerate into stress and anxiety.

The NUMMI production system thus gives managers enormous potential control over workers. With this potential power ready at hand, and under pressure to improve business performance, there is a real danger that the relationship will sooner or later slide back into the old coercive pattern.

The new system gives workers great positive power to improve production and great negative power to disrupt it.

But such a slide would have an immediate and substantial negative impact on business performance, because labor would respond in kind. An alienated work force wipes out the very foundation of continuous improvement and dries up the flow of worker suggestions that fuel it. And the lack of inventory buffers mean that disaffected workers could easily bring the whole just-in-time production system to a grinding halt. Alongside workers' positive power to improve quality and efficiency, the system also gives workers an enormous negative power to disrupt production.

In other words, NUMMI's production system increases the power both of management over workers and of workers over management.

A system this highly charged needs a robust governance process in which the voices of management and labor can be clearly heard and effectively harmonized on high-level policy issues as well as on work-team operating issues. The union gives workers this voice.

When, for example, workers felt frustrated by what they saw as favoritism in management's selection of team leaders, the union largely eliminated the problem by negotiating a joint union-management selection process based on objective tests and performance criteria.

As one UAW official put it, "The key to NUMMI's success is that management gave up some of its power, some of its traditional prerogatives. If managers want to motivate workers to contribute and to learn, they have to give up some of their power. If managers want workers to trust them, we need to be 50-50 in making the decision. Don't just make the decision and say, 'Trust me.'"

Union leaders and top management confer regularly on- and off-site to consider a broad range of policy issues that go far beyond the traditional scope of collective bargaining. The union local has embraced the NUMMI concept and its goals. But its ability and willingness to act as a vehicle for worker concerns adds greatly to the long-term effectiveness of the organization.

NUMMI's ability to sustain its productivity, quality, and improvement record now depends on workers' motivation, which rests, in turn, on the perception and reality of influence, control, and equitable treatment. It is in management's own interest that any abuse of management prerogatives should meet with swift and certain penalties. The contribution of labor's positive power depends on the reality of its negative power.

In this way, the union not only serves workers' special interests, it also serves the larger strategic goals of the business by effectively depriving management of absolute domain and helping to maintain management discipline.

Empowerment is a powerful and increasingly popular approach to reinvigorating moribund organizations. The NUMMI case points up two of empowerment's potential pitfalls and suggests ways of overcoming them.

First, worker empowerment degenerates into exploitation if changes at the first level of management are not continuously reinforced by changes throughout the management hierarchy. Strong employee voice is needed to ensure that shop-floor concerns are heard at all levels of management. Without it, workers' new power is little more than the power to make more money for management.

Second, worker empowerment degenerates into abandonment if work teams fail to get the right tools, training in their use, and support in their implementation. Standardized work, extensive training in problem solving, a responsive management hierarchy, and supportive specialist functions are key success factors for empowerment strategies.

Taylorist time-and-motion discipline and formal bureaucratic structures are essential for efficiency and quality in routine operations. But these principles of organizational design need not lead to rigidity and alienation. NUMMI points the way beyond Taylor-as-villain to the design of a truly learning oriented bureaucracy.

HUMAN RESOURCE INFORMATION SYSTEMS

INTRODUCTION

One of the competitive challenges that managers face is how to utilize technology to effectively manage human resources. Human resource information systems (HRIS) include software programs and computers that deal with the entry, maintenance, updating, and use of human resource information for decision making. Users, or customers of human resource information systems, include human resource professionals, executives, and line managers. HRISs are used to make strategic decisions (such as evaluating the impact of compensation plans on labor costs), to avoid litigation (e.g., identify the underutilization of women and minorities), to evaluate policies and practices (e.g., identify use of tuition reimbursement), or to support company operations (e.g., track job applicant's resumes).

Reading 38 by Renae Broderick and John Boudreau discusses three types of computer applications (transaction processing, expert systems, and decision support systems) and the ways they can help the company gain a competitive advantage. Transaction processing refers to computation and calculations used to review and document employee movement within the company. Transaction processing reduces paper handling and report accuracy. This helps employees and managers spend their work time more productively (e.g., problem solving) rather than on completing paper work and other administrative tasks. Decision-support systems help employees solve problems such as determining how changes in customer demands or product mix might affect human resource requirements (such as the type of skills employees need). Expert systems are designed to simulate the decision-making process of human experts. Expert systems provide recommendations or actions that the user could take based on the information provided. For example, if a manager has a problem employee, an expert system would ask the manager for information about the work environment, employee behavior, and training history. Based on the manager's responses to these questions, the expert system would suggest a course of action for the manager to consider (like enrolling the employee in a training program or beginning the discharge process).

Reading 39 by Terri Griffith discusses one of the most controversial uses of human resource information systems—computer monitoring of employees. Computers can be used to collect, process, and provide employees with feedback regarding their work in order to improve their performance. Unfortunately, computer monitoring has also been used to punish employees. Employees may also have concerns that computer monitoring violates their privacy. Griffith describes how one company, Hughes Aircraft, effectively used computer monitoring to improve productivity and quality. The article provides suggestions for managers regarding the design and effective use of computer monitoring systems.

READING 38

HUMAN RESOURCE MANAGEMENT, INFORMATION TECHNOLOGY, AND THE COMPETITIVE EDGE

Renae Broderick
John W. Boudreau

Executive Overview

Global competition is putting increasing pressure on U.S. managers to make faster and better business decisions. Investments in information technology are often touted as a critical means of speeding up and improving management decision making. Yet it has proved distressingly difficult to realize the potential of information technology investments. This is particularly so in business areas such as Human Resources (HR), though the longer lead times traditionally associated with changes in HR systems mean that it is a prime candidate to benefit from information technology.

To pull into the lead in global competition, managers must control labor costs, motivate employees to high quality, customer-oriented performance, and continuously search out new and better ways of doing both. These objectives must be met in the face of shrinking head count and a global environment in which employees are more culturally diverse and located throughout the globe. Even the relatively routine tasks of employee record keeping and legal and regulatory compliance are geometrically intensified in this context. Such complexity also demands more sophisticated applications of technology that go beyond simply improving the management of routine tasks.

All managers have a stake in exploiting information technology to better manage their human resources. We propose a framework to help managers consider how HR information technology can improve human resources management and contribute to competitive advantage.

Alice could never quite make it out in thinking it over afterwards, how it was they began: all she remembers is, that they were running, and . . . the Queen kept crying "Faster! Faster!" . . . till suddenly, as Alice was getting quite

Source: "Human Resource Management, Information Technology, and the Competitive Edge" by Renae Broderick and John W. Boudreau, *Academy of Management Executive*, 1992, Vol. 6, No. 2, 7–17.

exhausted, they stopped . . . Alice looked around in great surprise. "Why I do believe we've been under this tree the whole time! . . . in our country," said Alice, "you'd generally get somewhere else—if you ran very.fast . . ." "A slow sort of country!" said the Queen. "Now, here, it takes all the running you can do, to keep in the same place. If you want to get somewhere else, you must run at least twice as fast . . ." (Lewis Carroll, *Through The Looking Glass*).

Alice's run and its surprising results must strike a chord with many managers of U.S. firms. Accustomed to "getting somewhere else" when running fast in the competitive race, they are now finding that their best time only keeps them in place. Anxious to outrace others, managers search for the combinations of strategy, motivation, technology, and work method and design that yield a competitive edge: sustainable, above average business performance. Their search covers information technology and its management applications. Many managers are especially interested in applications designed to manage human resources better. They want investments in such applications to pay off by contributing to firm competitiveness.

No one has yet proved the effects of information technology on a firm's competitiveness, but the HR Information Technology Project in the Center for Advanced Human Resource Studies at Cornell suggests how technology can enhance HR contributions to competitiveness. Information technology has enormous potential to make HR more competitive. We base this on our basic research on the use of information technology in HR, interviews with Fortune 500 firms to discover what they've learned from their investments in Human Resource Information Systems (HRIS),[1] and our use of information technology in Human Resources (HR) training.[2] This article focuses on one issue involved in realizing this potential: the match between HR competitive objectives and the types of HR computer applications in which a firm invests. There are many other issues involved in realizing information technology's potential, such as planning and investments in work force skills, in databases and equipment, and in organization and work design.[3] Unfortunately, discussion of these issues is beyond the scope of this article; we will discuss them only in passing, as they relate to our major focus.

THE COMPETITIVE POTENTIAL OF INFORMATION TECHNOLOGY

The competitive advantage of information technology became widely accepted in the 1980s.[4] Computer technology had by then led to creation of new products and services. Citibank had raised the costs of entering the consumer deposit market by developing Automatic Teller Machines (ATMs). American Airlines had locked-in customers via its Semi-Automated Business Research Environment (SABRE). The ability of information technology to improve management decisions with better information had also been demonstrated. For example, computer applications designed to inventory all the parts used in specific manufacturing settings reportedly enabled managers to reduce inventory, purchasing and design costs, while also reducing the time needed to meet production and delivery targets. Such systems could propel a manufacturer into a strong market position by redefining the industry standard of "low-cost, high quality producer."

In HR, information technology can be used to develop competitive products or services,[5] but to date, it has mostly been used to improve HR decisions with better information. In interviews with the HRIS groups in ten Fortune 500 firms,[6] we found that the majority had invested in computer applications to manage employee records, payroll, and compensation and benefits administration. A common payoff to such investments was more efficient information management.

At NCR, automated pension record keeping applications eliminated several layers of "paper and pencil" entries and manual calculations, and helped cut pension administration costs by increasing the accuracy of pension payout estimates nearly ninety percent. Armstrong World's benefits management computer applications enabled the parent company to self insure and better control health benefit costs via targeted claims monitoring. ARCO's investments in computer systems to store and process HR information improved its accuracy and timeliness.

Better HR information has led managers to ask more questions about how head count, turnover, skills inventories, or performance ratings affect their units' business objectives. Mobil Corporation's managers developed computer applications that helped them select among several major work force relocation alternatives to choose the one that best met Mobil's cost reduction targets. NCR's finance and HRIS managers jointly developed a computer application that shows how decisions about hiring and training in sales units can affect sales revenues and profit. Now HR and line managers can more effectively hire and train sales forces to optimize these objectives.

These examples demonstrate that information technology can improve HR administrative, operational, and planning decisions. Unfortunately, most organizational investments in HR information technology support only a narrow range of administrative decisions, such as those associated with payroll and record keeping.[7] In many cases the competitive potential of even these narrowly focused investments has not been fully exploited. To reduce this investment myopia, we need a framework that helps managers think about how HR information technology—specifically different types of computer applications—can help achieve competitive objectives. We develop this framework in the sections that follow by:

- Defining HR competitive objectives and related decisions;
- Describing types of computer applications and the decisions they are designed to improve; and
- Matching HR competitive objectives with the computer applications that best support them.

HR COMPETITIVE OBJECTIVES AND RELATED DECISIONS

Schuler and Jackson's 1987 article in *The Academy of Management Executive*, identified three firm-level competitive strategies as primary drivers of HR competitive objectives: cost leadership, quality/customer satisfaction, and innovation.

In a cost leadership strategy, a firm strives to become the low-cost producer in its industry. Sources of cost advantage include economies of scale, proprietary technology, or favored access to important supply sources (people, raw materials, etc.). A quality/customer satisfaction strategy emphasizes improving existing work methods, products/services, and customer relations as a means of commanding premium prices. This strategy, like the cost leadership strategy is concerned with cost reductions, but only in areas that do not directly affect customers' perceptions of quality or value. The innovation strategy emphasizes differentiation through the creation of new operations and management methods, technology, or products/services. This strategy could yield long term results that support either cost leadership or quality/customer satisfaction strategies, such as a new technology that makes the firm the industry's low cost producer, or new work methods resulting in substantial increases in product or service quality.

To achieve these strategic objectives and realize competitive advantage for the firm, HR must first apply strategy within the HR function itself. Restructuring in most firms has left HR with a smaller work force, yet equal or greater responsibilities and new demands. Time has become as critical a resource as talent and money. HR must review its work to define strategic priorities. What work must continue to be done? Of that work, which can be done better by searching out efficiencies and economies of scale (cost leadership); which can be done better by delegating and collaborating with line managers and employees or other functional staffs (quality/customer satisfaction); and which would most benefit from creative time, talent, and resources (innovation)? In short, how can HR work harder, smarter, or with more vision?

Exhibit 1 illustrates how HR can divide its work and address related decisions for each competitive strategy. To achieve cost leadership, HR could streamline processing of employee records, payroll, and benefits by standardizing and eliminating unnecessary paper handling and reporting. HR thus becomes the low cost provider for critical administrative work, as well as a more accurate and timely provider of HR information. To achieve quality/customer satisfaction, HR can collaborate with line managers or other "clients," to become more responsive to their needs. For example, HR could replace a merit pay process requiring line managers to follow an imposed, standard set of guidelines with a system encouraging HR and line managers to customer pay increase plans jointly for their units. HR contributes the incentive design expertise. Line managers contribute their "hands-on" understanding of customer demands and the rewards that would best motivate employees to achieve those demands. Under an innovation strategy, HR could allocate fifteen to twenty percent of staff time to exploratory, creative projects with uncertain short term payoffs. Perhaps HR could reach new customers by providing expertise to other organizations, thus making HR a profit center.

Exhibit 1

HR COMPETITIVE OBJECTIVES AND RELATED DECISIONS

	Firm Level Competitive Strategies		
	Cost Leadership	*Quality/Customer Satisfaction*	*Innovation*
HR Competitive Objectives	Higher output for given labor cost PEOPLE WORKING HARDER	Continuous improvement PEOPLE WORKING SMARTER	Workable discoveries PEOPLE WORKING WITH VISION
HR Decisions and Actions	Streamline Standardize Decrease production time/headcount Reduce costs (e.g. increase accuracy	Educate line managers and other "clients" Delegate/share decisions Use customer driven performance criteria Increase flexibility	Define vision Attract creative talent Reward risk Provide opportunities/ tools for exploration
HR Division of Work	Administration	Operations	Planning/Creative

In most cases, work division will not be so clear cut as in Exhibit 1, but assigning HR work to cost leadership, quality/customer satisfaction, and innovation strategies reveals how resources might best be allocated to support one strategy over another.

TYPES OF COMPUTER APPLICATIONS AND THE DECISIONS THEY SUPPORT

Information technology encompasses hardware, software, and peripherals, providing management with increasing capacity to record, store, manipulate, and communicate information across wide geographic boundaries, with access by many users. We focus on computer applications that can improve HR's ability to access, manipulate, or present information. Such computer applications exist for all types of hardware—mainframes, stand alone PCs, or PCs operating as a network.

We consider three types of applications: transaction processing/reporting/tracking systems, expert systems, and decision support systems. In Exhibit 2 each type of application is briefly described, and classified in terms of the complexity of the decisions it is designed to address, and the demands it makes on a user's analytic and computer skills. Transaction processing/reporting/tracking

Exhibit 2

TYPES OF COMPUTER APPLICATIONS

Transaction Processing/Reporting/Tracking Systems

BEST AT:
High Volume Sorts, Lists, Merges
Editing
Simple Calculations
Displaying Information
Auditing & Spotting Discrepancies

Expert Systems

BEST AT:
Codifying Knowledge & Experience
Distributing Expertise
Recommending Action
Education

Decision Support Systems

BEST AT:
Supporting Research
Optimizing Decision Alternatives
Speeding Up Discovery

(Left axis: Decision Complexity Supported — Low to High; Right axis: Demands on User Skills — Low to High)

systems are associated with the least complex decisions, and the fewest demands on user analytic and computer skills. Decision support systems are associated with the highest decision complexity and demands on user skills.[8]

MATCH COMPUTER APPLICATIONS AND HR OBJECTIVES FOR COMPETITIVE ADVANTAGE

In Exhibit 3, we match HR objectives from Exhibit 1 with types of computer applications listed in Exhibit 2 to suggest how such matches offer competitive benefits for the firm. The cells in Exhibit 3 show the potential benefits of these matches. The diagonal shaded cells represent the matches with the highest potential benefits; the off diagonals illustrate other possible benefits.

In the sections that follow, we use HR examples of the three major types of computer applications in Exhibit 2, to illustrate the decisions these applications support. We then elaborate on the benefits of matching HR objectives and computer applications.

Transaction Processing/Reporting/Tracking Applications

Transaction processing/reporting/tracking applications best support routine high volume HR decisions with well-defined information needs and outcomes. The work associated with such decisions is very common in HR, including calculating overtime pay under the Fair Labor Standards Act, reviewing and documenting employee transfers, calculating employee pension benefits at different retirement ages, and comparing current payroll levels against budgets. The rules

Exhibit 3

MATCHING COMPUTER APPLICATIONS WITH HR COMPETITIVE OBJECTIVES

	Types of Computer Applications		
HR Competitive Objectives	*Transaction Processing/ Reporting/Tracking Systems*	*Expert Systems*	*Decision Support Systems*
Cost Leadership: People Working Harder	· Reduces paper handling · Standardizes entry and reporting · Increases processing accuracy · Increases report turnaround · Early warning of goal deviations	· Decreases need for HR experts · Helps spread database and training costs over entire workforce	· Increases chance of innovation for HR cost controls
Quality/Customer Satisfaction: People Working Smarter	· Increases time for HR quality initiatives · Enables custom reports and data entry · Increases awareness of HR information and can lead to its improvement	· Enables line employees to make HR decisions informed by HR expertise · Increases customizing of HR programs · Increases line satisfaction with/under-standing of HR	· Increases chance of innovations for HR quality/customer satisfaction
Innovation: People Working with Vision	· Increases time for HR innovation · Awareness of goal deviations sparks discoveries	· Increases time for HR innovation · Line Understanding of HR sparks collaboration and discovery	· Powerful support for discovery · Shortens discovery process · Fast testing, reporting and documentation of new finds

governing these decisions have been predetermined by the firm or by law. Transaction processing, reporting, and tracking applications can also be used effectively by people with minimal analytic or computer skills.

How do these applications improve the decisions associated with such routine tasks? Some of these applications directly improve transaction processing.

An application for managing information on employee pay and benefits can improve HR decisions by handling data processing and reporting quickly and accurately, thus improving aggregate estimates of the firm's pay and benefit obligations. Other applications increase information available to decision makers by providing easy access to information from many sources (including sources external to the firm), and reporting it in many formats (including graphs, tables, and charts). Such reporting applications are typically aimed at higher level managers and executives. For example, managers frequently ask about the distribution of employees in exempt pay grades by major business divisions. A sophisticated reporting application handles this question by allowing managers to type the question into their computer in English, and by reporting the answer back to them in simple summary sentences, statistics, and graphs.[9] HR tracking applications enable managers to compare unit or departmental performance against goals in areas such as performance appraisal completions, merit budget allocations, turnover, and hires.

Transaction Processing/Reporting/Tracking Applications MATCH Cost Leadership

As Exhibit 3 shows, transaction processing, reporting, and tracking applications primarily support cost leadership objectives—especially those that require reducing administrative costs. They enable HR to decentralize much administrative work and to eliminate layers of paper handling while increasing administrative standardization, accuracy, and auditing controls. Most transaction processing applications enable HR information to be entered directly into a computer at the point of transaction—new hire information would be entered by the hiring unit, for example. Direct entry can eliminate several layers of paper shuffling, yet still provide an aggregate record of transactions. These applications can thus free up some HR time to pursue other, more productive work, and may even decrease required HR head count.

Transaction processing applications typically have built-in audits that warn users when any information they input falls outside acceptable ranges, thus reducing errors at entry points, and minimizing later data checking. When tracking applications signal deviations from goals, they provide early warnings that allow faster and more effective corrections. For example, one application might tally total allocated monthly pay increases, compare them to targeted annual pay increase totals, and report the units where actual increases are running well ahead of target.

Such early warnings allow HR and line managers to act before variances become costly. In short, transaction processing, reporting, and tracking applications can support a firm's cost leadership goals by helping HR work harder with fewer people.

Exhibit 3 also suggests that these applications can support quality and innovation strategies. By reducing the time HR must spend on routine administrative tasks, transaction processing, reporting, tracking applications can free time for concentration on quality and innovation issues. The more advanced applications enable individual units to customize reports and maintain special databases, often increasing their satisfaction with HR, and potentially providing important information for the firm. By signaling deviations from current policy goals, tracking applications can even lead to discoveries supporting cost leadership or quality/customer satisfaction strategies.

Expert System Applications

Expert system applications improve decisions for which the "right" outcomes are determined through expert knowledge and experience. Like the applications described previously, expert system applications are based on rules, but the rules are complex, derived from careful analyses of expert decisions. Once programmed, these applications can distribute this expertise throughout a firm, without the presence of a human expert. Expert systems can be applied to many HR decisions. For example, using historical data on the number and quality of recruits from various sources, where should we recommend our new division recruit to meet its hiring goals? Do labor market factors justify higher professional salary offers in our West Coast offices? Should the content of performance appraisal training differ for managers in different units? There is no one right outcome for these decisions, but experience and expertise within the firm will dictate a specific set of alternatives.

The more advanced applications enable individual units to customize reports and maintain special databases, often increasing their satisfaction with HR, and potentially providing important information for the firm.

There are at least two kinds of expert system applications: black box and training. Black box applications simply provide a recommended decision outcome without educating users about how the decision is made. An example HR application is one that prompts employees covered by a flexible benefits plan to input personal information (such as their other sources of insurance or income), and then recommends a personalized package of options available for their fixed benefit dollars.[10] Such applications make only minimal demands on user analytic and computer skills.

In contrast, training applications guide users through a series of questions and information displays designed to educate them on the reasoning experts use in reaching a decision. For example, some expert system applications help line managers conduct better performance appraisals. The application prompts the manager to consider information that experts believe important to appraisal—employee performance history, sources of rater bias, firm or unit performance norms, special personal circumstances, and so forth. Given this information, the application suggests an "expert" appraisal outcome, which the manager may either use or override. This training application improved managers' appraisal decisions by providing both recommendations and interactive expert feedback throughout the decision process. Such applications require that users be analytic enough to diagnose their own situations, using the guidelines of the expert system. Often, only minimal computer skills would be required.

Black box systems are, to date, the most common expert systems. However, we believe that training systems have the most potential to improve HR decisions, by combining expertise with education.

Expert Systems Applications MATCH Quality/Customer Satisfaction

As shown in Exhibit 3, expert system applications allow firms to delegate some of the HR decisions that are critical to a firm's quality and customer satisfaction initiatives. Expert systems can also enable HR to track delegated decisions so that major deviations from expert opinion or approved designs can be investigated. These strengths are especially true of the training expert systems. Such systems could assist team building efforts, for example, in the form of training modules that apply and demonstrate the management and problem solving skills needed for effective team work. Individual team members could review these modules as needed. These systems could also help teams design "custom" performance evaluations or compensation programs that reflect goals tied to customer demands. Expert systems could assist team members conducting performance appraisals or allocating pay increases by letting them know when their decisions deviate from approved designs. Using expert systems, HR could delegate many traditional HR responsibilities to teams, while increasing the likelihood that team decisions are informed ones. Moreover, by using expert systems, team members may better understand how the firm's HR systems work, and thus be better prepared to suggest improvements based on the team's understanding of customer demands. Such suggestions then become part of the firm's HR expertise. This is the essence of people working smarter.

Expert system applications can also contribute to cost leadership goals. Earlier, we described a black box type expert system that recommended personalized option packages to employees covered by a flexible benefits plan. Such systems can provide recommendations that optimize employee demographic risk factors, thus controlling an employer's costs for any one benefit option. These systems also accurately record and quickly report employee choices. They may eliminate the need to train HR generalists to answer complex questions on benefits and pensions, or enable the firm to redeploy staff benefit experts and better use their time. The overall result could be an increase in HR productivity. It is not difficult to see how wide-spread use of expert systems—to assist line managers' decisions in hiring, performance appraisal, promotion, career development, and so forth— could decrease the number of HR experts needed by a firm, free up the time of remaining experts to support other issues, and thus enhance HR's ability to support cost leadership goals by working harder with fewer people.

Also, if expert systems liberate HR time and capture new information on HR practices from the line managers and others most directly involved in business operations, the new perspectives and information produced can support HR innovation objectives.

Using expert systems, HR could delegate many traditional HR responsibilities to teams, while increasing the likelihood that team decisions are informed ones.

Decision Support System Applications

Decision support system applications improve decisions for which the rules are changing or not well defined, and the "right" outcomes are unknown, such as: What is the right level of sales force hiring and training to maintain optimal sales?

Which combinations of people and skills will produce the most productive teams in our major business divisions? Which assignments and career development experiences produce executives best able to manage diversity and change?

Decision support system applications package computer tools that allow a user to pull together information, analyze it, and represent it in many forms (graphs, reports, etc.), and also assist the user with electronic memory aids and references. Although there are undoubtedly talented HR people currently using such applications, HR examples are scarce. Perhaps applications designed to facilitate group brainstorming offer a glimpse of decision support system potential.[11] These applications enable a group of users, working simultaneously on linked PCs, to call up a wealth of information on the issue of interest, display this information in many ways, and consider and capture new information as it emerges during brainstorming. An HR group charged with "defining the new competencies needed for effective HR management in the 90's might use a brainstorming application to help them more quickly achieve consensus on a concrete set of such competencies."[12] One such brainstorming session suggested that the set of HR competencies the group chooses will reflect a more thorough examination of the information and the alternatives than would otherwise be possible. Moreover, because the system allows everyone to talk at once by entering their ideas and having them displayed immediately to the entire group, substantial time savings can result.

Decision Support Systems MATCH Innovation

Exhibit 3 suggests that achieving innovative strategies in HR requires attracting creative people, and supporting their time for research and risk taking. User analytic and computer skills are critical to effective use of decision support system applications, but the applications themselves also represent powerful exploratory tools for such users. These systems can step up the pace of organizational discovery and learning. They can help attract creative, analytic talent, support innovative work, and make the fruits of innovation more readily available to HR and the firm.

For example, in the process of helping to set team performance targets based on quality goals, suppose an HR group starts to question those targets, guessing they are based on too narrow a view of customer satisfaction. Using a computer database from the firm's customer service group and a statistical analysis package, the HR group could design a statistical model to predict customer satisfaction from the narrow performance targets (time to delivery, low return rate, time to fill service requests). If their results suggest that these targets predict only a modest percentage of customer satisfaction, then the HR group might decide to explore other possible performance-related predictors of customer satisfaction, and to solicit ideas from the firm's marketing and sales groups. Using computer data from marketing, the HR group might revise its model to include two new variables: one representing sales force promises about what a product will deliver, and one representing problems reported during product installation. The revised model might substantially improve prediction of customer satisfaction.

Thus a creative and skilled HR group, armed with information from electronic databases in other functional areas of the firm and statistical packages that allow modeling and analysis, might make discoveries leading to a broader set of the team performance targets more likely to influence customer satisfaction, training indicators for sales and installation people, and a broader definition of desirable team skills. The original model could be tested in other parts of the firm, revised, and eventually made part of an expert system to assist teams in setting performance targets. Spinoffs from this modeling process might include external information systems that enable customers to input team performance assessments electronically to the firm's databases, or meetings between team members and major customer representatives in which important variables affecting team-customer relations are discussed and visually charted with the assistance of brainstorming software.

As Exhibit 3 shows, decision support system applications could also lead to discoveries that reduce costs, or to marketable innovations in technology, products, or services. These applications are tools that make the exploration involved in discovery less tedious and time consuming, that enhance the prompt dissemination of results, and that record learning. In short, decision support systems can speed up the organizational learning cycle from discovery, to expert judgment, to established facts that feed operating routine. They do require research, computer, and analytic skills, but they also offer considerable support to those who have these skills. They support HR people working with vision.

STAYING IN PLACE VERSUS GETTING SOMEWHERE

We began this article with a quote from *Through the Looking Glass*. That quote highlights the difference between staying in place and getting somewhere: running faster versus running twice as fast as that. We believe this is an apt characterization of the competitive business race, but even more so of the challenge managers face in applying information technology to win that race. Information technology appears to advance almost daily. Management needs to consider the role of information and information management in the firm's competitive strategy, to use these advances in ways that not only keep them in place, but add to the firm's ability to get somewhere, to sustain above average industry performance. We have focused on applications in HR, but our framework applies to all management areas.

Both survey work and our own research suggest that the majority of HR information technology investments are in transaction processing, reporting, and tracking computer applications. Though these applications can support cost leadership objectives, we believe that the competitive potential of investments in other types of applications has been neglected. We know that firms differ in competitive environments they face, and thus, in the strategic objectives emphasized. They should not overlook the advantages that matching investments in computer applications to strategically driven HR objectives could offer them.

Matching computer investments and strategic objectives, however, is only part of realizing information technology's potential. In our interviews with the HRIS groups in ten Fortune 500 firms, we found that those who were most successful in using information technology made additional system and organization development investments. These included developing good information databases, updating operating software, making computer equipment available to critical users, educating users about computers, developing the organizational expertise to manage information technology, building relationships with other information technology users in the firm, and so on. The magnitude and timing of these additional investments appeared to vary with HR's strategic emphasis, and with the firm's structure, culture, and work force.

Management needs to consider the role of information and information management in the firm's competitive strategy, to use these advances in ways that not only keep them in place, but add to the firm's ability to get somewhere, to sustain above average industry performance.

A complete treatment of these investments is beyond the scope of this article. We can offer some observations from our research about conditions critical to the successful implementation of the three types of computer applications we have discussed. First, transaction processing, reporting and tracking applications require comprehensive databases, and the applications, themselves, must be available and easy to use for a wide range of users. Expert system applications require good system builders, good experts, and user confidence in system recommendations. Decision support systems require good analysts and researchers, high quality comprehensive databases, and an organizational climate receptive to research and innovation.

Finally, estimating the true (net) valued added and the sustained competitive advantages possible from information technology investments requires concrete measures of their benefits and costs. Viewing these investments in terms of their contributions to cost leadership, quality/customer satisfaction, or innovation can point to potential areas of benefit measurement. The more difficult, but critical work of establishing concrete measures still remains.

Endnotes

[1]We define Human Resource Information Systems or HRIS as the composite of data bases, computer applications, and hardware and software necessary to collect/record, store, manage, deliver, present, and manipulate data for HR.

[2]See J. W. Boudreau, "Building a PC-Based Human Resource Management Curriculum at the School of Industrial and Labor Relations, Cornell University," *Proceedings of the Forty Second Annual Meeting of the Industrial Relations Association* (Madison, WI: Industrial Relations Research Association, December 1990), 441–453; R. Broderick and J. W. Boudreau, "Human Resource Automation for Competitive Advantage: Case Studies of Ten Leaders," Working Paper #90-04, Center for Advanced Human Resource Studies, School of Industrial and Labor Relations, Cornell University; G. T. Milkovich and J. W. Boudreau, *Personnel/ Human Resource Management* (Homewood, IL: Irwin, 1991).

[3]For more information on the dimensions of organization and system development considered important in successful HRIS investments see R. Broderick and J. W. Boudreau, endnote 2.

[4]There was a spate of articles on information technology, computer applications and their competitive potential in 1984 and 1985. For examples see F. W. McFarlan, "Information Technology Changes the

Way You Compete," *Harvard Business Review,* May-June 1984; M. Porter, *Competitive Advantage* (New York, NY: Free Press, 1985), 116–172; K. C. Laudon and J. P. Laudon, *Management Information Systems: A Contemporary Perspective* (New York, NY: MacMillan, 1988), 61–82.

[5]For example, Tesseract developed the first relational database management system designed specifically for HR and mainframes, and for many years has dominated the market for such systems.

[6]For more information on these interviews see R. Broderick and J. W. Boudreau, endnote 2.

[7]See surveys of HRIS in many firms, such as: C. Richards-Carpenter, "The Computerized Personnel Information Systems Survey Results, 1989," *Personnel Management,* August 1989, 21, 48–49; and KPMG Peat Marwick, *Computer Usage In Human Resources: A Competitive Advantage* (Dallas, TX: KPMG Peat Marwick, 1988).

[8]See K. C. Laudon and J. P. Laudon, endnote 4, 34.

[9]Developments in data capturing capabilities may soon enable users to ask questions using voice commands (voice recognition systems) or hand writing (optical character recognition systems).

[10]See J. M. Hannon, G. T. Milkovich, and M.C. Sturman, "The Feasibility of Using Expert Systems in the Management of Human Resources," Working Paper #90-19, Center for Advanced Human Resource Studies, School of Industrial and Labor Relations, Cornell University, for a more detailed description of expert system applications currently used in HR management.

[11]The brainstorming software used in the IBM Executive Development labs at Cornell is "GROUPSYSTEMS." It was jointly developed by IBM and the University of Arizona.

[12]Such a brainstorming session was recently conducted at Cornell with Center for Advanced Human Resource Studies researchers, and line managers, HR managers, and other functional staff representatives of a Fortune 500 firm.

READING 39

TEACHING BIG BROTHER
TO BE A TEAM PLAYER
Computer Monitoring and Quality

Terri L. Griffith

Executive Overview

*Computer monitoring should not be seen as a way of gathering information about work-
ers, per se, but rather as one part of a production and quality strategy that provides needed
information to a diverse team of workers. In its most powerful and effective form, computer monitoring is the use of computers to collect, process, and provide feedback information about work with the intent of improving performance and developing employees.
Unfortunately, computer monitoring has also been used to punish employees. Here, a
study of a successful computer monitoring system at Hughes Aircraft Company is
described. The study shows that computer monitoring can facilitate integrated production
and quality control strategies without negative effects on employee quality of work life.
Managers who wish to design and effectively use computer monitoring systems should:
(1) Use the monitoring system to provide feedback data to the workforce—not to gather
social information (e.g., time taken for bathroom breaks); (2) Determine the type of data
that employees believe will help them and be willing to adapt the system as they get ideas
about how to use the data; (3) Design a system that gathers integrated data—data that
will allow for useful comparisons between, as well as within, specific tasks; and (4) Realize that computer monitoring is only as noxious as the management system itself.*

Computer monitoring has a bad name. Consider the titles of some recent articles
in the business press: "Big Brother is Counting Your Keystrokes," "How Companies Spy on Employees," "Employee Performance Monitoring . . . or Meddling?",
"The Dark Side of Computing," "The Boss that Never Blinks."[1] These titles capture the primary way in which computer monitoring has been used in the workplace—as a surveillance technique to control employee behavior. Eavesdropping
is not acceptable behavior outside the workplace so it's not hard to understand
why electronic eavesdropping within it elicits negative reactions.[2]

Source: "Teaching Big Brother to be a Team Player: Computer Monitoring and Quality" by Terri L.
Griffith, *Academy of Management Executive*, 1993, Vol. 7, No. 1, 73–80.

The privacy issues inherent in computer monitoring have attracted the attention of the courts and Congress. For example, Mayor Robert Isaac of Colorado Springs, Colorado has been sued for reading the electronic mail messages that City Council members sent to each other from their homes during 1990. Isaac defended his actions by saying he was making sure that electronic mail was not being used to circumvent the Colorado "open meeting" law that requires most council business be conducted publicly.[3] Similarly, Epson America Inc. was named in a class action law suit concerning a systems administrator who eavesdropped on electronic correspondence.[4] These are not isolated instances and the problem is likely to grow worse. Sales of computer monitoring software hit $176 million in 1991 and are projected to grow fifty-percent annually through 1996.[5]

Many European countries have enacted anti-monitoring laws and, during 1991, H.R. 1281 and S.516—the "Privacy for Consumers and Workers Act"—were introduced in the U.S. Congress. Key components of these bills would require employers to provide prior written notice of:

- The forms of electronic monitoring to be used
- The types of personal data to be collected
- The frequency for each form of electronic monitoring which will occur
- The use to be made of personal data
- Interpretation techniques for collected information
- Existing production standards and work performance expectations
- Methods used for determining production standards and work performance expectations based on electronic monitoring statistics

The proposed legislation also would require that random or periodic monitoring be accompanied by a signal when the monitoring occurs, such as a signal light, beeping tone, or verbal notification.

Testimony at Congressional hearings also suggests that computer monitoring may detrimentally affect employee health. For example, a study by the University of Wisconsin and the Communication Workers of America found that computer monitoring was related to reports of physical complaints such as stiff or sore wrists, back pain, and headaches,[6] which also are associated with the fastest growing category of workers' compensation claims—repetitive stress injuries.

With this history, it is not difficult to understand why computer monitoring has a bad name. But does computer monitoring have to invade privacy or harm employee health? The answer is clearly, "No." In its most powerful and effective form, computer monitoring is the use of computers to collect, process, and provide feedback information about work with the intent of improving performance and developing, not punishing, employees. Work by Judith Komaki supports the idea that the most effective managers are involved in observing and improving the work process.[7] At AT&T, for example, computer monitoring technology is being used as part of a pilot project using self-managed teams to operate telephone call centers. The monitoring system allows experienced operators to listen in on less experienced operators' calls and coach them. Used in this manner, computer monitoring might be considered an electronic adjunct to Tom Peter's "management-by-walking-around," where managers gather information by observing employees working and then providing help when needed.

Computer monitoring can be an effective management tool in work settings when used as part of an entire production strategy—as part of a feedback system or by providing process information about how work actually gets done.[8] The competitive advantage of a computer monitoring system is that it can collect complex, interrelated data quickly, unobtrusively, and won't (usually) forget. The most effective strategy is when computer monitoring is an integral part of a production system and the focus is on improving the work process, rather than on controlling employee behavior.

THE CASE OF CVITS

> Setting: High technology clean room production facility. Workers dressed in sterile white "bunny suits" and booties. Powerful microscopes connected to computers and video screens. Wires running to straps on the workers' wrists.

This could be the opening scene from a science fiction movie where a computerized boss shocks workers' wrists whenever they are sensed to be slacking-off or making mistakes. The story is only partially fiction. These are microchip inspectors; the wrist straps are grounding wires so static electricity will not damage the delicate product—not torture devices. However, management is computer assisted.

Hughes Aircraft Company's Computerized Video Integrated Technology System (CVITS) provides an example of computer monitoring being used as an integral part of a production strategy, highlighting its "value added" potential. The system is used in their microchip production and inspection processes. The microchips produced in this system retail to the Department of Defense for more than $10,000. One inspector may see hundreds of parts per day. Much of what has been written about computer monitoring focuses on the importance of quantity versus quality.[9] Here, we show a system where the focus is clearly on quality and the use of a new tool by both managers and subordinates who are well versed in relating quality data back to the work process.

Thus, this example of computer monitoring is different from others[10] in that it is manufacturing oriented and provides data at a level where managerial issues can be closely examined. An Office of Technology Assessment report[11] summarizing the results of many computer monitoring attempts suggests that computer monitoring has negative effects. The limited results from more recent controlled studies, on the other hand, have not indicated negative effects on either worker performance or attitudes toward work.[12] Observing computer monitoring in a production setting where statistical process control and other empirical devices are better understood should help sort out these contradictions by illustrating the role of feedback and control as an integral part of work. This case describes a system that is both used and evaluated by the same work group that is in charge of identifying production process problems through data trends. Their familiarity with relating trend data back to the actual process should enable them to make long term effective use of the monitoring information.

Purpose and Design of the System

Strategic quality objectives drove the design of the CVITS at Hughes Aircraft Company. Hughes designed the system to collect information for the documentation of quality—increasing the convenience of the quality review process, creating a database of quality information, and developing a training and certification program using the information gathered about production. Digitized images from the inspection station microscopes are the basic technology for this system. A computer network connects these inspection stations to "WORM" (write once, read many) optical disks and video display monitors both at the inspection stations and upstairs in the supervisor's office. The system also allows for keyboard entry of text data onto the WORM disks.

The system provides two types of monitoring. One is the "real-time" video connection to the microscope stations used to inspect the microchips, which is also available remotely in the supervisor's office. The system achieves this real-time monitoring through simple video cables and a switch box that allows the supervisor to switch from one station to another. The other form of monitoring is archival. The inspectors take the digitized image of each defect and store the image and a text description (disposition) of the defect on the WORM disk. The supervisory and engineering staff then refer to this computer file to verify the disposition of each defect. If they change the verdict of the inspector, or if there are any other comments about the inspected part, this information is stored in the file. These data can be analyzed to identify consistent discrepancies between inspector/supervisor/engineering decisions or production trends.

Another feature of the CVITS is that its design was the impetus for the engineering staff to create an on-line library of "classic" examples for each defect an inspector might find. This library is available at each CVITS station and allows team members to compare questionable defects with the library definition. The library is indexed both by type of defect and by Department of Defense contract definition.

Quality within the manufacturing process is a collaborative effort where the final product is the joint responsibility of the entire production team. The Hughes team, consisting of the entire staff of inspectors, quality engineers, and production engineers, collectively identifies production problem areas and possible solutions. The CVITS supports their cooperative work by making information available to all members of the staff. The contribution of the system to quality is that all team members can use the information to solve production process problems. Additionally, the team is discussing the possible use of the accumulated database of digitized defects to teach a neural network how to further enhance the inspection process.

Exhibit 1

REACTION TO CVITS BY TEAM MEMBER ROLE

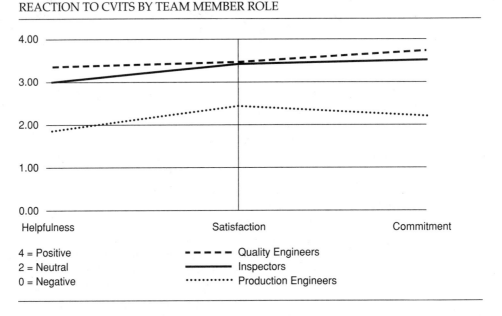

4 = Positive   – – – – – Quality Engineers
2 = Neutral   ———— Inspectors
0 = Negative   ············ Production Engineers

CVITS' Impact on Team Members

Discussion with team members[13] revealed that CVITS was implemented by what has been called "parachuting." Senior quality control staff built the system and actual users were not consulted or really informed before its appearance at their work stations. CVITS simply appeared (parachuted) into the inspection area without any prior introduction. Apparently CVITS is sufficiently user friendly and similar to the old method of inspection that this form of introduction was possible. However, as we show later, this form of introduction does have its drawbacks. Informal hands-on training was provided after CVITS' introduction and lasted for about five minutes per person. Users were asked in the interviews if they felt they needed any formal training. Only two felt they needed further information. Apparently they found no surprises about the system's capabilities, possibly because they had no idea about what to expect.

Questions in the interview were used to determine the degree to which team members perceived CVITS to be helpful, how satisfied they were with it, and how committed they were to using the system. The results provide some insight into this particular system and its effectiveness within this work group. As Exhibit 1 shows, there is considerable variation in team members reactions to CVITS. Inspectors and quality engineers saw the system as being more helpful and were more satisfied with and committed to its use than production engineers, whose reported reactions were neutral. Differences in these reactions are likely a result of differences in the way CVITS affects the tasks they perform. For example, inspectors find CVITS helpful in performing their jobs. Certainly the large digitized display of the microscopic image has advantages over looking through a microscope eyepiece and, on average, each inspector used the system about three hours per day. The biggest complaint heard from the inspectors was that there were not enough stations to go around. Some inspectors have 100-percent access to a CVITS station while others must share them. Another strength of CVITS, from the inspectors' perspective, is its archival database and ease of record keeping. However, these benefits have yet to be fully realized as the inspectors still have to maintain paper reports as well.

Quality engineers rated CVITS as helpful and, on average, used the system about 3.5 hours per day. They identify problems in production and the CVITS archival database increases the amount of information they have to work with. In contrast, production engineers, who have to work backwards to find solutions to those problems, are neutral in their perceptions of the system's helpfulness. As currently configured, the system does not provide much information that can be used to solve identified problems. This weakness may explain the production engineers' relatively low usage of the system—less than half an hour a day. However, they may increase their use of the system and become more positive about its helpfulness as the database evolves and provides information closer to their needs.

The satisfaction and commitment results parallel those for helpfulness. Quality engineers and inspectors are most satisfied with and committed to the system; production engineers are neutral. In short, it appears that team members' satisfaction with and commitment to the system are related to the extent to which they find the system helpful in performing their jobs.

The participants also were asked specific questions about computer monitoring. CVITS is configured such that the inspection supervisor and the engineers can directly monitor the inspectors through the video connection. All users have access to the archival information as it is entered by the inspectors. Five of the six inspectors volunteered that CVITS was used to monitor their work. Four of the inspectors also noted that they used CVITS to monitor other people's work (indeed, the data that they enter is a database about preceding production processes). In response to an item that asked, "How do you feel about the work being monitored," the five inspectors offered the following comments:

> "No problem."
> "Good for answering questions when you get stuck."
> "Doesn't bother me. They're going to see it anyway. They need to see it to disposition." (Dispositioning is the final "go/no go" test before passing a part.)
> "I think it's great. A way you find out where you're at."
> "I don't mind. At first I was nervous, or if I'm talking and you leave the [part just sitting there]—she can see if it's sitting there . . . if she has it on in her office."

These comments acknowledge that the CVITS does allow for surveillance. However, they also indicate (as do the satisfaction results presented in Exhibit 1) that CVITS is not creating an "electronic sweatshop" or Orwellian work environment. CVITS is acknowledged to have feedback as well as supervisory functions.

The Problem with "Parachuting"

CVITS is a technical success that paid for itself by simplifying the identification of defects. On another level, however, the system has not been as successful. As the study shows, people in different roles have different understandings about CVITS, which is probably true in most computer monitoring situations. Inspectors see it as pieces of equipment (monitors, keyboards, etc.). Engineers focus on either its dispositioning aspect or its statistical process control capabilities, depending on their particular role. However, team members do not uniformly see CVITS as part of an overall quality control strategy. This is perhaps the only problem caused in this setting by "parachuting" the system in, and it appears to be the biggest barrier to attaining the system's full potential.

An understanding of CVITS' role in the quality/production strategy is necessary for its full utilization. Team members need to understand the whole production process and how CVITS fits into this process to make full use of the system.

The parachute method of implementing CVITS allowed each of the different work groups to develop their own, bounded understanding of the tool—each group focusing only on how CVITS would affect their jobs. Training and participation in design and adaptation may be the key to developing shared sets of meaning between the different roles. A joint implementation effort, where inspectors, supervisors, and engineers all would be exposed to the system at the same time and in the same context, would have been more likely to support a common understanding of the system.

Such an implementation strategy would also help the three groups find synergies within and across their roles, as well as within the CVITS data. For example, production and supervision may have knowledge that would help inspectors better understand and predict problem areas, or, inspectors may have production hypotheses about patterns of problems that they identify in the microchips. Bringing supervision, production, and quality control closer together should create benefits throughout the production process.

CVITS was successful because it gathered quality information and feedback data for improving the workers' skills. The focus was on identifying areas to improve, not on finding reasons to punish employees.

A crucial point to make, both for the future use of CVITS at this site and within the general study of computer monitoring, is that the entire production strategy should be considered when planning for the system and its use. Monitoring of this type may include the capabilities of video monitoring, computer monitoring, and statistical process control. The role of the monitoring system, for example, is to allow inspectors, supervisors, and engineers to access and use detailed information about the production process. Successful monitoring is not just a surveillance tool for management. Instead, monitoring can be a part of a production strategy used by the entire work group.

It is likely that previous negative reports about computer monitoring describe issues that are not solely due to the technical design of the system. Both the Office of Technology Assessment report (which is full of warnings about computer monitoring) and this Hughes Aircraft/CVITS case examine computer monitoring without controlling for organizational or managerial factors. However, the lack of negative results here (e.g., inspector dissatisfaction or lack of commitment) is probably not due to the mildness of the CVITS technology. Rather, CVITS provides a full spectrum of monitoring capabilities and the CVITS users seem to be making justifiable choices about which data to collect and how to use it.

The implication is that computer monitoring is only as evil as the management system that employs it. The users were generally satisfied with it.

TEACH BIG BROTHER TO BE PART OF THE TEAM

Computer monitoring does not have to abuse workers by creating an electronic sweatshop environment. It is just another managerial tool that needs to be used responsibly. The following are some guidelines[14] for the effective use of computer monitoring, both from the perspective of employee privacy and the acquisition of useful production data.

1. Use the monitoring system to provide feedback data to the workforce—not to gather social information (e.g., time taken for bathroom breaks). CVITS was successful because it gathered quality information and feedback data for improving the workers' skills. The focus was on identifying areas to improve, not on finding reasons to punish employees. Data that is available to all members of the team is more likely to promote improved production processes. The CVITS inspectors participate in the collection of the data and understand that the data *must* be gathered to meet contract requirements. Engineers, as well as supervisors and inspectors have equal access to the files and can look for areas to improve. The idea is for the team to constantly consider new methods and techniques—as well as providing additional training to improve inspectors' skills. Moving away from systems where only supervision can access the data is certainly one way to improve both employee understanding of the system and encourage use of the data within the production team.

2. Determine the type of data that employees believe will help them and be willing to adapt the system as they get ideas about how to use the data. Most computer systems must be adapted to suit particular situational requirements. A critical feature of both computer-aided-manufacturing in general, and computer monitoring, in particular, is that the systems can be adapted as particular information needs are identified. CVITS' initial form was simply a computerization of tasks previously handled manually. As workers become more aware of other useful data, the system can be adapted to collect it. The CVITS users are aware of the flexibility of the system and have already requested that the tracking paperwork also be computerized. Training on and about computer monitoring systems should emphasize the

adaptability of the system and encourage workers to provide suggestions about important and useful data.

3. Design a system that gathers integrated data—data that will allow for useful comparisons between, as well as within, specific tasks. This should help increase the value of the system to employees, increasing their commitment to its use. CVITS combined video images of chip defects with a text database including the fault disposition provided by the inspectors. As CVITS is implemented in earlier production stages (i.e., production itself, rather than just inspection), production process variables can be linked to particular flaws. Integration between production and inspection can promote quicker solutions to production problems.

   As these changes occur, we expect that production engineers will perceive CVITS as more helpful and become more committed to its use. Integration between tasks is likely to increase employee perceptions that computer monitoring is a tool, not a punishment device. Providing integrated data will show that a specific group or individuals are not being singled out for monitoring. Integrated systems, such as CVITS, allow for complex relationships among tasks to be better understood and optimized.

4. Most important, realize that computer monitoring is only as noxious as the management system itself. Similar to time-motion techniques, computer monitoring provides managers with information that they can use for either good or ill purposes. Time-motion studies identified areas for more efficient production. They also provided information that could be used to decrease the rate paid for piece-rate compensation. Not surprisingly, workers focused on the later use and found ways to manipulate the data. Computer monitoring can identify areas for more efficient production, training needs, and production process improvements. However, if workers believe that management will use monitoring against them they may use their creative skills to find high-tech wrenches to throw into the "works." A Wang word processing representative acknowledged, for example, that ways around keyboard counts are as old as keyboard monitoring systems (e.g., computer programs that automatically enter huge blocks of text). A better outcome would be that they applied these skills to finding better production methods.

The common theme in these four suggestions is that modern quality control calls for the empowerment of the workforce for the improvement of the production process. The suggestions above build off ideas of employee understanding of the monitoring system and employee use of the data. Computer monitoring is developing at the same time as our management process is relying more and more on management roles being taken over by nonsupervisory employees or teams. The key may be to turn over computer monitoring to the workforce. With the data diffused throughout the production process, employees will better understand it, fear it less, and be more likely to find significant production process improvements. Workers are already learning statistical process control for their production areas. Why not let them use it to include themselves in the monitored processes? Better yet, create an incentive structure that rewards employee-driven improvements, then allow the employees the choice of tools to help them reach their goals. We don't have to lose Big Brother's skills, if he can learn to be a team player.

Endnotes

This research would not have been possible without the conceptual and practical assistance of Hughes Aircraft Company's Edson B. Gould, William Joyner, Geoff Hunt, and the users of the CVITS. I would also like to thank Raymond Zammuto and Gregory Northcraft for their invaluable comments and editorial assistance.

[1] W. Booth, "Big Brother is Counting Your Keystrokes," *Science, 238,* 1987, 17. G. Bylinsky. "How Companies Spy on Employees," *Fortune,* November 4, 1991, 131–140. S. Koepp, "The Boss that Never Blinks," *Time,* July 28, 1986, 46–47. M. C. Piturro, "Employee Performance Monitoring . . . or Meddling?," *Management Review, 78,* 1989, 31–33. T. Spain, "The Dark Side of Computing," *D&B Reports, 36,* 1988, 54–56.

[2] U.S. Congress, "The Electronic Supervisor: New Technology, New Tensions," Washington, D.C.: U.S. Government Printing Office, 1987.

[3] J. Markoff, *New York Times,* May 4, 1990.

[4] C. Casatelli, "Electronic Mail: Setting Ground Rules for Privacy," *Computerworld,* March 25, 1991, 47, 50.

[5] Ibid., *Fortune,* 140.

[6] M. J. Smith, P. Sainfort, K. Rogers, & D. Legrande, "Electronic Performance Monitoring and Job Stress in Telecommunications," University of Wisconsin—Madison, Department of Industrial Engineering, October 1990.

[7] J. L. Komaki, "Toward Effective Supervision," *Journal of Applied Psychology, 71,* 1986, 270–279.

[8] T. L. Griffith, "Monitoring and Performance: A Comparison of Computer and Supervisor Monitoring," *Journal of Applied Social Psychology,* (forthcoming).

J. L. Komaki, & M. L. Desselles, "Solution or Stepping Stone: The Role of Electronic Monitoring in Effective Supervision." Presented as part of a symposium, "Impacts of Electronic Monitoring," at the Academy of Management meetings, Anaheim, CA, 1988. D. Nebeker, & B. C. Tatum, "The Effects of Computer Monitoring, Standards and Rewards on Work Performance, Job Satisfaction, and Stress," *Journal of Applied Social Psychology,* (forthcoming).

[9] R. A. Grant, C. A. Higgins, & R. H. Irving. "Computerized Performance Monitors: Are they Costing you Customers?" *Sloan Management Review,* Spring 1988, 39–45.

[10] R. A. Grant, & C. A. Higgins, "The Impact of Computerized Performance Monitoring on Service Work: Testing a Causal Model," *Information Systems Research, 2,* 1991, 116–142. R. A. Grant & C. A. Higgins, "Monitoring Service Workers via Computer: The Effect on Employees, Productivity, and Service," *National Productivity Review, 8,* 1989, 101–112. U.S. Congress, "The Electronic Supervisor: New Technology. New Tensions," Washington, D.C.: U.S. Government Printing Office, 1987.

[11] U.S. Congress, "The Electronic Supervisor: New Technology, New Tensions," Washington, D.C.: U.S. Government Printing Office, 1987.

[12] J. Chalykoff, & T. A. Kochan, "Computer-Aided Monitoring: Its Influence on Employee Job Satisfaction and Turnover," *Personnel Psychology, 42,* 1989, 807–834. T. L. Griffith, "Monitoring and Performance: A Comparison of Computer and Supervisor Monitoring," *Journal of Applied Social Psychology,* (forthcoming).

D. Nebeker, & B. C. Tatum, "The Effects of Computer Monitoring, Standards and Rewards on Work Performance, Job Satisfaction, and Stress," *Journal of Applied Social Psychology,* (forthcoming).

[13]Several site visits to the CVITS site were made to gather information for the description of the system and to develop the structured interview for assessing the method of implementation and its success. The resulting interview included questions regarding the processes of implementation (socialization/training, rewards/helpfulness of systems, commitment to system) and multiple measures of implementation success (knowledge of system, use of system, attitudes about system). The focus was on perceived and actual outcomes relevant to the system. Each interview was conducted in a private office during work hours and took approximately forty minutes. Several hours were also spent simply watching the team use the system. The system's two designers also were interviewed. Their responses have not been included in the sample except as a measure of the technical capabilities of the system. This decision was made based on the designers' responses being singularly positive and showing no variance. For further information, please contact the author.

[14]A complementary set of guidelines appear in Grant, et al. (1988).